Welcome to

The New Laurel's Kitchen

Laurel Robertson
Carol Flinders &
Brian Ruppenthal

THE NEW
LAUREL'S
KITCHEN

A Handbook for Vegetarian Cookery & Nutrition

Ten Speed Press, Berkeley, California

TEN SPEED PRESS
P.O. Box 7123
Berkeley, California 94707

Library of Congress Cataloging in Publication Data
Robertson, Laurel.
The new Laurel's kitchen.
Includes index.
1. Vegetarian cookery.   2. Nutrition.
I. Flinders, Carol.   II. Ruppenthal, Brian.   III. Title.
TX837.R63   1986   641.3'03   86–14330
ISBN 0–89815–167–8
ISBN 0–89815–166–X (pbk.)

Printed in the United States of America

1 2 3 4 5 6 7 8 9 10   92 91 90 89 88 87 86

CAUTIONARY NOTE The recipes, instructions, and nutritional
information contained in this book are in no way intended as a substitute for medical counseling. Please do not attempt self-treatment
of a medical problem without consulting a physician.

Foreword

This wonderful volume goes way beyond nutrition, health, and the marvelous collection of recipes it contains. It is also a treatise on respect for the bounty of nature and an admonition that as residents of this planet, we must share it not only with each other but with all the living creatures, animal and plant alike. This is the message which permeates the book and sets its tone.

Laurel's Kitchen recognizes that food is the basis of nurturing and that nurturing is the process by which all things develop. It also addresses the science of food and nutrition and its role in preventing illness and maintaining health. That it so beautifully combines these often competing philosophies is one of the major strengths of the book.

I feel very fortunate that the authors asked me to review the material in this second edition, because I have consistently recommended *Laurel's Kitchen* to both professionals and non-professionals who are interested in nutrition.

I am often asked how I can recommend a book that completely ignores animals as a food source. After all, humans have consumed other animals for as long as we can trace the history of mankind. The truth is that millions of human beings have demonstrated that they can live long, healthy, productive, and spiritual lives without eating animal flesh. *Laurel's Kitchen* is based on such a philosophy and shows how simple it is to satisfy all the scientific precepts of nutrition with such a diet.

Laurel, Carol, and Brian live what they write. Because they believe it so deeply, they have produced a book that is at the same time accurate, informative, useful, and extremely loving. I want to thank them publicly for producing this important volume and for the friendship we shared during its final stages.

SHELDON MARGEN, M.D.

Professor of Public Health Nutrition
University of California, Berkeley

Table of Contents

A Handbook of Nutrition

Acknowledgments

The New Laurel's Kitchen shows the loving efforts of many, many friends who have wanted no thanks but that the book be as helpful as possible. Among them are readers who have written such thoughtful letters, good cooks willing to part with treasured recipes, testers unwilling to quit until the dishes turned out perfect, and friends who showed up at all hours to wash pots and pans. Doctors and health professionals, gardeners and scientists, secretaries and lab workers, all gave valued help when we needed it.

Special thanks go to George Briggs, Professor Emeritus of the University of California at Berkeley Department of Nutritional Sciences, who patiently shepherded us through the first *Laurel's Kitchen* and has continued to give us open access to his files of current literature on nutrition.

The nutrition section of this edition is deeply stamped with the influence and inspiration of Dr. Sheldon Margen, Professor of Public Health Nutrition at Berkeley's School of Public Health. We owe him a great deal, and hope that the joy of discussing matters scientific with him is reflected in what we offer here.

From Laurel

Through my window I can see the rambunctious excitement of the neighborhood preteens gathering to go off to the county fair. They formed a club a year or so ago, Friends of Wildlife (FOWL), when they found out that local sea lions were dying from a lung disease. FOWL raised money to help a group of volunteer veterinarians provide medical assistance, and the kids had the satisfaction of being invited to watch the last of the cured sea lions slide joyfully back into the sea. This year they have washed cars to finance their own booth at the fair: Save the Elephants. Their enthusiasm has attracted support from top people in the field around the world.

There is a saying in India that elephants think they are small because they have tiny eyes. Facing the threats to health and relationships today, we too may feel small. But seeing doors open for those children has been a real lesson. If school children can accomplish so much, how can we grownups say, "What can *I* do?"

This book has taught us a similar lesson, for it has shown us that we are not alone. Ever since we shipped out the first handbound copies some ten years ago, *Laurel's Kitchen* has continued to bring us new friends. Many of you have written us in beautiful letters that our book has made happy changes possible for you and your families, that it's provided the inspiration to keep the ball rolling. Well, *you* have helped and inspired *us* with your brave stories. There are a million of you all over the country and in many unexpected places around the world, valiantly struggling against junk food and junk living. It's a sort of secret society, whose strength is growing.

In trying to bring together good taste, good sense, and good science, *Laurel's Kitchen* was something of a pioneering effort. When we first wrote it, there were few popular books on vegetarian cooking and none with complete, reliable information on nutrition. Now vegetarian and whole foods cookery has become trendy, even gourmet, and nutrition handbooks head the best-seller lists. But we still think there's nothing like *Laurel's Kitchen*.

So what's different about *The New Laurel's Kitchen*? We try to put it all together: the satisfaction of good food, the importance of how it's prepared, the health of those who eat it and of the world they live in. Our recipes represent home-cooking at its best—the kind you want to do for people you care for, cooking that's tasty and healthful to eat and fulfilling to offer. We've improved old favorites and created dozens of great new dishes, and made a special effort to lower the fat while actually enhancing the taste.

Much has happened in the world of nutrition over the last ten years, and we're pleased to see that the way of eating we present here fits perfectly the recommendations of the American Heart Association, the American Cancer Society, and many other experts and scientific bodies around the world. With our nutrition section completely rewritten, you have a fresh, clear, workable guide to eating for health without hassle.

Finally, for all of us who love her writing, Carol has beautifully picked up her "Keeper of the Keys" theme in "The Work at Hand," taking on the challenges of the times with practicality, hope, and candor.

The book in your hands is a fresh interpretation of values that have always sustained life. If you're familiar with the first edition, you will see how much has changed—everything, in fact, except our goals and convictions. Writing this volume has renewed our belief that what is good for the planet, the creatures, and each one of us is the same, and that if we do our best to act in harmony with this unity, we can live long, healthy, happy lives, leaving the world a little greener for our having been here. What more can anyone ask?

Recently a friend reminded me that a century ago, slavery as an institution was wiped out all over the world in not much more than ten years. Perhaps, before long, we can help make the beginning of a gentler, more loving world too. Anyhow, let's start here, together, now.

LAUREL ROBERTSON

*For our teacher, Eknath Easwaran, who understood
the appeal in the eyes of a glossy black calf on its way
to the slaughterhouse many years ago and inspired us,
and thousands of others like us, to give the gift of life.*

The Work at Hand

The Work at Hand

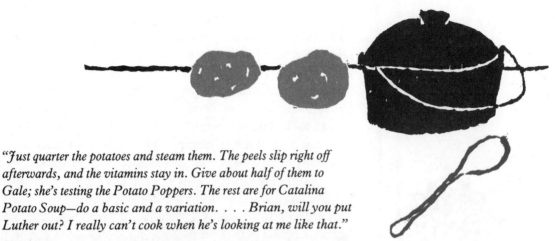

"Just quarter the potatoes and steam them. The peels slip right off afterwards, and the vitamins stay in. Give about half of them to Gale; she's testing the Potato Poppers. The rest are for Catalina Potato Soup—do a basic and a variation. . . . Brian, will you put Luther out? I really can't cook when he's looking at me like that."

The place is hopping. In the final crunch to check and double-check these recipes, every able-bodied cook we know has been drawn in. Two loaves of bread and a casserole just slid into the oven, and billows of ruby-red and green Swiss chard fill the sink. Someone's son has chosen this time to negotiate a late afternoon snack. Peanut-buttered toast? Too close to dinner. He settles for a carrot.

The spacious kitchen where we've gathered this afternoon is a far cry from the sunny cubby at the back of a dark Berkeley flat where Laurel and I first met. Long gone is the ancient gas range where she taught me to bake, and there's nothing quaint about the stainless steel, glass-fronted convection oven that replaced it. But a black crotchet of a cat still gazes balefully upward from the warm spot underneath—watch your ankles!

No Berkeley brownshingle this, and there isn't a sweet potato plant in sight. Soft green sunlight diffuses into the room from a walk-in kitchen greenhouse where eggplants, bell peppers, herbs, and trellised tomatoes grow. The sharp fragrance of basil and parsley permeates the kitchen; a fistful of each just went into the blender for Green Goddess dressing.

Overhead is a skylight and bare redwood beams; rose-pink quarry tiles are underfoot. At eye level are racks for everything that could possibly hang. No background music, just snatches of conversation and the rhythmic thunkety-thunk of knives on chopping boards. The crowded, bustly scene recalls a Thanksgiving dinner with all the aunts and sisters-in-law pitching in, except that you can almost feel everybody concentrating. We care mightily about this book, every one of us, and we want to get it right.

Laurel herself is working in a quieter corner of the Victorian farmhouse our families share. Her studio is a tiny room full of potted ferns and spider plants—foliage is supposed to detoxify the atmosphere around a VDT, you know. (Is there no end to what leafy greens can do?) But the terminal is covered and off to one side this afternoon, because she's started the new woodcuts. As you look about— the teal-blue paper lining the bookshelves, the perfect sand-dollar mounted like a jewel on black velvet, Laurel's purple kimonolike jacket lined with turquoise, worn over a silver gray turtleneck—it's clear that a natural, easy artistry governs just about everything she does.

(The door to *my* study I think we'll keep closed for now. Inspired by Laurel's example, hoping somehow to rescue my own working conditions, I have purchased several large sheets of rose-colored construction paper to line the bookshelves. The paper is probably on my desk somewhere, but to get to them I would have to dig through piles of clipped magazine articles, my son's art work, and drafts of upcoming columns. Maybe if you came back next week . . .)

"It's from Moosewood. I cut the butter in half and used yogurt instead of sour cream and cottage cheese instead of cream cheese and sunflower seeds instead of cashews. Do you like it? . . . Oh. Well, I guess even Molly Katzen doesn't get it right every time. . . ."

When I think about introducing the new *Laurel's Kitchen,* my mind keeps circling about one motif, a single bright thread that weaves its way through everything that seems to need saying. M. F. K. Fisher touched it deftly in a sketch she once wrote of the venerable Gare de Lyon, a train station built in Paris to celebrate the 1900 World's Fair. Sitting in a café there, waiting for her family to arrive, she suddenly realized that she "was not in a station, but in a place."

A *place*, she explains, invites you to come well before your departure, and to linger on after your arrival. Beauty is one element, of course; comfort is another. At the Gare, the food is splendid, your needs are met attentively and kindly, and a feeling of history is evoked which is personal as well as public, for you have come here many times over the years. "It comes down, I suppose, to a question of where one really chooses to be, and for how long."

"Well, yes," I thought, reflecting upon my own experience. As you stay someplace over time, because you *choose* to be there, you become part of that place, and it becomes part of you. You start to take responsibility for it. In Mrs. Fisher's case, you are distraught that the upstairs dining room, immense and lovely, has suffered deplorable neglect. You begin talking to people—by chance, the right people—and finally your beloved place is designated a national monument. The long lace curtains are cleaned and mended, the ceiling is repaired, the floor is strengthened; forty gorgeous *fin de siècle* murals emerge from sooty obscurity. All *you* have really done is to see the place for what it is, and impart that vision to others by whatever means come naturally to you. Nothing more, really, than what Ansel Adams did for Yosemite—or, for that matter, Woody Allen for New York.

Our good friend Alan Gussow, painter, sculptor, and writer, captured this in the title of his handsome book, *A Sense of Place*. Evoking that sense is the explicit objective of a good many artists and writers—Eudora Welty comes to mind; so do E. B. White, John McPhee, and many others. The impulse behind this kind of art seems often to be the yearning to *retrieve*: the feeling that something precious is about to be lost, if we don't recognize and save it.

My own slant on *place* is rural. Brought up on a farm, I respond immediately to the idea of committing yourself to a location and learning to live within its limitations—celebrating the foods that grow there and the beauties unique to the spot, forming relationships to the land, the animals, the people nearest you. But the sense of place is not relevant to farm and wilderness alone. My husband, Tim, remembers a particular bus in Berkeley

twenty years ago—the Dwight Way 76—that was truly a *place* in M. F. K. Fisher's sense. The driver had plied his route so long that he knew all his regular passengers by name and point of debarkation. He would stop in the middle of the block and honk his horn in front of elderly Mrs. Panofsky's house, then run up and walk her down the steps when she came tottering out. You felt at home as soon as you stepped on board, and the contentment you felt came right out of the driver's own.

When you walk into a workshop or studio, or the classroom of a dedicated teacher, you get the same magical feeling Mrs. Fisher describes. The key is that concentrated, conscientious work is done there regularly. In a *place*, something hangs in the air—a life, a spirit. You are held there not merely by comfort, but by interest and expectation: important things go on here. . . .

"Lynne, if we called Phil, do you think he could stop at Barindelli's farm on his way home? They've got kale and leeks and beets, but somebody needs to pick them up. . . Maybe he could pick Mark up at gymnastics too; he'll be finished at 4:30. Hey, why don't we have Recipe Test Potluck tonight? Just plan on having dinner here when the testing is done. Does anybody mind a kind of uncoordinated menu?"

The collection of friends who helped produce *Laurel's Kitchen* ten years ago has evolved into a strong network of kindred spirits whose lives touch at many points. We share a commitment to meditation which has enabled us to overcome inevitable differences in background and outlook and work together in increasing harmony. Our personal lives have gradually opened out and merged in a complex weave of bonds and reciprocities: the daughter of one marries the brother of another; an elderly parent is ill, and a friend takes your children while you go help. Sourdough starter, children's clothes, and power tools get passed around as they used to be in an old-fashioned extended family. Seeing little Nicholas in Chris's old denim jacket, you think for a minute he's yours—and that's probably as it should be.

Beyond this immediate circle of close friends, though, we feel closely connected with a much larger circle of families and individuals too—some that we know personally, others who have written to us over the years—who cherish values and ideas very much like ours, and who are working out their own ways of

living them out. They are married or single, elderly or young; they live alone or with friends or family, some in convents, some in condominiums. They run inner-city relief centers or tofu shops, farmsteads or farmer's markets; they work as carpenters, cooks, and computer programmers; students, lawyers, and storekeepers. You can find them in hospitals, libraries, auto repair shops, and plywood mills. Each in their own way, they too are testing and experimenting with these new–old values—creating around them, almost inevitably, a stronger, deeper sense of *place*.

"Diane, that's Phil on the phone. He's got the kale, but he can't find Mark. You think he went home with David? . . . Well, what's their number? . . . Ummm, no. I don't think we'd better ask him to get the mushrooms now. . . ."

The bread is just coming out of the oven, and the children are filling their plates: a little this, a little that, potluck style. The dining room is full, and we're spilling out into the living room—longtime friends, glad of each other's company. There is a feeling of calm, and warmth, and something more: the meals we share are sacraments, nothing less.

When *Laurel's Kitchen* first came out, in 1976, vegetarianism was still a vexing issue. Today, I don't think it is. The more fundamental question now is not so much "meat or no meat?" but "kitchen or no kitchen?" Indeed: "Place, or no place?"

The pressures of normal everyday life in the eighties push us toward a great deal of mobility and an extremely fast pace—a basically competitive outlook, and an unprecedentedly high level of getting and spending. And nowhere do those pressures converge more ferociously than on the kitchen and how we feel about being there. Everybody likes long-simmered soups and good whole-grain breads, but who in the world is going to provide them?

The obstacles are many. First, there is tremendous economic stress. The most affluent society in the world is not what it used to be. Real-dollar income in the middle class rose steadily between

1949 and 1973, but since then neither wages nor family incomes have grown in real terms, and for families with children real income has actually declined. Real income per family member has declined in most cases too, even though families are having fewer children and mothers are increasingly moving into the work force. People are having a much harder time purchasing homes, educating their children, and saving for the future—as you may have noticed.

Housing costs are an illuminating index. In 1949, a thirty-year-old worker could buy a median-priced home for about 14 percent of his gross monthly pay. In 1985, because of the higher cost of construction, high interest rates, and stagnant wages, the burden was 44 percent.

Small wonder that full-time jobs plus overtime have claimed so many of us. Small wonder we lurch in the door at 6 p.m.—later, if we stopped for groceries or cleaning—worn down by a full day's work and stupefied by commuter traffic. Miriam Burros, food editor for the *New York Times*, recorded a conversation last year with a friend who works for the Good Housekeeping Institute. "We used to feature a thirty-minute dish," said she. "Now it's a thirty-minute *menu*, and people keep writing to ask, 'Could you get it down to twenty minutes?'" Valiantly Mrs. Burros complied, with a suggested menu that was actually appetizing. But you could see she was rattled.

Subtler pressures are just as potent as economic ones. Someone asks you at a party what you "do." You tell them as vivaciously as you can that you run a household, and they simply don't know what to say next. From every quarter the message comes: housework is essentially demeaning, unmanly if you're a man, exploitive if you're a woman or child. (*Unless* you're running a trendy boulangerie or café or catering service. If you can make the car payments off those long-simmered soups and crusty French breads, you're an *entrepreneur*, and that gets you the blessing and admiration of everyone you meet.)

Finally, for those last holdouts who wonder how on earth their family is going to eat if no one's home to cook, there are the clamorous voices of our willing helpers: the producers of frozen dinners and delicatessen take-out salads, the purveyors of precut vegetables, ready-to-bake dinner rolls, and fried this and that to go. Their enormous advertising budgets (which we consumers pay for, don't forget) keep their products highly visible

and even alluring—so alluring, because of their convenience, that certain other considerations get overlooked.

A telephone survey in 1985 explored the growing takeout food market. Some 85 percent of the respondents said they engaged in some sort of physical activity because fitness was very important. But when asked about factors that influenced their purchase of carry-out foods, only 17 percent said they avoided such foods because of concerns about health, though typically such products are outrageously high in fat, salt, sugar, and preservatives.

Over the past ten years, the study of nutrition has burgeoned. Findings converge with amazing and well-publicized consistency. The diet which makes for a strong cardiovascular system is also the diet that protects against cancer, diabetes, diverticular disease, plain old obesity, tooth decay, osteoporosis, "tired nerves," the whole kaboodle. (Or should I say not "diet" but "regimen," because regular vigorous exercise now is almost a nutrient itself.) Whole cereal grains at the center, lots of fresh vegetables and fruits, legumes and low-fat dairy products if they suit you: eat a wide variety, eat seasonally, keep fat to a minimum, and you're there. Food for this diet, moreover, is what our planet is best equipped to provide: enough for all of us, and in full harmony with the environment. That it can be enjoyed without harm to animals, birds, or fish makes it almost too good to be true.

The one flaw with this otherwise perfect diet is that it runs headlong up against life as we would otherwise have it: food like this takes considerably more than twenty minutes a day to prepare. More even than thirty! Bean soups, whole-grain breads, appealing low-fat salads, fresh vegetables delicately cooked, and intriguing brown rice casseroles don't just happen. They take time. And so does the subtler side: the creation of a peaceful, loving setting, vital if those exemplary meals are actually going to be eaten and enjoyed.

Exactly how much time this has to take is of course an open question. It doesn't actually *have* to take *any*. Several years ago, for instance, I interviewed Dave Scott when he was reigning champion of the Ironman Triathalon. Six to eight hours a day of appallingly rigorous training put Dave's daily caloric intake into the five thousand range. He is a vegetarian who eats lots of brown rice and ungreased pasta—bananas, apples, veggies—and to get those calories on such a high-bulk diet, he had to be eating just about all the time he wasn't running, swimming, or cycling. Eating was in effect his fourth major event. Cooking, I imagined, must have been a fifth.

Wrong. At some point in our chat, Dave mentioned that he takes in quite a bit of tofu. I got right on the trail, hoping to make a Stop Press with "Ironman Tofu Delight." Breathlessly, I posed my question:

"And *how* do you eat your tofu, Dave?"

"Well, actually"—he giggled a little wildly—"I just spoon it up right out of the plastic tub."

For me and thee, though—for mine and thine—the story is probably a little different. If the meals are nutritious but not delicious, you can bet they'll be amply supplemented at the first available vending machine. To make your food both, you—or *some*body—has to put in some time.

This year, as we pummeled our recipe collection into compliance with current health guidelines, we concluded—with mixed feelings, you can be sure!—that once you have pulled back on fat, salt, and sugar, the one ingredient you can add to heighten appeal enormously is not fresh basil or lemon zest, though they both help, but time.

Some cooks can pare it to a minimum. Sultana, for instance, reared in village Greece, moves with unerring swiftness. Leans forward with the weight on the balls of her feet, and cooks *hard*. Julie, on the other hand, still doesn't feel entirely secure as a cook. She hesitates, she ponders the eggplant, she thinks a lot about whether she's chosen the right recipe. She takes probably twice the time Sultana does. Yet both cooks can turn out delicious meals—and even Sultana takes more than twenty minutes!

Then there's Alan Scott, who twice weekly takes time away from his blacksmithing to fire up his home-built backyard bread oven at dawn and then move food in and out of it all day: sourdough bread first, then baked potatoes and moussaka as it cools; then a rice pudding and baked pears, and finally, when the oven is lukewarm, yogurt. Meanwhile he's painting the back bedroom and riding herd on four-year-old Nicholas. How long does he spend on dinner? "Who's counting?" he grins wanly.

Any way you cut it, preparing a balanced and truly appetizing meal with unprocessed foods will take a chunk out of your day. If you're trying for healthful breakfasts and bag lunches too, the plot only thickens.

So there we are. Impasse. Collision. Gridlock, to use the dominant metaphor for our age. Life in the eighties really *does* militate against home-cooked wholesome meals —just as it does against friendships, marriage, parenting, and almost everything else that makes life worth living. It has to be like that, because the spirit of our time is to look only at the profit line.

It's good to clear the air on this point, and recognize that if you choose to live a different kind of life, it will take some doing. Think of yourself, then, as a pioneer. Celebrate the small, solid gains you *can* make, and don't dwell on the ones you can't make yet. And take heart from knowing that you are not alone.

No one can tell you how to fit those seemingly nonexistent hours into your own life, for the simple reason that it's your life. But I *can* tell you about some of the individuals I know who have managed to give priority to the kitchen, for whatever reasons and by whatever means, and about what has come of their choice.

Tragically, the turning point often comes when health—our own or that of someone we love—is threatened. Suddenly the games food advertisers play are no longer amusing. You find yourself angry now, seeing the damage they have done. Your priorities shift abruptly. And when you see that what you do in the kitchen might make the critical difference for someone you love, many of the subtler forms of resistance ("I'm being exploited," "This is tedious," or "But I cooked *last* night") lose their force. Life, we realize, is very short.

The change can be less dramatic and more positive. A baby comes. You nurse him or her, because there's no question today that it's the best possible start you could give your child. At first, all the sitting still and rocking might send you into paroxysms of restlessness. but then something in you gives way, relaxes, and your very reckoning of time alters. The present moment takes on an amazing luminosity. When the date you'd set to go back to work arrives, you may well let it pass. All that can wait; more is going on here than you'd anticipâtéd. And as you begin to give your child solid foods, you balk at anything but the purest and most wholesome. After all, that's what you've been giving up to now! You buy your first natural foods cookbook, and you're on your way. Short on money, maybe, and a little apprehensive, but quite certain, deep inside, that you're on the right track.

Whatever the actual turning point, something stops you and turns your attention inward—puts you in touch with your deepest beliefs and desires, so that for a time, the contrary and conventional messages from outside can't penetrate. With this inward shift there come, inevitably, ideas on *how* to change, too.

"So I take the cucumber, and I cut off the two ends. . . . I place the stem-end piece on the bottom and the bottom piece at the stem end, and I rub them together until I can see a milky substance. Then I set it aside, and gradually the bitter taste concentrated at one end goes? Hey, Laurel, do you believe *this?"*

During a recent interview, Laurel was asked, "One of the main things that I got out of both your books is how valuable the work in the kitchen is. How do you find the time to do everything ideally?"

Laurel's response was simple but telling: "We all have important other things we want to work on. When you come into the kitchen, the thing to remember is that you're going to be there for a certain time. Drop everything else and concentrate on doing the very best you can."

It sounds simple, but what she's really talking about is a take-a-deep-breath-and-swallow-hard act of acceptance. An opening of yourself to the work before you, and an agreement with yourself not to be obsessed with looking for shortcuts—not to hurry, or to let awareness of other responsibilities get you tense or even resentful.

It comes with practice.

Of all the things we said in *Laurel's Kitchen*, I don't think any subject brought more appreciative response than the section on working with one-pointed attention— sanctifying ordinary work by the state of mind you bring to it. Any work you do for a selfless purpose, without thought of profit, is actually a form of prayer, which unifies our fragmented energy and attention and calms the mind. In the words of a monk of the seventeenth century, Brother Lawrence:

> "The time of business does not with me differ from the time of prayer, and in the noise and clatter of my kitchen, while several persons are at the same time calling for different things, I possess God in as great tranquillity as if I were upon my knees at the blessed sacrament."

The approach may be catching on. Only last week I read of one homemaker's discovery that eggs are cooked to perfection after three Hail Mary's. "I use the boiling time," she adds, "to place myself in touch with earlier generations of cooks who measured their recipes with litanies, using time to get *beyond* time."

We are so oppressed by time these days—by "hurry sickness" and all its side effects. At moments of deep concentration, though, we are lifted clear *out* of time, and for a few minutes the stress of the day slips away. This may be why a very absorbing activity— chess, or fine needlework, or writing poetry—can leave us refreshed. Kitchen work, when it is undertaken in the spirit of Brother Lawrence, can heal and restore us in exactly the same way.

"I don't know, really, what changed," reflects my longtime friend Beth Ann. "I just know that one evening I walked in there grim as usual, determined to get it over with, and instead I found myself relaxing—accepting that I was there and willing to do it as well as I possibly could. And ever since then, it's been completely different."

"You know, partly I think it's the food itself. If you watch, so much beauty passes through your hands—of form, and color, and texture. And *energy* too."Abruptly her hands flew up into the air as if an electric current were passing between them. "Each grain of rice, each leaf of kale, charged with life and the power to nourish. It's heady, feeling yourself a kind of conduit for the life force!"

To be sure, everyday cooking ends up feeling more prosaic than this. Yet I suspect that what Beth Ann was groping to say has to do with an ancient, almost wordless truth. Long before institutionalized religions came along—and temples, and churches—there was an unquestioned recognition that what goes on in the kitchen is *holy*. Cooking involves an enormously rich coming-together of the fruits of the earth with the inventive genius of the human being. So many mysterious transformations are involved— small miracles like the churning of butter from cream, or the fermentation of bread dough. In times past there was no question but that higher powers were at work in such goings-on, and a feeling of reverence sprang up in response. I wonder sometimes whether the restorative effects of cooking and gardening arise out of similar—though quite unconscious—responses.

Gary Snyder has written compellingly about the importance of setting down deep roots wherever you live and forming a real relationship to the land itself. In his own way, he makes the same point M. F. K. Fisher does when he urges us to "find the holy places" where we live—the spring or grove or crest of a hill where you know that others have lingered before you and steeped themselves, like you, in its special stillness.

Perhaps, though, the real point is not so much to *find* the holy places as to *make* them. Do we not hallow places by our very commitment to them? When we turn our home into a place that nourishes and heals and contents, we are meeting directly all the hungers that a consumer society exacerbates but never satisfies. This is an enormously far-reaching achievement, because that home then becomes a genuine counterforce to the corporate powers-that-be, asserting the priority of a very different kind of power.

We balk at the "more than twenty minutes" clause. Yet it may well be that the time it takes to prepare good, wholesome food is as healthful and healing—for everyone concerned—as the food itself, for the simple reason that it requires us to "light down" for the duration. At first we may feel restless, wanting the quick fix, the fastest route. We want to skip the pregnancy and head straight for the delivery room, as if the preceding nine months were dispensable! But there are no shortcuts. If we want a home that is "not a station but a place," we must *be* there.

Time was—and not long ago—if you wanted to live in such a way as to be warmly connected with other people, the world supported your efforts. Today that really is not true. If you want community in any form, or family, or home, you just about have to invent it. Your version will be unique with you. But the first and all-important step is to dig in where you are and "make a place." When I suggested that we think of ourselves as pioneers, I wasn't being quaint. We are on a frontier, surrounded by wilderness, and the job at hand is to make a clearing—to clear a space and determine that what goes on within that circle will be a prototype of the world as you would like it to be. The thrilling thing is to see those small circles begin to touch upon one another here and there, and overlap—sturdy outposts, ground for hope.

I've gotten to be hypersensitive in recent years to the borrowed ruralism that sometimes creeps in when exponents of a post-industrial society are holding forth. Images of an idealized long-ago farm life swim vaguely and deliciously in the background of so many natural foods treatises that you'd think nothing bad ever happened on those farms. As someone whose family *left* the farm in 1958 because there was simply no more supporting us there, I know better. To suggest subliminally that all our troubles would be over if we just went back to the land is dishonest.

Yet there are good reasons why those images are so appealing. In the ten years since we first wrote *Laurel's Kitchen*, it's become clear to me that behind my contribution to that book, there is a driving force I never even talked about: someone who wasn't a vegetarian at all, and baked bread as white as the driven snow, but whose achievement of *place* was matchless.

Even when I was in college, my favorite way to doze off every night was to mentally reconstruct that place: the small Willamette Valley farm where my grandparents lived when I was a child. More particularly, the part of the farm that was enclosed by a half-circle driveway that curved away from the road and then back to it, containing the house, the gardens, and, really, a small universe.

There were primrose beds bright as mosaics, and gleaming white chickens; a red-painted swing that often held six or eight grandchildren at once; a whitewashed arbor with benches, where purple and green Concord grapes grew; three huge maple trees so moss-cushioned you could sprawl all morning in the lower branches with apples and books; a vast vegetable garden, and fruit trees of every kind. Animals—Siamese cats and an obese dachshund, twin goats, a foul-tempered goose, and (briefly) an even fouler-tempered donkey.

It was a place of unceasing activity: of planting and plucking, of pickling and freezing, of jam boiling down on the stove while a cheesecloth bag full of curds hung from the kitchen faucet to drain. From underneath the wood stove, a scratchy, scruffling sound was our clue that chicks or goslings were hatching. Over all of this my father's mother presided, Keeper of the Keys without parallel.

Life there had its rituals, seasonal, weekly, daily. On the hottest summer afternoons, for instance, my grandmother would bring out as many galvanized tin washtubs as she happened to have grandchildren around and place them in a sociable group-ing in the shade of a blue spruce. The tubs would be filled from the hose, and a stripped-down one of us would hop into each.

Grandma would disappear briefly and return with a homemade popsicle apiece. One could hardly have asked for more.

Sunday dinners were, in a way, similarly patterned. The dining room table was leafed out to its full length and all the sons and daughters and grandchildren who could make it were fitted around, and every square inch of lace tablecloth was covered: platters high-piled with Parker House rolls, bowls of coleslaw and green beans, cut-glass dishes of jelly and jam and more. If Uncle Herb was observed to enjoy the watermelon pickles, or Aunt Gertrude the garbanzos, you could count on seeing watermelon pickles and garbanzos on the table for the next forty-five Sundays running. She aimed to please.

In my mind's eye, still courting sleep, I walk on through the dining room and into the little-used formal "front room." Sunlight streams in a south window and spills across a yellow patchwork quilt stretched out on a frame. One of these quilts is in the works for each granddaughter. Some are blocked out with embroidered birds or butterflies, one with appliquéd Mistress Marys. This is mine, and its design —I'm sorry, but it's true—is "Grandmother's Flower Garden." The background color is the same butter-yellow as my graduation dress, and it couldn't be more beautiful.

Swathed by now in such unutterable security that nothing on earth could keep me awake, I would think fleetingly about what a perfect symbol quilts are for all that goes into making a home: the rescue of tiny scraps, the eye for where they might fit into a larger pattern, the charm of the pattern itself. And the patience. Good Lord, the patience. . . .

Today my respect is even more acute. I realize now what went into building that whole small universe. I see, for instance, the real function of those ritual Sunday suppers: the effect of "facing off" again and again, recognizing ourselves to be part of a clan, and feeling some pride in that; knowing that the bonds that held you together one-to-one were also part of that larger structure, so you didn't take them lightly. (If you did, or even *looked* as if you did, you'd be disappeared into the back bedroom for a highly effective talking-to.)

Blithely we ate and drank and basked our way through it all, taking it quite for granted. Not to say we didn't work. If there were any basic skills you didn't pick up by osmosis, an active 4-H program made sure you had them before you were twelve, and you were certainly expected to use them. But that feeling of

stepping into a charmed circle, where so many small things whispered that you were deeply and unqualifiedly valued: that we did take for granted until much later, when life had taught us how rare such a situation really is. Full awareness, and an ocean of gratitude, have finally come.

What did my grandmother draw upon to work the way she did? *Everybody* worked hard then, terribly hard; but that doesn't account for the restrained merriment we glimpsed in the way she went about things, or for the extras. I could say, "Oh, well, it was love." But that doesn't quite get it either. We all "love," after all. I think there was something more, and naming it comes as something of a shock in our supposedly liberated world: my grandmother knew her worth. She knew the value of everything she did there in the house and around it—knew that it was endlessly significant.

How did she know? How could she tell that all that giving made a difference? It's not an idle question; millions of women feel it deeply.

Twenty-one years ago this spring, a senior in college, I was asked to organize a faculty–student conference on what was then a breathtakingly new issue: "The Role of Women." Today it sounds incredibly naive that such a theme—in the singular, for heaven's sake!—would have gone unchallenged. But there it was, the spring of '65. Throughout the intervening years, as graduate student, college instructor, wife, mother, and columnist, but all along as a member of a community based on spiritual values, I have continued to struggle with the questions we took up so hesitantly. Is there such a thing as "a woman's place"? And do we really live in "a man's world"?

Today, I would have to throw out both questions and any others that stress the differences between us and ignore the underlying unity. Men and women alike, at home or "in the world," we face a common enemy: materialism, infatuation with *things*, and the competitive ethic it creates.

In a materialist culture, everyone loses: not just women but men, children, the elderly, the handicapped, and every minority in the book. Wherever the accumulation of wealth is enshrined, the resources of a society will always flow into the hands of the unscrupulous. You can spend your life fighting for equality and justice for one group or another; but if the entire frame of reference is wrong, nobody is going to win.

Today, wherever the complex issues surrounding "woman's place" are discussed, I have begun to hear a new maxim. Instead of fighting for a bigger share of the cake, women are concurring, let us see whether we can't bake a better cake. *All* of us, men and women alike. Let's make a world that has a *place* for every one of us—and that must surely start within our homes.

Those of us who share this perspective and want to live it out must go ahead and do so, however long drawn-out the battle turns out to be. Mahatma Gandhi's word for someone who sought to right wrongs without violence was *satyagrahi*, a "truth-seizer"—someone who, when he or she discovers something true, holds on and follows it out no matter how out of pace it seems with "normal" everyday life. Truth here means the enormous value of what goes on in the home—and it's just when the rest of the world seems to be denying that truth that those of us who perceive it have to take a stand, beginning where we are.

Connected with this higher purpose, cooking can be a high-status occupation. So can raising your own food. So is the teaching of our children, our next generation. Ordinary schooling, yes, but that's just the beginning. Only through our own lives—the examples we set—can we impart the values we're basing our lives upon.

Over the past ten years, it has become clear within our own circle of friends that nurturant work is not only for mothers, not only for parents even; it is the birthright of every man, woman, and child. Without it, we never grow to our full stature. This is an easy truth to discover when you start living it out. The only reason it is obscured from view in today's world is that supporting life is not a value on which our culture is based.

A tremendous amount of work has to be done. Even if we start now, much of the benefit will be felt only by our children or grandchildren. But that's no reason not to do it. There are no universal answers to the hard questions that fall between life as it is today and what we would like it to be. But answers need not be universal. Different individuals will find different solutions, answering to their particular needs. What's important is that each of us start trying.

Have I exaggerated the potential value of the Inhabited Kitchen? I don't think so. Every long journey begins with a single step, and the first step may be nothing more ambitious than learning to make whole wheat bread.

"So what are *you* doing here?"

"Not much. What are *you* doing here?"

It's ten p.m. and I've come back to the kitchen, because as I was putting my son to bed I remembered the garbanzos, still in the slow-cooker waiting for me to turn them into a sandwich spread. True to form, Laurel has already noticed and mashed them herself. Since she's here too, weighing out flour for tomorrow's baking and seeing to the kind of loose ends she alone seems to notice, I will go ahead and sauté the onions and spices now.

The floor gleams shiny wet and rosy where Ed has mopped it. Picking our steps cautiously, we are left in a companionable silence, friends of such long standing that sentences can hang between us half finished and we can meander from one *non sequitur* to another.

Laurel has remembered Brian's birthday, and she's baking a batch of cookies in his honor. She keeps a calendar where she's recorded everyone's birthdate. Personally, I'm glad if I can remember my husband's—my darkest fear is that some year Laurel will remember it and I won't. This sort of thing could get to you if you let it. But at some point very early in our relationship I decided that I could either drive myself crazy with invidious comparisons, or just enjoy her. Things have gone nicely since I chose the latter path.

Actually, that is one of the benefits of living in the sort of extended family we do. You stop feeling you have to play every role to perfection, and just do what you're best at. With everybody doing that, most bases get covered. There's a certain efficiency to it.

Which is what we ended up talking about finally.

"How did your talk in Petaluma go?" she asked. I had sat in on an InterFaith Forum panel on world hunger that afternoon.

"Fine, I think. I learned some things, and people had good questions. There was one that I didn't answer very well, though. I've been thinking about it all evening. A woman said, 'You've obviously made big changes in your lives. But could you have done it without the support of others who were making the same kind of changes?' She didn't mean it made things easy, you know, just *possible*. She said she'd tried to make changes herself, and kept falling back because she didn't have any immediate support. Some of the other people in the audience agreed. There's a tremendous yearning for community, I think, but nobody knows how to go about getting it."

No response for a minute. Laurel is feeding Luther and telling him what a splendid little creature he is. His eyes are mean yellow slits and he is gloating at me. Surely a less likable animal has never set foot on earth.

"Well, yes. That's hard. And it's true. But I think all people can do is start where they are—begin with small things they can manage, and build on those."

"I know. You wish there were a blueprint, or a guidebook, but really there isn't. . . ."

"Community" and even "family" are terms as nebulous today as they are compelling. No one's in agreement about what they will look like when we achieve them, and most people you read seem to agree that they won't bear much resemblance to the patterns of the past.

Or will they? Many of the quilts my grandmother made were very formal: tiny, precise geometric shapes held together in traditional patterns like stars, roses, daisy chains, and so on. Just so, around her lace-topped dining room table sat husbands and wives, aunts and uncles, children and grandchildren, bound together in the traditional fashion . . .

But she ran up other quilts too, of a more haphazard sort: bigger patches of sturdier fabric sewn together in apparently random patterns. Those were to keep the cold out. Exquisite they weren't, but brightly colored and warm and full of history ("*There's* my corduroy jumper, and that's a piece of mother's wool skirt!"). And they endured. As we strive to establish some semblance of community and family in today's fragmented world, the effect may well be patchwork too: not a uniform, regular pattern but something bold and colorful, diverse, but stitched together strong enough to keep us warm against the cold.

Hard-pressed settlers all—but we're not alone out here on the prairie. Another family lives a mile or two up the road, earnest vegetarians who'd love to share potluck. There's an older gentleman in your food-buying co-op who looks lonely, a beleagured single parent whose child is in the same school as yours; and downtown there's a houseful of teenagers, trying to be family for one another. There are a thousand things we can do to encourage and support each other. Taken one by one, they all seem so small. But look again— see how they fit together. Imagine what could come of it.

Recipes & Menus

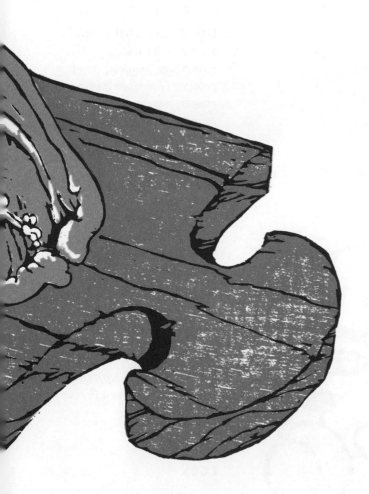

The New Laurel's Kitchen Food Guide

Every day

1 *Have 4 servings of whole-grain foods*
&
3 servings of vegetables
(including 1 of Super-Vegetables)

2 *Choose 1 serving of:*
    Super-Vegetables
    or Legumes
    or Dairy Foods

3 *Fill out your calorie needs with a variety of whole foods like these:*

The Food Families:

WHOLE GRAINS
Whole-grain bread (1 slice) or cooked grain—like rice— or noodles (1/2 cup)

SUPER-VEGETABLES
Dark leafy greens (3/4 cup cooked); edible-pod peas, brussels sprouts, broccoli, asparagus (1 cup); lima beans, peas (1/2 cup).

HIGH-CARBOHYDRATE VEGETABLES
Artichokes, potatoes, sweet potatoes (1 medium); beets, carrots, parsnips, winter squash, turnips (1 cup); corn (1 ear or 1/2 cup)

LOW-CALORIE VEGETABLES
A tomato; green beans, cabbage, cauliflower, leeks, cucumber, eggplant, okra, mushrooms, peppers (1 cup); lettuce (2 cups)

LEGUMES
Cooked dry beans, lentils, split peas (1/2 cup)

DAIRY FOODS
Milk or yogurt (1 cup); cheese (3 oz.); cottage cheese (1/2 cup)

NUTS & SEEDS

FRUIT

EGGS

Recipes & Menus

The recipes that follow are drawn from our own daily cooking —half a dozen families and many good friends. If you already eat along vegetarian, whole-foods lines, these dishes will fit easily into your repertoire, and should be especially helpful if you are trying for lower-fat meals. If whole-foods cookery is still new to you, the following pages will ease your period of transition. The food is delicious and varied—easy-to-eat home cooking.

On the facing page is an outline of our new Food Guide, which is explained at length in the chapter beginning on page 355. The Food Guide makes it easy to get all the nutrients you need for best health, no matter what your eating pattern is.

By choosing less-processed foods and avoiding meat, you have already escaped most of the witches' brew of chemical additives and the worst sort of fat as well. But many vegetarians are surprised to discover that they are still eating high-fat fare. Too much cheese, whole milk, oil, butter, nuts and nut butters, and rich desserts can raise anybody's diet up to or even beyond the national average: 40 percent of daily calories as fat, a level clearly linked with heart disease, cancer, and other serious health problems. Vegetarian or omnivore, unless you're unusually austere, eating less fat will probably mean better health and a longer life.

If you tote up your daily calories and find (as we did!) that you are eating more fat than you want to, the next question is where to cut. What does a 30-percent diet *look* like? How about a 25? *Is* it possible to eat this way without dreaming nightly of french fried onion rings?

Our answer is *yes!* We've developed some really satisfactory ways to make it work, and you will find relevant suggestions throughout the recipe section—not only recipes, but tips for giving zest to everyday foods without frying or slathering with butter. As with other reversals in life-style, especially if others in your household don't share your enthusiasm, it's usually a good idea to make changes slowly and artfully—but persevere. Here are some of the places that make the most difference:

⮞ Reduce or eliminate meat, processed foods, and fried foods. Whole grains, legumes, vegetables, and fruits are naturally very low in fat.

⮞ Choose lower-fat milk products, and substitute them for higher-fat ones in cooking.

⮞ When planning a meal, aim for balance: if you want to serve a rich dish, make the rest of the items on the menu especially low in fat. It isn't the dish that counts, but the whole meal, the whole day. (See menu suggestions, page 328.)

⮞ Instead of trying to use less of a problem food, sometimes out-and-out substitution is the most practical ploy. For some of us, using less Better-Butter on breakfast toast seemed a great deprivation (toast with a lot of butter gets 50 percent of its calories from fat; with only a little, 30 percent; with none, about 12). But switching to hot cereal with fruit and yogurt (less than 10 percent) was easy. What you spread on bread can really make the fat mount up, whether it is at breakfast or other times.

⮞ Sandwiches are another problem area: mayonnaise, cheese, and nut butters make a sandwich very rich indeed. Look for alternatives in our Lunch section, page 111.

⮞ Explore ways to flavor food without fat: parsley, lemon juice, exotic vinegars, citrus peel, yogurt, cottage cheese, shoyu, herbs, horseradish, spices. There are many suggestions in Sauces and Such, page 224.

⮞ Commercial salad dressings can be a mire of fat—and if not, of weird chemicals. Try our alternatives, pages 129–132.

Breakfast and lunch, of course, tend to be individual and varied. But when dinnertime rolls around, the responsibility for presenting a meal that is at once satisfying and healthful falls on the cook, who will rarely have time or inclination to add up how much fat is in each ingredient as the meal takes shape. How to do it? Here is a rule-of-thumb approach that has worked very well for us. It is rough, but over the long haul it keeps our dinners averaging less than 25 percent calories as fat without much extra fussing.

When planning a dinner meal, the cook allows 2 teaspoons of oil *or the equivalent* per person. (See the margin for "fat equivalents.") If you're serving four, you have 8 teaspoons to divvy up for sautéeing your onion, making salad dressing, and whatever else involves added fat. Any high-fat food like those in the margin should be measured as part of your fat allotment. In no time at all, you learn which combinations work and which are entirely outrageous: if you have muffins, for example, you don't put cheese on the broccoli. It works like that.

SHOPPING

Shopping for natural foods used to be a hurdle, but these days most supermarkets offer the basics, and natural food stores and food co-ops thrive everywhere. For saving money and meeting like-minded people, and for the freshest and best, no store can compare with a food-buying co-op; but if that isn't an option, or you haven't yet located a nearby source for freshly milled flour or other quality natural foods, write to the good people at Walnut Acres (Penn's Creek, PA 17862) for their superb catalog.

Vegetarians who prepare most of their food at home from unprocessed basics, and who avoid produce that has traveled very far, have relatively few worries about chemical additives, adulterants, and pollutants. If you do eat much out of packages, though, careful label-reading and keeping up on the safety of food additives is almost a survival skill. For keeping up to date,

1 tablespoon oil
  (= 3 teaspoons)
has as much fat as:

1 tablespoon butter,
  mayonnaise, or
  Better-Butter
2 tablespoons nut butter
3 tablespoons nuts
3 tablespoons sunflower seeds
3 tablespoons sesame seeds
⅓ cup sesame meal
⅓ cup grated cheddar
½ cup grated mozzarella
2 large eggs
¼ cup cream
1½ cups whole milk
3 cups low-fat milk
  ("2 percent" milk gets
  30 percent of its calories
  from fat)
½ cup dried shredded
  coconut
⅓ avocado

we recommend *The Nutrition Action Healthletter* (Center for Science in the Public Interest, 1501 16th St., NW, Washington, DC 20036).

What about "organics"? We think there are big changes coming in the next few years, as people become more and more concerned about what is being done to food. Everyone can help improve things by choosing better food, by insisting on better labeling laws and on regulations with teeth in them, and by buying from merchants with integrity who care about the quality and purity of the food they sell. One reason that we stress buying local produce is that the closer you are to the grower, the more you can learn about how the crops are grown. Home-grown is ideal, but few of us can grow all our food. Next best is to try to buy from people who grow food without pesticides, or from a co-op or sympatico storekeeper who buys from sources like these.

Integrity probably characterizes most of the organic food business—we immediately think of people like Paul and Betty Keene of Walnut Acres, Frank Ford of Arrowhead Mills, and the rice-growing Lundberg family. But sometimes you find carelessness too. When buying time comes, no one but you can decide how well-informed your storekeepers are, and how likely to be accurate in describing their products. There is so much misinformation about natural foods that you may find you actually know more than many storekeepers about the foods they sell.

≥●

The recipes on the following pages are not restaurant-style recipes, too rich for every day. They are delicious, healthful, satisfying home cooking from ordinary ingredients imaginatively prepared. These are the recipes we cook from regularly. We hope you will find them as useful as we do, both as they are and as springboards for your own creativity.

Bread

Breadmaking has held a special place in our lives for a long time, but it was when we took to vegetarian ways that the hearty brown stuff became the cornerstone of our diets—friendly and familiar as breakfast toast, sandwiches for lunch, after-school snack, and sometimes rolls or muffins at dinner. In some mysterious way it filled the gap that opened up when meat left the scene.

In the decade since *Laurel's Kitchen* first appeared, we've learned quite a lot about how to make our brown Staff of Life lighter and tastier. To tell the complete story would take a book—and did: *The Laurel's Kitchen Bread Book* (Random House, 1984) gives the full story on whole-grain breadmaking, ingredients, techniques, fancies, and all. Naturally, we recommend it with unreserved enthusiasm. In this chapter, we hope to tantalize you with some wonderful loaves; there is enough here to give you an excellent start as a breadmaker. Once you know how rewarding it is, there'll be no stopping you.

We have talked at length elsewhere about what a splendid food whole grains are. Good wheat bread may well be the whole grain *par excellence*. Where fiber is concerned, the fermentation of the dough in breadmaking softens rough bran without lessening its effectiveness. Fermentation also releases minerals that otherwise can be bound up in the grain by phytic acid. All the nutrients of the whole grain are present, of course, including the dozen or so that are not replaced in "enriched" white flour.

Fresh bread is so irresistible that it displaces a lot of less nourishing food, especially at snack time. Whole-grain bread is a good choice for dieters because it's low in calories but still nourishes, fills, and satisfies. (This is true even if you butter it, though as San Francisco gourmet Harvey Steiman opined while happily munching our homemade slices, "Bread that isn't good enough to eat without butter isn't worth eating.")

Besides the good food, though, something wonderful happens to your kitchen and your life when breadmaking becomes a regular activity. The fragrance and suspense of it, the sharing of its warm goodness at the end, the very fact that you care enough to take the time—all these remind us that home is a fine place to be. Though perhaps a small thing, breadmaking is one counter-

weight to the forces pulling family and friends away and apart. So it has been for us, and we hope you will find it so too.

𝒮

If you have children near at hand, let them take part in your baking days. It's a great way to spend time together, and no moppet is so small that he or she doesn't like to get fingers into dough, make a small shape to bake, and enjoy eating it, too. Bigger children can manage real jobs, beginning with greasing pans or measuring ingredients. Even before they were teenagers, some we know could handle a family baking all by themselves—a source of considerable pride.

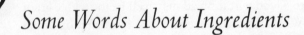

Some Words About Ingredients

Before we get into the recipes, there are a few things to know about the ingredients. If you are going to go to the trouble to make bread, you want to be sure that your efforts are supported by the quality of your flour and yeast. Even the most skillful baker can't get good bread from bad ingredients.

Flour

FRESHNESS   Unlike white flour, whole wheat flour is perishable and must be fresh to make good bread. If you buy packaged flour and can't decipher the "pull date" on it, ask your storekeeper. Don't try to make bread with whole-grain flour that has been on the shelf for more than two months. If you are in doubt, taste a pinch: there should be no bitterness. At home, store whole-grain flour in a cool place; if you are likely to have it around longer than a couple of weeks, keep it sealed airtight in the refrigerator. The day before you bake, take what you will need out of the refrigerator so it can come to room temperature before you use it.

To make a light, airy loaf, you have to have flour that is high in protein—specifically, gluten protein, because gluten is what makes a stretchy structure that lets your bread rise high. Only wheat, of all the grains, has enough gluten to make light yeasted bread; and good-quality whole wheat flour has plenty of it: you don't have to add refined flour to get a light loaf. When you shop, look for "bread flour" milled from *hard red spring wheat*, *hard red winter wheat*, or *hard white wheat*. Hard red spring wheat usually makes the highest loaves. If the bag doesn't have this information but does give a nutritional profile, the protein content should be 14 percent or more by weight. Whole wheat flours labeled "all purpose" or "pastry flour" are milled from low-protein wheat. They can make tender quick breads, muffins, and pancakes, but they do not have enough gluten protein to make light yeasted breads.

Stone-ground flour is often considered superior for breadmaking, and indeed we prefer it. The coarser grinds especially lend a delightful texture to the bread, and the rough fiber is ideal for digestive health. But if you want a *really* light loaf, very finely ground flour will help you achieve it. In past years, stone grinding was preferable because faster methods of grinding produced enough heat to degrade the flour. Nowadays, careful millers air-cool both stone mills and hammer mills so that nutrients and baking quality are protected, and you can choose the grind that will suit your recipe best.

Home mills offer many advantages, especially to people who do not have a reliable source of high-quality flour near at hand. Since all whole grains properly stored will keep perfectly fresh until they are ground, having a home mill means that you can store wheat, corn, rye, and buckwheat until you need them, then grind them to order. There is a big difference in baking performance and flavor when the flour is very fresh, no matter what you are baking.

Salt

Salt strengthens the gluten and regulates the growth of the yeast, helping to make a light, even-textured loaf. If you want to cut back, we suggest first reducing the salt in whatever you put *on* the bread rather than *in* it.

If you do want to make bread without salt, though, here are some tips: Don't omit the sweetener. Expect a much faster rise. Keep the dough a little stiff, and be sure to knead very well to compensate for the strength the salt would give the gluten. Put the bread in the oven a little early to ensure an even texture. Saltless loaves may not rise so high, but that's all to the good because denser bread has more flavor.

Sweeteners

We usually call for honey, but nearly any non-artificial sweetener will please the yeast and sweeten your loaf. Yeast, by the way, *can* make its own food from natural sugars and starch in the flour, so unsweetened loaves rise perfectly well.

Oil or Butter

Oil or butter will make your loaves tender and help them stay soft longer. If you add what bakers call a "conditioning amount"— 2 tablespoons oil *or* 1 tablespoon butter *per loaf*—the bread will rise higher for it. On the other hand, if you leave it out, few people will notice any difference. (Everyone will notice if the oil or butter was rancid, however; the bread will be horrid.)

Add oil along with the other liquids. To reap the full benefit of butter, though, add it soft *but not melted*, about halfway through the kneading time.

Grains Other than Wheat

As we mentioned earlier, wheat is the only grain that contains substantial amounts of the proteins that make gluten, the stretchy substance that lets your yeasted breads rise high. For quick breads, especially muffins, gluten is not essential, and other flours work well. (If no wheat flour is used, eggs help to keep the bread from being crumbly.)

Corn makes delicious quick bread and muffins. (See page 81.) In yeasted bread, we have best success using as much as a cup of polenta (coarsely ground cornmeal), softened first in a cup of boiling water and allowed to stand until cool. Knead into two loaves' worth of dough after the gluten is developed. (More about corn and its ways on page 286.)

Buckwheat, millet, rice, oats, and barley, added as whole cooked grains, lend interesting texture to yeasted breads and help keep the loaf moist and fresh. (See page 73.) Flours ground from these grains make heavy yeasted breads, but they shine in other places: buckwheat flour and oats make super pancakes, for example (see page 95).

Rye flour has a little gluten, and a rye-wheat mix from the field was probably the rule rather than the exception in most leavened breads until the last century—hence the magnificent traditional rye breads of Eastern and Northern Europe. Rye is harder to work with than wheat, but a little bit added to wheat flour can make a satisfyingly hearty loaf even for the beginning baker. (If you want people to think "rye," add caraway seeds.) (See page 71.)

Bean flours can be included in small quantities to increase the nutritional value of yeasted and quick breads alike, but they do not improve the flavor or texture. (More on page 72.)

Yeast

We call for *active dry yeast* because it is readily available and reliable, but if you like to use moist (or cake) yeast, that's fine too—use a ½-ounce cake wherever we call for ¼ ounce of active dry.

If you buy yeast in bulk, ¼ ounce of active dry yeast is now just 2 teaspoons, though a few years ago it was a full tablespoon. The leavening power, however, is about the same. Not all active dry yeasts are alike; it's worth shopping around for one that works best for you. The "fast-acting" yeasts, for example, have a special talent: they tolerate higher temperatures, which gives a faster rise. But if you aren't in such a hurry, lower-temperature rising, which is slower, gives superior flavor, nutrition, and keeping quality to your loaves.

In fact, the time your dough takes to rise is up to you, and depends entirely on how much yeast you use and how warm you keep the dough. The chart on the next page shows how you can arrange your rising times to make bread that accommodates your schedule.

Whatever kind of yeast you use, be sure it is fresh. If it isn't, it can't raise your bread. To check its leavening power, stir the yeast into the proper temperature water. For active dry yeast, follow directions on the package; if there is no recommendation, use water at 110°F. For moist yeast, about 80°F is good. Be sure that the yeast is completely dissolved; then stir in ¼ teaspoon honey or a tablespoon of flour. If the yeast hasn't foamed to the top within about ten minutes, it has lost its leavening power and you should throw it out. If you bake regularly and have a reliable source for your yeast, you won't need to test it every time.

STORAGE Store yeast airtight in the refrigerator. Active dry yeast in packets should be good until the date on the package. (Since air, light, and moisture damage yeast, bulk yeast is sometimes not such a bargain, depending on how it has been handled by the storekeeper.) Moist yeast is very perishable and will keep only about a week, even refrigerated. If you freeze it in foil-wrapped, baking-sized packets, it will be good much longer.

RISING TIMES FOR TWO LOAVES

Yeast	Rising temperature	First rise	Second rise	Shaping and proof	Time (plus bake)	Bread characteristics
4 teaspoons	90°F	1 hour	½ hour	½ hour	2½ hours	very light bland flavor poor keeper
2 teaspoons	80°F	1½–2 hours	1 hour	1 hour	4 hours	light good flavor moderate keeper
2 teaspoons	70°F	3–4 hours	1½–2 hours	1 hour	6–7 hours	excellent flavor very good keeper

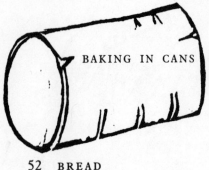

BAKING IN CANS We used to like to bake our bread in the big juice cans—they have many advantages over loaf pans. But a couple of years ago (science marches on) someone discovered that cans with seams down the sides sometimes leach lead solder into food stored in them. To be on the safe side, at least until unleaded cans are available, we recommend switching to regular pans, as we have ruefully done.

52   BREAD

Making Whole-Grain Bread

The method we present here is slightly different from what you might have encountered in other books (except our *Bread Book*). So far as we have been able to tell, written recipes for bread—even the ones for whole wheat bread—are based on the way *white* flour acts. But using whole wheat in a white-flour manner often doesn't work, and that has unfairly given whole wheat a bad name. White flour is not only milled to remove the bran and wheat germ, but blended and chemically treated to make it utterly uniform from bag to bag. Whole wheat flour can't be blended and standardized, so each batch has its own personality.

Our method is based on a traditional one developed long before white flour came along. It accommodates whole wheat flour's variability and makes the most of its great goodness. Beyond drawing on tradition, we have benefited a good deal from the knowledge and experience of professional bakers and bread scientists, who have helped make the whole process more understandable and controllable—especially in timing the risings and making the bread come out the way you want.

If you are a beginner, you will find the kneading easier if you make only one loaf. Divide the ingredients *and the kneading time* in half. Keep all the rest the same.

Some kind of a bowl, a pan, and a reasonable oven are all you really need by way of equipment. But because modern active dry yeast works best if it is dissolved in plain water at its favorite temperature, we suggest adding a thermometer to your supplies. A "chef's thermometer," with a steel spike and a dial that registers from 0° to 212°F, is the best.

GREASE: If you want to avoid using solid shortening, make super-grease: 1 cup oil blended with ½ cup lecithin. Great anywhere you need to grease; use just a thin layer.

Recipes for quick breads and muffins begin on page 79

Recipes for quick breads and muffins begin on page 79

USEFUL EQUIPMENT

*non-metal cup for
    dissolving yeast*
thermometer
*mixing bowl
    (about 4 quarts)*
small mixing bowl
measuring cups, spoons
rubber spatula
dough cutter or spatula
*comfortable kneading
    surface*
rolling pin (optional)
2 greased loaf pans, 8″ × 4″

Basic Bread Recipe

*2 teaspoons active dry yeast
(1 packet, ¼ oz, or 7 g)*
*½ cup warm water (about
110°F)*
*6 cups whole wheat
bread flour (2 pounds)*
2½ teaspoons salt

*2¼ cups lukewarm water
(2 tablespoons honey
or other sweetener)*
(2 tablespoons oil or butter)

Warm your yeast-dissolving cup by rinsing it with warm tap water; then measure the ½ cup warm water into it. If there are directions on the yeast package, follow them; otherwise, the water should be 110°F, which feels just-warm to your fingers. Sprinkle yeast into water while stirring with spoon, being sure each granule is individually wetted. Be sure the yeast is completely dissolved.

To get the best from your yeast, be sure the dissolving water has no salt or sweetener in it and that the temperature is right. If you need to test the yeast for liveliness, refer to page 52 for instructions.

Stir the flour in its container and measure 6 cups into your large bowl. (Freshly ground flour will be fluffier, so tap it down in the cup.)

Measure salt and stir it into the flour, making a well in the center. Mix oil and honey, if used, into the 2¼ cups water and pour it and the yeast mixture into the well you have made in the flour. Stir the liquid mixture into the flour, beginning in the center and working outward so that you first make a smooth batter, then gradually mix in the rest of the flour to make a soft dough. Squeeze with your wet fingers to make sure the dough is evenly mixed; it will be sticky.

Adjusting the Consistency

Now is the time to adjust the consistency of the dough. Because whole wheat flour varies in the amount of liquid it will absorb, the dough may be too soft or too stiff to make perfect loaves, and learning to adjust the dough at this stage makes all the difference.

Pick up the dough and squeeze it. Feel deep into the dough, not just on the surface. Just-mixed dough is sure to be sticky and wet, but is it soft or is it stiff? Does it resist your touch? Do you feel a strain in the muscles of your fingers? Then it is too stiff. Soft dough makes lighter loaves; but it can be too soft: it has to have enough flour to hold its shape. Does it feel waterlogged, sort of runny, as if the flour wasn't contributing much substance to it? Then it is too soft.

If the dough is too soft or too stiff, put it back into the bowl and flatten it out. If it is too soft, dust with ¼ cup more flour; if too stiff, sprinkle with 2 tablespoons more water. Fold the dough over, mix it again, and re-evaluate, adjusting until it does seem right. Even perfect dough will seem sticky at this stage, so don't try for a firm, clay-like touch or you'll end up with a brick.

Kneading

Kneading makes the dough resilient and stretchy so that the loaves can rise high. There are many styles and methods, but the thing to aim for is a pleasant, easy rhythm that doesn't tire you. What you are doing is knitting together the proteins from wheat that make gluten, and forming the gluten into a structure that can hold the gas released by the yeast. Depending on how much gluten protein is in the flour you use, it will take an efficient kneader about 20 to 30 minutes to knead two loaves' worth of dough to perfection. A food processor can do it in minutes (usually in two parts, sometimes three); a mixer with a dough hook takes 8 to 15 minutes.

If you like, you can use a little flour or a little water on the kneading surface to keep the dough from sticking. If you use flour on the board, try to use the tiniest amount possible; the commonest cause of bricky loaves is simply too much flour. (The next commonest is too little kneading.) You can avoid extra flour and water and just use a dough cutter or spatula as shown to pick up the dough and turn it over as you work, until the dough loses most of its stickiness.

Kneading is a matter of pushing and turning. Handle the dough lightly at first, until it loses some of its stickiness; then you can be more vigorous. Keeping the dough as much in a ball as possible, press down on it with the heel and palm of your hands, using your whole body rather than only your arms to give power to the push. Lift, turn the dough, and repeat in a rhythm that is natural to you. If the dough becomes stiff, add a little water by wetting your hands while you work.

It is hard to overknead by hand, but not by machine. Overkneaded dough gets gooey and can't regain its elasticity. Dough made from flour that is low in gluten, or flour that's not fresh, will break down after only a few minutes of kneading.

Somewhere around halfway through kneading, the dough loses its stickiness and begins to get springy and elastic, though if you try to stretch it out it still rips easily. If you look closely at the surface, especially if the flour is stone-ground, you'll see tiny flecks of bran against a beige background. Try pulling the dough out as shown. You should see little craters all over, and it still tears easily.

If you stopped kneading now, the bread *would* rise, but not nearly so well as if you continue kneading until the dough is silky smooth. Then, when you pull and tug gently, it will stretch without tearing. The surface will still be sticky, but the dough will have lost its wet quality. If the flour you used was coarse, when you look closely you'll be able to see that the dough itself is bright white, with the bran embedded in the gluten sheet like freckles on fair skin. Even with finely ground flour, the dough is bright and has a whitish cast. If you pull gently as illustrated here, the dough will make a paper-thin, translucent sheet without tearing. How satisfying!

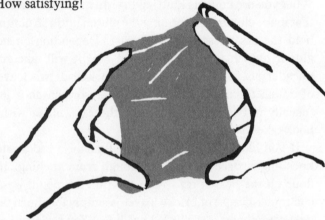

When you have finished kneading, it's time for you to rest while the yeast does its work. You can decide how long the rising times will be by how warm or cool you keep the dough: look at the chart on page 52 for your options.

Clean the bowl and shape the dough into a smooth ball, putting it in the bowl seam-side down. Cover with a platter or a plastic sheet to keep the dough from drying out, being sure that there's plenty of room for it to double or even triple. Don't oil or grease the bowl; unabsorbed fat can make holes in the finished loaf. Keep the bowl in a draft-free place at the temperature you need to give you the rising time you want.

Rising

When the dough has finished rising, it's time to deflate it. How to know when it is ready? Letting it double in volume is one way, but bakers know that doughs vary in the amount they can rise, so they use another test: wet your finger and gently poke it into the dough about one knuckle deep. Look at the hole you've made, and the dough around it. Does the dough begin to swell to fill in the hole? Then it needs more time. Does the hole remain, and the dough sigh slightly? Ready! (If the dough sighs profoundly and collapses, with alcohol on its breath, then you know that you have let it rise too long for the temperature it was resting in, and for the second rise, keep it in a cooler place, and/or allow *less than* half as long as the first rise.)

Deflating the dough and letting it rise again before shaping make a big difference in the the bread's texture, its keeping quality, and how high the final loaves will be. To deflate, wet your hand and press the dough flat; then form a ball again with the same top surface as before. Cover as before and let rise again. The second rise will take about half as long as the first at the same temperature.

At the end of the second rise, you should have what bakers call "ripe dough"—the kind that makes loaves which rise highest, taste best, and keep fresh longest. Feel the dough: it should have lost its stickiness and be pleasantly dry. When you pull on it, the strands of gluten should be thread-thin, where before they were thick and wet. Newly-kneaded dough is strong but not resilient; ripe dough is elastic. If you were to let it go even longer, the gluten would pass its prime and become brittle and "old," making grayish bread with poor flavor.

Turn the dough out on a very lightly floured board and flatten it with your hands. If you are making two loaves, divide it in half. Shape the dough pieces into smooth rounds again and cover them up while they rest. Use the time to rinse out the bowl and grease the pans: depending on the dough, it will take about 10 minutes for the dough to "relax" and be ready to shape.

Shaping

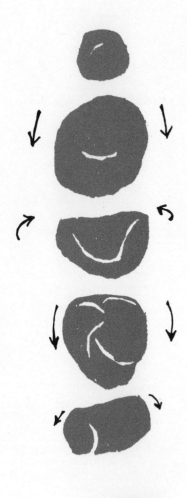

There are many ways to shape bread. Shape the relaxed dough gently, in easy stages. Dust the board lightly with flour if the dough seems sticky at all. (Honey, milk and some other ingredients, if they were included, will keep dough sticky even if it is ripe).

ஃ Turn the rounded loaf upside down and press or roll it into a circle about an inch thick.

ஃ Fold the top of the circle down not quite in half, making a smile. Press from one side to the other, letting the gas pop when it comes out the edge.

ஃ Fold in the sides, overlapping the ends slightly, so that the dough is about two-thirds the length of your loaf pan; press again, until the dough is about the length of the loaf pan.

ஃ Pull the top of the dough toward you as if you were curling it up jellyroll fashion. Since the piece is not very long, it may not roll up but just sort of fold in half. Either way is fine so long as it is tight and there's no air trapped in pockets.

ஃ Press the seam to seal it, and press the ends down to seal them.

ஃ Place the shaped loaf in the center of the greased pan, with the seam on the bottom, in the middle. Push the dough down with your hand to help it cover the bottom of the pan.

Perfect shaping takes practice, and if your early attempts aren't what they might be, take heart. Some of the most bizarre-looking loaves are most delicious, because they're so crusty.

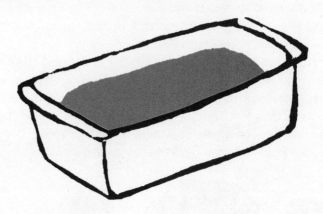

The Last Rise, or "Proof"

Let the loaves rise as before, protected from drafts, and contrive to keep the top surface of the dough from drying out. One way to do this is to set each loaf in a plastic bag that has been rinsed with water. Puff out the bag so the loaf can rise up; then seal it and set the balloon in its draft-free spot to rise. An ice chest (without ice) or even a roasting pan with plenty of room will also work well. This may seem like fussing, but a little more care at this last, most delicate part of the job can make all the difference in how high and even-textured your loaves come out.

This last rising will take a little less time than the one before if you maintain the same temperature. Keep the proof temperature about the same as before, or only a little warmer: otherwise the loaves will rise unevenly. About halfway along, preheat the oven.

Knowing when to put the bread in the oven is a learned skill. If the loaves have risen enough to arch above the top of the pan, well and good; but to be really sure, the best test is a gentler version of the finger-poke test you used before. Wet your finger and press lightly on the dough. When it's first shaped, it springs quickly back; as time passes, your fingerprint will fill in less quickly. The bread is ready for the oven when the dough returns slowly.

You have quite a bit of leeway here, but this is a moment for alertness because *underproofed* loaves won't be as high as they should, and may split drastically along one side in the oven; *overproofed* loaves will be holey at the top and dense on the bottom, and may even collapse.

Baking

A well-insulated oven that recovers its heat quickly after the door has been opened is a great boon for a baker. Ovens that recover slowly may allow bread to overproof before the heat can set the loaves. If yours is like that, put the bread in a little early. Another trick is to preheat to 400°F, turning the heat down just after the bread goes in. You can improve your oven for any kind of baking by lining the bottom with quarry tiles or firebrick. A less drastic step, but useful, is to set a pizza stone in the oven when you start to preheat. For sure, adjust the oven racks and tiles or whatever before you turn on the oven.

Handle the fully-risen loaves very gently. Center them on their racks in the oven, and *after half an hour* take a peek. Ideally it will take an hour to bake the loaves at 350°F, but ovens vary, and some of them bake unevenly. If the bread seems to need it, you can move the loaves around at this point, or lower the temperature to 325°F if the crust seems too brown. If you think the bread may be done a little early, check again after it's been in for 45 minutes.

Is it done? A tricky question, especially if you haven't been baking long enough to learn the quirks of your oven. Here are some characteristics of a loaf that has baked long enough:

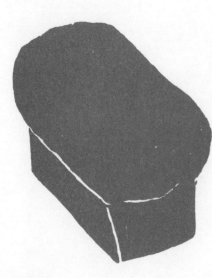

- it slides out of the pan easily
- it has an even, golden-brown color (darker if you included milk or much sweetener)
- if you tap the bottom sharply with your fingertips, the sound is hollow rather than thick
- when sliced, the crumb (all that's not crust is crumb) springs back to the touch rather than making a wettish dent that stays there*

*Some breadmakers are horrified at the very idea of slicing a loaf hot from the oven because any loaf, especially a fluffy one, can be mauled by all but the most skillful early slicing. But it *is* posible, with a *very* sharp, thin, long knife, to slice bread hot from the oven: use lots of gentle sawing and not much downward pressure.

French Bread

French Bread is just the opposite of "fast-rise" breads that get flavor from sugar, fat, and other added things. With only the essentials—flour, water, salt, and yeast—it develops its splendid flavor naturally during a long, cool rising period. A hot, steamy bake gives French Bread its high rise and crisp, chewy crust.

*2 teaspoons active dry yeast
(1 packet, ¼ oz, or 7 g)
½ cup warm water
(about 110°F)*

ھ

Follow the recipe for Basic Bread, omitting the sweetener and fat; make the dough soft by cutting back on the flour. Use icy cold water except for dissolving the yeast.

Let the dough rise in a cool place, 65 to 70°F, until it is ready to deflate; this should take 2½ to 3 hours. (You can give it more time in a cooler place, but if you let it get warmer, it won't have time to develop good flavor.) Deflate and let rise again, this time about 2 hours.

Press the risen dough flat and divide into pieces sized for the shapes you want to make. Round the pieces and set them to rest. Prepare the baking pans and then shape the dough, taking into account the suggestions below. Give the dough its final rise *in the same cool place as before*. It will take an hour.

*5½ cups whole wheat bread
flour (1¾ pounds)
2½ teaspoons salt*

*2¼ cups very cold water
(iced if you knead with a
food processor)*

ھ

Before you shape the dough, consider how to make the best use of the equipment you have so that you can give the bread the steamy-hot bake it needs. Because French Bread has no added milk or sugar, normal baking temperatures won't even brown the crust, let alone provide the characteristic beauty and flavor.

*"Reduce the oven heat,"
does not mean "turn the
thermostat down." If the
heat stays high after the
water is gone, the bread
will burn very quickly.
If your oven retains heat
well, you may want to turn
the thermostat down earlier
and even open the door for
a minute or so.*

*Whatever method you use
for steaming, please be
careful. The temperatures
are high and the presence
of steam makes the heat
intense. Before heating the
oven, put the racks in their
places and figure out where
you are going to put each
pan or dish when baking
time comes.*

What you want to mimic in French Bread is the traditional wood-fired brick oven, which has very high heat and humidity when the bread is put in and loses both slowly as the bread bakes out. Sounds impossible, but actually, there are simple and effective ways of coming close to these conditions in a home oven. Some suggestions are given on the next page. Choose one of them, and allow plenty of time for the oven to preheat.

Shape your bread or rolls and place them on the baking sheet or oven stone, or in the covered dish you will use for baking them. If the bread will be free form, you need only give the surface beneath it a moderate dusting of cornmeal. Casseroles or loaf pans, because the bread will touch their sides, must be greased, with cornmeal coming after.

Just before baking, wet your loaves or rolls, and slash their tops to encourage their best rise in the oven. It's the slashing that leaves the characteristic open-leaf pattern on the crust. Use a very sharp knife and hold the blade at an angle to the surface of the bread, rather than cutting straight downward, so that the slashed part will open up rather than spread out.

Bake big loaves as long as an hour; long thin ones, or rolls, need just 20 to 30 minutes, depending on their size.

Steaming Methods

COVERED CASSEROLE

This is the easiest and most surefire way of steaming, and the least nerve-racking. Glass, pottery, or even heavy metal works fine, so long as it is big enough to allow the dough to do all the rising it wants to (including a final "spring" in the oven). A clay baking cloche is great. The key is the snug fitting lid; if it has air spaces the steam will escape without doing its job. You can remedy leaky lids, and even fabricate a lid from foil. (Ceramic, by the way, tends to burn and stick: use plenty of grease and lots of cornmeal.)

Preheat the oven to 450°F. When the bread is ready to bake, pour ¼ cup of warm water over the loaf, slash, cover, and put into the oven. After about 20 minutes the crust should be a nice, rosy brown. Reduce the oven heat to 350°F and bake until done.

WETTING THE LOAF

If you want to bake loaves that won't fit into a covered casserole, and if your oven is a well-insulated one that quickly recovers the heat lost when its door is opened, here is the simplest way to wet the loaf: Preheat the oven to 450°F; then spray or paint the fully risen bread with warm water, slash it, and put it into the oven as quickly as calm efficiency allows. Repeat the spraying or painting every 3 to 5 minutes until the crust begins to brown nicely—probably three or four times, depending on your oven and your dough. Reduce oven heat to 350°F and bake until the bread is done.

STEAMING THE OVEN

This method requires a pretty well-insulated oven too, and also a heavy skillet or other flat pan that you don't mind possibly ruining for any other use. Preheat the oven to 450°F with the skillet on the bottom. When you put the bread in the oven, pour one cup of boiling water into the skillet and shut the oven door quickly. After ten minutes, peek. As soon as the water is gone, reduce the heat. You can use this method to heighten the effect of the previous one. And both are enhanced by lining the oven with quarry tiles or using a baking stone instead of a cookie sheet under the bread.

Raisin Bread, and Such

The simplest way to make raisin bread—or any fruit or nut bread, for that matter—is to spread handfuls of the goodies on the dough when you shape it and then curl it up jelly roll fashion, being careful not to let any air get trapped in the curl. Ease the roll into a a well-greased loaf pan or bake free-form on a cookie sheet, or cut the roll into swirly rolls with a loop of strong thread. The rising time will be a little longer than usual.

If you prefer, you can incorporate sweet dried fruits into the dough when you mix it up. To prevent active enzymes in the fruit from harming the dough, and to make the fruit softer and more appealing, steam raisins and other firm dried fruits long enough to heat thoroughly, then drain and cool before you start. Use the broth as part of the liquid measure. (Incidentally, soggy fruit will make holes in the bread and present difficulties in baking too, so swirly rolls are a better option if your fruit is wetter than the dough.)

Cinnamon, when added to the dough too early, can develop a metallic taste. It gives its best flavor if incorporated at shaping time, or sprinkled on the top of the moistened loaf just before baking.

You'll find much, much more about ingredients and techniques in The Laurel's Kitchen Bread Book (Random House, 1984).

Seeded Bread

Sprinkle seeds on the board while you shape any plain dough, letting them get folded and rolled into the loaf and stuck to the outside. You can use any seeds you like—sesame or poppy, of course, or sunflower, chia, caraway, cumin, fennel, dill, anise. Sesame and cumin really sing out if they are toasted in advance, and sunflower seeds have two entirely different personalities toasted and raw.

If you want stronger sesame flavor, include a tablespoon of unrefined sesame oil in the dough as part of the oil measure. To achieve a seedier crust, brush it just before baking with water, milk, or a mixture of a lightly beaten egg and a tablespoon of water; then sprinkle with seeds. The egg will make the loaf very shiny too.

Breads With Milk

You can use milk for part of the liquid in any loaf. Milk mellows the wheaty flavor, makes the crumb tender in texture, adds protein and minerals, enhances the keeping quality of the loaf, and gives a pretty, warm color to the crust. If scalded, it can also improve the rise.

Why scalded? Scalding denatures some of the proteins in milk which otherwise make bread dough sticky and keep it from rising high. To get the benefits without the drawbacks, scald the milk first, or else limit the amount you use to less than half the liquid measure. (With milk powder, this means using not more than ¼ cup powdered milk per 2 loaves. Stir dry milk powder into the flour along with the salt.)

Even more than fresh milk, we like buttermilk in bread—again, though, not contributing more than half the liquid. Buttermilk Bread is one of our top favorite recipes. It makes light, tender rolls too—fancy enough for royalty if you double the butter. Yogurt is good here too, but since it's much stronger-flavored than buttermilk, we recommend using even less: ⅔ cup for 2 loaves is a good amount. Follow the Basic Bread instructions, using these ingredients:

BUTTERMILK BREAD

2 teaspoons active dry yeast
  (1 packet, ¼ oz, 7 g)
1¼ cups warm water

1¼ cups buttermilk
¼ cup honey

5½ cups whole wheat
  bread flour
2 teaspoons salt

2 tablespoons soft butter

YOGURT BREAD

2 teaspoons active dry yeast
  (1 packet, ¼ oz, 7 g)
1⅔ cups warm water

¼ cup oil
⅔ cup yogurt
3 tablespoons honey

6 cups whole wheat
  bread flour
2 teaspoons salt

FRESH MILK BREAD

2 teaspoons active dry yeast
  (1 packet, ¼ oz, 7 g)
½ cup warm water

2 cups fresh milk,
  scalded and cooled
¼ cup honey

6 cups whole wheat
  bread flour
2½ teaspoons salt

2 tablespoons soft butter

Rolls & Breadsticks

We like to make some rolls whenever we bake, to hand around fresh out of the oven or to serve for dinner. Plain round cushion rolls are probably the best eating, but fancy shapes delight the eye and can make a meal special.

For grand occasions—especially if you are serving Aunt Agatha, who finds whole wheat so, well, *unrefined,* you know—you'll want to call up all your skills to make the rolls really light. Choose a dependably light recipe like Buttermilk Bread and double the butter; you can also include an egg if you want to. The buttermilk, the fat, and the egg will all help lighten the dough. Choosing fine flour helps too. But good kneading makes the biggest difference of all, and careful timing comes next. Let rolls have plenty of time in the last rising; unlike loaves, they don't run the danger of collapsing, because they're small.

If you are making rolls at the same time as a loaf, you can bake them at the same temperature; the rolls will take about half as long. If they are by themselves, rolls (smaller ones especially) and breadsticks will be crustier and less likely to dry out inside if you bake them at a higher temperature: as high as 400°F for the smallest ones. They're done when golden brown, about 15 minutes at these higher temperatures. Brush with butter, if you like, when they come out of the oven. You can make truly mouthwatering, featherlight rolls this way.

BREADSTICKS Breadsticks are just long, thin rolls. To make them crunchy, let them dry out at 200°F for an hour or so after baking. (How long it takes will depend on how big you make them.) We generally go for chewy-soft, which is how they turn out if you bake them just until done: about ½ hour at 350°F.

Pine Nut Pinwheels

This truly original recipe can be planned ahead to star for company, or just as happily use up the end-of-the-week Soy Spread for the delight of your Inner Circle. In a pinch, sunflower seeds can substitute surprisingly well for the pine nuts.

bread dough for one loaf

1½ cups Soy Spread
½ cup toasted pine nuts

ॐ

You will need half a recipe's worth of any not-too-sweet bread dough. If you are in a hurry, make up half a recipe using the full 2 teaspoons of yeast. Keep the dough quite warm and expect a very fast rise. Proceed as usual until shaping time. (See page 52 for timing.)

Roll the risen dough out on a lightly floured surface, making an 11″ × 14″ rectangle. Spread the dough with the soy spread and sprinkle with pine nuts. Roll up tightly and seal the seam. Use a sharp knife or a loop of strong thread to cut the log into 1″ slices. Place the swirls in a greased baking dish with their sides just touching and let them rise. The final rise, in a warm place, should take about ½ hour.

Preheat oven to 375°F. Bake pinwheels ½ hour or a little longer.

Makes 16.

CINNAMON ROLLS

Follow the directions for Pine Nut Pinwheels, only use a sprinkling of cinnamon and brown sugar instead of pine nuts and soy spread. Nuts and raisins can also figure in. After baking, brush with butter.

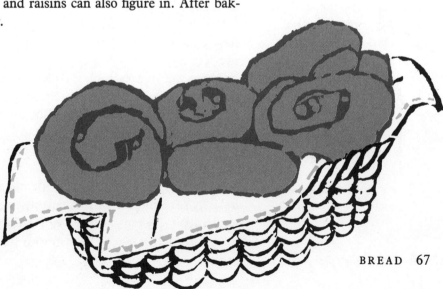

Pocket Bread (Pita)

Here the trick is the baking, and that isn't as tricky as it has been made out to be. Ovens differ, though, so it may take a little experimentation to figure out your own best setup. You need fast bottom heat, so bake the breads on the floor of the oven, with or without a cookie sheet or pizza stone. Electric ovens and many gas ovens work fine with a cookie sheet on the bottom rack.

Use plain Basic Bread dough. A good method for the first try is to make a normal loaf of half the dough and Pocket Bread out of the rest. That way you will have about a dozen pitas, which is probably plenty for the nerves if not for the cupboard. After you master the process, you can easily make dozens and stay calm and cool.

When the dough has nearly finished its second rise, preheat the oven to 450°F. When the dough is ready, divide it and shape your loaf and set it in its pan to rise in a cool, draft-free place. Of the remaining dough, form about a dozen small *smooth* balls. Keep them in order as you shape them, so that you can take them on to the next step in order too. Let the rounds rest about 10 minutes, protected from drafts. *This is essential.*

Use flour on the board to keep the breads from sticking. Roll the first three or five or so rounds into flat circles about as thick as a heavy wool blanket and 6″ or so across. Put the rolled-out circles on the floor of the hot oven, or on the cookie sheet or hot pizza stone, and quickly close the door. Roll a few more, but don't get distracted.

Check the breads in the oven in 3 minutes. They should have puffed; if they are brown on the bottom, open one up and check to see if the inside is done. It will be moist, but it shouldn't be shiny-wet. If you think your breads need a little more time, you can bake them for a minute more on the top rack while the next batch bakes on the bottom. But don't let them get crisp and brown or they'll break when you try to fill them. They bake from the steam inside them, which cooks very fast without browning the top.

From here on out, work as efficiently as you can, rolling and baking in a comfortable rhythm, adjusting your oven setup to get the ideal pita. When you finish all the pitas, you should have time to cool the oven a bit and have it ready to bake that loaf.

If they are too thick, they won't puff (though they will be nice buns). If they are too thin, or if you are too rough with the rolling pin, they may puff in places but not make balloons.

Making Rye Bread

Rye is the only grain besides wheat that has substantial amounts of gluten, so it has been used along with wheat for centuries to make the superb breads of Eastern and Northern Europe. But rye not only has a lot less gluten than wheat, it also has carbohydrates called *pentosans* which weaken the gluten, making the dough sticky and the bread heavy. To get the lightest and best-textured rye bread, a different technique from the standard wheat-bread method is helpful.

If you simply want to let the wheat gluten carry the bread, you can mix the liquids into the wheat flour, making a thick batter, and beat the batter until it is elastic; then mix in the rye flour to make your dough. But there is a way to get the rye gluten to help too. Mix the rye, wheat flour, and salt; then add the bread's liquid measure to the flour mixture in stages, beginning with just enough to get the dough to stick together. Knead this very stiff dough, using the rest of the recipe's liquid measure to wet your hands as you work, so that within about 10 minutes of kneading you have used most of it. Depending on the dough, 5 to 10 minutes more will finish the kneading—but stop when the dough becomes dramatically sticky, no matter how long you've been working.

The reason for the stiff first stage is that the rye's pentosans compete with the gluten proteins for liquids, and the gluten has a better chance if the dough starts out less wet. It is the pentosans glomming onto the water that makes rye dough so sticky. Adding acid to the dough, by the way, helps counter this, and that is why you'll see vinegar in the recipes.

Once the dough is mixed and kneaded, it can follow the usual pattern for bread dough—with the caution that rye dough is less tolerant of either very slow (cool) or very fast (warm) rising times than wheat dough. Handle rye dough gently, and don't expect it to rise sky-high. Bake it thoroughly.

About rye flour: you will see "light," "medium," and "dark" rye flours. All of them are refined: light rye has had all of the bran and germ removed, dark rye has only lost a good deal of it. If you want whole-grain rye flour, you need to ask for 100 percent whole rye flour, which usually means stone-ground. Rye flour is even more perishable than wheat flour, so try to get and use it

RYE FLOUR

when it is really fresh. If you like rye bread very much, we would go so far as to suggest home grinding; it makes a marvelous difference in the bread.

The following recipes are meant to be prototypes for the basic kinds of rye breads. You can flavor them with grated orange peel, use chili-flavored cumin seeds instead of the traditional caraway, or leave the seeds out altogether. Add raisins, following the suggestions on page 64; or darken the bread by using 2 tablespoons carob powder, Postum, or cocoa (but maybe not all at once!) Give your creation a fancy name and keep careful notes so you can make it again. This we can testify: if it has caraway seeds, people will think it is rye, whether it is or not; if it doesn't, they won't, whether it is or not.

Light Rye Bread

Dissolve the yeast in the warm water.

    Mix the flours, salt, and caraway seeds in a big bowl. Stir the honey, buttermilk, vinegar, and oil together and mix them into the flour mixture. Add the dissolved yeast next, mixing the whole into a stiff dough. Knead, adding the additional water gradually by dipping your hands into it as you work the dough. Kneading time should be 15 to 20 minutes. At the end you should have a soft, supple dough just beginning to become sticky.

    Let rise twice and shape as described in Basic Bread. Let rise once more. Preheat oven to 425°F. Before baking, spray or paint loaves with warm water. Place in hot oven and immediately turn heat down to 325°F. Bake about 1 hour.

2 teaspoons active dry yeast
   (1 packet, 1/4 oz, 7 g)
1/2 cup warm water

4 1/2 cups whole wheat
   bread flour, preferably
   finely ground
2 cups whole rye flour
2 1/2 teaspoons salt
1 tablespoon caraway seeds

3 tablespoons honey
1 cup cool buttermilk
2 tablespoons cider vinegar
2 tablespoons oil

about 3/4 cup water

Pumpernickel

This is a very old-fashioned rye bread, dark, tender, and hefty.

      ೢ

Dissolve the yeast in the warm water. Mix the flours, salt, and seeds together and stir in the molasses and vinegar. Add the dissolved yeast to make a stiff dough. Knead about 10 to 20 minutes, working the remaining water in gradually by wetting your hands, until the dough is supple.

    Let rise twice as described in the Basic recipe, shaping the bread into rounds. Let rise again and bake for about 1 hour, using one of the steaming methods described on page 63.

2 teaspoons active dry yeast
   (1 packet, 1/4 oz, 7 g)
1 1/2 cups warm water

4 cups whole rye flour
3 cups whole wheat
   bread flour
2 1/2 teaspoons salt
1 teaspoon caraway seeds

1 tablespoon molasses
2 tablespoons cider vinegar

1 to 1 1/2 cups more water

Bean Breads

GARBANZO BREAD

2 teaspoons active dry yeast
   (1 packet, ¼ oz or 7 g)
½ cup warm water

5 cups whole wheat
   bread flour
2½ teaspoons salt

2 tablespoons honey
garbanzo cooking broth,
   plus cold water to make
   2 cups liquid, about 70°F
(2 tablespoons oil)

2 cups freshly-cooked
   garbanzos, mashed

SOYBEAN BREAD

2 teaspoons active dry yeast
   (1 packet, ¼ oz or 7 g)
2½ cups warm water

5 cups whole wheat
   bread flour
2½ teaspoons salt

3 tablespoons honey
2 cups freshly-cooked
   mashed soybeans,
   or cooked soy grits

¼ cup oil

If you want to work beans into your family's diet but find resistance in the ranks, adding beans or bean flour when you prepare your bread dough can make a small but significant contribution. With a little art, not a soul will guess what extra nutrients that delicious slice contains.

Our preference is for cooked, mashed soybeans or garbanzos—up to a cup per loaf, kneaded into the dough after the gluten is formed. That way the beans really do disappear into the dough, and the bread has very good flavor.

BEAN FLOURS

Garbanzo flour will disappear too: add as much as ½ cup per 2-loaf recipe, along with the wheat flour. But soy flour is different. Not only can it be very bitter, soy (bean or flour) also has dramatic effects on bread dough because of enzymes it contains. Professional bakers make use of this quality by adding soy flour in minute quantities as a dough conditioner. But when you use enough to make its nutrients count, the loaf can be so "conditioned" that it can't rise. Here are some ways to get around this if you really want to work soy in.

USING SOY

Use a maximum of ⅓ cup fresh soy flour in a 2-loaf recipe, or add as much as 2 cups of cooked, mashed soybeans or cooked grits. Either way, if you want to counteract the binding properties of soy, you have to include fat: 2 tablespoons oil or butter per loaf, minimum, for a good rise. In addition, because of the conditioning effect, let soy-enhanced breads rise only once before shaping, instead of twice.

Soymilk, by the way, makes lovely bread. Dissolve the yeast in warm water and use soy milk for part or all the remaining liquid measure. Unless it is first-day fresh, be sure to scald and cool the milk before using. Here too, for a good rise, include butter or oil and let rise only once before shaping.

Cracked Wheat Bread

When most people dream of cracked wheat bread, it's the light, sweet honey–wheatberry type sold in supermarkets. If you want to duplicate this, you need a very light version of Basic—perhaps Buttermilk Bread—and maybe even an egg or two as part of the liquid.

For the cracked grain to make its best showing, use either very coarsely cracked bulgur wheat or sprouted wheat berries two to three days along, chopped with a knife. You can use as much as 1 cup cooked or sprouted grain per loaf, adding it either when you mix the dough or later as you knead. Sprouts probably do best, but chew carefully: the ones on the crust can be hard enough to crack a tooth.

2 teaspoons active dry yeast
  (1 packet, ¼ oz or 7 g)
½ cup warm water

¾ cup hot water
¼ cup honey
1¼ cups cold buttermilk

5½ cups finely ground
  whole wheat bread flour
2½ teaspoons salt
1 cup chopped sprouted
  wheat berries or
  1 cup cooked bulgur wheat

2 tablespoons butter
  or ¼ cup oil

Oatmeal or Barley Bread

With whole wheat flour, the taste of the oats or barley takes a back seat. Still, this is one of our most frequently-made breads, because it is so mellow and light and such a good keeper. We usually just use leftover oatmeal (or cooked barley cereal) as the "liquid" in Basic Bread, increasing the honey a little and decreasing the salt by whatever is in the cereal. Dissolve the yeast in plain water only, of course.

The only quirk is that at first the bread seems absurdly stiff and sticky at the same time, making it hard to resist the temptation to add extra water. After a little kneading, though, the dough smooths out and becomes almost normal. From there on it's smooth sailing.

To let the fans know it's Oatmeal Bread, sprinkle rolled oats in the greased pan before you put in the loaf. Soak a handful of rolled oats in warm milk, and just before baking, pat the mixture all over the top crust.

This bread takes kindly to the flavor of walnuts and sunflower seeds too. Knead them in when you shape the loaves.

2 teaspoons active dry yeast
  (1 packet, ¼ oz or 7 g)
½ cup warm water

5 cups finely ground
  whole wheat bread flour
2½ teaspoons salt

2 cups cooked oatmeal
  or barley cereal
3 tablespoons honey

(¼ cup oil)
(½ cup toasted
  sunflower seeds or
  walnuts)

English Muffins

English muffins—in fact, excellent English muffins—are not hard to make. It doesn't take special equipment, either, just your bread dough and a griddle. The secrets are in the mixing, kneading, and the final rising time.

Use any kind of dough that suits the mood of the muffin you would like to make. If you like 'em tangy, Yogurt Bread is a good choice; for *really* tangy muffins, even cut back the honey. Basic Bread with chopped wheat sprouts kneaded in makes a muffin that's nubbly and slightly sweet. Doughs with a lot of sweetener or milk will be very dark on top and bottom by the time they are cooked, but delicious nevertheless.

You can make eight muffins from one loaf's worth of dough—one loaf of bread and a batch of muffins from one 2-loaf recipe. Knead the dough as usual for bread; then divide it in two and set the loaf half in its draft-free place to rise. Put a cup or so of warm water in a small bowl, take the muffin half of the dough in hand, and knead more, wetting your hands as you do. Keep kneading until the dough is really quite *over*kneaded. It should become quite flabby, with no elasticity at all. It might stretch out like regular dough, but if so, it will pull apart gooily rather than tear the way unkneaded dough will. When you finish, you should be worried that you have kneaded it too much and that you might have worked in too much water: it should be pretty darn wet.

(Overkneading and making the dough wet are the first two of three Great English Muffin Secrets. Number three comes later.)

Let the muffin dough have its first two rises as if it were normal bread. Because it is so wet, though, the muffin dough will ferment much faster than its sister bread dough. If you want them to follow the same schedule, keep the muffin dough in a cooler place: for example, if the loaf is rising in the oven with the door propped open to keep it at about 80°F, then set the muffin dough on a countertop at about 70°F.

After the muffin dough has had its second rise, turn it onto a well-floured board, flatten it out, and divide it into eight parts. Form each into a round and set on a well-*floured* tray or cookie sheet for the final rise. Protect the muffins from drafts and let them rise until the rounds are quite saggy, not higher than an inch. This last step—a very, *very* full proof—is the third secret.

Heat your griddle or skillet moderately hot, a little cooler than you'd want for pancakes. Unless it is completely unseasoned, you won't need to grease the surface. Use a wide spatula to pick up the first muffin and, deft as a magician, transfer it flour-side-down to the griddle. Fill the griddle with the first four or so and let them bake until they are getting brown on the bottom; then turn over. Keep turning as they bake, to prevent them from getting too dark. They are done when the sides, which will not brown, are springy. If you are in doubt, split one open with a fork: when done, it will be moist but not wet. How long this takes depends a lot on the dough—very light, holey muffins bake the fastest. It's fine to make the second four wait for their turn on the griddle, so long as they aren't in a place that is so warm they'll overproof.

TROUBLESHOOTING

When they cool, the muffins will be impressively smaller than they were after baking. Eight muffins from this recipe should be the right size, but if you want them larger, next time make only seven—or even six.

If there aren't enough holes, next time knead longer and add more water. It's hard to believe how much it takes.

If the inside is a little gray and the flavor beery, you have let them rise too long or too warm. The wet dough ferments much faster than stiffer bread dough.

Sebastopol Pizza

2 or more cups whole wheat
flour
1 teaspoon salt
½ teaspoon cardamom

2 teaspoons active dry yeast
(1 packet, ¼ oz, 7 g)
⅞ cup warm water

1 tablespoon butter, soft

6 cups firm, tart apples,
sliced thin
1 cup apple juice
(2–4 tablespoons honey)
(2 tablespoons lemon juice)
1 tablespoon cornstarch or
arrowroot

⅔ cup chopped walnuts
2 cups grated mozzarella,
jack, or other favorite
cheese

In northern California, Sebastopol means apples: Gravensteins in particular, which folks who live anywhere nearby think can't be beat. But this recipe works well with any fresh local apple—best with a crisp, flavorful, sweet-sour variety that will counterpoint the cheese.

This concoction is both showy and surefire, the kind of thing you serve to provide conversation and good eating at a festive lunch. It also makes a great project to do with kids on a lazy Saturday morning.

&

Combine flour, salt, and cardamom.

Dissolve yeast in water.

Add yeast mixture to flour mixture, adding flour or water if necessary to make a soft dough. Knead about 5 minutes, and then work in the soft butter, kneading another 5 minutes or so, to make a silky dough. Set to rise, covered, in a very warm place (90°–95°F) about 1 hour. Deflate and let rise again ½ hour.

Cook sliced apples in ¾ cup of the apple juice just until tender, not quite translucent. Drain, reserving the liquid. You should have a cup of juice; if not, add more. Stir in honey if desired, and lemon juice if needed, to produce a balanced sweet-sour flavor. Dissolve cornstarch in remaining quarter-cup of cold apple juice and stir into the hot juice mixture. Cook over medium heat, stirring, until clear.

Preheat oven to 425°F.

Roll dough out to fill a 14″ greased pizza pan. Turn up an edge to hold sauce. Spread apples over crust, then pour thickened sauce over that. Sprinkle nuts over top and bake for 15 to 20 minutes, until crust begins to turn color. Spread cheese over the pizza and return to oven for another 5 minutes. Serve hot.

Find Pizza on page 266, along with some interesting variations.

Puffs

Puffs are light, airy, yeast-raised muffins, nutritious and easy to make in spite of the time they need to rise. The first version is for caraway puffs, but try the poppy and herb puffs too—and make up your own.

2 teaspoons fresh minced
*   onion*
1 tablespoon oil or butter
1 cup cottage cheese
2 tablespoons honey
1 teaspoon salt

Sauté onion in oil or butter. Add the cottage cheese, honey, and salt, and heat mixture to lukewarm (100°F).

In a medium-sized bowl, dissolve the yeast in the warm water. Stir in the egg, seeds, 1¼ cups of the flour, and the warm cottage cheese mixture. Mix this batter well, then add the remaining flour as needed to make a very soft dough. Knead lightly until elastic.

2 teaspoons active dry yeast
*   (1 packet, ¼ oz, 7 g)*
¼ cup warm water

Let the dough rise in a warm place (85°–95°F) for about 1½ hours. Grease a 12-cup muffin pan.

Flatten the dough and divide it into 12 balls. Place these in the muffin cups and let the dough rise again, about 40 minutes this time. Preheat the oven to 400°F. Bake for 15 minutes—a little longer if they are not terribly puffy.

Makes 12 puffs.

1 egg, beaten
2 teaspoons caraway seeds
2¼ cups whole wheat flour

POPPY PUFFS

Substitute poppy seeds for the caraway seeds, grated lemon peel for sautéed onion, butter for oil. Melt the butter and heat the cottage cheese gently in the same pan.

HERB PUFFS

Increase the onion to two tablespoons. For the seeds, substitute a selection of your favorite herbs. Dill weed, basil, parsley, and celery seed or leaves all make good puff flavorings.

Everyone's Muffins

OATMEAL VARIETY

2 teaspoons active dry yeast
  (1 packet, ¼ oz, 7 g)
1½ cups warm water

1¾ cups whole wheat flour
1½ cups rolled oats

1¼ teaspoons salt
2 tablespoons oil
2 tablespoons honey
2 pinches nutmeg

BUCKWHEAT VARIETY

2 teaspoons active dry yeast
  (1 packet, ¼ oz, 7 g)
1½ cups warm water

2 cups whole wheat flour

1¼ teaspoons salt
2 tablespoons oil
¾ cup buckwheat flour
½ cup raisins
¼ cup toasted sunflower
  seeds

Most muffin recipes call for eggs and milk, but not these! Like other muffins, they are at their best served hot from the oven.

For either variety, dissolve the yeast in the water in a large bowl. Mix in whole wheat flour (and oats, if desired) and beat well.

Add the remaining ingredients and beat vigorously. Cover the batter with a towel and let the dough rise for an hour in a warm place (about 90°–95°F). Stir down the batter and spoon it into greased muffin tins, filling each cup full. Let the muffins rise again.

Preheat the oven to 400°F. When the muffins have risen nicely rounded above the muffin cups, bake them about 25 minutes.

Each recipe makes 12 large, crusty muffins.

About Quick Breads & Muffins

Because they do not have the long fermentation of yeasted breads, quick breads and muffins require more fat and sweetener to give them flavor and texture. In addition, the use of soda destroys the B vitamin thiamin, which you have a right to expect to be richly supplied in a whole-grain food. Despite these nutritional drawbacks, though, quick breads aren't likely to disappear from the scene. Quick to fix, scrumptious, and often happily nonwheat in a wheaty world, muffins, corn bread, and their ilk provide variety and—well—people really *like* them.

For whole-grain muffins, smaller muffin cups succeed better than large ones, though either will do.

Ordinary double-acting baking powder is probably the most effective and the least bitter tasting. If you want to avoid aluminum, though, look for old-fashioned cream of tartar baking powders, or make your own: use ⅝ teaspoon cream of tartar plus ¼ teaspoon soda per cup of flour.

Poppyseed Muffins

Preheat oven to 375°F. Grease a 12-cup muffin pan.

Soak raisins 5 minutes in ¼ cup boiling water. Chop coarsely in blender or by hand.

Make the oats into a coarse flour in blender or food processor (in blender, do ½ cup at a time). You will need 2 cups of coarse flour.

Put oat flour in bowl and sift in the other dry ingredients. Beat eggs, oil, and honey together, then stir in the milk, raisins and water, poppy seeds, and lemon peel.

Add dry ingredients to liquid ones, stirring just enough to mix well. Spoon into muffin cups and bake about 15 minutes. The muffins will be a sunny yellow on top and delicate brown on bottom when done.

Makes 12.

½ cup raisins
¼ cup boiling water

2¾ cups rolled oats (about)
½ cup whole wheat flour
2½ teaspoons baking powder
½ teaspoon salt
¼ teaspoon mace or nutmeg

2 eggs
2 tablespoons oil or butter
¼ cup honey

1 cup milk
2 tablespoons poppy seeds
2 teaspoons grated lemon peel

Apple Bran Muffins

1 cup whole wheat flour
¾ cup wheat bran
¼ teaspoon salt
½ teaspoon baking soda
¼ teaspoon nutmeg
1½ teaspoons grated
    orange rind
½ cup chopped apple
¼ cup raisins
¼ cup chopped nuts
    or sunflower seeds

juice of ½ orange
⅞ cup buttermilk
    or sour milk
1 beaten egg
¼ cup blackstrap molasses
1 tablespoon oil

Moist, dark, and fruity, these are a long-standing favorite.

≥⋅

Preheat oven to 350°F. Grease a 12-cup muffin pan.

Toss flour, bran, salt, soda, and nutmeg together with a fork. Stir in orange rind, apples, raisins, and nuts or seeds.

Combine the orange juice, buttermilk, egg, molasses, and oil. Stir the liquid ingredients into dry in a few swift strokes. Pour into greased muffin cups, filling them at least two-thirds full, and bake for 25 minutes.

Makes 12.

Cinnamuffins

¼ cup oil
½ cup dark molasses
1 cup applesauce

1½ cups whole wheat
    (pastry) flour
½ teaspoon soda
1½ teaspoons baking powder
¾ teaspoon cinnamon
pinch cloves
½ teaspoon salt
½ cup raisins

Preheat oven to 375°F. Grease a 12-cup muffin tin—use the smallish-sized cups with this recipe.

Mix oil, molasses, and applesauce. Sift together the flour, soda, baking powder, cinnamon, cloves, and salt. Stir together wet and dry ingredients and raisins. Drop into muffin cups and bake 18 to 20 minutes.

Lynne's Muffins

Nutty in flavor and texture, these favorite unsweet muffins are wonderfully simple to make. Start them ahead of time, however, or they will taste of soda and not be so light.

2 cups rolled oats
1½ cups sour milk
  or buttermilk
1 cup whole wheat flour
1 teaspoon baking soda
1 teaspoon salt
¼ cup honey
1 or 2 beaten eggs

Soak the oats in the sour milk overnight, or at least several hours.
  Preheat oven to 400°F.
  Sift together the flour, baking soda, and salt. Combine dry ingredients, honey, and beaten eggs with the oats and stir lightly just until the batter is mixed. Drop batter into well-greased muffin tins, filling each cup two-thirds full.
  Bake for 20 minutes.
  Makes 12 muffins.

Corn Bread

Preheat oven to 425°F.
  In a large bowl stir the dry ingredients together, making sure there are no lumps of baking soda or powder.
  Mix liquids together and add to the dry ingredients, stirring smooth. Turn into a greased 8″ × 8″ pan. Bake 20 to 25 minutes. (Or make corn muffins: spoon into muffin tin and bake about 20 minutes.)

2 cups cornmeal
½ cup whole wheat pastry
  flour
1 teaspoon salt
½ teaspoon baking soda
1 teaspoon baking powder

1–3 tablespoons honey
1–2 large eggs, beaten
1–2 tablespoons oil
  or melted butter
2 cups buttermilk

(When you use 2 eggs or add grated carrot, reduce the buttermilk to 1¾ cup. When you add raw squash, reduce it to 1½ cup.)

VARIATIONS

For a grainy, Southern-style corn bread, use 2½ cups freshly ground corn and omit the wheat flour and honey. Use butter. If you want to use very coarse cornmeal, it is a good idea to let the batter stand for an hour before baking. Keep the eggs and leavenings to add, blended smooth, at the last minute.

For a light, delicate New England–style corn bread, use 1½ cups cornmeal and 1 cup whole wheat pastry flour, plus the maximum of eggs, honey, and butter. You can even separate the eggs, folding the whites in after mixing the rest.

A cup of grated raw carrot makes a sweet, pretty addition; a cup of grated raw yellow zucchini or winter squash will disappear completely. Parsley, peppers, grated cheese, onions sauteed in the oil measure with a teaspoon of chili powder . . . these are all tasty ways to add interest.

Boston Brown Bread

1½ cups whole wheat flour
½ cup rye flour
1 cup cornmeal
1½ teaspoons baking powder
½ teaspoon baking soda
1 teaspoon salt

2 cups buttermilk
¼ cup milk
½ cup blackstrap molasses
½ cup raisins
½ cup toasted sunflower
    seeds, lightly chopped

So moist and tender you'd imagine it to be terribly rich, but not so! The secret is in the steaming. This bread is easy to prepare and certainly easy to eat. It takes as long as three hours to cook, though, so start early.

꙳

Grease and dust with flour or cornmeal one 2-pound coffee can, or three 20-ounce cans, or five 12-ounce cans. *Use seamless cans;* the ones with a seam down the side may leak lead onto the side of the loaf.

Sift dry ingredients to make sure there are no lumps of soda or baking powder. If some bran or cornmeal stay behind in the sifter, tip them back into the mixture.

Stir liquid ingredients together with the seeds and raisins. Add to the dry ingredients, stirring just enough to moisten thoroughly. Fill cans to two-thirds full.

Cover the cans with greased foil or greased heavy paper and tie with string. Set the cans in a large pot or slow cooker on top of a trivet or a cooling rack. (Even crumpled foil will do, or old jar lids.) Fill the pot with boiling water to halfway up the cans. Cover the pot and let the bread simmer on very low heat for 3 hours—check after 1½ hours if you're using small cans.

Let the bread cool uncovered for 1 hour before removing it from the cans.

Boston Brown Bread keeps well wrapped in foil and refrigerated. To reheat it, steam lightly.

Oat Crackers

Place all dry ingredients in blender and blend until they are the consistency of cornmeal. Stop frequently to stir ingredients if they stick. (If you use a food processor, you may need to double the recipe.)

Stir in the milk. Use a frosting knife or rubber spatula to spread batter thinly and evenly on a well-greased baking sheet. Be sure the batter is not thicker at the center of the sheet.

Place in cold or preheated 325°F oven and bake slowly until delicately golden. After about 10 minutes, use a pastry wheel or sharp knife to score the dough in squares or rectangles. If the outside crackers bake faster, take them off and return the others to the oven.

Crackers become much crisper when they cool, so loosen them from the baking sheet as soon as they come out of the oven to keep them from crumbling.

½ cup walnuts, chopped
1¾ cups rolled oats
½ teaspoon salt
1 teaspoon baking powder

1 cup milk

To make sure that these come off the pan easily, use a few drops of lecithin along with the oil or shortening you use for greasing the pan.

Crispy Seed Wafers

These large, tasty, paper-thin crackers keep for several days if stored airtight.

Preheat the oven to 400°F.

Mix dry ingredients together. Add 2 tablespoons of the melted butter, the warm water, and the vinegar, and mix thoroughly. Knead for a minute or two in the bowl until the mixture forms a stiff dough.

Grease your hands lightly and shape the dough into a 12″ cylinder. With a sharp knife, slice the roll into 16 pieces.

For each piece spread ¼ teaspoon of seeds on a table top or counter and then press the dough into the seeds. Roll with a rolling pin into a paper-thin wafer. Spread another ¼ teaspoon of seeds and turn the wafer onto them.

When you've finished 4 or 5 wafers, slide them onto an ungreased cookie sheet, using a long, wide knife with a sharp edge. Brush the wafers lightly with the remaining butter or oil and bake them for 5 to 7 minutes, until golden brown. Repeat with the rest of the wafers.

Makes 16 wafers.

1 cup whole wheat flour
¼ cup cornmeal
¼ teaspoon baking soda
¼ teaspoon salt
1 teaspoon brown sugar

¼ cup melted butter or oil, divided
¼ cup warm water
1 tablespoon apple cider vinegar

poppy or sesame seeds

Chapatis

3 cups whole wheat flour
1 teaspoon salt
1½ cups warm water

USEFUL EQUIPMENT:

a rolling pin
a griddle
long thick oven mitts
a dish towel or other cloth,
    white linen or muslin

PLEASE BE CAREFUL!

*In India, even the youngest
cook can make chapatis,
but we who did not learn
these skills at mother's
knee have a challenge
before us. Protect your
hands with mitts and your
arms with long sleeves,
and go slowly at first.*

Chapatis are the North Indian version of tortillas, made from stone-ground wheat flour. They're a most delicious bread for eating with curries, or with peanut butter and honey, or cheese and tomato, or any which way.

❧

Mix the flour and salt in a bowl. Slowly add the water, working it into the flour until the dough comes together, soft but not wet. Knead until silky, about 20 minutes. If possible, let the dough rest at room temperature for an hour or so.

Pinch the dough into 12 balls, golf-ball size. Keep covered with a damp cloth while you round each one smooth and then, one at a time, flatten them with a rolling pin on a floured board, making each one about 7 inches across. Don't roll the pin off the edge of the round or the rim of the bread will get too thin. Stack with flour and waxed paper between. Heat the griddle medium-high—if it is too hot, the chapatis will burn; if too cool, they won't puff up. Best of all is to work together with a friend, one rolling and the other baking.

If your griddle is not well seasoned, put a thin film of oil on it. You will be using the dish towel for pressing on the chapatis to encourage them to puff up, so make the towel into a smooth wad that is easy to hold.

Place the first chapati on the hot griddle and let it sit for one second, then turn it over. Use the cloth to press on the top of the bread as it cooks. The object is to help the chapati form steam pockets. Ideally each chapati will puff up round like a balloon, filled with its own steam, though at first it may blister in just a few places. Press gently on the small bubbles to enlarge them. Turn the chapati over as soon as the bottom browns lightly. It won't brown evenly, but will be a pretty pattern of brown and beige. It is done when delicately beige and brown on both sides, with no wet-pinkish places. (Flour will accumulate on the griddle as you cook; wipe it off so it doesn't burn.)

These wonderful breads are best served immediately, but you can wrap them in towels and keep them warm in the oven until time to eat. Don't let them dry out, though.

Breakfast

To eat or not to eat a hearty breakfast is something that goes in and out of fashion. Most important is to work out a way to get your nutrients in a pattern that's comfortable for you, whatever the fashion is. There is some scientific evidence in favor of a good breakfast, though, and our own experience supports it.

For one thing, metabolism is most efficient when we are moving around. Calories, and even demon fat, taken when you'll be exercising, are more likely to be used instead of being stored as fat. The fact that the digestive system rests when we sleep, working slowly or not at all, argues against eating a heavy supper: anyone can attest that going to bed stuffed makes for a sour, sluggish awakening.

Maybe the key to enjoying a substantial breakfast is to be up and around for at least an hour beforehand. There are hidden dividends in getting up early. The first hours of the day are the loveliest. The air is fresh then, and once you've broken free of the pillow your mind is likely to be at its clearest too. The silence of early morning is a perfect background for studying, writing letters, or taking a walk or run. In many traditions, it is the time of day thought to be most auspicious for meditation.

The earlier you get up, the more leisurely your morning can be. That's all-important, because the pace you set in the morning is the pace you'll maintain all day. If there are children about, try especially to keep breakfast time as slow and tranquil as can be. If eyelids are heavy, offer them some incentive: a fresh camellia, or a bowl of bright purple plums.

If you've been up long enough to get breakfast well underway before the family appears, you can actually sit down and eat with them instead of flying around the kitchen bagging lunches, burning toast, and feeding the cat. Children are much more likely to eat a well-balanced breakfast if their parents eat with them. Beyond a few gentle queries, it doesn't seem to matter if you say much. Just being together in a peaceful, warm atmosphere makes all the difference in how everyone gets through the day. Food eaten calmly, without hurry, will be digested much better than when one eye is on the plate and the other on the kitchen clock.

Our own breakfast mainstay during the week is hot whole-grain cereal and toast. Eggs we have only seldom. Buttermilk or

Oatmeal Pancakes turn up maybe one morning a week, or sometimes bagels. We like dry cereal, and granola is a favorite, but we think of such foods more often for snacks than for breakfast because of the nutritional advantages of cooked cereal. Dry toasting, whether of bread or of grains for cereal, destroys substantial amounts of the B vitamins thiamin and folacin and the amino acid lysine, all of which are protected in the kind of cooking that porridge gets. Since low, light toasting minimizes such losses, making your own granola (see page 88) and toasting your bread lightly can make a real difference.

If you can't find time to make your own granola, try to find a local bakery that prepares it with low heat, and without added fat. Nutrition-conscious people often turn away from big-name breakfast cereals to buy granola, only to realize that most commercial granolas are simply loaded with fat—often highly saturated fat—and sugar. Homemade granola can be custom-tailored to your family's needs. It'll taste better, too, because all the ingredients are fresher—and the money saved is impressive.

HOT BREAD

Leftover muffins or rolls, or even not-so-fresh bread, can be revived for breakfast by steaming. Wrap the bread in a damp towel and put it in a covered glass pan in the oven for 20 minutes at 325°F. (Quicker but trickier is to steam the wrapped-up slices on top of the stove in a steamer basket.) If you get your setup worked out, the results can be nearly as appealing as fresh-baked.

BREAKFAST BEANS

Beans for breakfast might seem odd. Our first adventure with them was many years ago, during a visit to the Tassajara Monastery near Santa Cruz. We were startled to encounter a steaming hot bowl of adzuki beans at the breakfast table, served with a pungent pickled radish and a chunk of Tassajara's hefty, whole-grain bread. Maybe it was the mountain air, but nothing could have tasted better, and since then, beans have become a staple breakfast item. Electric slow-cookers cook them perfectly overnight. Strange as it sounds, morning is the ideal time to eat beans, because problems digesting them are minimized by the physical activity of the day.

Besides breakfast recipes, this chapter includes some miscellaneous recipes that might be used throughout the day—instructions for preparing yogurt, buttermilk, and soy milk, and for toasting nuts, wheat germ, and seeds.

Porridge

Hard to believe that anything so satisfying could also be nourishing, inexpensive, and simple to prepare. But then, half the appeal does seem to come from what you put on top. We make our choices from a smorgasbord of healthful garnishes, so every bowl looks a little different.

The cereal we eat most often is an earthy commercial nine-grain, milled nearby, and very fresh. Probably we'd be satisfied if it were the only cereal we ever had. But since receiving a little electric stone mill, we have discovered how amazingly different, and delightfully better, *really* freshly milled grain tastes. Some mixtures that seem especially good to us are listed here for you to try. Some can be mixed from already-cracked grains in your pantry. Rice Cream, though, whose delicate flavor is truly remarkable, can be had only by those who grind their own.

Usually breakfasters expect their porridge to be softer than a dinner grain, and so it is cooked with extra water. As a general rule, unless the cereal is rolled, use 3 to 4 cups water to 1 cup cereal, making about 4 cups of porridge. For rolled cereals follow the directions on the package, or start with 2 cups water to 1 cup grain.

Finely cracked cereals tend to settle in the pot and burn more easily than bigger grains do. For long-cooked porridge with no burning, use a double boiler. Cook and stir over direct heat for just a few minutes first, until the cereal thickens; then put the pot over water. Allow 20 minutes or more, depending on how fine the grain is: the smaller the pieces, the faster they'll cook. If you are pressed for time in the morning, try the thermos method: bring cereal to a boil and stir till it thickens; then put it into a preheated wide-mouthed thermos, cap it, and let it stand overnight. By breakfast time the cereal will be cooked and piping hot. If it's thick, thin it to your liking with more hot water.

SOME GARNISHES FOR BREAKFAST PORRIDGE

*toasted sunflower seeds,
    sesame meal, nuts
    wheat germ
stewed prunes or other
    dried fruit
dates or raisins
fresh fruit in season
yogurt, cottage cheese
    milk or buttermilk
beans*

CEREAL MIXES TO TRY

LIGHT AND BRIGHT

*Equal parts lightly
    toasted millet, cracked
    barley, rice, and oats*

ALL—GRAIN

*Equal parts (or not!)
    cracked wheat, rye, corn,
    barley, rice, oats,
    millet, triticale*

RICE CREAM CEREAL

*7 parts cracked brown rice
1 part cracked brown
    basmati rice*

STUART'S CHOICE

*2 parts cracked wheat
1 part coarse cornmeal*

Granola

4 cups rolled oats
1 cup toasted wheat germ
½ cup chopped toasted nuts
½ cup raisins or
  chopped dried fruits
(½ cup warmed honey)

We have listed the ingredients so simply because granola can be good in so many different variations, and your own will be the very best of all.

❧

Toast the oats in a 300°F oven in a big baking pan. Stir them often until they are fragrant and barely beginning to turn golden. How long this takes will depend on how thick your oats are.

When the oats are done, stir in the other ingredients. *Let cool completely* and store airtight in the refrigerator.

Makes 5½ cups.

TIPS

OATS You can buy rolled oats (and other rolled grains) in several thicknesses, from very thin (Instant) through Quick, Regular, and the thickest, Old-fashioned. If you are making granola for small children, choose one of the thin kinds; children often don't chew well enough to render the thicker ones digestible. Some of our crustier friends really do prefer the chewy natural-foods-store kind, but for most of us a big bowl of that sort of granola can mean a pretty tired jaw. Maybe start with Regular?

TOASTING Once you get your timing down, you may be able to toast oats, nuts, and even wheat germ together, adding each one at the right time so that they are all done at the same moment.

FRUIT Adding the fruit while the other ingredients are still hot lets the fruit get extra-dry and chewy. We like it this way, and it has the added advantage of preventing moisture in the fruit from softening the cereal in storage. If you want fruit that is soft, best add it when you eat.

Raisins or currants are obvious choices, but apricots add something really special, too. For very fancy cereal, add bits of dried pineapple, monukka raisins, chopped pitted prunes, or whatever you think is special.

Nuts add flavor and crunch. Almonds or filberts are our first choice. Or try peanuts, soy nuts, and pumpkin and sunflower seeds. All of these are most flavorful if toasted.

Bran is often added to granola, and if you feel the need to add extra fiber to your diet, this is a good a place to do it—though a diet that includes plenty of whole grains, vegetables, and fruits, probably has adequate fiber already.

For sweeter granola, stir warmed honey into the oats before toasting, or brown sugar or date sugar after toasting. How much to use is up to you, but ½ cup is a good place to start. Honey toasted with the oats has the advantage of making the cereal crunchier, too, which can make the difference between thumbs-up and thumbs-down on homemade granola. You'll want to adjust the amount to your family's tastes. Less is better *unless* it means that they reach for the sugar bowl to take matters into their own spoons! Then less usually means more.

A high percentage of fat calories is one of the most telling arguments against most commercial granolas. When you make your own, it will be delicious without added oil. If you do add oil, however—or shredded coconut—keep the granola in the refrigerator and use it soon; oil that has been treated this way doesn't keep its freshness long.

Toasting Wheat Germ

Raw wheat germ, with its abundance of unsaturated oil, goes rancid very quickly. The low heat of careful toasting helps preserve freshness in two ways, by inactivating enzymes that speed rancidity, and by reducing moisture content.

Unless you can get wheat germ that is freshly milled (very rare indeed), we recommend buying the kind that is toasted where it is milled. If you want to toast your own, the secret to preserving nutrients is to keep the oven temperature low, about 300°F. Use a wide, flat baking dish and stir the toasting wheat germ away from the sides and bottom frequently—it will brown there the fastest. When it is all golden brown, remove from the oven and allow to cool completely before storing airtight in the refrigerator.

Nuts & Seeds, Butters & Meals

TOASTING

Toasting brings out the flavor of nuts and seeds, and makes them crunchier. If it is done carefully, damage to the protein and unsaturated oils is minimal. Always toast *before* chopping. Use a big shallow pan, and keep the oven heat low, not above 325°F; stir often. Roasting in a pan, and oven toasting at higher temperatures, are quicker, but more nutrients will be destroyed and neither flavor nor texture will be quite as good.

NUT AND SEED MEALS

For garnishes, and for some recipes, nut and seed meals are called for. A grain mill with cleanable grinding plates—not most stone mills—or an electric blender or food processor will make meals quite easily. The trick with the blender is to chop the nuts first if they are smooth ones like almonds or filberts, and then do just ½ cup at a time, blending briefly, stopping the motor, stirring from the bottom, and repeating until the grind is right and you have the amount you want.

BUTTERS

Nut and seed butters offer a delicious whole-food alternative to butter and margarine, though keeping them on hand may result in eating *more* fat calories rather than less, because people like them so much and spread them so thick. Still, unlike butter or margarine, they are real foods and do provide nutrients. Fresh, locally-made nut or seed butters often cost less to buy than the nuts or seeds would, to buy and do it yourself. Just read the label to be sure the one you buy has no added oil, salt, sugar, or additives.

Peanut butter presents a special concern. Commercial peanut butter is often made from poor-quality peanuts that are dirty or broken in harvest or storage. Such nuts may be contaminated with the potent liver carcinogen aflatoxin. Whole, sound, clean nuts are likely to be safe, because the mold that produces the toxin requires damaged tissues to grow. Peanuts, which grow under the ground, are especially susceptible to infection when harvested by machine, because so many of them get broken or crushed. Whole, sound nuts are usually reserved for selling as peanuts, while the "splits" are used for making peanut butter. There are ways of checking for the presence of mold, but how carefully this is done is largely up to the processor. (Irradiation of food, incidentally, does not inhibit this mold but greatly stimulates its growth.)

Many natural foods suppliers are extremely conscientious about their peanuts. If you like a particular brand, write or call the company and ask them what precautions they take to protect the consumer. Do they use broken peanuts? Are the nuts tested for presence of the mold that produces aflatoxin? How are they stored? How is the equipment kept clean? If their answers satisfy you, you can probably eat their peanut butter with confidence. Otherwise, we suggest grinding your own from peanuts you know are clean and whole, or switching to almond butter. Happily, bumper crops of almonds in California in recent years have made almond butter an affordable, and delicious, alternative. (Since almonds do not grow under the ground, they are much less subject to damage and to contamination by molds that produce aflatoxin.)

To grind your own peanut or almond butter, use a grinder as described above for making nut meals, but grind finer; or use a food processor, following the manufacturer's directions. Most ordinary blenders are not powerful enough to make smooth nut butter.

SEED BUTTERS

Sesame is wonderfully flavorful, and uniquely resistant to rancidity, so sesame butter—tahini—has been enjoyed in other cultures for many centuries. Tahini is available in various degrees of toastedness in natural foods stores. Usually it is made from hulled seeds, because they make a smoother, less bitter spread. As you would expect, much is lost with the hulls, including B vitamins and minerals. (More about sesame seeds on page 116.) Sunflower seeds make tasty butter, too, but they don't contain a natural antioxidant, as sesame seeds do. Unless preservatives are added, sunflower seeds become rancid quickly after they are ground, so grind just what you'll use in a few days.

Stewed Prunes

An old-fashioned favorite, stewed prunes are a regular item on our breakfast menu. Some of the few remaining prune orchards in California are just a morning's drive away, so we can buy fresh dried prunes in bulk at a good price. Any food cooperative can probably do the same.

For a nutritional bonus, stew the prunes in an iron pot. They take up perfectly usable iron, making them an even richer source of this important mineral.

❧

Cover a pound of dried prunes with cold water and bring to a boil. Simmer for about 20 minutes, until puffy; then, if you like, add a piece of cinnamon stick or half a lemon, scrubbed and sliced, and cook for another 10 minutes or longer, depending on your prunes and your taste. Some of us like to let them stand long enough to make the juice really thick and syrupy—good enough for pancakes, even.

Makes 3½ cups.

Fruit Compote

This sweet treat, a dressier version of stewed prunes, can be elegant or simple. Put about a pound of dried fruit—apricots, peaches, pineapple, prunes, pears—whatever takes your fancy—in a non-iron pan, cover with water, and simmer slowly until all the fruit is tender and the broth is rich and deeply flavored. Lemon or orange slices can be included to good effect. One of the best versions of this dish is just figs with a handful of raisins or prunes and a sliced lemon, simmered an hour and then kept hot on the pilot light (or in a slow cooker) overnight to develop the broth to its syrupy best.

Spoon over hot cereal or pancakes; for dessert, serve compote with yogurt or vanilla pudding—or all by itself in tiny cut-glass dishes. For quick, flavorful homemade jam, puree stewed fruit with some of its juice. Store in the refrigerator.

Better-Butter

This is surely one of the most popular of all our recipes. It offers an easy-spreading alternative to margarine, which can otherwise be the most highly processed—and salted—food in a natural foods kitchen. (For more about margarine and its problems, see page 448.)

Better-Butter combines butter (for flavor) with the unsaturated fats of good-quality oil. The result is a spread that's as low in saturated fat as margarine, but without hydrogenation, processing, and additives. You probably won't need to add the salt unless you have been using a salty margarine up until now.

1 cup safflower or corn oil
1 cup (½ pound) butter
2 tablespoons water
2 tablespoons powdered nonfat milk
¼ teaspoon lecithin
(½ teaspoon salt)

≥å

Use butter that is soft but not melted. One version of Better-Butter can be made by simply blending equal parts of oil and butter together, pouring into covered containers, and storing in the refrigerator. By including the other ingredients, though, you will have a spread that stays firm a little longer at room temperature.

Blend all ingredients until smooth. Refrigerate. Makes just over 2 cups.

Apple Butter

Here is another kind of "butter"—strangely, it really does work as a spread all by itself. Adjust the honey and the cider vinegar to the tartness of the apples you have.

2 pounds flavorful apples
½ cup apple juice or water
¼ to ½ cup cider vinegar
2 to 3 tablespoons honey or brown sugar
1 teaspoon cinnamon
¼ teaspoon allspice
dash cloves

≥å

Core and quarter apples and place in a saucepan with apple juice (or water), and vinegar. Bring to a boil, then lower heat, cover, and simmer until apples are soft—perhaps as long as ½ hour.

Press apples through a food mill or strainer and return to saucepan along with honey, cinnamon, allspice, and cloves. Bring to a boil, then lower heat to a brisk simmer, stirring frequently, as mixture reduces. When it "sheets" as you drop it from a spoon, it is ready. Refrigerate to store.

Makes 2 to 3 cups.

Old-Fashioned Pancakes

2 cups whole wheat flour
½ cup wheat germ
  (or just use more flour)
2 teaspoons baking powder
1 tablespoon brown sugar
1 teaspoon salt

2 large eggs
2½ to 3 cups fresh milk

2 tablespoons oil

Add interest to these or other kinds of pancakes by sprinkling the the griddle first with sesame, sunflower, or poppy seeds. Using wheat germ is optional, but it does improve the pancakes' texture, especially if your flour is finely ground. (Bran works too.) Coarser flours—like most stone-ground flours—make tender, light pancakes.

With coarse flour, it is entirely possible to make light, tasty pancakes without dairy products: simply use the dry ingredients as listed, plus water in place of the egg and milk measure. Leaving out the oil is also an option, though there, the character of the cakes is quite different. Let oil-free pancakes cook longer, over slightly lower heat.

Friends who make pancakes often like to stir up 3 or 4 batches of dry ingredients and store them airtight in the refrigerator, ready to mix with liquid as the occasion arises.

૭ৡ

Stir together all the dry ingredients.

Beat the eggs lightly and combine with the milk, then add to the dry ingredients and stir briefly. Stir in oil.

Heat the griddle. It should be hot enough so that when you sprinkle water drops on the surface, they dance. Unless the griddle is hopelessly unseasoned, it shouldn't need any grease. Pour the batter onto griddle by large spoonfuls. Cook over medium heat, turning once when bubbles come to the surface and pop, and the edges are slightly dry.

Makes 18 pancakes.

BUTTERMILK PANCAKES

Replace baking powder with 1 teaspoon baking soda and substitute buttermilk for sweet milk. These tender delicacies are a great favorite.

FRESH CORN PANCAKES

Add a cup of cooked corn kernels to either of the above.

Oatmeal Pancakes

Combine the milk and rolled oats in a bowl and let stand at least 5 minutes.

Add the oil and beaten eggs, mixing well; stir in the flour, sugar, baking powder, and salt. Mix just until the dry ingredients are moistened.

Bake on a hot, lightly oiled griddle, using ¼ cup of batter for each pancake. Turn them when the top is bubbly and the edges are slightly dry.

Makes 10 to 12 four-inch pancakes.

WHEATLESS OAT CAKES

Make 1¾ cups of flaky meal by spinning 2 cups or so of rolled oats in blender. Use instead of the combined oat and wheat measure.

Mix ingredients and let stand about 5 minutes. If griddle is not well seasoned, oil it lightly, as these pancakes tend to stick.

Makes 12.

1¼ cups milk
1 cup rolled oats

1 tablespoon oil
2 eggs, beaten

½ cup whole wheat flour
1 tablespoon brown sugar
1 teaspoon baking powder
¼ teaspoon salt

Buckwheat Pancakes

Sift the buckwheat flour (it tends to be lumpy) and stir the other dry ingredients in lightly with a fork.

Add the oil, beaten egg, and milk, and mix briefly. Include orange peel for a gourmet touch.

Cook the pancakes on a medium-hot, lightly oiled griddle. Buckwheat pancakes take a little extra cooking, so wait until bubbles appear all over the surface before turning them.

Makes 18 four-inch pancakes.

1 cup buckwheat flour
2 teaspoons baking powder
1 cup whole wheat flour
(use whole wheat pastry flour for very tender cakes)
½ teaspoon salt
1 tablespoon brown sugar

1 tablespoon oil
2 eggs, beaten
2 cups fresh milk
(grated peel of 1 orange)

Potato Latkes

1 tablespoon onion, or more
1 tablespoon oil

2 teaspoons active dry yeast
1 cup warm milk, stock,
   or water

1 medium potato
1 egg, beaten
1 teaspoon salt (scant)
1/2 cup whole wheat flour
1/4 cup wheat germ

These richly flavored yeast-raised potato pancakes are light, delicious, and not at all greasy—wonderful not only for breakfast, but at any time of day. Easy to make, too—a favorite for Sunday supper with a big spinach salad.

Sauté onion in oil. Dissolve yeast in liquid. Grate potato and mix together with egg, salt, flour, and wheat germ. Add the onion with its oil.

Let rise 30 minutes. Stir down. Cook over medium heat on lightly oiled griddle until browned on each side, about 6 to 7 minutes.

Serve with applesauce and yogurt or Mock Sour Cream.
Makes 8 pancakes.

Stewed Apples or Applesauce

6 flavorful apples
handful raisins
1/2 cup water or apple juice

(lemon juice or peel)

Core apples and cut into chunks. Add raisins and water or apple juice, bring to a boil, and simmer until tender. To make applesauce, mash with a fork.

Lemon lends a piquant touch to complement the raisins' sweetness.

Makes 3 or 4 cups.

Fresh Fruit Sauce

4 ripe bananas
1 orange, peeled
juice of 1 lemon
1/4 cup raisins
1/4 cup boiling water

A pancake topping that really can compete with syrup, this is quick to prepare, too. Since bananas tend to darken, eat this soon after preparing it.

Pour boiling water over raisins and let stand a moment until raisins are plump. Combine all ingredients in blender and puree until smooth.

Makes 1 1/2 to 2 cups.

Dosas

Dosas are a classic South Indian pancake and an adventure in a whole other way of thinking about meal preparation. They must be set up two days in advance, and brought along in stages, and the cook—usually a mother, grandmother, or aunt—proudly insists on serving them hot from the griddle, so she doesn't get to sit down until the happy eaters can eat no more.

1/3 cup hulled split
* black gram (*urid dal*)*
* or garbanzo beans*
pinch whole fenugreek seeds
1 cup brown rice
scant 1/2 teaspoon salt
1/3–1/2 cup water
oil

≈

Soak the dal (or garbanzos), fenugreek, and rice overnight in ample water to cover.

The next morning, drain most of the water off and, using only as much water as necessary, grind the mixture in blender or processor to make a paste that is light and frothy. When smooth, add the salt and water to make a thick pouring consistency—a little thinner than normal pancake batter. Let stand about 24 hours, loosely covered, at warm room temperature.

To cook the dosas you will need a griddle, a serving spoon with a round, shallow scoop, a saucer with a small amount of oil in it, and a pancake turner.

The griddle should be a little cooler than for pancakes, or the batter will "pick up" and you won't be able to make the dosas thin enough. Unless the griddle's surface is very well seasoned, wipe it with a cloth dipped in oil. Stir the batter as you make the dosas.

Pour about 3 tablespoons of batter in the middle of the pan. Using the back of your big spoon, and starting in the center, spread the batter in a spiral from the center outwards to make a very thin pancake about 9″ to 10″ across. It will show a slight pinwheel from the track of your spoon. Next, dip the tip of your spatula in the oil and flick tiny droplets over the dosa—that helps it cook. When the top surface has dried, loosen the cake from the griddle with your spatula, and turn it over. You can turn it more than once. Dosas can be made paper-thin and very crisp or slightly thicker and soft. They are done if you can press the dosa with the back of your spatula, without a sizzling sound. Thin dosas cook much faster than thick ones.

Serve hot from the griddle with Tomato or Coconut Chutney; or make MASALA DOSAS: spoon a couple of tablespoons of Masala Potatoes or Dal (next page) on the dosa, and fold it in half.

Makes about 12.

Masala Potatoes

3 large potatoes

1–2 large onions,
1 tablespoon minced ginger
1 green chili
   (or ¼ green bell pepper)

1–2 tablespoons oil
1 teaspoon black mustard
   seeds

1 teaspoon turmeric
½ teaspoon salt

juice of ½ lemon
chopped fresh coriander
   leaves

The proportions of onion and potato in this dish can vary. If you want to serve it as a vegetable dish, tasty but not overpowering, use the measures as they are given; if it is to be a relish for dosas or a filling for stuffed eggplant, use more onion and less potato.

Steam the potatoes until tender. While they are cooking, cut up the other vegetables: the onions should be cut in ½″ cubes; the ginger and chili minced. (If you use a whole chili the dish will be fiery beyond belief. To make it merely hot, take out the seeds; use only part, and it will be nippy. Green pepper without any chili at all is fine for most Western palates.) Peel and mash the potato, or cut into cubes.

Heat the oil in a heavy skillet and drop in the mustard seed. Cover and let the seeds pop; the moment the sound of popping quiets down, add the onions. Stir and sauté until the onions are soft; then add the ginger and chili or green pepper, continuing to sauté gently for about a minute. Stir in the turmeric and salt, then the potatoes, and half a cup of water or so. Cook and stir until the water evaporates and the mixture is dry. Add lemon juice and coriander leaves, stir well, and remove from heat. Serve with Dosas or Chapatis; or use as a side dish, or as a stuffing for peppers or small eggplants.

Makes about 3 cups.

Dal

1½ cups yellow split peas
1 teaspoon salt
1 onion
½ green pepper
1 teaspoon turmeric
½ teaspoon curry powder
2 tablespoons oil
1½ teaspoons black
   mustard seeds
juice of 1 lemon

In one form or another, this simple, delicious dish is popular all over India—and anywhere else it has been served.

Boil the yellow split peas for about 30 minutes—until they are tender, but not so long that they lose their shape. They should be rather dry, like mashed potatoes. Stir in salt. While the peas are cooking, chop onion and green pepper. Combine with turmeric and curry powder.

Heat oil in a large, heavy pan with a lid. When oil is hot, add mustard seed and cover. The seeds will pop noisily; when the sound quiets down, immediately add onion mixture. Sauté until onion is transparent and golden, and stir into peas along with the lemon juice. Serve with Dosas or Chapatis or over rice or other grains. Makes about 4 cups.

About Cultured Milk

Culturing milk—letting carefully chosen bacteria grow in it, producing various magical changes—is one of the oldest methods of food preservation, practiced by dairying people all over the world. Products like yogurt, buttermilk, and most kinds of cheese, make use of the talents of one or more microorganisms.

Since 1908, when the Nobel Prize-winning Russian scientist Elie Metchnikoff suggested that Bulgarian peasants owed their unusual longevity to the large amounts of yogurt in their diet, scientists have studied the benefits that yogurt offers for health. One discovery is that the microorganisms which culture dairy products make them more digestible: proteins are partially broken down and thus more easily assimilated.

Yogurt is similar to milk in its vitamin and mineral content except that the fermenting bacteria do consume some vitamins—especially B-12, which is reduced by about half. On the other hand, folic acid is synthesized in yogurt by the lactic cultures so that the amount is greatly increased. Calcium, phosphorus, and iron are easier to absorb.

Cultured milk bacteria can supply a digestive enzyme, *lactase*, that most people—except those of northern European stock—cannot make for themselves after childhood. Lactase is responsible for breaking down the natural sugar in milk, *lactose*. People who are deficient in the enzyme find that milk gives them stomachache, gas, and diarrhea. The lactase enzymes in yogurt (and to some extent in other cultured milks) slightly reduce the amount of lactose. Yogurt usually contains *Lactobacillus bulgaricus* and *Streptococcus thermophilus*. These two remain active for some time after they have been eaten, continuing to help with the digestion of milk sugar in the small intestine. *S. thermophilus* has about three times as much lactase as *L. bulgaricus*. If you have trouble digesting milk products, look for the names of these cultures on the label when you buy yogurt.

Buttermilk and sour cream are cultured, but with different organisms that don't reduce lactose. In cheese and cottage cheese, lactose may be diminshed both by the culturing bacteria, if any, and by the removal of whey in cheesemaking.

Cultured dairy products can inhibit the growth of harmful bacteria that cause intestinal infection, diarrhea, flatulence, and

LACTOSE INTOLERANCE

other problems. *Lactobacillus acidophilus* culture (contained in some but not all yogurts) may also help to reestablish a beneficial balance in the intestines after the natural flora have been destroyed by antibiotic medication.

Research has shown that milk lowers blood cholesterol levels, and that cultured milk is more effective in this than uncultured. Other studies indicate that some cultured dairy foods are anticarcinogenic: in animals, eating yogurt has dramatically reduced tumor cell proliferation; and in both animal and human studies, bacterial enzymes associated with bowel cancer were reduced by eating *L. acidophilus*.

The ways microorganisms work for us—in yogurt, wine, miso, tempeh, bread, cheese, and many other foods—is a vast topic for study. A great deal remains to be learned.

Foolproof Yogurt

Homemade yogurt is cheaper than the commercial kind, and can be as good as the best. Because your own yogurt is fresher, the culture will be more vigorous and enzyme activity greater. And when you make your own, you can control the flavor and tartness to suit your taste.

If you use commercial yogurt as your starter, be sure that it has an active culture. If the label says it's pasteurized or stabilized, the contents won't make new yogurt. Best is if the label says "active culture"—unless the container has been on the shelf for weeks. Once you get your own yogurt-making system going, you will always have a lively starter, and the time each batch of yogurt takes to set will be less.

Using powdered milk makes the process much simpler because there's no milk to heat, no pan to wash; you just use tap water at the right temperature. To us, yogurt made this way is so good that there's no need for the added fat and cholesterol of whole milk. But yogurt made from fresh milk *is* delicious. To make low-fat or whole milk yogurt, use the same recipe, but scald the milk and cool it to 120°F beforehand. Heat the milk gently because scorching spoils the flavor; a double boiler is best, if you have one. Fresh milk makes tender yogurt; if you want it firmer, blend in 2 tablespoons of milk powder along with the starter.

If your oven has a pilot or electric light, the temperature inside may be just right for incubating yogurt during times when you have nothing to bake. Or keep the yogurt on a heating pad in a warm nook, covering it with towels or newspapers to keep in the warmth. Some people like to use a Styrofoam box filled with warm water, and set the jars in that. Many things work, so long as the temperature stays steady long enough: 90° to 120°F. Above 120°F the culturing bacteria will die.

MISCELLANEOUS TIDBITS

Powdered low-fat and whole milks are available, but there is concern that the drying process damages the cholesterol in these products, making it especially harmful.

POWDERED WHOLE MILK

We recommend using non-instant milk powder because sometimes the instant kind is tricky for making yogurt. If you can get only instant, you will need more powder than we call for here. For making yogurt, use one-eighth more milk powder than the package directs for mixing regular-strength milk. (1½ cups milk powder instead of the normal 1⅓ to make a quart, for example.) If you find that you have trouble making yogurt, try reconstituting the milk and letting it stand overnight in the refrigerator. Warm it to temperature the next day to make yogurt.

INSTANT POWDERED MILK

To keep your starter free from stray organisms, sterilize the jar before you start. A run through the dishwasher will do it, or you can soak the container in this bleach solution for 30 seconds or more. Rinse thoroughly, because residual bleach can kill the yogurt culture. (By the way, this solution will sanitize eating utensils, too.)

STERILIZING CONTAINERS

1 tablespoon 5% chlorine bleach
2 gallons warm (not hot) water

1/4 cup plain yogurt
1 cup non-instant powdered
* skim milk*
3 1/2 cups water, 100–110°F

EQUIPMENT

1 one-quart glass
* or plastic jar with lid*
electric blender
a warm place

Fill the jar with warm water to about 2 inches from the top. Pour 1 cup of the warm water into the blender. Turn the blender on low and add the milk powder and the yogurt. The instant the mixture is smooth, stop blending and return it to its jar. This prevents the milk from foaming.

Set the filled jar in a warm place and leave undisturbed for 3 1/2 to 8 hours. The livelier the culture and the warmer the place, the more quickly the yogurt will set. Check from time to time. As soon as the surface of the yogurt resists a light touch of your finger even slightly, it is ready; but if you want a tart flavor, leave it another hour.

Refrigerate and let cool completely before you dip into it.

The first spoonful of yogurt from each jar can be set aside to be the starter for the next batch. To keep your starter fresh, plan your amounts to make yogurt at least once a week.

TROUBLESHOOTING YOGURT

The yogurt didn't set up

—Is your milk powder fresh? Fresh dried milk is odorless—take a sniff to see.

—Was the water too hot? Below 95°F the yogurt bacteria are not active; above 120°F, they die. The water should feel just warm to your hand. A dairy or chef's thermometer can be helpful here.

—Was your culture too old, or was your starter from a stabilized commercial brand? Try again with a different kind. Cheap local brands are often fresher and livelier than their more expensive and long-traveling colleagues.

—Did you sterilize the container with bleach and not rinse it well enough?

The yogurt tastes chalky

—The milk mixture might have been too concentrated. If you allow foam to build up when you're mixing powdered milk, it will fill your container and can trick you into including less water than is needed.

The yogurt is very soft or tender

—Either the milk solution is too dilute or the yogurt needed more time to set up. You can make yogurt extremely firm, if you want to, by increasing the amount of milk; but skim milk yogurt that is made very concentrated may taste chalky.

The yogurt separates and tastes sour

—Probably it was warm too long. Sometimes this happens if your refrigerator can't cool it fast enough; try cooling as suggested for soymilk on page 107, or just remove it from the heat promptly as soon as it has set.

—Another possibility is that your heat source is too intense. Prop the oven door open with a roll of towel or turn the heating pad down a notch.

The yogurt tastes off

—Some stray bacteria might have set up housekeeping. Start over with a new culture, and be careful to keep your starter and containers absolutely clean. Merely gamy yogurt isn't harmful, but if your batch smells really hideous, don't taste it, toss it.

Yogurt Cheese

Yogurt cheese made with low-fat yogurt is a slim version of sour cream or cream cheese (depending how stiff you make it), useful in many ways. The nonfat version can taste overwhelmingly yogurty by itself, but still be useful for such dishes as Jaji (page 118), Yogurt Cheese Pie (page 326), or Topping (page 318)—anywhere there are other flavors going.

❧

Line a colander or strainer with a large cloth napkin. Turn a quart of yogurt into it and allow to drain until the cheese is as stiff as you want, anywhere from 6 to 24 hours. You can hang it over a sink by tying the napkin closed and fastening it to the faucet, but outside the refrigerator the cheese will become very tart. Another option is to suspend the yogurt over a bowl in the refrigerator.

No matter how stiff it is, when yogurt cheese is beaten hard it becomes liquid, so handle it gently when mixing.

Makes about 2 cups.

Buttermilk

We find that powdered milk doesn't make tasty buttermilk. If you can get good buttermilk for about the same price as fresh skim milk, there may be no reason to culture your own. But if splendid unsalted or skim-milk buttermilk is hard to find in your area, here's a dependable, simple method for making it:

❧

To 2 quarts fresh skim milk, add ⅓ cup delicious buttermilk. Let stand at 65°–70°F for 24 to 36 hours. How long it takes will depend on how vigorous your starter is and whether the milk was straight from the refrigerator. When it tastes good to you, refrigerate it.

Soymilk

Soymilk is not a whole food, and it is far from being a nutritional substitute for milk, but for people to whom milk is not acceptable, what a boon!

Bottled soymilk has improved a lot in the last few years, and if you can get fresh liquid soymilk from a soy dairy nearby, you may find it quite good. The unflavored kind can be used in cooking wherever milk is called for; the flavored versions provide a reasonable alternative to milk for drinking. We really can't recommend any powdered variety we know of: the flavors are either too strong and beany or overly sweet. The list of additives can be amazing, and the price sky-high. Highly commercialized liquid soymilks have some of these problems too: more incentive for buying from a small local soy dairy, or making your own. The homemade version is wonderfully cheap and far more delicious than any you can buy, though it's decidedly not a "quick and easy" recipe.

COMPARING SOYMILK

1 cup	Calories kcal	Protein g	Riboflavin mg	B-12 mg	Calcium mg	Fat g	% cals as fat	Sat. Fat g	Unsat. Fat g
Soymilk: plain	73	7.5	0.1	0	46	3.3	40	0.5	2.4
sweetened	115	7.5	0.1	0	46	3.3	30	0.5	2.4
Skim milk	86	8.4	0.3	0.9	300	0.4	10	0.3	0.1
Whole milk	150	8.0	0.4	0.9	290	8.2	50	5.0	2.7
Goat's milk	168	8.7	0.3	0.2	320	10.0	50	6.5	3.1
Broccoli	46	4.6	0.3	0	140	0.4	10	0.1	0.2

Soymilk is a food in its own right, and maybe it's unfair to compare it with cow's milk. Still, since people use it as if it were cow's milk, knowing the nutritional differences is important, especially when considering the needs of children.

Soymilk has the same amount of protein as cow's milk and less fat than low-fat milk; almost all its fat is unsaturated. So much carbohydrate is removed from the soybeans when soymilk is made that almost none remains. One reason we suggest adding honey or barley malt syrup is that many people who drink soymilk are vegans—that is, vegetarians who avoid all foods of animal origin, including milk—and one of their nutritional needs is plain old *calories*. Soymilk is low or lacking in certain other nutrients richly supplied in milk: calcium, vitamin B-12, and riboflavin. (See suggestions for fortification on page 108.)

The basic procedure for making soymilk is to soak the beans in water for 4 to 16 hours until they are saturated, then grind them up fine in a blender, with more water. The "milk" is then strained off, flavored, cooked, and refrigerated.

Soymilk can have a bitter beany taste, the result of an enzyme (lipoxygenase or lipoxidase) that goes into action when the bean is broken in the presence of air and water. Scientists at Cornell University developed a way to inactivate the lipoxidase, and it is on their method—along with our own years of weekly soymilk production—that the following recipe is based.

&

METHOD

The secret of the Cornell process is to grind the beans in *hot* water, at least 180°F, which inactivates the lipoxidase. (Cooking the beans first and *then* grinding them inactivates lipoxidase too, but the protein is thereby rendered insoluble, so it won't make milk.) This boiling–water grind process yields a soymilk that is bland and pleasant-tasting. But you have to be careful that the water you use is at a good rolling boil; it won't work if you let the water boil and then set the kettle aside for even a few minutes. This takes extra effort and time, but the result is well worth it.

1 cup dry soybeans
6 cups boiling water
 (plus 2 cups boiling
 water to heat blender)

FOR FLAVORING

¼ cup honey
 OR
2 tablespoons honey and
2 tablespoons barley malt
 extract

The quality of the soybeans you use will affect the amount and flavor of the milk they yield, so choose beans that are clean and sound. Wash them thoroughly and soak in 3 cups cold water for 4 to 16 hours; in warm weather, you can leave them in the refrigerator. The beans will double in size, so allow room in the container. If the water bubbles a little, it means that the beans fermented slightly: no problem.

Drain the beans well and rinse them in warm (not hot) water. If they were kept in the refrigerator, rinse them long enough to warm them through; this will help you maintain the required heat while the beans are in the blender.

Put a large kettle full of water on to boil. Divide the beans into three equal parts. Preheat the blender by blending 2 cups of boiling water for approximately 1 minute. Stainless steel blender containers are the best. Plastic ones cannot withstand boiling water. Glass tops should be warmed before pouring in boiling water to prevent their cracking.

Grind each portion of beans with 2 full cups of boiling water for 2 to 3 minutes. During the grinding, insulate the blender with a towel to keep the temperature high.

Strain the mixture in a muslin bag to remove the insoluble residue. Squeeze the bag to get as much of the milk as you can.

Mix in the sweetener and take note of the quantity. Heat the milk uncovered for 30 minutes in a double boiler, stirring occasionally to keep it from forming a film on top. Add water to the original quantity, replacing the amount lost to evaporation. This extra heating is important because it deactivates enzymes that interfere with the digestion of protein, soybean trypsin inhibitors (SBTI). Their presence in soybeans makes thorough cooking of any soy product essential.

This recipe makes 6 to 7 cups of soymilk.

A couple of tips to help your soymilk keep fresh longer:

[1] What makes the milk turn sour near the end of the week is the presence of bacteria. Be very careful to keep all your soymilk equipment extremely clean, and sterilize anything that will touch it after it is cooked, even the funnel, if you use one. This should extend the "sweet life" of your soymilk by several days.

[2] If you make a large quantity of soymilk at once, or if your refrigerator isn't up to cooling it in an hour or so, pre-chill the milk by setting it in its jar or pitcher in a dishpan of cold water for about half an hour. Keep the water cold by icing it, or by letting the faucet run in it. If the soymilk is in a plastic or glass container, this process will take longer; metal is best.

A NOTE ON CLEANING
UP AFTER

For easy cleanup, soak the muslin bag and all your equipment in a solution of washing soda immediately after you are through using them. Soda is very strong, so wear rubber gloves, and rinse everything thoroughly.

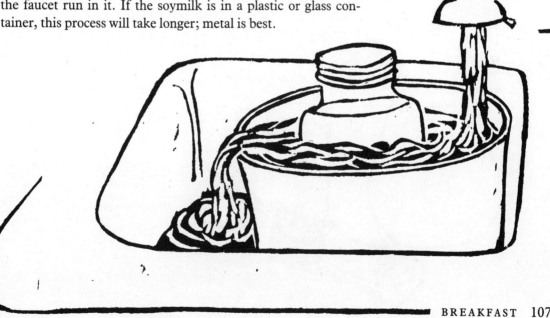

FORTIFICATION

Because of the nutritional differences mentioned above, soymilk can't entirely take the place of milk. If you don't use dairy products, be sure to eat plenty of green vegetables each day for calcium and riboflavin, and include a source of vitamin B-12 also. Special care is necessary in planning food for the vegan child, since children often resist eating vegetables.

Soymilk can provide an alternate source of some nutrients. It is not practical to add riboflavin to soymilk, but you can add B-12 by crushing and stirring in one tablet (the smallest size is 25 milligrams, which is far more than two quarts of milk would supply). Calcium can be added by mixing calcium carbonate, which is available in drug stores, into the soymilk, ½ teaspoonful per cup. The amount of calcium will then be comparable to that of milk, though it will not be absorbed so well and may cause constipation. Calcium lactate can also be used—it dissolves, which is an advantage over carbonate—but if the soymilk is heated, calcium lactate will make it curdle.

FLAVORING

The flavoring we suggest makes a drink that is sweet and delicious to our taste, but there's no reason not to experiment with other sweeteners and flavorings too: molasses, brown sugar, maple syrup; vanilla, or a pinch of cardamom or nutmeg. Keep some unflavored if you want to use it in place of milk in soups, cream sauces, quick breads.

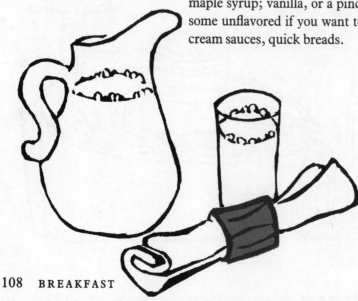

Lunch

Not so long ago most people either ate at home or carried a brown-bag lunch. It's not uncommon now to stop at a deli or fast-food place for something quick that goes down easy. Americans spend 40 cents of their food dollar eating out—an average of 3.7 meals a week. But eating out, while it can be an enjoyable change of pace, isn't the best way to get your nourishment on a regular basis.

The chief nutritional complaints against restaurant food, from fast food to gourmet cuisine, are excessive fat and salt. Fast food in particular is loaded with both. One burger can exceed an adult's recommended daily maximum of salt, and a fast-food meal is not unlikely to have considerably more than half the day's allotment of fat—usually of the worst kind. (That rare vegetarian option, the "cheese"-stuffed potato, may have even more fat and calories than a burger.) Fast-food means frying, often in beef tallow or lard (even for fries, doughnuts, and turnovers), and the fat is used over and over again. Fast-food companies also employ the full array of additives: colorings, thickeners, flavorings, preservatives, emulsifiers. There is consumer pressure to require ingredient labels on fast foods, but at this writing, even if you ask, it's hard to discover what's in a particular item.

The best restaurant meals, of course, are to be had in individually owned places that use fresh, natural ingredients and cook without inordinate amounts of salt or fat. Next best may be a salad bar, where with care you can select a genuinely nutritious meal. But much depends on who's running the show. If the management is not committed to freshness, salad fixings—even lettuce—may be laced with preservatives of many kinds, and the dressings and cheeses can be of the most processed, chemicalized sort.

For such reasons, we and most of our friends prefer to bag our own: it's tastier, cheaper, and more nutritious, and you can take just what you want.

Incidentally, if lunchtime for you means a perfunctory affair with nobody else around—grabbing some bread and whatever, eating between jobs, paying no attention—why should the brown-baggers get all the delights? Even if you don't need much food in

the middle of the day, take the time to treat yourself to some of these suggestions; a home luncher needs pick-me-ups too. If you are tired of sandwiches, a fresh, tasty soup or a really worthy vegetable, grain, or fruit salad takes just moments to prepare. Everyone deserves a lunch that satisfies aesthetic as well as nutritional needs, however simple it may be—and even aside from the food, it's worth taking time to make a break.

Carry-Out Lunches

Even for brown-baggers who like a streamlined lunch, with nothing to carry home when you're done, there are lots of possibilities beyond the standard sandwich and apple. Carrot and celery sticks, of course, but why not green peas in the pod, cherry tomatoes, whole little lemon cucumbers (easy to grow, very digestible)? Besides fruit bars and "real" cookies, try a simple bag of dried fruit and toasted nuts—whether its raisins and peanuts or medjool dates and pecans. Toasting the nuts yourself saves money, avoids oil and salt, and guarantees freshness.

If a small plastic container will come home afterward, a substantial salad—potato, grain, or pasta—makes an interesting break from the usual fare. Or pack some chilled, lightly steamed vegetables from the night before, with a little salad dressing. One of our friends takes a really righteous green salad every day, with the dressing packed separately in a tiny jar. It travels fine.

Moving up another step in the box lunch business brings us to thermoses. Soups, pasta dishes like spaghetti or macaroni with a good sauce, and many vegetables (the less fragile ones are best)— nearly anything, really—will keep its temperature and much of its goodness for hours in a widemouthed thermos. The trick with thermos jugs is to wash them well and never store them empty with their lids on; they get smelly.

Whether you go in for thermos jugs or not, special mention goes to grain salads—Tabouli, Yogurt Rice, and the like—which pack well and go down easily. Any grain left over from the night before can make a scrumptious salad with the help of a tad of yogurt and maybe a little olive oil and lemon, some chopped celery or pepper, and chives. Or skip the grain and use some crisp-tender broccoli with a few leftover noodles, a lace of red bell pepper, and a little Vinaigrette or a sprinkling of grated

Parmesan or toasted sesame seeds. It can taste awfully good around noontime, and makes a cheering change from the routine lunch.

Sandwiches

Sandwiches are a practical favorite, the challenge being to make them delicious and easy-to-eat without lots of mayonnaise or butter. Made with bean spreads, and even with moderate amounts of cheese, they're quite respectably low in fat. Soy spread on whole wheat, for example, is 19 percent fat without mayonnaise; add a tablespoon of mayo and it becomes 41 percent fat. A sandwich with 1 ounce of jack cheese on rye is only 32 percent fat without, 48 percent with. Our conclusion: try to cut back on the mayo. Tomato slices, alfalfa sprouts, sunflower greens, lettuce, pickle, mustard, sliced olives, and such all add juiciness without so many fat calories.

If you do want to use mayonnaise, try cutting it half and half with yogurt, or try our tofu mayonnaises on page 241 for a version much lower in fat. Careful packing, with a double wrap of waxed paper if needed, helps keep bagged sandwiches from drying out.

OTHER PLOYS:

≈ For cheese sandwiches, include lots of goodies—tomato, lettuce, sliced mushroom, cucumber, onion, whatever—and then slice the cheese with the potato peeler, using enough to taste great but not enough to add much fat.

≈ Make cheese spreads by mixing cottage cheese with grated hard cheese for a slightly lower-fat and less expensive cheese filling. (See page 118.)

≈ For egg salad, lower the fat by adding low-fat cottage cheese or chopped firm tofu. You can even substitute tofu for the egg altogether, but since tofu is only slightly lower in fat, its main advantage is that the fat is less saturated and there is no cholesterol.

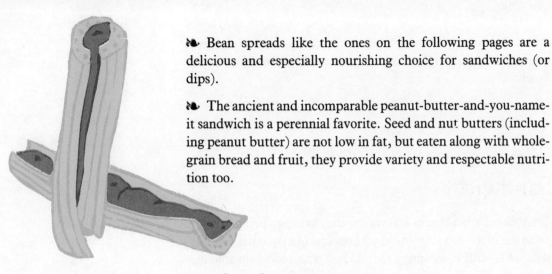

 ❧ Bean spreads like the ones on the following pages are a delicious and especially nourishing choice for sandwiches (or dips).

 ❧ The ancient and incomparable peanut-butter-and-you-name-it sandwich is a perennial favorite. Seed and nut butters (including peanut butter) are not low in fat, but eaten along with whole-grain bread and fruit, they provide variety and respectable nutrition too.

Sandwich Suggestions

Peanut butter and: chopped dates, sliced apple or banana, raisins, or stewed prunes; lettuce and tomato, or pickle

Almond butter and any of these; or try it with Dijon mustard, raisins, spinach leaf, dill pickle

Tofu Bars with pickle and lettuce on Whole Wheat

Pizza sandwich: on a slice of bread, Pocket Bread, or English Muffin, spread fresh tomato slices, pepper ring, oregano; sprinkle with olive oil, add grated cheese and grill until melted

Soy Spread, sprouts, tomato, on any whole-grain bread

Jaji and cucumber slices on Pumpernickel

Lentil Loaf slices, thinly shredded cabbage, and Dijon mustard on Light Rye

Walnut Oatmeal Burgers, mustard, ketchup, pickles, lettuce on a bun

Soy Pâté, cucumber slices, grated carrot on Pumpernickel

Split Pea–Parmesan Spread, red pepper rings, spinach leaves on Cracked Wheat

Garbanzo Spread, cucumbers, and lettuce on Whole Wheat

Reuben's Revenge: Swissy Spread and Vegetable Relish on Rye

Ricotta cheese, toasted walnuts, and Apple Butter on Oatmeal Bread

Yogurt Cheese, chopped dried apricots, and toasted almonds with a dash of cinnamon on Raisin Bread

Refrito Spread, tomato slices, and lettuce rolled in a Chapati

Jaji, grated carrot, cherry tomato, cucumber slices, and Tempeh Bars in Pocket Bread

Sesame spread and banana slices on Buttermilk Bread

Sliced mushrooms, tomato, spinach leaves, and Tofu Mayonnaise on Garbanzo Bread

Chili-Cheddar Spread, sliced olives, tomato, lettuce on Sesame Bread

Bean Spreads

Sandwiches with spreads made from cooked, mashed beans are a delicious addition to the lunch scene. Soy spread has been a staple at our house for years now. We like it best with lettuce or alfalfa sprouts and sliced tomato or pickle.

Beans—even soybeans if they are well-cooked—are easy to mash with a potato masher if you drain them hot from the cooking pot and set to work at once. (If you can't mash them right away, use a meat grinder or food processor; but drain them hot or the spread will be too runny.)

Bean spreads keep for about a week in the refrigerator. If you've made more than you can use up in sandwiches, stir the rest into soups or make Neat Balls or Pine Nut Pinwheels.

Soy Spread

Sauté onion and garlic in oil until onion is soft; then add celery (and green pepper if desired) and continue to cook until onion is transparent. Crush the garlic glove with a fork. Add tomato paste and herbs. Simmer briefly. Stir the sauce into the mashed beans and add vinegar, salt and pepper to taste.

Makes about 1½ cups.

½ onion, minced
1 tablespoon oil (or less)
1 clove garlic
1 small stalk celery,
  chopped fine
(¼ cup chopped green
  pepper)

ZIPPY SOY SPREAD

Omit basil. When onion is nearly cooked, stir in ½ teaspoon cumin and a dash of cayenne. If you have coriander powder, add 1 teaspoon of that, too.

2 tablespoons tomato paste
1 teaspoon basil
½ teaspoon oregano

QUICK SOY SPREAD

Stir ¼–½ cup flavorful tomato sauce into mashed beans; correct for salt.

1 cup cooked, mashed
  soybeans
1–2 teaspoons vinegar
½ teaspoon salt
dash pepper

SOY SPREAD WITH PARSLEY

Omit the tomato paste and herbs. Add ¼ cup chopped fresh parsley to the onion and celery before taking off heat. Add 1 teaspoon soy sauce and the juice of ½ lemon as you mix the ingredients together.

Garbanzo Spread

½ onion, chopped
1 clove garlic
1 tablespoon oil
dash cumin
salt to taste
1 teaspoon basil
½ teaspoon oregano
½ bunch parsley,
    chopped fine
juice of 1 lemon
3 cups cooked garbanzo
    beans, mashed

(⅔ cup toasted sesame
    seeds, ground)

Garbanzo Spread is an enduring favorite. Try it as an open-face sandwich with cucumber and tomato slices, or thin it with a little vegetable or bean stock and serve as a dip with whole wheat crackers.

Sauté onion and garlic in oil until onion is transparent. Add cumin and cook until fragrant. Crush garlic with a fork. Add herbs and parsley at the last minute, cooking just enough to soften parsley. Mix with the lemon and mashed beans (and sesame), stirring together thoroughly.

Makes about 3 cups.

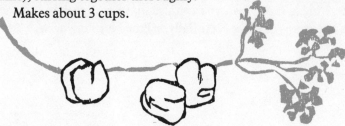

Refrito Spread

1½ cups cooked,
    well-drained pinto,
    kidney, or black beans

1 bunch scallions
    or a big onion
1 tablespoon oil

1 or 2 cloves garlic
½ teaspoon cumin powder
1 teaspoon chili powder
¼ chopped green pepper
    or chopped green chili
    peppers

½ cup grated cheddar cheese
½ teaspoon salt

Mash the beans. You should end up with about a cup.

Chop the onion and sauté with whole garlic cloves in oil. When the onion is done, crush the garlic with a fork. Add the spices and the green pepper. (If you are a chili fan, you can use green chilies instead of pepper.) Cook until the pepper is softened and the spices are fragrant.

Remove from heat and cool slightly. Add beans and mix. Add cheese and salt, and check the flavor: if the beans were unsalted, you may need more salt.

Makes about 1¾ cups.

Split Pea Spreads

When you make these spreads, you can use either plain cooked split peas (cooked with less water than you would use for soup) or very thick leftover pea soup (much tastier!). In either case, the peas should be cool when you mix the spread so that you can judge the consistency accurately. If you don't use soup, you can make the spread tastier by sautéeing onion and garlic in the oil measure before adding the peas, or by adding shoyu or miso to taste.

&

Mash split peas and mix with other ingredients. Refrigerate.

SPLIT PEA—PARMESAN

1 cup cooked green split peas
2 tablespoons oil (or less)
2 tablespoons Parmesan cheese
2 tablespoons cottage cheese
¼ teaspoon basil
salt to taste
dash pepper

SPLIT PEA—SUNSEED

1 cup cooked green split peas
2 tablespoons oil (or less)
¾ to 1 cup toasted
*   sunflower seeds, ground*
salt to taste
dash pepper
(2 tablespoons lemon juice)
(2 tablespoons whole
*   toasted sunflower seeds)*

SPLIT PEA—TOFU DIP

1 cup cooked green split peas
2 tablespoons oil
1 pound firm tofu
1 cup toasted sunflower
*   or sesame seeds, ground*
1 tablespoon light miso,
*   or salt to taste*

Soy Pâté

This delicious and very savory pâté makes a sophisticated sandwich spread, very easy to make once the soybeans are at hand.

&

Sauté the onion in oil, adding the garlic once the onion is transparent and beginning to turn golden. Continue to sauté briefly, taking care not to burn the garlic. Remove from heat. Put the seeds in the blender, whirling them until they are ground. (You can grind them any way you want, but this is very fast.)

Mix all the ingredients together. The pâté will be stiff, which is fine if you are going to serve it on pumpernickel bread; otherwise, stir in water or stock until the consistency is more to your liking. Adjust salt.

Without the optional added liquid, the recipe makes a little over a cup.

1 onion, chopped fine
1 tablespoon oil
2 cloves garlic, minced

½ cup toasted
*   sunflower seeds*
1 cup cooked, mashed
*   soybeans*
¾ teaspoon salt
pepper

Sesame Seeds

Natural sesame seeds are sometimes called "brown" because they are a darker color than the hulled and bleached supermarket variety. They lose some important nutrients along with the hulls. Looking at food charts, you'd think the most important loss is calcium, which is present in very large amounts in sesame hulls. But the calcium in the hulls is in a form that is unavailable, so calcium is really not the issue: probably you get the same small amount whether the seeds are hulled or not. More significant are the losses of folacin and vitamin B-6; and thiamin if the seeds are alkali processed. Minerals go, too, especially iron and potassium.

Since most sesame seeds grow in Latin America, what about pesticide residues? Arizona sesame producer Ray Langham told us that sesame seeds grow well without pesticides in Arizona and northern Mexico, but farther south, where a large part of the supply comes from, this is not usually possible. Importers seldom distinguish which batch comes from where. The tiny seeds are difficult to clean, too, and so may have traces of natural as well as chemical activity. To ameliorate both problems, toast before using. Conserve nutrients by using low heat, 300° to 325°F, stirring often. They are done when a shade darker, and too hot to hold in your hand.

Some natural foods companies are beginning to market domestic, organically grown seeds. Why not see whether your co-op or store carries them?

Sesame Spread

¾ cup natural sesame seeds
1 tablespoon honey
   or other sweetener
¼ cup water
   or apple juice
⅛ teaspoon salt

Toast sesame seeds and grind into a meal in blender; remove to bowl and add honey, water, and salt. The mixture will thicken as it cools, so you may want to thin it by adding more water or juice.

Slightly less quick, but very good, is to use raisins for sweetener. Pour boiling water over ½ cup raisins, and let them stand until cool. Blend or process the soaked raisins along with the seeds, adding the soaking water as needed to achieve a reasonably smooth grind.

Makes ¾ cup with honey, 1 cup with raisins.

Tofu or Tempeh Bars

The saucy bars are delicious hot from the pot over rice or toast, and the remains may be even tastier the next day or two in sandwiches. Leftover tempeh bars are good to crumble and stir into spaghetti sauce or chili.

Use either tofu or tempeh in this recipe. The difference is that tempeh takes longer to absorb the flavors of the sauce. It tastes best and is tenderer after a really long simmer, so its sauce needs extra liquid at the beginning.

ह

If you are using tofu, rinse it first. For sandwiches, slice tempeh or tofu into bars about ¼" thick and somewhere around the size of half the slice of bread. If you are serving the dish hot, cut the pieces any size that appeals to you.

Chop onion and sauté in oil in a large skillet until golden. Stir in the shoyu, vinegar, tomato paste, water or broth, and mustard. Bring to a boil. Arrange tofu or tempeh slices in the pan, spooning the sauce over them as you do. Be sure they are covered with sauce.

If you will be serving the dish hot, cover and simmer about 20 minutes for tofu, ½ hour or longer for tempeh. Serve over toast or rice.

If you want to use the bars for cold sandwiches, cook uncovered until the sauce is evaporated and absorbed, making a glaze on the bars. Keep an eagle eye on them while you do this to prevent their sticking and burning.

FOR A PEPPIER SAUCE add a clove of garlic and pinch of cayenne to the onion when sautéeing. Toward the end of the sautéeing time, crush the garlic with a fork and add a tablespoon of chopped fresh ginger.

SERVE OVER RICE or noodles, or with spaghetti: When the onions are nearly done, add 2 cups or so of sliced mushrooms and ½ cup diced celery if desired. Increase the broth or water and add more salt or shoyu to taste.

1 pound firm tofu
 or tempeh

1 onion
2 tablespoons oil

2 tablespoons shoyu
2 tablespoons vinegar
¼ cup tomato paste
1½–2 cups water or broth
¼ teaspoon mustard
pepper

Cheese Spreads

1 cup grated natural cheese
1 or more cups
   low-fat cottage cheese

OPTIONAL ADDITIONS

finely chopped celery or
   green or red pepper
minced parsley, chives
chopped tomatoes
paprika
mustard powder
dill weed

Cheese is high in fat and natural cheeses are expensive, but cost and fat both go down when you grate the cheese and mix it with low-fat cottage cheese to make a flavorful spread. Start with a half-and-half mixture and experiment. You can raise the portion of cottage cheese much higher and still have good results.

Below are some spreads fancy enough to serve on a buffet platter. For everyday sandwich making, a plain mixture is fine: Swiss, jack, or good sharp cheddar with low-fat cottage cheese. The spread will keep as long as the cottage cheese stays fresh, and it can be used to make sandwiches of many moods.

≈

Mix the ingredients together and refrigerate. If you add fresh vegetables—tomatoes, for example, or peppers—make only what you will use in a day or two.

SWISSY SPREAD

½ cup grated Swiss
½ cup low-fat cottage cheese
¼ cup chopped green pepper
½ teaspoon dill weed
salt and pepper to taste

JACK AND DILL SPREAD

½ cup grated jack cheese
½ cup low-fat cottage cheese
½ teaspoon dill weed
1 tablespoon chopped
   toasted almonds
1 tablespoon minced chives
   or scallion tops
(½ teaspoon Dijon mustard)

CHILI–CHEDDAR SPREAD

½ cup grated cheddar
½ cup low-fat cottage cheese
1 small onion, chopped
   and well sautéed with
   a clove of garlic and
1 teaspoon chili powder

Jaji

1 cup cottage cheese
1 cup yogurt cheese
⅓ cup finely chopped
   green pepper
3 scallions, chopped
⅓ cup finely chopped celery
½ teaspoon dill weed

Jaji is Armenian and unabashedly oniony, so if your tastes are for milder fare, start with only the inner leaves of one scallion rather than three whole ones, or use chives. Nippy as it is, Jaji is very refreshing. It can be either a dip or sandwich spread, depending on how stiff you make the yogurt cheese.

≈

Blend cottage and yogurt cheese with potato masher or put through food mill. Add green pepper, scallions, celery, and dill weed.

Makes 2½ cups.

Smoothie

This versatile summertime beverage easily accommodates many needs. It can be a quick, light lunch when you're at home; when you're packing a meal, smoothie travels better in a thermos than plain milk does. Dieters can enjoy the low-calorie version made with skim milk or buttermilk, while those who need to gain weight find that a smoothie (made calorie-rich with nut butter) goes down easily when other food might seem overwhelming.

1 cup milk or buttermilk or soymilk
½ cup or so fresh fruit: one banana, a peach, strawberries, apricots; or combinations: orange and banana, date and banana, etc.

EXTRAS

(1 or 2 of the following, —or none—but not all!)
1 tablespoon almond butter
1 teaspoon nutritional yeast
2 tablespoons wheat germ
1 tablespoon soy powder
1 tablespoon milk powder

Blend in blender until smooth. Makes one serving, about 1½ cups.

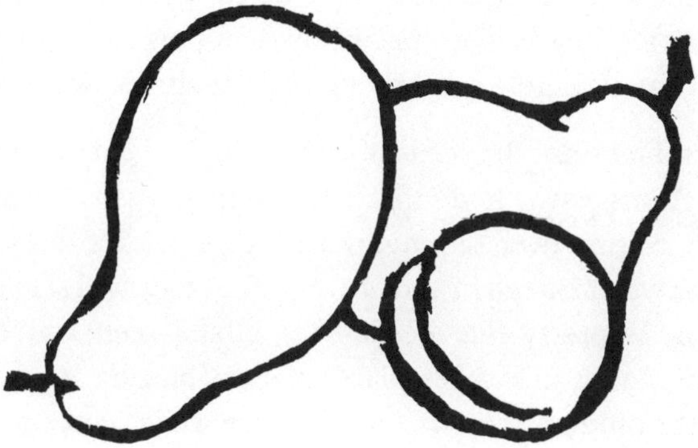

Mock Rarebit

Serve this rather zippy sauce over toast or as a dip for chunks of French Bread, fondue-style. Not bad on veggies either.

1 tablespoon cornstarch
1½ cups milk, divided

¾ cup cottage cheese
¼ teaspoon salt
1 teaspoon mustard powder

½ cup grated sharp cheddar cheese

Mix the cornstarch into ½ cup of the milk and set aside.

Blend the cottage cheese smooth in blender with 1 cup of the milk, or heat cottage cheese in the top of a double boiler until melted, stirring until it is smooth. Stir in the remaining ingredients except the cheddar and heat gently, letting them simmer very slowly for 10 minutes. Stir in the grated cheese and serve.

Makes 2¼ cups, enough for about 6 slices of toast.

Sprouts

The classics for sprouting are mung beans, garbanzos, lentils, wheat berries, and alfalfa seeds; but if you get into sprouting, try fenugreek, watercress, sunflower, radish, or mustard seeds, or other whole grains or beans. Be sure that the seeds you sprout were meant for food and haven't been treated for planting. For best nutrition, use your sprouts within a couple of days.

[1] Check your seeds or beans and remove rocks or other interlopers. Soak about ⅓ cup of your selection in a quart jar of cool to tepid water overnight. Choose a wide-mouthed jar if you have one. A quart jar is big enough to hold the ⅓ cup of most seeds or beans after they are sprouted, though not big enough for mung sprouts (if you want to grow them long) or alfalfa (see below).

[2] Next day, rinse the seeds in cool water and drain them thoroughly. An easy way to do this is to fasten a piece of cheesecloth or nylon netting over the mouth of the jar with a thick rubber band: the water can go in and out, but the seeds will stay behind. (You'll need pretty fine netting for alfalfa seeds, of course!) Keep the jar in a darkish place—if possible, on its side—and protect the mouth with a damp towel; the seeds want air but they don't want to dry out.

[3] Rinse the sprouts two times a day—three if the weather is hot. Be sure to drain them well each time.

[4] Depending on what you are sprouting, your crop may be ready by the second or third day. Sunflower seeds are sweetest when the sprout is only one-third the length of the seed. Sprouts from mung beans, lentils, and most other beans can be eaten the third day. Alfalfa sprouts take about five.

SOME SPECIAL CASES:

ALFALFA SPROUTS

During the winter when the lettuce supply isn't the best, we are grateful for the freshness of alfalfa sprouts in salads and sandwiches. Their virtues may have been overpraised, but their nutritional assets are respectable—they compare quite favorably with lettuce!

The sprouter trays sold in natural foods stores are terrific because you can rinse and green your sprouts in the same tray. It's easy to do a good job with everyday home equipment, though, and here's a simple method.

For the first three days, follow the method suggested for other sprouts, above.

The third day, pour the sprouts into a 3–quart (or bigger) bowl and flood with water. If the sprouts have clumped, separate them gently. Pour the sprouts and water into another bowl, leaving the unsprouted seeds behind at the bottom of the first bowl. Strain and drain well, letting them grow as before. Keep the bowl covered with a small towel or with plastic.

Continue to rinse the sprouts a couple of times a day and keep them in a darkish, cool place until each one has two tiny leaves. Now, when you flood them with water, you can swish them gently to wash off the brown seed casings—not required, but elegant.

Drain the sprouts for the last time and spread them out on a glass or plastic dish (a 9″ × 13″ baking dish is fine). Cover with clear plastic or waxed paper and set them in a *cool* place where they have a source of light. (Don't let them get too warm or they will quickly rot.) In a few hours they will be bright green and ready to enjoy. Store in the refrigerator, closely covered.

Alfalfa sprouts are delicate and pretty, delightful on a sandwich or salad. But don't eat pounds a day. Alfalfa contains small amounts of a natural toxin, saponins. Such natural toxins do occur in foods; usually, as with alfalfa sprouts, they do no harm if the food is not eaten in abnormally large quantities.

BEAN SPROUTS

Sprout soaking water is vitamin candy for houseplants.

Soybeans require special attention because the sprouts mold easily. Remove the nonsprouters as soon as they make themselves known. Rinse the sprouting beans *at least* three times daily, and disentangle them when you do. Don't expect a long tail to develop. Sprouted soybeans are ready to eat after three days.

To get longer tails on mung bean sprouts, keep them in utter darkness while they sprout. Seed casings will float off if you swish sprouts gently in a basin of water during the last rinsings.

Soy sprouts must be cooked at least 5 minutes to destroy harmful enzymes. Other bean sprouts do not require cooking, but they will have better flavor if you dip them for 5 seconds or so in very hot water just before adding them to your salad or sandwich. Rinse quickly in cold water, pat dry, and serve.

Dinner

"This whole business of family meals," a very popular writer on nutrition remarked recently, "has gone by the bye for most families. It's rare, during the week, that we're all four of us home at the same time. So I keep meals ready in the freezer, and take them out in the morning."

It is true, of course, that the competing claims on our evening time are many and powerful. Meetings, workshops, dates, dance lessons, exercise classes, late work at the office or just Wanting to Get Away pull family members in different directions. There is more going on now, for people of every age, than a generation ago, and none of us wants to miss out. Little by little, the family dinner hour has indeed fallen on hard times.

The drift is clear, but that we're happier this way —that we'd really have *chosen* it—is not clear at all. Life has skidded dramatically toward the mechanized and impersonal in recent years. We bank with automated tellers, we assess political leaders by their performance on television, we accept finally that most of our telephone conversations will be with recorded message devices. Surely the personal relationships we do have today are more precious than ever. Surely they are worth sustaining—and to date, no one's come up with a more universally effective way to achieve this than by sharing a meal.

Granted, there will be nights when you look back at the time you just shared—maybe it wasn't all grace notes —wince a little, and wonder whether it's worth the effort. Maybe that one evening you *would* have been better off at haunts of your respective choices. But the rewards don't come on any one evening, and really can't be measured over the short run. It's the cumulative effect you're after: the continuity itself, and what comes with it. By setting off that one hour and drawing a circle around it, you are creating a situation where, over time, some very important processes can take place: where subtle connections can be forged, and the kind of wordless understandings established that allow human beings to be of real use to one another.

Just as there is an art to breadmaking and gardening and other old-timey skills, there is also an art to the convivial dinner hour. Don't be discouraged if everyone comes off a little callow at first. Gradually, you learn to draw one another out about the day's adventures, and to keep an eye open during your own day for table-worthy anecdotes. An eight-year-old's version of such stories can be pretty roundabout, but an attentive listener asking the right questions can gradually make him a real spellbinder—and give him convincing proof that you do care.

It's an institution too valuable to be reserved for "families" strictly defined. In the days before singles apartments and frozen entrees, most families had a single aunt or uncle to supper regularly—or just a friend of long standing—and it worked to everyone's advantage, especially the children's. We know individuals who get together once or more a week for potluck suppers—especially helpful for people who love "from-scratch" meals but find it's a lot to do for just one person.

We don't just differ politely, then, from those who would dismiss the family dinner hour without a backward glance. We flat-out *adamantly* protest. Eat late if you must, if that's what it takes to get everyone together. Keep the menus simple, and involve every able body in the preparation. Buy a gorgeous new tablecloth, go the candlelight route if you have to, but get them ranged 'round that table and eating what*ever* it takes.

The single most insidious opposition to a civilizing meal hour, incidentally, is probably television. Besides absorbing attention so we don't really see or hear one another, it fills the mind with trivia, and its backdrop of continual violence exerts a disintegrating influence on personal relationships and family unity. Whatever you think of TV, it surely doesn't have a place at the dinner table, and wonderful things happen when you start easing it out of your life. For a delightful rundown on other families' experiences, read *What to Do After You Turn Off the TV*, by Frances Moore Lappé and her children, Anthony and Anna (New York: Ballantine, 1985).

Salads

Whether you like yours at the beginning of the meal as most Americans do, or served just before dessert in the Italian fashion; whether it makes a graceful complement to the meal or *is* the meal, salad makes a vital nutritional contribution to anyone's diet. Raw leafy greens provide the essential B vitamin folacin in abundance. When salad greens are homegrown, or at least really *green*, they supply other members of the B vitamin complex, too, and vitamins A, C, E, and K, as well as a respectable amount of minerals: calcium, iron, and magnesium.

Fresh-picked greens require only light and simple dressing, but there is always some odd or end that will make the salad special: a bit of cheese, a spark of bell pepper, a handful of new green peas. If you aren't already a salad nut, do experiment with some of the fancies on the next page and see whether a little extra pizzazz doesn't make twice as much salad disappear.

Use our ideas as a springboard for your imagination, and you will come up with dozens of variations on our variations. I like remembering the lady who rushed up and told us, "I just *love* your book! Your recipes are wonderful." Then looking a little abashed, she added, "Of course, I never *follow* them." Hurray for her! I bet she makes great salads.

Making Irresistible Salads

&. Use salad greens that are fresh, crisp, clean, cold, and dry. Wash lettuce in cold water and dry gently by spreading it out on a clean terry towel and rolling it up, or by putting it in a lettuce spinner. You can wash and dry lots of lettuce and put it in its towel in a plastic bag or crisper in the refrigerator, ready to be cut (or torn) and dressed as needed just before serving.

&. For zest and variety, use a medley of salad greens in your bowl. Romaine, red, green leaf and butter lettuce, escarole, napa cabbage, watercress and spinach are seasonally available in most supermarkets. Gardeners and farmer's market shoppers will have even more of a selection.

❧ Don't toss salads until you're ready to serve the meal. Use dressing at room temperature; it spreads further and coats the greens more evenly. Start with a little and toss well—a lot of extra salad dressing gets eaten just because it's dumped on top.

❧ To make a salad into a light meal that's perfect for lunch or dinner on a hot summer evening, select some of these additions:

Cooked chilled garbanzo or kidney beans

Sprouted garbanzos, lentils, or red beans

Small chunks of cheese or marinated tofu

Lightly cooked vegetables like fresh corn, string beans, sliced carrots, broccoli florets and slices, or beets (Chill with or without a marinade and add to the salad before tossing)

Raw vegetables like thinly sliced zucchini, celery, cucumber, cabbage, green or red pepper, parsley, finely grated carrot, avocado chunks, or (best of all) tiny fresh green peas

Croutons (page 158)

❧ Fresh herbs add a lot to salads, and to other dishes as well. Grow them in a window box or in a plot near your kitchen. Mince fresh herbs and crush dried ones to bring out all their flavor.

❧ Nasturtiums grow easily nearly anywhere, and their bright petals add color to salad long before the tomatoes ripen. Nasturtium leaves too can be chopped for peppery zest in salads. (Other flowers add color too—johnny jump-ups, calendula, borage—but nasturtiums *taste* especially good.) For best effect, sprinkle on top after dressing.

To get salad greens in really dazzling variety, try growing your own. Lettuce is particularly easy, and seed catalogs provide countless gorgeous and tasty varieties you'll never find for sale commercially. Many of the smaller seed companies offer interesting varieties that aren't available anywhere else. For a directory of small companies with locally special seeds, write to:

Seed and Nursery Directory
Rural Advancement Fund
P.O. Box 1029
Pittsboro, NC 27312

Oil for Salads & Cooking

From a nutritional standpoint, by far the most important thing about salad oils is not what kind you use but how little. Make sure that what you do use is fresh; beyond that, what oil to buy is mostly a matter of taste. We use corn oil for salads and sautéing and for making Better-Butter; for flavoring salads and sauces, good olive oil. Here are the main options with some of their distinguishing characteristics. All are high in polyunsaturated fatty acids and low in saturated ones. If refined, all are pale and nearly tasteless.

Safflower oil: Highest in polyunsaturates, therefore somewhat more prone to rancidity unless it has preservatives added. The smoke point is very low, so safflower oil is not good for frying. It has a greasy texture when used in salads.

Corn oil: A versatile all-around oil.

Soy oil: Unrefined soy oil has a very strong flavor and is especially prone to rancidity.

Peanut oil: Higher than other oils in saturated fats, lower in polyunsaturated ones. If you do fry (we don't), peanut oil is best because it has a high smoke point. Research on rabbits and primates has shown peanut oil to be uniquely atherogenic—more so than butter. These results have not been supported by studies with humans, but the finding has cast a shadow on peanut oil's reputation.

Sesame, walnut, avocado, sunflower, and other special oils: Refined, these are as stable and mild in flavor as other refined oils. Unrefined, each has its own distinct flavor from the nut or seed of its source. All unrefined oils have to be protected from light, air, and heat. Don't expect them to keep for a long time.

Olive oil: For flavor, nothing can match good olive oil. There is evidence that nothing can match it nutritionally either. The top grades are labeled "virgin," which means that the oil is pressed from the fruit (rather than extracted by solvents) and unrefined. "Pure" means only that all the oil in the bottle is from olives, usually solvent-extracted. Very much less expensive are blends of some cheap refined oil with a very small amount of good olive oil for flavor, which can be called "blended olive oil." We think it's worth getting a small bottle of the real thing for flavor; if you like, you can blend it yourself with an all-purpose oil like corn oil for salad making. As the demand for good-quality domestic olive oil increases, it should become more widely available and cheaper. Our co-op now carries really good California virgin olive oil (under the Co-op label) at a rather moderate price; maybe your co-op can get it too.

"Salad oil" blends containing cottonseed oil, palm oil, or the preservatives BHA, BHT, or EDTA, are best avoided.

Vinegar & Lemon

One good way to cut back on oils in salad dressings is to use a really fine wine vinegar—raspberry is a big favorite—and skip the oil altogether. Of course, these tasty vinegars do a lot to make any salad special even *with* oil.

Juice from homegrown lemons can vie with the most exquisite vinegar in nearly any dressing, especially if you include the finely grated peel. If you have sunshine and a place you can protect from frost, a dwarf lemon may be the most rewarding thing you plant. One small tree, even in a tub, can provide plenty of its delicious lemons nearly all year round. Fragrant and pretty to look at, too. Ask your nursery to help you choose the right variety for your climate.

Salad Dressings

We suggest making these quickly-mixed dressings fresh each day or two. One good no-muss way to blend up just the right amount is to lay in a supply of half-pint-sized blender jars so that instead of using the usual big blender container, you can just put all your ingredients in the little jar, screw on the blade unit, invert, and blend. Any dressing left over can be stored right in the jar, ready for the next day. (The small glass jars make it easy to grind spices in the blender too.) There have been some awful accidents when people used ordinary jars in this way, however, so get ones made for your own blender.

Marinade

Sometimes cooked beans and vegetables are marinated for extra flavor before being used in salads. Most often, the marinade is a combination of oil and vinegar or lemon juice with salt and herbs, or perhaps the same dressing that will be used on the salad. We find that you can get excellent flavor by skipping the oil and simply tossing the cooked beans or vegetables in fresh lemon juice, with salt and pepper, herbs, and perhaps a little garlic. The taste is great, and there's a considerable saving on the fat quota.

Lowering the Fat

In experimenting with dressings that make a mouth-watering salad with less oil, we have found two basic extenders. One is cultured dairy products—especially buttermilk, but also cottage cheese and yogurt. The other is vegetables, especially tomatoes, blended smooth. Mixing one of these into a well-seasoned normal dressing will usually make a tasty dressing that covers much more salad with fewer calories from fat. The catch is that when there is a lot of liquid that is not oil, the dressing doesn't keep well, so these dressings need to be made fresh in small quantities.

On the next page are some of our favorite dressings with variations. If you are very serious about lowering fat in your diet, most of these taste fine without any oil at all.

Our own approach might be of interest here. We discuss on page 45 our usual way of keeping control of the amount of fat that goes into dinner. By the time soup or sauce is done, the meal's fat allotment leaves maybe ½ teaspoon of oil per person to use in salad dressing. That's the amount that goes in, no more. You can experiment in the same direction by adjusting the recipe to your own limit (or by using only a part of the dressing). One nice thing about this approach is that it leaves room even for the classic vinaigrette.

Vinaigrette

Mix the vinegar or wine, mustard, and salt. Add other herbs if desired.

When salad-making time comes, measure the amount of oil you want to use for the whole salad. Either mix in the flavored vinegar to taste or, for the freshest possible salad, toss the oil with the greens first and follow that with the vinegar mixture, to taste. Even a tiny amount of oil will cover a lot of lettuce that way, and protect it from the wilting effects of the vinegar too.

*2 tablespoons wine vinegar
    or ¼ cup dry red wine
½ teaspoon Dijon mustard
¼ teaspoon salt*

*olive oil
pepper*

Favorite Salad Dressings

We draw on these dressings every day in all possible variations. Mix the ingredients by hand, chopping as necessary, or put everything in the blender.

We often call for lemon zest. "Zest" is the colored part of the citrus peel only; the white inner peel is bitter. To get the zest, either use a potato peeler and then chop the peeling fine, or take advantage of technology and use a *zester*.

1 medium lemon
= 3 tablespoons juice
and 1 tablespoon zest

LEMON-PARSLEY DRESSING

2 tablespoons oil
zest of one lemon
2 tablespoons lemon juice
1/2 cup parsley, chopped
1/4 teaspoon salt
1 tablespoon chopped
  green pepper
dash black pepper

Makes about 1/2 cup.

ॐ

BLUE CHEESE DRESSING

1 ounce blue cheese
1 tablespoon oil
  or mayonnaise
2 tablespoons cottage cheese
1/4 cup buttermilk
pinch salt and pepper
a drop of pressed garlic
(chopped scallion leaves,
  chives, and/or coriander
  leaves)

Makes 1/2 cup.

ORANGE-PARSLEY DRESSING

IN BLENDER:
1 orange, cut up, and
  1 tablespoon zest
2 tablespoon oil
1 tablespoon cider vinegar
1/4 teaspoon salt

ADD:
2 tablespoons chopped
  parsley

Makes 2/3 cup.

ॐ

SESAME DRESSING

1/4 cup freshly toasted
  sesame seeds, ground
  in blender into meal
1 tablespoon oil
1 tablespoon lemon juice
  (or more, to taste)
1/8 teaspoon salt
1/4 cup buttermilk
  or orange juice

Makes 1/3 to 1/2 cup.

BASIC BUTTERMILK DRESSING

2 tablespoons oil
1/2 small lemon,
　　juice and zest
1/3 cup buttermilk
(2 or 3 chives
　　or a scallion leaf)
(1/4 cup tender parsley
　　and/or other fresh herbs)
(drop of pressed garlic)
pinch salt, dash pepper

Makes 1/2 cup.

CURRY DRESSING

*Make Buttermilk Dressing
but omit herbs and use
cider or white wine vinegar
instead of lemon. Add 1/4
teaspoon curry powder.*

ARTICHOKE DRESSING

*Make Buttermilk Dressing,
using olive oil if possible, and
include garlic. Add cooked,
cut-up artichoke hearts and
leaf-scrapings, letting the
mixture marinate for an hour
or more before tossing salad.
Allow 1/4 cup dressing and
1/4 cup artichoke per person.*

FRESH TOMATO DRESSING

1 tomato, fresh and ripe
2 tablespoons olive oil
1 tablespoon vinegar
1/8 teaspoon salt
1 teaspoon fresh
　　or 1/2 teaspoon dry
　　chopped basil

Makes about 3/4 cup.

EVERYDAY DRESSING

*Make Fresh Tomato
Dressing, using
red wine vinegar and
great handfuls of
fresh basil and parsley.
Add pepper and dry
mustard, a dash each.*

FEROZ'S DRESSING

Blend smooth:
1 medium lemon, juice
　　and zest
1/2 teaspoon salt
1 large peeled tomato
dash cayenne
2 small cloves garlic
2 tablespoons olive oil
1/4 teaspoon each
　　ground coriander,
　　cumin, dry mustard,
　　paprika
1/2 teaspoon brown sugar

Makes 3/4 cup.

COTTAGE DRESSING

1/4 cup cottage cheese
1/4 cup buttermilk
2 teaspoons lemon juice
1 tablespoon oil
pinch salt
pinch pepper
1 teaspoon fresh herbs

Makes 1/2 cup.

GARDEN COTTAGE DRESSING

*Make Cottage Dressing and
mix in a tomato (cut up),
1 tablespoon fresh chopped
basil, and a pinch more salt.*

RUSSIAN DRESSING

1 tablespoon mayonnaise
1 tablespoon tomato paste
1 tablespoon cottage cheese
1/3 cup buttermilk
1 tablespoon wine vinegar
1/4 teaspoon salt
1/8 teaspoon each
    mustard and paprika

Makes 1/2 cup.

THOUSAND ISLAND DRESSING

Make Russian Dressing;
chop and add pickles,
celery, and hard-boiled egg.

AVOCADO DRESSING

1/2 large ripe avocado
1 tablespoon lemon juice
1/8 teaspoon salt
1/8 teaspoon chili powder
squeeze garlic
1/4 cup buttermilk

Makes 1/2 cup.

AVOCADO DIP OR SANDWICH SPREAD

Omit the buttermilk and
double the recipe (except
the salt).

YOGURT SALAD DRESSING

1/2 cup yogurt
2 tablespoons oil
    or mayonnaise
1 tablespoon lemon juice
1/8 teaspoon salt
grate pepper

Makes 2/3 cup.

BRIGHT MINTY DRESSING

Add to Yogurt Dressing
    and blend smooth:
1/2 cucumber, sliced
2 tablespoons fresh
    mint leaves
2 scallion leaves

GREEN GODDESS DRESSING

1/2 cup yogurt
2 tablespoons oil
    or mayonnaise
1/4 cup chopped parsley,
    basil, and/or
    coriander leaves
1 teaspoon chopped chives
1 tablespoon lemon juice
1/4 teaspoon salt
(scallion leaf)
(squeeze garlic)

Makes about 3/4 cup.

Astonishing Salad

A truly impressive, unusual, and delicious salad.

ᴈ

In a small pot, heat wine and lemon juice to a bare simmer. Turn off the heat and add the apricots. Cover and let apricots soak for about ½ hour, turning occasionally if liquid doesn't cover.

Wash spinach and drain well. Quarter and core apples and slice paper-thin. If the salad won't be eaten right away, cover apples with orange or other fruit juice, draining thoroughly before you add them to the salad.

Over a bowl, drain the apricots through a sieve. Reserve liquid and cut apricots into bite-sized pieces. Add the oil, salt, and pepper to the apricot liquid and whip with a fork. In a salad bowl, mix spinach and apple slices, add dressing, and toss thoroughly. Sprinkle apricots and walnuts on top. Toss again just before serving.

Makes 4 servings or a light meal for two, with muffins and a creamy soup.

½ cup dry white wine
2 tablespoons lemon juice
½ cup dried apricots

1½ pounds fresh tender
  spinach leaves
2 apples
2 tablespoons olive oil
¼ teaspoon salt
pinch pepper
½ cup chopped walnuts

Greek Salad

Like our other Greek recipes, this one comes from our friend Sultana, and provides an utterly satisfying balance of flavors, colors, and textures.

ᴈ

Wash and cut lettuce. Crumble cheese over the top and add the olives, tomatoes, cucumber, and green pepper.

Pour olive oil over salad and toss well to coat; then add the wine vinegar, salt, and pepper and toss.

Serves 4—or two salad connoisseurs.

leafy lettuce or mixed greens
2 or more ounces feta cheese
1 handful black olives
  (Greek, if available)
1 tomato, chopped
1 small cucumber, sliced
1 green pepper, diced
1 tablespoon olive oil
2 teaspoons wine vinegar
salt and pepper to taste

Dilled Cucumber & Yogurt Salad

1 cup water
1/4 cup vinegar
1 teaspoon dill weed
1 slice raw onion
2 cucumbers, thinly sliced

1 cup yogurt
1/2 teaspoon salt
dash pepper
1/8 teaspoon turmeric

leafy lettuce, or mixed greens

Combine water, vinegar, dill, and onion. Add cucumber slices and let stand half an hour or longer. Drain, and discard the onion.

Mix yogurt, salt, pepper, and turmeric. Stir cucumbers into the mixture and serve on beds of salad greens, cut into bite-sized pieces.

Serves 4.

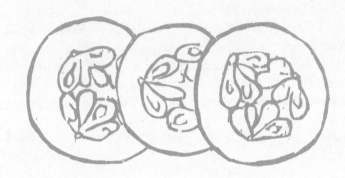

Ceci Salad

2 cups raw garbanzo beans
1/3 cup wine vinegar
2 tablespoons olive oil
1/2 teaspoon salt
1/4 teaspoon paprika
1/4 teaspoon oregano
pinch cayenne
1 clove garlic
1/4 cup chopped chives
    or 1 minced scallion

4 quarts tender fresh
    spinach leaves
1 small avocado
black pepper

Cook garbanzos until tender. Drain and toss with vinegar, oil, and seasonings. Marinate for an hour or more. (If you want to use already-cooked beans, warm them first or just allow them longer to marinate.)

Wash and dry spinach leaves, and cut or tear to bite-size. Cube avocado and toss all together. Check salt.

Makes salad for 4 or more. Served with crackers and chilled tomato juice, Ceci Salad also makes a fine, light meal.

Some Good Salad Combinations

MEXICAN SALAD BOWL

MARINATE:

¾ cup cooked kidney beans
juice of 1 lemon
salt and pepper

TOSS:

leafy lettuce or mixed greens
¼ cup Everyday Dressing
¼ teaspoon crushed oregano
¼ teaspoon lightly toasted
  cumin seeds or ground cumin

TOP WITH:

½ avocado, cubed
½ green pepper, diced
1 tomato, cut up

(½ cup grated cheddar)

SHADES OF GREEN SALAD

MARINATE:

½ cup green peas
½ cup cooked lima beans
lemon juice, salt, and pepper

TOSS TOGETHER:

leafy lettuce or mixed greens
  and tender spinach leaves
¼ cup toasted sunflower seeds
Green Goddess Dressing

CHEF'S SALAD

MARINATE:

½ cup cooked garbanzos
juice of 1 lemon
salt and pepper

TOSS:

Big bowlful romaine lettuce
dressing of your choice

ARRANGE ON TOP:

8 cherry tomatoes
½ cucumber, sliced
½ bell pepper, in rounds
cheeses in strips
1 hard-cooked egg, quartered
fresh black pepper

SPINACH AND MUSHROOM SALAD

Big bowlful tender spinach
leaves
raw mushrooms, thinly sliced
Parmesan cheese
garlic-flavored whole-wheat
  Croutons
Fresh Tomato Dressing
  (or your choice)

CALIFORNIA TOSSED SALAD

leafy lettuce or mixed greens
¼ cup watercress leaves
½ avocado, cut up
½ cup sliced cucumber
8 cherry tomatoes, halved
1 cup herbed croutons
2 tablespoons Parmesan cheese
Vinaigrette

TOMATO PEPPER SALAD

DICE AND TOSS TOGETHER:

fresh and ripe tomatoes
crisp green peppers

parsley and/or fresh
  basil, finely chopped

NAVY BEAN AND CASHEW SALAD

MARINATE TOGETHER:

1 cup broccoli or cauliflower
  pieces, steamed
½ cup cooked navy beans
juice of 1 lemon
salt and pepper

TOSS WITH:

leafy lettuce or mixed greens
¼ cup chopped toasted cashews
Avocado or Blue Cheese
Dressing

Antipasto

whole small mushrooms
broccoli florets
   and sliced stems
cauliflower pieces
asparagus spears
whole green beans
artichoke hearts
zucchini
green pepper
celery sticks
scallions
tomato wedges
   or cherry tomatoes
olives
garbanzo or kidney beans
cubes of cheese

BABA GANOUJ

Peel and mash a baked egg-plant, add a few tablespoons tahini, a minced garlic clove, and the juice of half a lemon; salt to taste; let stand half an hour, at least. Just before serving, sprinkle with a few drops of olive oil and dashes of ground cumin. Wow.

Traditionally served to whet the appetite, any of a number of beautifully arranged and tasty dishes can be an antipasto. In American translation, the appetizer may grow to become most of a light meal, perhaps preceding a good soup and fresh bread. The idea is to present a feast for the eye as well as the palate, so indulge your artistry to its utmost in arranging the vegetables and other dishes. The choices can be light or rich, and as varied as you choose, so Antipasto Americano offers a splendid answer to what to serve when dieters come or when your guests have widely different eating preferences. ("Adelaide, it's all low-cal except the pâté." "Vergil, there's no dairy in anything except the cheese sticks!")

Some antipasti are traditional: *Misto*, fried vegetables (we substitute lightly steamed ones, marinated or not); Greek Peppers (next page); Caponata (also next page), *crostini* (toasted slices of bread, with spicy or cheesy toppings, served hot); stuffed artichokes or tomatoes; deviled eggs; mushrooms; and, for their beauty, an assortment of young, fresh raw vegetables, olives, and scallions.

Some other ideas: any of the spreads from our Lunch section, stuffed into small tomatoes or celery boats or mounded and garnished for spreading on bread or dipping. Or make the classic dip, Baba Ganouj. Hot food is quite welcome, especially if it is bite-sized—for example, trays of hot Potato Poppers or Neat Balls.

Caponata

Caponata is a traditional antipasto dish, but it can hold its own as a dip for crackers or vegetables any day.

ঌ

If you are able to get the long, thin Japanese eggplants, steam them in their jackets until tender. The most effective way to deal with the fat, round, normal kind is to halve and bake it at about 350°F. When tender, set aside to cool.

Chop the onion rather fine and sauté it in the olive oil. Chop the celery similarly and stir it in when the onion is beginning to get translucent. Cook until the onion is soft and barely golden.

Add the bell peppers, if used, and tomatoes, capers, honey, vinegar, and olives. Simmer, stirring frequently, until most of the liquid has evaporated.

Meantime, peel and dice the eggplant. When the tomato mixture has lost most of its liquid, remove it from heat and add the eggplant, salt, and pepper. Correct the salt: how much you need will depend on how salty your olives were. Serve chilled.

*4 long thin eggplants
  or one big one
  (about 1 pound)*

*1 big onion
2 tablespoons olive oil
8 center stalks of celery
  (1 cup chopped)*

*(1 bell pepper, diced)
1¼ cups tomatoes,
  peeled, seeded, chopped
¼ cup capers
1 tablespoon honey
¼ cup red wine vinegar
½ cup olives, chopped
¼ teaspoon salt
fresh black pepper*

Grilled Peppers

Roast green, red, or yellow peppers under broiler or directly over a gas flame, turning frequently, until the skin turns black. Place in a covered dish or pot for a few minutes to steam and cool, making them easier to peel; then rub and wash off the blackened skin and remove the seeds and stem. Peppers smell heavenly while roasting, and they will taste just as good; you can use them anywhere that canned chilis or cooked peppers are wanted. To make them into GREEK PEPPERS, chop coarsely and marinate lightly with olive oil, lemon juice, and pepper.

Coleslaw

*½ head cabbage,
  green or red (about
  4 cups shredded)*
*½ cup Basic Buttermilk
  or Yogurt Dressing*

Cabbage is a rich source of vitamin C and is available year-round at low cost. For slaw, use any kind of cabbage and shred coarse or fine as suits you. The dressings suggested are considerably lower in fat than the standard mayonnaise dressing, and you can extend them even more with extra yogurt or buttermilk.

Unlike green salad, coleslaw can be dressed ahead of serving time—in fact, it is still very good the next day. When the cabbage is fresh, slaw is good made very plain; but you can alter its mood in many ways. We list some tasty additions below.

Serves 4 to 6.

dill weed
tarragon
caraway seeds
poppy seeds
toasted sunflower seeds
chopped walnuts
slivered almonds

chopped fresh pineapple
orange chunks
grated apples
raisins
dates or dried apricots

minced green pepper
chopped celery
minced parsley
grated carrots
cooked green beans
shoestring beets
corn off the cob
pickle

Slaw Chez Nous

2 tablespoons almonds
2 tablespoons sesame seeds
*2½ cups shredded cabbage,
  white or Chinese*
(2 scallions or chives)
½ small red bell pepper

1 tablespoon oil
*1 tablespoon rice vinegar
  or ½ teaspoon cider
  vinegar*
1 teaspoon honey
⅛ teaspoon pepper
¼ teaspoon salt

Toast nuts and chop them; toast seeds. Allow to cool. Shred the cabbage, chop the scallion, and dice the pepper. Toss the vegetables together.

Mix oil, vinegar, honey, pepper, and salt. Just before serving, combine vegetables, dressing, seeds, and nuts.

Makes 3 cups.

Red Rogue's Delight

This pretty slaw can be exceedingly zippy unless the red onion is just-picked. If you aren't a raw onion enthusiast, the salad's good without it, or with just a thin slice. (Sweet white onions will do the trick too.)

❧

Shred cabbage thin or grate coarse and combine with onion. Mix oil, lemon juice, orange juice, mustard, salt, and pepper and stir them into the cabbage and onion. Sprinkle sunflower seeds on top.

Makes 4 servings.

½ medium red cabbage
   (3 cups shredded)
¼ cup chopped
   red bermuda onion
2 tablespoons oil
1 tablespoon lemon juice
¼ cup orange juice
1 teaspoon Dijon mustard
½ teaspoon salt
freshly ground black pepper
¼ cup toasted
   sunflower seeds

Carrot Salad

We used to drown carrot salad in mayonnaise, but we like this version much better. If the carrots aren't very sweet, grate apples in too. Or, for a carrot slaw, substitute grated cabbage for half the carrots. For a savory version, omit the raisins and orange zest and add finely chopped parsley and chives instead.

❧

Mix well. To be fancy, top with nuts before serving.

Makes 3 cups, to serve 4.

3 cups carrots, grated fine
½ cup raisins or currants
½ cup orange juice
1 tablespoon lemon juice
1 teaspoon each: zest of
   orange and lemon
(¼ cup nuts,
   toasted and chopped)

Disappearing Carrot Salad

Almost a light chutney, it's so gingery and sweet. Very good packed up in tomorrow's lunchbox too.

❧

Toast walnut pieces and coconut in a low (300°F) oven. The walnuts will take about 10 minutes and the coconut 5. Chill.

Combine grated carrots, apple, lemon zest, orange and lemon juices, currants, salt, and ginger. Add walnuts and coconut and serve.

Makes 3 cups, to serve 4.

¼ cup walnut pieces
1 tablespoon shredded
   coconut
2 cups grated carrot
1 apple, cored and grated
zest and juice of ½ lemon
½ cup orange juice
½ cup currants
dash salt
1½ teaspoons grated
   fresh ginger

Russian Salad

2 cups diced cooked potatoes
2 cups diced cooked beets
½ cup peas
2 tablespoons chopped
    fresh parsley
2 scallions, thinly sliced

2 tablespoons mayonnaise
6 tablespoons yogurt
2 tablespoons vinegar
dash black pepper
½ teaspoon salt

A classic that eclipses plain old potato salad.

All vegetables should be cold; if you use frozen peas, let them thaw. Put potatoes, beets, peas, parsley, and scallions in salad bowl. Mix together mayonnaise, yogurt, vinegar, salt, and pepper. Toss together.

Makes 6 servings (4½ cups).

Fruity Beety

4 beets
3 oranges
2 tablespoons coconut
1 teaspoon honey
juice of ½ lemon
grated peel of ½ lemon
2 tablespoons currants
(1 teaspoon vinegar)
pinch salt

This sweet and deeply colorful salad adds a bright touch to any plate; it's especially fine alongside green vegetables and rice. Many people who ordinarily avoid beets will eat an astonishing amount of Fruity Beety.

Wash beets and steam whole until tender; then peel. Grate on ripple-shaped grater or slice in long, thin sticks.

Peel, seed, and cut up oranges. Place half the oranges in blender with coconut, honey, lemon juice, and peel, and blend 2 minutes.

Mix all ingredients, balancing the sweetness with the additional vinegar if needed. Chill, letting the flavors blend for 2 hours or so.

Makes 3 cups.

Sweet Potato Salad

Place sweet potato, green pepper, celery, scallions, and walnuts in a small salad bowl.

Stir together mayonnaise, yogurt, lemon zest and juice (about 3 tablespoons), and salt. If you're fond of fresh ginger, try it in this dish: peel it, cut in three pieces, and press the pieces in a garlic press to extract the juice. (It will well up in the upper part of the press—pour from there, loosen with a fork, and squeeze again.) Mix the juice into the dressing, adding to taste. Combine with sweet potato mixture and adjust salt and lemon juice to taste.

Makes 3 cups, to serve 4.

2 cups cubed cooked
sweet potato
1/2 cup chopped green pepper
1/2 cup chopped celery
3 scallions, sliced thin
1/2 cup chopped walnuts

2 tablespoons mayonnaise
1/4 cup yogurt
zest and juice of 1 lemon
1/4 teaspoon salt
(nubbin of ginger, thumb-tip size)

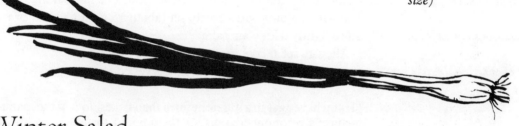

Winter Salad

Quarter potatoes lengthwise and steam only until tender. Remove peel if you want to and cut in 1/2-inch chunks.

Steam broccoli pieces ever so briefly, until they cook just tender. The scallions can be added either raw or cooked. If you want to sauté them, use some of the oil to do it.) Place broccoli, scallions, and potatoes in a salad bowl.

Combine olive oil, sesame seeds, ginger, honey, salt, and vinegar. Pour over the potatoes and broccoli and toss lightly. Taste to see whether it needs a little more vinegar. Serve at room temperature.

Makes about 4 cups, to serve from 4 to 6.

2 medium potatoes
(red if possible)
3 cups broccoli florets
(and peeled, sliced stems)
1 bunch scallions, sliced thin

1–2 tablespoons olive oil
2 tablespoons toasted
sesame seeds
1 1/4" fresh ginger, minced
1/2 teaspoon honey
3/4–1 teaspoon salt
3 or more tablespoons
vinegar

WINTER SALAD WITH ARAME

Before starting the potatoes, soak 1/2 cup dried arame sea vegetable in water to cover. Let stand 15 minutes while you prepare the potatoes and broccoli. After you mix the dressing, drain the arame and stir it in. Combine with the vegetables as described above.

Tomato Aspic

¼ cup agar flakes*
1 quart tomato juice
    or 1 cup tomato paste
    dissolved in 3 cups water
1 teaspoon honey
½ teaspoon curry powder
1 teaspoon dried basil
1 teaspoon salt

1 cup chopped celery
¼ cup chopped green pepper
1 cup grated carrot
3 green onions, chopped

3 tablespoons lemon juice

1 cup chopped walnuts

A flavorful vegetarian version of the classic aspic usually made with animal gelatin. The quantities given here produce a slightly soft, spoonable result; if you like yours stiffer, increase the agar to 6 tablespoons.

Because Tomato Aspic is usually considered holiday fare, this recipe is sized for a crowd. But it's simple enough to prepare for everyday use in half-size amounts.

Dissolve agar in 1 cup tomato juice and let stand 1 minute. Put remaining juice in saucepan with honey, curry powder, basil, and salt. Heat to boiling. Mix in vegetables. Add dissolved agar and chopped onions and boil for 2 minutes. Cool slightly, add lemon juice, and pour into a 2-quart bowl or flat baking dish. Top with walnuts when partly set (about 15 minutes) and press down lightly with your palm.

Allow to set at cool room temperature for 1 hour.

Cut into squares, or spoon out. Serves 6 to 8.

*If you have agar in a different form than flakes, follow the manufacturer's recommendation for the amount to use for jelling 4 cups of juice.

VARIATIONS

A teaspoon of grated fresh ginger adds zest.
1 teaspoon soy sauce lends a deeper, heartier flavor.
2 tablespoons of fresh parsley gives a springy lift.
Try Florence fennel instead of celery; or use ¼ teaspoon fennel
    seeds with or without celery.

Finocchio Salad

An especially mouth-watering pasta salad.

ද

Cook macaroni until tender in salted boiling water. Cool and combine with fennel, parsley, bell pepper, mushrooms, chives, and olives.

Mix 2 tablespoons lemon juice, olive oil, salt, and pepper. Toss salad in dressing, taste, and add remaining tablespoon of lemon juice if desired.

Makes 5½ cups.

No fennel in sight? Substitute raw celery or blanched green beans, or crisp-tender broccoli.

1½ cups raw whole wheat macaroni
½ cup sliced Florence fennel*
¼ cup chopped Italian parsley
¼ cup diced bell pepper
1 cup sliced raw mushrooms
2 tablespoons chopped chives
(⅓ cup sliced black olives)

2 to 3 tablespoons lemon juice
2 tablespoons olive oil
½ teaspoon salt
freshly ground black pepper

Yogurt Rice

Traditional in South India for tiffin, and as delicious at home as on the road.

ද

Heat the oil in a heavy skillet that has a lid. Add the mustard seeds to the hot oil and cover the pan. As soon as the wild sound of popping dies down—it only takes a few seconds—add the ginger, the chili if used, and then the rice, yogurt, and salt. (If you use rice that was already salted in cooking, use less salt than the recipe calls for.) Stir and cook gently for 5 minutes; then remove from heat and chill. Serve cool.

Makes 4 cups.

1 tablespoon oil
2 teaspoons black mustard seeds

2 teaspoons finely minced fresh ginger
(1 small green chili, seeded and minced)
4 cups well-cooked, cooled brown rice
1½ cups yogurt, beaten smooth
1 teaspoon salt

Tabouli

3 cups water
¾ teaspoon salt
1½ cups raw bulgur wheat
½ cup cooked white beans
2 tomatoes, chopped
3 tablespoons olive oil
pepper to taste
1 garlic clove, minced
2 tablespoons chopped chives
2 teaspoons chopped
   fresh mint leaves
juice of at least 2 lemons
¼–½ cup chopped parsley

This classic Lebanese salad makes a truly delicious luncheon dish. The combination of garlic, lemon, and fresh mint reverberates delightfully on the palate. Beans are not traditional but definitely tasty; omit them if you prefer.

Bring water to a boil with salt. Add bulgur and return to boil. Remove from heat, cover pot tightly, and set aside for 15 minutes.

Drain off any excess water and chill the grain. Toss thoroughly with all ingredients, adjusting salt and lemon if needed.

Makes 6 generous servings (6 ½ cups).

Pineapple-Bulgur Wheat Salad

1 cup water
¼ teaspoon salt
1 cup raw bulgur wheat

1 medium avocado
1 cup fresh pineapple chunks
½ cup chopped red bell
   pepper
2 inside stalks celery,
   chopped, or
   ½ cup cucumber,
   chopped
3 or 4 scallions, thinly
   sliced
chopped chives
1 tablespoon oil
3 tablespoons lemon
   juice, or
   2 tablespoons cider
   vinegar

This fresh and sweetly satisfying salad makes a friendly lunch all by itself. If you need to prepare it ahead, try to leave at least the avocado and pineapple till the last moment; this one doesn't keep.

Bring water to boil with salt. Add bulgur and return to a boil. Remove from heat, cover pot tightly, and set aside for 15 minutes or until water is absorbed. Cool to room temperature.

Peel and cube avocado and stir into pineapple chunks so that the juice from the pineapple will keep the avocado from discoloring. Combine with bell pepper, celery, scallions, oil and lemon juice or vinegar. Stir in bulgur wheat and serve.

Makes 6 generous servings.

Sideways Sushi

Not to be confused with the more familiar Nori Maki Sushi (page 274), this is "O-sushi" or "Big Sushi." It comes to you "sideways" because we have taken some liberties with this classic dish, which we first tasted at the hands of an honored and beloved friend, Fukuda-Sensei, many years ago.

❧

Bring water to boil with salt. Add rice and boil uncovered 5 minutes. Cover and reduce heat to low. Cook for 45 minutes. Turn off heat, cover, and allow to rest for another 10 minutes.

While rice is cooking, steam carrot until crisp-tender and prepare cucumber and almonds.

Spread hot rice out quickly on the biggest tray or platter you have (but not one made of metal!). Toss rice with a fork for several minutes while you or a helper fan the steam away with a fan or a folded newspaper. This helps make the rice as dry and fluffy as possible.

Sprinkle vinegar over rice as you toss it. Lightly stir in the cucumber, carrot, and almonds. Taste and add more vinegar if you like. Do not refrigerate. Cover with a damp cloth and serve warm or at room temperature.

Makes 8 servings.

3¾ cups water
1 teaspoon salt
2 cups raw long-grain brown rice

1 medium carrot, diced
1 cucumber, peeled and diced
½ cup chopped toasted almonds
⅓ cup rice vinegar

Other options for additions (use three or four only, about 2 cups total):

tiny strips of omelette
diced sautéed mushroom
thin-sliced steamed green beans
minced scallion
diced green bell pepper
nori sea vegetable, toasted and crumbled

Persian Rice Salad

This sophisticated salad is sweet and tangy. Perfect for carry-outs too.

❧

Dress rice with combined olive oil, lemon juice, and dill weed. Add salt to taste. Combine with scallions, cashew pieces, and dates and serve immediately. (If you can't serve right away, set the cashews aside and add them just beforehand.)

Makes 4 servings (2½ cups).

2 cups cold cooked long-grain brown rice
1 tablespoon olive oil
3 tablespoons lemon juice
¼ to ½ teaspoon dill weed, by taste
½ teaspoon salt, optional
3 thin scallions, sliced thin
⅓ cup toasted cashew pieces
4 to 6 medium dates, cut up

Soups

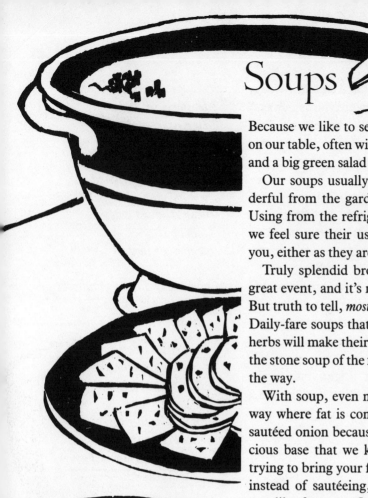

Because we like to serve light suppers, soup appears frequently on our table, often with nothing more than fresh bread or muffins and a big green salad alongside.

Our soups usually take form around what is fresh and wonderful from the garden (or sometimes it's What Really Needs Using from the refrigerator). The recipes here reflect that, and we feel sure their usefulness for us will make them helpful to you, either as they are or as inspiration for your own creations.

Truly splendid broth can transform an ordinary soup into a great event, and it's not hard to make; some suggestions follow. But truth to tell, *most* of the time, plain old water is all you need. Daily-fare soups that have a dose of onion and celery, garlic, or herbs will make their own broth in the pot and be delicious. Like the stone soup of the fairy tale, they develop their character along the way.

With soup, even more than most dishes, there is a lot of leeway where fat is concerned. Most of the soups here start with sautéed onion because that is the surest, quickest way to a delicious base that we know. But if you have more time and are trying to bring your fat intake to a real minimum, boil the onion instead of sautéeing, adding seasonings or other vegetables if you like for extra flavor. When the onion is very well cooked, you can use it and its broth, or puree them, or strain out the onion and use just the broth by itself. The onion's flavor will be different than if it had been sautéed, but still sweet and satisfying. A variation on this theme is spelled out in the Corn Chowder recipe.

Because soup is so good the next day for lunch, either at home or in a thermos, we have scaled many of the soup recipes generously. Check the serving size before you start; if your household is very small, you may want either to cut the recipe in half, or plan to freeze part for using another time.

INSTANT SOUP A little leftover sauce, thinned with broth or milk or tomato juice (whichever seems appropriate) and heated with leftover vegetables and/or noodles, makes fine soup in a trice.

Basic Vegetable Soup

In a big soup pot, sauté a chopped onion until golden, adding garlic and some chopped celery or green pepper if you like. Add stock or water and bring to a boil. Stir in whatever vegetables are in season, chopped attractively—start with slower-cooking ones like potatoes, carrots, and green beans, and end with delicate greens like spinach or parsley and fresh herbs. Leftover grains, beans, or noodles are welcome and contribute substance to the pot; so does tomato sauce or other leftover sauce. A simple and low-calorie way to make the soup thicker is to put part of its cooked vegetables (and grain) into the blender and blend smooth, returning the puree to the pot.

Especially when you're preparing soup for more than four people, you may prefer to cook all or part of the vegetables separately, adding them with their cooking water to the pot toward the end. This insures that each one will be perfectly cooked, and preserves individual colors—especially helpful when the soup is tomato-based. Cooking separately like this can save time too, because the vegetables can be simmering while you prepare the rest.

This simple soup is a perfect way to use up odds and ends from the garden, but made with a delicately flavored broth and just the right herbs, it can be superb.

Stock

When you simmer vegetable trimmings to make stock, you preserve both useful nutrients and rich flavors that would otherwise be lost. It's a thrifty procedure that can become such a habit that the little work involved slips unnoticed into your routine.

Collect clean vegetable trimmings for a week, storing them in a covered jar in the refrigerator. To make stock, take stock: what kinds of trimmings have you collected? Balance the flavors: if it's all spinach and parsley stems, for example, slice in some carrot or potato or winter squash to sweeten the pot. Don't include anything that is over the hill, and take time to add whatever extras you think will insure that your brew tastes great. Cover with cold water and add a small spoonful of salt, if you like, to draw out the flavors. Bring to a boil and simmer gently about half an hour, or until the vegetables are very soft. Let the pot sit as long as is convenient, or until cool. Drain, discarding the vegetables. Use at once, preferably, or keep in the refrigerator for a day or two at most.

TIPS   ❧ Some things can tolerate more cooking than others. Onions, potatoes, and the like can simmer for hours. But don't overcook the green things; their flavors become drab and harsh. Grate the carrot and potato when you are in a hurry; smaller pieces cook faster.

❧ Very good for stock are pea pods, trimmings of green beans, squashes of all sorts (including their seeds) parsley, carrot and potato bits (but not eyes and bad spots!), any edible part of any member of the onion family, celery leaves, and mushroom bits.

❧ Take advantage of the the sea vegetable kombu, which has a wealth of minerals and also a natural glutamic acid which MSG was invented to imitate. Wash and soak a piece of kombu in cold water for several hours or overnight, or put a four-inch square in a quart of cold water and heat slowly, removing the kombu as soon as the water comes to a boil. You can include a small piece of kombu with other vegetables when you make stock in the normal way, but don't let it stay in after the stock boils.

🍂 Some things do more harm than good: artichoke trimmings and bell pepper innards, for example, are bitter, and the whole brassica family from cabbage to cauliflower overcooks quickly, giving a heavy, sulfury taste.

🍂 Adjust the stock to its purpose, seasoning or flavoring it according to its proposed use. Try adding one or more of the following: a few fennel or cumin seeds, peppercorns, turmeric, bay leaves, onion, garlic, ginger.

Special Broths

BROTH FOR PEOPLE WITH COLDS OR FLU

"Get lots of rest and drink plenty of *fluids*." Fruit juice and herb teas are fine, but after a while what tastes best is good, hot broth. Golden Broth (page 151), strained and thinned, is good for colds. Or try Rasam (next page) if your snuffly patient has good digestion and an adventurous palate. The broth described below, with onion, garlic, cumin, and perhaps tomato added for extra flavor, also hits the spot when you have a cold.

But when the patient is recovering from flu and has a sore, touchy stomach, a light, soothing broth seems to help most. These ingredients can be varied to suit, but when nothing else seems good, this mild broth can be heavenly just as it is.

🍂

Wash and cut up the vegetables. Place in a saucepan and cover with cold water, adding salt if desired—even a little bit makes a big difference in flavor. Bring to a boil and simmer gently until the vegetables are very soft—about 20 minutes or so, depending on how small they were chopped. Add the leaves and simmer 10 more minutes, then drain, discarding the vegetables. Serve soon, refrigerating and reheating the rest as needed—but this broth is best when used within a day or two.

2 small zucchini
  or use winter squash,
  potatoes, or carrot
handful green beans
handful parsley stems
  and/or spinach stems
⅛ teaspoon salt
2 quarts water

1 cup parsley and/or
  spinach leaves

Rasam

4 small cloves garlic
1/4 teaspoon cumin powder
1/2 teaspoon black
    peppercorns

1 tablespoon oil
2 teaspoons black mustard
    seed
1/2 teaspoon cumin seed

2 tomatoes, quartered
1 cup water
1 teaspoon turmeric
1/2 teaspoon salt
2 teaspoons tamarind
    concentrate dissolved
    in 1 cup hot water
        OR
    juice of one lemon
    in 1 cup hot water

1 cup well-cooked yellow
    split peas

(chopped coriander leaves)

This exceedingly spicy broth is credited with curing colds in South India, and if it seems to do the same in North America, who can complain? The cures are undocumented, but the brew is breathtaking, no doubt about it. For a less fiery version (and more soup) use 6 tomatoes and add extra water. For LEMON RASAM, omit the tomatoes—and stand back!

❧

Crush the garlic, cumin, and peppercorns with a mortar and pestle or in a blender, using just enough water to cover the blades.

Heat the oil in a very heavy small pan. Add the mustard seeds, coating the bottom of the pan evenly. Cover the pan quickly and listen for the moment when the furious sound of popping slows dramatically. Then add the cumin seeds so that they brown, but almost immediately *turn off the flame* and add the tomato, water, and turmeric, then the garlic mixture.

Bring to a boil and add the tamarind or lemon and salt. Mash the peas and add them too. Simmer gently until the tomatoes are soft, about ten minutes. In Kerala they take advantage of the way this soup separates, serving the liquid top part over rice at the beginning of the meal and the thick bottom part over rice at the end of it. If you want a uniformly creamy soup, give the finished version a spin in the blender. Serve with a garnish of chopped coriander leaves on top, if you have them.

Makes 2 cups as written, 6 cups with extra tomato and water.

Golden Broth

This is a hearty broth that is useful wherever you think you need chicken stock. If you want to make it without the fat, the flavor is quite satisfactory with everything just boiled together. You can't strain it, however.

1 onion, chopped
1 clove garlic
½ cup yellow split peas
2 tablespoons oil

½ teaspoon turmeric
2 quarts hot water

୬

Sauté onion, whole garlic clove, and split peas in oil until delicately brown. Stir in turmeric and add water. Simmer at least half an hour. Strain for a thin stock, puree for a thick one.

GREEN BROTH: substitute green peas for yellow. Add a bay leaf and omit the turmeric. For a very full flavored broth, add a carrot and potato, cut up. Celery leaves are good too.

Golden Noodle Soup

Golden Noodle Soup is our answer to Mother Campbell, and to all the colds, malaises, and depressions usually remedied at the expense of our feathered friends. This is wonderful, elemental, satisfying soup. Easy, too.

2 quarts Golden Broth
big handful whole wheat
  ribbon noodles
1 cup each diced celery,
  potatoes, carrots
1 teaspoon salt
½ cup finely chopped
  parsley

୬

Bring broth to a boil in a heavy pan. Add noodles, celery, potatoes, carrots, and salt. Reduce heat and simmer gently until the vegetables are tender, about half an hour. Stir in the parsley, adjust seasoning, and serve.

Makes about 10 cups of soup (and you won't be sorry.)

TIMESAVING VARIATION: If you don't already have the broth, cook the noodles and vegetables in another pot while the broth simmers, combining them after you puree or strain the broth. Total cooking time is about half an hour.

Gumbo

1 onion, chopped
3 cloves
2 tablespoons oil
1 green pepper, diced
2 cups diced tomatoes
4 cups vegetable stock
1 cup cooked lima beans
1 cup fresh corn
1½ cups sliced okra
1 teaspoon salt
¼ teaspoon allspice

(½ cup cooked brown rice)

You won't feel diffident about serving a vegetarian gumbo when you taste this soup. (Who says it isn't gumbo, anyway?) Fresh tomatoes are wonderful, but canned work fine.

❧

Sauté the onion and cloves in oil until the onions are soft. Remove the cloves.

Add green pepper and stir over medium heat for several minutes; then stir in the tomatoes. Bring the mixture to a boil, turn down the heat, and let simmer for 5 minutes.

Add the rest of the ingredients. Bring soup to a boil again, cover, and simmer for 15 minutes. Add rice if desired.

Makes about 8 cups.

Whole Beet Borscht

1 small onion
1 clove garlic
2 teaspoons oil
2 tablespoons flour
5 cups stock or water

1 bunch beets and greens
   (3 large or 6 small)
1 potato
1 carrot
1 stalk celery
½ small cabbage
1 bay leaf
1½ teaspoons salt
¼ teaspoon pepper
1 teaspoon honey
2 tablespoons tomato paste
   or 2 fresh tomatoes,
   chopped

This is *good*, especially served with Mock Sour Cream.

❧

Chop onion and sauté with garlic clove in oil. Mash garlic clove when onion is translucent and browning. Stir in flour and cook gently for a minute. Add stock or water and bring to a boil.

Meantime, trim roots of beets, saving the good leaves and stems. Slice potato, carrot, and celery thin. Add these and simmer 10 minutes while you shred the cabbage and chop the beet leaves and stems small. Add these and bay leaf, salt, pepper, honey, and tomato to the vegetable mixture. Simmer until all vegetables are tender. Remove bay leaf.

Makes 10 cups.

Minestrone

Minestrone is a general name for a richly flavored tomato-based soup that welcomes infinite variation, according to the season's taste and needs. It can appear as a light, fragrant vegetable soup on summer evenings or, most memorably, as a hearty stew for a cold winter day. Either way, minestrone is a wonderful meal in itself with green salad and crusty fresh bread. Begin with the tomato soup base and include any of the suggested grains, beans, and vegetables.

≥●

Sauté onion, garlic and celery in oil until soft. Crush garlic. Add tomatoes, or tomato paste and stock, and herbs. Simmer the soup gently while you prepare whatever vegetables, beans, or grains you wish to add.

At least 30 minutes before serving soup, add beans, noodles, and/or the grain.

Minestrone welcomes leftover steamed vegetables, but if you are cooking them fresh, we suggest steaming or simmering them before adding to the soup because vegetables cooked with tomato will lose their color. Incorporate the vegetable cooking water into the soup. Parsley and tender greens will keep their color and not be overcooked if you add them just a few minutes before serving. Don't count them as part of the 2 cups of vegetables because they cook down so much; just add them as extras.

After combining all the ingredients, bring the soup to a boil, simmer briefly, and correct the seasonings. If you like, garnish each bowl with a spoonful of Parmesan cheese.

Makes about 10 cups—all to the good because it's even better the next day. Serves 6 generously.

1 onion, finely chopped
1–2 cloves garlic
1½ cups chopped celery
1½ tablespoons olive oil
4 cups chopped tomatoes
  with juice, or
  1 six-ounce can tomato
  paste and 3 cups
  vegetable stock
2 bay leaves
1 teaspoon oregano
2 teaspoons basil
pinch fennel seed

2 cups or more, chopped:
  carrot, zucchini, potato,
  broccoli, green
  beans, green pepper,
  cabbage, peas, corn,
  sautéed mushrooms

1 cup cooked beans:
  lima, kidney, pinto,
  black, or garbanzo

handful of raw or cooked
  whole wheat pasta

(½ cup cooked grain)
salt to taste
plenty of pepper

(tender greens, cut up)
½ cup chopped parsley

Puree

"Puree" means to reduce whatever it is to a smooth, thick liquid. You can do this with a food mill (or a strainer and spoon), or a blender or food processor—whichever you find most convenient. A few recipes specify one of them if the others aren't practical for that particular step. If a food mill is called for, you can always use the strainer-and-spoon method, but food mills are inexpensive, and so handy that we can hardly imagine cooking without one.

Blender companies are very stern in their instruction booklets about the danger of blending hot liquids. *They're right!* If you are making soup or sauce and can't wait for the temperature to go down to lukewarm before popping the brew in the blender, *please* fill the container not more than half full, cover tightly, and hold the cover in place with a large, half-folded towel. Stainless steel blender jars won't break, but besides cracking glass and plastic blender jars, hot liquids can cause bad burns if they come spewing out the top.

Xergis

3 cucumbers
3 scallions or
   1/2 small onion
(1 clove garlic)
5 cups yogurt
(1 teaspoon oil)
4 teaspoons dill weed
1 teaspoon salt
dash pepper

On hot summer evenings, this flavorful Levantine beverage is a refreshing first course.

Peel cucumbers and remove seeds. Chop cucumbers, onion, and garlic. Mix all ingredients and divide in 3 parts. Place in blender one part at a time and blend very smooth. Chill.
    Makes 6 to 8 cups.

Creamy Green Soup

At its simplest—and some say its best—Creamy Green Soup is just cooked, garden-fresh zucchini blended with its own broth with salt, pepper, and a dab of butter. You can enliven it if you like with bright red bell peppers or corn off the cob, sautéed scallions or chives, parsley or chopped greens. For added heft, you can blend in a spoonful of milk powder, cottage cheese, cooked green split peas, or a little nutritional yeast.

Vary the texture by blending some ingredients and leaving others chopped or shredded. Thin with good vegetable stock or milk, or thicken by adding half a cup or more of well-cooked brown rice that has been blended smooth with a small amount of the soup.

To complete its versatility, Green Soup can be served chilled. Top it with a spoonful of yogurt and add crackers with Garbanzo Spread for a refreshing supper on a hot summer evening.

The following versions are some current favorites.

Old Favorite Green Soup

Sauté the onion and celery in oil until soft. Add 4 cups of stock, split peas, and bay leaf. Bring to a boil; then cover loosely and simmer over low heat for about 40 minutes.

Add zucchini, remaining stock, and seasonings. Cook for another 10 minutes, until zucchini is tender.

Remove bay leaf and discard. Puree soup, return to the soup pot and stir in the spinach and parsley. Cook over medium heat for several minutes. Adjust seasonings and serve.

Makes 7 to 8 cups.

1/2 onion, chopped
2 stalks celery, diced
1 tablespoons oil

6 cups vegetable stock
3/4 cup green split peas, rinsed
1 bay leaf

6 cups diced zucchini
1/4 teaspoon basil
1/8 teaspoon pepper
1 teaspoon salt

1 pound spinach, washed and chopped
1/4 cup chopped fresh parsley

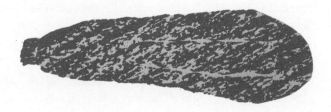

New Favorite Green Soup

1 onion or 1 bunch scallions
1 tablespoon oil or butter
2 or 3 potatoes, cut up
6–8 cups chopped fresh
    greens—chard, spinach,
    etc.

broth or milk
salt and pepper

Sauté onion in oil or butter until very soft. Add the potatoes and water to cover. Cook until tender and remove peels if you desire. Add greens and simmer until they wilt. Puree all. Add broth or milk to thin and extend as desired, then add salt and pepper to taste.

Asparagus Soup

½ onion or 6 scallions
1 tablespoon oil or butter
1 medium potato
2 cups vegetable stock
    or water

1–1½ pounds fresh
    asparagus
4 stalks celery
1–1½ teaspoons salt
⅛ teaspoon pepper
(milk or broth)

For an elegant touch, set aside the asparagus tips and stir them in just a little before serving. This delicate, spring-fresh soup makes good use of slender, stringy asparagus as well as fat, succulent spears.

෧

Sauté onion in oil or butter. Dice potato and add along with 1 cup of stock. Simmer until potatoes are soft.

Wash the asparagus and snap off the tough ends. Slice. (If you have a lot of tough ends but the spears seem fresh and good, peel and include the tender inside parts, or cook the spears along with the rest and put the finished soup through a food mill to remove the tough fibers.)

Chop celery small, including leaves. Add asparagus, celery, and remaining vegetable stock to potatoes and onions. Cook for 10 minutes, until the vegetables are quite tender. Add salt and pepper and puree. Add milk or broth to thin or extend soup as desired.

Makes about 6 cups.

Creamy Cauliflower Soup

The cauliflower disappears completely, making a warm-flavored soup as thick and white as heavy cream—but much tastier and better for you!

ᡓᢩ

Cook the potato in the broth. Chop the celery and add. When the potato is nearly done, add the cauliflower and cook until tender. As always in blended soups, the potato must be very well cooked; otherwise the soup will be gluey.

While the vegetables are cooking, chop the onion and sauté it and the garlic clove in the olive oil. Cook them gently until very well done but don't let them brown.

Puree all the cooked vegetables and the onion and garlic in blender or food processor until smooth. To get a very smooth soup, blend or process in small batches.

Stir in the wine, if you choose, and the salt and pepper. Reheat gently, adjust seasoning as needed, and serve.

Makes 10 cups.

ᡓᢩ

This soup is lovely as is, pure white. If you want to add color or other interest, though, stir in one or more of the following a few minutes before serving:

*1/2 pound fresh mushrooms, sliced and sautéed,
   with 1 teaspoon each marjoram and savory*

1/2 cup chopped fresh parsley

1/2 cup diced red bell pepper

1 cup fresh corn off the cob

*1 1/2 cups potato
   chunks (no peels)*
4 cups light broth or water
*1 1/4 cups chopped pale
   celery*
*5 cups cauliflower
   pieces (1 head)*

1 small onion
1 whole clove garlic
*1 tablespoon olive oil
   or butter*

(1/2 cup dry white wine)

1 teaspoon salt
pinch pepper

Lynne's Spiced Pumpkin Soup

1 small pumpkin
  (about 10 cups diced)
3 carrots

1½ tablespoons oil
¾ teaspoon black mustard
  seed
½ onion, chopped
½ teaspoon turmeric
½ teaspoon cumin
½ teaspoon cinnamon
¼ teaspoon ginger

¾ cup powdered milk
2 teaspoons honey
1 teaspoon salt

Truly remarkable with pumpkin, but if you haven't any, substitute winter squash. A light, flavorful soup that finds favor even with squash haters. It's worth growing pumpkins for.

Peel and chop pumpkin and carrots, and simmer in water to cover until tender.

Toward the end of the cooking time, heat oil in a small, heavy skillet. When hot, add mustard seeds. Cover pan and keep over high heat until the sound of popping dies down a bit, then *immediately* add the onion and reduce heat. Cook and stir until onion is clear. Measure the spices while the onion is cooking; then stir them into the mixture and allow to cook on low heat for a minute or so until they are fragrant. Turn into the pumpkin pot, using a cup or so of cooking water to rinse the spice pan into the soup pot.

Puree the seasoned pumpkin and carrots in their cooking water, adding the milk, honey, and salt to the mixture in the blender or processor. Add salt to taste.

Makes 10 cups.

ALTERNATE METHOD: If you have leftover cooked pumpkin, or prefer to use fresh milk, warm the squash and milk and then puree them, using the milk instead of the cooking broth to provide the liquid.

Croutons

The best croutons come from bread that is airy and not too sweet. Light sourdoughs are great.

For croutons in a hurry, toast bread slices, butter them, and cut into cubes. Croutons made in this way will be soft in the middle and are not meant for storing, but for eating up right away.

To make plain croutons that will keep a long time, cut bread into ½″ to 1″ cubes, spread on a shallow pan, and bake very slowly until they become 100 percent crunchy. (Chomp on one; there's no other way to be sure that we know of.) Cool thoroughly and store airtight.

Squash Soup

A wintertime standby of many interpretations, this hearty soup provides a useful role for leftover baked squash.

❧

If you use raw squash or pumpkin, simmer in water until tender. Puree the cooked squash.

Sauté the onion in the oil. When the onion is golden, add the parsley. Cook just long enough to soften parsley; then combine with squash and add salt.

Bring the soup to a simmer—don't boil or it will stick.

Near the end of the cooking time, if you like, add fresh spinach or other tender greens, chopped bite-size. Colorful and tasty too.

Makes about 7 cups.

5 cups cubed raw winter
   squash or pumpkin, or
   3 cups cooked winter
   squash
2½ cups water

1 cup chopped onion
1 tablespoon oil or butter
½ cup chopped parsley
2 teaspoons salt
(2–4 cups tender greens)

Carrot Soup

Cut carrots in 1″ chunks, quarter the potatoes, and place both in a 2-quart sauce pan. Add just enough water to cover. Bring to a boil and simmer, covered, until vegetables are tender. Remove and discard potato peels.

Meanwhile, wash leeks thoroughly and chop them coarsely. If they are very muddy, chop them first and rinse well in a sieve after chopping. Sauté in butter along with the tarragon. Use blender or food processor to puree the vegetables in batches, adding the milk, stock, and salt. Return soup to pot; add pepper and wine, and reheat.

Makes 8 cups.

5 medium-large carrots
2 small potatoes or one large
1 bunch leeks
   (or 1 large onion)
2 tablespoons butter or oil
1 teaspoon dry tarragon
   leaves, or
   1 tablespoon fresh
   tarragon
2 cups milk
2 cups vegetable stock
   or water
1 teaspoon salt
pinch black pepper
½ cup dry white wine

Kale-Potato Soup

1 large onion
1 tablespoon butter
1 clove garlic

2 big potatoes
1 large bunch kale
5 cups hot water or stock

1/2 teaspoon salt, to taste
black pepper

An utterly satisfying soup. How many winter nights does this seem to be the only possible choice? A classic, a favorite, a stand-by. With fresh young kale, it is, perhaps, even a world-class soup.

ॐ

Sauté onion in butter, cooking and stirring until clear and slightly golden. About halfway, add the garlic; when the onion is done, crush the garlic with a fork.

Add the potatoes and 2 cups of water. Simmer, covered, until potatoes start to soften around the edges. Meantime, wash the kale, remove stems, chop, and steam. (Don't try to cook it with the potatoes; the flavor will be too strong. Really.)

When the potatoes are very well done, puree half of them with remaining water and the salt and pepper. Combine all and heat gently, correcting the consistency if necessary by adding hot water or milk.

Makes about 6 cups and serves 4 if no extra water is added.

Potato-Cheese Soup

4 medium potatoes
2 carrots

1 onion, chopped
(1 whole clove garlic)
1–2 tablespoons oil or butter

3 cups milk
1/2–1 cup grated sharp
    cheddar
2 teaspoons salt
1/4 teaspoon pepper
1 tablespoon chopped parsley

"Your Potato-Cheese Soup gets us through the Minnesota winter," writes a friend. What a tribute! What a soup!

ॐ

Cook the potatoes and carrots in water to cover in a large, heavy pan. Remove potato skins. Meantime, sauté the onion—and garlic, if desired—in the oil or butter and combine with potatoes, carrots, and cooking water. Puree in batches.

Return puree to pan and add milk, cheese, and seasonings. Heat until cheese is melted and soup is piping hot—but don't let it boil.

Makes 8 to 10 cups.

Corn Chowder

When a recipe has been with you as long as you can remember, and enjoyed so much, it can be hard to think what to say about it. This is an elemental, wonderful chowder.

≈

Simmer the water, onion, celery, potato, and parsley until half cooked, about 10 minutes.

Add the corn. Simmer gently with the other vegetables until nearly done, not more than a few minutes.

Add the milk or Cream Sauce, and bring the soup just to the boiling point without actually boiling. Add seasonings and correct to taste.

Serve piping hot, with a dot of Better-Butter. Serves 4 to 6.

VARIATION: Instead of milk or cream sauce, you can use 1 cup tomato sauce and 1 cup broth. Presto, MANHATTAN CORN CHOWDER!

2 cups water
½ chopped onion
½ cup chopped celery
½ cup diced potato
½ cup chopped parsley
1 cup fresh raw corn
*   off the cob*
2 cups milk
*   or light Cream Sauce*
1 teaspoon salt
¼ teaspoon pepper
Better-Butter

Cream of Celery Soup

A warming, soothing brew for chasing chills on cold winter evenings. Homey and good.

≈

In a large soup pot, sauté onion and garlic in oil until soft. Add 4 cups stock and bring to boil.

Stir in potatoes, celery, and celery seed. Cover and simmer for 10 to 15 minutes, until potatoes are very soft. Add cabbage if you want and simmer 5 more minutes. Puree half of the soup mixture. (If you use a blender, do it in 2 portions of 2 cups each.) Add pureed soup, salt, parsley, pepper, and paprika to soup pot and reheat. Thin with milk or broth if desired.

Makes about 8 cups, to serve 4 to 6.

½ onion, chopped
1 garlic clove
1 tablespoon oil
4 cups water or broth

2 medium potatoes, diced
½ bunch celery, diced
¼ teaspoon celery seed
(¼ head cabbage, chopped)

1½ teaspoons salt
¼ cup finely chopped
*   parsley*
dash pepper
¼ teaspoon paprika
(2 cups milk, or more broth)

Tomato Soup

1 medium onion
2 stalks celery
1 carrot
1 tablespoon oil

¾ teaspoon oregano
1½ teaspoons basil
4 cups cut-up tomatoes★

2–3 cups hot vegetable stock
¾ teaspoon salt
pepper to taste

★Here and anywhere we call
for tomatoes, use fresh
if you have them, canned
if you don't.

A fine basic tomato soup, spectacularly good when the tomatoes are garden-fresh and ripe. Delicious as is, or a fine base for any kind of red-brothed soup.

෨

In a big soup pot, sauté the onion in oil, adding the celery and carrot when the onion is partly cooked. Cook together until the onion is soft.

Add oregano, basil, and tomatoes to the pot and simmer gently until the tomatoes are very soft. If you want a smooth, creamy texture, puree the soup. (Using a food mill for pureeing will remove the tomato seeds and skins, making a velvety soup.)

Add the hot stock, adjusting the amount to get the quantity and thickness you want. Bring to a boil and simmer on low heat for 5 minutes. Season with salt and pepper to taste.

Makes about 8 cups.

Cream of Tomato Soup

Follow the Tomato Soup recipe but tone down the herbs, using just ¼ teaspoon oregano and ½ teaspoon basil—and perhaps a little extra salt.

Blend 1 cup of dried skim milk with part of the stock or with the tomato mixture. Pour it back into the pot, add salt and pepper, and heat thoroughly (but *don't boil*). For a heartier soup, add a cup of cooked brown rice.

Makes about 8 cups.

Gingery Tomato Soup

A tangy, fruity soup, very light and refreshing.

২

Sauté shallots or onion and whole garlic in oil; add ginger. Add tomatoes and stock and simmer until tomatoes are soft. Put through sieve or food mill.

Add black pepper and shoyu to taste, starting with 1 teaspoon shoyu.

Makes about 5 cups.

2 teaspoons oil
3 shallots
    or 1 onion
2 cloves garlic
1 tablespoon minced ginger
3 cups tomatoes
2 cups stock
1 tablespoon shoyu
fresh black pepper

TOMATO–PEPPER SOUP

Make Gingery Tomato Soup, omitting ginger and shoyu. While soup simmers, roast, peel, seed, and chop 2 red bell peppers (see page 137). Sieve the tomato soup as described in the recipe, then puree the peppers with part of the soup. Mix together, adding ½ cup sherry. Simmer 10 minutes gently, then adjust seasoning.

TOMATO–PEPPER SAUCE: Don't add extra stock; simmer soup gently to reduce volume to 2 cups.

Fresh Corn & Tomato Soup

A thick, creamy, coral-colored soup with truly superb flavor.

২

Sauté onion, celery, cayenne if desired, and garlic in oil in a heavy 2-quart pan until tender. (This amount of oil will be enough if you keep the heat low and stir frequently.)

Strip corn from cobs with a small, sharp knife. Remove stem end of tomatoes and cut up coarsely.

Add corn and tomatoes, water, and salt to sautéed vegetables. Bring to a boil; then reduce heat to low and simmer, covered, until corn is tender, about ½ hour.

The soup is pretty now, but even better if you take your courage in hand and proceed with the next step: puree it all. Return to pot, thinning with a little more water if you want, and correct the salt. Heat, stirring in coriander leaves just at serving time.

Serves 4.

½ onion, chopped
1 stalk celery, chopped
(dash cayenne pepper)
1 whole clove garlic
1 tablespoon oil

5 ears corn
    (4 cups off the cob)
4 good-sized tomatoes
½ cup water
½–1 teaspoon salt

(handful fresh coriander
    leaves, lightly chopped)

Miso Soup

How much salt does miso have?

½ teaspoon salt
= 2 teaspoons shoyu
= 1 tablespoon salty miso:
    (red, barley, light-yellow,
    soybean, or Hatcho)
= 1½ to 2 tablespoons
    "mellow miso"
= 2½ to 3 tablespoons
    sweet miso

SOURCE: *The Book of Miso, by William Shurtleff and Akiko Aoyagi (Berkeley: Ten Speed Press, 1983)*

Flavorful and salty, miso is a brown, golden, or reddish paste made by fermenting soybeans with or without rice or other grains. A staple in Japanese cuisine, it is a versatile seasoning with considerable nutritive value—one that Americans are finding increasingly useful.

In traditional Japanese families, hot miso soup is served every morning alongside a steaming bowl of rice cereal. In their splendid *Book of Miso*, Bill and Akiko Shurtleff describe the place miso has in the Japanese consciousness: its warming aroma is as nostalgic and comforting as the fragrance of baking bread is to us of European extraction. They also describe miso's versatility: to give just an idea, one Japanese firm publishes a calendar with a different seasonal miso soup for each and every day! Here and elsewhere in this book we present some simple ways to let miso work its magic.

Like yogurt, miso contains beneficial organisms—and like yogurt, it is often pasteurized, so that these organisms are not available to the eater. If you can buy unpasteurized miso, cook it as little as possible so that you don't pasteurize it yourself: if you want to use it to flavor a soup, for example, stir the miso smooth in a small amount of broth and add at the last possible moment before serving.

In this context, researchers who have spent decades studying miso at the USDA Northern Regional Research Center in Peoria, Illinois, say that although miso bacteria may well be helpful to the eater while they are present in the digestive system, they are not the kind of organisms that would be able to colonize the intestines with beneficial flora after a course of antibiotic drugs, as is sometimes claimed.

Store miso airtight in the refrigerator; it can spoil.

Some Ways to Use Miso

Traditional soups are composed of miso broth with one main vegetable and two garnishing vegetables, the latter being freely interpreted to include such things as tofu pieces or lemon zest besides zucchini, spinach, mushrooms, and the like. The ingredients are cut with mindful artistry and simmered in stock; then the miso is stirred in as described above and the soup is served. With unsalted broth, 1 or 2 teaspoons per person of miso is about the right amount, depending on the variety.

Untraditional soup can be literally any liquid that tastes better with miso in it. Its flavor in soup is deep and hearty, with the darker varieties almost like a vegetarian bouillion.

Since miso is flavorful and salty, it can be used to enhance many dishes where you would use salt or shoyu. Sandwich spreads made from beans or tofu would be a good example.

A more concentrated version of miso soup, thickened with flour or cornstarch or with cooked rice or vegetables pureed smooth, makes a very convincing brown gravy.

Some of our friends swear by miso as a coffee substitute. A spoonful stirred into hot water makes a satisfying hot drink, with or without a garnish of crumbled, toasted nori. Commercial instant miso soups that come in packets may lack the living cultures of unpasteurized miso, but they travel easily and need no refrigeration, so they are convenient pick-me-ups when you're away from home.

TO MAKE SOUP

AS A SEASONING

TO MAKE GRAVY

AS A HOT DRINK

Catalina Soup

1 onion
1 clove garlic
1 tablespoon oil

¼ cup tomato paste
4 cups water or stock
2 large potatoes
½ teaspoon oregano
1 teaspoon salt
black pepper

(handful of fresh
   chopped coriander leaves)
½–1 cup grated jack cheese

Like all often-made favorite dishes, this soup adapts to the needs of the day. For tomato paste, you can use tomatoes—or less, or much more—and the amount of potatoes can go up or down to make the soup heartier or lighter.

ᐧᕑ

Chop the onion and sauté it and the garlic in oil until the onion is soft; then crush the garlic with a fork. Add the tomato paste and water or stock, stirring to mix. Bring to a boil.

Meanwhile, cut potatoes into ½″ cubes and add to the soup pot. Simmer until potatoes are tender but not mushy. Add oregano, salt, and pepper (if you used seasoned broth, you may want less salt).

Just before serving, stir in the coriander leaves, if desired, and the cheese.

Makes about 7 cups, a meal for 4 or more.

VARIATION: Before adding cheese and coriander, stir in a quart of chopped fresh spinach or tender chard leaves. Simmer just until tender.

Black Bean Soup

1½ cups black beans
6 cups water
1 onion
2 tablespoons oil
2 large cloves garlic
2 stalks celery
1 potato
1 carrot
1 bay leaf
1 teaspoon oregano
¼ teaspoon savory
2 teaspoons salt
⅛ teaspoon pepper
2 lemons

Wash the beans and put them in a saucepan along with the water. Cover loosely, bring to a boil, and simmer for 2½ hours or so, until beans are quite tender.

Meantime, chop the onion and sauté in the oil with garlic until soft. Crush the garlic. Chop the celery, including the leaves. Dice potato and carrot or grate on large grater. Add celery, potato, and carrot to onion and heat for several minutes, stirring all the while.

Add the vegetables to the beans, along with the seasonings, in the last hour of their cooking. Bring the soup to a boil and lower the heat to simmer until the beans and vegetables are done. Puree half or all the soup if you want a thick, hearty broth.

Juice one lemon and slice the other. Stir in juice and add slices just before serving.

Makes about 9 cups, to serve 6.

Hearty Pea Soup

It's easy enough to make plain pea soup with just onion, potato, and carrot—and it's good, too. But this fine soup is the perfected model, worth the extra hour of simmering.

ॐ

Sauté onion in oil until soft, along with bay leaf and celery seed. Stir in peas, barley, and limas. Add 2 quarts water and bring to a boil. Cook on low heat, partially covered, for about an hour and a half.

Add salt, pepper, vegetables, and herbs. Turn heat down as low as possible and simmer another 30 to 45 minutes. Thin with additional water or stock as you like. Correct seasonings.

Makes about 8 to 9 cups.

1 onion, diced
2 tablespoons oil
1 bay leaf
1 teaspoon celery seed

1 cup green split peas
¼ cup barley
½ cup lima beans
2 quarts water

2 teaspoons salt
dash pepper
1 carrot, chopped
3 stalks celery, diced
½ cup chopped parsley
1 potato, diced
½ teaspoon basil
½ teaspoon thyme

Greek Lentil Soup

A thinner, more flavorful version of lentil soup than the usual stewy kind.

ॐ

Pick over lentils and wash.

Mix all ingredients except the vinegar in a soup pot and cook until the lentils are very soft, about one hour. Stir in vinegar at the end and serve.

Makes about 8 cups, to serve 6.

2 cups uncooked lentils
8 cups water or
* vegetable stock*
½ onion, chopped
1 small carrot, chopped
1 celery stalk, chopped
1 small potato, chopped
2 tablespoons olive oil
2 bay leaves
1½ to 2 teaspoons salt

2 teaspoons red wine vinegar

Fruit Soups

Fruit soups are sweet, but not very. They are a whimsical, enjoyable way to start just about any meal—like brunch, for instance. There's a distinctly Old European mood about fruit soups. In Scandinavia they are likely to be made with buttermilk and fresh raspberries, then topped with meringue and slivered almonds. That's in the summertime. Come winter, a mixture of dried fruits is stewed—a happy commingling of apples, prunes, pears, raisins, lemon peel—then sweetened lightly and pureed. Cinnamon, allspice, nutmeg, or cardamom are often added.

Fruit soups are a great way to use fruit that isn't quite showy enough to serve as is. They can be delicate and modestly caloried or downright devastating. Whatever recipe you use, you'll want an accompanying crunch: a crisp wafer or cookie, or a sprinkling of toasted nuts on top. Use full-flavored cooking apples and pears for the following recipe.

Early Autumn Fruit Soup

*1 pound ripe cooking apples
  and/or pears
1 quart water
strips of peel from ¼ lemon
  and ¼ orange
1 tablespoon cornstarch
¼ cup cold water
3 tablespoons light honey
¼ teaspoon ground
  cardamom
½ teaspoon orange zest
2 tablespoons lemon juice
juice from one orange*

Cut apples and pears in chunks. Place in a pan (cores, peel, and all) with quart of water.

Use a potato peeler to take a strip from the orange and lemon peel; use a zester or fine grater to take zest from the rest of the orange, making ½ teaspoon. Juice the orange and lemon and combine the orange zest and juices, setting them aside. Add the strips of orange and lemon peel to the cooking soup and bring to a boil. Lower heat and simmer for 10 minutes, or until the fruit is soft.

Remove strips of rind and put the soup through a food mill or strainer.

Mix the cornstarch with ¼ cup cold water and stir it into the puree. Add honey and cardamom.

Return soup to clean pan, bring to a boil again, then lower heat and simmer for five minutes, stirring frequently. Allow it to cool slightly, then add grated orange rind, lemon and orange juice. Chill and serve with a dollop of yogurt or a thin slice of orange on top.

Makes 5 cups.

Vegetables

Soon after people become vegetarians, they are likely to make a marvelous discovery: vegetables. No longer relegated to the role of second-class citizens, these best of foods can shine out as the fascinating individuals they are: stalwarts like broccoli and butternut squash, arty types like asparagus and artichokes, gnarly characters like rutabaga, and the town zany, kohlrabi.

Quick on the heels of that discovery comes a second: the spiffiest recipes in the world won't compensate for lack of freshness. Then the chase is on for the freshest, most flavorful vegetables you can lay hands on. That chase can take you in some unexpected directions: to the early-morning uproar of a big city produce terminal, armed with the buying power of a cooperative food buying club; to the merry hubbub of a farmer's market; or, best of all, to your own backyard, newly dug and ready to plant exactly the vegetables you want.

The produce section in a typical supermarket has doubled in size over the past ten years. If looks were everything, no one would need to go further; these aisles heaped and banked with bright eggplants and peppers, gleaming onions and ruffled lettuce, are a feast for the eye. Actually, the quality *can* be quite good too. But often it isn't. For one thing, the produce sold to supermarkets is generally bred to travel well cross-country. It is sturdy, often to a fault. If, in addition, it has been grown in one of those countries where winter never comes, it has not only spent a long time on the road but might have residues of pesticides not permitted in this country. Third, a really knowledgeable produce manager is a rare treasure, and without someone who knows a lot about how to do it, produce isn't always stored or handled well, particularly the more fragile things like leafy greens and uncommon varieties of fruits and vegetables. Finally—and this drawback you won't see or taste—much out-of-season produce comes from places in the Third World where giant multinationals grow export crops on land that's needed for staple foods for the local people. The price may seem right, but the hidden costs are high.

The answer to all these problems is to strengthen our food supply system at the local level: to learn to use and enjoy what your region will produce. Support your local farmers by being

faithful customers. Even among supermarkets there are some that try to buy from local farmers. Patronize them, and tell them why you're doing it.

Implicit in the mandate to buy local is a corollary: buy seasonal. Far from being a constraint, the choice to eat foods in season can enhance your life. The first warmth of spring brings fresh asparagus to mind, and then peas and new potatoes. With the chill of autumn you start to hanker after heartier fare—baked winter squash and cabbagey stews. Even if you can't grow your own vegetables, it's satisfying to feel in tune with the growing cycle of the year.

Having said this, though, we'd like to put in a special word for home gardening. The vegetables are incomparably better, you'll save oodles of money, but above all, the work is a joy. If you are a latent gardener who needs encouragement, or if you're deterred because you think you have to have a back yard, or if you're already gardening and just want a host of practical ideas, try some of the inspiring reading listed in the margin.

How to Grow More Vegetables Than You Ever Thought Possible on Less Land Than You Can Imagine, by John Jeavons (Berkeley: Ten Speed Press, 1982)

Designing and Maintaining Your Edible Landscape Naturally, by Robert Kourik (Metamorphosis Press, 1986)

Organic Gardening magazine (write to Rodale Press, Emmaus, PA 18049)

STORAGE

Even the most vitamin-rich, mineral-rich, organically grown, vine-ripened tomato or string bean can be denuded of its nutritional value if not treated properly. Good handling starts with harvesting: when you're picking vegetables, don't let them stand in the sun to wilt; whisk them into the refrigerator right away, or at least into the shade. If you're harvesting them from a supermarket, the principle is the same: even if the price is right, don't buy wilted-looking produce. It's no bargain. If possible, buy only a few days' supply of perishable things like greens and eggplant. If you buy for a week, plan to eat the most perishable things first.

Store potatoes, onions, and uncut winter squashes outside the refrigerator in cool, well-ventilated cupboards or cellars. To keep other vegetables crisp and vitamin-rich, store them in the refrigerator in plastic bags or in a humidifier. Tomatoes that are not overripe may be stored at cool room temperature (not on a hot windowsill) for up to a week. Keep bunches of especially fragile green things like spinach, parsley, and coriander upright in a cottage cheese carton in the refrigerator—line the cartons with a moist cloth beforehand and cover the top with a plastic bag. You'll find other storage suggestions where we talk about each vegetable in turn.

The nutrients that are most likely to be lost in cooking are the water-soluble vitamins: vitamin C and the B vitamins folacin, riboflavin, and pyridoxine. Air (oxygen, to be exact), light, heat, and water are the vitamin thieves, so try to protect vegetables from these four as you work. Wash vegetables as quickly as you can, and avoid soaking them. If you aren't going to cook them immediately, cover them and put them back in the refrigerator.

Peeling vegetables is usually unnecessary and a waste of time and food, as well as nutrients, which usually concentrate just beneath the skin. Try to peel only when the skin is unpalatably tough (most broccoli stems), bitter (oldish turnips), or so rough-skinned that it can't be thoroughly scrubbed (an infrequent twisty carrot). To preserve nutrients, you can cook potatoes and beets first and peel and chop afterwards.

Cutting vegetables in large chunks exposes minimum surface area to the vitamin thieves and preserves flavor and juices as well. On the other hand, smaller pieces cook more quickly; so if they're called for, chop away, especially if you're careful to preserve cooking liquids. Broth from cooking many vegetables —corn, winter squash, zucchini, carrots, string beans, spinach —is delicious and contains significant amounts of the water-soluble vitamins. Save it to use in place of water for cooking grain or making soup or sauce. (Broth from some other vegetables may be vitamin-rich but too strong-tasting to use.)

Some vegetables are so attractive in their native shape that it's nice to steam them and serve them whole: not only artichokes but tiny crookneck and patty pan squashes, carrots, beets, asparagus, and broccoli spears. Tender green beans can be cooked whole or with just the ends snipped off. Serve an assortment of these vegetables with Mock Sour Cream and crackers for an ultra-simple dinner.

We've found that carefully cut vegetables are appealing to the eye and therefore more appetizing. You can cut a carrot in at least eight ways, each one appropriate for a particular dish. Vegetable chopping has never been quite the same for us since we watched a Japanese friend prepare a lavish supper for twenty-five people. As her knife flashed swiftly and rhythmically across the board, her expression was completely concentrated. She didn't say a word. In just half an hour she had filled several big bowls with vegetables, all cut in pretty, perfectly uniform little shapes. In other parts of the world, like India or China, this humble art is taken for granted. You don't need to worry about the swiftness, but the artistry is certainly worth emulating: proof again that even the simplest daily act is worth our full attention.

It might seem that the best way to preserve nutrients in vegetables would be to eat them raw. It's true that vitamin C and folacin are both vulnerable to heat (hence the importance of fresh fruit and green salads). Fortunately, though, it's easy to defend cooked vegetables too. Cooking breaks down a food's cellulose structure and makes other vitamins, as well as minerals, *more* accessible than they would be otherwise. Proper cooking methods can preserve 90 percent of the nutrients your food offers.

The cooking methods we prefer are steaming and the so-called waterless method, where vegetables actually steam in their own juices. In both these methods, steam fills the space in the pan around the vegetables so that oxygen can't rob them of their vitamins. Since the vegetables aren't standing in water, the water-soluble vitamins and minerals stay put.

Pressure cooking is an alternative that offers real advantages to anyone constrained by time. Grains and beans can be ready in half their usual time, and vegetables often in just seconds. An added advantage of pressure cooking is that it conserves some vitamins better than ordinary methods can. The color of cooked vegetables is preserved too. If you are thinking of buying a pressure cooker, try to get one of the newer stainless steel models with a safety gauge that absolutely prevents the kind of messy and even tragic explosions that some of us remember all too well in connection with the old-fashioned models.

One of our favorite kitchen gizmos is the collapsible steamer basket, the kind that opens flowerlike to fit small or large pots. Nothing could be simpler to use. Bring ¾″ of water to boil in a saucepan. Plunk your magic basket into the pan, put the vegetables into the basket, add a close-fitting lid, and reduce the heat so that it is just high enough to keep the water simmering. Vegetables cook quickly this way and require a minimum of fussing.

172   VEGETABLES

For the waterless method, the vital equipment is a pan which conducts heat well and has a close-fitting lid. Most vegetables contain enough water to steam by themselves once they are heated, as long as the heat is coming from all sides. Best of all for most kinds of vegetables is a good iron pot. This does entail the loss of a certain amount of vitamin C, which reacts with iron; but the gain in usable iron is so great—and dietary iron so much more critical for most of us—that it outweighs the partial loss of C. Watch out for acidic foods like tomatoes and walnuts, though; they interact more with iron and may get discolored or begin to taste rusty if you leave them in the pot very long.

To cook by the waterless method, preheat the pot and place two tablespoons of water in it, to provide steam until the vegetables release their own. When the water boils, add the vegetables, stir, and cover. Turn the heat down after a couple of minutes. Cooking time is a little longer than with steaming, and the amount of water that different vegetables need will vary too; so give a stir from time to time, and keep a watchful eye and ear to prevent burning.

One thing to remember when using heavy cooking pots is that they retain heat for a long time. If you have to hold the vegetables for tardy biscuits or a late diner, take the pots off the flame well before the vegetables are cooked through. Left in the pots with the lid on, they will continue to cook gently.

Another waterless method is stir-frying, where the vegetables are placed in a hot pan with a little oil and sautéed before they are covered to steam, with a little added water if needed. Tenderer vegetables, especially spinach and the like, may not even need the steaming period, but can cook directly as you stir.

The one disadvantage of this quick and tasty method is that it is easy to find yourself using a lot of oil. A happy answer is a *wok*, which is especially suited for stir-frying. Its round bottom keeps the oil where the heat is, so your vegetables cook neatly in the smallest possible amount of fat, and the depth and round shape make vigorous stirring easy too. In our experience, the wok is most effective when used on a gas stove with fairly large burners.

It isn't possible to give precise cooking times for vegetables. There are so many variables, not the least of which is that what is "done" is really a matter of taste. Suppose you're cooking green beans. How old are they? Were they picked young and tender, or tough and stringy, or in between? What size pieces were they cut into? How heavy and how big is the pan? What kind of burner are you using? With all this to consider, the cooking time can vary by half in either direction.

Generally, though, we encourage you to push back the timer little by little when cooking vegetables. You may discover that you have been missing a great deal of taste, to say nothing of vitamins, by overcooking. This is particularly true of the brassica family (cabbage, cauliflower, brussels sprouts, broccoli), whose sulfur compounds break down with very long or harsh cooking to release obnoxious flavors and aromas. Aim for tender, or crispy-tender, rather than mushy.

Cooking time for different vegetables will vary. Try 8 minutes or less for sliced asparagus, garden peas, or corn; roughly 10 minutes for ¼" pieces of zucchini, 12 minutes for ¼" pieces of carrot or broccoli stems, and up to 20 minutes for reasonably tender green beans or broccoli spears. Artichokes will take anywhere from 30 to 45 minutes, depending on their size.

When you are steaming *mixed* vegetables, simply cut the ones that require longer cooking times into thinner pieces. If you want similar-sized chunks, add them at intervals, longest-cooking first.

With vegetables, in terms of nutrition and aesthetics too, simple is beautiful, especially if a vegetable is garden-grown. Freshly harvested spinach is so sweet and delectable that it begs to be enjoyed steamed as it is, with only the tiniest hint of flavoring. When we steam vegetables we like to serve them with just a little lemon and parsley, or salt and pepper, or a sprinkle of Parmesan cheese. Broccoli spears, new young chard, or the first harvest of garden zucchini are good eating with no embellishment at all. Growing your own vegetables, of course, is a good way to help your family enjoy them for themselves. Serving them with an eye to their visual appeal helps too.

Serve a wide variety of vegetables. If your local paper runs a greengrocer's column, check it regularly to learn about vegetables new to you, and new ways to prepare the familiar ones. These columns can help you keep abreast of what's available in the stores too, and make suggestions for using seasonal produce. If you are a gardener, you know there are many delicious varieties of vegetables that simply aren't available in the supermarket, though many do find their way to farmer's markets.

Now we'd like to sing out the glories of our favorite friends from the vegetable patch one by one, and tell some of the ways they can be enjoyed. We've tried to stick to ingredients that are easily available and not expensive. Radicchio and enoki mushrooms may well add a lot to a salad, but you won't find them in our recipes. "To make something out of something is nothing," a friend who lived at Findhorn used to say. "To make something out of nothing—*that's* something!" Succulent "somethings" are possible every day from ordinary, inexpensive seasonal produce, when you stir them up with imagination.

Mingled here and there among the recipes and serving ideas that follow, you will find some intentionally rough suggestions. Don't be frustrated by their vagueness. When amounts are unspecified, it's because you have a lot of latitude and know better than we do how much squash you can eat at a sitting. We include these suggestions to convey our own approach to vegetables, which has almost nothing to do with recipes. Once you acquire a feel for characteristics and cooking times—and that doesn't take long—your imagination can take over. Then you won't be bound to recipes at all; they'll just be useful for inspiration, or as points of departure.

Artichokes

Artichokes are California's own. The highway south from Berkeley to Big Sur takes you through Castroville, with its funky banner telling you that you've finally made it to the Artichoke Capital of the World. Well might they brag. They're on to a good thing.

Trimming isn't necessary, but it reduces the mess at the table and prevents you and the eaters from getting stuck by those nasty little thorns. Use a sharp knife to cut off the top, with most of the thorns; use the knife or scissors to remove thorns from the remaining leaves. While you're at it, you might as well take off the tiny outside leaves—the great eating begins where the leaves are large—and trim the stem near the base too.

Steam artichokes (trimmed or not) upside-down in a steamer basket, or in a saucepan with an inch or so of boiling water. Depending on the size of the artichoke, it may take half an hour to a whole hour to steam. That's a long time, so check the pot now and again to be sure the water level is up. If you aren't going to be serving them whole, chokes will cook in half the time if they're cut in half. They are done when the outer leaves come off effortlessly or when a fork slides easily into the heart. Serve them hot or chilled. (To keep chilled artichokes or their cut parts from darkening, douse exposed places with lemon juice.)

Artichoke leaves dipped in mayonnaise or drawn butter are marvelous, but so are artichoke leaves dipped in absolutely nothing, or in one of the many delicious low-fat sauces in the next section. If artichokes become a regular item in your diet, this could be a critical discovery!

Although extracting the edible parts from an artichoke may seem a tedious task for a cook, it's really not bad, and the flavor is so rich that one or two artichokes can make good eating for up to four people. The following dishes are well worth the effort.

Artichokes Tellicherry

2 large artichokes, steamed
2 medium potatoes, steamed

3 shallots or 1 small onion
(1 clove garlic)
1 tablespoon butter

(½ teaspoon ground cumin
or fennel seed)

(½ cup tiny peas)
(1 big, fresh, ripe tomato,
chopped)
salt and plenty of pepper

Tellicherry in South India is famous for black pepper. Artichokes have probably never been seen there, but toasted cumin and fennel seeds often scent a vegetable dish. We use this combination in many ways to take full advantage of the long artichoke season. Some of the possibilities are outlined below. The ingredients in parentheses are optional, but they add a lot.

Prepare cooked artichokes by removing the outer leaves and scraping them with a spoon to get the tender meat. The middle leaves will come off together and the tender portion can be cut off and chopped. Discard the leaves. Pull or spoon out the thistly top from the center of each choke and discard. Trim away the stringy stem and dice the heart, putting it with the other good gleanings from the artichoke parts. All together, this should measure about a cup.

Peel and dice the steamed potatoes. They should measure about a cup or a little more.

Sauté the shallot or onion (and garlic) in butter in a sizable skillet, cooking until soft. Add the cumin or fennel if desired and heat and stir until fragrant. Lightly stir in the remaining ingredients, and heat through.

This is a very flexible recipe, as you can see, and the quantities are changeable. Plain—without the optional additions—it makes 2 cups or stuffs 4 medium tomatoes, which will serve two people generously or four as a tidbit. With the peas and whatnot, you'll have more.

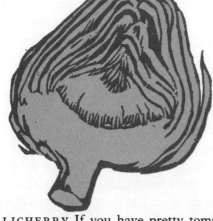

VARIATIONS

TOMATOES TELLICHERRY If you have pretty tomatoes, instead of chopping one, hollow out one for each person and use the artichoke mixture to stuff them. Cut the top off the tomatoes and scoop out the insides with a spoon, leaving at least ¼" of tomato on the skin. Fill with hot artichoke mixture and top with buttered bread crumbs; heat in moderate oven about 15 minutes.

ARTICHOKE PATTIES With the optional ingredients (but without the tomato), the mixture can be formed into patties. Adding a beaten egg helps hold them together but isn't really necessary. Press both sides of each patty into a dish of whole grain bread crumbs and cook them on a lightly buttered griddle or in the oven, turning once.

STUFFED ARTICHOKE HEARTS Instead of chopping the heart, trim it and scoop it out carefully; then dip in lemon juice to keep it from darkening. Mix the rest of the ingredients (no tomatoes) to make the filling. Pile it into the heart and decorate the top with sliced olives, tiny pearl onions, pine nuts, or sliced cherry tomatoes. Small artichokes work well for this version, but if yours are large you can quarter the choke after you stuff it. Good hot or cold.

Asparagus

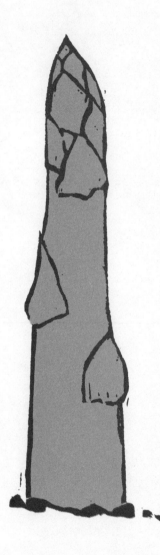

Asparagus ranks right alongside the hyacinth as a sure, spriggy herald of spring. Its season is so brief (at least, its affordable season!) that we never have time to tire of its delicate appeal.

Have you considered growing asparagus? Even a narrow strip against a wall at the back of a flower bed is a good place, because by midsummer, asparagus makes tall, feathery ferns that provide a beautiful backdrop for decorative plantings. Needless to say, homegrown asparagus is wonderfully special. You can pick it when the shoots are less than six inches long and closed up tight, so sweet that cooking seems superfluous.

Whether you grow your own or find it in the supermarket, the fattest spears will be the most succulent. Look for heads that are tightly closed, firm, and fresh-looking; the bottoms shouldn't be dried up or moldy. Break the stalks just above the white part at the place where they choose to snap. Save the bottom for making stock, or if there is a sizeable green portion, peel it and cook it along with the tops. Use your steamer basket or a skillet with a tight lid (and a minimum of water!) to steam the asparagus; or try the old-fashioned trick of standing the spears straight up in a coffeepot with an inch of water in the bottom. Never overcook asparagus.

Serve fresh spears with Lemon Butter (or just lemon) or a sprinkle of Parmesan cheese. If you want the piquancy of hollandaise with less fat, try Sunshine Sauce or Dijon Sauce, or Mock Sour Cream. Sliced toasted almonds make a pretty and harmonious garnish.

For ASPARAGUS PATTIES, slice an onion very thin, and sauté with a couple of cloves of garlic. Crush the garlic gloves with a fork. Add a cup each of lightly steamed, thin-sliced asparagus and steamed, grated potato. Grated cheese is optional; salt and pepper to taste. A beaten egg helps hold the mixture together but isn't necessary. Cook on bread crumbs on a buttered griddle, turning once onto more crumbs. An easy way to form the patties is to put a tablespoon of crumbs into a ⅓–cup measure and press the mixture into that, turning it out onto crumbs on the griddle.

Chinese Asparagus

A classic dish that fits in anywhere. Use tiny snow peas or sliced sugar snap peas instead of asparagus later in the season.

Have you ever tasted *fresh* water chestnuts? They are as much better than the canned ones as fresh asparagus is better than canned. Chinese groceries often have them even if others don't, and they are worth looking for. Choose firm nuts that haven't shriveled at all. Peel and rinse, then use as you would the canned ones, allowing a couple of extras for the cook to nibble raw.

ଛ

Combine the shoyu, honey, cornstarch, and water and set aside.

Trim the asparagus and cut diagonally into 1″ slices. Have the remaining ingredients ready. Heat a wok or big heavy skillet; when hot, add the oil and then the leek. Cook just a minute, then add ginger and garlic, stirring for only a few seconds. Add water chestnuts and asparagus, stir once more, and add the broth. Reduce heat, cover, and simmer gently only until the asparagus is tender.

Stir the sauce to dissolve the cornstarch completely. (If you have Chinese sesame oil, add that to the sauce.) Turn the heat to high, uncover vegetables, and pour the sauce over them. Bring to a boil, stirring constantly about a minute or until the sauce is thick. Serve at once, sprinkled with sesame seeds if you like.

Serves 4.

1 tablespoon shoyu
½ teaspoon honey
2 teaspoons cornstarch
1 tablespoon water

1 pound asparagus
2 teaspoons oil
1 medium leek, sliced thin
1 tablespoon ginger, minced
2 cloves garlic, minced
8 water chestnuts
½ cup flavorful broth

2 teaspoons toasted
sesame seeds or
Chinese sesame oil

Green Beans

Green beans are one of the most versatile and delicious of vegetables. They are incomparably good when freshly picked, and their growing habits are varied enough that you can have them early and late, tall and short, green or yellow, in whatever clime and soil and space is available.

But store-bought beans are plenty good too. Look for the young and crisp. The tender, tasty Blue Lake variety that used to be available only to home gardeners now appears in produce sections from time to time. And don't think of them as "string beans"—the stringiness was bred out years ago, thank goodness.

Green Beans Hellenika

1 pound green beans,
   cut bite-size
   (about 4 cups)
1 small onion, chopped
3 tomatoes, chopped
½ bunch parsley, chopped
1 tablespoon olive oil
½ teaspoon salt
dash pepper
about 1 cup water or stock

Cook all ingredients together at least 20 minutes, until the beans are tender, using just enough water to prevent sticking. Stir from time to time.

   Makes 3 cups, to serve 4 to 6 people.

Green Bean Stroganoff

Take yogurt (and buttermilk, if used) out of refrigerator to warm to room temperature. Wash green beans and cut into bite-sized pieces. Steam until tender.

While the beans cook, chop the onion and sauté in oil or butter. Slice mushrooms in thick pieces and add them to the onion. Cook and stir until tender.

Cube eggplant and add to mushrooms. Cover and steam until tender, stirring as necessary to prevent sticking. Add green beans and season with salt and pepper.

Beat yogurt (or yogurt and buttermilk) smooth. Stir cornstarch into the beaten yogurt and bring it to a boil, stirring vigorously; it will separate and then smooth out again. Add to the bean mixture.

Serves 4 to 6 over rice, noodles, or kasha.

CABBAGE STROGANOFF Use a whole large onion and substitute 2 cups packed shredded cabbage for the beans and eggplant.

2 cups yogurt, or yogurt and buttermilk

1 pound green beans

½ large onion
2 tablespoons oil or butter
½ pound mushrooms

2 small or ½ large eggplant (½–¾ pound)
1 teaspoon salt
pinch pepper

2 teaspoons cornstarch

Spicy Green Beans

Bring water, garlic, onion, bay leaf, tomato, and green beans to boil. Cover pan and simmer over low heat for about 20 minutes, or until the beans are tender. Remove garlic and cloves and stir in vinegar, salt, and cinnamon. Cook, uncovered, for 2 to 3 minutes.

Serves 4 to 6.

½ cup water
1 clove garlic, studded with 3 whole cloves
½ onion, chopped
bay leaf
1 small tomato, peeled and diced
1 pound green beans, cut in 1" pieces

2 teaspoons cider vinegar
½ teaspoon salt
¼ teaspoon cinnamon

Beets

Charmed by the rich red of its root, most people give short shrift to the beet's greatest asset: its leaves, where an abundant store of vitamins and minerals is tucked away. Cook the greens like chard: they are tart and lovely.

Beet leaves, incidentally, share their red color liberally with whatever is cooked along with them—a quirk that can take you off guard in mixed vegetables, but one you can turn to your advantage in a tomato-based soup. (For that matter, beet greens or a little grated beet root will correct the color of any tomato sauce that's turned out too orangish. Don't add so much that it goes purple, though!)

If you are a gardener, do you know about golden beets? They are sweet and as pretty as the red ones without that uncontrollable red juice. Especially good for salads.

If you steam mature beets until they're tender, the skins slip off in the most cooperative way you could imagine. Slice them and serve hot with a dollop of Mock Sour Cream or a sauce of a little warmed honey and orange juice. Chilled and marinated, they are good cut up in green salad or simply served as is.

The following recipe is meant to use beet thinnings from the garden. We like it so much that we now pluck many more of our baby beets than we would normally, and just keep planting new ones. Mature beets too can be cut up and cooked in the same way.

Whole Beets

*12 to 15 tiny beets,
    tops and all
2 tablespoons oil
juice of 1 lemon
1 green onion, chopped
½ teaspoon dill weed
½ teaspoon tarragon
½ teaspoon salt
(a squeeze of garlic)*

Wash beets well and remove inedible parts, leaving them whole and keeping the skin and leaves.

Heat oil, lemon juice, onion, and seasonings in a heavy pan with a tight-fitting lid. Add beets and steam over medium heat. Check after 5 minutes, and add a small amount of water to prevent burning if necessary. Cook until tender.

Serves 4 to 6.

Broccoli

We don't usually think of green vegetables as a source of protein, but 1 cup of steamed broccoli provides 5 grams, not to mention that it also has 140 milligrams each of calcium and vitamin C! We serve plain spears, or bite-sized chunks with a little lemon, very often. Here's a vegetable that is universally loved in its simplest manifestation—a special boon for balancing dinners with some other dish that's a little rich.

Fresh broccoli is one vegetable that almost always needs some peeling. The outer skin of the stalk can be quite fibrous and tough, and if you cook broccoli long enough to cook the skin tender, you risk overcooking the other parts, losing more vitamin C in the process than you've saved by keeping the skin. On the other hand, do save the leaves; they are a mine of vitamins and minerals. Cook them along with stems and tops; or, if they look untidy to you, snip them off and save them to add to a soup or casserole the next day.

If you peel the stem and cut it into ¼" slices, it will cook right along with the flowers in the same amount of time. Serve broccoli cut up or in spears with salt and fresh-ground black pepper; with lemon, Lemon Butter, Sunshine Sauce, or Potato Dill Sauce; with a sprinkling of Sesame Salt, or with any cheese or cheese sauce. But don't be surprised if you find yourself coming back to the simplest and very best: fresh, bright green, crispy-tender spears with no ornament but their own reputation.

King Cole Curry

1 bunch broccoli, cut into
   flowers and sliced stems
½ head cauliflower, cut
   into florets
1 medium potato, sliced
   small

SAUCE

½ onion, chopped
1 tablespoon oil
2 tablespoons whole
   wheat flour
¾ teaspoon curry powder
1½ cups water
¾ pound tofu, rinsed
   and mashed
2–4 tablespoons lemon juice
1 tablespoon shoyu
¾ teaspoon salt

TOPPING

½ cup bread crumbs
pinch salt, pepper, paprika

This colorful vegetable curry looks and tastes as creamy and rich as it could be, but it has no dairy products at all; its creaminess comes from tofu. Serve it with bulgur wheat or whole wheat noodles, marinated beets on a bed of romaine, and a fresh fruit salad.

Steam broccoli, cauliflower, and potatoes.

Sauté onion in oil. Add flour and curry powder and stir two minutes over medium heat. Stir in 1 cup of the water and cook until thickened.

Preheat oven to 350°F.

Blend or mash tofu with lemon juice, shoyu, and remaining ½ cup water until smooth. Stir into onion mixture. Add more salt or lemon juice to taste.

In a 2½-quart casserole dish, spread half the vegetables. Top with half the sauce and repeat. Mix topping ingredients and sprinkle over casserole. Bake covered for 10 to 15 minutes, uncovered for 10 minutes more or until the sauce is bubbly.

Serves 4 to 6.

Brussels Sprouts

These days the visual glories of fresh vegetables are well established; whole calendars are given over to translucent cross-sections of cucumbers and interior shots of bell peppers. But when vegetable art was in its first blush, one photographer with a sense of whimsy circulated a striking picture of a cabbage perched atop a grater box while tiny brussels sprouts tumbled out from underneath. Mini-cabbages they may be, but aristocrats for all that, and delectable.

Arresting, too, is the brussels sprout *plant*: a mighty three or four-foot stalk stuck all over with round knobs peeking out from where the long leaf connects. You pick from the bottom up as they ripen, and one plant can supply a whole family. You end up with an elegant miniature palm tree, complete with little green "coconuts." (There are reasons why gardeners are a little daffy about the whole affair.)

Sweet, tender young brussels sprouts can be cooked intact, but if the core seems hefty, you will want to trim it off. Score any but the tiniest brussels sprouts by cutting an × in the bottom ¼″ deep, to ensure a quicker, evener cooking time. The outermost leaves should go if they are yellowish or spotty.

Steamed whole, or simmered gently in milk, brussels sprouts are delectable, and when they're first in season it never occurs to us to eat them any other way. After the initial thrill subsides, we start dressing them up: a light sprinkling of grated hard cheese, or Cream Sauce or Potato Dill Sauce (with nutmeg or thyme replacing the dill) to complement their very special flavor.

One of our favorite fancy winter dishes is BRUSSELS SPROUTS WITH CHESTNUTS. Roast and peel chestnuts and cut them into chunks; then stir them into steamed sprouts with the tiniest bit of Better-Butter. The mild, nutty flavor and somewhat mealy texture of the chestnuts complements the sprouts beautifully. Try the following recipes too; the first one has a real holiday air.

Brussels Sprout–Squash Casserole

1 pound brussels sprouts
1½ cups winter squash,
    peeled and cubed
1 medium onion, minced
1 cup chopped celery
1 tablespoon butter
2 tablespoons oil
¼ cup whole wheat flour
2 cups milk
½ teaspoon salt
½ teaspoon marjoram
dash pepper
dash nutmeg

Clean, trim, and score brussels sprouts; cut large ones in half. Steam sprouts and squash separately until barely tender. Set aside.

Preheat oven to 350°F.

While squash and sprouts cook, chop onion and celery. Sauté onion in butter and oil. Add flour and cook slowly for about 3 minutes, stirring continually. Add milk and spices slowly, stirring to keep mixture smooth. Bring to a boil and remove from heat. Correct seasonings.

In a greased 8″ × 8″ baking dish, arrange cubed squash on bottom and spread over it an even layer of brussels sprouts. Sprinkle chopped celery over the top. Pour the sauce over the vegetables and sprinkle with nutmeg.

Bake for 30 minutes. Serves 4 to 6.

Brussels Sprouts & Bell Peppers

1 pound brussels sprouts
2 small red bell peppers
½ small onion, chopped
2 teaspoons oil
1 bay leaf
¼ cup vegetable stock
    or water or milk
1 small potato, cubed
salt to taste

The bright sweetness of red bell peppers complements the nippy taste of brussels sprouts perfectly.

෪

Clean, trim, and score brussels sprouts. Cut large ones in half. Cut peppers into ½″ pieces.

Sauté onion in oil with bay leaf until onion is soft; add pepper pieces and stir for a few seconds. Add the brussels sprouts and stir again.

Add ¼ cup of stock and simmer, covered, until just tender. (Probably about 7 minutes, but keep checking.)

Steam or boil potato cubes separately and puree, using some of the juice from the vegetables if needed. Stir together with sprouts and peppers. Season with salt.

Serves 4 to 6.

Cabbage

Because cabbage can endure a certain amount of winter storage, most people think of it as strong-flavored, and often it is served in a sweet or sweet-and-sour sauce or dressing that makes it even more assertive. But try another tack. Steamed and cooked in milk, especially when freshly picked, cabbage can be as sweet and pleasing as you'd ever want a vegetable to be, and as digestible as well. Always cook it gently, not too hot and not too long. Simmered in milk, then tossed with a dab of butter, salt and pepper, and maybe a handful of chopped parsley, cabbage gets surprised requests for seconds even from devout cabbage-loathers.

Chinese Cabbage

Chinese cabbage has pale, curly leaves and is taller and far more elegant than its plump occidental cousins. With its lighter, subtler flavor it is delicious raw, and it makes a truly fluffy slaw. Or try it Chinese style, sliced thin and stir-fried in a little oil, a dribble of shoyu, and sesame salt or Chinese parsley for garnish. Very good added to mixed Chinese vegetables, too.

Bubble & Squeak

Traditionally, Bubble and Squeak is a thick "pancake" of mashed potato and cooked cabbage, fried in lots of fat. The fat bubbles, the cabbage squeaks. Listen closely, and you might hear the cabbage squeak as you stir-fry this much lighter contemporary variation. The flavors combine splendidly.

&

Cut the cabbage in strips. Quarter leeks and slice in ½" pieces. Cut potato in ½" pieces.

If you have a wok, use it to cook this dish; otherwise a heavy skillet or dutch oven is good (not iron, though, if possible). Stir-fry the cabbage and leeks over medium-high heat for 3 or 4 minutes. Add garlic. Cover and reduce heat to low until cabbage is crispy-tender, about 5 minutes. Add the potato and stir another minute or so until warmed through.

Sprinkle with shoyu and vinegar and serve immediately.

Makes about 4 servings (5 cups).

1 medium head curly-leafed cabbage (about 7–8 cups)
3 medium leeks
1 tablespoon oil
1 or 2 cloves garlic
1 large potato, quartered, steamed, and peeled
2 tablespoons shoyu
1 tablespoon cider vinegar

Carrots

Carrots are one of those staples we always have on hand for soups and mixed vegetables, but which we don't have real recipes for. That's probably because we more often use winter squash, which grow more easily in our gardens, to provide that spot of sweetness or color in winter menus. Carrots often substitute very nicely for winter squash—they have a smoother, less sweet presence. The lacy green tops, by the way, are great for soup stock.

Orange or lemon juice gives a boost to carrots that aren't garden fresh: add a tablespoonful or so for 2 cups of carrots while you're cutting or grating. It enlivens their flavor considerably and keeps them from turning brown if they have to wait a while before cooking or serving.

Most people are fond of carrots. Try them in some of these ways, which we like very much:

&- Cut in thin sticks and cook by the waterless method. Just before serving, stir together with a small dab of butter and a handful of chopped parsley.

&- Glaze just-cooked carrots lightly by stirring in a tablespoon or two of honey; remove from pan and add a handful of chopped, lightly toasted walnuts.

&- Glaze with orange juice, honey, and a small spoonful of minced fresh ginger, or with applesauce and lemon.

&- Grate carrots and cook, seasoning with tarragon, nutmeg, dill weed, or chervil.

&- Sauté chopped onion in oil, stir in cut carrots, cover, and cook on low until tender.

Crumby Carrots

A surprisingly delicious dish, much more so than you would think from the simplicity of the ingredients. If you want to make more than one recipe, plan to do it in batches, because the breaded carrots can't cook properly if they are deeper than one layer in the skillet.

3 medium carrots
(about 2 cups cut)
1 clove garlic, minced
¼ teaspoon cumin powder
2 teaspoons butter

Cut carrots in ½″ sticks and steam until crispy-tender. Meantime, mince garlic and add with cumin to butter in a large skillet. Heat briefly and gently to cook the spices, being careful not to brown the garlic. Stir in the bread crumbs and set aside.

⅔ cup whole wheat
bread crumbs

Use two shallow bowls, one to mix the flour and salt, the other for the egg and milk. Line the bowls up, with the skillet making number three, and dip the carrot sticks a few at a time, first in the flour and salt mixture, then in the egg and milk; then roll them in the bread crumbs. Try to get each one completely covered. When you are finished, put all the carrots in the pan and cook over low heat, turning occasionally with a spatula. When all sides are crisp, they are ready to serve.

¼ cup whole wheat flour
pinch salt

1 beaten egg
2 tablespoons milk

Serve the carrots at once in a warmed dish, with the yogurt as sauce.

⅓ cup plain yogurt, beaten
smooth

Cauliflower

Snowy white it is, but don't be fooled: cauliflower is a good choice nutritionally. It's a versatile addition to mixed vegetables because of its color, mild flavor, and pretty shape, but it's also good on its own with parsley or basil, a little sesame salt, chopped toasted cashews or almonds, seasoned bread crumbs, or a grating of hard cheese.

For an impressive entrée, steam a head of cauliflower whole and serve it surrounded by green vegetables on a platter, topped with a generous grating of sharp cheddar cheese.

Cauliflower is tasty raw too, or lightly cooked to serve on relish trays or in salad.

Greek Cauliflower

1 head cauliflower
juice of ½ lemon
(about 1 tablespoon)
1–2 teaspoons olive oil
¼ teaspoon salt (scant)
2 tablespoons chopped
parsley

Our favorite way of serving cauliflower.

Wash, trim, and cut cauliflower into bite-sized florets. (From a smallish head you will get about 4 cups.) Steam gently until tender. Sprinkle with lemon juice, olive oil, salt, and parsley. Toss gently and then adjust the flavorings to taste. Heat gently, just to soften the parsley, and serve at once.

Serves 4.

Celery

We keep celery on hand for soups, Chinese-style vegetables, casseroles, sandwich spreads, and stuffings for this or that. With its assertive flavor and negligible nutritional contribution, it is really more of a seasoning than a vegetable. For crunchiness, though, nothing is so handy. And when the larder is nearly bare, or the winter seems very long, sometimes a light, creamy celery soup can provide just the break you need from strong greens and sweet squashes.

Swiss Chard

Gardeners all know chard because it grows undaunted from spring through the first hard frosts, letting its outer leaves be taken while the plant continues on. For sheer beauty, there may be nothing quite like a big tender ruby chard leaf against the morning sun, with the light shining through its red stem and showing up the deep curly forest-green of the leaf. Not all chard is red-veined, of course, and most of what you buy in the market has white stems. It may be less gorgeous, but it can be a lot more useful in vegetable combinations or soups where the red color isn't wanted. Chard doesn't have quite the delicacy of spinach, but it is so much easier to grow that we find ourselves using its leaves virtually everywhere we would use spinach.

When the leaves are very young, the stems can be chopped and cooked along with them. But as they get more mature, the stems become thicker and need extra cooking time; trim them off the leaf, chop them, and give them a head start in the pan or steamer basket. Chard stems are similar enough to celery that they can substitute for it in many cooked dishes. Like spinach, chard contains oxalic acid and will discolor if cooked in an iron pot.

For a simple and very tasty chard dish, sauté chopped onion and stir in chard, cut bite-size, and a handful of raisins. Cook until chard is tender; then toss in a handful of toasted sunflower seeds.

Or sauté onion and garlic and add a tablespoonful of minced fresh ginger; add chopped chard, and when it is tender, add a tablespoon of shoyu and a cup of chopped tomato. This dish is good with steamed diced potato, or over rice.

Nearly any sauce is good on chard, particularly those with a milk or cheese base. For a real treat, try Stuffed Chard Leaves—they don't take as much time as you'd think—or Chard Pita.

Chard can sub in any kale or spinach recipe too—and don't overlook the chard variation of Hijiki Stir-Fry.

Chard Cheese Pie

6 cups lightly cooked chard,
   well drained
2 cups low-fat cottage cheese
2 eggs, beaten
juice of 1 lemon
½ teaspoon salt
½ cup whole-grain
   bread crumbs
paprika

We developed this fine recipe when the garden produced its first enormous chard crop, and we've cooked it regularly ever since, throughout the long chard season. If you are enjoying a bumper crop, you can make Chard Cheese Pie with leaves only, but it is good with some stems included too. Either way you will need a scant 6 cups of cooked, well-drained chard.

ૐ

Preheat oven to 350°F.

Beat together the cottage cheese, eggs, lemon, and salt. Stir a cup of this mixture into the chard and press it down in a well-greased 8″ × 8″ pan. Spread the remaining cottage cheese mixture evenly over the top and sprinkle on the bread crumbs and paprika.

Bake for about half an hour, or until set. Allow to stand for several minutes before cutting into squares.

Serves 4 to 6.

VARIATIONS

Chill and serve with red-ripe garden tomatoes and a sprinkling of crumbled blue cheese.

Add ¾ cup grated Swiss cheese to the chard mixture. Omit lemon.

To make more from less, add a cup of buttermilk and another egg.

Substitute spinach or kale for the chard.

Add a chopped, sautéed onion.

Corn

Remember all that stuff about how the only way to eat corn is to pick it at five minutes to six, *run* from the garden, shucking all the way, drop it into a pot of boiling water, snatch it out again, and skid into the dining room by six sharp? Remember? Well, it was all true until a couple of years ago when science broke through corn's tendency to convert sugar to starch as soon as it was picked, and managed to produce a whole new breed of corn—now available to gardeners, and probably very soon in stores. Its sugar stays unstarched for hours and days after picking. Meantime, even with the old-fashioned kind, the arrival of the first corn is one of the great events each summer.

For the first week or two, no one thinks of eating corn any way but straight off the cob. But when the enthusiasm begins to flag, try gilding the lily in any of the following ways. Remove the kernels from the cob with a sharp knife, being careful not to cut down deeply into the cob. Then, using the back of the knife, scrape the cob to force the nutritious germ of the grain out into your bowl.

&. Chop an onion, a bell pepper, and a tomato. Sauté the pepper and onion in oil until soft, then stir in fresh corn and tomato. Cover and cook briefly. Add salt and pepper to taste.

&. For a summer garden treat, sauté sliced green onions; add snow peas and then fresh corn. Cover and cook till tender— just the twinkling of an eye.

&. Cook cabbage in milk, add fresh corn and parsley.

&. For a corny liquid to flavor pancakes or sauces—or to make the base of a delicious soup with red and green peppers—sauté a big white onion, adding a spoonful of chili powder once the onion is soft. Stir in 2 cups corn kernels and add water to cover. Simmer until tender; then puree. (To get a smooth liquid, strain through a sieve or put it through your food mill.)

Eggplant

These jewel-toned fruits are a traditional and delicious substitute for meat. They are so spongelike that they absorb whatever oil or juices are nearby while they're cooking, so eggplant dishes can be heavily greasy. We have designed our recipes to take a minimum of oil, usually by steaming or baking the eggplant rather than frying it.

It isn't hard to adapt old favorite recipes that call for frying. Use the guidelines in the recipes that follow, or try the simple technique of cutting the eggplant in half and baking it face down on a greased baking pan at 350°F until it's tender—about half an hour for a medium eggplant. At that time it can be cooled and chopped or sliced or scooped out for stuffing. Eggplants cooked this way have marvelous flavor without any fat at all. An added advantage is that if the eggplant is a little over-mature, the bitter seeds separate out easily after baking and you can discard them. A medium eggplant will give about a cup of well-cooked pulp. (The peel will be tough and you'll probably want to discard it).

You will see the most amazing tips about choosing eggplants, but it isn't all that hard. The skin should be firm and glossy, and if you press the eggplant, it should give and then bounce back. If it doesn't give, it's immature (only gardeners are likely to encounter that); if it doesn't bounce back, it's over the hill. Unfortunately, this is not unusual in market eggplants, since they don't keep very well.

Some cooks like to slice and salt eggplant, letting it drain for an hour, before cooking. This removes some of the liquid, which makes frying easier, but that's not necessary when you are using other cooking techniques. Salting also removes some bitterness when you have to use an eggplant that is older than you would like.

Eggplant Parmesan

This is a truly delicious Eggplant Parmesan, and easily the lowest in calories. To make an even lighter dish, you can use 3 egg whites instead of the 2 whole eggs, or omit the mozzarella—or both.

If you use cracker crumbs, adjust the salt to compensate for the saltiness of the crackers. This recipe is written for the moderate saltiness of bread, and normally crackers are much saltier.

ᐌ

Prepare three bowls for dipping the eggplant:

[1] ½ cup whole wheat flour
     ½ teaspoon salt

[2] 2 eggs, slightly beaten
     ¼ cup milk

[3] 2½ cups crumbs
     ½ teaspoon salt
     pepper and oregano

Preheat oven to 350°F.

Cut eggplant into ¼″ rounds and dip slices in each mixture in turn, coating them completely.

Layer slices in a greased 9″ × 13″ glass baking pan. Slices may overlap but should not cover each other completely. Sprinkle each layer with tomato sauce and Parmesan cheese. Cover tightly and bake for 30 to 45 minutes, or until a fork pierces middle slices easily. Remove from oven, top with mozzarella, and return dish to oven until the cheese melts and bubbles.

Serves 6.

½ cup whole wheat flour
1 teaspoon salt, divided

2 eggs
¼ cup milk

2½ cups whole wheat
  bread crumbs
  or cracker crumbs
¼ teaspoon oregano
dash pepper

1 medium-sized eggplant
2 cups Tomato Sauce
½ cup Parmesan cheese

1 cup grated mozzarella
  cheese

Florence Fennel

"Common" fennel is an herb: you use just the seeds and young leaves. Cousin Florence (also called finocchio) is actually a vegetable, one that looks like a cross between a teardrop and a head of celery, with fancifully feathery headdress. This is one of the peasant-hearty vegetables which gourmets claim but won't be able to keep from ordinary folks like us because it's so easy to grow. In Italy, where fennel is a great favorite, it is enjoyed raw like celery or cooked in tomato dishes where its mildly aniselike flavor can add a lot. It's often served raw for dessert with creamy cheeses, too; its sweet crunchiness clears the palate.

Fennel is available throughout the fall and into the winter, but quality deteriorates after December. Serve it as you would celery in salads, on platters of "finger food," or in tomato soup or sauce. Very lightly cooked, its unusual flavor can add a graceful dimension to simple stir-fried vegetables or rice or lentil pilaf. Cooked longer, the flavor becomes pretty strong.

Kale

Trying to talk about kale is a little like describing a very dear friend: there are so many nice things to tell, and yet all of them together don't really add up to what is so endearing. Kale is delicious and spectacularly nutritious, especially because it has little oxalic acid to prevent absorption of its rich supply of minerals. Besides that, it is *pretty*: its lacy, ruffled leaves, the subtlest grayed-down green, are beautiful enough to make a border for a flower bed, if you are into edible landscaping. Northerners, Scottish or not, have a special fondness for kale because it grows bravely all winter, surviving even snow and frost to provide its goodness when nothing else is fresh. (In fact, the Scottish word for kitchen garden is "kailyard.") Its nippy flavor makes a perfect foil for the sweetness of starchy winter vegetables like potatoes and winter squash.

Like most vegetables, kale is exceedingly good straight from the garden. (As with other greens and leaf lettuce, you can pick the outer leaves and let the plant keep growing.) But if you're at the grocery store and the kale looks a little tough and gray, don't be deterred. Unless the leaves are actually yellowish, it will cook tender and reward you with a bright green, ruffly vegetable dish that is simply unbeatable.

Before some of our favorite serving suggestions, a few general words on preparation. Wash the leaves by submerging them in a sink full of water, swishing them around to remove dirt and any incidental aphids. Bugs are a problem only in late summer; one drop of detergent in the water usually sends them to the bottom of the sink. Rinse very well. (This method works well with any kind of buggy vegetables.) Strip and discard the stems; they are tough and stringy. You can cook very young, tender kale by the water-less method or stir-fry it, but steaming is better for kale slightly older than baby-size because of its strong flavor. Kale cooks down as all greens do—though less than most—and keeps its ruffly texture. A one-pound bunch will serve two kale fanatics, or a family of four in a dish that includes potatoes or other mitigations.

Since kale is so rich in flavor and nutrients, we frequently combine it with other vegetables, especially the sweet ones: for example, with potatoes and Tangy Cheese Sauce; with potatoes, tomatoes, ginger and soy sauce; with winter squash or yams, and a handful of raisins; chopped fine and floated in Squash Soup or Potato Cheese Soup; sauced with Potato Dill Sauce, Stroganoff Sauce, Sunshine Sauce. . . .

If you have both kale and spinach, for example, cooking both and serving them mixed together makes a third dish with quite a different flavor—and the virtues of both.

MIXING GREENS

Colcannon

Quarter potatoes and put them on to steam; put kale also on to steam separately. Meantime, chop leeks or onion and sauté in butter, stirring frequently to prevent sticking. If they start to stick, add a little water and cook them until soft.

When potatoes are tender, peel and mash them. When kale is tender, drain it very well. Combine potatoes, kale, leeks, milk, parsley, salt, and pepper. If you need to reheat, you can do it by stirring in the skillet you used for the onions, or by the traditional method of making a mound of colcannon on a platter and baking it in the oven with a dollop of butter on top. Since the dish is plenty good without the extra fat, we use the nontraditional method.

4 medium potatoes
3–12 cups chopped kale
3 leeks or 1 large onion
1 tablespoon butter

⅓ cup milk
¼ cup chopped parsley
¾ teaspoon salt, to taste
black pepper to taste

Tomato Kale

1½ bunches kale
  (1–2 pounds)

1 small onion
(1 clove garlic)
1 tablespoon olive oil
1 teaspoon cumin seeds
  or ground cumin
½ cup tomato paste
1 cup tomatoes, chopped

½ cup peas

salt if needed

Wash kale, strip off stems, and chop. You should have 12 cups, more or less. Steam until tender and drain.

Meantime, sauté onion (and garlic, if desired) in oil, adding cumin when onion is soft. Continue to cook a moment more until the cumin is fragrant. Add the tomato paste and tomatoes, and stir to heat through. Add peas, cooking until tender, then add kale. If you have used canned tomatoes or frozen peas, you may not need to add more salt; check, and adjust salt to taste.

Makes about 4 cups.

VARIATION: Instead of peas, add a cup of cubed steamed potato or winter squash.

Crumby Greens

1 leek or a medium onion,
  chopped
1 tablespoon oil
½" slice of fresh ginger,
  minced fine
1½ cups cooked chard
  or kale
  or other greens, very
  well drained
1 cup lightly toasted
  crumbs
salt and pepper to taste

A delicious way to use garden greens, whether you serve as is, use it to stuff tomatoes or steamed ripe bell peppers, or make into patties.

ଽ

Sauté the leek or onion in the oil until soft. Remove from heat and stir in the remaining ingredients.

If you want to make patties, add a beaten egg, form 6 small patties, coat with more crumbs, and grill on a lightly greased skillet until the crumbs are nicely browned; turn once.

This recipe is a happening; add whatever sweet vegetables are in season. These are good: fresh corn off the cob, diced red bell pepper, chopped coriander leaves.

Serves 4 to 6.

Okra

Okra has a tendency to yield a mucilaginous goo as it cooks—a plus or minus, depending on the dish! But with a little art in cooking, this nutritious and wonderfully tasty vegetable can become a favorite.

Choose fresh okra carefully. It should be a really clear green, with no dark spots, and if you press the pointy end slightly, the tip shouldn't bend over. As with mushrooms, wiping is better than washing, because water is what makes okra gluey. (If you do wash them, dry at once with a towel.)

In soup, where a little glueyness does no harm, okra is enormously good, and its little wheels make a sparky point of interest in rice or millet pilaf. One of our favorite ways of serving okra eludes formal recipe-writing: slice it thin and toss with a beaten egg white, then gently coat with fine cornmeal. Cook very slowly in a very lightly oiled skillet, until nicely browned. Season with salt and pepper. Utterly delicious.

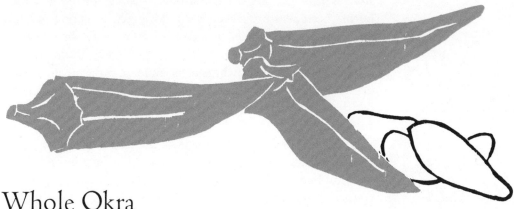

Whole Okra

Clean okra and trim it as needed. Cutting a tiny bit off the tip tells you whether that pod is tender or tough.

Sauté the onion and garlic in oil, cooking gently until soft. Crush garlic with a fork. Add okra and stir and cook until it changes color slightly, about 5 minutes. Add just enough water to cover the bottom of the pan, cover, and cook gently until the okra is almost tender. Add tomatoes, salt and pepper, and cook uncovered until the okra is tender and tomatoes are done.

Serves 6.

1½ pounds small young okra
1 large onion, minced
3 whole cloves garlic
1 tablespoon oil
1½ cups tomatoes, peeled,
* seeded, chopped*
1 teaspoon salt
pepper

Onions

The most common crime against onions is to undercook them so that they have a harsh aftertaste. People who don't like onions have often been victims of this kind of cookery.

For the record, the word *sauté* means to cook something in a little fat while stirring. *Fry* requires more fat; no stirring required. Sometimes you will hear that you can sauté with water instead of oil. Cooking without oil isn't sautéeing: the effect on flavor is different. But you *can* sauté in less fat than you are used to. The trick is to keep the fire lower, use a heavy skillet, and stir vigorously, with attention. If the onions begin to brown before they cook as much as you want them to, lower the heat; *then* add a little water and keep stirring until the water evaporates. Do this more than once, if necessary; it's called "candying" and makes a sweet, deeply rounded flavor. Scallions (green onions) and shallots cook quickly, so they are easy to sauté in very little oil.

From winter to spring, the onions you see are varieties that store well, which are usually stronger tasting. In the fall, big purple bermudas are sweet and mild; green or spring onions (scallions are the smaller version) give nip and freshness year-round. Both are great for salads. Scallions are welcome in any vegetable or grain dish where color and zip, rather than sweetness, is wanted. Delicate and less oniony than scallions are chives, which grow easily even in pots and lend zing to salads or soups with no cooking needed.

On the other end of the scale is the gourmet's onion, the shallot, which combines sweetness and pungency in one tiny, flavorful bundle. Shallots grow easily wherever there is full sun, so there is no reason for them to be so rare, except that unlike their larger cousins, they do not store well. You can use the leaves of shallots as you would chives or scallions—an added bonus for the gardener.

The onion that is an eating vegetable—and another easy-to-grow member of the family—is the leek. Leeks are sweet and mild and green in their flavor, so they often don't play a supporting role but star in dishes like leek soup, patties, or pita.

Garlic

Is there anyone who doesn't have a strong opinion about garlic? Some people believe it will cure anything, and that life without it is a hollow shell. Others can't abide even a hint of its strident flavor and would rather starve than meet a whiff in dinner. If you are a fan, you know how you like to use it; if you are a foe, you will know how to leave it alone. The following paragraphs are addressed to everyone else.

Garlic gives heft and heartiness as no other ordinary seasoning can. Its warmth enhances certain vegetable dishes where a deeper, rounder flavor is wanted; it provides a bass note in bean dishes and an added dimension to both bean and grain concoctions.

The most common crime against garlic is to use garlic powder or salt, both of which invariably taste rancid and have a characteristic sour afterbite that is quite horrid. The second most common mistake is to add minced garlic along with onions while you sauté them. Garlic is fragile and burns easily; once burned, it makes the whole dish bitter. Try these techniques and see whether you don't find that they work better for you:

[1] Add the whole uncut clove of garlic while you sauté the onion. When the onion is done, use a fork to mash the clove, which should be perfectly cooked.

[2] Mince the garlic and add it once the onion is done; then continue to sauté only briefly to cook the garlic.

[3] Use a garlic press, squeezing the garlic into the onion as in method [2].

[4] A drop or two from the press can add a lot to salad dressings—but this is controversial.

Parsnips

Parsnips are one of those old-fashioned vegetables being redis-covered now that complex carbohydrates are high chic. Their sweetness combines well with other root vegetables, as well as with sharp-flavored greens or with green beans in mixed vege-table dishes. They add an unmatchable note to winter stews. Young, tender parsnips can be steamed but older ones will get rubbery, so stir-frying is better. If the top center is pithy, cut it out.

Sesame-Glazed Parsnips

1–1½ cups parsnips, peeled
  and cut in ¾" chunks
1–1½ cups carrots,
  cut in ¾" chunks
1 tablespoon sesame seeds
2 teaspoons butter or oil
2 tablespoons maple syrup
½ teaspoon salt
juice of 1 orange (½ cup)

Sweet and scrumptious.

౩

Steam parsnips and carrots together until barely done.

Toast sesame seeds in a medium-sized skillet over medium flame. When they begin to turn color slightly, add oil or butter, maple syrup, salt, and orange juice. Stir in carrots and parsnips. Turn heat up to medium high and cook, stirring with increasing frequency, until liquid is reduced to a glaze.

Makes 4 servings (about 2 cups).

Parsnip Patties

4 cups raw parsnips, peeled
  and cut in chunks
1 onion, minced
1 tablespoon oil
1 teaspoon dried tarragon
2 eggs, beaten briefly
1 teaspoon salt
½ cup finely chopped
  walnuts
2 cups whole-grain bread
  crumbs

These are truly outstanding. *Don't* leave out the walnuts. Along-side broccoli, green beans or kale, and a dollop of applesauce, very fine eating indeed.

౩

Steam parsnips until tender—10 or 15 minutes. While parsnips are cooking, sauté onion in oil. Add tarragon.

Mash parsnips with potato masher (a few lumps are okay). Stir onion into mashed parsnips with egg, salt, and walnuts.

Preheat oven to 350°F.

Form parsnip mixture into patties, using about ⅓ cup for each. Spread half the bread crumbs on a greased baking sheet and place patties on crumbs. Press remaining crumbs on top. Bake for 20 minutes.

Makes 12 patties. Serves 6.

Bell Peppers

Green peppers are a familiar favorite, quite indispensable for dishes of Spanish or Creole persuasion. Red bell peppers, though, are really special. They're the same vegetable, only riper, and hence much more quickly perishable. Their season is brief—just a few months in autumn—but how we treasure their bright, sweet tartness and color! They combine perfectly with the quieter autumn vegetables like squash and brussels sprouts. Wonderfully good too are golden yellow peppers, pretty for salads, stuffing, or light cooking, like their red counterparts.

If you want to enjoy peppers of any color year-round, you can find them at amazing prices in specialty groceries, imported from places as far away as Holland—or you could consider giving them growing space indoors. One of our greenhouse pepper plants is three years old, and our very most prolific bearer. Even without a greenhouse, some of the smaller peppers will grow happily in pots. Commercial peppers, especially imported ones, are usually coated with a pesticide-impregnated wax, and the peels are very tough and sometimes bitter. We usually peel them with a sharp potato peeler—or roast them; see page 137.

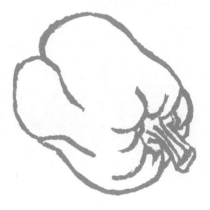

Stuffed Peppers

Pepper cases give a sense of purpose to untidy grains and miscellaneous mixtures, and they make leftover Spanish Rice a feast. Or try filling them with Stuffing, Rice-Lentil Polou, Bulgar Wheat Pilaf, or any similar dish. Filled with lightly creamed greens, pretty red or yellow cups are dazzling—one of those little touches that make a meal special.

If the filling wants the extra baking, the peppers can be stuffed raw, but usually you'll want to steam them first. For small ones, just cut the top off; otherwise, cut in half lengthwise. Remove the seeds and membranes and cook upside down in a steamer basket until barely tender—about 5 to 10 minutes, depending on the pepper.

To keep the surface of the filling from drying out, and for artistic effect, top the filled peppers before baking. If you steam them along with the peppers, you can use the tops you cut off; or try almost any combination of bread or cracker crumbs, nut or seed meal, grated cheese, and tomato slices.

Chinese Peppers & Sprouts

1 pound fresh mung bean
    sprouts
½ each, large red and
    green bell peppers
(1 head baby bok choy)
1 leek

2 tablespoons sherry
½ teaspoon honey
1 teaspoon salt

1 tablespoon oil

Crunchy, pretty, and fresh-tasting, this dish graces a Chinese dinner or an American one equally well. Bean sprouts are very perishable, so buy them only if they show no signs of brown and use them right away. (Or sprout your own: see page 120.)

Rinse the sprouts in cold water and drain. Cut the peppers into thin strips somewhat the size of sprouts; do the same with the bok choy, if you use it. Slice the leek into thin strips also, and rinse in cold water until clean. Drain well.

Mix sherry, honey, and salt in small dish.

Heat oil in a wok or large skillet; when hot, add the leek and stir-fry for about a minute, letting it soften but not brown. Add peppers (and bok choy, if desired); stir about half a minute, until hot. Add sprouts, tossing as they cook, until hot—another half minute. Pour sauce over all, again stirring and tossing. Vegetables are ready when they are coated with sauce.

Serves 4 to 6.

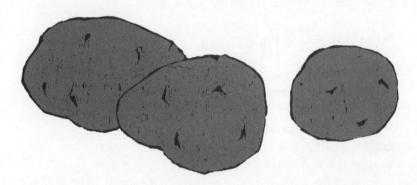

Potatoes

Potatoes have gained prestige recently because of the discovery that complex carbohydrates are Good For You. Partly because of this renewed interest, friends who didn't grow up back in the last century have asked that we tell a few basic things about this wonderful vegetable—such as, for example, what's the secret of really fluffy mashed potatoes (Cook them well, mash with milk and some of the cooking water, and never, never let them cool off. We like to use buttermilk instead of the standard milk and omit the butter: it makes a rich-tasting mashed potato with much less fat.)

Besides their other nutritional virtues—vitamin C and minerals, modest calorie count, etc.—potatoes are *versatile*. For example, cooked very well and blended smooth, they thicken sauces and soups in place of cream sauce. The flavor is good, the fat much less.

Another useful ploy for those trying to cut back on eggs is to use grated potato (raw or lightly steamed) in patties; they'll hold things together well enough for most occasions. (See pages 177–178.)

We've also found that with their sweet, mellow taste, potatoes (either chunky or saucy) are a perfect balance for the assertiveness of dark greens.

In late spring, wherever you shop, there'll be "new" potatoes: small, freshly-dug potatoes with a flavor that's unbeatable, especially after the tired winter-storage potatoes that you've had for months before. With fresh peas, or maybe a little parsley, what could be better?

GREEN POTATOES: If a potato's skin is green, the toxin solanine may be present. It's bitter and can cause slight to serious illness. Peeling deeply will remove most of the poison, but if more than half of the skin is green, it's much better to throw the potato away.

French Bakes

These are a favorite around our house. They are enough like fries for most of us, with or without Homemade Ketchup.

3 *large potatoes*
1 *tablespoon oil*
½ *teaspoon salt,*
   or to taste

ั

Preheat oven to 400°F.

Scrub potatoes and cut into french fry–sized pieces. Put them in a bowl with the oil and toss very well, so that each piece is coated with the oil. Spread them on greased cookie sheets one layer deep, and sprinkle with salt. Bake about 35 minutes, or until done to your taste.

Serves 4.

Parsley Stuffed Potatoes

4 baking potatoes

1 bunch scallions
   or 1 onion
1 tablespoon oil or butter

½ to 1 cup yogurt
   (not tart*)*
1 teaspoon salt
dash nutmeg
⅛ teaspoon black pepper
½ cup chopped parsley

Prepare potatoes as described in Green Potatoes for Six.

Meanwhile, sauté the scallion or onion in the oil. When the potatoes are done, scoop out their insides and mash while still hot with enough of the yogurt to make them fluffy—moist, but not soggy. Mix in the sautéed scallion and the remaining ingredients. Return the potato mixture to its jackets and bake for another 20 minutes.

Makes 8 stuffed potato halves—4 or more servings.

Green Potatoes for Six

6 medium or 3 large baking
   potatoes
3 stalks broccoli
   (about a pound)
¾ cup grated cheese
1 teaspoon salt
⅛ teaspoon pepper
¼ cup milk

This is a simple recipe, most enthusiastically received by the children.

Preheat oven to 400°F.

Scrub potatoes. Butter skins and make shallow slits around the middle as if you were cutting the potatoes in half lengthwise. Bake until done, 45 to 60 minutes depending on size.

Peel broccoli stems. Steam whole stalks until just tender and chop fine.

Carefully slice the potatoes in half (the slit helps) and scoop the insides into a bowl with the broccoli. Add ½ cup of the cheese and the salt, pepper, and milk. Mash all together until mixture is pale green with dark green flecks. Heap into the potato jackets and sprinkle with remaining cheese. Return to the oven for about 10 minutes.

Serves 6.

Ishtu

This South Indian dish is almost a sauce. You serve it over rice with a green vegetable, curried or not, alongside. Add mint chutney, which makes a perfect foil for Ishtu's soothing sweetness, and you have a truly special meal.

1½ cups dried, unsweetened coconut
5 potatoes
3 medium onions
1 teaspoon salt
3 tablespoons chopped fresh ginger

&

Soak coconut in 1 cup very hot water.

Peel potatoes (alas, yes) and cut them into 1″ cubes. Put them in a 3–quart saucepan with about 2 cups water. Bring to a boil and lower heat to a simmer. Meanwhile, cut onions in big chunks—about 1–1½″, cutting away the very top and bottom so the layers separate. Add to the potatoes after the first few minutes. Cover pot and cook potatoes and onions until they are just tender, about 15 minutes altogether.

Put chopped gingerroot in blender (use a small blender jar if you have one) with just enough water to cover, and blend smooth. Add to potato-onion mixture along with salt when potatoes are just about done (ginger is best when it's barely cooked). Check occasionally to be sure there's still enough water to prevent sticking.

Place coconut and its water in blender and blend for 2 to 3 minutes, stopping frequently and pushing coconut down into blades with rubber spatula. Use a cloth napkin, or your hands and a strainer, to squeeze out the milk and set it aside.

Return squeezed coconut to blender with another cup of very hot water. Blend for another few minutes and repeat the squeezing process. Add the second coconut milk to cooked potatoes and onions. Stir. Bring stew to a boil, then add the first milk (it is delicately flavored and best if not boiled). Add more salt if you think it needs it.

Makes 6 servings.

Potatoes Tarragon

1 large onion
1 tablespoon olive oil
3 large potatoes
1 bay leaf
3 tablespoons vinegar
1 teaspoon dried
    tarragon leaves
1 teaspoon salt
¼ teaspoon black pepper

A variation on hot potato salad, but much lower in fat.

Remove top and bottom of onion and slice down through center into long strips ¼″ wide. Sauté in olive oil in a good-sized skillet until transparent.

Slice potatoes in half lengthwise, then in semicircles ¼″ thick. Add to onions along with bay leaf, vinegar, tarragon, salt, and pepper. Add just enough water to barely cover potatoes. Bring to a boil, then cover and reduce heat. Simmer for 30 to 45 minutes—long enough to cook potatoes very well, so well they're beginning to crumble. Stir gently from time to time to make sure they aren't sticking. The pan sauce and potatoes should be commingling deliciously when you serve the dish.

Makes 4 generous servings.

Buttermilk Scalloped Potatoes

2 very large baking
    potatoes (1 quart packed
    when thinly sliced)
¼ cup whole wheat flour
1 teaspoon salt

1 medium onion, chopped
2 tablespoons butter
2 cups buttermilk
freshly ground black pepper
    to taste

Here's a delicious, rich-tasting scalloped potato dish with much less fat than you'd guess.

Peel potatoes and slice very thin. Combine salt and flour and dredge potato slices in that. Place them in a 9″ × 13″ casserole dish. Sauté onion in butter until tender, then add buttermilk to pan just long enough to warm but not boil. Pour mixture over the potatoes, grind pepper or paprika over them, and bake in a 350° oven for 1 hour or until potatoes poke tender with a fork.

Makes 6 servings.

Papas Chorreadas

If you include the green beans, this Latin American potato dish is a meal unto itself, needing only a pile of steamed tortillas to sop up the juices. Add a salad of lettuce, oranges, and avocadoes, with a pinch of cumin in the dressing, and you have a festive feast.

☙

Quarter potatoes lengthwise and steam them. Remove skins and slice into ½" pieces. Cut green beans in 1" pieces and steam separately until barely done.

Meanwhile, heat butter in a skillet. Sauté onion over low heat until tender, then add green onions and garlic. Add chili if desired, along with cumin and oregano, and sauté a minute more. Add tomatoes and salt and simmer 10 minutes; then stir in cottage cheese, cheese, and coriander. Heat until cheese melts. Combine with potatoes and green beans and serve immediately.

Makes 4 to 6 servings.

4 medium potatoes
(½ pound fresh green beans)

1 tablespoon butter
1 medium onion, chopped
4 green onions, chopped
1 clove garlic, minced
(1 green chili, seeds out, minced)
½ teaspoon cumin
½ teaspoon oregano
2½ cups chopped tomatoes
1 teaspoon salt
½ cup cottage cheese
¾ cup grated jack cheese
(2 tablespoons chopped coriander leaves)

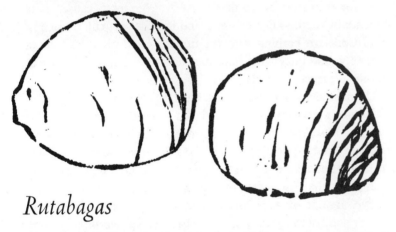

Rutabagas

A down-home Complex Carbohydrate if there ever was one. Peel and boil rutabagas until they turn orange, then mash them and beat in some salt and pepper (and milk, if you like), or mix them with equal parts of mashed potatoes to make Roota-Roota, the way Grandma Bauman used to do. Very good indeed on cold winter nights, whether you are in Sweden or the U.S.A.

Like parsnips, rutabagas make a flavorful addition to winter stews. Northern gardeners leave them in the ground all winter—no storage problem at all!—to use as needed. Dill and fennel are complementary seasonings.

Sea Vegetables

Most people think of edible seaweed as a characteristically Japanese food, but maritime cultures all over the world have made use of the tasty and nutritious vegetables collected from their shores. In Scotland, for example, dulse is used to make a cream soup not unlike New England clam chowder. In fact, Americans eat a lot of seaweed—mostly derivatives like agar, algin, and carrageenan that are used as thickeners in convenience foods.

Here we give only a brief introduction to some of the sea vegetables you can find in your natural food store. For the adventurous palate, these foods offer a new realm of flavors and textures; but even conservative cooks will find useful material here. Agar, for example, offers a vegetarian alternative to gelatin. Nori, the thin black wrapper around sushi, can be lightly roasted over a flame to make a blameless snack food that children love.

Sea vegetables have a lot to offer nutritionally, particularly for their trace mineral contribution. Kombu, for instance, has been used for centuries in China for treating goiter because of its dependably high iodine content, and laver is particularly rich in iron. Constant bathing with the mineral-rich waters of the sea probably guarantees to all marine vegetables a full spectrum of the elusive trace minerals.

Unfortunately, however, most sea vegetables available in stores today are grown in the polluted waters of the Japan Sea, and available research shows that heavy metal pollutants, pesticide residues, and other contaminants do find their way into edible seaweeds and algaes. From the extremely limited data available, it appears that the levels of heavy metals in products on the shelves are not greater than those found in land vegetables. Still, at this point we are wary of any vegetables grown in areas with significant pollution problems. We suggest that you buy from domestic growers, such as those whose sea vegetable farms are in Maine, and that you join in the efforts to cut down on the tragic pollution of our oceans. Ask your local oriental or natural foods stores for the names of companies that grow sea vegetables in domestic waters.

AGAR (also known as agar-agar or kanten) is a seaweed derivative that works like gelatin to make molded salads and aspics (pages 142 and 323) or can replace eggs in thickening anything that doesn't have to be served hot. Agar comes in bars, granules, or flakes, the flakes being the easiest to use. Unlike gelatin, which has to be chilled, agar thickens at 98°F and has nearly no calories.

KOMBU (*Laminaria*) is a member of the kelp family whose special talent is making soup stock (see page 148). It contains glutamic acid, the natural version of MSG. Added to beans, it reduces cooking time and may help to prevent flatulence.

HIJIKI (*Hizikia fusiforme*) is black, piney-looking, and exotic. Its hearty, salty marine flavor tastes best with sweet vegetables like carrot, squash, and onion, or with tofu. Try it in our Hijiki Stir-Fry (next page).

ARAME (*Eisenia bicyclis*) is fibrous and needs to be soaked before using. Try it in Winter Salad (page 141).

WAKAME (*Undaria pinnatifida*) is green and leafy and has a mild flavor close to that of leafy land vegetables. Like kombu, it tenderizes foods cooked with it.

DULSE (*Palmaria palmata*) is salty and makes a good snack food right out of the bag. It comes in thin sheets and has a beautiful purple color.

NORI has been cultivated by the Japanese for three hundred years, and was collected wild before that. The characteristic thin black sheets have a high concentration of nutrients, though the amounts are very small. Nori can be eaten as is, but it is usually toasted over a flame. We like it cut up and floated in miso broth as an instant snack. To preserve flavor, store airtight.

Many sea vegetables (particularly nori) can be toasted and then crushed or rolled into a flaky powder to use in the salt shaker. Nori has much less sodium than table salt, but equals it in flavoring strength: much of its salty flavor comes from potassium rather than sodium.

Hijiki Stir-Fry

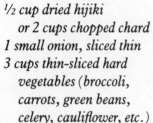

1/2 cup dried hijiki
   or 2 cups chopped chard
1 small onion, sliced thin
3 cups thin-sliced hard
   vegetables (broccoli,
   carrots, green beans,
   celery, cauliflower, etc.)

2 tablespoons white or
   yellow miso
1 tablespoon honey
1 teaspoon fresh ginger,
   grated
3/4 cup water
dash cayenne

2 tablespoons oil
   (corn or sesame)
(1/2 cup tofu cubes)
1 tablespoon toasted
   sesame seeds

If you aren't up to hijiki yet, use chard instead. Either way, we guarantee one of the tastiest stir-fry meals you can make. A very adventurous palate—or one that has developed a taste for sea vegetables—will enjoy the hijiki version. It makes a completely different dish, and a very good one also.

❦

If you use the hijiki, cover it with water to soak for ten minutes. Meanwhile, chop the vegetables.

Mix together in a cup: miso, honey, ginger, water, and cayenne. Drain and rinse the hijiki.

Stir-fry the sliced vegetables in oil for about 4 minutes, then add the hijiki or chard and stir-fry another minute. Add the miso mixture, and the tofu if you like. Stir briefly and cover. Steam over reduced heat another 5 minutes, or until the vegetables are cooked to your taste.

Sprinkle with sesame seeds and serve with brown rice. Makes 4 cups, enough for 4 people.

Spinach

It's hard to figure out how spinach ever got such a bad press, because fresh spinach is an enormous hit among the people we know, *especially* the children. Maybe the hangup is some primal recollection of canned spinach: gray, slimy, gritty stuff with its own unique bitterness.

Fresh spinach deserves to be handled with delicacy. Wash it carefully, especially if it is sandy or muddy, swishing it gently in a sinkful of cold water, draining, and repeating until the water is clean. Don't soak it or handle it roughly, or you'll get dark, soggy places where the vitamins have up and gone.

Cook and serve it whole, with just the roots taken off, or chop it before or after cooking to make the forkwork easier. Even a big pot of spinach leaves will cook in the water that clings after washing, if you stir from time to time. If you aren't used to cooking it, you'll be amazed to watch a bunch of spinach that makes 4 quarts of leaves cook down to a cup or so when it's done.

Like chard and beet greens, spinach contains oxalic acid, which makes the taste slightly sharp. To minimize this, you can cook it in milk or serve it with a creamy sauce (real cream isn't necessary), or accompany it with blander vegetables like potato or zucchini or with other salty or tart foods like shoyu, tomato, or lemon. Beyond the flavor problem, however, oxalic acid does bind minerals like calcium so that a portion of what such greens offer isn't available to the eater. Spinach, chard, and beet greens are excellent foods, but if you depend on greens for your calcium—that is, if you don't include much milk in your diet—emphasize greens from the cole family. Kale, collards, broccoli, bok choy, and such have very little oxalic acid, and they contribute calcium generously.

Spinach and eggs seem to have an affinity, and for special occasions we like to make Spanakopita, Quiche, or Crepes. For simpler "nutrient-dense" fare, garnish a serving of spinach with chopped hard-boiled egg along with a dash of vinegar. Or do it the way our friend Josh invented many years ago: pile up a lot of cooked, diced potatoes, about as much as a nine-year-old can eat and still have room for apple crisp; dot them with Better-Butter; add a layer of lightly cooked chopped spinach, and top with a poached egg. Perfect for filling a growing kid's "hollow leg."

Creamed Spinach

3/4 cup milk
2 tablespoons powdered
    milk

1/2 small onion
1–3 tablespoons butter
3 tablespoons whole wheat
    flour
3 quarts fresh spinach,
    washed, dried, and
    chopped
    (3 small bunches)
1/4 teaspoon salt
pinch nutmeg

(1/2 cup grated Swiss cheese
    or 2 tablespoons
        Parmesan
    or 1/4 cup cream cheese
        crumbled with a fork)

It's normal to cook the spinach separately and add it to the sauce, but here's a method which preserves nutrients that would be lost in the cooking water, and leaves one less pan to wash too.

This recipe has considerable sauce for the amount of spinach. When a very *spinachy* version is needed, we find we have better results cooking sauce and greens separately, and draining the spinach well before combining it with the sauce.

❧

Blend the milk and powdered milk and set aside. Chop onion fine and sauté in the butter in a large, heavy skillet. When the onion is clear, stir in the flour and cook and stir for about 2 minutes very gently. Don't let the flour brown. Add the milk and bring to a boil, stirring.

A handful at a time, stir in the spinach, adding more as the greens cook down. Simmer gently until tender, seasoning with salt and nutmeg. Add the cheese if wanted.

This recipe will make about 3 cups, enough for 4 generous servings. It is not a soupy creamed spinach but goes nicely on the plate by itself, or with mashed potatoes, or in crepes.

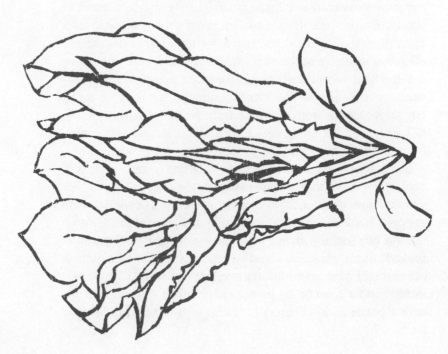

Summer Squash

Summer squashes are similar to each other in flavor and texture, but they vary in shape and color, so we like to cut up whatever's fresh and cook them together in chunks, perhaps with sautéed green onion and ripe tomatoes. Cooked crispy-tender, these bright yellow or dark or pale green squashes are light and refreshing after a hot summer day.

In the last few years, the yellow zucchini called "Goldrush" has replaced crooknecks in our patch. They fruit earlier, taste better, keep better, and produce longer. Because they are straight, they're easier to cut evenly, and they don't have big seeds like the crookneck. Whichever kind you have, the golden yellow squashes are pretty in tomato dishes and hide cleverly in corn bread and similar adventures if you happen to grow too much.

Patty pan squashes are fanciful, with their scalloped parasol look, and they are the sweetest-flavored too. We like them best picked when they're only 2″ to 2½″ across, steamed plain and served with a piquant sauce; or, at the 3″ stage, scooped out and stuffed with herbed bread crumbs.

And then—zucchini. What hasn't been said about this versatile vegetable? Welcome and delicious, and so outrageously productive in the garden that around the middle of August people start thinking of ways just to use it up. That's why you see zucchini recipes so farfetched as to boggle the imagination in every newspaper's late-summer food pages. Still, it may be at its best served simply—stir-fried, or sliced lengthwise and baked, then topped with cheese, herbs, crumbs, or just freshly ground pepper; or blended smooth in the dozen versions of Green Soup.

_ço_

ZUCCHINI PATTIES Slice and sauté a bunch of scallions (or slivered onion); add a grated potato, and let it cook about halfway, then add the same amount of grated zucchini, and a big handful of chopped parsley or coriander leaves. Mix well; salt and pepper to taste. (You can add beaten egg or grated cheese, if you want.) Form or spoon onto buttered crumbs on a griddle, and cook until the crumbs brown. Turn onto more crumbs, and brown the other side. You can make SPINACH PATTIES the same way.)

Zucchini Provencal

1 bunch green onions
1 whole garlic clove
1 tablespoon olive oil

1 potato, cubed
3 smallish zucchini, cubed
½ cup chopped celery
2 medium ripe tomatoes,
 in 1" chunks or
  ½ cup tomato sauce
1 teaspoon basil
½ teaspoon salt
pepper

Use a large skillet or stewpan. Chop the onion and sauté with the whole garlic clove in oil. When onions are transparent, crush garlic with fork. Add potato and a little water. Cover and simmer gently, stirring occasionally, for about 10 minutes. Add the zucchini (and the celery, if you want it soft rather than crunchy) and cook another 10 minutes, until tender. Stir in the celery (if you haven't already), tomatoes, and basil. Heat uncovered, stirring as necessary, until tomatoes are soft. Check seasoning.

Makes about 4 cups. Serves 4 to 6.

Baked Zucchini

5 to 8 small zucchini
1 egg
1 cup cottage cheese
(3 tablespoons buttermilk)
paprika or cayenne

EXTRAS

Add to the topping:
 ¼ cup grated cheese
 or this sautéed mixture:
 ½ onion, 1 clove garlic,
 and 2 tablespoons finely
 chopped parsley

Sprinkle on top before
 the second bake:
 Toasted bread crumbs
 Parmesan cheese

Another standby, dependable and infinitely variable.

Preheat oven to 350°F.

Slice zucchini in half lengthwise and place as many as will fit cut side up, sides touching, in a greased 9" × 13" glass baking dish (metal pans can give a metallic taste where they touch the zucchs). Cover with a cookie sheet and bake until half done—about 15 to 20 minutes, depending on the size of the zucchini.

Meantime, beat the egg and cottage cheese together (if you want it smooth, add the buttermilk and blend in blender). When the zucchini are ready, remove from oven and spoon the cottage cheese mixture over the top. Dust with paprika or cayenne and return uncovered to the oven for 15 minutes. When done, the zucchini will be tender (poke with fork) and the topping melted and bubbly-browned.

Greek Stuffed Zucchini

Yet another Macedonian specialty from the repertoire of our friend Sultana. This may just be the world's most delicious zucchini dish. If you don't have time for all the coring and stuffing, you can just chop the would-be stuffees into the rest and bake.

ð

Hollow out the zucchini. Make cylinders with an apple corer, or slice in half lengthwise and scoop out the insides to make little boats. In either case, you will need a pan large enough to arrange them side by side for baking.

Chop all of the vegetables very small. Chop insides of zucchini too, but keep separate.

Cook rice with water, onion, celery, salt, pepper, and oil for 25 minutes.

Add chopped zucchini and cook 5 minutes more.

Add parsley, bread crumbs, juice from 2 of the lemons, and slightly beaten whites of the eggs.

Preheat oven to 350°F.

Put the filling into the scooped-out zucchini shells. (If you chose the cylinder style, pack the filling in firmly with your fingers, keeping a bowl of cold water nearby to cool your hands.)

Arrange zucchini in a baking dish. If there is extra filling, spread it over and around the zucchini. Cover and bake for about 40 minutes.

Beat the egg yolks with remaining lemon juice. Spoon out some of the juices from the baking dish. Add slowly into egg yolk–lemon mixture, stirring briskly. Pour this sauce over the zucchini and bake for another 5 minutes.

Serves 6 to 8.

10 six-inch zucchini

1½ cups chopped onion
2 cups chopped celery
½ cup raw brown rice
1 cup boiling water
1 teaspoon salt
pepper
3 tablespoons olive oil

1 cup chopped parsley
1 cup bread crumbs
3 lemons
2 eggs, separated

Winter Squash

Easy to grow, easy to store all winter and use as needed, these golden squashes provide reliable good food from October through April. Their warm sweetness is a nice complement to the other standard winter vegetables from broccoli through kale and on to cabbage, whether combined or served side by side.

Although most winter squashes are generally interchangeable in recipes—even in pumpkin pie—each has particular strengths that can make a difference. For example, small squashes like delicata, Lady Godiva, and acorn make the best individual-serving stuffers, especially with savory fillings. Sweet-meat and butternut are richly flavored and mealy, wonderful for baking in chunks. Pumpkin has its characteristic flavor, with a smooth, non-mealy texture; by itself it has only a few more calories than zucchini, where butternut and acorn have double. Even so, any winter squash is a calorie bargain: a good complex carbohydrate with lots of vitamin A and potassium for under 100 calories per cup. Satisfying fare for all of us who want to lower our fat intake: the really tasty varieties are good enough to eat plain.

Here is a bonus for small children on rainy winter days: take the seeds from a big pumpkin, and in a bowl of warm water, clean off all the slimy strings. Put the seeds on a towel to drain, then on a baking sheet to toast until crisp. A delicious treat very high in protein and minerals.

Sandy's Gingered Squash

3 cups hot, cooked,
  mashed winter squash
1½ teaspoons butter
pinch salt
2 tablespoons finely minced
  fresh ginger
juice of 1 lemon
2 tablespoons honey

A light, bright dish to serve alongside any dark green vegetable.

❧

Mix all ingredients, adjusting the amount of lemon and honey as required for balance. (It will depend on how sweet your squash is.)

Makes about 3 cups, or 4 to 6 servings.

Cranberry Squash

The pungency of the cranberries is a perfect foil for the mellowness of the squash. A pretty and lively variation on baked squash.

❧

Arrange pieces of squash in one layer in a baking dish with a cover (or use aluminum foil). Scatter cranberries, chopped apple, and raisins over and around squash. If you use acorn, butternut, or other small squash, you can halve them, mix all the other ingredients together, and pile the mixture into the cavities. Otherwise, mix orange juice, grated peel, honey, butter (if desired), and salt together and pour over squash.

Cover baking dish and bake until squash is tender—25 to 45 minutes, depending on variety.

Makes about 4 servings.

1 1/2 pounds raw winter
* squash, unpeeled,*
* cut in serving-size chunks*
1/2 cup raw fresh cranberries
1 small apple, chopped
* in 3/4" pieces*
1/4 cup chopped raisins

juice and grated peel of
* 1 small orange*
1 1/2 tablespoons honey
(1 tablespoon melted butter)
dash salt

Stuffed Acorn Squash

Use acorn squash, delicata, Lady Godiva, or any other small variety of winter squash. A handsome, colorful presentation.

❧

Preheat oven to 350°F. Halve and clean squash. Place cavity face-down in a greased baking dish and bake for 25 to 45 minutes, until tender to a fork. The time will depend on which squash you choose.

Meantime, sauté onions in oil until soft. Add chopped celery. Cover and simmer on medium heat until just tender. Add spinach; stir to wilt.

Stuff squashes with vegetable mixture. Sprinkle with salted bread crumbs. Return to oven for 10 to 15 minutes.

Serves 4 to 6, depending on size of squash.

3 small winter squashes

3 green onions, chopped
2 tablespoons oil
1 cup diced celery
1 bunch spinach, coarsely
* chopped*

1/2 to 1 cup whole wheat
* bread crumbs*
1/2 teaspoon salt

Hungarian Squash

1 small onion, chopped fine
(1 clove garlic)
2 tablespoons butter
1 quart cubed winter squash

1 teaspoon paprika
1 teaspoon dill weed
2 tablespoons chopped
    parsley
1 cup yogurt, beaten smooth
1 teaspoon salt

Best with a truly sweet and mealy squash so that you get a piquant, sweet-and-sour taste when combined with the yogurt.

೩

Sauté onion (and garlic, if desired) in butter. Add squash and cover; simmer for 15 to 20 minutes on low heat. If the squash is very starchy, it might need ½ cup water added midway. If any liquid is left after squash is cooked, uncover and cook and stir until it evaporates.

When squash is tender, stir in remaining ingredients. Heat very gently until warmed through. If you heat it too much, the yogurt will separate—still tasty, but less attractive.

Serves 4 to 6.

Squash Malagushim

⅓ cup coconut
½ cup very hot water
1 teaspoon ground cumin

½ cup yellow split peas
1 cup water

2¼ pounds winter squash
    (6 cups cut)

½ teaspoon turmeric
½ teaspoon salt

1 teaspoon black mustard
    seeds
2 teaspoons oil

This South Indian dish goes as beautifully with Western food as it does as part of an Indian dinner. We like to serve it in winter alongside broccoli or other green vegetables and rice.

೩

Cover coconut with very hot water. Add cumin and set aside.

Cook split peas in water until soft, about half an hour. Be sure they are covered with water as they cook, but try to end up with as little extra water as possible.

Peel squash, remove seeds, and cut in ¾″ cubes. Cook in as little water as possible. When half cooked, add turmeric and salt.

Mash split peas with cooking water.

Puree coconut and soaking water in blender 3 minutes or until very smooth. (This step can be omitted, but it makes a much nicer dish.)

Mix peas, coconut, and squash. Simmer a few minutes.

In a small, heavy pan, heat oil and add mustard seeds. They will begin popping like popcorn. Cover and listen: the instant the frantic sound of popping dies down, turn the seeds into the squash dish and mix well.

Serves 4.

Butternut Tostada

Artist Alan Gussow works in several media, including vegetables. This hands-across-the-border dish reflects his eclectic approach nicely. The combination may sound strange, but this is one fine dish, a revelation for people who love Mexican food but can't eat beans.

❧

Cut and quarter the butternut and steam for 20 minutes. Meanwhile, toast the tortillas over gas burner or on a griddle until just softly crisp.

Remove the squash pulp from the skins. Heat oil in a heavy pan and sprinkle with chili powder, cumin, and garlic. Stir and fry until the spices are fragrant. Add squash and oregano, stirring while mixture heats through.

Place squash on tortillas, sprinkle with shredded cheese, and place under broiler until cheese melts. Remove, cover with lettuce or sprouts, and dot with salsa. A handful of toasted pumpkin seeds makes a delicious final touch.

Makes 4 rather unusual but very tasty tostadas.

*1 butternut squash
  (to make 2 cups cooked
  pulp)*
4 tortillas
1 tablespoon oil
1 teaspoon chili powder
½ teaspoon ground cumin
1 clove garlic, minced
*1 teaspoon well-rubbed
  oregano*
*1 cup shredded cheddar
  or jack cheese*
*4 cups shredded lettuce
  or alfalfa sprouts*
salsa (see below)
(toasted pumpkin seeds)

Salsa

Dice tomatoes, chop onions, mince garlic and chili; combine all these with herbs and mix well. If you are not an old chili hand, see page 236 for some tips about using them.

3 ripe, red tomatoes
4 green onions
2 cloves garlic
*1 jalapeño or yellow
  hot chili pepper*
*¼ cup chopped fresh
  coriander leaves*
1 teaspoon oregano

Sweet Potatoes & Yams

The controversy continues, so we looked them up. Yams proper are tuberous roots of tropical plants of the genus *discorea*, hardly ever available north of the tropics. All our so-called yams are probably really sweet potatoes, but when people say yams, usually they mean the moist, dark orange varieties that taste so terrific. Bake them in their jackets and serve piping hot, with or without Better-Butter. Some brown-baggers we know like to take the leftovers for lunch, to eat like fruit. But the competition for leftovers is keen because yams are so delicious chunked into dinnertime greens or used for Sweet Potato Salad.

For baking, allow about twice the time you'd give for similar-sized normal potatoes: 2 hours at 375°F for big ones. Scrub and trim as necessary, removing black spots. Since they are full of natural sugar, which tends to burst out in the oven, covering the baking sheet with clean brown paper or cooking parchment makes clean-up a lot easier.

South Indian Sweet Potatoes

3 cooked sweet potatoes
    or yams (2 cups mashed)
2 teaspoons oil
1/2 teaspoon mustard seeds
1/2 cup green pepper, finely
    chopped (1/2 large pepper)
(1 fresh green chili, minced,
    or dash cayenne)
1/2 teaspoon ground cumin
lemon juice to taste
1/2 teaspoon salt, to taste

What could be better than plain baked yams? Maybe nothing, but this dish would definitely get votes. Why not bake extras and use them this way? Very different, and utterly delicious. Warm them up before proceeding with the recipe.

৵

Peel and mash the yams and set aside.

Heat oil in a small skillet until faint lines form on the surface.

Sprinkle in mustard seeds and keep covered over high heat while they pop. When the wild noise dies down, immediately add the chopped green pepper. Return to a medium-low flame and sauté, adding chili (if desired) and cumin.

When green pepper is tender, add mashed sweet potato and heat through. Add lemon juice to taste. (A tablespoon or more is delicious, but if you're serving the dish with anything else that's piquant, you might want to use less.)

Makes 4 servings.

Tomatoes

Tomatoes are so basic to year-around cooking that it's hard to imagine doing without them. We give them much of our tiny greenhouse space, so that we have some fresh all year. Still, we use them so much that tomatoes are the one vegetable we buy canned. If you, like us, have to rely on canned tomatoes sometimes, be sure that you remove all the contents once you open the can. Most cans are still lead-soldered, and lead leaches into the food once the can is open. (That goes for tomato paste too, and any other food or juice in soldered cans.)

Much has been written lately about the poor eating quality of commercial fresh tomatoes, and all of it is true. The happy result of the flack is that local growers are actually bringing real home-grown tomatoes to market—red, ripe, luscious, and in season, mind you; the real thing. Ask for them if you can't grow them yourself. The salmon-colored, cubical lumps of papier-mâché that agribusiness calls tomatoes add nothing to any salad, sandwich, or casserole.

Our own tomato season is so short that we can seldom bring ourselves to cook with fresh tomatoes. Instead we enjoy them in salads, or stuffed with Tabouli, or in sandwiches. But sometimes, at peak of season, we get a chance to make Tomato Soup—simple, but what more satisfying?—or grilled tomato halves, with maybe a drizzle of olive oil, a sprinkling of parsley or fresh basil, and a grating of black pepper or hard cheese. Fresh-picked tomatoes usually inspire our version of a Mexican feast at least a few times each summer: fresh steamy-hot tortillas, Refritos, shredded lettuce, Mock Sour Cream, sliced tomatoes, Salsa, Avocado Dip, grated jack and cheddar cheeses, so everyone can construct tostadas to taste. (See pages 276–277 for more.)

Mixed Vegetables

The next few recipes are for mixed vegetable dishes, most of which draw their inspiration from other cultures. Besides these, and too simple to be treated as real recipes, are the many delicious combinations of garden-fresh vegetables that one stumbles upon from day to day as the seasons change. Serve them in a colorful heap just as they are, or accompanied by lemon wedges or shoyu, or topped with Sesame Salt, chopped nuts, grated cheese, Lemon Butter, or your favorite sauce. Serve them with brown rice or millet, or fresh whole wheat rolls. Add a salad and your meal's complete.

You may choose to start with a sautéed onion, but from there on almost anything goes, though most cooks prefer to keep the number of vegetables down to three. Choose them with color, texture, and flavor in mind. Vary the way you cut the vegetables, and you'll be amazed what a difference it can make. Chop them, dice them, slice thin or thick, in rounds or diagonals or matchsticks; shred or grate them; fix some one way, some another; but make them as pretty as you can. If some will cook quicker than others, you can adjust the thickness of the slices or give the slower ones a head start.

The following combinations are a few that we enjoy often. Treat these suggestions as a jumping-off place: invent your own medleys, a different one each time.

🌢 Zucchini and stems of broccoli cut in thick rounds (florets bite-size), carrots in thinner rounds

🌢 Cauliflower and green beans with red bell peppers for accent

🌢 Winter squash or leftover yams cubed, with celery crescents and chopped spinach or chard

🌢 Green beans, diced potato, and sautéed onion

🌢 Zucchini coarsely grated or sliced very thin, with corn and parsley (that's a quickie)

🌢 Carrots and zucchini grated large, with shredded cabbage and finely chopped parsley (add salt and lemon juice at serving time)

Ratatouille

Ratatouille (the word means "stew" or "soup" in French) makes use of a savory vegetable combination which is a favorite the world round. The exotic dishes from the Middle East which follow are variations on this basic theme.

If you can use fresh, perfect ingredients—not only the vegetables but the herbs too—this dish can be truly wonderful.

୬

Dice eggplant into 1″ cubes and slice zucchini in ½″ rounds. Chop onion coarsely and cut green pepper into squares.

Use a heavy-bottomed saucepan with a lid. Sauté the onion, garlic, and green pepper until they are soft; stir in eggplant and zucchini and sauté a few minutes more. Crush garlic clove with a fork. Add tomato and seasonings. Cover and simmer gently for about 30 minutes or until all the vegetables are well cooked.

Uncover and turn the heat up to evaporate some of the liquid, stirring as necessary.

Serves 6 to 8.

VARIATIONS

IMAM BAYILDI: Preheat oven to 350°F. Add a large potato cut in chunks, some sliced mushrooms if you wish, and a cup of hot water or stock. Instead of simmering on top of the stove, bake in a covered dish for 45 minutes.

GVETCH: Include not only potato chunks and sliced mushrooms, but also 4 carrots sliced in rounds and the juice of 1 lemon. Use only 2 tablespoons water instead of a whole cup and bake as for Imam Bayildi.

1 large eggplant
2 medium zucchini
1 large onion
1 green pepper
1 whole clove fresh garlic
2 tablespoons olive oil
3 fresh, ripe tomatoes,
  chopped or
    5 tablespoons tomato paste
    and 3 tablespoons water
1 teaspoon salt
⅛ teaspoon pepper
½ teaspoon basil
½ teaspoon oregano

Aviyal

¼ pound green beans
2 large carrots
2 large potatoes
2 medium zucchini
1 teaspoon turmeric powder
1 teaspoon salt

1 cup unsweetened
   coconut flakes
1 cup hot water
1 cup yogurt, beaten smooth
(1 small green chili)
juice of 1 lemon,
   if yogurt is not tart

Aviyal means "miscellaneous," so if this list isn't in season when you prepare your feast, choose from winter squash, broccoli stems, asparagus, or plantains. Serve with rice, other vegetable curries, and chutney.

Cut vegetables into strips the size of your little finger and cook in as little water as possible. Start with the green beans, then add carrots and potatoes after a few minutes. Zucchini should go in last, when the other vegetables are half cooked. Add turmeric. Stir the vegetables so they will cook evenly, but be careful not to break them. Add salt. Add water if necessary.

Grind coconut in blender or food processor with the hot water, adding the chili if you like things fiery. When all the vegetables are tender—not mushy—stir in the blended coconut. Remove from heat. There should be just a little water left. Stir in yogurt, adding lemon juice if needed: the sauce should be a little tart.

This makes 6 cups or more, to serve 4 to 6.

Cauliflower Eggplant Curry

1 cauliflower
1 eggplant
2 tablespoons oil
1 teaspoon black mustard
   seed
½ teaspoon turmeric powder
1 teaspoon curry powder
1 teaspoon salt
¼ cup water
2 potatoes
1 cup peas
1 tomato, chopped
juice of 1 lemon

One of our favorite mixed vegetable dishes, whether the meal is Indian in mood or not.

Remove thick stems of cauliflower and cut them into small pieces. Separate the head into florets and slice.

Cut eggplant into ½″ cubes.

Heat oil in heavy pot with a lid. When very hot, add mustard seed and cover quickly. The seeds will pop wildly; when the sound dies down, turn off the flame, open the lid, and immediately add the spices and the cauliflower. Stir to coat with spices and oil. Add ¼ cup water and eggplant. Cube potatoes and boil them separately until partially cooked before adding them.

Continue cooking over medium heat, adding 1 or 2 tablespoons of water from time to time, stirring gently. Add peas about 5 minutes before serving. At the last minute, add finely chopped tomato. Turn off heat and add lemon juice.

Serves 6 to 8.

Middle Eastern Vegetables

Preheat oven to 375°F.

Dice potato, carrot, and apple small. Separate cauliflower into small florets. Cut zucchini into chunks.

Sauté onion in oil with bay leaf, mustard seed, celery seed, and dill.

Stir in vegetables in this order, leaving 2 minutes or so between each addition: potato, carrots, cauliflower. Then add apple.

Add tomato and zucchini. Heat quickly and transfer to oven for 20 minutes. Sprinkle with salt and paprika.

The trick of getting vegetables to bake evenly is to cut the longest-cooking vegetables (potato, carrot, and cauliflower) quite small.

Serves 4 to 6 over rice, bulgur wheat, or millet.

1 potato
1 carrot
1 medium green apple
1/2 head cauliflower
2 zucchini
1/4 onion, chopped
1 tablespoon oil
1/2 bay leaf
3/4 teaspoon yellow
  mustard seed
1/4 teaspoon celery seed
1/2 teaspoon dill weed
1 tomato
1 teaspoon salt
1/2 teaspoon paprika

Chinese Vegetables

This recipe is not very authentic, but we make it often and enjoy it very much. Where amounts are given, they are for 4 to 6 people.

Allow at least 1 cup of vegetables per person. Cut attractively in diagonal shapes; cut the onion vertically in thin wedges. If a vegetable doesn't lend itself to the diagonal cut—cabbage, for example—dice or cut in square pieces.

Heat the oil in a wok or a large skillet. Stir-fry the onion, then add minced garlic and ginger, stirring in the other vegetables in turn, beginning with the longer-cooking ones and ending with such quick-cookers as peas and bean sprouts. If you want to use tofu, rinse and cut into 1″ cubes and place on top of the vegetables before they are completely cooked. Cover and steam until tofu is hot and vegetables crisp and tender.

Add shoyu to taste. Sprinkle with toasted sesame seeds and serve right away, with a steaming bowl of brown rice.

THE MUSTS

1 onion
minced garlic
1 teaspoon minced ginger
2 tablespoons oil
green pepper, celery
1/2 cup water
shoyu to taste

THE VARIABLES

mushrooms
snow peas or green beans
carrots, peas
broccoli, cauliflower
zucchini
bok choy or chard
Chinese or Western cabbage
tofu chunks
mung bean sprouts

Mushrooms Petaluma

3 potatoes
3 carrots
¾ pound fresh mushrooms
  (ideally buttons)
2 bell peppers
1 large onion, chopped
2 tablespoons butter or
  butter and oil combined
2 tablespoons mustard
  (Dijon best)
3 tablespoons shoyu
3 tablespoons brown sugar
1 cup mellow red table wine
½ cup chopped fresh parsley
salt and pepper to taste

This rather purple stew may look odd, but it's quite delectable.

ᶥᴥ

Trim potatoes, quarter lengthwise, and slice in ½" pieces. Slice carrots the same thickness. Steam potatoes and carrots together.

Clean mushrooms with a damp cloth and cut larger ones into good-sized chunks. Remove seeds and stem from peppers and cut in 1" squares.

Sauté onion in butter in a heavy 2-quart pot until translucent. Add mushrooms and bell pepper and sauté, stirring, until mushrooms begin to sweat.

Mix mustard, shoyu, brown sugar, and wine. Add sauce to sautéed vegetables along with carrots, potatoes, and a cup of the water they steamed over (or other vegetable stock).

Bring mixture to a boil and add parsley. Reduce heat and simmer, covered, until vegetables are all quite tender. Cook uncovered then, if you want to, to reduce and thicken sauce. Serve with whole-grain noodles.

Makes 6 servings.

Winter Stew

8 cups kale, chopped
1 large or 2 small parsnips
1 rutabaga (¾ cup)
1 smallish turnip (½ cup)

SAUCE

1 onion, chopped
2 whole cloves garlic
2 stalks celery
2 tablespoons olive oil
3 tablespoons shoyu
1–2 tablespoons molasses
2 tablespoons lemon juice
2 teaspoons dried basil
2–4 cups stock

Just the thing to perk up a jaded winter appetite.

ᶥᴥ

Steam kale until nearly tender. It may take more or less time than the rest of the recipe ingredients, depending on whether it is tender or tough; if it cooks quickly, take it off earlier. You should have about 2 cups. Drain well. While kale is cooking, peel roots and dice in ½" cubes.

Sauté onion, garlic, and celery in olive oil. Mash the garlic cloves with a fork and add the remaining sauce ingredients, as well as the parsnips, rutabaga, and turnip. Simmer 10 minutes. (Adjust the amount of stock to suit the way you will be serving the stew.) Simmer until parsnips etc. are nearly tender, about 20 minutes. Add kale and cook briefly, until everything is tender. Serve with grain, potatoes, hot rolls, or (maybe best of all) Spoonbread, page 286.

Makes about 5 cups, to serve 4 to 6.

Sauces & Such

What better way than a fine sauce to brighten the flavors of your vegetables, or to join otherwise disparate ingredients in a happy marriage? But is there sauce after fat?

To enhance what is already good, and to make appealing what is nutritious but maybe not so immediately welcome, a little fat can be a big help for the magic it works in a skillet. But when you begin to lean on cream, butter, or even good olive oil, you soon notice that the stuff is addictive. Fortunately, there are alternatives.

There is, for example, the time-tested combination cherished by Greek cooks: parsley and lemon juice. Nothing simpler, nothing more appetizing, and nothing in the world more innocent. Always add lemon juice and parsley (and any other fresh herbs) at the last minute; they don't take kindly to long cooking.

The sauces that follow are meant to make good food even better without sending you to an early grave. Even so, use a light hand. We sauce only one dish per meal, as a rule, and do the saucing in the kitchen; it's tempting to ladle on too much at the table. Everyone can discover the exquisite flavors of vegetables and grains—but not when the food is drowned in sauce.

If you have a tiny bit left, it's well worth keeping. Those few spoonfuls might be just what tomorrow's soup needs for extra sparkle, or combine with leftover beans to make a delicious spread.

Flavoring

When your appetite is keen and the green peas were picked moments ago, it's a travesty to reach for the spices. But when you're trying to simplify your family's diet, or introducing them to Complex Carbohydrates, or when the midwinter gleanings from the garden seem monotonous beyond relief—at times like these, imaginative saucing and seasoning can change everybody's feeling about dinner, and make the difference between good nutrition and a secret raid on the local fast foods outlet. With this in mind, we have collected some of our favorite ways of adding appeal to praiseworthy dishes that might otherwise not get the top billing they deserve.

SALT Try to use just enough in the kitchen that no one reaches for it at the table. Our recipes use the amount of salt that seems right to people who are used to lightly salted food. If you can use less, by all means do it!

PEPPER Nicer when freshly ground. Pepper is aromatic when added just before serving; it becomes hot-tasting when it sits in cooked food.

BAY A bay leaf adds dimension to soups, sauces, and stews. Be sure to remove it before serving time.

GINGER Ginger adds nip and brightness. Use it to enhance dishes that already have a fruity mood, such as winter squash or tomato soups or sauces. Ginger gives ping to vegetables that might otherwise taste flat or heavy, and is often included along with garlic in Chinese and Indian cooking. Wonderful stuff. Don't overcook.

Growing Your Own

Few of us have time or space to grow all our own spices and herbs. But anybody who wants to can grow at least pots of basil, parsley, and chives. Garlic and onions are practical for gardeners, and oregano, marjoram, savory, rosemary, and thyme grow easily. Lemon thyme makes a beautiful green-and-yellow ground cover. Coriander, even more than basil, is best fresh, and its pretty, lacy flowers have a bonus: they support very tiny wasps that help keep the aphid population down. Growing herbs is a very satisfying thing.

PARSLEY

Parsley must be the friendliest herb of all. We keep it planted just outside the kitchen door, but it will flourish even in a pot (use a deep one) and provide plenty for salad dressings and more. Where many other herbs seem too strong-flavored for vegetarian fare, parsley adds freshness and sparkle to just about anything that isn't green already. To our taste, the tender Italian kind with flat leaves has the best flavor. No parsley wants much cooking, and the color is preserved too if the chopped leaves are added at the very end of cooking time.

To say that parsley is very nourishing may seem silly considering how little you use at a time, but there you are: it is. Good for freshening the breath after a garlicky dinner, too—just chew up a sprig.

CHINESE PARSLEY

Also called coriander or cilantro, these leaves make a brightly green topping for many Mexican, Indian, and Chinese dishes. It is one of our favorites for adding freshness to salads and grain dishes. Buy it in the produce section of supermarkets or in Mexican or Chinese groceries.

BASIL

Fresh or dried, basil adds perky sweetness to any tomato dish, as well as to peas and salad dressings. Its mild, sweet flavor is a perfect complement to the lighter flavor of meatless sauces and vegetables. The large-leafed kind grows and harvests easily and has a lovely, mellow flavor.

Seasoning Blends

Commercial blends can be a godsend for cooks who feel diffident about using herbs and spices. Try to choose for freshness, and read the label: some have a lot of salt (which you can add more cheaply in the kitchen!) and some contain MSG—an additive worth avoiding. It may be just as easy to create your own blends, either on the spot or at convenient times; they are likely to be fresher than commercial mixes and certainly will taste better.

MEXICAN FLAVORING

Cumin powder is the essence of Mexican flavoring. Add cayenne for hotness (to the extent that you want it), oregano, and garlic. Cayenne is what gives Mexican food that fine red color, but if you want to go light on cayenne you can add quite a lot of paprika instead; it's made of dried ripe bell peppers instead of chili peppers, and gives color without hotness. Cumin and chili powder give their best flavor when you add them as you sauté the onion.

Add fresh, chopped leaves of cilantro to salsa, and top your chili beans or guacamole with it.

ITALIAN FLAVORING

If spaghetti is a spur-of-the-moment standby, you may want to keep Italian Blend on hand. Mix 6 parts basil, 2 of oregano, 1 of thyme; use about a teaspoon per cup of sauce (for example), to taste. Include fresh garlic in your sauce too, and a bay leaf.

Indian cooks blend spices differently for each dish, but in the U.S. we have the convenience of prepared curry powder (coriander, cumin, ginger, cardamom, turmeric, etc.), a dash of which can save a vegetable stew from disaster or give interest to sauces that lack pizzazz. Shop around to find a curry blend that you particularly like. Most of the spices in curry powder require cooking to give their best flavor, so include it at the sauté-the-onion stage.

A spice blend often made in advance even by Indian cooks is *garam masala*. This mixture is sweeter than curry powder and wonderful for dishes with spinach or peas. Indian specialty stores stock different masalas in various degrees of hotness, but if you often use Indian recipes that require it, you may want to grind your own, using a recipe from a good Indian cookbook like Madhur Jaffrey's *World-of-the-East Vegetarian Cookbook* (Knopf, 1981). If you're caught short when a recipe calls for garam masala, use allspice.

Many South Indian dishes call for black mustard seeds. These are smaller than the familiar yellow seeds, and must be popped like popcorn for best flavor. Don't let them burn. Black mustard seeds give an unmatchable warmth to many vegetable curries and to Raita, page 239.

Three spices from the Indian palette that work together to make bean dishes and soups special are coriander powder, cumin, and turmeric. Use them as a team, a quarter to a half teaspoon turmeric, a teaspoon of cumin, and two or even three of coriander. Added when you sauté the onions, the mixture makes an event of a pot of pintos. All three are believed to help prevent flatulence, and all should be cooked well to give their best flavor.

Turmeric is an acrid yellow powder encountered mostly in prepared mustard, which would be only pale tan without it. Used in most curries in small amounts, it adds interest, an assertive curl, and a sunny color.

Cumin is familiar to anyone who enjoys Mexican cooking, but it appears as frequently in Indian dishes. It gives bright, warm piquance to bean and tomato dishes and greens.

Ground coriander seed may be a stranger, but once you try it with beans, you'll want to have it around regularly. Its sweet warmth rounds out the flavor of cumin, and when sautéed and added to bean dishes and such, it thickens the liquid into sauce.

Soy Sauce, Shoyu & Tamari

For counting sodium:
2 teaspoons shoyu
= ½ teaspoon salt

"Soy sauce" is a general term for the dark-brown flavoring liquids with a soybean base. *Shoyu,* the term we use throughout this book, is the naturally-fermented kind whose ingredients include soybeans and wheat (in nearly equal portions) and salt. Made in the traditional way by long fermentation, it has especially good flavor. Some of the finest of commercial Japanese shoyu is now available in the United States. When you are shopping, check the label for the ingredients mentioned, and be sure there are no preservatives.

The "other kind" of soy sauce is an unfermented preparation made from hydrolyzed vegetable protein (HVP), corn syrup, caramel color, salt, and monosodium glutamate. We don't use or recommend it.

To add to the confusion in terminology, for a decade or so some natural foods firms have been calling their shoyu *tamari.* Tamari is also a flavorful brown liquid, and not so different from shoyu that you couldn't use it as a substitute; but real tamari, a by-product of miso making, is not usually available commercially. What you may find called tamari is usually a Chinese version of shoyu that *may* be made without wheat. Again, the thing to watch for on the label is preservatives.

Aside from providing their own characteristic and delightful flavor, shoyu and tamari can be helpful to people who are trying to cut back on salt. The salty flavor of these products *does* come from actual salt, but they seem somehow saltier-tasting for an equivalent amount of sodium, enabling you to use less. You still have to be careful, though: it only works if you use less!

Homemade Ketchup

We like this version better than store-bought. It's free of additives and sugar, and much lower in salt—and cheap.

❧

Mix all the ingredients together. Store in a jar in the refrigerator. Makes 1¾ cups.

1 twelve-ounce can tomato paste
½ cup cider vinegar
½ cup water
½ teaspoon salt
1 teaspoon oregano
⅛ teaspoon cumin
⅛ teaspoon nutmeg
⅛ teaspoon pepper
½ teaspoon mustard powder
squeeze of garlic from press

Sesame Salt

A flavorful seasoning to add at table.

❧

Toast sesame seeds and grind in blender with salt, one part salt to eight *or more* parts seeds.

Quick Vegetable Relish

A crisp, tangy relish that goes well in sandwiches. Try it with Swiss cheese and mustard for a Vegetarian Reuben that's a real knockout; or use a spoonful alongside simple fare to add interest.

❧

Combine all ingredients and pack into a pint-size jar. Add enough water to cover, if needed—about ¼ cup. Cover tightly and refrigerate overnight.

Makes 2 cups (the vinegar shrinks the vegetables). Store in refrigerator.

2 cups shredded green cabbage, packed
½ cup grated carrot, packed
½ cup very thinly sliced red onion
½ cup very thinly sliced green pepper
2 teaspoons salt
dash pepper
6 tablespoons distilled vinegar

Margarita's Salsa

4 fresh medium tomatoes
½ smallish onion
1 mild jalapeño pepper*
½ teaspoon (rounded)
   oregano
½ teaspoon (level) cumin
½ teaspoon (scant) basil
½ teaspoon salt
dash black pepper

This is freshness itself, and best served shortly after its creation. A perfect garnish for any dish with Mexican antecedents, or with vegetable or bean concoctions where a little fire is called for. Even with mild jalapeno, however, this is a hot salsa by many people's standards. For a milder version, use just a few chives or one small scallion top instead of the onion; you might also omit the chili, or substitute ¼ green pepper.

Puree in blender or food processor, or just chop everything very fine and mix.

   Makes about 2 cups.

*An aside to anyone who isn't used to chilis: the seeds and membranes are the hottest parts, and you can get flavor with less ferocity if you discard them. Cut the chili in half, being careful to handle it by its skin and trying not to touch the inside. Remove the seeds with knife or spoon—and don't flip one up into your eyes! After you have chopped the chili, wash your hands, knife, and chopping board, and don't touch your face for at least half an hour.

Chutneys

The recipes on this page are for fresh chutneys of the sort made daily in Indian homes; the bottled ones in stores are more in the category of pickles. Both can serve to pick up the palate and complement the other dishes at a meal.

If you have fresh coconut, remove the white flesh and grate it before you start. If not, use dried: soaking it beforehand in hot water to cover makes the chutney smoother; use part of the water from the recipe to do that.

Coriander Chutney

Place all the ingredients in the blender and blend smooth, using a minimum of water. This chutney should not be runny, so you will have to stop the blender frequently to stir, especially at first. Makes ¾ cup, enough for 4 at a feast or for 2 for Dosas.

MINT CHUTNEY: Substitute ¾ cup coarsely chopped mint leaves for the coriander. (For another delicious mint chutney, see the recipe on the next page.)

1 cup coriander leaves
½ cup shredded coconut
1 small shallot, chopped
*   or 2 tablespoons onion*
1 tablespoon chopped ginger
(½ green chili)
¼ teaspoon salt
1 tablespoon lemon juice
1 teaspoon brown sugar
about ¼ cup hot water

Coconut Chutney

This chutney comes from Tamilnadu, and is good for Dosas or —if you have our Bread Book—Iddlis. Blend all the ingredients except oil and seeds, using enough hot water to grind easily but well; it should be a thick smooth paste. Rinse the blender, using about ¾ cup hot water, and add that to the chutney to make about 2 cups.

Heat the oil in a small, heavy pan and add seeds. They will pop frantically; the moment the sound of popping dies down, add the chutney. Reduce heat and bring the chutney just to a simmer. Makes 2 cups.

1 cup coconut
1 tablespoon minced ginger
1 medium shallot, chopped,
*   or 3 tablespoons onion*
(½ small green chili)
½ teaspoon salt
¾ teaspoon brown sugar
1½ tablespoons lemon juice
hot water

1½ teaspoons oil
1 teaspoon black mustard
*   seed*

Tomato-Ginger Chutney

3 cups red ripe tomatoes,
    peeled, seeded, and diced
½ teaspoon turmeric
1 tablespoon minced ginger
3 garlic cloves, minced
½ teaspoon salt

1 tablespoon oil
1 teaspoon black mustard
    seeds
½ teaspoon cumin seeds

A very tasty general-purpose chutney, not too hot. If you want fire, add a dash of cayenne when the cumin seeds begin to brown.

ая

Combine tomatoes, turmeric, ginger, garlic, and salt, and set aside. Or, for a quicker, rather liquid version, put tomatoes in blender or processor along with the turmeric, ginger, and garlic; whirl briefly, then force the mixture through a food mill to remove seeds and skin. Add salt.

Heat a heavy skillet; when hot, put in oil. When the oil is hot, add mustard seeds. They will pop wildly. When the noise of the popping dies down slightly, remove the pan from the heat and add the cumin seed. Heat slowly, stirring, until the cumin is slightly darkened, then immediately add the tomato mixture. Simmer gently about 10 minutes to reduce and thicken.

Makes about 1¼ cups.

Apple Chutney

2½ cups (or more)
    diced tart apples
1 cup cider vinegar
½ lemon, chopped
¾ cup raisins
¾ cup brown sugar
⅓ cup minced ginger
1 or 2 cloves garlic,
    chopped
½ teaspoon salt
(dash cayenne)

Here is an easy "Anglo" chutney that can go alongside nearly anything that wants perk. We like it especially with kale.

ая

Combine all ingredients and simmer until fruit is soft, about ½ hour if the apples are crisp. Makes 2⅓ cups.

Mint Chutney / Raita

A cooling chutney, quite runny; delicious spooned next to any sort of rice or spicy vegetable dishes. If you are short on mint, you can use coriander leaves or spinach. Mint and coriander are used raw, but cook the spinach first and squeeze it dry, then chop small. Being milder, this dish is much more like raita than chutney.

≥

Combine all the ingredients. Makes ⅔ cup, plenty for 4 at a feast; if you use it on iddlis (you really *should* have the *The Laurel's Kitchen Bread Book*), this will make enough for about 6 iddlis.

½ cup chopped mint leaves
½ cup mild yogurt,
    beaten smooth
(thin slice green chili,
    or 1 teaspoon ginger)
½ shallot, chopped, or
    1 tablespoon onion
¼ teaspoon salt

Raita

Raita is an Indian side dish that complements the flavors of the rest of the meal, adding tartness where needed for balance. It can do the same for Western-style meals.

Rai means mustard, and authenticity demands that raita include mustard seeds "popped" in the traditional way. You will see many raita recipes without the seeds, though, and as elsewhere, omitting them doesn't mean the dish won't turn out. However, there are few flavors so delicious.

If you omit the popped mustard seeds and use skim-milk yogurt, the raita can sometimes taste a little chalky. If you have this problem, stir in only a little cream, or a *little* oil.

≥

Beat yogurt smooth and mix with all the vegetables. Heat a tiny, heavy pan very hot; add the oil and, when hot, the mustard seeds. Cover and listen for the sound of frantic popping. As soon as the sound diminishes, uncover the pan and turn its contents into the raita. Mix, and serve cool.

Makes about 2½ cups: enough for 4 people, more or less, depending on how much else there is for dinner.

BANANA RAITA: Use bananas instead of tomatoes and cucumber. Omit ginger. Wow.

RED ONION RAITA: Use red onions and tomatoes for the vegetables. Add ½ teaspoon of honey and ½ teaspoon lightly toasted ground cumin. This one stands nicely with or without the mustard seed.

1½ cups yogurt, beaten
    smooth
½ cup diced tomato
½ cup diced cucumber
2 teaspoons minced fresh
    ginger
¼ teaspoon salt, or to taste

(½ green chili, seeded and
    minced, or dash cayenne)
chopped coriander leaves

1 teaspoon oil
½ teaspoon black mustard
    seed

Mock Sour Cream

*1 cup low-fat cottage
  cheese*
2 tablespoons lemon juice
2 tablespoons mayonnaise
¼ cup buttermilk
zest of ½ lemon
pinch of salt if needed

Mock Sour Cream is easy to fix; it's dramatically lower in fat, saturated fat, and cholesterol than sour cream itself, and it's not half bad as a source of calcium. We make it often to serve with vegetables, on baked potatoes, Blintzes, and Whole Beet Borscht, with Mexican-style dinners, and for dressing potato salad. The taste is distinctly lemony; if you plan to use it with other flavorings, you can omit the lemon zest and reduce the juice.

Mock Sour Cream works reliably in most recipes that call for sour cream. Other options are to use soft Yogurt Cheese (page 104), stirred smooth; or thick Buttermilk Sauce (page 244).

❧

Place cottage cheese, lemon juice, mayonnaise, buttermilk, and lemon zest in blender and blend thoroughly until creamy smooth.

Makes 1½ cups.

Homemade Mayonnaise

1 egg
½ teaspoon salt
½ teaspoon mustard powder
2 tablespoons cider vinegar
1 cup oil

This recipe has just as much fat as normal mayo, but it tastes better and has no harmful additives.

❧

Put egg, salt, mustard, and vinegar in blender with ¼ cup of the oil. Blend on low, uncover, and slowly but steadily pour in the remaining oil.

Atmospheric conditions will occasionally cause mayonnaise to curdle as you make it. If this should happen, remove it from the blender, put another egg in the blender, turn it on, and slowly pour in the curdled mayonnaise.

Makes 1¼ cups.

Tofu Sour Cream

This makes a tasty substitute for sour cream in cooking and other places that call for plain sour cream. For more emphatically flavored tofu-based concoctions to use as dips or in place of mayonnaise, see below.

You won't need the water with soft tofu, but with firm tofu you probably will.

❧

BLENDER: place all ingredients except tofu in blender. Add tofu bit by bit, blending smooth with each addition. If the mixture stops moving, turn off blender and stir, then blend again. Add tofu and repeat until all is included.

PROCESSOR: put it all in and process until creamy smooth.

Makes 1½ cups.

¼ cup lemon juice
2 tablespoons oil
1 tablespoon light miso
¼ teaspoon mustard
(2 tablespoons water)
1 tablespoon shoyu
  (or other flavoring)
1 cup tofu (½ pound)

Tofu Mayonnaises

Follow the directions for Tofu Sour Cream above, using the ingredients listed.

RUSSIAN

1 tablespoon white miso
1 tablespoon prepared
  mustard
2 tablespoons oil
3 tablespoons cider vinegar
dash pepper
pinch chili powder
½ teaspoon dill weed
⅛ teaspoon paprika
½ pound tofu

ORIENTAL

1 tablespoon shoyu
  or dark miso
3 tablespoons rice vinegar
white part of 2 scallions,
  minced
2 teaspoons ginger, minced
sliver fresh garlic, minced
2 tablespoons oil
½ pound tofu

FRENCH ONION

2 tablespoons oil sautéed with:
  ½ small onion, minced
  1 clove garlic
  ½ small carrot, grated
  pinch chili powder
  ⅛ teaspoon paprika
2 tablespoons cider vinegar
⅛ teaspoon black pepper
½ pound tofu

Cream Sauce

*1, 2, or 3 tablespoons
each butter and flour
(for thin, medium,
and thick sauces)
1 cup hot milk
¼ teaspoon salt
pinch nutmeg*

Cream sauce is unarguably delicious and versatile. We seldom use the whole amount of butter, and find that although cooking the flour with less butter requires more determined stirring, the sauce comes out tasting great. The best flour is whole wheat pastry flour, but any whole wheat flour works fine.

ʔ⟨

Melt butter in pan. Stir in flour and cook 3 minutes over low-medium heat, stirring constantly. Add milk slowly while stirring, and bring to boil to thicken. If you can, set the pan over a very low heat or even in the oven for a while; the sauce will get richer and thicker. If the sauce lumps up, a spin in the blender will set it right.

Makes 1 cup; less if you simmer it afterward.

SWEET AND SOUR MUSTARD SAUCE: To 1 cup basic Cream Sauce, add this mixture: 1½ teaspoons cider vinegar, 1 teaspoon honey or brown sugar, 1 teaspoon mustard powder (or 1 tablespoon Dijon mustard). Very good on sweetish vegetables like carrots or green beans or on greens, especially chard.

SAUCE DIJON: Make the sauce above, omitting the sweetener and vinegar. Add 2 tomatoes, quartered, a sautéed onion, 2 cloves garlic, and ½ cup of Madeira or port. Simmer until tomatoes are tender, stirring often, and put through a sieve or food mill. Try this on asparagus!

CHEESE SAUCE: Stir ½ cup sharp grated cheese into 1 cup Cream Sauce, either the basic version or that which follows. If you're using cheddar cheese, you can enhance the cheddary flavor by adding ¼ teaspoon (or more) of chili powder, cooked briefly in a teaspoon of butter. Half a teaspoon of prepared mustard works to the same end. With Swiss cheese, a tablespoon of Parmesan rounds the flavor nicely, and a little dill weed complements it well. Either version can be further garnished with chopped parsley or peppers.

Cream Sauce with Onion

Even if you are going to use 3 tablespoons of flour for a very thick sauce, when you start with the sautéed onion it is easy to get away with using just 1 tablespoon of butter, because the onion will let the flour cook nicely without lumps. The onion supplies flavor too—a help with lower-fat sauces.

ે

Melt the butter as in the Cream Sauce recipe and add ¼ to 1 cup chopped onion. (Add garlic with the onion if you want to.) Sauté the onion in the butter very gently, until onion is soft and slightly golden—this takes some time and some stirring. Stir the flour into the sautéed onion and cook them together for 3 minutes, again stirring. Add milk and proceed in the usual way, bringing the milk to a boil—more stirring—and then simmer gently to enhance and marry the flavors if you have time. Puree if you like.

Cream Sauce without Butter

A cream sauce made without butter isn't really a sauce, but it can make a working base for cheese sauces or sauces with other very flavorful additions. If it lumps up on you, blend it.

ે

Toast flour lightly in a dry pan, then add the milk and boil to thicken. The flour needs toasting or it will taste raw, but if you toast it very much, the sauce will get brown. The more the flour is toasted, the less it will thicken your sauce. You can brown the flour and use this method to make brown gravy—a flavorful way to go—but you will need twice as much flour for the thickness you want.

For creamy sauces, you can also use corn flour (untoasted); or thicken milk with cornstarch, as suggested in the Buttermilk Sauces on the next page. As with the above, this makes a working base; it isn't flavorful enough to be a sauce on its own.

Buttermilk Sauces

Here is a genuinely satisfying alternative sauce. Good buttermilk has a taste reminiscent of sour cream, and in sauces this works very nicely, whether you make a normal cream sauce (using buttermilk instead of milk) or the cornstarch version below. If you use flour, the sauce will stand up better to reheating. The cornstarch version is a little quicker because you don't have to cook cornstarch before adding the liquid, as you do flour. If you prefer, you can use arrowroot instead of cornstarch, but arrowroot sauces can become gluey.

BASIC SAUCE

1 cup cold buttermilk
1 tablespoon cornstarch
2 teaspoons shoyu, to taste

For a medium sauce, mix ingredients and bring to boil in a heavy skillet. Use a spiral whisk or a fork and keep stirring vigorously as you bring the sauce to a boil. Let it simmer gently to thicken. It will curdle, but don't panic: as you stir, it will smooth out and come back together.

This quietly tangy sauce can stand on its own with anything interesting or flavorful—potatoes, say, or a pasta dish that has tasty vegetables in it and sesame crumbs or cheese on top.

Stroganoff Sauce

1 cup buttermilk
1 tablespoon cornstarch

1 small onion, chopped
(1 clove garlic)
1 tablespoon butter
1/3–1 1/2 cups mushrooms,
   sliced

1/4 teaspoon salt
   or 1 tablespoon shoyu
black pepper

Combine buttermilk and cornstarch and set aside. Sauté onion and garlic in butter until soft. Crush the garlic with a fork. Stir in mushrooms and cook just until tender. Remove mushrooms and juices from the pan and pour in the buttermilk mixture. Stir and cook until thickened, then return mushrooms and their juices to the pan. Season with salt (or shoyu) and pepper. This really tastes like a sour cream sauce, even with only a few mushrooms.

Tomato-Buttermilk Sauce

This delicious sauce is well received by the younger set. Its fruity, cheesy taste is especially good on noodles. Great for vegetables too.

☙

Mix buttermilk and cornstarch and set aside. Sauté onion and garlic in oil. Crush garlic with a fork. Add tomato paste and basil, then buttermilk mixture. Bring to a boil, stirring, and cook until thick and smooth.

Makes 1 cup.

1 cup buttermilk
1 tablespoon cornstarch

½–1 small onion, chopped
(1 clove garlic)
2 teaspoons oil or butter

2 tablespoons tomato paste
½ teaspoon basil

Sunshine Sauce

Sauté onions in oil just until soft. Add turmeric and cook gently for a minute.

Stir cold buttermilk into cornstarch, then add to the spiced onions and bring to a boil, stirring. Cook and stir until smooth. Stir in the cheese, and when it has warmed enough to melt into the sauce, check to see if salt is wanted. Just before serving, stir in the coriander leaves if you have them.

A lovely piquant sauce for vegetables, especially those that are a little sweet, like broccoli.

2 green onions with tops,
  chopped
2 teaspoons oil
⅛ teaspoon turmeric

1 cup buttermilk
1 tablespoon cornstarch

1 tablespoon grated
  Parmesan cheese
(1 tablespoon chopped
  fresh coriander leaves)

Tangy Cheese Sauce

Mix the buttermilk and cornstarch and stir while you bring to a boil. Simmer to smooth and thicken. Stir in cheeses and check for salt. Good additions: dill weed with Swiss cheese; chopped parsley with anything. Very good on greens, any of the cole family (broccoli, cauliflower, kale, etc.), on green beans, or even on toast.

1 cup buttermilk
1 tablespoon cornstarch

½ cup cottage cheese
¼ cup grated sharp cheese
  (but not cheddar)

HUNGARIAN SAUCE: Halve an onion lengthwise and slice it crosswise paper-thin. Sauté in butter or oil until golden. Set the onion aside while you prepare the sauce above, with or without the cheese. When the sauce is smooth, stir in the onions. Garnish the final serving liberally with paprika.

Potato Dill Sauce

½ onion, chopped
1 clove garlic
1 tablespoon oil or butter
1 cup vegetable stock
1 potato, cubed
1 teaspoon dill weed

½ teaspoon salt, to taste
black pepper
1 tablespoon chopped parsley

Excellent on any winter greens: broccoli, Swiss chard, brussels sprouts, kale. This sauce, and Cheddy (below), are so low in fat that you can use rather a lot without getting too much. Both are good thinned with broth or milk to make soup.

ɝ

Sauté onion and garlic in oil. Add stock, potato, and dill weed. Cook partially covered until potato is soft, then puree. Add seasonings and parsley. Thin with stock or milk if desired.

Makes 2½ cups.

CHEDDY SAUCE: A delicious sauce that seems very rich and cheesy, even when you don't include the cheese!

ɝ

Follow the directions for the sauce above, except that when the onion is nearly done, add ½ to 1 teaspoon chili powder and cook about 1 minute. Add a small carrot, cut up, to the cooking vegetables. Omit dill weed.

Puree. Stir in ¼ cup grated cheddar cheese and check salt.

Makes 2¾ cup.

Mushroom Sauce

½ onion, chopped
1 clove garlic
1 tablespoon oil or butter
1 cup sliced mushrooms
3 tablespoons flour, toasted
1–1½ cups water
1 tablespoon shoyu
½ teaspoon molasses
¼ teaspoon savory
¼ teaspoon thyme
dash pepper

Sauté onions and garlic in oil or butter until soft. Mash the garlic with a fork. Add the mushrooms and simmer 5 minutes over low heat. Stir in the flour and add water, shoyu, and molasses. Cook, stirring, until thickened. Season with herbs and spices. Adjust to taste.

Makes 1 cup thick or 1½ cups medium.

Wickedly Good Sauce

Sauté onion in oil with the whole garlic. When the onion is tender, crush the garlic with a fork. Add the ginger and pepper and cook gently a minute more.

Stir in the peanut butter and shoyu, then water and celery leaves. Stir until smooth; then simmer about 5 minutes.

Add the tofu and cashews and heat through. Serve over steamed vegetables.

Makes ¾ to 1 cup.

¼ onion, chopped
1 teaspoon oil
1 clove garlic
½ teaspoon minced ginger
¼ green pepper

1 tablespoon peanut butter
1 tablespoon shoyu
½ cup water (or more)
*2 tablespoons celery
  leaves, chopped*

¼ pound firm tofu, cubed
*2 tablespoons toasted
  cashew pieces*

Yogurt Sauce

Serve this simple, surprisingly delicious sauce cold, at room temperature, or *gently* heated. Don't boil! Very good on vegetables, with falafel in Pocket Bread, or as a dip for raw vegetables. Makes a tasty dressing for potato salad too.

Sauté onion in oil. Toast sesame seeds in another skillet, stirring often to keep them from burning. Put all ingredients in blender or food processor and puree until smooth. Thin with additional yogurt or buttermilk if desired.

Makes 1 to 1½ cups.

1 chopped onion
1 tablespoon oil

¼ cup sesame seeds

1 tablespoon lemon juice
⅛ teaspoon salt
dash pepper
½–1 cup yogurt

Tomato Sauce

½ onion, chopped
1 clove garlic
2 tablespoons oil

1 small carrot, grated
2 tablespoons chopped
  green pepper
1 bay leaf
½ teaspoon oregano
½ teaspoon thyme
1 teaspoon basil
2 tablespoons chopped
  fresh parsley
2 cups tomatoes,
  coarsely chopped
1 six-ounce can tomato paste
1 teaspoon salt
⅛ teaspoon pepper
(¼ teaspoon honey)

One of our most praised recipes. Use vegetable broth to thin it to the right consistency for spaghetti, or use it "as is" for dishes like pizza.

Fresh tomatoes are wonderful, of course, but if they aren't in season, use canned. (Check the label to avoid added salt and sugar.)

❧

Sauté onion and garlic clove in oil until onion is soft. Crush garlic with a fork.

Add carrot, green pepper, bay leaf, and herbs. Stir well, then add the tomatoes, tomato paste, and seasonings. Simmer 15 minutes. Remove the bay leaf.

Makes about 3 cups.

VARIATIONS

MEXICAN SAUCE: When onion is nearly done, stir in 1 teaspoon cumin and 1 teaspoon chili powder, or to taste. Increase oregano to 1 teaspoon.

ITALIAN SAUCE: Add a pinch of fennel. Increase oregano to 1 teaspoon.

Quick Spicy Tomato Sauce

½ cup chopped shallot
  or red onion
2 cloves garlic
1 tablespoon oil
1 tablespoon coriander
  powder
1 teaspoon cumin
¼ teaspoon turmeric
½ teaspoon salt

3 cups chopped tomatoes

Sauté shallot or onion with whole garlic cloves until soft. Add spices and continue cooking and stirring for a minute or so, until spices are fragrant and onion begins to brown. Stir in the tomatoes, cover, and cook gently at least until tomatoes have turned to liquid. Force through food mill or sieve.

Makes 2 cups.

Good Gravy

Delicious, rich-tasting gravy, brown and fragrant with or without the mushrooms. If you cook beans for Soy Spread, you'll have plenty of the makings: the thick broth strained off after the beans are tender. Perfect with potatoes or on grain, even on vegetables.

❧

Toast and stir the flour in a dry pan until it is quite brown. Remove the flour and sauté the onion in oil, adding garlic and mushrooms if desired. Mash the garlic with a fork. Stir in the toasted flour, then the stock. Bring to a boil and simmer for a few minutes, adding the salt, marjoram, and pepper. Check the seasonings. Thin with water, broth, or more soy stock if desired.

Makes 1 to 2 cups.

¼ cup whole wheat flour
1 small onion, chopped
(1 or more whole cloves garlic)
(¼ to 1 cup mushrooms, sliced)
1–2 tablespoons oil

1 cup soy stock (cooking water from soybeans)
½ teaspoon salt
½ teaspoon marjoram
black pepper

YEAST BUTTER We were going to let this sinfully rich sauce slink into oblivion with this edition, and no doubt it deserves the fate. But its advocates insist that Yeast Butter alone has made life possible on many a day. So here it is, just on the QT: the "health food" of the sixties, become the wild indulgence of the eighties.

Melt a cube of (yes) margarine (½ cup). Add 2 tablespoons torula yeast and stir. Drizzle over broccoli or summer or winter squash; or let it cool and use on your toast the next day. Phew.

Lemon Butter

This is one of the nicest things that could happen to a pile of fresh, steamed asparagus spears. Try it on carrots, too, and broccoli, but use a light hand. It's rich.

❧

Juice the lemon and zest half of the peel. Melt the butter and pour it into a small blender jar along with the lemon juice and peel. Blend smooth and fluffy.

Makes about ⅓ cup.

1 lemon, well scrubbed
¼ cup butter

Heartier Dishes

In this section are one-dish meals, international delicacies, casseroles—generally, fanciful or traditional preparations that are definitely greater than the sum of their parts. These are the recipes you pull out when you are stumped, when the refrigerator is full of leftovers, or when wary nonvegetarian relatives are coming to dinner. This section in particular really highlights the marvelous good fortune of today's vegetarian cook, who has access to such an array of ethnic cuisines that the possibilities are endless.

In their traditional form, many of these dishes are loaded with calories and fat. We have reduced butter, eggs, and cheese wherever possible, and substituted low-fat milk products. These dishes are unquestionably special, but they will let you walk away from the kitchen with a clear conscience—and from the table with clear arteries.

Whole-Grain Pasta

Whole-grain pasta is available everywhere now, and you can use it anywhere you used to use white-flour pasta, giving all the advantages of whole grain over white. If it is made from normal hard red wheat, the color of the noodles is a light brown. This makes tasty spaghetti and lasagna, and the ribbon noodles are very good. It usually needs longer cooking than its paler counterparts.

But just as hard red wheat is good for bread, and soft white wheat (the grains themselves are white, not red) good for pastry flour, there is durum wheat for pasta. (Semolina, from which the best white-flour pasta is made, is durum's refined version.) Durum wheat's grains are yellow instead of red, so it makes noodles that are a pale creamy-golden color—something that seems to reassure those who are new to whole-grain pastas. The noodles keep their shape well, and they are tender and mellow in taste. There *are* some who object to red-wheat whole wheat pasta, but nobody has anything but praise for durum whole wheat pasta. Try it—and if you make your own pasta, ask for whole wheat durum flour; you won't believe the difference there.

Pasta-making is challenging fun when you are just learning, and easy fun once you have mastered the art. There are pasta-making machines plain and fancy now, and if you hanker for exotic varieties or like to serve noodles often, they are a bargain. We have the oldest, simplest kind of machine, and use it frequently for some of the dishes that follow. Store-bought noodles are perfectly adequate substitutes, however, so if you are thrifty with your time, don't pass up the noodle recipes just because they say to make your own.

Buckwheat noodles deserve special mention. Their assertive flavor is an old favorite in Japan, but new to many of us in this country. If you get the 100 percent buckwheat flour noodles, expect them to be very fragile and *very* flavorful. For a milder-flavored noodle that is more resilient, look for a mixture of buckwheat and wheat flours. Serve them with Chinese Vegetables or in miso soup, or just stir into the cooked, drained noodles a cup or so of stir-fried vegetables like onion, peas, celery, or cauliflower; add shoyu and a sprinkling of sesame seeds.

Cooking Noodles

Cook noodles uncovered in a *big* pan with 1 quart of briskly boiling water and 1 teaspoon salt for each ¼ pound of dry noodles. Adding oil to the water helps keep the pot from boiling over, but isn't necessary if there is enough water and you keep it boiling. How long it takes will depend on the thickness of the pasta: 5 minutes for very thin, 20 minutes for thick! There are classic tests, including throwing the noodles against the wall (if it sticks, it is done); but the best is to bite a piece. There should be a trace of resistance to the teeth—*al dente*, as the Italians say. Drain the noodles, keeping them wet. No need to rinse unless they're to be used in a salad. Serve—or at least sauce—at once.

As a rule of thumb for a main dish, allow ½ pound of dry noodles and about 1 cup of sauce (depending on the sauce) for 4 people.

½ pound raw noodles = 4 cups cooked, approximately.

Homemade Noodles

It is easy to make good noodles, and in fact, fresh homemade noodles are as much better than the store-bought kind as your own bread is better than store-bought. If you are content with simple ribbon noodles, you need no more equipment than a rolling pin, a knife, and a table, and that's a good place to start.

Including whole eggs in your pasta adds a rich flavor, and noodles are surely one of the more delicious ways to eat eggs. Egg helps noodles hold their shape; to lower the fat and cholesterol, egg white serves this purpose as well as whole eggs. For simple noodling with a flavorful sauce—spaghetti, for example—the egg is completely unnecessary; and once you are adept at making noodles, even Canneloni and other ambitious performances can be achieved perfectly well without eggs.

❧

FOR FOUR CUPS COOKED NOODLES

1½ cups fine whole wheat flour
1 teaspoon salt
2 eggs
2 tablespoons water
   OR
1½ cups fine whole wheat flour
1 teaspoon salt
¾ cup medium-hot water

Measure the flour and salt and mix them in a bowl or on the tabletop, making a mound with a well in the center. Put the liquids (water and/or egg) in the well, and beginning in the center, mix them with flour to make a stiff dough—stiffer than bread dough. If it is too soft, you'll have trouble rolling them out, trouble moving them around, and trouble drying. If it is too stiff, however, there is a lot more work for you in rolling—so don't aim for a rock.

Knead the dough until it is supple, about 10 minutes. Large batches take more time. For easier rolling, cover the ball of dough after kneading and let it rest for about an hour. Use your rolling pin (if you don't have a machine) to roll the dough thin. If you are making more than just a small amount, keep the part of the dough you are not actually working on covered up so that it doesn't dry out. Use as much flour on the board (or with the machine) as you need to keep the dough from sticking—no harm done by that. In fact, as you come to the finishing stages, keep the noodles floury; they won't be likely to stick together.

Cut into ribbons or whatever shape suits your recipe. By hand, the little zig-zag rolling cutters make life easier in this department (even a pizza cutter is better than a knife). Cook at once, or let them rest a couple of hours; or dry thoroughly on cookie sheets, after which they will keep for weeks if stored in an airtight container kept in a cool place. Fresh is best of all, though. (Quaintly appealing as wooden chairbacks draped with drying noodles may be, we haven't found the practice very useful. If the noodles are thin enough to be tender, they are also fragile enough to break.)

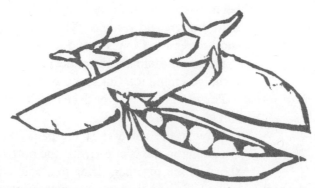

Hungarian Noodles

This delicious noodle dish is one of our longtime favorites. For everyday, we use vegetables on the sweet side—diced carrots, green beans, broccoli—but this dish really rises to magnificence with artichoke hearts (or asparagus), tiny fresh peas, and lots of coriander leaves.

Cut the onion into thin slivers and sauté in the butter until soft. Add the flour and cook, stirring, for 2 minutes. Stir in the buttermilk and cheeses and gently heat just until the mixture comes to a boil.

Preheat oven to 350°F.

Cook the noodles and drain them. Stir them and the vegetables (and coriander, if desired) into the sauce. Put into a greased baking dish and bake about 15 to 20 minutes, until bubbly.

Serves 4.

1 large onion
2 tablespoons butter
1/4 cup whole wheat flour
2 1/2 cups thick buttermilk
2 cups low-fat cottage cheese
1/4 cup grated Parmesan cheese

noodles to make 2 cups cooked (1/4 pound raw)
1 1/2 cups cooked diced vegetables

(1/4 cup chopped coriander leaves)

Vermicelli Florentine

1 large onion
1 tablespoon butter

3 medium red-ripe tomatoes
2/3 cup small peas
1–2 bunches spinach
(12 oz; 3–4 quarts of
leaves)

2¼ oz thin whole
wheat vermicelli or
linguine

½ cup buttermilk
2 teaspoons cornstarch
1–2 teaspoons shoyu
or ¼ teaspoon salt

(grated Parmesan, if desired)

This is a delicate, satisfying dish that can be exceptional with excellent tomatoes and homemade noodles. As written, it makes a light meal for two; if you want to double the recipe, use a wide dutch oven instead of a skillet.

Cut the onion in half and slice paper-thin. Use a large, heavy skillet to sauté the onion in the butter, keeping heat low and stirring very frequently until the onion is golden. If the pan begins to brown, turn the onion out, wash the pan, add a little more butter, and resume. When the onion is soft and evenly cooked, remove from heat and set aside.

Prepare the tomatoes by removing seed and juice (and the peel, if you've a mind to). Cut into 1″ chunks.

Put water on to boil for the pasta. Wash and stem the spinach. Cut leaves into ¼″ strips.

Remove the onion from the pan, and with the golden film remaining in the cool pan, stir the buttermilk, cornstarch, and shoyu or salt together. Bring to a boil, stirring all the while. It will curdle and then come together into a smooth sauce. Add tomatoes and peas. Heat gently.

Add salt to the boiling noodle water and then add the noodles. Start stirring the spinach gently into the sauce and tomato mixture. When noodles are done, drain and stir them in also, working to get the spinach and noodles evenly dispersed. (A couple of oversized forks are useful here.) Taste for salt. Add cheese if desired and serve *at once*.

Serves 2 handily with salad, French Bread, and dessert.

Canneloni

These are large homemade noodles with a delicately flavored cheese filling. The saving grace of this admittedly time-consuming marvel (wait till you taste it!) is that it can be done in several steps ahead of time. The whole dish can be assembled early and baked later.

ॐ

To make the filling, combine Parmesan, mozzarella, and cottage cheese or ricotta with 1 beaten egg, nutmeg, and ¼ cup of the cream sauce. Reserve remaining cream sauce for topping.

Wash spinach and steam briefly to wilt. Drain well and chop fine. Combine with cheese mixture and refrigerate.

To prepare noodles, mix flour and salt together and place in a mound on a flat surface. Make a well in the mound and drop in the 2 unbeaten eggs and the water. Use your fingers to work these ingredients together swiftly and knead well until smooth. This will take about 10 minutes. Cover the dough and let it rest 10 minutes before rolling it out.

Bring 3 quarts of water to a boil in a wide, shallow pan, and add a teaspoon of salt and a tablespoon of oil to keep the noodles from sticking together as they cook.

Divide dough into two balls. On a floured surface roll dough out paper-thin, turning it around and over frequently. Keep turning and rolling dough until it's about 1/16″ thick; or roll with a pasta-making machine at the second-thinnest setting.

Cut dough into ten 4″ × 6″ rectangles and drop a few at a time into simmering water. Keep pushing the noodles back under the water. When the noodles are tender, remove with slotted spoon. Put them carefully on a wet baking sheet.

Preheat oven to 350°F.

Fill noodles with a generous ¼ cup of filling each and roll them up. Place seam-side down in a greased casserole. Spoon the remaining cream sauce on top and dribble tomato sauce over all. Bake for 20 minutes, then sprinkle with parsley.

Serves 4 to 6.

FILLING

¾ cup grated *Parmesan cheese*
½ cup grated *mozzarella cheese*
2½ cups *low-fat cottage cheese and/or ricotta*
1 *egg*
¼ teaspoon *nutmeg*
1 cup medium *Cream Sauce (page 242) seasoned with 1 bay leaf and a pinch of nutmeg*

1 bunch *spinach*

NOODLES

1¾ cups *whole wheat flour*
½ teaspoon *salt*
2 unbeaten *eggs*
4 tablespoons *water*

TOPPING

reserved *cream sauce*
1 cup *Tomato Sauce (page 248)*

½ cup chopped *parsley*

Lasagna al Forno

¾ pound whole wheat
   or whole wheat–soy
   lasagna noodles
6 cups Tomato Sauce,
   Italian Style (page 248)

2 cups cottage cheese
3 cups grated mozzarella
   or Swiss cheese (10 oz)
1–3 bunches spinach
½ cup grated Parmesan
   cheese
¾ cup chopped toasted
   walnuts or almonds

Perhaps the most favorite of all our casseroles, this lasagna is lighter than most but plenty fancy for company, and a sure hit even with nonvegetarian guests.

The spinach can be added either raw or cooked. If raw, one large bunch will be enough: wash, shake dry, and chop fine. Cooking ahead lets you use a larger amount—three big bunches or even more. Cook very briefly with only the water that clings to the leaves, drain well; chop fine.

For everyday dinners, the greens can be Swiss chard or even nippier ones like kale. Any kind of cheese is fine. In fact, crumbled tofu can be good, provided your sauce is very flavorful. A topping of bread crumbs tossed with a little olive oil is delicious and keeps the top from drying out. You can lower the fat further by cutting back on the cheese and using less oil in the sauce.

᠀

Cook noodles in a very large pan of boiling, salted water until *almost* tender: they will cook more in the oven, absorbing liquid from the sauce as they do, and if they are slightly undercooked at this point, they'll hold together better while you're assembling the dish. After draining the noodles, it can be helpful to spread them out on a towel or waxed paper, or submerge them in cold water.

Grease a 9″ × 13″ × 2½″ baking dish. Spread a thin layer of sauce in the bottom, and then a layer of noodles, lengthwise. Keep the best of the noodles for the top and use broken ones in the middle. Each layer of noodles should lie crosswise to the one below it.

On the layer of noodles, spread the first layer of filling: one half the cottage cheese, one third of the nuts, one fourth of the Parmesan; then a coating of sauce. Layer noodles again, then the spinach and most of the mozzarella, and sauce. More noodles, another cheese and nuts layer, and your prettiest noodles across the top. Add sauce and the rest of the nuts and cheese for the top.

Bake at 350°F for 30 to 45 minutes (if your ingredients were hot, the shorter time will be enough); then let stand 10 minutes before cutting—otherwise it will be too runny to hold together, and too hot to eat.

Serves 8.

Poppyseed Noodles

Quick and zippy. To make a dairy-free version, replace the Mock Sour Cream with Tofu Sour Cream (page 241).

❧

Cook noodles in boiling salted water until tender and drain.

Preheat oven to 350°F.

Combine Mock Sour Cream, poppy seeds, and noodles. Place in greased 9″ × 13″ baking dish. Sprinkle with Parmesan and paprika if desired.

Bake about 20 minutes.

Makes 4 servings.

½ pound whole wheat ribbon noodles
1½ cups Mock Sour Cream (page 240)
1 tablespoon poppy seeds
½ teaspoon salt
(grated Parmesan cheese)
(paprika)

Lazy Pirogi

A scrumptious cabbage dish to serve over whole wheat noodles. Many people who find cabbage hard to digest have no trouble with sauerkraut—the pickling fermentation has done some of the work already! Buy sauerkraut in jars rather than cans to prevent the possibility of getting lead from the can's seam. We suggest also that when you use a brand you haven't tried before, taste it before using. The salt level may be different from what you expect. If it's too salty, you can drain and rinse before using, if necessary—but often it will be going over potatoes (or noodles, as here), when it might supply the salt for the whole dish.

1 large onion
1 stalk celery
6 fresh mushrooms
2 tablespoons oil
1 cup (packed) drained sauerkraut
¼ pound whole wheat ribbon noodles

❧

Chop onion, celery, and mushrooms. Starting with onion, sauté in oil until onions are tender. Add ½ cup hot water and simmer for 10 minutes.

Meanwhile, cook noodles until tender in unsalted boiling water; drain.

Stir together sautéed vegetables with sauerkraut and noodles. Heat through and serve.

Makes 4 servings.

Sandy's Macaroni

1 small bunch scallions,
  sliced thin
1 or 2 garlic cloves, minced
1 bell pepper, diced (red,
  green, or some of each)
½ cup sliced mushrooms
1 stalk celery, diced
2 tablespoons butter
¾ teaspoon salt
dash black pepper
¼ cup chopped parsley

¼ cup whole wheat flour
2 cups low-fat milk
(2 tablespoons grated
  Parmesan cheese)
½ pound whole wheat
  macaroni or noodles

This is a very light, low-fat alternative to macaroni and cheese—one we serve often. Toasting the flour separately lets you use about half the fat you'd need otherwise. The long, slow simmering draws the flavors of the vegetables out into the sauce.

❧

Sauté scallions, garlic, bell pepper, mushrooms, and celery in butter in a heavy pan for 5 minutes; then add 1 cup of boiling water, salt, pepper, and parsley. Bring to a boil, reduce heat, and simmer covered for 20 to 30 minutes.

Meanwhile, toast flour in a small, dry skillet over low heat, stirring constantly, for 5 minutes or so—just until it starts to smell toasty. It shouldn't change color.

Add some of the vegetable–water mixture to the flour, stirring to avoid lumps; then add this back to the pot along with the milk (and cheese, if desired). Bring just to a boil; then reduce heat and simmer uncovered for 10 or 15 minutes, until sauce is creamy and reduced to about 2½ cups. Cook pasta; drain and mix with sauce. Serve immediately.

Makes 4 generous servings.

Blini

2 teaspoons active dry yeast
  (1 packet, ¼ oz or 7 g)
¼ cup warm water

½ cup buckwheat flour
½ cup whole wheat flour
1 cup milk, lukewarm
1 teaspoon honey
2 tablespoons oil
¼ teaspoon salt
2 egg whites and one yolk,
  beaten slightly

These are buckwheat crepes, served in Russia (long ago, at any rate) during the week before Lent. Serve with Mock Sour Cream, chopped hard-boiled egg, and chopped sweet onions. Very good alongside steamed beets or cabbage.

❧

Dissolve yeast in water. In a medium-size bowl, stir together buckwheat and whole wheat flour, milk, honey, oil, salt, eggs, and yeast mixture. Beat until smooth, cover, and let rise in warm place free from drafts until bubbly—about 1 hour.

Stir down. Heat a 6″ crepe pan or griddle, lightly oiled, until a drop of water dances on its surface. Drop batter by spoonfuls onto griddle, spreading it around by tilting the pan. If batter seems thick, more like pancake than crepe batter, add a bit more milk to thin it down. Cook crepes until top is beginning to look dry, then turn over and brown on second side. Keep blini warm in a damp towel placed in a warm oven until ready to serve.

Makes about 12.

Crepes

Crepes can turn nearly any vegetable dish into an event: not just creamed spinach but Ratatouille, or asparagus with grated Parmesan, or even more mundane choices like chopped broccoli and cauliflower, nicely cooked and seasoned. Top with a light cheese or mushroom sauce. Add tiny peas to nearly any filling if you need to make it go farther.

As soon as you roll them up in a crepe, vegetables become interesting to children (and others) who might otherwise not find them so, and since the batter is so easy to prepare, and nutritious, that's a bargain. Keep extra batter in the refrigerator to use in the next couple of days. If it turns dark on top, just shake the jar and forge ahead.

1 cup milk (or half water, half milk)
¾ cup whole wheat flour (finely ground or with bran sifted out)
2 eggs or 3 egg whites
½ teaspoon salt

ેર

Put all crepe ingredients in blender and mix on low speed, or use an electric or rotary beater. For best results let batter stand an hour, or refrigerate overnight.

Use a 7″ skillet with sloped sides, or a nonstick pan or seasoned griddle. Heat over medium-high flame as for pancakes. If there's any chance of sticking, use a little butter or oil spread thin with a paper napkin between pours.

Pour a scant ¼ cup of batter on the pan. Tilt pan as you pour so the batter spreads evenly on the bottom. Brown the bottom of the crepe lightly, and as the top becomes visibly dry—about 1 minute—turn it over and cook the second side until it too is lightly browned. Let each one cool, and overlap them on a platter. The pretty spotted side is the traditional outside for the crepe. (If you think the crepes could be thinner, add more milk or turn the pan faster.)

Makes about 12.

DAIRY-FREE CREPES

Both the egg and the milk make a significant contribution to the flavor and character of crepes, but you can produce a very satisfactory crepe without them, using the ingredients listed here. (If you really want *delicious* non-dairy crepes, though, learn to make Dosas, page 97.)

1 cup finely ground whole wheat flour
1½ cups water
½ teaspoon baking powder
½ teaspoon salt
1 tablespoon oil

ેર

Beat or blend very well. Follow the directions for pouring given above.

Blintzes

1 recipe Crepes

CHEESE FILLING
2 cups baker's cheese,
   ricotta cheese, or
   low-fat cottage cheese
1 tablespoon brown sugar
1 tablespoon melted butter
½ teaspoon salt
2 tablespoons chopped
   toasted almonds
1 tablespoon raisins
(Add ½ teaspoon cinnamon
   or ½ teaspoon vanilla
   or 1 tablespoon lemon
   juice.)
OR
(Substitute a dash of pepper
   and ½ teaspoon paprika
   for sugar and raisins.)

We like to serve cheese-filled blintzes with yogurt and apple-sauce. Tangy Cheese Sauce (page 245) goes well with either the savory or the simple vegetable fillings. Mock Sour Cream (page 240) is a fine topping for all three versions.

❧

Prepare crepes as described in the recipe above, but *do not cook them on the second side, and don't stack them.*

Combine filling ingredients. Preheat oven to 400°F.

Put 2 big tablespoons of filling on the cooked side of each crepe. Turn in opposite sides and then roll up. Place seam-side down in a well-buttered baking pan and bake for 20 minutes. After the first 10 or 15 minutes, when the bottom is brown, turn to brown the other side. Some filling may escape from the crepes, but they will be just as good. Instead of baking the blintzes, you may brown them on a nonstick or iron skillet if you prefer.

Each filling recipe makes enough for about 12 crepes, which will serve 4 to 6.

SIMPLE VEGETABLE FILLING FOR BLINTZES

Prepare 1½ cups of your favorite combination of vegetables. Cut them quite small or grate them. Cook and season to taste. Try any of these:

   Creamed spinach and celery
   Asparagus and green onion
   Green pepper and eggplant or okra
   Shredded cabbage, carrots, and onions
   Fresh corn, green onion, and parsley

Sauté onions in oil just lightly. Stir in green beans. Add stock and bring to a boil. Simmer for 10 minutes or more, until beans are tender. If there is too much liquid, drain and save for the sauce topping.

Combine beans and onions with remaining ingredients. Cool until ready to fill the blintzes.

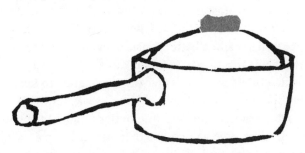

*3 small green onions,
    sliced fine*
1 tablespoon oil
1 cup finely cut green beans
*¼ cup vegetable stock
    or water*
*½ cup baker's cheese,
    ricotta cheese, or
    low-fat cottage cheese*
½ teaspoon salt
*1 tablespoon grated
    Parmesan cheese*
*½ cup well-cooked green
    split peas*

Spinach Crepes

This dressy, delicious dish is always well received, and because it can be prepared in stages ahead, it's great for special occasions. For every day, though, unless you cut some corners along the way, it is not a low-fat presentation. There *are* corners to cut: use whites instead of one or both yolks in the crepes; make a lower-fat cream sauce (we often use the Cream Sauce with Onion here, keeping the butter to a bare minimum.) Balance the meal by serving low-fat foods alongside: baked yams or winter squash, for example, and fruit salad for dessert.

❧

Preheat oven to 350°F. Grease a 9″ × 13″ baking dish. Place a generous ⅓ cup of creamed spinach across the lower middle of each crepe, roll it into a cylinder, and place in the baking dish, making two rows of 6 each. Pour the sauce over the top, down the middle of the rows of crepes—or, if you like plenty of sauce, thin the sauce with more milk and cover the crepes completely. Sprinkle with cheese and nutmeg, if desired.

Bake about 15 minutes—long enough to heat through. Makes about 12 crepes, enough for 4 to 6 people.

1 recipe Crepes
*1 double recipe Creamed
    Spinach (page 214)*
*1 cup thin Cream Sauce
    (or more) (page 242)*
*(grated Parmesan
    or Swiss cheese)*
(nutmeg)

*A little lemon zest blended
into the crepe batter gives a
nice lift to the flavor.*

Piroshki

*4 cups whole wheat bread
  flour, finely ground*
*2 cups whole wheat pastry
  flour*
2½ teaspoons salt

*2 teaspoons active dry yeast
  (1 packet, ¼ oz, 7g)*
½ cup warm water

1 teaspoon honey or sugar
2 cups buttermilk

more water as needed

This makes 20 each of 2 fillings. The piroshki are about 4″ across, with maybe 3 tablespoons of filling in each one. The dough makes a crust that, while not crispy like piecrust, is nevertheless not thickly bready, and doesn't toughen even if it sits awhile.

❧

Mix the flours and salt in a large bowl, making a well in the center. Dissolve the yeast in the warm water. Mix the sweetener into the buttermilk and pour it into the well in the flour. Stir the liquid in the well to make a batter consistency; then add the yeast and mix the whole together to form the dough. It should be very soft; so while you knead, use water on your hands to keep the dough from sticking, adding water to it in this way until you have a supple, well-kneaded ball. With the buttermilk and the pastry flour, the kneading time will be less than usual. Keep at it until the dough is smooth and elastic, though, or it will not have enough strength to perform its required feats.

Let the kneaded dough rise in a warm place, protected from drafts. If it is kept at 80°F, the dough will be ready in about 1½ hours. (You can let it rise slightly cooler and longer, but this dough will not tolerate a really long rise.) When a ½″ hole made with your wet fingertip does not fill in, deflate the dough. (Don't wait until your fingerpoke makes the dough sigh.) After deflating, let rise again as before. At the same temperature, the second rise will take about half as long.

Deflate the dough and round it into two or three balls, keeping them covered while you work. Roll very thin and cut into 5″ squares, using plenty of pastry flour on the board. If you're not the speediest worker, chill the dough that you aren't actually working with and do this part in stages. The easiest way by far to do the rolling is to use a pasta machine, if you have one; end with the next-to-thinnest setting.

Fill the squares as shown, or any way that strikes your fancy. If you have a ravioli cutter, you can cut and seal the edges nicely with that. Use about 3 tablespoons of filling for each. Put them on greased cookie sheets and bake in a preheated 375° oven for as long as it takes to brown the crust nicely—about 10 minutes. Since the filling is already cooked and contains no egg, you don't need to worry about cooking it. Nevertheless, the filling should be warm when you put it in so that the crust browns nicely.

FILLINGS

Any zesty mixture of vegetables, cut small and nicely cooked, is a candidate. The following combinations have worked well for us, either as they are or with white or any harmonious kind of bean in place of part of the potato.

ARTICHOKE FILLING

4 shallots, chopped
1 tablespoon oil or butter
1 garlic clove, minced

1 cup cooked mashed
* artichoke hearts and*
* leaf scrapings*
* (about 2 large or 4*
* small artichokes)*
2 cups mashed or diced
* cooked potato*
1 cup fresh tender peas

1½ teaspoons salt
pepper to taste

Sauté the shallots in oil or butter, stirring constantly until soft. Add the garlic about halfway. Stir in the other vegetables, and cook gently until the peas are hot through. Season to taste.

MUSHROOM FILLING

Substitute 1 cup sautéed mushrooms for artichoke hearts.

ASPARAGUS OR GREEN BEAN FILLING

1 bunch scallions
1 tablespoon olive oil

2 cups cooked diced
* asparagus*
* (or green beans)*
2 cups cooked mashed or
* diced potato*
¼ cup chopped parsley or
* coriander leaves*
* and/or ¼ cup grated*
* Gruyère cheese*

1¼ teaspoons salt
pepper to taste

Sauté the scallions in the oil until soft. Add the other vegetables and heat until the parsley is wilted, if used. Add the cheese when the vegetables are hot. Season to taste.

SPINACH FILLING

1 small onion, chopped
1 tablespoon oil
¼ cup each chopped
* bell pepper, green and*
* red, and celery*
(1 green chili, with seeds
* removed, very finely minced*
* or ½ teaspoon chili powder)*

1 cup cooked, finely
* chopped spinach*
2½ cups cooked potato
* (mashed or boiled)*

½ cup grated cheddar cheese
1¼ teaspoons salt
pepper

Sauté the onion in the oil, stirring. Add the green pepper, then the red pepper and celery. Add the chili, if desired. Cook until they are crispy-tender. Add the other vegetables and stir. When they are warm, stir in the cheese and salt and pepper.

Spanakopita

FILLING

2 or 3 bunches spinach
½ teaspoon salt
3 cups low-fat cottage cheese
3 eggs

DOUGH

2½ cups whole wheat
  flour (fine-ground is best)
1 teaspoon salt
1 cup warm water

½ cup melted butter

When Specially Honored Friends are offered whatever they want for supper, they almost always ask for Sultana's Spanakopita. There is a knack to making it, but it's a knack you'll be glad to have developed—and even before you've quite got it the results will be most acceptable.

You will need a pizza pan and a 4-foot piece of ¾″ or 1″ dowel to roll out the dough. If you have neither a pita pan nor a pizza pan, don't be daunted. Use pie plates or tins: one recipe will make two 9″ or 10″ pie-sized pitas. Divide the dough into *four* balls instead of two in the instructions below; and since your pitas will be smaller, you can use a rolling pin instead of the dowel to make the dough paper-thin.

Wash and dry the spinach and chop it fine. Sprinkle with salt and squeeze or wring to wilt it. Add the cottage cheese and eggs. Mix very well and set aside.

Sift the flour and save the bran for tomorrow morning's porridge. Mix flour, salt, and water, and knead briefly until you have a soft dough.

Divide dough into two balls, one larger than the other. Pat the larger ball flat and roll it into an 8″ circle, using your dowel or rolling pin.

Now, beginning with the edge closest to you, roll the dough over the dowel as shown. Use the sifted flour as needed to keep dough from sticking. Start with your hands in the center and move them forward and backward, working outward toward the ends of the dowel. When your hands reach the edge of the dough, unroll it gently so that it is flat again. Turn the crust (larger now, but lopsided) a ⅛ turn, and repeat this rolling operation until the dough is very round, paper-thin, even, and 3 inches bigger all around than your pan. The tricky part is to do all this without making holes in the dough.

Grease your pan. Preheat oven to 400°F.

Place the dowel with the dough wrapped around it on one edge of the pan, and unroll the dough over the pan. Gently fold the excess edge of the crust in toward the center, so that it won't break while you're preparing the second crust.

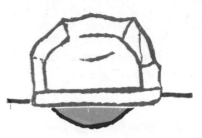

Now roll the smaller ball similarly, until it is slightly smaller than the other. Set it aside carefully.

Unfold the edges of the dough in the pan and spread with a tablespoonful or two of the melted butter. Put in the filling and drizzle again with a little butter. Place the second piece of dough over the top, leaving it loose with plenty of wrinkles. Pour half the remaining butter over the edges and fold the under-crust edge around the upper-crust edge as shown.

Drizzle the last of the butter over the top, particularly around the edges. Be sure to poke holes all over the top crust with a fork or a sharp paring knife.

Bake the pita on the bottom rack of the oven for 45 minutes, until just brown. Cover it with a towel and let it stand for 10 minutes before serving. Cut in wedges.

Serves 6 properly, though many of us could easily eat three pieces each.

Chard Pita

We're very fond of chard, which grows abundantly in our gardens. With a few changes, the Spanakopita recipe adapts very nicely. The crust is the same; here is the filling:

❧

Sauté green onions in oil in a large pan until soft. Mix with the chard. Combine all ingredients and mix well. Prepare crust and then fill and bake just as you would Spanakopita.

1 bunch green onions, chopped
1 tablespoon oil
4 quarts chopped chard leaves
3 cups low-fat cottage cheese
3 eggs
1 teaspoon salt
pinch pepper
¼ cup grated Parmesan or other sharp cheese

Pizza

2 teaspoons active dry yeast
  (1 packet, ¼ oz, or 7g)
1⅔ cups warm water
  (110°F)

4 cups whole wheat flour
¼ teaspoon black pepper
2 teaspoons salt

3 cups Tomato Sauce
  (page 248)
½ pound grated mozzarella,
  jack, Swiss, or other
  cheese
¼ cup Parmesan cheese

GARNISHES

pepper rings
sliced mushrooms
sliced olives
onion
crumbled bits of Soy Pâté,
  tofu, or Neat Balls

This recipe is a prototype, and you can vary it as you see fit. It makes two rather thin pizzas; if you like yours thicker, either halve the sauce and make only one, or double the dough and make two. The thicker version will take somewhat longer to bake. Be sure to let it rise after rolling out before you bake it. If you use sliced mushrooms on top, rubbing them with a *little* olive oil first makes a delectable difference.

ð

Dissolve yeast in the warm water and set aside. Mix the flour, pepper, and salt together, making a well in the center. Add the yeast liquid and mix together. The dough should be quite soft. Knead until silky and elastic. (Double dough will take double kneading, by the way.)

Cover and set in a warm, draft-free place to rise. You can adjust the rising times to suit you (see page 52); if you keep the dough in a warm spot, it will be ready to deflate in about an hour and a half. Carefully press the air from the dough and let it rise again. The second rise should take half the amount of time the first one did.

Preheat the oven to 375°F.

Press the twice-risen dough flat and divide in two. Form two balls and let them rest, covered, while you warm your sauce and gather cheeses and garnishes. Grease your pizza pans and dust them with cornmeal. Roll the dough into circles just a little bigger than your pizza pans (this takes some patience if the dough is good). Roll until the dough tenses up, then wait, then roll again. Take consolation from the fact that really elastic dough will rise better in the oven. Avoid forcing it though, that might crush and tear the structure of the dough.

Transfer the rolled-out dough to the pans. (If you have time, let it rest now another 15 to 20 minutes in its warm place; the bread will be lighter.) Spread the sauce on, add the garnishes, and pop the pizza in the oven. When the bread is delicately brown—about 10 to 15 minutes, depending on the oven—spread the cheeses and return to the oven until bubbly.

If you need only one pizza today, make the second completely except for the cheese; bake just until the bread is beginning to brown. Sprinkle with cheese, cool, and wrap in plastic and freeze to warm up when needed.

Use any size piece of bread dough, or else a slice of bread, a Pocket Bread, or an English Muffin. Arrange with thick slices of raw, red-ripe tomatoes, peppers, mushrooms, etc. Sprinkle with oregano, a little basil, and grated cheese. If you use bread dough, of course, the little pizza has to be baked; but with the other choices, just slip the pizza under the broiler until the cheese is melted.

A Pretty Corny Pizza

If you detect the hand of Analee the Summer Squash Queen —inventrix of Crookneck Chiffon Pie and other early-September wonders—you're right on the money. This one goes over very well with kids and other smart eaters.

Cut squash in large chunks and steam until tender. Puree; you should have 2 cups. Mix honey, eggs, and oil with the puree. Combine the cornmeal, salt, and baking powder. Mix the dry ingredients and wet, stirring until smooth. Turn into a greased 12″ × 18″ baking pan or a large pizza pan (mixture should be about ¾″ deep) and bake 12 to 15 minutes, just until corn bread begins to pull in from the sides of the pan.

While corn bread is baking, sauté onion in olive oil along with chili powder, oregano, cumin, and coriander. Spread onion mixture across top of corn bread, then scatter tomato atop that. Sprinkle with basil, then cheese. Return to oven for 10 minutes.

Serves 6 generously.

CRUST

1¾ pounds summer squash
1 tablespoon honey
2 eggs, beaten
2 tablespoons oil

2¼ cups cornmeal
1 teaspoon salt
2 teaspoons baking powder

TOPPING

1 large onion, chopped
2 tablespoons olive oil
1 teaspoon chili powder
1 teaspoon oregano
1 teaspoon ground cumin
½ teaspoon ground
    coriander seed
3 large ripe tomatoes,
    chopped
1 teaspoon dried basil
1½ cups grated jack cheese

Good Shepherd's Pie

TOPPING

2 cups leftover mashed
    potatoes
    OR
3 medium potatoes,
    ¼ cup milk, and
    ½ teaspoon salt

pinch paprika

FILLING

1 onion, chopped big
1 tablespoon oil
1 pound broccoli
1 green pepper, diced
4 medium carrots, diced
½ teaspoon basil
1 bay leaf
¾ cup chopped fresh
    tomatoes
    or ¼ cup tomato paste
    and ½ cup water

1 bunch spinach or Swiss
    chard
1 teaspoon salt

Here's a happy home for leftovers. The vegetables will vary according to the season. A small amount of leftover lentil, pea, or bean soup may be stirred in with the vegetables to good advantage too.

≈

Unless you have leftover mashed potatoes, steam potato chunks or cook them in fast-boiling water until soft. Mash well, adding milk and salt. Save the potato water for breadmaking.

Cut broccoli into florets and stems. Peel and slice the stems in ¼″ rounds. Wash spinach thoroughly and cut into bite-size pieces.

Preheat oven to 350°F.

Sauté onion in oil. Add broccoli, green pepper, and carrots, then the basil and bay leaf. Stir well and add tomatoes. Bring to a boil, cover, turn heat to low, and simmer for 15 minutes or until vegetables are just tender. Stir in spinach. Add salt.

Put vegetables into a 9″ × 13″ baking dish. Spread potatoes over top and shake paprika over all. Bake for 10 or 15 minutes, until the potatoes are piping hot.

Serves 4 to 6.

Potato Carrot Kugel

A kugel is a pudding, and it comes in many forms. This delicious version is almost a meal in itself: serve with a green vegetable and salad and you're there.

≥

Preheat oven to 300°F.

Sauté onion in oil until well done, and add garlic. Add stock, carrots, and potatoes and cook for 3 minutes. Remove from heat and stir in eggs.

Mix together the flour, wheat germ, baking powder, and seasonings and add to vegetables. Pour into a greased baking dish and bake for 1 hour.

Serves 4 to 6.

1 onion, chopped
2 tablespoons oil
1 clove garlic, pressed
   or minced
¾ cup vegetable stock
   or water
1 cup grated carrots
   or 2 cups winter squash
3 cups grated
   potatoes
2 beaten eggs

¼ cup whole wheat
   flour
¼ cup wheat germ
1 teaspoon baking
   powder
pinch pepper
1½ teaspoons salt

Potato Poppers

So easy and so much loved, especially by the younger set.

≥

Preheat oven to 350°F.

Sauté onion and celery in oil. Combine all ingredients and form into 1½" balls. Place on greased baking sheet and bake on the top rack of oven for about 20 minutes, until delicately browned.

Makes 12 balls.

½ onion, diced
1 celery stalk, diced
½ tablespoon oil
1¼ cups mashed potato
1 cup cooked brown rice
¼ cup tomato paste
½ teaspoon salt
½ cup whole-grain bread
   crumbs
¼ cup grated Parmesan
   cheese

Cabbage Rolls Normande

FILLING

*1 medium onion, chopped
   fine*
1 tablespoon oil
1 clove garlic, minced
1 large stalk celery, diced
1 medium carrot, diced
*1 teaspoon ground
   coriander seed*
3 cups cooked brown rice
2 tablespoons shoyu
*½ cup chopped toasted
   filberts or almonds*

SAUCE

*3 tablespoons whole wheat
   flour*
2 cups apple juice
*1 cup vegetable stock
   or water*
¼ cup fresh lemon juice
zest of 1 lemon
½ teaspoon salt
½ cup raisins

*12–14 large cabbage leaves
   (1 large cabbage)*

Cabbage rolls are a traditional Eastern European favorite, but this version is an original (and mighty good) presentation. Vary the filling by using kasha instead of rice.

Make filling first: Sauté onion in oil until soft, then add garlic, celery, carrot, and coriander. Sauté briefly, then add ¼ cup water, bring to a boil and cover. Cook over low heat for 3 minutes, then stir in rice, shoyu, and nuts.

To make sauce, toast flour a minute or two in a skillet over low heat, stirring constantly, until it's just beginning to brown. Slowly add apple juice and stock or water, bring to a boil, and simmer until sauce thickens. Stir in lemon juice, peel, salt, and raisins.

Wash cabbage leaves carefully and steam them in a large pot over a steamer basket for no more than 3 minutes. With a small, sharp knife, remove the most inflexible central stem from each leaf (don't cut too high up into the leaf, though).

Preheat oven to 350°F.

Place about ¼ cup of filling on each leaf (less if the leaf is small) and roll the leaf around it into a fat little packet. Place the rolls in a 9″ × 13″ baking dish, pour sauce over them, and place in the oven. Bake covered for 30 minutes, and uncovered for another 10 or 15.

Makes about 12 to 14 rolls: serves 4 hungry eaters, 6 restrained ones.

Stuffed Chard Leaves

This dish is one of our very favorites.

಄

Preheat oven to 350°F.

Sauté onion in oil. Mix all ingredients except chard.

Wash and dry chard leaves and remove stems, including the fat part of the rib if it extends rigidly up into the leaf (select leaves that are not too "ribby"). Place 2 tablespoons or more of filling on the underside of the leaf, a third of the way from the bottom. Fold over the sides of the leaf and roll up into a square packet. Place seam-side down in a greased casserole. Cover and bake for about 30 minutes. Alternatively, steam the rolls in a steamer basket over boiling water until the leaves are tender, about 20 minutes. Bake any extra filling and serve with stuffed leaves.

Serves 6 to 8.

VARIATION

Stuff chard with Bulgar Wheat Pilaf (page 284) and serve with Sunshine Sauce (page 245).

1 onion, chopped
1 tablespoon oil
2½ cups cooked brown rice
1½ cups low-fat
cottage cheese
1 egg, beaten
½ cup chopped parsley
¾ cup raisins
1 teaspoon dill weed
¾ teaspoon salt

16 large leaves Swiss chard

Simple Cheesy Bread Pudding

This is a standby for us, very useful when there is stale bread around. A flexible recipe which you can adjust as you like to suit the rest of the menu and the mood of the bread that wants using. (Sweet or fruity breads do better with a more desserty treatment, like the one on page 314.)

಄

Use part of the butter to grease an 8″ × 8″ pan and put the bread cubes into it. Mix the milk, egg, and cheese and pour them over the bread. Dot with the remaining butter. Bake in a moderate oven, about 350°F, until the custard is set and the top nicely brown.

Let it cool before you eat; it is incredibly hot when it comes out of the oven.

FANCIES

Use cheddar cheese and top with toasted sesame seeds.
Rye bread, especially sourdough, is particularly good with Swiss cheese. Add a sautéed onion and ½ cup chopped celery for a delicious casserole.

1 tablespoon butter
4 cups of cubed light bread
(4–8 slices)
2 cups warm milk
1 egg, slightly beaten.
⅓–½ cup grated sharp
cheese

Quiche

3 eggs, slightly beaten
2 cups warm milk
½ teaspoon salt
pinch each pepper
    and nutmeg
¾ cup grated Swiss cheese
1 teaspoon butter

piecrust (either Whole
    Wheat Piecrust, page
    324, or one of the
    lighter versions on
    the next page.)

TIMBALE
Omit crust; bake at 325°F,
set in a pan of very hot
water.

Quiche is not for every night, or even every *other* night, but recognizing what a beloved dish it is, we offer this relatively prudent version. It calls for half the cheese that's normally used, and low-fat milk in place of cream. It is shy one egg, too, and a mere teaspoon of butter replaces the usual generous dots on top (with *no* butter, a bothersome "skin" forms over the surface.) Use the Lighter Whole Wheat Piecrust recipe on the next page and enjoy thoroughly.

Quiches are favored for other reasons than their palatability. They are dependable, not tricky; they can wait; and they can be served hot, cold, or in between. The simplest version, made from just the ingredients listed, is perhaps the most delicate. Use a fine Gruyère cheese and you have a dish that can stand proudly anywhere the American Heart Association hasn't penetrated.

For a more complete meal, add a cup of nicely cooked, *well-drained* vegetables: spinach, asparagus, sautéed mushrooms, even zucchini. The recipe gives proportions for an 8″ pie shell, or 9″ with vegetables. Larger shells are possible: 10″, for example, or the deeper special quiche pans. To adapt the recipe, measure the capacity of your pan with water beforehand. Keep the 2:3 ratio of liquid to egg—it is the minimum for being sure the quiche will set up. As long as there are enough eggs to set the milk, you can increase the vegetables to two or more cups. Larger, especially deeper, quiches will take longer to bake. If the crust seems to be in danger of browning too much, cover it with a strip of aluminum foil.

ɔ৯

Preheat oven to 350°F. Combine eggs, milk, salt, and pepper. (Use white pepper, or omit, with plain quiche.) Spread the cheese evenly in the bottom of the pie shell and pour the milk mixture over it. Sprinkle the top with nutmeg and dot with butter. Place pie plate on a cookie sheet and bake for half an hour, or until set. Remove when the outside is set and the middle couple of inches still jiggles if you tap the pan—quiche must stand for 10 or 15 minutes before it is cut, and in that time the center will set. Try not to overbake, as the texture will be less smooth.

Serves 6.

Lighter Whole Wheat Piecrust

Not the tender, flaky, buttery version for sure, but plenty good for all that.

28.

Stir dry ingredients together. Mix in oil and enough of the water to make the dough form a ball. Roll flat between sheets of waxed paper and lift into pan. Make decorative edge. Bake at 400°F for 10 minutes, or until slightly browned and crisp. Makes one 9″ shell.

1 cup whole wheat pastry flour
½ teaspoon salt
3 tablespoons oil
¼ cup water

Oat-Nut Crust

Preheat oven to 400°F.

Blend oats and walnuts in blender or food processor until the mixture is floury, with only a few visible oat pieces. Turn into bowl and mix in water and salt (try just 2 tablespoons of water at first, and add the third only if needed to hold dough together). Press into 9″ or 10″ pie tin and bake just 10 minutes.

2 cups rolled oats
½ cup chopped walnuts
3 tablespoons water
½ teaspoon salt

Analee's Crookneck Chiffon Pie

Analee is legend for her success at using beautifully what might otherwise be considered a surfeit of summer squashes.

28.

Preheat oven to 350°F.

Press bread crumbs into a liberally buttered 9″ pie plate. Steam squash until barely tender and puree, making it very smooth. You should have 3 cups.

Sauté onion in oil. For a very smooth filling, puree the onion, eggs, cottage cheese, cornmeal, salt, and Swiss cheese and combine with the squash. Add dill weed. Pour into lined pie plate and decorate with tomato and/or pepper slices. Bake 40 to 45 minutes, until set. Let stand at least 10 minutes before cutting.

Serves 6.

2 cups whole-grain bread crumbs
6 cups crookneck squash or yellow zucchini, in chunks
½ cup chopped onion
1 tablespoon oil
2 large eggs, beaten
½ cup cottage cheese
2 tablespoons cornmeal
½ teaspoon salt
⅓ cup Swiss cheese
1 tablespoon dill weed
tomato slices, pepper slices for garnishing

Nori Maki Sushi

1 cup short-grain brown rice
2 cups water

4 sheets dried nori

½ teaspoon salt
2–4 tablespoons rice
vinegar
2 teaspoons honey

FILLING INGREDIENTS
(choose three for each roll)
grated raw carrot or jicama
cooked chopped spinach
toasted sesame seeds
strips of scallion, bell
pepper, celery, omelette,
lightly steamed asparagus,
carrot or green bean
pickled umeboshi plum
(use just a bit)
avocado
chopped watercress
mushrooms (see below)

CONDIMENTS

Shoyu, sweet-and-hot
mustard,
pickled ginger

A perfectly vegetarian sushi, as good as the best. The outside wrapper *nori*, is made from seaweed. It has best flavor when freshly toasted and eaten soon after, but even so, sushi makes fine lunchbox fare.

If you want to include mushrooms, shitakes are traditional, but normal ones work too, sautéed and cut in strips. If you do come upon some dried shitakes, soak several in water, then simmer in 2 teaspoons each shoyu and sherry. Chop fine or cut into strips.

❧

Cook rice uncovered in boiling water for five minutes, then cover, and reduce heat to low. Simmer for 45 minutes.

While the rice is cooking, select and prepare your choice of fillings. You'll be making four rolls—it's fun to vary the fillings in each. Combine about three of the suggested ingredients in each—or whatever seems good to you.

Unless the nori sheets you have are pre-toasted, wave each one over a flame (a gas burner is ideal), holding it with tongs or fingertips, so that each sheet changes color and texture slightly, becoming lighter and coarser.

Dissolve salt in rice vinegar in a small saucepan and add honey; heat gently to liquefy. When the rice is cooked, turn it out onto a large platter or baking dish with sides. Pour the vinegar mixture over it, stirring as you do, and fanning the steam away—a folded newspaper works nicely. When the rice has cooled to room temperature, it is ready.

For rolling the sushi, a traditional bamboo mat is great, but not essential: a big cloth napkin works fine—just a little bigger than the nori sheets. Place the mat or cloth flat in front of you and put the first sheet of nori on it. Moisten your fingers with water or vinegar and spread one-fourth of the seasoned rice on the mat, covering it except for an inch or two at the top, which you'll use to seal the roll.

The rice should be not quite ½″ thick. Across the middle, parallel to the top, form an indentation and place the filling materials there, forming a thin line from one end to the other. For example: a strip of omelette, a line of chopped watercress, and strips of red bell pepper. Aim for beauty, and harmony too.

Grasping the nearest side of the mat, roll it up and away from you toward the top, pressing the whole thing together tightly and pushing the filling ingredients into place if necessary. Dampen the remaining "flap" of nori and seal the roll by presing the flap along the length of the roll. Place the roll on a cutting board and slice it with a very sharp knife into 1″ segments. Arrange cutside up, and serve.

Makes about 6 servings.

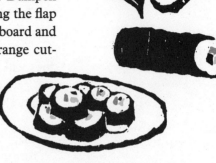

Chillaquillas

Here is a traditional Mexican way to dispose of leftover tortillas—not that it isn't good enough to send us to the store for new ones, but less fresh tortillas hold up better in the cooking. If you don't have tasty, *ripe* tomatoes, use canned ones.

1 dozen corn tortillas

1 bunch green onions, chopped
2 cloves garlic, minced
1½ teaspoons chili powder
½ teaspoon ground cumin
1 tablespoon oil

Tear the tortillas into 2″ pieces. In a big, heavy skillet, sauté the onion, garlic, chili powder, and cumin lightly in the oil; then stir in the tortilla pieces, coating them with oil and spices.

½ teaspoon oregano
1 teaspoon basil
¾ teaspoon salt
2 cups tomatoes, chopped

Turn the tortillas out of the pan into a bowl (don't worry about where the onions and spices go) and add the herbs, salt, and tomatoes to the pan. Bring to a boil, stirring, and simmer about 5 minutes.

Stir the tortillas, sauce, buttermilk, cheese, and chilis together, reserving a little cheese to sprinkle on top. (If you aren't used to chilis, see page 236 for tips.) Cover and cook over low heat until the mixture is bubbly and the cheese melted.

2½ cups buttermilk
¾ cup grated cheddar
(⅓ cup chopped green chilis or green peppers)

The dish needs to sit for about 20 minutes before serving—ideally, in a low (325°F) oven, covered. If your skillet and lid aren't ovenware, turn the mixture out into a casserole first.

Serves 4.

Fiesta

When summer's tomato crop is at its peak—and at other times of year for a change of pace—we put together an impromptu Mexican feast and let friends create the tostadas, tacos or burritos of their dreams. This meal is delicious, pretty, and easy. It is also perfect for potlucking. For dessert, serve papaya halves with lime wedges, or a giant, luscious fruit salad.

Tortillas are available in supermarkets now, in the deep freeze if nowhere else. But any town that has a sizeable Mexican community will have a source of fresh, locally-made tortillas, and they will taste *much* better: ask at a Mexican restaurant how you can get some. We like the corn variety best; the flour ones are nearly always made from white flour and contain lard. For a good flour tortilla, make our Chapatis (page 84) without pressing on them while they cook.

Tortillas are often deep-fried for tacos and chips. An alternative that is at least as authentic and plenty delicious is to heat them on a griddle or directly over a burner flame, turning them once or twice with deft fingers (or tongs) as they begin to brown. If you want the tenderness that fat adds, rub a dot of butter or oil onto both sides of the tortilla with the palms of your hands before warming it as described above. To heat a lot of tortillas for serving soft, wrap them in a damp towel and put them in a covered casserole. Warm in 325°F oven for 15 minutes, until hot through.

To make TORTILLA CHIPS, tear the tortillas into smallish triangles, spread them on cookie sheets, and bake for 30 minutes at 325°F. If you rub each tortilla first with a tiny bit of butter—¼ teaspoon to a side—the flavor steps up; cut down the baking time to 20 minutes. Either way, they will be delicious even though unsalty.

POSSIBLE OFFERINGS

Hot tortillas
Refritos (page 307) or
   Chili con Elote (page 308)
Shredded lettuce
Steamed vegetables:
   green beans and corn
   broccoli and cauliflower
   zucchini, scallions,
     and peppers
Mexican-style Tomato Sauce
   (page 248)
   or Salsa (page 221 and 236)
Mock Sour Cream (page 240)
Avocado Dip (page 132)
Grated jack and cheddar
   cheeses
Tomato wedges
Olives
Grilled Peppers (page 137)
   or chiles
Chopped raw scallions
   or red onions
Fruit punch

TACO

crisp corn tortilla
   (folded in half while hot)
filled with:
   Refritos
   cheese
   shredded lettuce
   Salsa

ح

TOSTADA

crisp corn tortilla flat
   on plate topped with:
   Refritos or Chili
   shredded lettuce
   cheese
   Salsa
   Avocado dip
   tomato wedges
   Mock Sour Cream

QUESADILLA

soft tortilla folded in half
   over slices of grilled pepper
   or chili
   chopped scallion
   jack cheese
heated on griddle to melt cheese
(serve with Salsa)

ح

ENTOMATADA

soft tortilla dipped in hot
   Tomato Sauce
topped with
   shredded lettuce
   grated cheese
   Salsa
   (any other vegetables)
   fried egg, sunny side up

ح

BURRITO

soft tortilla folded around
   Refritos and cheese

Grains & Beans

The next time you bite into a cinnamon roll or a tortilla, or while you're dishing out a bowl of oatmeal at breakfast, pause and pay your respects. Cereal grains are the stuff on which great civilizations are built. Wherever humanity is locked into a hunt-and-gather food supply system, life consists mostly of moving around. A basket might get woven, the wall of your cave might sport a sketch or two; songs will be sung and stories told: but Athens would never happen, or Chartres, or the Globe Theatre, or a Taj Mahal. For these and much, much more, we have cereal grains to thank in part, because grander possibilities really only open out when food can be cultivated and stored from season to season. And that, of course, means grains 'n' beans.

It's funny to realize that cereal grains were the first convenience foods, but there it is. Forty-five minutes for a pot of brown rice to cook might seem like an eternity to today's homemaker-on-the-run, but measured against a day gathering acorns, it looks terrific.

The leisure that's let us develop art, music, and laser beams has also allowed us to tease out of those cereal grains a wondrous variety of dishes. Have couscous on Monday, chapatis on Tuesday, pasta on Wednesday, bulgur on Thursday, biscuits on Friday; buttered toast on Saturday, and steamed dumplings come Sunday: all these from one grain—wheat—alone. The list from rice would be much longer.

The marvelous thing about being a vegetarian today is that you have access to the traditional grain dishes of just about every ethnic cuisine. This makes for endless variety, and the great fun of slipping into another culture—another world—for the time it takes to prepare and eat those dishes.

It also makes for superb nourishment, for whole grains turn out to contain nearly everything we need for glowing health: vitamins, minerals, complex carbohydrates, and good-quality protein, present in just the right percentage. What more could you ask of a food?

Speed? Well, some whole-grain foods actually *are* convenience foods. Kasha and bulgur wheat cook in just 15 minutes. Whole-grain pastas take between 10 and 25 minutes, and even brown rice, once put on to simmer, cooks itself while you do other things. Once cooked, it can be kept for days and reheated quickly.

Store whole grains in a cool dry place, protected from bugs and mice, and they will keep indefinitely—and that does mean nearly forever. Archaeologists have sprouted a grain from a Minoan palace of ancient Crete—four thousand years old, and suddenly full of life. After grains are cracked or ground into flour, though, their freshness begins to wane, so keep flour and the like in the refrigerator if you won't be using it within a couple of weeks.

Beans are also an ancient foodstuff, about twice as dense in nutrients. Beans keep a long time (store them like grains), but after a year or so you'll find they won't be so tasty and will take longer to cook.

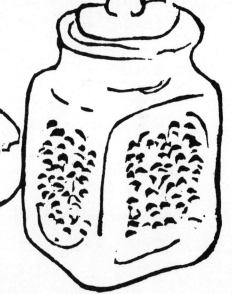

Grains

Most often, the rice takes its place quietly on the plate, waiting for the stewy vegetables, or whatever, to come alongside or land on top. You don't need a recipe for that! In the following pages, though, we talk a little about the grains we find ourselves choosing most often, and give some recipes for fancying them up, too.

Cooking Times & Proportion for Grains & Beans

Grain (1 cup dry measure)	Water	Cooking time	Yield
Barley (whole)	3 cups	1 hour 15 minutes	3½ cups
Brown rice	2 cups	1 hour	3 cups
Buckwheat (kasha)	2 cups	15 minutes	2½ cups
Bulgur wheat	2 cups	15–20 minutes	2½ cups
Cracked wheat	2 cups	25 minutes	2⅓ cups
Millet	3 cups	45 minutes	3½ cups
Coarse cornmeal (polenta)	4 cups	25 minutes	3 cups
Wild rice	3 cups	1 hour or more	4 cups
Whole wheat berries	3 cups	2 hours	2⅔ cups
Quinoa	2 cups	15 minutes	2½ cups
Black beans	4 cups	1½ hours	2 cups
Black-eyed peas	3 cups	1 hour	2 cups
Garbanzos (chickpeas)	4 cups	3 hours	2 cups
Great northern beans	3½ cups	2 hours	2 cups
Kidney beans	3 cups	1½ hours	2 cups
Lentils and split peas	3 cups	45 minutes	2¼ cups
Limas	2 cups	1½ hours	1¼ cups
Baby limas	2 cups	1½ hours	1¾ cups
Pinto beans	3 cups	2½ hours	2 cups
Red beans	3 cups	3 hours	2 cups
Small white beans (navy, etc.)	3 cups	2½ hours	2 cups
Soybeans	4 cups	3 hours or more	2 cups
Soy grits	2 cups	15 minutes	2 cups

Barley

Normal barley, like rice and oats (and unlike wheat and rye), does not grow "naked"; its indigestible hull clings tenaciously to the grain. To remove the hull, the grain is milled. In the case of *pearl barley*, the milling is repeated over and over until the germ as well as the chaff is gone. *Scotch* or *pot barley* has been milled fewer times and so is more nutritious. Sometimes you will find a special hull-less variety that grows naked like wheat and needs no milling to render it deliciously edible.

Hull-less barley is often sold as "barley for sprouting." But beware: some suppliers sell normal unmilled barley—not hull-less at all—"for sprouting", and unless you have a grain mill, barley with its chaff is not very useful. Keep asking for the real thing: demand creates supply.

If you can't get it hull-less, buy the other kind and mill it yourself. Here's how: crack the grain to the coarseness you want, and just before you cook it, flood it with water in a deep pan, letting the grain settle in the bottom and the hulls float off. To save the "fines" (flour) which would otherwise be lost along with the chaff in washing, sift the milled grain with a fine sieve before you wash it. Then you can make these great crackers:

Barley Crackers

Using a lecithin spray or the greasing formula on page 53, grease a *flat* 12″ × 18″ cookie sheet or the back of one with sides. (The crackers will stick otherwise.) If you want them especially thin, use the same amount of batter on *two* sheets.

Sift the flour, salt, and soda. Stir in the buttermilk. Spread the batter on the cookie sheet(s) as if it were frosting on a cake, making it quite even.

Bake at about 300°F until *very* delicately brown. About halfway through the baking—some 10 minutes along—score the dough in squares or rectangles or whatever you like, so the crackers will break apart easily when they are done.

1 cup barley fines (or flour)
½ teaspoon salt
½ teaspoon baking soda

1 cup buttermilk

Spinach and Barley Dumplings

*1 cup barley, finely
cracked
1 to 1½ pounds spinach
(1 cup cooked)
(chopped leaves from
1 bunch coriander)
1 egg or 2 whites, beaten
½ teaspoon salt
barley flour as needed*

*good broth, simmering 3″
deep in a big shallow pan
with a tight lid*

Delicious floating in any tomato soup, lovely bathed in Cheddy Sauce or Tomato Pepper Sauce.

In a large, heavy skillet, toast the barley until it is just barely golden and becoming fragrant. Keep stirring so the toasting is even. (If necessary to get rid of chaff, wash now—see previous page.) Add water to cover and bring to a boil. Cover tightly and remove from heat.

Cook the spinach and drain dry. Chop, adding coriander leaves if you like. Mix in the barley. Allow to cool to lukewarm, then add the egg and salt.

Add just enough barley flour to make the mixture capable of being formed into balls, and make balls about as big as a walnut, rolling them in more barley flour. When you have about 10, drop them in the broth. Cover the pan and form the rest.

It's a help if the pan has a glass lid, because you want to keep the dumplings simmering or they won't cook, but you don't want them to boil hard or they may fall apart. Peeking is required if you can't see through the lid. The dumplings cook quickly. Allow about eight minutes, then use a slotted spoon to remove them to the sauce or soup you'll be serving them in and cook the second half.

Makes 18, which will serve 4 to 6.

WITHOUT EGG: By adding a little extra barley flour when you mix the dough, you can make these dumplings without the egg. Make the mixture pretty stiff and allow extra cooking time. This is tricky, but not impossible.

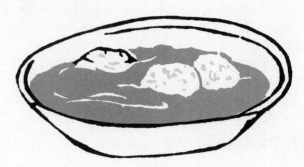

Buckwheat

Like wild rice, buckwheat is not really a grain. Botanically it's a fruit, growing on a pretty, hardy plant with heart-shaped leaves and white flowers that bees love. It has a nearly perfect amino acid balance and is rich in calcium and riboflavin and low in fat and sodium. Because it is blight-resistant, it is one commercial grain almost always grown without pesticides. Most of the buckwheat we eat is grown in the U.S.

Partly for its hardiness, but also for its heartiness, this "grain" is a staple in Russia and the Balkans. The seeds are usually toasted before cooking; if so, you have kasha. Roasting brings out the robust flavor; it is milder raw. Buckwheat flour, of course, is for pancakes. We keep the grain on hand and grind it in the blender when we want flour: it keeps fresher that way, and there's no problem grinding it because the grains are both soft and brittle.

Rinse the buckwheat grains in cold water and drain well before you cook. If you want to toast the grain before cooking, either toast and then rinse or follow the traditional cooking method: Mix a cup or so of rinsed groats with a beaten egg and then heat dry, stirring in a heavy skillet. Add water—about 1½ cups per cup of grain—and bring to a boil. Cover, and steam over very gentle heat about 15 minutes. (Iron pans will give a dark gray cast to the cooked grain.) Serve kasha with any of the winter vegetables, especially cabbage and sweet squash; mix it with sautéed onion, garlic, and whole wheat bow tie noodles to make KASHA VARNITCHKES.

Buckwheat pancakes, page 95, Blini, page 258

Bulgur Wheat

Quick-cooking bulgur wheat, with its nutty flavor and persistent fluffiness, is one of the most useful grains for pilaf and grain salads like Tabouli. When time is short, bulgur also fills in admirably for any of the longer-cooking grains in "serve over" dishes (serve over rice, serve over noodles, serve over mashed potatoes. . .).

Bulgur groats come in small, medium, and large. We like the largest size for nearly everything we make. Since it is precooked, bulgur needs only a short time on the stove; in fact, if you want it chewy, just cover with boiling water and let stand until the water is absorbed. Cooking it like rice is a little faster: use 1½ cups water to 1 cup bulgur.

Here is a very simple basic pilaf that you can vary freehandedly:

Bulgur Wheat Pilaf

1 small carrot
1 medium stalk celery
   or Florence fennel
½ green pepper
2 green onions
(¼ cup chopped mushrooms)
(1 cup tiny peas)
1 tablespoon oil
1 bay leaf
1 cup bulgur wheat
1¾ cups boiling water
½ teaspoon salt

Dice carrot, celery, pepper, and onion. Heat oil in a heavy pot and add all the vegetables and the bay leaf. Stir over medium heat for several minutes, then stir in the bulgur. Add the boiling water and salt. Reduce heat, cover, and keep over very low heat for 15 minutes.

Makes about 4 cups, to serve 4 to 6.

Uppuma

This flavorful dish was our first exposure to South Indian cuisine, and it remains one of our favorites. Uppuma ("*oopma*") is popular in India for high tea, but it is very satisfying and suitable for breakfast, lunch, or dinner.

ॐ

Toast the grain in a big, heavy-bottomed pan, stirring until the grain is fragrant and just beginning to brown. The toasting ensures that the uppuma will be flaky rather than gummy. Remove from heat.

In the same pot, emptied, or in another heavy and sizeable one, heat the oil very hot and add the mustard seeds. Cover the pan and let them pop. As soon as the sound of wild popping slows down a bit, remove from heat, uncover, and add the cashews, stirring quickly until they are golden. Add the onion, ginger, and chili in succession, giving the onion a bit of a head start. Sauté until tender.

Add the water and salt and bring to a boil. Add the grain, stirring as you do to mix evenly. Cover tightly and allow to cook over very low heat until the grain is tender. (How long depends on the grain, but 10 minutes is about par.) When the water is all gone, the grain should be tender and flaky. If the grain isn't done when the water has evaporated, stir in a quarter cup more boiling water and cover again, keeping over lowest heat for 5 more minutes. If the grain is tender but gummy, or if the water is not gone, turn up the heat and stir vigorously with a fork while the excess water evaporates.

Chop the coriander leaves and mix them and the lemon juice into the grain just before serving. Serves 4.

ॐ

Like most beloved dishes, this one admits a lot of variation. To simplify, for example, you can omit the nuts and/or the coriander leaves. Try also cooking a cupful or so of finely chopped vegetables along with the grain: potato, carrot, green beans, or peas. Sometimes a few tablespoons of fresh grated coconut is stirred in just before serving.

*1 cup finely cracked wheat
  or rice or barley*

1 tablespoon oil
*½ teaspoon black mustard
  seeds*
5 cashew nuts
1 small onion, minced
½ tablespoon minced ginger
*½ green chili, seeded
  and minced, or
  ¼ green pepper, minced*

1½ cups boiling water
½ teaspoon salt, to taste

leaves of ½ bunch coriander
¾ teaspoon lemon juice

Corn

Almost everybody likes the warm color and sunny flavor of corn, and Corn Bread is certainly the quick bread we make most often. Cornmeal mush is good breakfast cereal, and the leftover sets up temptingly to slice and fry in a little butter or oil to eat at supper, or as a treat with maple syrup at another breakfast.

Corn is a native American, but Italians have made it their own. In Italy, coarse cornmeal is cooked long and slow, then spread out thin, cooled, and topped in any number of ways—often with farmer's cheese or tomato sauce—to make POLENTA.

If you have noticed a slight bitterness in the things you make from cornmeal, here's the cause: because of plant breeding, corn contains so much polyunsaturated oil that it goes rancid soon after it is ground. For really sweet, sweet corn bread and polenta, grinding your own is the surest way; if you're not set up to do that, buy the freshest you can and keep it airtight in the refrigerator. Freezing of course postpones rancidity, but it does destroy vitamin E.

Here are two excellent recipes using polenta, the coarse-crack version of cornmeal.

Spoonbread

1 cup coarse cornmeal
  (polenta)
1 cup skim milk powder
1 cup cold water or whole
  milk
3 eggs, beaten
1¼ teaspoons salt
(1 tablespoon butter)

Perfected under the tutelage of a beloved Virginian who knows her spoon breads, this simple dish is irreplaceable.

❧

Put the cornmeal and 1 cup of cold water in a heavy saucepan. Bring to a boil, stirring in 2 cups of boiling water as the mixture thickens. Stir as needed to prevent the corn from sticking as it simmers for about 20 minutes. When very thick, set aside.

Preheat oven to 400°F. Butter a deep 2-quart casserole dish.

Blend smooth the milk powder and cold water or milk. Combine with eggs and salt. Mix in about one cup of the cooked cornmeal, then combine all together, adding butter if wanted. Pour into the prepared baking dish.

Bake uncovered for 30 minutes, or until golden brown on top. Spoon out hot, alongside vegetables or for breakfast.

Makes 6 servings.

Helen's Polenta with Eggplant

Place polenta in top of a double boiler with 4 cups of boiling water and ½ teaspoon of the salt. Bring to a boil, reduce heat to low, and cook for 30 to 40 minutes, until mush is quite thick. Pack into round, straight-sided containers that are, ideally, the same diameter as the eggplants. Refrigerate.

Meanwhile, sauté onion, pepper, and garlic clove in oil until tender. Crush garlic with a fork. Then add tomatoes, parsley, basil, and remaining 1 teaspoon of salt. Bring to a boil and simmer, stirring often, for 15 minutes, breaking up tomatoes as you stir.

When polenta is chilled, slice it in ½″ rounds. Do the same with the eggplants. Oil a 9″ × 13″ baking dish and overlap alternating slices of eggplant and polenta in a pretty, fish-scale design (if the eggplant is too large to do this, simply layer it lasagna-style). Pour tomato sauce over the whole works and sprinkle cheese on top. Cover the dish and bake in a 350° oven for 45 minutes, or until eggplant tests done with a fork.

Serves 6.

*1 cup raw polenta
(coarse-ground cornmeal)*
1½ teaspoons salt

1 large onion, chopped fine
1 green pepper, chopped fine
1 whole clove garlic
1 tablespoon olive oil
3 cups chopped tomatoes
¼ cup chopped parsley
1 teaspoon dried basil
*2 medium (or 1 large)
eggplants (1½ pounds)*
*¾ cup grated jack or
mozzarella cheese*

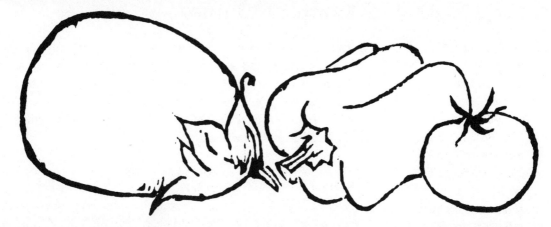

Millet

While millet is perfectly good food, it has not, so far as we know, inspired any deeply beloved ethnic dish. You can use millet where you want a mild-flavored grain accompaniment to something spicy, or for a light, rather nice breakfast cereal. Prepare millet soon before you mean to eat it, as it tends to solidify as it cools.

Quinoa

Quinoa ("*keen*wa"), sacred staple of the ancient Incas, still grows on the high slopes of the Andes—but also, nowadays, on the high slopes of the Colorado Rockies. New-age entrepreneurs are cultivating it for the small but rapidly growing American market. Quinoa appeals to natural foods enthusiasts for its good nutrition (its balance of essential amino acids is close to ideal) and to gourmets for its unique texture and delicious flavor. Purists will insist that like buckwheat, quinoa is not a proper grain—but it sure cooks and eats like one!

Quinoa cooks in just fifteen minutes, and it's so delicate, so light and fluffy, that you can hardly believe it is a whole food. The flavor is appealing, and not quite like anything else, either. It bears some resemblance to couscous, and can be used in much the same way. It shines in dishes where you'd normally use bulgur wheat or millet.

Confetti Quinoa

1 cup raw quinoa
2 cups water
¼ teaspoon salt
½ medium onion, finely chopped
¼ each, red and green bell pepper, seeded and finely chopped
1 teaspoon olive oil
2 tablespoons chopped toasted almonds or
¼ cup sliced water chestnuts
2 tablespoons chopped fresh coriander leaves

Rinse quinoa thoroughly in a fine sieve. Bring two cups of water to a boil, then add salt and quinoa and bring to a boil again. Cover, reduce heat to a low simmer, and cook for 15 minutes.

Meanwhile, sauté onion and pepper in olive oil. Combine with grain. Just before serving, stir in almonds or water chestnuts and coriander leaves. Check salt.

Makes 3 cups.

Rice

To half the world, "rice" means "food," and several of the great cuisines on the planet are built around the subtle delicacy of this nourishing grain. The more familiar it gets, the better we enjoy it. No other dinner grain bears repetition so endearingly.

Rice is not native to this hemisphere, but it grows well in the southern states and in California. Not long ago, supermarkets just carried "rice." Now we can count varieties: long, short, and medium grains; sweet "glutinous" rice, used for making *mochi;* perfumey Indian basmati; the new texmati and warmly ruddy wehani—and, of course, wild rice, which is another story altogether.

Brown rice, whether long, short, or medium, should look clean and uniform. Our friend Meera wouldn't consider preparing rice without picking out the discolored grains and unhulled "paddy." In this country we take for granted that the cleaning has been done for us, but sometime you may find you've bought poor-quality brown rice full of green, broken, and even moldy grains. These are far from pleasant to eat; if you don't want to pick them out, please take it back, and insist on better stuff.

We present here some recipes that reflect the enthusiasm of rice-appreciating cuisines from the four corners of the world—including our own.

The basic formula for cooking brown rice is simple enough: boil 1 cup rice in 1¾ cups water for 5 minutes; reduce heat and cover, allowing about 45 minutes in all. That's it, essentially, but certain factors can make a difference. You should use a heavy pan, and if it is *really* heavy and has a tight-fitting lid, you may need even less water—especially if the rice you are cooking is this year's rather than last's. For some reason, a larger quantity of rice also seems to need less water. If you like your rice a bit on the chewier side, cutting back the water somewhat will do it. One final tip: one friend of ours found that she couldn't cook rice on her gas stove until she spread and subdued the flame with a "flame tamer."

Spanish Rice

3 cups cooked brown rice

1 onion, chopped
4 stalks celery
1 large green pepper
2 cloves garlic
1 tablespoon oil
1 teaspoon chili powder
1 teaspoon cumin

1 cup chopped tomatoes
1 teaspoon salt
½ teaspoon oregano
¼ teaspoon pepper

Rice should be warm.

Sauté onion, celery, pepper, and garlic in oil. Add chili powder and cumin. When fragrant, add tomatoes, salt, oregano, and pepper. When tomatoes are cooked through, stir in the rice.

VARIATIONS: For a rich, cheeselike taste, include ⅓ cup cornmeal with the rice when you first cook it. Then, when making the Spanish Rice, increase the tomato a little.

Top the rice dish with grated jack and/or cheddar cheese, and put in the oven long enough to melt the cheese.

Teresa's Spanish Rice

1 small onion
2 teaspoons oil
1 clove garlic

1 teaspoon cumin
1 teaspoon paprika
½ red bell pepper

½ teaspoon oregano
1 cup raw brown rice
½ teaspoon salt
2 cups water

A flavorful and very different version.

Chop onion and sauté in oil with garlic clove. When onion is translucent, add cumin, paprika, and red bell pepper and cook a moment more, until spices are fragrant. Mash garlic clove with a fork. Add oregano, rice, salt, and water. Bring to a boil, then reduce heat and simmer on lowest flame for about an hour, until done.

Pilaf Avgolemono

Avgolemono sauce is another fine offering from our Greek friend Sultana. It goes well on vegetables too, but here it is on rice, for a delicious, rich-tasting grain dish that's one of our favorites.

ॐ

Make a cream sauce (see page 242) with butter and flour, milk, stock, and salt. Remove from heat and allow to cool to lukewarm.

Beat egg with lemon juice and slowly add to the sauce, stirring constantly. Return pan to the stove and continue cooking and stirring until the sauce thickens. Stir in half the cheese and pour sauce over grain. Top with remaining cheese.

Makes about 4 cups, to serve 4 to 6.

2 tablespoons butter
2 tablespoons whole wheat flour
1/2 cup milk
1/2 cup hot stock, or water
1/2 teaspoon salt

1 egg
juice of 1/2 lemon
1/3 cup Parmesan cheese
4 cups hot, cooked brown rice

Green Rice Casserole

Preheat oven to 350°F. Chop scallions and sauté with garlic in oil until soft; crush the garlic with a fork. Combine with remaining ingredients in a greased 2-quart casserole. (Be sure to reduce the amount of salt if you use rice that's already salted.) Bake about 45 minutes.

Serves 4 to 6.

1 small bunch scallions
1 small clove garlic
1 tablespoon oil
2 1/2 cups cooked brown rice
1/3 cup chopped parsley
1/2 cup grated Swiss cheese
2 eggs, beaten
2 cups milk
1 teaspoon salt
(1/2 teaspoon dill weed)

Sarah's Super Curried Rice

This dish is so simple that you can halve the recipe easily for smaller amounts. A very satisfying way to use up leftover rice.

ॐ

Cook rice in water with salt. Meantime, chop and sauté the onion in the butter, adding the curry powder when the onion is soft and cooking them together for a minute to remove the raw taste of the spices. Combine rice, onion, raisins, and peas. Heat, stirring—or bake, covered—until hot through. Garnish with toasted cashews on special occasions.

Serves 6.

2 cups brown basmati (or long-grain) rice
4 cups boiling water
3/4 teaspoon salt
2 large onions
1 1/2 tablespoons butter
1 tablespoon curry powder
2/3 cup raisins
2/3 cup golden raisins
2/3 cup peas

Wild Rice

1 cup wild rice
⅓ cup brown rice
1 carrot
1 large stalk celery
6 green onions
1 garlic clove
2 tablespoons oil
5 cups boiling water
1 teaspoon marjoram
¼ teaspoon thyme
pinch rosemary
1 teaspoon salt
dash pepper
⅓ cup toasted almonds

Wild rice, along with corn, is a native American. It is unarguably nutritious, and so delicious and special that even its outrageous price doesn't stop us from making this fine dish on special occasions.

❧

Rinse grain well.

Chop carrot and celery in ¼″ cubes. Chop green onions and sauté them with garlic in oil. Crush garlic clove with a fork. Add water and bring to a boil. Stir in the vegetables, rice, herbs, salt, and pepper. Bring to a boil, cover, reduce heat, and cook gently for an hour or more, until the rice is tender. Chop the almonds and add them about 20 minutes before serving.

Makes about 5 cups.

Beans

Beans are eminently nutritious, admirably ecological, low on the food chain, available everywhere, wonderfully versatile, dependably delicious, and very, very cheap. In fact, if any food (besides grains) could claim to have all the virtues, it'd have to be beans.

But. There is that annoying little problem, impossible to ignore: eating beans does cause intestinal gas in many people, especially those who are not accustomed to them.

Decades of research at the USDA have unearthed a probable set of contributing factors. Scientists have identified two sugars, with the splendidly disreputable-sounding names "raffinose" and "stachyose," which our digestive system can't break down. Bacteria that live in our intestines can and do break them down, however, producing gas as a by-product. Whether there is so much gas that it is uncomfortable, and whether it has odor, is determined by other things.

A lot of people, however, do eat beans without physical or social discomfort. How to join their enviable number? Here are some suggestions that seem to work for us. Another, more radical approach is outlined in Preparing Beans on the next page.

&ate; When you eat beans, keep the meal light. Eating beans with a lot of fat, or eating a lot of beans at once, or eating a lot of anything when you eat beans—these three are sure to bring trouble.

&ate; Morning (bizarrely enough) is the best time to eat beans because when you are active, your digestive processes work better. Nighttime is worst. Eating them at breakfast is an acquired skill for adults; children can take to it easily.

&ate; Getting plenty of exercise is a good way to improve your digestion in general.

&ate; Some beans are less gas-producing and some more. This varies from person to person, but in general, adzuki beans are considered the most digestible, with "unbean" legumes like mung beans, split peas, and lentils close behind.

&ate; Thorough cooking helps. So does sprouting.

&ate; Folk wisdom suggests some additions: garlic, cumin, ground coriander, and certain other spices or a little vinegar added near the end of the cooking time.

&ate; Fermented soy foods like tempeh and miso are more easily digestible than the plain cooked beans. Tofu is not fermented, but since it contains only a fragment of the soybean, with most of the fiber removed, it doesn't cause problems for most people.

&ate; Beans are a rich source of fiber, and when you aren't used to them, high-fiber foods will cause gas. But most people find that such troubles diminish as the body accustoms itself to high-fiber foods. Give yourself time by eating small amounts at first.

Preparing Beans

The old-fashioned procedure of sorting through beans before cooking them makes an enormous difference in how they taste. Since they come to us directly from the field, without any kind of processing at all, it isn't surprising to find perhaps a couple of rocks, a few dirt clods, and a couple of moldy or otherwise disreputable individual beans in any given cup or two. An easy way to find the offenders is to spread the beans out on the far end of a big, shallow baking pan, using your fingers methodically to flip the good ones toward you and lift the bad ones out.

After sorting, rinse beans well to remove dirt and dust. You can soak them, if you like, for several hours; it reduces cooking time about 15 minutes for quick-cooking beans and as much as half an hour for slow-cooking ones. Soybeans tend to ferment, so soak them in the refrigerator in hot weather.

SCIENTIFIC SOAKING

A more drastic soaking procedure has been developed by USDA scientists to address the flatulence problem. They claim that their method removes 90 percent of the sugars that cause intestinal gas. If you want to try it, here's how: Boil the beans for 10 minutes in 5 to 10 times their weight in water. (Beans weigh about half as much as water, so that'd be 5 to 10 cups of water for a scant 2 cups of beans.) Allow them to cool and soak for 24 hours at room temperature in the same water. Discard the soak water, rinse the beans, and cook. This method does not affect protein content significantly, but there is considerable loss of minerals and vitamins.*

*Alfred C. Olson, et al., "Nutrient composition of and digestive response to whole and extracted dry beans," *Agricultural and Food Chemistry* (Jan.-Feb. 1982), pp. 26–32.

Cook beans in two or more times their measure of water, simmering until tender. Add salt toward the end of cooking time—added at the beginning, salt toughens the beans and makes them take longer to cook. (Our rule of thumb is ½ teaspoon of salt per cup of raw beans.) A good heavy pot helps prevent scorching. Beans cook fastest if the water is simmering all the time.

The easiest way to cook beans is in an electric slow cooker, because you can leave it to its own devices and the beans will cook perfectly overnight or while you are at work. The clay pot lets the beans keep their color and shape beautifully. Soybeans seem to cook only if the water is really at a slow boil; for some crocks, this means on "high" the whole time. Putting a thick folded towel on top of the lid helps conserve heat.

When thinking beans, maybe the most helpful thing to keep in mind is that these are natural super-foods and having a small quantity often is much better and easier than trying to center a meal around them once in a while. Add a few to soups or casseroles, or have bean spread sandwiches, or use a handful in salad; nearly all the problems people have with beans disappear when they are consumed in small quantities. Several friends with small households tell us they cook a pot of beans, then freeze the unused portion in ice cube trays. The little squares are easy to store and easy to thaw for use here and there.

Who's Who

ADZUKI (also *azuki* or *aduki*) beans are considered the most digestible of all. Their flavor is not what Western bean-fans are used to, but they are especially delicious served with rice or millet. Flavorful enough to stand on their own, but try adding a little shoyu, some green pepper, and ginger.

BLACK—EYED PEAS gained a lot of attention recently when everyone was looking for a good natural source of selenium—but Southerners needed no incentive. In the South, these quick-cooking, easily digested legumes have long been a favorite, and just tomato and a little onion are all that's required for embellishment. Serve with rice or Corn Bread, page 81) or add them to vegetable soups. (See Black-eyed Peas Virginia Style, page 309)

KIDNEY BEANS cooked gently and chilled, are wonderful in salads because of their bright color and light flavor. Most kidneys, though, find their way into chili dishes, and there they are the stars of the show. With a sautéed onion, garlic, oregano, and chili powder, you're in business. Kidneys, incidentally, cook quickest of the big beans: unless they are very old, you can boil them up in a little over an hour. (See Chili con Elote, page 308; Refritos, page 307; Refrito Spread, page 114; Tennessee Cornpone, page 309; Tamale Pie, page 307; Mexican Salad Bowl, page 135)

BLACK BEANS have long been the staple food in parts of Latin America, and they figure large in Japanese and Chinese cuisines as well. Super-nutritious Black Beans and Rice may be one of the most delicious of all classic bean-grain combinations. Black Bean Chili is one of the best-known dishes at Greens, the famous gourmet vegetarian restaurant of San Francisco; but if you don't want chili, season black beans with onions and plenty of garlic and add lemon just before serving. (Black Bean Soup, page 166; Refritos, page 307)

GARBANZOS (also known as chick-peas or ceci) are versatile, mildly nutty-flavored beans that keep their baby-chick shape and beige color when cooked, making them ideal for salads. Mashed, they make wonderful spreads; in vegetable and grain dishes they play a variety of parts, usually supporting roles rather than starring ones. (See Garbanzo Spread, page 114; Ceci Salad, page 134)

LENTILS take as little as half an hour to cook. They make delicious, saucy soup and stew, and they welcome flavorings of many sorts: from onion and garlic, explore tomato, potato, and eggplant; head east with green pepper, ginger, and shoyu; or try a little curry powder and yogurt for an Indian dal mixture that's surprising and soothing. Lentils can cook along with rice to make a tasty high-protein combination. Don't cook lentils in an iron pot— they turn black. (See Greek Lentil Soup, page 167; Lentil Loaf, page 306)

RED LENTILS are bright coral color when raw, but cook quickly to a soft yellowish-beige, rather like yellow split peas but more delicate.

LIMAS are two. Baby limas cook quickly but otherwise act pretty much like any white bean. Large limas or "butter beans," however, are truly one of the great beans of all time. All by themselves they make a delicious soupy sauce, to serve alongside vegetables and bulgur or rice—or to make into BUTTER BEAN SOUP with plenty of celery and sautéed green onion and maybe a dash of dill weed or parsley—one satisfying soup.

MUNG beans are familiar to everyone as Chinese bean sprouts. Cooked as beans, they are delicious and very digestible. In Indian cooking they are called *moong dal* or green gram. *Urid dal* or black gram is a close relative. (Sprouts, page 120; Kichadi, page 305)

PINTOS, if there were a bean popularity contest, might win hands down. For chili they are classic, and Refritos are pintos most pinto-y. Good in soups, too. They take a long time to cook, but they don't smoosh. (See Refritos, page 307; Refrito Spread, page 114; Tamale Pie, page 307; Tennessee Cornpone, page 309)

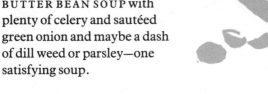

SPLIT PEAS are two, too: green and yellow. Green split peas are comfortably familiar, even to People Who Never Eat Beans. Digestible, tasty, and pretty, split peas make soup in half an hour or a little more, and though there are fancier versions, the very best may be the simplest: just a little sautéed onion and a bay leaf, salt, and pepper . . . well, celery, carrots, and potato are

good additions, and maybe a handful of parsley. (See Hearty Pea Soup, page 167; and Split Pea Spreads, page 115)

YELLOW SPLIT PEAS have a very different flavor, much warmer, better at supporting chords than at playing the melody. We use them often, cooking them along with rice (2 rice to 1 pea) to make DAL RICE; to add heft to broth and stock, to make soups heartier, or to warm and round greens dishes. (See Golden Broth, page 151; Rasam, page 150.)

WHITE BEANS—small navy beans, great northern, even baby limas—make fine additions to soups and stews. When cooked with plenty of water, they provide a smooth, saucy broth. One of the best of all stewy soups is GREEK BEANS: cook white beans along with cut-up carrot, celery, onion, and oregano, then add a dash of olive oil, salt, and paprika.

SOYBEANS are power-packed nutritionally, with more of nearly everything than the other beans—except flavor. But their very lack of personality enables them to become many things: tofu, tempeh, miso, shoyu, TVP, and other commercial products; in the kitchen, cooked and mashed soybeans make a base for tasty spreads, disappear into bread, or thicken soup. (Pine Nut Pinewheels, page 67, Soy Bread, page 72; Spreads, page 113 and 115)

Most of the enthusiasm about soy has centered around its abundant and very high quality (complete) protein. But science marches on: we now know that for most of the people who will be reading this book, getting too much protein is more likely to be a concern than getting too little. One serving of tofu may provide a quarter of your daily protein needs—rather a lot, if you will be eating other protein foods that day.

Furthermore, soy is the one bean that has a high enough fat content that you need to watch it: about 38 percent in plain soybeans, compared to less than 5 percent for most other beans. Half the calories in tofu come from fat.

TEMPEH A bright note on the soy foods scene is tempeh ("*tem*pay"), which, unlike tofu, uses the whole bean and so contains all its nutrients. Often prepared from a mixture of grain and soybeans, tempeh can have a lighter fat and protein profile than straight soybeans too. Until recently, it was hard to find really fresh tempeh, and freshness is essential for good flavor; so if you tried it and didn't like it, give it another chance. Tempeh is like fresh cheese or yogurt: a culture makes it happen, and there's a time when it's at its best; after that things go downhill. Tempeh's culture shows white at first, then black; so if you see many black spots, don't buy. At home a few black spots are okay, but the flavor won't be so mild as if you'd eaten it a day earlier.

When you prepare a tempeh dish, remember that the culture will grow very fast in a warm environment. Plan to cook it fast at a high temperature or marinate it before using. Usually tempeh is fried—it is a perfect meat substitute for new vegetarians—but since we don't ever recommend frying, our recipes offer other fast-cooking techniques that really work.

We have mentioned earlier that tempeh is more easily digestible than plain soybeans because of the fermenting culture. Commercial tempeh is produced under very carefully controlled conditions, but in its native Indonesia tempeh is made at home as we make yogurt, and the cultures (to say nothing of the flavors) are much more varied and complex. Some samples of tempeh that have been tested have contained the vitamin B-12, and you may see the claim that tempeh is a vegetarian source of B-12. *Sometimes* it may be; but the organism that makes tempeh (*Rhizopus oligosporus*) does not make vitamin B-12. If the vitamin is present, it means that bacteria have been at work too, either by accident or design. Read the label to see if B-12 is present.

For much more about this fine food, including directions for making your own, we recommend the superb *Book of Tempeh* by William Shurtleff and Akiko Aoyagi (New York: Harper and Row, 1985).

Tofu is not a fermented food like tempeh, but it is a form of bean that many people find quick to prepare, pleasant to eat, and easy to digest. Because of its high fat and protein content, and because it is not a whole food, we don't use tofu as often these days as we used to. But it is so versatile and popular that it has an important role in a transitional diet, when you're trying to edge out less desirable foods like meat, cheese, and eggs. An important consideration when you're buying tofu: although tofu is often touted as an excellent source of calcium, it is so *only* if the coagulant used is calcium sulfate. The label will tell you.

TOFU

MISO *and* SHOYU *are fermented soybean condiments that find many uses in a vegetarian whole foods kitchen. For more about miso, see page 164; shoyu, page 234.*

Tempeh à la King

2 cups vegetable broth
8 ounces tempeh

1 medium onion, minced
2 tablespoons olive oil
1/2 cup chopped red bell
    pepper, or
    1/4 cup drained canned
    pimientos
1 cup sliced fresh
    mushrooms

3 tablespoons whole
    wheat flour

(1 teaspoon light miso)
2 tablespoons sherry
freshly ground black pepper
1/4 cup blanched slivered
    almonds

Bring broth to a boil. Cut tempeh in small cubes and simmer in broth for about 10 minutes. Drain, reserving liquid, and set aside.

Sauté onion in oil until clear, then add bell pepper and mushrooms and continue to sauté over low heat, stirring often, until mushrooms are tender. (If you use pimientos, add them after mushrooms are cooked.)

Stir flour into sautéed vegetables and continue to cook and stir a minute or two. Meanwhile, add water to the reserved vegetable stock to bring it back up to 2 cups liquid and stir gradually into sautéed vegetable–flour mixture. Bring to a boil, reduce heat, and simmer for 5 minutes. Stir together miso and sherry and add to sauce along with pepper and cubed tempeh. Simmer briefly, adding almonds just before serving. Serve over brown rice or on triangles of whole-grain toast.

Makes 4 servings.

Tempeh Cacciatore

1 medium onion, slivered
1/2 cup chopped green
    bell pepper
2 tablespoons olive oil
1 clove garlic, minced
1 cup sliced fresh mushrooms
2 1/2 cups tomatoes,
    peeled and chopped
1/3 cup red wine
1 bay leaf
1/2 teaspoon oregano
1 teaspoon basil
8 ounces tempeh, cubed
2 tablespoons shoyu

Sauté onion and pepper in 1 tablespoon olive oil over low heat until onion is translucent; then stir in garlic and mushrooms and cook another 5 minutes or so. Add tomatoes, wine, bay leaf, oregano, and basil and bring to a boil. Reduce heat and simmer for 10 minutes.

Meanwhile, in another small skillet or wok, sauté tempeh in remaining 1 tablespoon oil, stirring frequently, until it browns slightly. Add to sauce along with shoyu and simmer over low heat to marry the flavors (best if it can simmer at least half an hour). Serve on a bed of whole-grain spaghetti or brown rice.

Makes 4 servings.

Tempeh à l'Orange

This is about as haute as a soybean's gonna get. And *good*.

❧

Cut tempeh in ½″ chunks and sauté in 2 tablespoons oil for about 5 minutes. Drain on paper towels. (Tempeh will soak up all the oil you give it, so save half the oil to sauté the second side.)

Chop onion coarse. Slice celery stalks once lengthwise, then cut across in ½″ slices. Sauté onion and celery in remaining oil until celery is tender. Stir in flour and keep stirring over medium heat just a minute or so; then add boiling water gradually.

Cook, stirring, while mixture thickens. Add orange juice, salt, honey, orange zest, pepper, parsley, and wine. Stir, bring to a boil, and simmer 4 or 5 minutes. Add tempeh chunks and simmer a few minutes longer to let flavors be absorbed.

Serves 4, over brown rice, quinoa, or bulgur wheat.

8 ounces tempeh
3–4 tablespoons oil

1 large onion
2 stalks celery
3 tablespoons whole wheat flour
2 cups boiling water

½ cup orange juice
1¼ teaspoons salt
1½ teaspoons honey
zest of 1 orange
dash black pepper
¼ cup chopped fresh parsley
½ cup white wine (or more orange juice)

Swedish Bean Balls

1½ cups cooked,
    well-drained beans
    (kidney, pinto, or red)
1 cup chopped onion
1 bay leaf
2 tablespoons oil

1 teaspoon lemon zest
1½ teaspoons lemon juice
1 slice whole wheat
    bread, soaked in
    milk or water
1 egg, beaten
¼ teaspoon thyme
dash nutmeg (and
    cardamom)
¾ teaspoon salt (divided)

(¼ cup dry whole wheat
    bread crumbs or cooked
    brown rice, if needed)

⅓ cup whole wheat flour
¼ teaspoon black pepper
2 cups milk
1 cup water

Preheat oven to 350°F.

Mash beans with potato masher, processor, or meat grinder. Sauté onion and bay leaf in oil in a large skillet until the onion is golden. Remove about ¼ cup of the sautéed onion with a slotted spoon and add it to the beans along with lemon peel and lemon juice. Squeeze all the liquid out of the bread (save it for the gravy) and work the bread into the mashed beans along with egg, thyme, spices, and ¼ teaspoon of the salt. (Omit salt if beans were already salted.)

If you have time, chill the mixture; it's easier to shape the balls when cold. If it seems too loose, add the dry bread crumbs or rice to stiffen it. Form 1½″ balls and place on greased baking sheet. Bake 20 minutes, until balls are dry and firm.

Meanwhile, make the gravy. Stir flour into reserved sautéed onions and cook, stirring, until flour starts to brown. Add remaining ½ teaspoon salt, pepper, and milk and water. Cook over medium-high flame, stirring frequently, until mixture begins to boil and thickens. Reduce heat to low and simmer another 7 or 8 minutes, stirring frequently.

Remove bean balls from baking sheet and place in the skillet, spooning gravy over them. Cover and let stand for 10 minutes before serving; they need time to soak up some gravy. Serve with mashed potatoes or ribbon noodles.

Makes 12 balls, to serve 4.

Walnut Oatmeal Burgers

An oatmeal-walnut "burger" that makes a satisfying sub for the nonvegetarian sort in several dishes, including the Cuban favorite Picadillo below. So that you can try the burgers as such and enjoy Picadillo too, here's a double recipe of the basic mixture. Both recipes are quite flexible. Using the smaller amount of walnuts and eggs makes for a less rich but still excellent result.

ᔈ

Grind walnuts in blender and combine with oats, eggs, milk, onion, sage, salt, and pepper. Set half the mixture aside and refrigerate, to be used as suggested below. Form patties with the rest: 4 or 6, depending on the size of buns you'll be using.

Brown patties on both sides in a lightly oiled skillet, then pour the stock into the skillet and bring to a boil. Reduce heat and simmer, covered, for 25 minutes. Serve on buns with "the fixin's" or crumble and use as you would hamburger in chili beans, spaghetti sauce, etc.

Makes 4 to 6 burgers plus:

1½–3 cups walnut pieces
2 cups rolled oats
3 or 4 eggs, slightly beaten
½ cup skim milk
1 large onion, chopped fine
1 teaspoon sage
1 teaspoon salt
freshly ground black pepper
  to taste
oil to brown patties
3 cups vegetable stock

Picadillo

This spicy mixture is traditionally served with Cuban black beans and rice, accompanied by mixed greens. It serves admirably well, too, over brown rice or whole wheat buns in the "Sloppy Joe" manner.

Form burger mixture into patties and brown on both sides as above. Dilute tomato paste in vegetable stock (if you have tomato sauce on hand, use 2 cups of that and 2 of stock). Add bay leaf and pour into the skillet. Bring to a boil break up burgers with a fork (*picadillo* means "bits and pieces"), and reduce heat to a simmer. Cook uncovered, stirring often, for 20 minutes. Add chilis, olives, apple, and raisins, bring to a boil again, and simmer just until apples are tender.

Serves 4 generously.

½ recipe for
  Walnut Oatmeal Burgers
oil for sautéeing
½ cup tomato paste
3½ cups vegetable stock
1 bay leaf

½ cup cooked green chilis
  (or a 6-ounce can)
½ cup (1 small jar) stuffed
  green olives, cut in two
1 large, tart green apple,
  peeled and chopped
(¼ cup raisins)

Neat Balls

1 cup cooked bulgur wheat
   or brown rice
½ cup Soy Spread (page 113)
¼ cup cottage cheese and/or
   grated Swiss cheese
½ cup whole-grain bread
   crumbs
1 teaspoon shoyu

Easy, tasty, and whimsical. No one will take them for their look-alike, but in spaghetti with Tomato Sauce, or with gravy, or even just alongside vegetables, they provide a welcome bit of chew.

❧

Preheat oven to 350°F.

Combine all ingredients and form into 1½″ balls. Bake on greased cookie sheets for about 20 minutes. (Place them in top third of oven, or else turn them over after 10 minutes.)

Makes 12 to 15.

Sweet and Sour Tofu

½ cup large walnut pieces
2 blocks tofu (about
   22 ounces)
4 tablespoons shoyu
2 tablespoons sherry or saki

1 large onion
1 large green pepper
1 stalk celery
1 large or 2 small carrots
2 tablespoons oil
1 heaped cup fresh pineapple
   chunks

1½ tablespoons honey
2 tablespoons vinegar
1¼ cups vegetable stock
   or water
1½ tablespoons cornstarch

Toast walnut pieces in a dry skillet over medium heat, and set aside.

Cut tofu into 1″ cubes and marinate in 2 tablespoons of the shoyu and the sherry.

Cut onion across center and down through the middle into wedge-shaped slices. Cut green pepper in pointy wedges and celery and carrots in thin diagonal slices. Stir-fry in oil until crispy-tender, adding pineapple after the first 2 or 3 minutes. Use a wok or heavy pan that has a lid—but not one made of cast iron; the acidity of this dish will cause it to discolor and taste metallic.

Combine honey, vinegar, and 1 cup of the vegetable stock, and add to vegetables along with tofu. Bring to a boil and simmer for a few minutes to heat tofu thoroughly.

Dissolve cornstarch in remaining ¼ cup stock and the remaining 2 tablespoons soy sauce. Stir into vegetables. Heat, stirring, while sauce thickens and clarifies somewhat.

Just before serving, adjust balance of sweet and sour to taste. Stir in the walnuts. Serve with brown rice.

Makes 6 servings.

Rice Lentil Polou

This recipe will have its best color if you cook it in a nonferrous pot.

❧

Chop onion and sauté in oil until soft. Add rice and stir for several minutes. Combine tomato paste with water and cinnamon. Add this mixture, along with the rinsed lentils, to the rice. Bring to a boil, cover tightly, turn heat very low, and simmer for 30 minutes.

Preheat oven to 350°F.

Stir in salt, raisins, and nuts. The mixture should still have a little water; if not, add ¼ cup. Place in greased baking dish. Cover and bake for 20 to 30 minutes.

Serves 4 to 6.

½ medium onion
1 tablespoon oil
1 cup raw brown rice
1 tablespoon tomato paste
2½ cups water or
*   vegetable stock*
¼ teaspoon cinnamon
¼ cup raw lentils
1 teaspoon salt
½ cup raisins
(½ cup pine nuts
*   or chopped almonds)*

Kichadi

A traditional dish that is served in many versions all over India. If you prefer, you can use 1 teaspoon curry powder instead of the whole spices and turmeric—Western guests may not expect to remove the cloves and sticks as they go along!

❧

Soak the mung beans for half an hour.

Cut onion in paper-thin slices. Sauté in oil until golden; then, using a slotted spoon, remove the onions and set aside. Using the oil remaining in the pan, sauté the mung beans and spices for 5 minutes, stirring madly. Stir in the rice; when it begins to stick, add 5 cups of the hot water and bring to a boil. Turn to low and simmer very gently about half an hour. At that point, check to see if you think the remaining cup of water will be needed, and stir in the salt. Continue to cook for 15 minutes or longer, until rice and beans are tender. Garnish with onions.

Makes 6 cups.

1 cup mung beans
2 medium onions
1½ tablespoons oil
1 cinnamon stick
4 cloves
1 pod cardamom (seeds only)
¼ teaspoon turmeric

2 cups raw brown rice
6 cups hot water
1½ teaspoons salt

Lentil Nut Loaf

l onion, chopped fine
1 tablespoon oil
2 cups cooked, drained lentils
½ cup whole wheat bread
    crumbs
½ cup chopped toasted
    walnuts, or
    toasted sunflower seeds
½ teaspoon sage or thyme
2 tablespoons whole wheat
    flour
2 eggs, beaten
½ cup broth or water
2 teaspoons vinegar
2 teaspoons shoyu
1 tablespoon toasted
    sesame seeds

A flavorful and nourishing (if somewhat rich) loaf. This recipe is a favorite from our first edition, much simplified and improved. Quick to prepare using leftover lentils, and very well received at lunchtime with mustard or Homemade Ketchup or at supper with sauce or gravy.

≥•

Preheat oven to 350°F.

Sauté onion in oil until translucent and slightly browned.

Mix ingredients except sesame seeds and place in greased loaf pan. Sprinkle top with the seeds. Bake for 30 minutes covered, then for 10 minutes uncovered.

If you are in a hurry, you can shape patties and cook them on the griddle, with bread crumbs and/or more sesame seeds on top and bottom.

Makes one loaf, or 8 patties.

Stuffing

1 small onion, chopped
1 tablespoon oil
2 stalks celery, chopped
    (about 1 cup)
1 teaspoon basil
½ teaspoon oregano
¼ teaspoon thyme
⅛ teaspoon sage
½ teaspoon salt (adjust
    if salted stock is used)
shake of pepper

⅔ cup water or stock
4 cups whole-grain bread
    cubes
(½ cup coarsely chopped
    pecans or hazelnuts)

Use this to stuff tomatoes, green peppers, oversized zucchinis, winter squash, or just yourself and your friends.

≥•

Sauté the onion in the oil and add the celery and herbs, cooking until the celery is crispy-tender. Add the water or stock, then the bread, stirring to be sure it is evenly moistened. When hot through, add the pecans if desired.

Serve at once, or bake to make a crispy top.

Serves 4 as a hearty grain dish at lunch or dinner.

Tamale Pie

Tamale Pie is a satisfying main dish that can take a lot of variation.

If you have a double boiler, you can start the polenta cooking first, stirring it only occasionally. (In a regular pan it is likely to burn if left to itself while you prepare the filling.)

ঌ

Sauté onion and garlic in oil. When nearly soft, add chili powder (and cumin, if desired) and crush garlic with a fork. Continue to cook and stir until spices are fragrant. Meantime, mash beans and mix them and the tomato paste into the onion, along with the other filling ingredients. When hot, adjust seasonings and set aside.

Stir cornmeal slowly into boiling water. (If you use regular cornmeal instead of coarse it is likely to lump: stir it first into 1 cup *cold* water, then into 2 cups boiling water.) Cook and stir until thick, adding the salt and chili powder once the mixture comes to a boil.

Grease an 8″ × 8″ pan and spread two thirds of the cornmeal mixture over the bottom and sides; then pour the bean mixture into this cornmeal crust and drop and spread the remaining third of the cornmeal on the top. (Don't worry if it doesn't cover completely.) Sprinkle the top crust with grated cheddar cheese and cook in a 350° oven for half an hour.

Serves 4 generously.

FILLING

1 onion, chopped
1 clove garlic
1 tablespoon oil
2 teaspoons chili powder
(½ teaspoon cumin)
2 cups cooked pinto
   or kidney beans
1 teaspoon salt (less if beans
   were salted already)
2 tablespoons tomato paste
½ cup whole ripe olives
(½ cup fresh corn)
½ green pepper, chopped
½ cup chopped celery

CRUST

3 cups boiling water
1 cup coarsely ground
   cornmeal, or
   1½ cups regular
   cornmeal
1 teaspoon salt
½ teaspoon chili powder
¼ cup grated cheddar cheese
   (more if desired)

Refritos

Heat oil in a heavy pan. Put in the beans and heat, mashing them with a potato masher. Add pepper, and salt if the beans were not salted in cooking. Delicious served with a sprinkling of cheese on top.

Makes 4 cups.

1 tablespoon oil
   (olive is best)
4 cups cooked pinto beans
black pepper
(1 teaspoon salt)

(¼ cup or so grated jack
   cheese)

Many Bean Stew

1 onion, chopped
1 tablespoon oil
(1 clove garlic)
1½ teaspoons paprika

½ cup pinto beans
5 cups boiling water
1 bay leaf
1 teaspoon celery seed
½ cup kidney beans
½ cup limas
½ cup yellow split peas
1 teaspoon dill weed
2 teaspoons salt
¼ teaspoon pepper
2 cups cubed vegetables:
　　potatoes, carrots, etc.

A good, hearty stew, adaptable to endless variations.

Sauté the onion (and garlic) in oil along with paprika.

If you have a slow cooker, put all the ingredients in and simmer about 8 hours. If not, add the pintos and water, bay, and celery seed, and bring to a boil. Simmer, partially covered, about an hour. Add kidneys and limas and simmer another hour, then add remaining ingredients. Check and stir occasionally, especially toward the end, to make sure there is enough liquid to prevent burning. Simmer gently another hour, until done.

Makes about 6 cups.

Chili con Elote

1 onion, chopped
1 clove garlic
2 tablespoons oil
1 green pepper, diced
1 teaspoon chili powder
1 teaspoon cumin powder
1 cup chopped tomato, or
　　2 tablespoons tomato
　　paste
1 cup fresh corn
4 cups cooked kidney,
　　black, or pinto beans
1½ teaspoons salt
1 teaspoon oregano

Basic and classic. The corn adds a lot, but when it isn't in season we make the dish without and it's just great.

The chili powder here is just enough for flavor without fierceness. If chili without tears isn't chili to you, use more, or add cayenne.

Sauté onion and garlic clove in oil until onion is soft. Crush garlic clove. Add green pepper and spices. Sauté another 2 or 3 minutes. Add tomatoes and corn if you have it. Mash 2 cups of the beans and add to pot along with whole beans and salt and oregano. Simmer 30 minutes.

Serves 6.

Boston Baked Beans

This classic, richly-flavored version is irresistible whether you have time to bake it or not—but the baking does marry the flavors in an especially splendid way.

&

Preheat oven to 325°F.

Sauté onion in oil. Mix all ingredients. Place in a greased, shallow glass or ceramic casserole. Bake covered for 45 minutes.

Makes 6 servings (about 3½ cups).

1 onion, chopped
1½ tablespoons oil
3 cups cooked navy beans
*   and liquid*
⅓ cup molasses
2 to 4 tablespoons
*   shoyu, to taste*
1 tablespoon prepared
*   mustard*

Tennessee Corn Pone

A homesick friend from Knoxville described a dish his grandma used to make. He says this one is juuust like grandma's. It's certainly one of our favorites.

&

Heat beans until quite hot and pour into a lightly greased 8″ × 8″ baking dish. Preheat oven to 450°F.

Mix the cornmeal, baking soda, and salt in a large bowl. Melt the butter and combine with buttermilk and egg.

Stir the wet and dry ingredients together until smooth, and pour them over the hot beans. Bake on the top rack of your oven until bread is a rich golden color and the sides of the corn bread pull away from the sides of the pan—about 30 minutes.

Serves 4 to 6.

2 cups very juicy cooked
*   and seasoned beans*
*   (especially pinto or*
*   kidney)*
1 cup cornmeal
1 teaspoon baking soda
½ teaspoon salt
2 tablespoons butter
2 cups buttermilk
1 egg, slightly beaten

Black-Eyed Peas Virginia Style

Sauté onion in oil, add celery and green pepper, and sauté another 2 minutes. Add tomato, beans, and salt and pepper to taste (½ teaspoon salt is about right if the beans weren't already salted.) Cook another 5 minutes and serve.

Serves 4.

1 small onion, chopped fine
1 tablespoon oil
¼ cup chopped celery
¼ green pepper, chopped
⅔ cup tomato, chopped
2 cups black-eyed peas,
*   well cooked, with liquid*
salt and pepper

Dessert

A keen sweet tooth tells a monkey whether the fruit in his hand will nourish or give him stomachache. Even an amoeba will go toward sugar in solution. Something very deep in us responds to sweetness, and no category of food taps such passion. (A lot of people have told us that it was easy to give up meat, but *sugar*—!)

Well, there *is* a time and place for a child's birthday cake, for oatmeal cookies slipped into a lunchbox, or for pie or cobbler to celebrate a cache of fresh-picked blackberries. But when those special gestures start to slip in several times a week, they begin to pose a real threat to health. Annual per capita sugar consumption in this country has risen to 127 pounds. Clearly, Americans are in trouble.

So, our basic premise: keep special occasions special by reserving fancy sweets for them, and let daily desserts and snacks be mostly fruit, with all its natural goodness.

In this section we offer sweets that are real alternatives. Our cookies *are* cookies, but with a lighter touch; our pound cake *is* pound cake, but with less butter; our cheese pie is *almost* cheesecake, but with a tiny fraction of the fat—and so on. Many natural food dessert books claim that because their confections are made with unbleached flour, pure honey, natural butter, and fertilized eggs, they are "healthy." How we wish we could agree! Using natural ingredients is good; you avoid many additives. But "healthy"—well, it's still the same amounts of butter, sugar, and eggs.

A dessert concoction can delight and satisfy without astronomical amounts of fat and sugar calories; but if you want "healthy," you can't come closer than fresh, ripe fruit. Plain, cut up with yogurt, made into salad, or cooked in imaginative ways when the season is on the wane, fruit really is the ideal way to say yes to a sweet tooth. Search out local sources; you may be able to get grapes, apples, peaches, apricots, berries, ripe from the tree or vine. What a difference!

Less obvious, there's a subtle magic about the rhythm of fresh fruit. Eating plenty of what is in season means that you can welcome eagerly something you haven't had all year. Enjoy it every which way until the season is finished, so you're even a little glad to see the end of it and ready to greet like a long-lost friend the next fruit that comes along.

If you have the kind of self-control that lets you enjoy sumptuous desserts when the rare occasion demands it, but never feel tempted at other times, this section is not necessary for you. But if you don't, or your family doesn't, and you are looking for ways to decelerate the sweets roller coaster, the following recipes should prove helpful.

Innocent Sweets

STUFFED PRUNES OR DATES

This works best with large fruit ("colossal" prunes are amazingly good). Stuff with Yogurt Cheese or a mixture of cottage cheese and ricotta, blended smooth with a little honey; add pizzazz with finely grated lemon rind or minced crystallized ginger and decorate with a perfect walnut half. (Chill before serving; the cheese mixture will firm up.) A festive offering at holiday time.

BAKED PEARS

In winter, Bosc pears and Winter Nelis are often available at bargain prices. Even if they are rock-hard, bake them like yams for the sweetest, most delicious, and easiest dessert imaginable. They don't want stuffing like apples; you just stand them on their bottoms in a pan (line it with brown paper if you want to save scrubbing later) and bake at about 350°F for 45 minutes or so, until the syrupy juice has broken out and the pear is soft. We usually serve them as is, but you might want to make a gingery sauce or pass toasted nuts or feta cheese to nibble alongside.

FRUIT POPS

Make fruit pops by blending equal parts of mild yogurt and ripe berries or other sweet fruit. These can be rather horrid if the yogurt is tart and the fruit not sweet, so add some honey when needed. Freeze in popsicle molds.

FRUITED YOGURT A perfect combination that can be plain or fancy: just fruit with a dollop of yogurt. You can alternate layers in parfait glasses, or in small jars for bag lunches. You can even make your own fruit yogurt: just place a layer of dried or cooked fruit in the bottom of several containers, pour in the milk and starter, and culture as usual. All these ideas work best when the yogurt is mild.

Here are some easy and tasty suggestions, with approximate amounts to use for one cup of yogurt:

½ cup stewed apples and a dash of cinnamon

½ cup Fruit Tzimmes

1 large, ripe persimmon, peeled and cut up,
   and a tablespoon of raisins

3 or 4 chopped dried apricots (add a little honey if
   apricots are tart) or a mixture of apricots and pineapple

4 big dates, pitted and chopped, with a dash of cinnamon

¼ cup chopped prunes, with a slivered slice of crystallized
   ginger

any amount of fresh strawberries or other sweet berries,
   or fresh ripe peaches, pears, apricots, plums . . .

3 tablespoons raisins, with a dash of cinnamon

Desserts from Apples

Since apples grow nearly everywhere and store well, they are inexpensive and good during the cold months. For winter desserts, they take many roles. Here are a few of our favorites.

Baked Apples

Preheat oven to 350°. Core apples and place in a greased baking dish with a cover. It's good if the apples are a snug fit: if not, cut up a fifth apple in quarters and tuck it around.

Mix the wheat germ, raisins, nuts, lemon zest, cinnamon, sugar, and salt and press lightly into the apple cores. Mix the flour and apple juice and pour over the apples.

Bake 40 minutes, or until the apples are very soft. Let cool slightly before serving for best flavor.

Serves 4.

VARIATION:

Substitute 2 tablespoons toasted sesame seeds for the nuts, and use 6 tablespoons of raisins instead of 4. (This is a delightful combination.)

4 large flavorful apples

¼ cup toasted wheat germ
¼ cup raisins
*¼ cup chopped walnuts
  or filberts*
zest of ½ lemon
⅛ teaspoon cinnamon
1 tablespoon brown sugar
pinch salt

1 tablespoon flour
¾ cup apple juice

Diane's Apple Crisp

This homey, quickly-made favorite, with perhaps a little yogurt alongside, can stand proudly next to the most exotic dessert.

Preheat oven to 375°F. Slice apples until you have enough to fill a greased 9″ × 13″ baking dish. Mix the apples in a bowl with lemon juice, cinnamon, flour, and raisins. Return them to the baking dish, adding enough water or apple juice to cover the bottom.

Mix topping in a bowl and press onto top of apples. Bake for 25 minutes, or until apples are soft.

Serves 8.

*8 apples (green pippins
  are best)*
juice of 1 lemon
1 teaspoon cinnamon
*2 tablespoons whole
  wheat flour*
¾ cup raisins
water or apple juice

TOPPING
1 cup rolled oats
⅓ cup toasted wheat germ
½ cup whole wheat flour
½ teaspoon salt
2 teaspoons cinnamon
½ cup brown sugar
½ cup butter (or oil)

Appley Bread Pudding

2 cups grated apples
juice of 1 lemon

4 cups whole-grain bread,
    cubed small
½ cup cottage cheese
⅓ cup raisins
¼ teaspoon cinnamon

2 cups milk
¼ cup dried skim milk
1 egg
¼ cup brown sugar

1 tablespoon butter

The best bread pudding we have tasted. Besides being a super way to use up stale bread, the dish is so nutritious and high in protein that it can supply all the heft that is needed with a light dinner.

Of course, bread pudding can be even simpler. If you are out of apples, or in a hurry, all you actually *have* to have is the cubed bread with the milk and egg, plus sugar and spice (and a dot or two of butter) for flavor. It bakes while you eat dinner, and is ready when you want dessert.

❧

Preheat oven to 350°F. Grease an 8″ × 8″ pan.

Grate the apples and mix in the lemon juice.

Put ⅓ of the bread in the bottom of the greased pan. Cover with half the apple, half the cottage cheese, half the raisins, and a sprinkle of the cinnamon.

Blend the milk, milk powder, egg, and sugar together and pour half over the ingredients in the baking dish. Now repeat the layers of bread, apples, and liquid, ending with more bread. Pour the last of the milk mixture over the top, sprinkle with cinnamon, and dot with butter.

Let the pudding sit for 20 minutes if you can, especially if the bread is not light. Bake, covered, for 45 minutes, then let stand for at least ten minutes at room temperature before serving.

Serves 4 to 6.

Fruit Tzimmes

1 pound (3 cups) dried
    fruits: raisins, prunes,
    apricots, but not dates
    or figs
2 grated carrots
2 grated apples
1 lemon or lime, thinly sliced
1 teaspoon salt
1 tablespoon butter
water for soaking fruit

Tzimmes is a favorite fruit dessert in Jewish cookery: sweet but piquant, delicious with Blintzes or Latkes, or with yogurt, or as a kind of chutney with brown rice and vegetables.

❧

Wash dried fruit and soak in water, covered, for 1 hour. Drain water and reserve. Combine all ingredients in a pot with ½ cup of the soaking water. Bring to a boil, then cook over very low heat for 1 or 2 hours, adding more liquid as needed.

Makes 4 cups.

Vanilla Pudding

Serve this simple, wholesome dessert with fresh peaches or berries, figs, or orange slices, garnished with chopped toasted nuts—or serve it plain. It's nearly as easy as instant pudding and a whole lot cheaper. Using honey instead of sugar gives a delightful flavor, but *some* honeys can make the pudding thin out—most frustrating.

2 cups fresh milk

1/4 cup brown sugar
1/8 teaspoon salt
2 tablespoons cornstarch
 or arrowroot
1 teaspoon vanilla

꙾

Gently heat 1½ cups of the milk in a heavy pan. Stir in the sugar and salt.

Combine the cornstarch or arrowroot with the reserved milk. Add to the milk when it is very hot; cook and stir over low heat until thick. If you are using cornstarch, continue to cook and stir over very low heat for a few minutes more. (If you want a richer version, you can stir a beaten egg into ½ cup of the pudding, then beat that into the whole pudding while it is still very hot.) Cool somewhat and add vanilla.

Makes about 2 cups to serve 4—in theory. (Sometimes it actually serves two.) Good warm or cold.

Payasam

Literally food for the gods—at least, in Indian myths—this creamy rice pudding is the required finale for a South Indian feast. To make rice meal, grind brown rice fine in blender.

1/4 cup rice meal

1 quart milk
1/4 cup brown sugar

꙾

Make a paste with rice meal and ½ cup of the cold milk.

Heat remaining milk and stir in rice mixture and sugar. Bring gently to a boil, stirring to prevent sticking, and continue to cook gently until mixture thickens slightly, 5 to 10 minutes, depending on how fine the rice was.

3 cardamom pods
1 tablespoon butter
1/4 cup cashews
1/4 cup raisins

Remove pods from cardamom and discard. Crush seeds in a mortar and pestle or with two spoons. Heat butter in a small skillet; add cardamom and cashews, and when cashews are just beginning to toast, add raisins. When nuts are nicely brown and raisins puffy, add them to the thickened milk.

Cool. Payasam is quite soupy when it's "just right."
Serves 4 to 8.

Apple Spice Ring

2½ cups grated apple,
    peeled and cored first
2 cups raisins
1½ cups boiling water
3 tablespoons oil

1 cup + 2 tablespoons honey
1½ teaspoons cinnamon
1½ teaspoons allspice
½ teaspoon cloves
1½ teaspoons salt

3 cups whole wheat pastry
    flour
1½ teaspoons baking soda
¾ cup chopped walnuts

Moist, rich, and spicy, a favorite for festive occasions. Keeps for a week in the refrigerator, if no one knows it's there.

Preheat oven to 350°F.

Pour boiling water over apples and raisins. Top with oil and let stand 10 minutes. Add honey and spices (including salt), then allow to cool.

Sift together the flour and baking soda, add walnuts, and combine with the other ingredients. Pour into well-greased tube pan (or 8″ × 8″ pan or two 4″ × 8″ loaf pans).

Bake for 45 minutes to 1 hour.

CARROT FRUITCAKE

Replace apples with 1½ cups grated carrots. Use 1½ cups raisins and 2¼ cups boiling water. Cook the carrots and raisins in the water 10 minutes; then add oil, honey, salt, and spices and allow to cool. Proceed as above, beginning where the dry ingredients are sifted together.

Pound Cake

2¼ cups whole wheat
    pastry flour
1½ teaspoons baking
    powder
½ teaspoon baking soda
½ teaspoon salt

⅔ cup honey
½ cup butter
1 teaspoon vanilla

2 eggs
¾ cup buttermilk

Traditional versions of this gloriously understated dessert require a pound of butter, a pound of sugar, and a pound of eggs. Yet this one is delicious.

Preheat oven to 350°F.

Ingredients should be at room temperature. Sift flour before measuring, then sift with baking powder, baking soda, and salt.

Cream honey and butter. Add vanilla.

Separate eggs. Whip egg whites until stiff. Beat yolks and add to honey and butter. Add sifted ingredients to this mixture, a third at a time, alternating with buttermilk.

Fold in egg whites and turn into a 4″ × 8″ loaf pan.

Bake 1 hour.

Banana Bread

Preheat oven to 375°F.

Mash bananas and mix them with lemon juice until smooth. Cream butter or oil and sugar together and add the banana mix, stirring well.

Sift together flour, salt, baking powder, and baking soda. Mix in wheat germ. Add to the banana mix and stir in the dates and nuts if desired.

The dough will be very stiff. Turn it into a greased 4″ × 8″ loaf pan and bake for about 45 minutes. To test for doneness, insert a knife into the loaf: if it comes out clean, the bread is done.

Makes 1 loaf.

(You can also bake banana bread in an 8″ × 8″ pan, or make 12 cupcakes. Bake these for about ½ hour.)

3 very ripe bananas
  (1 cup mashed)
juice of 1 lemon
⅓ cup oil or butter
½ cup brown sugar

1½ cups whole wheat flour
½ teaspoon salt
½ teaspoon baking powder
½ teaspoon baking soda
½ cup wheat germ
(1 cup chopped dates)
(1 cup toasted nuts)

Gingerbread

This may well be the definitive gingerbread. We certainly tested enough alternative versions before we agreed upon it. (In fact, this whole chapter of recipes has been extraordinarily well tested.)

❧

Preheat oven to 350°F.

Mix butter and molasses. Beat in egg and add buttermilk or orange juice.

Sift together the dry ingredients and combine everything together.

Turn into a greased 9″ × 9″ square pan. Bake 40 minutes.

⅓ cup soft or melted butter
1 cup dark molasses or
  ⅔ cup blackstrap and
  ⅓ cup honey
1 egg
1 cup buttermilk or orange
  juice

2½ cups whole wheat flour
1 teaspoon soda
1 teaspoon cinnamon
2 teaspoons powdered ginger
½ teaspoon salt

½ cup raisins
(1 tablespoon orange zest)
(½ teaspoon mustard
  powder)

Figgy Pudding

2 tablespoons soft butter
½ cup honey

3 eggs

1 cup chopped dried figs,
   packed
1 apple, peeled and sliced
1 cup apple juice

zest of 1 lemon
1 teaspoon vanilla
1 cup raisins
1 cup finely chopped walnuts
2 cups soft whole wheat
   bread crumbs

1 cup whole wheat flour
· 1 teaspoon baking powder
½ teaspoon salt
¼ teaspoon baking soda
1 teaspoon cinnamon
½ teaspoon nutmeg
¼ teaspoon ground cloves

Traditional as can be, and delicious, Figgy Pudding contains lots less fat than pie, though you'd never guess it.

≈

Cream butter and honey. Separate eggs, setting whites aside. Beat egg yolks until creamy. Add to butter-honey mixture.

Use a blender or food processor to grind figs and apples with apple juice to jamlike consistency. Combine with lemon rind, vanilla, raisins, walnuts, bread crumbs, and the egg yolk mixture.

Sift flour with baking powder, salt, soda, cinnamon, nutmeg, and cloves. Beat egg whites until stiff. Combine wet ingredients with dry, then gently fold in egg whites. Turn batter out into a greased 2-quart casserole or pudding mold with a lid. You can use parchment or foil for a lid, securing it with twine, but be sure to allow room for expansion: the pudding will rise to about half again its uncooked size.

Place pudding on a rack inside a pot large enough to give 2 inches of space all around for the steam to circulate. Pour boiling water into the pot halfway up the sides of the casserole. Cover the pot and let water boil briskly a few moments, then turn heat to low. Keep an eye on the water and replenish it if the level goes down. Steam for 2½ hours or until top springs back when touched.

To unmold, turn out carefully onto a plate. Splash with brandy and ignite, if you like, and serve with a scoop of vanilla ice cream or with the topping below.

Serves 12.

Yogurt Cheese Topping

1½ cups yogurt cheese
2 tablespoons honey
lemon juice to taste
zest of 1 lemon, minced

This topping is adaptable to many roles, and can be made entirely successfully with low-fat or even skim-milk yogurt. If you have good oranges or tangerines, they can sub for the lemon—try that on strawberries!

≈

Gently stir cheese smooth with a fork and add the other ingredients, adjusting the sweetness to taste.

Spicy Pattern Cookies

These are quite austere when freshly baked, so if you want to eat them right away, plan on at least a little frosting. But they improve in airtight storage so that two weeks later, they are fine even without decoration.

❧

Preheat oven to 350°.

Cream butter and sugar and beat in the molasses. Sift the flour, setting aside any bran that remains behind to add later. Sift again with the soda, salt, and spices, then stir in wheat germ and reserved bran. Mix dry ingredients into molasses mixture, adding enough of the water to make a workable dough.

Roll dough out about ¼" thick (or thinner if you prefer) and cut into shapes. Transfer to greased cookie sheets and bake for about 10 minutes, until just barely beginning to brown. Makes 4 dozen 2" cookies.

Decorate by pressing in currants, filbert halves, etc., before baking or with a simple powdered sugar frosting after the cookies have cooled. (If you are working with children and want to tint decorative frostings with food coloring, remember that artificial food colors shouldn't be ingested in anything but truly minute quantities.)

¼ cup butter
¼ cup brown sugar

½ cup dark molasses

3 cups whole wheat flour
1 teaspoon baking soda
½ teaspoon salt
1 teaspoon ginger
½ teaspoon cinnamon
¼ teaspoon cloves

½ cup wheat germ

about ½ cup water

Anise Seed Cookies

Light, delicate cookies, softly crisp.

❧

Sift together flour, baking powder, and salt. Cream butter and sugar. Beat in egg, lemon peel, anise seeds, vanilla, and water. Gradually add dry ingredients to liquid, mixing well. Divide in half and roll into logs 1½" in diameter. Wrap each in waxed paper and refrigerate several hours or overnight.

Preheat oven to 375°F. Cut dough into slices about ¼" thick. Dip in powdered sugar if desired and bake on greased cookie sheet for 10 to 12 minutes.

Makes 3 to 4 dozen.

1½ cups whole wheat flour
1½ teaspoons baking powder
½ teaspoon salt
3 tablespoons butter (room temperature)
½ cup brown sugar
1 egg, slightly beaten
1 teaspoon grated lemon peel
1½ teaspoons anise seeds
1 teaspoon vanilla
3 tablespoons water
(powdered sugar)

Oatmeal School Cookies

½ cup butter (¼ pound)
¾ cup brown sugar, packed
1 lightly beaten egg
1½ teaspoons vanilla
½ teaspoon salt

1 cup whole wheat flour
¾ teaspoon baking powder
½ cup toasted wheat germ
¾ cup rolled oats
¾ cup raisins
¾ cup chopped walnuts or
  toasted sunflower seeds

When we make cookies, it is almost always these. They are *Cookies*: utterly satisfying. One would wish they could be maybe a little lower in fat and sugar, but there, that's *Cookies* for you—don't make a habit of 'em.

❧

Preheat oven to 375°F. Cream butter and sugar until fluffy. Add egg, vanilla, and salt, and beat well.

Stir flour, baking powder, wheat germ, and rolled oats together with a fork. Blend well with other ingredients, adding a tablespoon or more of water if necessary to hold the mixture together.

Place by tablespoonful on greased cookie sheets. Flatten them slightly. Bake for 10 to 12 minutes.

Makes 24.

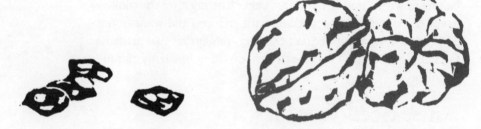

Graham Cookies

2 cups whole wheat flour
½ cup wheat bran
½ cup wheat germ
1 teaspoon baking powder
½ teaspoon baking soda
¼ teaspoon salt

½ cup butter
½ cup brown sugar

½ cup milk or buttermilk

This delicious version of graham crackers is too rich to be called a cracker, but too good not to include.

❧

Stir together the dry ingredients. Cream the butter and brown sugar until fluffy. Add flour mixture alternately with milk, mixing well after each addition.

Chill dough for several hours or overnight.

Preheat oven to 350°F. Roll dough out thin, directly onto greased cookie sheets, and cut into squares or shapes. Prick with fork and bake 10 to 12 minutes, until brown.

Makes about 4 dozen 2½″ cookies.

Raisin Bars

This recipe is a gift from master whole-foods baker Manuel Freedman. It has no sugar or honey, and needs none! The taste is reminiscent of an old favorite, those giant flat cookies with smooshed raisins inside.

ૐ

Preheat oven to 325°F.

Blend the flour, oats, salt, and oil with fingers until evenly mixed. Add raisins, nuts, and water, and mix them in, pressing together with the fingers. (Use larger amount of water only if absolutely necessary to make it all hold together.) Press down very well into a greased 8″ × 8″ pan and cut into squares with a spatula before baking.

Bake ½ hour. Makes 16 two-inch bars.

1 cup whole wheat pastry flour
1 cup rolled oats
½ teaspoon salt
¼ cup oil
1¼ cups finely chopped or ground raisins
1 cup chopped walnuts
⅓ to ½ cup water

Sunshine Bars

Well, here they are, "health food bars"—but much tastier than the ones you can buy.

ૐ

Preheat oven to 350°F.

Heat orange juice to a boil. Put dried apricots in pan, bring to a boil again, and turn off heat. Cover pan and let apricots absorb juice until tender enough to cut with a sharp knife, but not really soft.

Meanwhile, mix honey and oil. Stir oats, flour, wheat germ, cinnamon, and salt together.

Drain apricots and add the juice to the honey-oil mixture. Chop apricots coarsely and stir into dry ingredients along with raisins and almond meal. Combine wet and dry ingredients and press mixture into an oiled 9″ × 13″ baking dish. Bake about 30 minutes. Keep an eye on them! Cookies made with honey brown quickly.

Allow to cool completely before cutting.

Makes about 2 dozen large squares.

1 cup orange juice
1 cup dried apricots, loosely packed

½ cup honey
½ cup oil

1½ cups rolled oats
1 cup whole wheat flour
½ cup wheat germ
1 teaspoon cinnamon
½ teaspoon salt

1 cup raisins, partly cut up
⅔ cup toasted almond meal

Honey-Peanut Butter Cookies

1 cup natural peanut butter
   (*crunchy is best*)
1 cup honey
1 egg, beaten
1½ teaspoons vanilla

½ teaspoon salt
½ teaspoon baking soda
2 cups whole wheat flour,
   preferably pastry flour

These cookies, and the following almond version, are natural-foods alternatives to the very rich and sugary standard editions. The flavor is different: the honey really sings out. It also makes the cookies softer rather than crispy, and (sad truth) prone to burn if not watched carefully while they bake. They're worth it: these are *very* good cookies indeed.

❧

Preheat oven to 350°F.

Cream peanut butter and honey together. Stir in egg and vanilla. Sift together salt, soda, and flour, and stir into peanut butter mixture.

Drop by teaspoonfuls onto oiled cookie sheets. Mash each cookie slightly with the back of a fork, wetting the fork frequently to prevent sticking. Bake for 10 or 12 minutes, until they just begin to turn golden brown on the rims. Keep a close eye on them! Cookies made from honey pass very quickly from golden brown to black.

Makes 3 or 4 dozen. Very good keepers.

HONEY–ALMOND COOKIES

The Adult Version: light, flavorful, pretty.

❧

Substitute smooth, toasted almond butter for peanut butter, and almond extract for vanilla.

To form the cookies, roll the dough into balls about walnut-size. Press a blanched almond down in the center of each one.

Another way to use these recipes is REFRIGERATOR COOKIES: form the dough into a cylinder, and refrigerate, slicing off what you need to bake in smaller batches. Or make pinwheels: Work ¼ to ½ cup chocolate or carob powder into half the dough; then roll both halves out thin on waxed paper and, using your rolling pin to lift the dough, transfer one onto the other. (It's tricky, because there's no moving 'em once they're together!) Roll up tightly and refrigerate overnight. Cut into thin cookies with a sharp knife or strong thread (dental floss works very nicely).

Bake as above.

Summer Fruit Mold

Molded salads are a traditional favorite for summer, but many people write them off when they become vegetarians because they don't want to use gelatin. Agar, made from seaweed, puts molded salads back on the map. The following recipe is simple, pretty, and adaptable to any number of fruits—and dressy enough for the fanciest wedding buffet. (Look for white grape juice at the supermarket if you don't want to pay a fortune for the gourmet kinds.)

2½ tablespoons agar flakes
2 cups white grape juice
2 tablespoons lime juice
   (1 big lime)
1 cup fresh raspberries or
   blackberries
1 cup sliced fresh peaches

Dissolve agar in grape juice and add lime juice. Let sit a few minutes, stir, and heat to just shy of boiling. Reduce heat and simmer for 3 minutes, stirring frequently. Pour into 4 warm wine glasses and allow to cool for just 15 minutes. Gently stir in berries and peaches, and refrigerate until ready to serve. (It will set firm in about 30 minutes.) Decorate with a sprig of mint and a few raspberries, or whatever seems pretty to you.

   Makes 4 servings.

Cashew Cardamom Balls

Cashew Cardamom Balls have an oriental ambience. Sophisticated, sweet, and sinfully rich-tasting, they qualify easily as gourmet fare; but they're so easy to make that you can turn them out for lunchbox treats.

1 cup lightly toasted
   cashew pieces
cardamom seeds from
   2 to 4 pods
   (⅛ to ¼ teaspoon
   powdered)
1 cup finely chopped dates
finely grated peel of
   one orange
½ cup dried coconut, toasted
   and then powdered in
   blender

Chop cashews rather fine (the blender chops them *too* fine). Remove cardamom from pods and grind with a mortar and pestle or between two spoons. Combine cashews and cardamom in a bowl with dates and orange peel. Knead mixture with fingertips until uniform, then roll in 1″ balls and coat them with coconut.

   Makes 18.

Whole Wheat Piecrust

1½ cups whole wheat flour
½ cup wheat germ
　(or ¼ cup flour)
¾ teaspoon salt
10 tablespoons butter,
　chilled

4 to 6 tablespoons cold water

Keep an eye on the baking pastry; whole wheat piecrust tends to brown easily. When we bake pumpkin pie, for example, we keep strips of aluminum foil on hand to put around the crust at the half-way point. Baking the pie on a cookie sheet helps too.

Whole wheat flour gives piecrust a rich flavor that makes the white kind seem insipid. This recipe is not difficult to prepare, and it gives a flaky, mouth-watering result, especially if you use the wheat germ. (If there's none in the house, or if you want a less overtly wheaty flavor, using a little extra flour works fine too.)

Use all-purpose whole wheat flour, or half bread flour and half pastry flour. Using all pastry flour makes a tender, crumbly crust rather than a flaky one.

❧

Stir together flour, wheat germ, and salt. Grate the cold butter on a coarse grater or cut into small pieces, tossing it with the flour as you go. Use a pastry cutter or two knives to combine the flour and butter until it is the consistency of rolled oats. Sprinkle with the water, using just enough to hold the dough together.

Using cupped fingers, form the dough quickly and gently. As soon as it will hold together, make it into a ball.

Press the dough out into a thick disk. Roll to size on a lightly floured surface, or between sheets of waxed paper, or on a pastry cloth. Gently roll the dough over the rolling pin and onto the pie plate, easing it loosely into the plate. If it sticks to the table, slide a long, sharp knife underneath; if it tears, patch with extra dough once it is in place. Gently press the dough into the plate so there are no air pockets. Cut off the excess with a sharp knife, but make the rim double thick to keep it from burning.

If you are making a bottom-shell-only pie, form an attractive rim on the crust and prick the shell all over with a fork. To keep the pastry from shrinking, and to get the flakiest crust, refrigerate it for about 2 hours or overnight before filling.

To prebake, place in a preheated oven (400°F) for 10 to 12 minutes; cool and fill. For a partly baked shell (for quiche, for example) bake only until the pastry is set, about 7 minutes.

If you are making a pie with a top crust or lattice, preheat the oven to 400°F. Fill the bottom shell and put the top crust or lattice in place, baking according to the directions in the recipe you are using.

Makes one 10″ bottom crust or crust and lattice for one 8″ pie.

Mock Mince Pie

This simple, scrumptious recipe is our Thanksgiving favorite.

❧

Pare and slice apples, chop raisins, and mix with apple juice. Scrub the orange, then grate the peel and squeeze the juice. Add peel and juice to the apple mixture and simmer together in a covered pan until the apples are very soft. Stir in the sugar, cinnamon, cloves, and the brandy extract if desired. This mixture will keep for several days if you want to prepare it ahead.

Preheat oven to 450°F.

Line a 9″ pie pan with pastry and make the extra dough into a lattice. Reheat the filling, if it has been chilled, and pour it hot into the shell. Cover with lattice and bake for 30 minutes.

Makes one 9″ pie.

4 medium apples
½ cup raisins
⅓ cup apple juice
1 orange

¾ cup brown sugar
½ teaspoon cinnamon
½ teaspoon cloves
½ teaspoon brandy
  (or extract)
dough for a 10″ piecrust

Berry Pudding Pie

For a scrumptious summertime dessert, fill a prebaked pie shell or crumb crust with 3 cups or so of fresh blackberries, raspberries, strawberries, blueberries, or sliced peaches. Pour Vanilla Pudding (page 315) over them while it's still warm. Sprinkle with toasted nuts if you like, and chill.

If you have fruit too pretty to hide, fill your pie shell with pudding and let it cool slightly. Arrange sweet berries or slices of ripe, sweet peach, kiwi, or apricot on top. (You can prevent sliced fruit from turning brown by dipping it in orange juice, or by heating it briefly as described in the Blueberry Cheese Pie recipe, on the next page.)

Yogurt Cheese Pie

graham cracker crust
  (page 327)

This delicious dessert is very like cheesecake, but a more innocent one you won't easily find. And it is easy.

❧

¼ pound dried calimyrna
  figs (¾ cup chopped)
⅓ cup honey

Chop figs and place in small saucepan with honey. Add boiling water to cover. Bring to a boil, reduce heat, and simmer, stirring occasionally, for 10 minutes. Cover and let sit until figs are fully rehydrated; boil off extra water until the remaining liquid is quite thick.

1½ teaspoons vanilla
zest of 1 lemon, finely grated
2 cups stiff yogurt cheese
  (page 104)

Stir stewy figs, vanilla, and lemon zest into yogurt cheese and pour into crust. Sprinkle with walnuts. Chill for a couple of hours before serving.

¼ cup chopped walnuts
  for topping

BLUEBERRY CHEESE PIE

2 cups berries, or a
  combination of fruits

Leave out the figs and vanilla. Sweeten and flavor the yogurt cheese with honey and lemon zest, adding extra honey as needed to taste. Spread it into the crust and top it with berries or a beautiful arrangement of other prime summer fruits, such as sliced peaches, raspberries, strawberries, and blueberries.

For extra elegance, you can glaze the fruit very lightly to bring up its flavor and give it shine. Kuzu powder gives the best shine, but you can use arrowroot if you have that. (Cornstarch doesn't thicken as quickly, so the fruit may overcook.)

GLAZE

juice of 1 lemon
2 tablespoons honey
1 tablespoon kuzu powder
  or arrowroot

Dissolve the kuzu powder in lemon juice and stir in the honey. Heat the fruit in a non-iron skillet, shaking or stirring gently to ensure even heat. When hot, add the mixture of lemon juice, honey, and thickener. Stir gently as before, letting the liquid coat the fruit evenly. As soon as the thickener has cooked, remove from heat. Allow to cool somewhat, then place topping on cheese filling. If you are using a combination of fruits, cook in separate batches to keep each one's color clear.

Graham Cracker Crusts

This crust holds together well, tastes good, and has no fat beyond what is in the graham crackers.

❧

Mix ingredients very well and press into a buttered 8″ or 9″ pie pan or quiche pan (the kind with scalloped vertical sides and pop-out bottom). The mixture is sticky; it helps to wet your fingers.

Bake 15 minutes, until delicately brown.

*1½ cups finely crushed
   graham crackers
3 tablespoons yogurt
1½ tablespoons honey
¼ teaspoon cinnamon*

❧

This version is much more sinful and doesn't hold together as well as the first, but it has the slight advantage of not needing baking.

❧

Mix ingredients and press into 9″ pie pan.

*1 cup finely crushed
   graham crackers
3 tablespoons warm honey
3 tablespoons melted butter
½ cup finely chopped
   walnuts*

Peanut Butter Bars

A calorie-packed treat. Candy is what it is, and "PB Bars" probably should have been exorcised from this book long ago. But they seem to fill a need—emergency rations, if you will. They are the *only* way some among us (who want to) can gain weight; and friends testify that they are an effective last-ditch defense against chocolate truffles. Too much fat, assuredly. But not empty calories. . . .

Use peanut butter that's 100 percent peanuts, and not hydrogenated. The amount you need to use varies somewhat, depending on whether the peanut butter is off the top or bottom of the jar.

❧

Mix wheat germ, milk, sugar, raisins, salt, and optional ingredients. Add enough peanut butter to make the mixture stiff but not crumbly.

Roll mixture into balls, or press on flat surface by hand or with a rolling pin until it's about ½″ thick. Cut into 1½″ squares. Cover with coconut or sesame. Store in a covered container in refrigerator.

Makes about 3 dozen bars.

2 cups crunchy peanut butter

*⅓ cup toasted wheat germ
½ cup dried skim milk
⅓ cup brown sugar or honey
½ cup raisins
½ teaspoon salt*

*(chopped dried fruit)
(toasted chopped nuts or
   sunflower seeds)*

*¾ cup toasted unsweetened
   coconut flakes or
¾ cup toasted sesame seeds*

Menus

Well and good, a book bulging with fresh new vegetarian recipes—but what about combining those delicious sounding dishes into meals? What does a well-balanced vegetarian meal *look* like? What combinations of flavor and texture work well together? Here are some that work for us:

BREAKFAST

Breakfast, of course, is a somewhat personal matter, but these are some of our favorites:

*Hot whole-grain cereal
    with low-fat milk,
    toasted sunflower seeds,
    and stewed prunes
Grapefruit*

*Homemade Granola with
    sliced fresh figs and
    buttermilk*

*Spoonbread
Black-eyed Peas Virginia Style
Fresh peaches*

*Cheese Blintzes
Applesauce*

*Boston Brown Bread
    with ricotta cheese
Boston Baked Beans
Pears*

*Masala Dosas
Yogurt
Orange slices*

LUNCH

After a while, favorite meal patterns emerge—for us, nowhere more than at lunch. Basically, there are two:

🍃 Sandwiches accompanied by raw vegetables or fruit

🍃 Soup, salad, or a pot of beans with fresh bread, muffins, or tortillas

DINNER

Dinner too has its patterns, without anyone getting tired of the variations. Ours are always accompanied by a salad, with fresh fruit for dessert.

Here are a few sets of menus for lunch and dinner. Following our Food Guide, each day includes at least three servings of vegetables, one of which is a "super-veggie." Assuming that you've dispatched two servings of some kind of whole-grain food at breakfast—a bowl of cereal, for example, with a slice of toast— these lunch and dinner pairs illustrate ways of filling out the rest of the Food Guide plan.

The dishes in parentheses are optional: you can omit them or substitute something simpler. For instance, whole-grain rolls may be easy on baking day, but you could certainly serve brown rice, muffins, or noodles instead. Don't feel constrained by these menus—they are illustrations, meant to inspire and set your imagination free.

> *A casserole or "hearty dish," flanked by a vegetable unless the casserole is already laced with them*

> *A medley of steamed or stir-fried vegetables, served over or alongside rice, bulgur wheat, pasta, or potato (see page 224)*

> *Soup with muffins, bread, rolls, or breadsticks*

> *Two or more vegetables cooked separately, along with something hefty: the "vegetable plate" pattern. (The trick is to keep your sauces and garnishes simple and harmonious)*

SUMMER

Summertime, and the livin' really *is* easy: fruits and vegetables are at their best now. Think about meal-in-a-bowl salads made with perfect lettuce, or stir-fries of the newest arrivals in the garden: fresh tomatoes, corn, zucchini, eggplant, green beans, peas, tender chard, oh, my . . .

LUNCH FROM THE GARDEN
Creamy Green Soup
Tomato-Pepper Salad
Oat Crackers

SOUTH INDIAN DINNER
Cauliflower Eggplant Curry (Aviyal)
Brown rice
Coriander Chutney
Payasam

SIMPLE LUNCH
Sandwich of almond butter, sprouts, and tomato with Dijon mustard on whole-grain bread
Apricots

GARDEN DINNER
Broiled half tomatoes
Baked Zucchini
Potatoes Tarragon
Spinach-Mushroom Salad

SOUP & SALAD LUNCH
Fresh Corn and Tomato Soup
California Tossed Salad
Whole-grain bread
Blackberries and yogurt

CHINESE DINNER
Sweet and Sour Tofu over brown rice
Chinese Asparagus
Stir-fried Bok Choy
Plums

AUTUMN

With the fall, temperatures drop and appetites quicken. Many of the summer vegetables—eggplants for instance—stretch on into October. Local apples come in, streaked with red, then ripe yellow pears and golden pumpkins.

LUNCH

Ceci Salad
Breadsticks
Fresh figs

DINNER

(Early Autumn Fruit Soup)
Mushrooms Petaluma over
*   whole wheat noodles*
Slaw Chez Nous

SUNDAY LUNCH

Sebastopol Pizza
Green salad, Curry Dressing

DINNER

Eggplant Parmesan
Chard with Lemon Butter
Green Salad
(Whole-Grain Dinner Rolls)

SOUP & SANDWICH LUNCH

Soy Pâté sandwich on
*   whole-grain bread*
*   with mustard and sprouts*
Carrot Soup

SOUP & SALAD DINNER

Creamy Cauliflower Soup
Shades of Green Salad
Cracked-wheat Rolls

LUNCH

Black Bean Soup
Light Rye Rolls with
*   Jack and Dill Spread*
Fresh pears

DINNER

Bulgur Pilaf
Mustard greens
*   (with Wickedly Good Sauce)*
Carrot Salad
Baked Apples

WINTER

Hearty appetites need food to match: substantial soups, assertive root vegetables, squash and potatoes and broccoli and kale. Variety is limited during the cold months, but your presentation doesn't have to be.

LUNCH

Sarah's Curried Rice
Spinach sautéed with
*   ginger and garlic*
(Raita)
Orange slices

DINNER

Lentil Nut Loaf
Steamed collards
(Red Onion Raita)
Sandy's Gingered Squash
Baked Pears

HOT LUNCH

Lynne's Spiced Pumpkin Soup
Boston Brown Bread
*   with ricotta*
Apples

DINNER

Poppy Seed Noodles
Glazed carrots
Broccoli Spears
Green Salad with
*   Lemon Parsley Dressing*

SOUP & SALAD LUNCH

Catalina Potato Soup
Green salad, Avocado Dressing
Whole-grain crackers

DINNER

Tempeh à l'Orange
*   over bulgur wheat*
Savoy cabbage sauté
Green salad with
*   Bright Minty Dressing*

SPRING

Just when you think you'll come undone at the sight of one more coleslaw or rutabaga, a break in the weather brings a welcome change in fare. Now you can think fresh and young again: tender asparagus, crisp green spinach, new potatoes and peas, tiny whole beets and baby carrots. Fruits, of course, are citrus and winter-storage apples until the first strawberries appear.

BAKE–DAY LUNCH

Pine Nut Pinwheels
Asparagus Soup
Orange and grapefruit slices

DINNER

Artichokes Tellicherry
*Whole-grain pasta with
    Stroganoff Sauce*
Spinach Salad

LUNCH

*Mock Rarebit on
    whole-grain toast*
Russian Salad

DINNER

Spinach Crepes
*Green salad with
    Orange-Parsley Dressing*
Fresh raspberries and yogurt

MIDDLE EAST LUNCH

*Pita Bread
    stuffed with Neat Balls,
    shredded lettuce, red
    cabbbage, grated carrots*
Xergis

DINNER

Asparagus Spears
Green Rice Casserole
(Sesame-glazed Parsnips)
Butter lettuce salad
Fresh strawberries

HOLIDAY FEASTS AND ETHNIC DINNERS

FOURTH OF JULY

*Vegetable platter with French
    Onion Tofu Mayonnaise*
Finocchio Salad
Boston Baked Beans
(Corn on the cob)
(French Bread)
Watermelon
(Blueberry Cheese Pie)

ITALIAN DINNER

Antipasto
Canneloni
*(Peas with mushrooms
    and fresh basil)*
(Breadsticks)
Fresh fruit with Marsala

CHRISTMAS DINNER

Relish tray
Cranberry Squash
*Brussels Sprouts with
    Chestnuts*
Wild Rice
Pineapple-orange ambrosia
Herb Puffs
Figgy Pudding

PASSOVER DINNER

*Spinach and Barley
    Dumplings in broth*
(Cabbage Rolls Normande)
Potato Carrot Kugel
*Dilled Cucumber &
    Yogurt Salad*
Braised Beet Greens
Yogurt Cheese Pie

THANKSGIVING DINNER

*Tomato Aspic on lettuce leaves
    (with Mock Sour Cream)*
Creamed Spinach
*Large mushroom caps filled
    with Stuffing*
*Mashed Potatoes with
    Good Gravy*
Cranberry sauce or relish
Buttermilk Rolls
Mock Mince Pie

GREEK DINNER

Spanakopita
(Green Beans Hellenika)
Greek Salad
Melon and figs

The Search for an

Optimal Diet

The next chapter is an introduction to our nutrition section, presenting some of the research behind current ideas of an optimal diet and other ideas we present in this book.

The real heart of this section is a food group plan that is easy to follow and allows limitless tailoring to your own needs:

The Search for an Optimal Diet

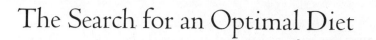

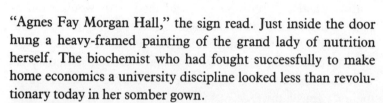

"Agnes Fay Morgan Hall," the sign read. Just inside the door hung a heavy-framed painting of the grand lady of nutrition herself. The biochemist who had fought successfully to make home economics a university discipline looked less than revolutionary today in her somber gown.

Other reminders of the past—relics of public nutrition campaigns, the tired old USDA food group charts, posters about drinking enough milk—blended with the building's drab appearance. A stab of doubt entered my mind. I wanted a career in the health sciences, but had I been right to choose nutrition?

Yet on this first day of classes in the early seventies, with memories of antiwar protests still fresh on the Berkeley campus, the unrevolutionary nutrition department was mobbed with students. Change was in the air. After decades of a high school home-economics image, nutritionists were actually making changes in the American way of life, and idealistic young people were lining up to join them.

George Briggs was my introduction to the profession. I soon found that this kindly, relaxed, and seemingly disorganized man was an achiever in overdrive, dedicated to public education on nutrition and health. His office was always busy—students needing help, the phone ringing with a call from Washington, visitors from the U.N., someone wanting his endorsement (which he would refuse) or a statement on a topic of public concern, which he would give calmly with his wry yet gentle smile.

The drama of the department, however, was upstairs. The top floor of Morgan Hall, dubbed "the penthouse," hummed with the excitement of something big. Scientists, grad students, lab assistants, secretaries, even the janitors, were working together around the clock while researchers cooped up volunteers for weeks and months and subjected them to endless weighing, pricking, probing, prodding, and deprivation, trying to account for every molecule going in or out. Even the rinse water from toothbrushing was collected and analyzed. Privacy was gone, forfeited in the name of science in the search for an optimal human diet. We never knew what might happen as patience wore thin and commitment wore out. Desperate subjects had once fashioned paper kites, reeled them out the window on contraband strings to waiting conspirators, and tried to pull them in again with illicit foods tied to the line. . . .

But it had a purpose. The world food crisis would soon be making headlines, and in the metabolic research units above our classrooms, scientists like Sheldon Margen and Doris Calloway, who were advising U.N. committees on basic nutritional needs, were establishing the international standard for protein requirements. Clearly, my fears of a moribund profession were groundless. These were men and women motivated by compassion, taking on issues of public health that affected many millions of lives. Nutrition *was* making a revolution, and Berkeley was a perfect place to join it.

≈

For a thoughtful overview of these trends in nutrition science, see D. M. Hegsted, "Nutrition: the changing scene," Nutrition Reviews 43(12):357–367 (Dec. 1985).

In a sense, the search for an optimal diet began long before history. As a science, however, it made a rather late appearance. Today we know that each kind of animal has a characteristic balance of proteins, carbohydrates, fats, vitamins, and minerals that is best for longevity and health, but only recently have many biologists thought that the same might be true of the human being.

Even in the early years of the twentieth century, when nutrition was a fledgling science, it took courage, imagination, and the willingness to be branded a medical heretic to crusade for the idea that the *absence* of something in the body might cause a disease.

One such nonconformist was Joseph Goldberger, chief epidemic sleuth of the U.S. Public Health Service in the early 1900s. Pellagra, the disease of the "four *ds*"— dermatitis, diarrhea, dementia, and often death—had been vexing public health officials on and off for decades, but by 1908 it had reached epidemic proportions, with some ten thousand new cases annually. It looked like another Great Plague brewing, right in the United States.

A commissioned report by a group of physicians, noting similarities between the skin lesions of pellagra and those of syphilis, had concluded that pellagra must be an infectious disease, perhaps caused by a variant of the syphilis spirochete. Sometimes, Goldberger observed, past success can blind us to future progress. Those were the heady years of "magic bullets," when inoculation and vaccination were ridding the earth of previously incurable infectious diseases. By the prevailing bias, every unexplained malady was presumed to be germ-caused.

Goldberger, however, was sure that pellagra was not infectious. It just didn't spread like an infectious disease. Not everyone in a family would get it, nor every child, or even most, in a public school. And it was too selective. A disease which afflicts adults and children alike, which strikes male and female alike and is not associated with a specific occupation or activity, would normally find its way to every class of society if it were infectious. Pellagra afflicted only the very poor.

At the Georgia State Sanatorium for the Insane, while meeting the staff and inspecting the premises, it dawned on Goldberger that only the patients were getting pellagra. If it were infectious, the staff would get it too.

Aside from mental stability, the most obvious contrast between staff and patients at the Georgia sanatorium was their diets. The patients got what was then standard fare for poor people all over the South: a monotonous round of grits, molasses, sowbelly, and gravy. Goldberger had no idea what might be lacking from such a diet—the presence of vitamins was still unsuspected by the medical sciences—but he felt sure it was woefully inadequate. He immediately organized a supplemental feeding program including milk, meat, and eggs. Within days the pellagra was on the mend.

Despite an impressive series of similar cures, Goldberger met tremendous resistance from the medical establishment. He was, he realized, fighting against success, against dazzling displays and miracle cures of Pasteur and his successors. Well, so be it. He would fight on his opponents' own terms.

Goldberger staged his definitive experiment at a "diet camp" set up at a prison farm. He began by inducing pellagra in a group

Goldberger's story and other dramatic discoveries in nutrition can be read about in Milestones in Nutrition, *by Samuel Goldblith & Maynard Joslyn (N.Y.: AVI, 1964);* A History of Preventive Medicine, *by Henry Wain (Springfield, Ill.: Thomas, 1970);* Drugs, Demons, Doctors and Disease, *by Perry A. Spencer (St. Louis: Green, 1973)*

of volunteers by feeding them the inadequate diet he'd seen so often in institutions in the South. Then sixteen more volunteers, including Goldberger and his wife, set about to disprove the infectious disease theory in the most dramatic way imaginable: by injecting, ingesting, and otherwise exposing themselves to blood and other biological samples straight from the pellagra victims. Not one of the sixteen developed the disease.

Goldberger had won his case. Physicians did not yet know the cause of pellagra—it proved later to be the absence of niacin, a B vitamin—but at last they knew its cure. One by one, researchers began to build up a list of other factors in food that are absolutely required for life and health. With their discoveries, it finally became possible to talk scientifically about what kind of food a human being really needs.

੨ঌ

These newly discovered deficiency diseases were largely diseases of poverty. By 1945, when the U.S. emerged from the Second World War with a standard of living unequaled in the world, the American diet—epitomized in the Department of Agriculture's Four Food Groups of breads and cereals, milk, meat, and vegetables and fruits—seemed the answer to all nutritional problems, at least for those who could afford it. But complacency in science kills interest. Throughout the fifties and into the sixties, nutrition was something you learned in grade school and then ignored.

The bubble of complacency about the American way of eating was punctured dramatically in 1967 and has been deflating ever since. In its place came a fresh sense of urgency as old assumptions came under question.

We can date the event precisely: April 10, 1967, Jackson, Mississippi, the first field meeting of the Senate Subcommittee on Employment, Manpower, and Poverty. Weeks of previous testimony had not prepared the senators for what they were to see and hear: families without income or chance of work, suffering from actual starvation; vivid testimony from local officials on the magnitude of hunger in Mississippi; children with kwashiorkor and other diseases of starvation thought to be found only in the third world; families going days or even weeks without food.

Senators Joseph Clark and Robert Kennedy were deputed by the committee to tour three representative counties. Kennedy observed conditions as bad as anything he had seen in extensive

Let Them Eat Promises: The Politics of Hunger in America, by Nick Kotz, with an introduction by George S. McGovern (Garden City, N.Y.: Doubleday, 1969)

tours of South America. A medical expert with him, with decades of experience in Africa, compared malnutrition in Mississippi to that in Kenya or Aden.

The subcommittee wrote to the president, and emergency measures went into effect with commendable swiftness. But more important, their work—especially the field tour by Kennedy and Clark—caught the public eye. Evidence of crippling poverty and malnutrition in other parts of the U.S. was reported in a gathering storm of public concern. With the appearance of a shocking documentary on national television, "hunger in America" became a major concern.

One of the bolder steps the government took was the establishment in 1969 of yet another investigative body, which would prove to be a real agent of change: the Senate Select Committee on Nutrition and Human Needs, chaired by Senator George McGovern. Many good scientists, including Berkeley's George Briggs, objected rightly that setting nutritional guidelines for a nation isn't a job for politicians; it is the province of scientific groups like the Food and Nutrition Board of the National Research Council. But guidelines were needed, and no expert body was preparing any. It is to the great credit of Congress that it did act, and act effectively. More than anything else, it was probably the McGovern committee that sparked the change in public thinking about the American diet. For although it set out to investigate the causes of hunger in the United States, the committee quickly found that malnutrition in this country covers not only diseases of deficiency, but also diseases of excess.

ᘐ

Senator Hubert Humphrey sat hollow-eyed through the sessions of 1976. He was not likely to live much longer, and he knew it. But among the members of the McGovern committee, he in particular was a man with a mission. Over years of expert testimony, the committee had accumulated piles of evidence linking nutrition with heart disease, stroke, and diabetes. Humphrey wanted to look into diet and cancer. It would be too late for him to benefit personally, but his own fight with the disease had charged him with the desire to raise public consciousness.

Expert after expert argued before the committee that some ways of eating are associated with a high incidence of cancer, while others might help prevent it. Humphrey listened in dawning amazement. His generation had been raised on the "eat your meat

A moving account of one of the citizens' inquiries can be read in Hunger, U.S.A: A Report, *by the Citizens' Board of Inquiry into Hunger and Malnutrition in the United States, with an introduction by Robert F. Kennedy (Boston: Beacon Press, 1968).*

Almost twenty years later, after considerable progress, the problem has returned in full force: see see Hunger in America: The Growing Epidemic, *by the Physician Task Force on Hunger in America (Middletown, Conn.: Wesleyan Univ. Press, 1985).*

and drink your milk" message of the USDA, which had contained no hint that there is anything *not* to eat. "If only someone had told us," he told one witness poignantly. "If only we'd known . . ."

Gradually, from the mass of evidence before the McGovern committee, a bigger picture emerged. With the industrialization in Europe and America, it seemed, once-rare diseases had arisen to take the place of the defeated plagues of previous times. Totally different from infectious diseases, these problems crept up without prior warning of illness, and attacked average and otherwise healthy people whose modern life-style should have guaranteed personal health.

Puzzles like the rising rates of heart disease and cancer, scientists found, were not amenable to the kinds of investigation that had led to the conquest of infectious disease. In these modern plagues, no bacillus was to be found. In place of labs testing for vaccines, an essentially descriptive branch of medicine was pressed into investigative use: epidemiology, which looks at the patterns of disease in large populations. A new kind of medical detective took to the field.

The first big breakthrough was in heart disease. Up through the nineteenth century, heart disease was so uncommon that it had no specific name. But in the twentieth century, its rate of occurrence in industrialized countries rose in a crescendo, reaching epidemic proportions within a few decades. By the late forties it had become the chief cause of death in the United States and Western Europe and a baffling, serious public health concern.

In 1948, to isolate the underlying causes of heart disease, physicians in the U.S. Public Health Service designed and set in motion a study of epic proportions. In Framingham, Massachusetts—to all appearances, an almost perfectly average American town—they proposed to follow over five thousand healthy adults for at least thirty years to see if any factors in their medical histories or daily lives were statistically associated with heart disease. After an exhaustive initial examination, each subject came to the clinic every two years for follow-up—an endeavor that has engaged a small army of medical workers for almost forty years.

Even today, the Framingham study continues to yield useful new data. But well before the first thirty-year phase was completed, the preliminary results had begun to rock the medical community and catch the public's imagination. The first pub-

The Framingham story is told by one of the principal investigators in The Framingham Study: The Epidemiology of Atherosclerotic Disease, by Thomas R. Dawber (Cambridge: Harvard Univ. Press, 1980).

lished findings—the five major risk factors that increase the odds of developing heart disease—have defined the scope and direction of heart disease research ever since. Every physician in the United States knows about the Framingham reports, and virtually everyone over the age of twelve is probably aware of at least three of the risk factors this study clearly linked with heart disease: high blood pressure, a high level of blood cholesterol, and cigarette smoking.

The Framingham results marked the first time that life-style factors entered the public understanding as possible causes of disease. It was a major turning point in the progress of medical science: people began to realize that what they like and dislike, what they choose and avoid, can affect their health and longevity. The message is both unpleasant and inspiring: unpleasant because it means that some of our enjoyable habits may be harmful; inspiring because it means that we have a measure of control over our own health.

This had never been true before—certainly not in the centuries before public hygiene, when rat-borne pestilence periodically decimated whole populations; not even after the discoveries of vaccination and antibiotics had brought cures for the majority of infectious diseases. In practical terms, the Framingham study suggested that by influencing blood pressure and cholesterol levels, what we eat and how much we exercise may well govern whether we live free from heart disease or die from it.

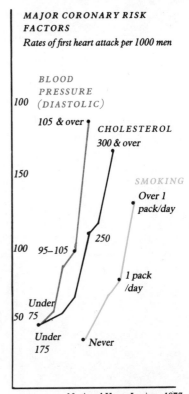

MAJOR CORONARY RISK FACTORS
Rates of first heart attack per 1000 men

DATA FROM *National Heart Institute 1977*

ᘒ

"The first duty of a physician at a medical school," Dr. Hugh Trowell told the Senate committee in 1977, "is to teach students to diagnose commonly the common diseases, and not to diagnose commonly the rare diseases." Dr. Trowell had taught medicine in Kenya and Uganda at medical schools whose standards qualified their students to be placed on the British Medical Register. He was referring to an anomaly that western-trained physicians in Africa cannot fail to notice: the majority of common diseases in the developed countries, which naturally receive the most attention in western medical training, are often rare or absent in unwesternized African populations.

Dr. Trowell had taught medicine in Africa for twenty-six years before diagnosing the first case ever recorded of coronary artery disease in a black African. "He was, of course, leading a partially westernized life," said Trowell—"eating our food, working as a high court judge."

Dr. Denis Burkitt, a surgeon and colleague of Trowell's, had been intrigued for decades by this difference in disease incidence between whites and blacks in South Africa, his home country. How could a surgeon help but notice that no African in his practice over the years had ever required surgery for hemorrhoids, acute appendicitis, deep vein thrombosis, or varicose veins, each fairly common problems among whites?

Some years before the Senate committee launched its investigations into the American diet, Burkitt's interest had led him to a systematic inquiry of his own: a comparison of disease incidence in traditional versus westernized peoples. Laboriously he compiled data, sending a monthly letter to over one hundred hospitals scattered through the rural areas of many countries in Africa and Asia. Gradually he compiled a list of thirty-three diseases, currently of unknown cause, whose incidence is common in the West yet rare in unsophisticated areas of the world.

What could account for the difference? These societies had very little in common with each other except that they all belonged to the preindustrial third world. Shorter life span could not be responsible; studies had repeatedly shown that elevated blood pressure and altered arteries, not uncommon among westernized males in their thirties and even twenties, are not found at any age in the traditional societies of Africa and Asia.

Independently of Framingham, Drs. Burkitt and Trowell concluded that what made the difference in the disease patterns of these cultures and those of the industrialized nations was diet. Whatever they ate—and the physicians found the widest possible range of variations—traditional peoples got little or none of the highly refined carbohydrate foods like white flour products enjoyed by industrialized societies. Their diets were naturally high in fiber, especially the bran types of fiber from the husks and hulls of unrefined grains.

Of course, western diets too had much more bran and other types of fiber from whole grains just a few generations back—at least a third more in the United States at the turn of the century. Over the years, Drs. Burkitt and Trowell noted, the incidence of these chronic diseases had risen more or less in step with the consumption of refined carbohydrates and fat, as the consumption of whole-grain products declined.

Not proof, of course, just a pattern. But since Dr. Burkitt's first paper on the subject appeared in 1970, studies have been bearing out his hypothesis that a particular way of eating—in Trowell's words, "high fiber, very high unrefined complex carbohydrate, low-fat, low cholesterol, low sugar diets"—may protect against many of the chronic diseases that afflict industrialized societies today.

For more on the "diseases of civilization," see Western Diseases: Their Emergence and Prevention, *by H. C. Trowell and D. P. Burkitt (Cambridge: Harvard Univ. Press, 1981).*

ཀ

The unfortunate feature of modern dietary treatment of diabetes, Dr. James W. Anderson of the University of Kentucky observed in 1974, was that it seemed to make the disease worse rather than better, and the dreaded complications—atherosclerotic heart and artery disease, stroke, blindness, kidney disease—more likely and more virulent. As yet, few colleagues agreed.

Anderson had rediscovered something about diabetes that doctors had believed on and off since ancient times: that the disease is better controlled with *high* carbohydrate intake than with low. If contemporary medical science found this difficult to accept, it was because it contradicted common sense. Diabetes is a disease involving high blood sugar levels, and starch is made of sugar; to keep blood sugar down, therefore, one should limit the intake of starch and sugar. The conclusion was so obvious that few bothered to test it. Those who did reported that the standard dietary treatment actually led to higher blood sugar values rather than lower. But their reports went ignored.

Dr. Anderson's own studies confirmed that diabetics on diets high in starch maintained consistently better blood sugar control. Subjects on a standard low-carbohydrate diabetic diet had blood sugar values that were way out of control; when the groups were switched, the results were the same.

Anderson began to suspect that other features of diabetes might be exacerbated by the current treatment. Why, for example, are diabetics as a group typically at high risk for developing heart and artery disease? Might the Framingham risk factors be involved? As a group, the diabetics he'd studied tended to have higher than average blood cholesterol levels, placing them more at risk for arterial disease. Could it be that the standard diet for treating diabetes actually *worsens* such complications?

It had to be considered. After all, atherosclerotic heart disease had been linked with diet in studies since the 1950s, especially with diets high in fat. Since energy in the diet can only be sup-

AN OPTIMAL DIET 343

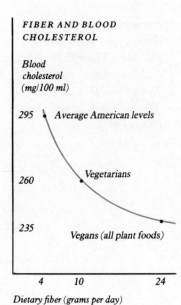

FIBER AND BLOOD CHOLESTEROL

Blood
cholesterol
(mg/100 ml)

295 Average American levels

260 Vegetarians

235 Vegans (all plant foods)

4   10   24

Dietary fiber (grams per day)

DATA FROM: *H. Trowell 1972,
"Ischemic heart disease and dietary fiber,"
American Journal of Clinical Nutrition
25(9):926–932*

plied by carbohydrate, fat, or protein, and since most high-protein foods—meat, cheese, nuts—contain generous amounts of fat as well, the low-carbohydrate diet prescribed for diabetics was almost invariably high in fat. Worse, in the case of meats and cheeses this meant saturated fat, which had been especially implicated in high blood cholesterol levels.

Anderson knew of Burkitt's theory that dietary fiber might protect against diabetes. But Burkitt's work at this point amounted to nothing more than an attractive hypothesis. No experimental verification had yet been attempted. In the first of a series of clinical trials, Anderson tried treating diabetics with fiber supplements and measuring the effect on blood sugar curves.

The results were dramatic. Anderson found that most vegetables, and many kinds of fruit, had beneficial effects on diabetics' blood sugar control—due, he concluded, to the pectin and other soluble fibers they contain. These foods not only lowered blood sugar but drew down blood cholesterol levels as well.

Today physicians recognize that Dr. Anderson's "HCF" diet—high complex carbohydrate, high fiber, low-fat—helps control diabetes. Since it accords so well with other studies linking diet and disease, the American Diabetes Association now recommends a variant of the HCF diet for almost anyone in this country "interested in good health."

❧

However, medical opinion is nothing like unanimous about causal links between diet and chronic disease in general. The Framingham results carry considerable weight, but critics point out the inevitable truth: epidemiologic data can never show what *causes* a problem, but only that some factors appear to be linked with it.

Yet if the data are detailed enough, the time span long enough, and the study populations big enough, the power of statistical association becomes strong enough to convince every reasonable person that certain conclusions are all but proved. The data on smoking and lung cancer now show, through sheer volume, an overwhelmingly positive association. If the Marlboro man says "It ain't *proved*," he'd be right—dead right—but intentionally ignorant. The association is so well established that to ignore it flies in the teeth of the evidence.

In May 1985, at the annual meeting of the American Society

for Clinical Nutrition, health scientists listened to the first reports of a monumental public health survey conducted in China—a study which, in terms of vastness of sample size and care of data collection, promises enough statistical power to confirm diet–cancer links as conclusively as this imperfect world will allow.

Basically, the whole population of China has served as the experimental group, with regional dietary patterns and their correlations with cancer the topic under investigation. The study period: ten years. A study of this size and breadth is unique in the history of public health investigation. It could only have happened in the context of China's highly controlled social conditions, and even there it could probably never be repeated.

The study began between 1973 and 1975, when the government of China surveyed more than 840 million Chinese to find out who had died from cancer. In 1980 Dr. Jun-shui Chen was sent by his government to Cornell University with the compiled results. At first he and T. Colin Campbell of Cornell were only looking at variations in the intake of the trace mineral selenium from province to province, trying to see if there was any correlation with cancer incidence. But as they got into the analysis, it dawned on both men that they had stumbled on a gold mine: the possibility of an epidemiological study vastly greater than anything ever done before.

Chen and Campbell arranged a series of tests in sixty-five randomly selected counties in China—food analyses, blood samples, and extensive interviews to provide variables to correlate with cancer incidence. Blood samples were drawn from thirteen thousand subjects, and complete nutritional analysis obtained of thousands of indigenous foods. The amount of data is staggering; it will take years to analyze. One thing is not in doubt: this study will generate conclusions as influential as those from Framingham, which permanently changed our concepts about heart disease. The very magnitude of the China study gives even its preliminary findings a stamp of reliability. Through it, clear relationships have come into focus between eating habits and the incidence of cancer—relationships which amplify and confirm the more limited previous studies.

The conclusions? A diet that is low in fat, high in complex carbohydrates, high in fiber, and rich in fresh vegetables seems to protect humans from cancer. Or is "protect" the right word?

Chen and Campbell's preliminary report has not been published as we go to press, but one physician's account of their announcement can be read in "Diets That Protected against Cancer in China" (Medical Mailbox), by Cory SerVaas, Saturday Evening Post, July-Aug. 1985, pp. 107–110.

*EFFECT OF COMPOUNDING THE
FRAMINGHAM RISK FACTORS*

*Probability that a 35-year-old man will
have coronary heart disease in 6 years,
related to the major Framingham risk
factors*

*Nonsmoker, no relevant physical
abnormalities**

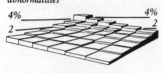

*Cigarette smoker, diabetic, heart
abnormalities**

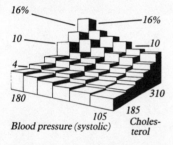

Blood pressure (systolic)   *105*   *185
Choles-
terol*

**The major "relevant physical
abnormalities" are glucose intolerance
(diabetes) and abnormalities of the left
ventricle of the heart. FROM N. O.
Borhani 1977, "Primary prevention of
coronary heart disease," American
Journal of Cardiology 40(2):251–259, in
Diet Related to Killer Diseases, vol. 6,
Hearing before the Select Committee on
Nutrition and Human Needs
(Washington: U. S. Govt. Printing
Office, 1977)*

Might it not be more accurate to say that such a diet seems natural for the human organism, so that deviations from it are likely to produce problems?

&.

What we look for often governs what we see—and, conversely, what we do not suspect often gets overlooked. In experimental science, the experimenter has to choose a focus. But how do we determine what is irrelevant? The China study began with a focus on selenium intake and cancer. A fortunate leap of imagination enabled the researchers to look for broader relationships. Yet even in this study we may ask, what about the data that were *not* collected? Might diet be only part of the picture?

The Framingham study demonstrated some statistically powerful connections between the variables it followed—smoking, blood levels of cholesterol and glucose, blood pressure, and condition of the heart. Later in the study, the design was modified to include dietary intake and exercise habits. This seems to cover the whole territory, all the physical factors that might be relevant. Yet in certain ways, what the Framingham researchers did not look at may be as significant as what they found.

To William Kannel, Thomas Dawber, and the other physicians who designed the study in 1948, the small, peaceful, stable town of Framingham seemed a near-ideal mirror of average America. Its inhabitants were mostly white middle-class. There was a strong community feeling in those days, and few people either moved in or moved out. The citizens were churchgoers with a low divorce rate. All these characteristics were attractive to researchers, who wanted dependable people they could easily keep track of.

But how representative *was* Framingham? That very stability, the community feeling, the homogeneity, the religious beliefs— in other words, the factors that reflect life-style—might not these too be variables in the heart disease risk equation? What about family ties, personal relationships, job satisfaction, personality makeup, and all the other factors related to what we loosely call stress? These questions were not asked by the designers of the Framingham study, but they suggest the commonsense conclusion that diet is only part of a much larger territory begging to be explored.

Most American cities today, of course—even Framingham— are not like Framingham in 1948. As the second decade of data began to come in, investigators like Dr. Stewart Wolf of the University of Oklahoma noticed that although the link between heart disease and risk factors remained as strong as ever, the *incidence* of heart disease in Framingham—the actual number of people afflicted—was far below what the initiators of the study expected. This aspect of the Framingham study is not widely commented on, yet it is distinct in the data: after twenty years, one-third fewer people in Framingham had heart disease than Dr. Kannel and his colleagues had predicted from national rates.

Life expectancy in general in this quiet town also proved to be substantially greater than nationwide for people in similar categories of age, sex, and race. Furthermore, fully half of the Framingham subjects who did die from heart disease were *not* in the most risk-prone category according to the study's own measurements. What had been overlooked?

ح

Even without statistics, it seemed clear to Dr. Benjamin Falcone that heart attacks were oddly rare in another small American town: Roseto, Pennsylvania. Patients in Bangor and Nazareth, very similar towns just a bike ride away, were struck down much more commonly, mirroring the national average. Something, Dr. Falcone reasoned, was protecting Roseto from heart disease.

At his alma mater, the University of Oklahoma, Falcone caught the attention of Drs. John G. Bruhn and Stewart Wolf of the university's Health Sciences Center. The men decided to go to Roseto and examine the medical records. The data from the town's only hospital were simple and convincing: myocardial infarction (heart attack) rates of 1 per thousand males, 0.6 per thousand females, roughly one-fourth the national average.

Some of the differences were obvious. Roseto lies in east-central Pennsylvania, a part of the state that had been decimated by logging when settled by Italian immigrants in 1882. Severe hardships greeted the would-be settlers: discrimination, harassment, swindling by unscrupulous countrymen, severe economic hardship. Few stayed, but those who did were drawn close to each other by their trials. Through sheer industry they survived and even thrived. Others from their native town in Italy joined them, and over the years Roseto became a close-knit, almost entirely Italian community. When Bruhn and Wolf arrived, they found a busy, relatively prosperous ethnic enclave retaining many of the Old World ways.

Mormon communities in Utah have kept very clear family records. Researchers studying familial high blood cholesterol in Mormons note that men with this condition today suffer heart attacks in their early forties and die from heart attack at an average age of 45. Ancestral males born before 1880 with the same genetic tendency for heart disease lived to between ages 62 and 81. Researchers believe that high-risk men can "avoid early coronary death in the same manner as their great-grandfathers even without drugs."

R. R. Williams et al. 1986, Journal of the American Medical Association 255:219–224

The Roseto Story: An Anatomy of Health, by John G. Bruhn and Stewart Wolf (Norman: Univ. of Oklahoma Press, 1979).

A landmark study in Alameda County, California, related health to 7 regular habits in life-style:

*adequate sleep

*breakfast every day

*snacks rarely or never

*maintain proper weight

*physical activity

*moderate drinking

*never smoke cigarettes

Physical health index
(0 is best)

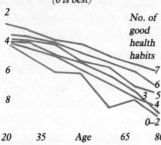

No. of good health habits

20   35   Age   65   80

Researchers found a remarkable correlation between health and the number of these practices followed—independently of which ones. Everyone's health declined with age, but "the physical health status of those who reported following all seven good health practices was consistently about the same as those 30 years younger who followed few or none. . . ." (N. B. Belloc & L. Breslow 1972, "Relationship of physical health status and health practices," Preventive Medicine 1:409–421)

Another Alameda study showed the same pattern between health habits and longevity, but also found that "people with social ties and relationships had lower mortality rates than people without such ties." (L. F. Berkman & S. L. Syme 1979, "Social networks, host resistance, and mortality," American Journal of Epidemiology 109(2):186–204

Yet these characteristics, though they set Roseto off from most other towns and cities in the United States, did not seem helpful in accounting for Roseto's remarkably low rate of heart attack. Bangor and Nazareth, where rates were much higher, were also almost entirely Italian—in fact, many of the families came from the same genetic stock. Demographically, the three towns were remarkably similar.

Bruhn and Wolf began to look for the usual suspects: the Framingham risk factors. What they found was equally perplexing. Rosetans actually had a greater prevalence of obesity than the national average, which should have made them more susceptible to heart disease, not less. They ate at least as much animal fat as did the inhabitants of Bangor and Nazareth. High blood pressure and diabetes were about equally prevalent in all three towns. Patterns of smoking and exercise were similar. In sum, not one of the conventionally accepted risk factors accounted for Roseto's freedom from heart disease.

What did make Roseto different from its neighbors, as Bruhn and Wolf observed and the townspeople themselves testified, was the quality of life, and especially the stability of personal relationships. The incidence of crime, notably violent crime, and suicide was startlingly low. Rosetans also had distinctly fewer psychiatric admissions to the hospital. Like Framingham, the town was small and remarkably stable. Few people moved in and few moved out, though enough of the latter had moved to Nazareth to be able to comment on the differences they felt. Roseto, they observed, was slow and old-fashioned, but there was something satisfying in its Old World values. Its pace was slower, and daily life seemed far less stressful in its simplicity.

"Family relationships" in Roseto, Drs. Bruhn and Wolf summarized, "were extremely close and mutually supportive," even by Italian standards. This cohesiveness "extended to neighbors and to the community as a whole." The positions of man and woman, children and grandparents, in the family was clearly defined. The elderly were cherished and respected, and their authority was obeyed. Finally, the researchers commented, "the atmosphere of Roseto was gay and friendly and reflected an enthusiastic and optimistic attitude toward life."

Clearly, nutrition is only part of the story of heart disease. James J. Lynch, professor of psychology at the University of Maryland medical school, believes that the protective factor in

Roseto is its close, supportive personal relationships. But there may be other ways of looking at the same information, ways that suggest still further complexities: behavior, social values, the very makeup of personality. To what extent *does* the way we live—perhaps even the way we think—affect our physical health?

ح

"You know," the upholsterer commented to Dr. Meyer Friedman, "your armchairs wear out different from other people's." He handed over the work order to sign and date. "The only places that are worn are the front parts—right on the edge of the seat and the front of the arms. Most people's chairs get worn in the middle of the seat and on the chair back. Funny thing, isn't it?"

Something in that remark caught Friedman's imagination. "The fronts of the chairs," he kept thinking on the way home. "You mean, our patients never lean back? They sit on the edge of their seats like racehorse jockeys?" Friedman shared his office with another San Francisco cardiologist, Dr. Ray H. Rosenman.

During the next day he observed his patients as they sat in the waiting room. It was true: they sat on chair's edge, as if ready to spring into emergency action. These were hard-driven men. He'd known that for a long time, and over the years he had noticed that those who had had a heart attack or suffered from anginal chest pains were especially impatient and short-tempered. They were usually men, usually aggressive high-achievers, often hard on their wives and tyrannical at the office. Could these common behavior traits underlie their heart disease? Could heart disease, in part at least, be due to a personality disorder? And if so, could you treat it by helping patients to change their emotional responses and behavior?

Dr. Friedman made a note to himself to talk again to Rosenman about these questions. They had speculated about a behavioral theory of heart disease before, but the upholsterer's comments sparked a decision. They should do a study. . . .

"In the fields of observation," Louis Pasteur once told a rapt gathering of scientists, "chance favors only the prepared mind." He was describing his own discovery of the chicken cholera vaccine, when an error in the course of an experiment sparked the insight that led to preventive vaccinations.

Often, in the development of science, the ideas that block progress were once revolutionary themselves. Pasteur and others had had to fight bitterly to convince the medical community of

For Framingham and Roseto in a larger context, see The Broken Heart: The Medical Consequences of Loneliness *by James J. Lynch (N.Y.: Basic Books, 1977).*

STRESS AND SUSCEPTIBILITY TO ILLNESS

Number of streptococcal infections in families, related to stressful events (100 children in 16 families over 1 year)

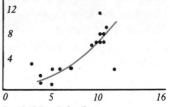

Level of chronic family stress

FROM R. J. Haggerty 1980, "Life stress, illness and social supports," Developmental Medicine and Child Neurology 22:391–400

the bacteriological nature of many diseases; yet their discoveries were so overwhelmingly successful that within a generation, pioneers in nutrition like Joseph Goldberger had to fight to convince colleagues that some unknown diseases were *not* infectious. In the 1960s, Friedman and Rosenman found most of their colleagues interested only in Framingham risk factors, especially cholesterol. To fellow cardiologists they were renegades; to psychologists and social scientists they were interlopers, poaching on others' turf.

Friedman and Rosenman did not dispute that high blood cholesterol was linked with heart disease. But their clinical observations, and the trained physician's intuition, suggested that something more was involved. Was cholesterol or saturated fat *in the diet* the only possible factor determining cholesterol levels in the blood? Some intriguing data—a study, for example, which showed that accountants' blood cholesterol levels rose during the stressful weeks before the tax deadline, April 15, and then fell again afterward—suggested that an unknown but powerful psychological factor was present too.

Friedman and Rosenman embarked on a long-term study of behavior as it affects heart disease risk. After ten years the two were able to conclude that certain personality characteristics are more strongly associated with heart disease than blood cholesterol levels or even smoking. The main elements of the heart disease–prone personality are "hurry sickness," the impelling need to do everything fast if not faster; a perfectionism and need to control others—family members, underlings, colleagues—so that they do what one wants the way one wants it; an inability to admit one's errors; free-floating anger and hostility; competitiveness in almost every endeavor; and a tendency to "catastrophize" or to see even minor events or needs as overwhelmingly urgent. Such people, not surprisingly, have difficulty maintaining close relationships with others; so Friedman's work and the Roseto observations may converge.

Faulty diet does of course play a role, as do the other risk factors. But as Friedman puts it, when someone is felled by a heart attack, "Diet and cigarettes are the bullets, but behavior is the gun." Friedman and Rosenman labeled the syndrome of heart disease–prone behavior the "Type A personality."

Dr. Meyer Friedman is a remarkable man and an ideal physician. Once Type A himself, he has taught himself through great

"After more than 30 years of studying heart attack patients, [Rosenman and Friedman] realized that such suspected causes as smoking, diet and exercise accounted for less than half the cases seen. They were impressed with a poorly defined factor which appeared to relate to a quality of 'maleness,' and indeed, more than two thirds of heart attack victims in the United States were men. Curiously, this was not the case in Mexico or southern Italy where the incidence of heart attacks was equally divided between the sexes, or in northern Italy where the male/female ratio abruptly shot up to 4 to 1. These findings would be difficult to account for on the basis of diet or environment. What did appear to be relevant were sociocultural differences in . . . behavior between the sexes."

P. J. Rosch 1983, "Effects of stress on the cardiovascular system," Physician and Patient (Nov.), pp. 36, 41

effort to become an inspiring model of the Type B personality: tolerant, relaxed, humble, genuinely interested in others, highly motivated and professionally productive.

When my father had a coronary a couple of years ago, he enrolled in a course taught by Dr. Friedman and Diane Ullmer for teaching Type A's to become Type B's. My father's enthusiasm made him a star pupil, and eventually brought me the good fortune of meeting Dr. Friedman myself. Over dinner, I asked him something I had long wondered about. "Dr. Friedman, your work has documented a strong connection between behavioral traits and heart disease. But what about other ailments?" I mentioned some studies I knew he too had seen: research suggesting that anger and fear might be part of a "cancer-prone" personality, and that stressful life events like loneliness and depression can have harmful effects on health and the course of illness; studies of emotional factors affecting diabetic control and the incidence and progress of other diseases. "Do you think the Type A personality might lead not only to heart attack but to other chronic diseases as well?"

Dr. Friedman said with a twinkle in his eye, "Let's just start with heart disease." At least twenty-five years of work and struggle had gone into establishing that one connection, and the battle still is not won; the Type A hypothesis is not undisputed. "Let's make sure that the point is not lost. Let's make the connection between heart disease and behavior so clear that it can't be ignored, that it demands serious attention from everybody who deals with this problem or suffers from it. After that we can look for other diseases that Type A behavior might cause."

❧

When the three major nutrients—protein, carbohydrate, and fat—were discovered, scientists thought they had found everything food requires to sustain life. Yet laboratory animals fed exclusively on these life-giving chemicals always died. Only the discovery of vitamins and minerals, needed in such tiny quantities, brought an explanation: the purified diet was leaving something out.

In a sense, we go on finding that we are leaving things out of the picture of human health. At the turn of the century, few people suspected that diet might be related to health and disease. Next came the discoveries of individual nutrients, without which we fall ill; now it seems clear that illness also follows if we eat

Friedman's story is told in Type A Behavior and Your Heart, *by Meyer Friedman and Ray H. Rosenman (N.Y.: Knopf, 1974), and continued in* Treating Type A Behavior–And Your Heart, *by Meyer Friedman & Diane Ulmer (Knopf, 1984).*

Many studies have suggested a connection between stress and illness, but some indicate that it is how one views stress that makes the difference. In one study of high-stress executives, researchers found it possible to predict who would be illness-prone and who would not. They report that "high-stress/low-illness executives" feel committed rather than alienated, have "a greater sense of control over what occurs in their lives" (as opposed to "those who feel powerless in the face of external forces"), and "view change as a challenge [rather than] as a threat." Such people "have a belief system that minimizes the perceived threat of any given stressful life event."

S. C. Kobasa 1979, "Stressful life events, personality, and health," Journal of Personality and Social Psychology 37(1):1–11

"The time may have come when it would be enlightening to introduce 'life situations' in the scientific study of clinical nutrition. In a pilot experiment one might consider, for example, placing two groups . . . on a rich and abundant diet. . . . The members of one group would be directed to eat either alone or in a dreary Second Avenue restaurant. The members of the other group would be selected for their ability to enjoy their food in a jolly Roseto kind of social situation. I am willing to volunteer for the experiment, but only if I can be part of the second group, because it might well give me a better chance to observe the final results in a good state of health."

R. Dubos 1979, "Nutritional adaptations," *American Journal of Clinical Nutrition* 32:2623–2626

them in excessive amounts. In the future, the idea of rigid daily requirements is likely to give way to a much more dynamic view in which *balance,* the whole diet, is emphasized over individual chemical constituents.

Yet even this framework is too small. Today, approaching the problem from different directions, experts have converged on a way of eating that helps guard against chronic disease. It is a pleasant surprise to discover that this same way of eating is also easy on the environment and on other creatures: it does no harm; it fosters life. In this view, the word *diet* regains some of its original meaning: a way of life, a way of thinking, not just a matter of food.

Every choice a person makes—what he eats, how she does business, how we think and act—has consequences for health. The food we choose to put on the dinner table is one factor in the well-being of farm workers thousands of miles away. The industries we encourage with our buying are major influences on the quality of our water, food, and air. And as the Roseto experience shows, our environment is not merely physical but emotional; it includes the way we relate to those we live and work with. Love, patience, goodwill, and generosity are healing factors, for us and for those who come in contact with us. Anger, hostility, greed, and prejudice are hazardous even to health.

Today, we in the developed nations face an epidemic of diseases which evidence links increasingly with our life-style, while the rest of the world races to follow our example. If it succeeds, heart disease, cancer, and other degenerative diseases will be a global plague. To do anything to ameliorate such immense problems seems far beyond the power of ordinary citizens like you and me.

Yet big problems do get resolved, often in unexpected ways and with unexpected rapidity. Often, too, answers come not through the efforts of governments, but through the quiet choices and adaptations of ordinary people.

Twenty years ago, if you had predicted that so many adults would be giving up smoking that smokers might feel antisocial, people would have called the idea absurd. If you had told the Framingham researchers in 1948 that in just twenty-five years so many Americans would be jogging for health that housewives would be entering marathons, they would have objected, "Impossible!" Twenty years ago it was odd to be a vegetarian even in Berkeley; now a Rand study announces that the majority of Americans may be vegetarian for health reasons by the year 2000. Revolutions in ways of thinking do come, and often so quietly that what seemed impossible is, in retrospect, simply taken for granted. What doesn't ever happen is that things stay the same.

Technological medicine has captured public hopes for a healthier future, but CAT scanners, the new drugs, and organ transplants have done nothing to stem the crisis of chronic disease. These problems are for us to solve as individuals. The next revolution in medicine may well be in our very ways of thinking and relating to others. Diet will then be seen as just a corner of a larger picture, in which the human being fits harmoniously into an indivisible environment and is much more than a biochemical entity.

ABBREVIATIONS: *Scan.*, Norway, Sweden, & Finland[1]; *AHF*, Amer. Health Found.[1]; *Neth.*, Netherlands[1]; *Can.*, Canada[1]; *UK*, Royal College of Physicians[1]; *Sen. Comm.*, "Dietary Goals," Senate Select ("McGovern") Committee[2]; *Austral.*, Australia[3]; *Surg. Gen.*, U.S. Surgeon General[2]; *AMA*, Amer. Medical Assoc.[2]; *NCI*, Natl. Cancer Inst.[2]; *NAS-FNB*, Food & Nutrition Board, Natl. Acad. of Sciences[2]; *USDA-DHHS*, Dept. of Health & Human Services, USDA[2]; *NAS-DNC*, Comm. on Diet, Nutrition & Cancer, Natl. Acad. of Sci.[2]; *ACS*, Amer. Cancer Soc.[2] ADAPTED FROM: [1]R.W.D. Turner 1978, Postgraduate Medical Journal (54):141–148; [2]S. Palmer 1985, Nutrition & Cancer 6:274–283; [3]Journal of Food & Nutrition 39:206, 1982

DIETARY GOALS
The Emergence of Consensus on an Optimal Diet

Generally recommended ■
Only on physician's advice ■
Implicit in other recommendations ■ ■

	Scan. 1968	AHF (US) 1972	Neth. 1973	Can. 1976	UK 1976	Sen. Comm. 1977	Austral. 1979	Surg-Gen. 1979	AMA 1979	NCI 1979	NAS FNB 1980	AHA 1982	NAS DNC 1982	ACS 1984	USDA-DHHS 1985
Variety of foods							■			■	■				■
Limit or reduce fat	■	■	■	■	■	■	■	■	■	■	■	■	■	■	■
Reduce saturated fat	■	■	■	■	■	■	■	■	■		■	■			■
Limit cholesterol			■	■	■	■	■	■	■		■	■			■
Limit sugar	■	■	■	■	■	■	■	■			■	■			■
More complex carbohydrates						■	■	■			■	■	■	■	■
More fresh fruits, vegetables							■						■	■	■
More fiber						■	■	■		■	■	■	■	■	
Restrict salt						■	■	■	■		■	■	■	■	■
Moderation in alcohol						■	■	■	■	■	■	■		■	■
Ideal weight; exercise				■	■	■	■	■	■	■	■	■	■	■	■

The New Laurel's Kitchen Food Guide

Every day

1   *Have 4 servings of whole-grain foods*
&
3 servings of vegetables
(including 1 of Super-Vegetables)

2   *Choose 1 serving of:*
      Super-Vegetables
      or Legumes
      or Dairy Foods

3   *Fill out your calorie needs with a variety*
of whole foods like these:

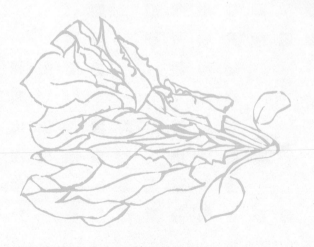

The Food Families:

WHOLE GRAINS
Whole-grain bread (1 slice)
or cooked grain—like rice—
or noodles (½ cup)

SUPER-VEGETABLES
Dark leafy greens (¾ cup
cooked); edible-pod peas,
brussels sprouts, broccoli,
asparagus (1 cup);
lima beans, peas (½ cup).

HIGH-CARBOHYDRATE
VEGETABLES
Artichokes, potatoes, sweet
potatoes (1 medium); beets,
carrots, parsnips, winter
squash, turnips (1 cup);
corn (1 ear or ½ cup)

LOW-CALORIE
VEGETABLES
A tomato; green beans,
cabbage, cauliflower, leeks,
cucumber, eggplant, okra,
mushrooms, peppers (1 cup);
lettuce (2 cups)

LEGUMES
Cooked dry beans, lentils,
split peas (½ cup)

DAIRY FOODS
Milk or yogurt (1 cup); cheese
(3 oz.); cottage cheese (½ cup)

NUTS & SEEDS

FRUIT

EGGS

The New Laurel's Kitchen
Food Guide

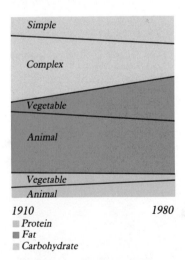

"Eat your spinach"—or rice, or beans, or tempeh. "It's good for you." The idea that certain foods make a good diet has probably been around for thousands of years. Only with the discovery of vitamins and the unfolding of knowledge of other nutrients, however, did it become possible to talk scientifically about an optimal diet for human health.

Food grouping schemes were devised in the 1930s as an attempt to synthesize the new knowledge into a consumers' guide. Today's professional recommendations draw on a range of information unavailable in earlier decades: epidemiological research of national diets around the world, experimental work with animals and humans, and the relatively new field of nutritional anthropology, which studies the diets of traditional societies. These findings and recommendations converge on an international consensus, summarized in the table on page 353: human beings live healthiest and longest on a varied diet that is adequate but not excessive in calories, high in complex carbohydrates and vegetables, and low in fat (especially animal fat) and salt.

This is not to say there is only one right way to eat. A great variety of dietary styles can be consistent with health. The human body is capable of extraordinary adaptation—learning to absorb more of a particular nutrient, for example, when it is in short supply—and biological needs vary considerably from individual to individual, and even within the same individual at different times as the body responds to its environment. In broad outline, however, it is now possible to describe scientifically a kind of diet on which the human being thrives.

This chapter presents a simple three-step plan for such a diet.

TRENDS IN FOOD CONSUMPTION IN THE U.S.

DATA FROM: *S. O. Welsh & R. M. Marston 1982, Journal of the American Dietetic Association 81:120–125*

The plan is almost infinitely flexible; you can tailor it easily to your own needs. Yet it allows you to forget about the supposed problems of a meatless diet—including protein!—and concentrate on preparing and enjoying new kinds of meals.

A VARIETY OF WHOLE FOODS IN MODERATION

The heart of our plan can be summarized in one phrase: *A variety of whole foods in moderation.*

VARIETY

Four foods provided the foundation of the Englishman's diet in the nineteenth century: bread, beer, beef, and cheese. In the big cities, the diets of the poor—that is, the majority—centered mainly on the first two.[1] Why beer? There are other reasons, especially if you are poor, but even the poorest in the cities of those days did not drink water if they could help it: the water in London and other big cities was rightly suspected of spreading diseases.[2] The science of nutrition did not exist then, of course, and few observers connected the widespread ill health in urban England with a poor diet. Today, however, we would look upon this particular four-food-group diet with alarm, for one paramount reason: it is so seriously lacking in variety.

Variety in eating provides far better health insurance than any health maintenance organization can offer. At its most basic level, it means eating foods from many different categories or families of foods—fruits, root vegetables, grains, and so on. The Londoner's diet mentioned above rarely included vegetables or fruits of any kind, though on very special occasions the commoner might have had pie or pudding that included fruits or vegetables. We know now that a diet without vegetables or fruits is bound to be lacking in nutrients like vitamin C, vitamin A, and magnesium. In fact, vegetables are by far our most nutrient-dense foods, as you will see in the next section.

Each major category of food has its special strengths, and the task of balancing a diet becomes more difficult the fewer food families you have to choose from. The first principle of variety, then, is: *choose foods from as many different families as possible.* The second principle is to vary your choices even within food families.

Variety not only ensures that your nutritional bases are covered, it also makes up for unnoticeable variations in quality. Food tables, for example, will tell you that the average rutabaga supplies a

THE TOP 10 SOURCES OF CALORIES IN THE U.S. DIET

1. *White bread, rolls, crackers*
2. *Doughnuts, cookies, cakes*
3. *Alcoholic beverages*
4. *Whole milk*
5. *Hamburgers, cheeseburgers, etc.*
6. *Beef steaks, roasts*
7. *Soft drinks*
8. *Hot dogs, ham, lunch meat*
9. *Eggs*
10. *French fries, potato chips*

G. Block et al. 1985, American Journal of Epidemiology 122:13–40

[1] *J. L. Mount 1975, The Food and Health of Western Man (N.Y.: Wiley), p. 2*

[2] *P. A. Spencer 1973, Drugs, Demons, Doctors, and Disease (St. Louis: Warren H. Green)*

certain amount of iron. But iron content is dependent on a great many factors, including growing conditions—soil, weather, and so on—and handling, including processing and cooking methods. The rutabaga you just ate might have delivered only half as much iron as the mythical average item on the chart. Fortunately, however, the string beans served with it happened to be rich in iron. A wide variety in food choices provides insurance against such fluctuations in nutrient content.

Finally, of course, variety makes for interest, for cooks and eaters alike. No small consideration: nobody likes a monotonous diet. Either we lose appetite and start eating less, or we find snacks to fill the gaps.

Nutritional well-being in nineteenth-century urban England was marginal, but people managed if they got enough to eat, since bread, beer, beef, and cheese are in fact nutritious foods. Scurvy and rickets, diseases resulting from lack of vitamin C and vitamin D, were common among the poor, but the struggling middle class managed to avoid frank deficiency diseases—at least, until late in the century. After the roller-milling of flour came into vogue, though, this picture began to change.

Roller mills are large cylinders which crush wheat kernels between them. The flour, germ, bran, middlings, and other fractions come off in "streams" that can easily be separated from each other, which is why these products are called separated foods. Though roller mills were patented as early as 1753 by Wilkinson, it was not until porcelain was introduced in 1870 that the machines could be used for large-scale operations. In 1877 Lord Radford of Liverpool set up roller mills in several parts of England, and from then on they proliferated so fast that in a few years the stone mills were almost completely superseded. The inexpensive white flour produced by the new mills was very popular. Not coincidentally, the thirty years following 1880 saw "perhaps some of the worst malnutrition [England] has ever known."[3] The same phenomenon occurred much earlier in the Far East as rice milling became more efficient.[4]

It is also no coincidence that the science of nutrition was born in this period. Prior to the industrial revolution (and even after it in rural areas) there was hardly any need for knowledge of nutrition. Since separated foods could not be produced efficiently enough to make them widely available, most people ate whole

WHOLE FOODS

VITAMINS LOST WHEN WHOLE WHEAT IS REFINED

86% *Vitamin E lost*
81 *Niacin**
80 *Riboflavin**
77 *Thiamin**
70 *Vitamin B-6*
67 *Folic acid*
50 *Pantothenic acid*

Replaced commercially after refinement.
SOURCE: H. A. Shroeder 1973, The Trace Elements and Man (Old Greenwich, Conn.: Devin-Adair), p. 57

[3] Mount 1975, p. 6
[4] S. Davidson, R. Passmore, & J. F. Brock 1972, Human Nutrition and Dietetics (Edinburgh: Churchill Livingston), p. 169

EFFECT OF A FULL
CONVERSION TO
ORGANIC FARMING

*Percentages of the estimated total value of
production, cost, and net income from
organic farming methods compared with
results from conventional high-export
agriculture, assuming no government
programs and near full use of land*

■ *Less than 100% (net loss with conversion)*

■ *100%–400% gain in net income*

■ *1480% gain in net income*

	Value of prod.	Cost of prod.	Net income
A	112%	79%	390%
B	84	73	118
C	77	74	86
D	132	95	217
E	117	78	250
F	145	131	184
G	127	81	332
H	76	70	92
I	123	111	128
J	199	153	1481
U.S.	116	86	214

DATA FROM *J. A. Langley, E. O.
Heady, & K. D. Olson 1983, "The macro
implications of a complete transformation
of U.S. agricultural production to organic
farming practices," Agriculture,
Ecosystems and Environment*
10:323–333

foods. With efficient milling came efficient loss of nutrients—and severe malnourishment. After roller mills came steam-driven screw presses for oil production and other food processing machinery. Separated foods became cheap and plentiful, and deficiency diseases became widespread.

In this country, too, the deficiency diseases struck hard, especially after roller milling became common. It took several decades to understand that the new food processing methods helped cause these alarmingly widespread diseases. When it became clear that certain nutrients were lacking in the milled flour, the government issued laws in 1941 requiring that this product be "enriched" with four of the twenty-five or more nutrients lost in processing. This has helped us avoid pellagra and beriberi from niacin and thiamin deficiency, but there is evidence that many Americans still do not get enough of several other nutrients, such as vitamin B-6 and some of the trace minerals, partly because of the use of highly milled flour.

Separated foods also include the other "empty-calorie" or "calories-only" foods—oil, sugar, and alcohol—as well as salt. Some use of such items is still consistent with health, so long as the amounts in the diet are minor compared to more wholesome foods. The basic problem with all separated foods is that they tend to fill you up while making only a marginal contribution—or none at all—to your nutritional needs.

A whole-foods diet means a cook-it-yourself-from-basic-foods style of eating, with all the benefits—and inconveniences—that implies. The difference between buying preprocessed food and preparing it from scratch yourself is that you naturally tend to make wholesomeness and nourishment your first priority, while most manufacturers care first and foremost about profit. They tend to eliminate parts of a food that do not store well and to add chemicals that mimic freshness and flavor, since these steps reduce costs, increase sales, and lengthen shelf life.

The precious quality of whole foods is not just aesthetic, or economic, or that they help avoid the chemicals that are added to processed foods. Whole foods have a balance of nutrients, a completeness, that matches our needs beautifully—not surprisingly, perhaps, considering that human beings have been eating such foods for millions of years.

Fresh and *local* are two other watchwords that deserve mention here. Since vegetables steadily lose vitamins from the time they are harvested, the fresher the vegetable, the higher its vitamin content will be. Seek out sources for local produce and encourage local stores to do the same. Best of all, of course, look into the pleasures of a kitchen garden of your own. Even if you do not have a yard, you can do amazing things with a sunny kitchen window or front porch. In some cities, people have been getting together to sharecrop the roof of their apartment building or even a vacant lot.

"Buy fresh" is a goal, however, not a rigid rule. Some processing techniques don't interfere much with the nutritional value of produce but add greatly to the variety of what is available—an important consideration in colder climates. Freezing technology is a second-best alternative. Canning is also a useful art, and even dried fruits and pickled vegetables provide interest and variety. (See page 453 for guidelines on preserving nutrients in vegetables.)

By contrast, fresh foods that are totally out of season (such as grapes in March) are often not desirable. They are usually flown in from the southern hemisphere, often from places that do not regulate pesticides. Apart from the effect on your own health, what such cash crops do to workers' health and local economies in these countries can be severe.

"Moderation in all things": in how much we eat, how fast, how often, how spicy or salty or sugary or oily the food. Much of this book is devoted to putting this simple principle into practice.

The New Laurel's Kitchen Food Guide

Our three-step plan for a meatless diet is based on one simple but very recent realization in the field of nutrition: *all known nutrients are adequately supplied by a varied diet of whole foods which meets your energy needs.* In particular, if you get enough calories from a reasonable variety of unrefined grains and vegetables, it is difficult to get too much fat and almost impossible to get too little protein, vitamins, or minerals. That is the nutritional power of variety and whole foods.

This plan emphasizes whole grains, with vegetables a close second. The other food categories are useful, tasty additions. They help provide variety and the full spectrum of nutrients, but grains and vegetables are the stars. Together they supply the major share of all the nourishment needed in a vegetarian diet.

Even today the first concern of a prospective vegetarian—or of his or her family—is often protein. We hope to convince any worried readers, and well-meaning relatives or friends who might be alarmed, that the decades-old obsession with protein is overdone. It is very easy to get enough high-quality protein even on an all-plant or vegan diet. Anyone who follows our three-step plan and gets enough calories or food energy can hardly avoid getting enough well-balanced protein. For most vegetarians, no additional planning for protein is necessary.*

Whole-grain cereals and breads are the basic stuff of a meatless diet. Grains have been staple foods since ancient times, and for good reason: their nutritional contribution is balanced and reliable. They contain starch and protein roughly in proportion to our energy and protein needs, and the whole-grain package contains the micronutrients (vitamins and minerals) needed for metabolizing that starch and protein too.

Even outside vegetarian circles, whole grains are coming into their own. No one these days has to be told that carbohydrate—that is, starch—is good for you. Whole grains deserve even more acclaim for their fiber content. Whole grains and legumes also supply many nutrients that omnivores get from meat, which refined grain products do not have in comparable amounts. (More on fiber on page 424 and under Diabetes, page 403).

Grains are not strangers to the American diet, but they have taken a back seat in recent decades. During the Second World War our government embarked on a conscious policy of encouraging meat intake as a way to boost agriculture, a policy which remains in place today. Ever since then we have been feeding a large share of the grain we produce to beef cattle, in the context of a grain-hungry world. In our own country the results of this policy have shown up in the grim statistics of heart disease and of certain other chronic health problems. These effects can be reversed by reorienting the national diet—starting with

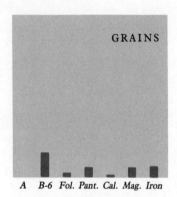

GRAINS

A   B-6 Fol. Pant. Cal. Mag. Iron

NUTRIENT PROFILE

Jean Pennington's seven Index Nutrients (see p. 432) are a reliable guide to how well a food supplies all known essential nutrients. Our Nutrient Profiles show what proportion of the adult RDA *is supplied by each Index Nutrient, on the average, in a food family.*

*If you are sick (when your body needs to repair damaged tissues) or if you are a teenager or pregnant (when new tissues are growing at a rapid rate), protein needs are still easily met with a whole-foods diet, but you do need to be more careful. (See the chapters on protein, page 412, and pregnancy, page 368.)

ourselves—by discovering anew the food that has sustained the human race for millennia: whole grains. We have been told it was "just starch" and "fattening." Now we know that grain is an important food in a well-balanced and ecologically harmonious diet, the worthy staff of life.

"Whole grains" doesn't just mean sober little heaps of buckwheat groats or brown rice. Bread is grain too, with added nutritional advantages from the fermentation of the yeast, which makes some minerals more available than they are in less sophisticated grains. And whole-grain pastas are available now in a wonderful variety of shapes.

Our Food Guide calls for a minimum of four servings of grain a day: wheat, rice, barley, millet, what have you. It can be bread, cooked breakfast cereal, noodles, pasta, or even cakes on a special occasion—or any of a hundred possible variations.

When you see the serving size we are talking about—the equivalent of one slice of bread or half a cup of cooked rice—we think you will agree that four servings is not very much for the staple food of your diet. Naturally, you can eat more if your caloric needs require it. However, we strongly recommend that you not eat less, because whole grains supply nutrients (particularly B-6 and zinc) not readily supplied by other kinds of foods.

The vegetable groups include the whole glorious range of edible roots, shoots, stems, leaves, florets, and fruits that nature provides. Ideally, they are the freshest food in our diet.

Most food group systems just say "vegetables," as if they were all about the same nutritionally. (In fact, the old Four Food Groups of the USDA not only tosses vegetables together but throws in fruits as well.) If you look at the nutrient profiles of the most commonly eaten vegetables, however, you will see that they fall naturally into three groups: high-protein leafy greens, high-starch root vegetables, and low-calorie vegetables.

For nutritional contribution, the high-protein dark green leafy vegetables reign supreme. This group is a nutritional powerhouse. Even the dairy group can't match "super-veggies" in key nutrients like folacin and magnesium. For plant foods, these vegetables are surprisingly good sources of protein too: one stalk of broccoli, for instance, provides approximately 5 grams of good-quality protein.

In this group are many of the foods that have shown specific

SUPER—VEGETABLES

A   B-6   Fol.   Pant.   Cal.   Mag.   Iron

ability to protect against chronic diseases—cancers especially, but also heart disease and diabetes. But these foods are not just healthy; they are delicious. They're so useful in the kitchen that our recipe section goes overboard on ways to bring out their best: the delicacy of spinach, the spicy heartiness of kale, and the sheer fresh exuberance of broccoli, green peas, or asparagus.

Sea vegetables can be classified as dark leafy greens based on their nutrient content. Some of them—kombu, nori, carrageenan (from Irish moss)—can lower blood cholesterol levels, and many have mild anticoagulant properties. The amino acid laminine, found in the *Laminaria* species (which includes kombu), acts as an antihypertensive medication in humans when given in a purified form.[5] Extracts from red, green, and brown algae (again including kombu) show the ability to inhibit tumor growth in mice.[6] And sodium alginate extracted from *Laminaria digitatis*, a brown seaweed, is used medically to treat acute heavy metal poisoning.[7] Sadly, coastal waters around the world are becoming progressively more polluted. For this reason we recommend sea vegetables grown in relatively nonpolluted waters, such as offshore Maine.

In some parts of the world, root vegetables and tubers such as potatoes and yams are staple foods and serve as an alternative to grains. Their principal contribution in this regard is their energy value—calories. Yet they provide respectable amounts of important minerals and vitamin C. The orange pigment in carrots and sweet potatoes is beta-carotene, which the body converts to vitamin A. The richly colored winter squashes, with orange or golden flesh, are also colored by provitamin A: the deeper the color, the richer the provitamin content. In fact, along with the dark green leafies, these orange and yellow vegetables provide our most important sources for vitamin A activity. Both carotene and vitamin C in vegetables like these have been associated with lower cancer risk.

Potatoes, incidentally, are popular foods, but they are often put in the "forbidden" category because of the persistent notion that they are fattening. At around 100 calories, however, the average baked potato is a caloric bargain, full of nutrients and no more blameful than a medium-sized apple. The problem, of course, comes with high-fat toppings.

[5] S. Arasaki & T. Arasaki 1983, *Vegetables from the Sea* (Tokyo: Japan Publications)

[6] J. Teas 1981, "The consumption of seaweed as a protective factor in the etiology of breast cancer," *Medical Hypotheses* 7(5):601–613

[7] Y. Tanaka et al. 1972, "Application of algal polysaccharides as in vivo binders of metal pollutants," in K. Nisizawa, ed., *Proceedings of the Seventh International Seaweed Symposium,* Sapporo, Japan (N.Y.: Pergamon), pp. 602–604

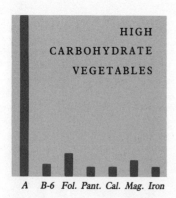

HIGH CARBOHYDRATE VEGETABLES

A   B-6   Fol.   Pant.   Cal.   Mag.   Iron

This family contains the most widely used vegetables in this country: lettuce, celery, green peppers, and the other crisp favorites listed in the Food Guide on page 354. While these foods are not remarkable in their nutrient content, they are very *dense* in nutrients because their calorie contribution is so low—that is, you get a lot per calorie. These vegetables also contain several different kinds of dietary fiber, each with its own beneficial effects on health.

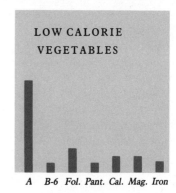

LOW CALORIE VEGETABLES

A   B-6 Fol. Pant. Cal. Mag. Iron

Most vegetarians include dairy foods—milk products and cheese—in their diets. This makes it very easy to keep the diet balanced, because milk is a rich source of a large spectrum of nutrients, including some otherwise hard-to-get vitamins (riboflavin, vitamin B-12) and minerals (calcium and magnesium). The protein in milk is abundant and complete in all the essential amino acids. A rich source of these nutrients can make the difference between good and poor health for certain groups, especially older people, children, and pregnant women. We recommend dairy products for people in these groups.

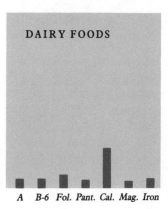

DAIRY FOODS

A   B-6 Fol. Pant. Cal. Mag. Iron

Around the world, people who live on traditional cereal-based cuisines include some form of supplementary animal food. To us, this seems to be the best role for dairy products in our diet too. New vegetarians often feel more comfortable eating cottage cheese and yogurt than less familiar foods like adzuki beans or pilaf. In time, however, many find that their use of dairy products declines. Large quantities of dairy foods can make the diet higher than it should be in protein and saturated fats, and often lower in fiber and iron.

Animal foods like milk products—and eggs, a separate category in our scheme—also provide vegetarians with the one essential nutrient that is not normally available from plant sources: vitamin B-12. One cup of fresh milk (or one egg) supplies about 1 microgram of B-12: half the daily allowance recommended by the United Nations, and ten times the calculated minimum requirement of 0.1 microgram per day. Some cultured milk products are lower in B-12 than fresh milk, as you can see from the table on page 376, so it takes more of them to meet the requirement.

Some people find that a glass or two of milk leads to stomachache, a bloated and gaseous feeling, and diarrhea. These are

[8] *International Dairy Federation 1983,
Cultured Dairy Foods in Human
Nutrition (Brussels: I.D.F.; FIL-IDF
Document 159), p. 22*

A   B-6   Fol.   Pant.   Cal.   Mag.   Iron

symptoms of lactose intolerance or lactase deficiency, a lessened ability to digest milk sugar or lactose. Lactose intolerance is quite common among anyone not of Northern European stock. After childhood the body easily loses its capacity to digest lactose, making it intolerant of milk and other dairy products containing this sugar, though small amounts such as ¼ to 1 cup at a time usually present no problem. Buttermilk seems to be no better than fresh milk in this regard; yogurt may be tolerated and so may cheese, including cottage cheese, because the lactose-rich whey has been removed. Because of milk's reputation as "nature's most nearly perfect food," lactose intolerance used to be considered a serious problem for vegetarians. To us it seems more of a nuisance. If you have trouble with foods from this group, you can skip them in part or entirely and still be completely well nourished, *if you follow the Food Guide.*

Generally speaking, it is a good idea to use low-fat or skim milk products to keep fat intake low. Those whose blood cholesterol levels go up when challenged by saturated fat and cholesterol in the diet should use skim milk only. Milk itself, you'll be pleased to know, has a cholesterol-lowering effect, which is enhanced if the milk used is either low-fat or skim and enhanced even more by low-fat or skim milk yogurt.[8]

The legume family includes a large assortment of protein-rich beans, peas, and other pod-growing pulses. Generally, foods in this group also provide starch for energy and a kind of dietary fiber that helps keep blood glucose levels and blood cholesterol low. Legumes also supply lysine, an amino acid that grains tend to be low in. Legumes are often rich in folacin and are good sources of several minerals.

We are impressed with the versatility of beans in the kitchen, but it has taken some years of experimentation to cultivate this appreciation. Take your time in making their acquaintance, to attune your digestive capacities. You will find that legumes have rich flavors, and that they can also be flavored richly according to your mood. Yet it is wise to start with small quantities at a simple meal, and not a huge bowlful right away. Through experimentation you will find which beans taste best and agree with your body, and in what quantities. Some of these variables will depend on the season or on other factors: how much exercise you are getting, other foods and flavors in your meals, and so on.

We give a collection of helpful suggestions in the recipe section, pages 293–297.

While legumes are nutritious foods, they are not absolutely essential on a vegetarian diet. It is possible to cover nutritional needs without them, even in the context of the milk-free or vegan diet. If you are not acquainted with these rich vegetables, however, by all means get to know them. In taste and nutrition alike, they can do wonderful things in main dishes, soups, salads, and spreads.

Nuts and seeds add a whole range of flavors and textures to the meatless diet, and they can make a significant nutritional contribution too. Those old familiar munchies, sunflower seeds, for example, are a rich source of vitamin B-6. This group is generally a good source of magnesium and especially of trace minerals such as zinc. Unfortunately, nuts and seeds contain too much fat to be sprinkled liberally through the day's menu. Chestnuts, with only 15 percent of their calories from fat, are a welcome exception.

Many nuts and seeds can be ground, for use in sandwich spreads or as a topping for other dishes. If you do not grind them, do chew them well. Otherwise, members of this group that don't cook soft—sesame seeds, for example—will not get digested at all.

NUTS & SEEDS

A   B-6   Fol.   Pant.   Cal.   Mag.   Iron

Fresh, local fruit in season has to be one of the greatest pleasures of the table. It's also the easiest and best of snacks—best because it provides a quick boost without the subsequent quick letdown some people get from even natural fruit *juices*, not to mention candy and refined sweets. Nutritionists once allowed fruit only grudgingly, largely because it supplies so much vitamin C. Yet many fruits contain significant amounts of provitamin A and good amounts of magnesium, both of which seem to offer some protection against chronic diseases. The recent flood of research on fiber makes fruit today look even more respectable, for pectins and other soluble fibers supplied by fruits help to lower blood cholesterol. All these features make fruit therapeutic as well as enjoyable.

We see only one problem with fruit: it is so delicious that you can forget to eat enough of other foods more dense in nutrients. People who try completely fruitarian diets (which traditionally

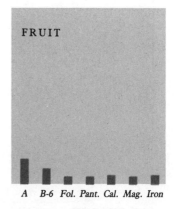

FRUIT

A   B-6   Fol.   Pant.   Cal.   Mag.   Iron

EGGS

A B-6 Fol. Pant. Cal. Mag. Iron

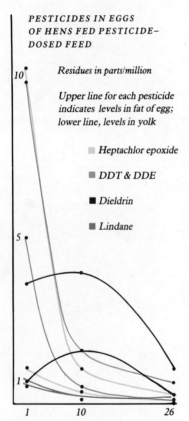

PESTICIDES IN EGGS
OF HENS FED PESTICIDE-
DOSED FEED

Residues in parts/million

Upper line for each pesticide
indicates levels in fat of egg;
lower line, levels in yolk

■ Heptachlor epoxide

■ DDT & DDE

■ Dieldrin

■ Lindane

Eggs laid 1, 10, and 26 weeks after
pesticide dosage ceased (5–10 parts/million
in feed for 5 days). Concentration is in the
fat of the egg yolk, since most pesticides are
fat-soluble. FROM T. C. Byerly 1975[9]

include seeds and nuts) court protein, vitamin, and mineral deficiencies if they don't expand their definition of fruit to include grains and legumes and take other precautions described in the chapter on vegans, page 397.

Eggs have figured large in the controversy about cholesterol. Most scientists today agree that for most people, eating cholesterol is not as likely to endanger the heart and blood vessels as eating too much fat, and to that extent eggs have come out from under a cloud. The catch is that there is a minority—perhaps as many as a third of us—who *are* sensitive to dietary cholesterol, which means that eating foods high in cholesterol does raise blood levels significantly. Probably it is still a good idea to keep dietary cholesterol reasonably low, by using low-fat and skim milk products instead of their full-fat equivalents and by limiting your consumption of eggs (by the usual recommendation, four per person per week is considered moderate). If you have someone at your table who is in the high-risk group for heart and arterial disease, save eggs to use occasionally for the magic they can work in recipes. Egg *whites* are cholesterol-free and work fine in most recipes that call for whole eggs.

One other depressing message about eggs. If you use very many of them, try to find someone who sells eggs from free-ranging hens, or at least hens that are given unadulterated foods. Traces of the hormones and antibiotics administered daily to commercially reared chickens show up in their eggs, and the effects of low doses of these on human beings are unknown but probably not good.[9] In addition, the necessities of the profit margin impose horrible living conditions on commercially grown chickens, including cramped quarters and forced laying. You may be able to buy from families and small farms, whose chickens still range free.

AEROBIC EXERCISE AND ENERGY NEEDS

Why talk about exercise in a food book? Because regular aerobic exercise actually changes the way your body uses nutrients and burns calories. It's so important to nutrition that it's almost a nutrient itself.

The third step of our Food Guide says to fill out your caloric needs with a variety of whole foods. But what *are* your caloric needs? Basically, you need to get enough energy from food to maintain your body's basic functions (your basal metabolism) plus whatever more the body needs for daily activities. Basal metabolism varies from individual to individual, and of course daily activity does too.

Here's one startling fact: if your body doesn't really need much in the way of calories—for example, because it's geared to a low level of physical activity—you can meet your physiological energy requirement with so little food that what you eat *doesn't supply the full range of nutrients you need for health.* Either you eat more (and put on weight) or you eat very little and stay malnourished.

In this connection William Dietz, an authority on childhood obesity, is currently investigating the metabolism of children viewing television. He reports that the first child he tested, a twelve-year-old boy, exhibited a drop in basal metabolic rate of 200 calories an hour while he watched cartoons, as though he were in a trance or stupor.[10] If that boy watches TV just five hours a day—considerably less than the average, according to a 1986 survey—his body needs *1000 calories* less per day than a doctor's chart would show. How is he going to get the nutrients he needs without gaining weight?

What is the answer? Raise your metabolism high enough that you *need* all the calories a varied diet supplies. And the best way to do that is through a program of vigorous exercise. We are talking specifically about aerobic exercise because it is aerobic exercise that increases fat metabolism. *Aerobic* means the use of oxygen. Aerobic exercise lets you take in more oxygen, and moves its invigorating presence efficiently throughout the body. When exercise is too gentle, you are not burning fat fast enough to change your metabolic rate. When exercise is more strenuous, as in sprinting and weight-lifting, your body shifts from fat as a major fuel and draws on faster-burning glucose instead.

For these reasons, the kind of exercise that most benefits your body's utilization of food (as well as your heart and lungs) is not brief spurts of high-intensity activity, but moderately demanding activity over a period of time—jogging comfortably for half an hour or more, for example, instead of going all out for ten minutes. The longer you exercise at this pace, the greater the benefit. More than this a food book need not say; there are so many good books about aerobic exercise today.

[9] C. A. Sáenz de Ródrigues, A. M. Bongiovanni, & L. Conde de Borrego 1985, "An epidemic of precocious development in Puerto Rican children," Journal of Pediatrics 107(3):393–396;

M. Sun 1984, "Use of antibiotics in animal feed challenged," Science 226(4671):144–146 (Oct. 12)

A. M. Pasquino et al. 1982, "Transient pseudo-precocious puberty by probable oestrogen intake in three girls," Archives of Disease in Childhood 57(12):954–956;

M. J. van Logten, F. X. van Leeuwen, & R. W. Stephany 1981, "Toxicological aspects of the use of hormones as anabolic agents," Tijdschrift voor Diergeneeskunde 106(7):353–356;

T. C. Byerly 1975, "Effects of agricultural practices on composition of foods of animal origin," in R. S. Harris & E. Karmas, eds., Nutritional Evaluation of Food Processing (Westport, Conn.: AVI)

[10] G. Kolata 1986, "Obese children: A growing problem," Science 232(4746):21 (Apr. 4);

W. Dietz, Jr., & S. L. Gortmaker 1985, "Do we fatten our children at the television set?" Pediatrics 75(5):807–812

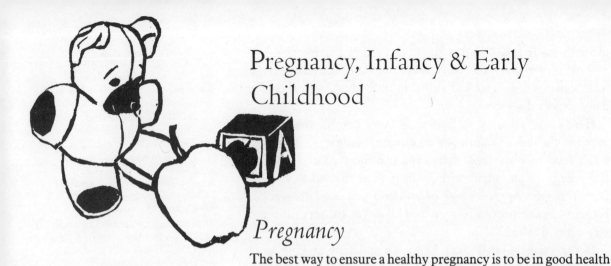

Pregnancy, Infancy & Early Childhood

Pregnancy

The best way to ensure a healthy pregnancy is to be in good health to begin with. If you have been eating and exercising well before becoming pregnant, that will help the whole birthing process and also improve the health of the baby. But if your diet hasn't been what it should be, or if you're not sure about the importance of good nutrition during pregnancy, now is a good time to learn. When you realize that your baby will share and grow on whatever you eat, it becomes easier to make the right choices about food.

Actually, nutrition for a pregnant woman is not very different from nutrition for everyone else. The basic advice remains the same: *variety, whole foods, moderation.* But there are five nutritional needs that deserve special attention during pregnancy: calories, protein, iron, calcium, and folacin.

At term, even a big baby accounts for only one quarter or so of the weight you gain in pregnancy. The rest is nutritional stores for lactation, protective cushioning, added blood, and new tissues.

ENERGY NEEDS AND WEIGHT GAIN

A woman needs extra energy throughout pregnancy to accommodate the growing baby and her own increased physiological needs. About 100 more calories per day for an average woman is recommended during the first three-month period or trimester, increasing to 400 by the third trimester. This does not translate into a very large amount of extra food, since even one banana provides an extra 100 calories.

Not long ago physicians used to advise pregnant women to restrict their food intake so they wouldn't gain too much weight, in the mistaken belief that this helped to make labor easier. Since then it has been demonstrated that not gaining enough weight actually poses greater risks than gaining too much. Dieting during pregnancy is a dangerous practice that can lead to low birth weight babies, and low birth weight is implicated in about 25 percent of infant mortalities. Today it is a

WHERE YOU GAIN WEIGHT AS YOUR BABY GROWS

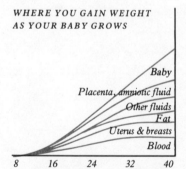

Weeks from last menstrual period

FROM *R. Pitkin 1976, "Nutritional support in obstetrics and gynecology,"* Clinical Obstetrics & Gynecology 19:489

rare doctor who tries to restrict a pregnant woman's gain in weight. Later on, breast-feeding will help get rid of unwanted pounds—as, of course, will a good exercise routine when you are ready for it.

As you can see from the margin, not all of this gain in weight is accounted for by the baby; most comes from your own physiologic changes. In a 27-pound gain, some 3 to 5 pounds is stored as fat, as a protective mechanism for both mom and baby in case food becomes scarce. The fat storage also comes in handy for providing some of the extra calories needed when breast-feeding.

Most women will gain between 25 and 35 pounds, but if you gain more than that gradually, there is no need for alarm. Women who begin their pregnancy underweight or have not been pregnant before often gain more than the average. On the other hand, women who begin pregnancy *overweight* need not gain so much. The amount a woman gains due to water retention varies from person to person, and this leads to wide variations. In other words, weight gain is an individual matter. The maxim is: instead of counting calories, make the calories you eat count. Then your weight gain should adjust itself to what is best for you.

Usually not much weight is put on during the first three months, the average being between 2 and 4 pounds. Most of your weight will be added during the second and third trimesters, when ½ to 1 pound per week is common. People who are 20 percent or more overweight at the beginning of pregnancy will still put on more weight as the pregnancy proceeds, but will not need to gain as much as others—one study suggests that such women need to gain only 15 pounds or so.[1] In speaking of women who begin pregnancy 35 percent or more overweight, another study concludes that "recommendations for a minimum weight gain for obese women are unnecessary."[2]

PROTEIN

Protein is the basic structure of all the cells in your body. In pregnancy, extra protein is required for the increase in blood volume, breasts, and uterus, and for building your baby's body.

The current recommended dietary allowances advise getting 30 grams of protein per day above your ordinary requirement. A typical vegetarian diet usually supplies plenty of high-quality

*SERVINGS SUPPLYING
15 GRAMS OF PROTEIN*

2 large eggs
2 ounces firm cheese:
        swiss, cheddar
½ cup cottage cheese
1¾ cups milk:
        whole, skim, yogurt,
        buttermilk
¼ cup peanut butter
        or ½ cup peanuts
1 cup cooked beans
¾ cup cooked soybeans
¾ cup tofu
½ cup sunflower seeds
3 cups cooked grains:
        rice, millet, oats
6 slices whole wheat bread
3 cups cooked broccoli
6 tablespoons pumpkin seeds

[1] *A. Gormician, J. Valentine, & E. Satter 1980, "Relationship of maternal weight gain, prepregnancy weight, and infant birthweight," Journal of the American Dietetic Association 77:662–667*

[2] *B. F. Abrams & R. K. Laros 1986, "Prepregnancy weight, weight gain, and birth weight," American Journal of Obstetrics and Gynecology 154(3):503–509*

[3] E. Letsky 1980, "The haemato-logical system," in F. Hytten & G. Chamberlain, Clinical Physiology in Obstetrics (Oxford: Blackwell Scientific), pp. 43–78

[4] E. Beutler 1980, "Iron," in R. S. Goodhart & M. E. Shils, eds., Modern Nutrition in Health and Disease, 6th ed. (Philadelphia: Lea & Febiger), pp. 324–354 (p. 341)

[5] J. King 1983, "Dietary risk patterns during pregnancy," in J. Weininger & G. M. Briggs, eds., Nutrition Update, vol. 1 (N.Y.: Wiley), pp. 205–225 (p. 219)

[6] Beutler 1980, p. 326

protein; still, it makes sense to check how much you are getting and to increase your intake if it is less than the recommended amount. The list in the margin can help you do this; each serving listed supplies about 15 grams of high-quality protein. If you would like to be more precise about the protein content of your present diet, check the tables in the back of the book.

IRON

Iron is essential for the production of hemoglobin, the substance in blood that carries oxygen. During pregnancy your need for iron increases markedly because you make up to 4 pints of extra blood, provide iron for your baby's reserve stores, and fortify yourself against blood loss during delivery. Iron is one of the few nutrients where the fetus actually drains your nutrient stores. If you don't have enough, you could become anemic.

In addition to the 18 milligrams recommended for women of childbearing age, most physicians would like a pregnant mother to get an additional 30 to 60 milligrams of iron every day: a whopping daily total of 48 to 78 milligrams. Even 18 milligrams is hard for most women to get from food alone. Physicians in the United States generally prescribe iron supplements as a matter of course, but this practice is not followed in several other countries with equally high standards of health care.[3] We recommend that you look on your iron pills as insurance, and try to get at least the normal 18 milligram requirement from food. Vegetarian women should be especially careful, since they do not get the highly absorbable iron found in meat.[4] If you prefer to avoid supplements, have your blood level checked by a physician. Ask that the test include a serum ferritin measurement, since this actually gauges your body's iron stores; the familiar pinprick hematocrit and hemoglobin blood tests can only measure anemia.[5]

Generally, whole and unprocessed foods are richer in organically bound iron than are processed foods. In addition, you can increase the amount of iron your body can absorb by including a source of vitamin C, such as orange juice or fresh vegetables, with your iron-rich foods or your supplement tablet. Cooking in iron pots also adds significant amounts of iron to your diet.[6] Leaf tea, coffee, and certain foods high in phytate (see page 426) limit iron absorption.

CALCIUM

Because calcium is one of the three major minerals in teeth and bones, the need for calcium is most crucial during the last three months of pregnancy when the baby's bones are developing. Even if you don't get enough calcium in your diet your baby's bones will be fine, because you will mobilize your own stores of calcium to serve its needs. But this calcium drain can increase the likelihood of osteoporosis later in your life, especially if you are not getting enough weight-bearing exercise (such as running or walking), which increases bone strength, and enough exposure to sunlight to promote vitamin D, which helps calcium absorption. (More on osteoporosis on page 407.)

The recommended allowance for calcium for a pregnant mother is 1200 milligrams, slightly more than what you can get from one quart of milk. Leafy greens, legumes, and cottage cheese can provide the rest of the calcium you need. The foods listed on this page have the same amount of calcium as one cup of milk. If for some reason you simply can't take in enough calcium-rich foods and feel you need a supplement, calcium carbonate pills are effective and not very expensive. Avoid dolomite and bone meal, which can contain lead. There is no benefit in getting much more than the recommended total of 1200 milligrams per day.

SOURCES OF CALCIUM

RDA for pregnancy and lactation is 1200–1600 mg

302	milk, skim, *1 cup*
302	yogurt, *1 cup*
300	milk, low fat, *1 cup*
300	buttermilk, *1 cup*
290	milk, whole, *1 cup*
280	blackstrap molasses, *2 tablespoons*
270	collard leaves, *¾ cup*
260	cheese, swiss, *1 ounce*
210	cheese, jack, *1 ounce*
196	tortillas, *2*
176	ice cream, *1 cup*
160	broccoli, *1 stalk*
150	kale, *¾ cup cooked*
150	okra, *1 cup cooked*
148	turnip greens, *¾ cup cooked*
135	parmesan cheese, *2 tablespoons*
120	bok choy, *¾ cup cooked*
120	carob flour, *¼ cup*
115	cottage cheese, *½ cup*
112	mustard greens, *¾ cup*
108	acorn squash, *1 cup baked*

FOLACIN

Folacin is needed for making DNA and RNA, the molecules that transfer genetic information and translate it into tissue production. Because this role is so basic to the life process, a folacin deficiency can have far-reaching consequences.[7] The current recommendation for a pregnant woman is 800 micrograms, twice as much as the nonpregnant adult. It is not difficult for a vegetarian to get this much folacin in a day's food intake. Think "foliage": dark leafy greens are the richest source of folacin for vegetarians, and one cup of cooked spinach or asparagus contains one fourth of your daily needs during pregnancy. Other good sources include green beans and peas, legumes, nuts, fresh oranges, and whole wheat products. Your vitamin–mineral formula should contain folacin, but again, please look upon this as insurance and not a substitute for eating folacin-rich foods.

[7] *K. A. Winship et al. 1984, "Maternal drug histories and central nervous system anomalies,"* Archives of Disease in Childhood *59(11):1052–1059; editorial comment by R. W. Smithells, 1059–1060*

*Tobacco smoke
(including others');
car exhaust;
organic solvents (turpentine,
paint thinner, oven
cleaners, lacquer thinner);
oil-base paints and stains;
contact cement,
model airplane glue,
and fiberglass emulsion;
hair spray;
pesticides and herbicides;
diagnostic X-rays unless
there is no alternative.*

*Be sure each dentist or doctor
you see knows that you are
pregnant.*

[8] *H. Niederhoff & H. P. Zahradnik
1983, "Analgesics during pregnancy,"
American Journal of Medicine
75(5A):117–120*

[9] *S. L. Ink & L. M. Henderson 1984,
"Vitamin B-6 metabolism," Annual
Review of Nutrition 4:455–470 (p.
466)*

[10] *M. A. Dubick & R. B. Rucker 1983,
"Dietary supplements and health aids:
A critical evaluation; Part 1: Vitamins
and minerals," Journal of Nutrition
Education 15(2):47–53 (p. 48)*

[11] *S. L. Nightengale & W. G. Flamm
1983, "Caffeine and health," in
Weininger & Briggs, Nutrition
Update, vol. 1, pp. 9–12;*

SUBSTANCES TO AVOID

There are a few substances that you will want to avoid entirely during pregnancy: alcohol, cigarettes, and drugs of any kind (except under your physician's direction). Alcohol in moderate to large daily quantities causes fetal alcohol syndrome, which includes mental retardation and physical defects of various kinds. Recent research shows that even small amounts of alcohol taken every day can cause a reduction in birth weight. Binge drinking is potentially disastrous.

Cigarette smoking has been clearly linked to low birth weight, a condition linked with many health problems in infancy, including increased mortality. Now is the time to quit smoking. If you absolutely cannot quit, it is extremely important to cut down as much as possible. It may be hard to be motivated for yourself alone, but when what you do so clearly affects your unborn baby, it becomes easier to find the willpower to do what is best.

Except what your doctor is currently prescribing for you during pregnancy, drugs of any kind—even over-the-counter products, including aspirin[8]—should be avoided. Megadoses of vitamins—amounts ten or more times the recommended daily allowance—can be as harmful as drugs. Vitamin B-6 in large doses can cause neurological problems,[9] and too much vitamin C can cause rebound scurvy in the newborn.[10] The amounts in an ordinary one-a-day pill, however, should not be harmful, and a reliable source for vitamin B-12 is necessary for anyone who cannot eat dairy products or eggs.

Another substance you should moderate your intake of is caffeine. In the range supplied by five to ten cups of coffee per day, caffeine has been linked to birth defects.[11] Lesser amounts have not been proven harmful, but common sense advises caution. Caffeine is also found in leaf tea, cocoa, chocolate, and cola drinks. Instead of these beverages, try fruit juices or coffee substitutes made from grain.

FIRST TRIMESTER

During the first three months the embryo is implanted in the uterus and develops into a three-inch, one-ounce individual. At three months it is called a fetus and is no longer an "it" but either a boy or a girl. Your baby can open and close its mouth. The arms and legs can kick about, though you probably won't feel the movement yet.

These early months are a time of rapid and critical growth. It is very important that you avoid all the substances that were mentioned earlier. You should also try to develop healthy eating habits if you haven't already done so: they will serve you well throughout your pregnancy, and during lactation if you breastfeed. Later on, your good example will also make it easier to teach your little one to eat well.

Constipation is a common problem during the early months of the pregnancy, due to increases in a hormone that prevents expulsion of the embryo. It is also common during the third trimester, as the available abdominal space becomes more cramped and compressed. (Turn to page 376 for some suggestions.)

The biggest impediment to eating healthily in these early months is what is commonly referred to as morning sickness. The "morning" part is a misnomer: some women may be more affected in the morning, but others feel sicker in the evening and still others experience it all day long. Some, of course, never have the problem. But if you aren't one of these lucky few, whether you have just a little queasy feeling upon awakening or are outright throwing up many times a day, morning sickness can make it difficult to eat three healthy meals in a given day.

Every mother you speak to will tell you that this, that, or the other thing worked for her nausea. That is basically all we can suggest to you: try many ploys to see what helps you most. One common approach is to keep some food in the stomach at all times. Small meals with high protein content may feel the most soothing, and many women find that dry, starchy foods and cool foods work best. For instance, crackers and cheese before you go to bed and when you get up in the middle of the night can help prevent the early morning queasies, since hunger itself can trigger the problem. Fresh fruit that you can pop easily into your mouth, such as grapes, counteracts the drops in blood sugar that contribute to nausea. But try to keep your snacks healthy: remember, your little one eats what you eat.

One mom we know found that Mexican food was the most appetizing during this time. Others find themselves yearning for long-forgotten childhood favorites. Sipping mint tea may help, but note that a few herbal teas should be avoided in pregnancy (see margin). If heavily spiced dishes turn you green around the gills, try bland foods like cornstarch pudding, tapioca, and homemade fruit yogurts. Eat smaller, more frequent meals if you have

---

CAFFEINE CONTENT OF BEVERAGES
Milligrams per cup

100–150	*Coffee (brewed)*
60–80	*Coffee (instant)*
3–5	*Sanka*
40–100	*Tea*
17–55	*Cola drinks*

Virtually all herb teas have medicinal properties. Though they are "natural," some may not be innocuous in pregnancy.

Herbs causing adverse hormonal effects:

Devil's claw; Licorice root, Papaya leaf, Pennyroyal oil, Raspberry leaf, Squaw tea (Ephedra viridis)

Herbs causing adverse effects on nervous system:

Burdock root, Catnip, Cohash, Hydrangea, Jimsonweed, Juniper, Lobelia, Wormwood

Cathartics, diuretics, and irritants:

Aloe leaves, Buckthorn bark, Dock root, Juniper berries, Senna, Shave grass (horsetail)

Stimulants:

Hydrangea, Kola nut, Maté, "Mormon tea", (Ephedra nevadensis)

M. Abramowicz, ed., 1979, "Toxic reactions to plant products sold in health food stores," Medical Letter 21(528):29–32;

R. K. Segal 1976, "Herbal intoxication," Journal of the American Medical Association 236(5):473–474;

J. F. Morton 1974, "Is there a safer tea?" Morris Arboretum Bulletin 26:24–30

As little as 10 grams of alcohol daily (about 1 drink) in the very early stages of pregnancy leads to a small but significant decrease in birth weight.

R. E. Little et al. 1986, "Fetal growth and moderate drinking in early pregnancy," American Journal of Epidemiology 132(2):270–278

CAFFEINE IN PREGNANCY
Percentage of complications (spontaneous abortion, stillbirth, premature birth, or death of the baby within 48 hours) in 489 pregnancies, related to caffeine consumption of mother and father. These data do not show a cause–effect relationship, but they do suggest caution for mothers and fathers whose coffee consumption is high. (Caffeine content of beverages in mg on page 373.)

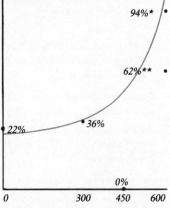

94%*
62%**
22%
36%
0%

0   300   450   600

Estimated daily caffeine in mg per day

*600 mg/day or more by mother
**more than 600 mg/day by father, less than 400 by mother

FROM *P. S. Weathersbee, L. K. Olsen, & J. R. Lodge* 1977, "Caffeine and pregnancy," Postgraduate Medicine 62:64

to, and eat more when you feel less nauseous so that you can get in your recommended allotment of nutrients. But if you do throw up a lot or are unable to eat the recommended amounts, don't worry too much: your body's stores will carry you and the baby through this trying time.

First-time moms may think that this will never end, and that nothing could be worth this awful feeling. But it does pass, and your spirits will revive. Most women feel better by the end of their third month; and when the baby is placed in your arms at the end of the ninth month, you will remember those difficult days and think they could have been twice as long and twice as hard and it would still have been worth it.

SECOND TRIMESTER

At the end of the sixth month your baby will be moving actively, especially at night when you are trying to sleep. It will weigh about one and a half pounds, have eyebrows and eyelashes, and may even suck its thumb. Ten or more rhythmic bumps in a row means that baby probably has the hiccups.

Months three to six are called the golden months by physicians. For most women the nausea will have faded away. Instead of merely looking a little plump, your tummy will finally become gloriously round.

If you found exercise difficult in the first trimester, try to get back into a routine now. Regular daily exercise will give you the endurance needed for labor and delivery and help you to get back into shape faster after your baby is born. There is some evidence now that increasing aerobic exercise beyond what you have been used to can lead to a lower birth weight, so we recommend the less mechanically stressful kinds of exercise such as swimming, cycling, or walking. Stretching and calisthenic activities specifically designed for pregnancy are also beneficial.

Eating in the second trimester is easier, though the growing baby may cramp your usual stomach capacity. If eating smaller meals more frequently helped before, go ahead and continue now.

THIRD TRIMESTER

The last three months may seem like the longest in your life. Those friendly, reassuring kicks now become a little tiresome; they may even give you sore ribs. It is hard to take a deep breath and it is impossible to tie your shoes. By the eighth month all of the baby will be formed. It will take its birthing position, usually head down, and fatten up until it is time to be born. During the ninth month, weight is put on and antibodies are stored up. Although you may feel you will be pregnant forever, the long-looked-for event is not far off.

For some women, the cramping of stomach space brings back the nausea of the first trimester. For the majority, however, the bane of these last three months is heartburn. There are two causes. First, an increase in certain hormones during pregnancy causes smooth muscle relaxation so that the sphincter between stomach and esophagus is relaxed, allowing stomach contents and acid to come back up more freely. Second, the capacity of your stomach has been reduced: there seems to be no room for both food and stomach juices.

If you have heartburn, there are several things you can try.

IRON CONTENT AND IRON COOKWARE

Iron content after cooking (mg/100 g)

■ *Glass cookware*
■ *Iron cookware*

■ 1.7	Scrambled eggs
■ 4.1	(Cooking time: 3 min.)
■ 1.4	Rice casserole
■ 5.2	(20 min.)
■ .45	Fried potatoes
■ 3.8	(30 min.)
■ .47	Apple butter
████ 52.5	(2 hrs.)
■ 3.0	Spaghetti sauce
████ 87.5	(3 hrs.)

DATA FROM *Data from C. V. Moore, "Iron," in R. S. Goodhart & M. E. Shils 1973, Modern Nutrition in Health and Disease, 5th ed. (Philadelphia: Lea & Febiger), p. 300*

Food Guide for Pregnancy & Lactation

Every day

1 *Have 4 servings of whole-grain foods*
&

3 servings of vegetables
(including 1 of Super-Vegetables)

2 *Choose 1 of the pathways*

3 *Fill out your calorie needs with a variety of whole foods*

Pathways

DAIRY FOODS
4 servings, plus:
2 protein servings, p. 371

LEGUMES
1 serving, plus:
4 servings Dairy Foods
1 protein serving, p. 371

SUPER-VEGETABLES
1 serving, plus:
3 servings Dairy Foods
2 protein servings, p. 371

(For food families and serving sizes, see page 354. Iron can be increased by cooking in iron cookware; see chart above.)

Some mothers report that sipping a glass of milk slowly eases the burning sensation; others swear by a tablespoon of cream or ice cream. Avoid stimulating the production of excess acid with caffeine, alcohol, spices, or anything else that you find exacerbates your heartburn. Smaller, more frequent meals will help this problem, as will avoiding liquids at meals. Don't eat or drink too close to bedtime or before lying down, since a reclining position can wreak havoc while your food is digesting; when you do lie down, try elevating the head of your bed or sleeping on two or three pillows. If, despite these precautions, the burning sensation makes it hard to sleep, ask your doctor for an antacid to use at night.

Another dietary problem of the last trimester is constipation. Again, the cause is smooth muscle relaxation as well as cramped quarters. Regular daily exercise, plenty of fluids, plenty of fiber, and answering nature's call promptly can all help with this problem. Don't take any stool softeners or laxatives without consulting your physician.

A few lucky women have no nausea or heartburn whatsoever. If you do find eating unpleasant, however, you may appreciate the assurance that your baby will be healthy even if you can't eat heartily. Almost as soon as the baby is born your appetite will return to normal, and food that you couldn't think about before will become appetizing.

Lactation

Once the baby arrives, you might find that preparing meals and eating regularly become trickier. In that sense, it may be even more difficult to eat well at this time than it was when you were pregnant. But it is important to make the effort. Unless you are very undernourished, the milk you produce will be quite adequate for the baby's needs, for your body will give lactation—the milk-making process—top priority. For just that reason, however, you need to eat enough of the right foods to protect your own nutritional stores.

The best diet for breast-feeding is similar to that for pregnancy, except that you need more calories and less protein. In general, you need only follow the guidelines in the previous chapter. However, there are a few details of nutrition while nursing that deserve a different emphasis.

CALORIE NEEDS

Women who eat too little while breast-feeding tend to produce less milk, although the nutrient content of the milk remains just as good. If you gained weight adequately while pregnant, you can probably lactate well as long as you get more calories. Don't try to lose weight at this stage by eating less! Since the fat stored during pregnancy is used for making milk, breast-feeding itself is an excellent (if slow) method for losing weight. You can safely lose from ½ to 1 pound a week, but please do not try to speed up weight loss beyond that. Even women who have been successfully breast-feeding for a while can lose some of their milk supply by cutting calories.

The recommended allowance set by the National Research Council calls for 400 extra calories a day while breast-feeding. This can be difficult to manage, but not usually because of lack of appetite or heartburn as in pregnancy, but because of the time-consuming demands of your new baby. Especially during those first two or three weeks, it may seem like all you can do just to care for the little one and still squeeze in enough sleep. Nevertheless, you need to eat well to keep up your energy and to maintain a good milk supply. For the early days, have your partner take over preparing meals. If he can't or won't cook, try to enlist the aid of a friend. You might also consider stocking the freezer with casseroles and soups before the baby comes. You may find it easier to grab several small meals than to arrange to sit down to three larger ones.

FLUIDS

In the excitement and fatigue of a new baby, it is easy to neglect drinking enough fluids to ensure an adequate milk supply. While there is nothing to be gained from drinking much more than feels comfortable, it is still necessary to pay close attention to your fluid needs. Some women find it helpful to drink something every time they nurse. Water, fruit juice (preferably unsweetened), vegetable juices, soup, and milk all help to meet your need for liquids. Although it is not necessary to drink milk to make milk, cow's milk is a good source of calcium, protein, and riboflavin, all nutrients you need plenty of while breast-feeding.

Nursing Mothers Counsel
P. O. Box 50063
Palo Alto, Calif. 94303
(408) 272–1448

Nursing Mothers Council
Boston Association for
*   Childbirth Education*
P. O. Box 29
Newtonville, Mass. 02160
(617) 244–5102

La Leche League International
91616 Minneapolis St.,
Franklin Park, Illinois 60131
(312) 455–7730

Check with local hospital and community groups for classes, support groups, and hotlines for nursing mothers. Write your letters and make contacts before the baby is born!

Nurturing Your Child

When our children were infants, a mother of teenagers advised us, "Whatever you do, teach them from the start to eat all kinds of foods. Once they get older, it's impossible; they will only eat what they like." We all know adults in that very predicament: able only to eat what they like and finding themselves helpless to change. Our approach to establishing good eating habits, based on the combined experiences of several families who have raised a passel of kids, is rooted in the following convictions:

❧ Flexibility in eating, as in other areas, gives a person a tremendous advantage in life. The child who learns not to take likes and dislikes in food too seriously will find that capacity translates into freedom over many other potentially rigid habits.

❧ In a world where there is such unequal distribution of material wealth, it is helpful to grow up feeling a personal responsibility not to waste resources like food, which (like water and air) should be available for all.

❧ Mealtimes are central to the experience of family, so it is important that meals be pleasant and harmonious.

Today, when we look back on the trying experiences of fostering good eating habits among our children, we can say with a sigh, "Somehow we managed it." Our kids, now sliding into their teens, calmly eat eggplant and kale, don't leave their bread crusts, and can be satisfied with a snack of fruits, nuts, or a smoothie. They love pizzas, of course, but they clamor with equal enthusiasm for Chard Cheese Pie and Spanakopita, and have been known to ask for seconds of cabbage. In the years to come, we expect them to experiment with junk food—after all, once you leave the home it's all around you! But we will continue to provide a healthy base at home, and we're confident that we have given them a good start. Their tastes and outlook are formed, and by and large, they disdainfully turn down substitutes for the real thing. Later, when they settle down to lives of their own, they will have these skills and training to draw upon.

INFANCY

The preceding pages looked at the breast-feeding mother's nutritional needs. What about the needs of the infant?

Thirty years ago, formula feeding was the dominant fashion in infant care. It was considered clean and "modern," and was touted as a triumph of science over nature. Since then, however, widespread experience with many types of formula and whole generations of babies and mothers has established that even the best formulas are no real match for mother's milk. Today experts agree that mother's milk is the ideal food for the newborn, and that no other food is required for six months or so.

To name just a few of the differences, formula-fed infants are more likely to develop allergies to cow's milk, and possibly to other substances too.[12] Breast-fed infants have better protection against infectious illnesses, because the mother's antibodies are supplied in her milk and particularly in the pre-milk fluid or colostrum that first comes after the baby is born.[13] Later, after teeth have appeared, bottle feeding can lead to tooth decay if the baby is left to fall asleep with bottle in mouth.[14] The incidence of a much more serious problem, childhood diabetes, was associated with bottle feeding in one epidemiological study.[15]

Finally, in addition to nutritional differences, many mothers who breast-feed count convenience and economy among the bonuses.

In the last ten years there has been an increasing awareness of the advantages of breast-feeding all over the world, for which much credit is due to groups like La Leche League. In the United States, the percentage of mothers nursing their babies went from 25 percent in 1970 to 54 percent in 1980.[16]

To ensure successful breast-feeding, however, more may be required than simply recognizing the advantages of mother's milk. First, even though a huge volume of scientific research has accumulated which strongly favors breast-feeding, residual prejudices against it remain. Also, busy schedules and work situations often mitigate against this most natural practice. For these reasons, it can be immensely helpful for a new mother to make contact with others who can give support and encouragement. La Leche League has done a fine job fulfilling this role, and there are many smaller local groups as well. A new mother may need reassurance about the quality of her milk, the well-being of her baby, and a hundred other small questions that arise. For instance, most new mothers are surprised and chagrined at how frequently their babies want to nurse. It is not uncommon for an infant to want even hourly nursing sessions, sometimes throughout the night. Obviously, more is involved here than hunger: the other vital function of breast-feeding, the bonding pro-

[12] C. Briggs 1983, "Infant feeding and nutrition," in Weininger & Briggs, Nutrition Update, vol. 1, pp. 236–48 (p. 240)

[13] T. Beaudette 1986, "Infant feeding practices," Seminars in Nutrition 5(2):1–18;

C. Briggs 1983, pp. 236–248;

J. Metcoff 1982, "Nutrition and the development of the child," Journal of Food and Nutrition 39(4):193–197 (p. 194)

[14] L. W. Ripa 1978, "Nursing habits and dental decay in infants," Contemporary Nutrition 3(5)

[15] K. Borch-Johnson et al. 1984, "Breast feeding and diabetes," Lancet 2(8411):1083–1086 (November 10)

[16] S. M. Oace 1982, "Infant feeding practices," Journal of Nutrition Education 14(2):51

cess. The infant has a deep need for intimate contact with the mother, which is fulfilled naturally by nursing.

Mothers today are sometimes concerned too about baby fat, perhaps because some researchers have traced adult obesity to obesity in childhood. Chubbiness in *infancy*, however, is a completely different matter, having little or no correlation with overweight problems later in life. A chubby little baby is more likely to be healthy and happy than actually obese.[17] If you feel worried about your baby's weight, however, regular checkups and comparison with standard growth charts should tell if there is a problem brewing. More than likely you will find, as we have with our children, that a roly-poly toddler is destined to grow into a tall, slender youth.

If you are breast-feeding yet concerned with the apparent chubbiness of your infant, keep in mind that breast milk is a fairly dilute solution, and a certain amount of effort is required of the baby to suck it from the breast. For this and perhaps other less tangible reasons, it is unlikely that breast milk will produce excessive weight if no other foods are given.

Of course, once infancy has passed, there *is* a danger that a child will be overweight. Fat children are more likely to be obese as adults than are children of normal weight, and unfortunately, childhood fatness is on the rise in our very sedentary society.[18] We feel that children who grow up in an active environment, with parents and other adults who enjoy keeping fit, are not likely to become obese. If fatness is creeping up on your family, consider storing the television in the closet and enrolling the whole family in an enjoyable and physically active program.

Mothers are often concerned that a baby is not thriving on breast milk alone. Here again, consult the growth chart with your family physician if you have any doubts. Your own observations will provide valuable clues: if your baby looks healthy and is lively and responsive, he or she is likely to be well nourished. But any sign of listlessness or apathy lasting more than a day or two should definitely be checked out. The first thing to examine is your own diet. Are you cutting back, trying to lose those pregnancy pounds quickly? Or is your demanding new schedule leaving you little time to address your own nutritional needs? Make sure you're getting adequate nutrition—still for two—and plenty of liquids, including milk. A good rule is to drink something whenever you sit down to nurse. If meals are scarce and

[17] E. Satter 1983, Child of Mine (Palo Alto: Bull Publishing Co.), p. 376

[18] S. M. Garn & M. LaVelle 1985, "Two-decade follow-up of fatness in early childhood," American Journal of Diseases of Children 139(2):181–185

sparse, have a snack as well. You will certainly slim down gradually and safely during the nursing months.

Contrary to medical consensus, the experience of many mothers we know is that foods eaten by the mother *can* cause distress to the baby through her milk. One friend, who lived on an apple farm when her first baby came, didn't dare indulge in the fresh, juicy apples that hung so temptingly from the trees: if she did, her baby had a sleepless night. Others have had trouble with chocolate, coffee, and other foods. The sensitivity varies from baby to baby, and many never experience it. But if you suspect that what you eat may be causing colic or other reactions, watch for the foods mentioned above and in the margin.

Although breast-feeding is more accepted now than it was in the recent past, barriers remain. But the climate is changing. Today even a nursing mother who works full time may find it possible to arrange to leave work for nursing periods. If that is impossible, the mother can store bottles of her own milk in the refrigerator for feedings when she has to be away, and still nurse the child herself after work hours. This phase of the infant's life is so crucial, and so precious to the mother as well, that it is worth overcoming a few hurdles for. Most mothers who have nursed their babies will probably agree that breast-feeding is a rich, satisfying, strengthening process for both mother and child.

Of course, there are some instances when it really is impossible to nurse a child. If this is so, we want to point out that the love and tender, intimate contact with their mothers that babies need to thrive on can also be supplied by bottle-feeding parents. But if you can breast-feed, by all means do: it is an opportunity that is not to be missed.

We recommend continuing to nurse for many months, holding off on supplementary food until at least the fourth month but not later than the sixth, unless your baby is underweight and not thriving. By delaying the introduction of solids, you reduce the potential for allergies, excessive weight gain, and decreased milk supply.

Usually the baby will tell you when he or she is ready to begin eating solid food. You will see longing eyes watching your food on its way to your mouth, and little hands reaching toward your plate for some tempting morsel. This begins the new phase, the start of a lifelong process. There is a good chance that you will be

Foods eaten by the mother that are most often associated with colic in some babies include coffee, chocolate, coles (foods in the cabbage and broccoli family), onions, red wine, tomatoes, black beans, and chili.

Ellyn Satter adds milk to this list, but also cautions, "It is probably the unusual child who reacts to his mother's diet. Further, it is hard to sort out whether infant behavior is a true reaction to food or simply a coincidence, since all babies are fussy, get congested, or appear colicky at times. But if you have a fussy or colicky baby, it is probably worth a try to see if your food could be causing it. . . . Stop eating [the suspected food] a couple of times, see if the symptoms disappear, then reintroduce it and see if they reappear . . . but check to make sure you are not unnecessarily limiting your food selection before you cut it out completely."

E. Satter, p. 189

FIRST FOODS

VEGETABLES HIGH
IN NITRATES[19]

celery
beets
rutabaga
broccoli
kale
turnips
cucumbers
squash
carrots
soybeans
lettuce
radishes
corn

Do not feed these and other
high-nitrate foods to infants
under 3 months, or to infants
under 12 months who have
diarrhea; nitrites, which form
from nitrates after vegetables
are picked, are harmful to
infant hemoglobin.

M.S. Yelvigi 1982, "Implications of
spinach consumption in infants,"
Lawrence Review of Natural Products
3(8):1–3;
J. P. Keating et al. 1973, "Infantile
methemoglobinemia caused by carrot
juice," New England Journal of
Medicine 288(16):824–826 (Apr. 19);
Rose Ann Soloway of the National
Capital Poison Center also reports
a case of a 3-month infant with
methemoglobinemia induced by beets
[letter to Carol Flinders, Jan 9, 1986]

[19] *J. M. Keating 1964, Poisonous Plants*
of the United States and Canada
(Englewood Cliffs, N. J.:
Prentice-Hall), pp. 42–43

feeding your child even into early adulthood, and will always feel a sense of responsibility for his or her well-being. You will certainly find that nurturing your child involves a great deal more than factual knowledge. Along with nutritional know-how must come generous amounts of love, understanding, artful discipline, timing, and judgment, for you are helping your child establish the nutritional habits of a lifetime. If you can instill good habits now, you'll save your child a lot of misery later in life.

Mashed-up banana makes an ideal first food. Start with a small piece and mash it with a fork until all the lumps are out. Plan to introduce it about midway between normal nursing periods so the baby is not too full, but not desperately hungry either. Hold the baby in your arms in a half-sitting position and slip in a tiny spoonful. Sometimes that's all it takes; but don't be surprised if the food comes spitting back out. The baby may seem more interested in this new sensation as a plaything for the tongue. It may take several sessions before any amount is swallowed, but if you take your time and are relaxed and pleasant, your baby will soon be enjoying the new snack.

Once you have succeeded with bananas, you can go on to mild fruits that are cooked and mashed: applesauce, pear sauce, peaches. You can move on to cereals shortly thereafter, and the first to try should be rice, since it is least likely to irritate. Baby cereals are easy to use and not very expensive, but it is easy to make your own. Grind a handful of uncooked brown rice in a blender; then cook it well, using plenty of water, until it is very soft and smooth. Another method is to blend very well-cooked rice with water or with pureed fruit. Once rice is well established, you can introduce oats, barley, corn, and other grains.

Always begin with a small amount of a new food and only introduce one new food at a time, so you can observe any adverse reactions your baby may have. Discontinue any food that seems to cause rash or gastric distress and try it again after several weeks. Generally it's best to wait past the fifth month to introduce wheat, cow's milk, citrus fruits, and other likely irritants. Start with mild, pleasant-tasting vegetables such as potatoes, carrots, sweet potatoes, peas, and green beans, cooked well and mashed smooth. Stronger-flavored vegetables like broccoli, cabbage, dried beans, and spinach and other greens can wait until the baby can handle finger foods and a little chewing, as these vegetables are not very appealing in mashed form.

As with cereals, you really don't need to purchase specially processed baby foods. It is simple, less expensive, and more healthful to feed the baby a milder version of the varied whole-food diet that the rest of the family eats. All you need is a blender or a small baby-food grinder, which can be used right at the table to mash up a few bites at a time so there needn't be a lot of waste. There is no need to add seasonings such as sugar, spices, or salt. In fact, at this stage it is easy and prudent to keep your child from developing an early taste for such additions.

Throughout this period your child is refining the skills of good eating, and should be deriving great pleasure from experimenting with an array of new sensations. It's important, if you're not to come to grief over these feeding sessions, to be prepared for what can only be called a holy mess. A certain air of abandon on the child's part combined with the perfectly mushy texture of the food makes this inevitable. You can try several approaches. Some mothers spoon-feed the child, carefully scooping up any spills. Some babies tolerate this, but sooner or later the urge to try it oneself will become irresistible—as it should. Then the best you can do is provide an area which is easily cleaned, protect your clothes and furniture as best as you can, and have plenty of water close at hand for afterwards. Since the process can severely disrupt the family meal, it might be better to offer a cracker or breadstick if you want the baby to join in at dinnertime, and save the real fun for a more private moment.

This is one of those intense periods of childhood which, though brief, seem endless at the time. Since milk is still a major source of nourishment, your main concerns are to encourage and promote learning, and to introduce a wide variety of well-prepared cooked and mashed fruits, vegetables, grains, and (by the end of this period) wheat bread, cheese, and a few raw fruits and vegetables. Be careful when introducing raw carrots and apples, as they can cause choking and might be aspirated into the lungs. You should be especially wary of nuts for the same reason; it's better to give them as nut butters.

Somewhere between the ages of eighteen months and two years, your child will have acquired the skills and digestive maturity to handle most foods without much special preparation. At this point he or she needs the widest possible variety of fruits, vegetables, grains, and legumes to supply the demands of

Do not feed honey in any form to infants under 1 year of age. Serious food poisoning (infant botulism) may result.

S. S. Arnon et al. 1979, "Honey and other environmental risk factors for infant botulism," Journal of Pediatrics 94:331–336

TWO TO FIVE

increased physical and mental activity. This brings about a personality change as well; the toddler experiences and expresses a growing sense of separate identity taking shape within, and strong likes and dislikes begin to form. All this requires a great deal of skillful management on your part. You'll be walking a fine line between encouraging growth and setting limits, and much of this will center around food. In this connection, it is as important to avoid distressing power confrontations at mealtimes as to provide a nutritious diet. Here are some suggestions that helped us through this challenging period.

We wanted to give the training in good food habits that would help our children make healthful choices in later life, while at the same time avoiding those distressing food battles where everyone loses. So while family mealtime is set aside as a special occasion where certain standards of behavior are expected, we planned frequent snack periods for youngsters to allow them freedom to choose and reject. There we offered a more tantalizing array of nutritious options so as not to have to rely on mealtimes to provide everything we wanted the young ones to have.

These ages mark a period of slowing growth rate, so the need for quantities is less; quality and variety are more crucial. At mealtime, everyone in the family is served a portion, but for the youngest this can be just a tiny dab of each course. Once he or she has eaten some of everything, it's all right to have more of any item—you can have more spaghetti when you finish your broccoli. This applies to everyone in the family, but you don't need to press quantities on anyone.

Youngsters have much more sensitive palates than adults do, and at this age the flavor, smell, and texture of foods is vividly experienced. You will have much more success offering a few steamed carrots than a dish of creamed carrots with mushrooms and scallions; three portions of separated foods than a bowl of minestrone soup; a tortilla and plain beans than enchiladas. Onions, avocados, eggplant, strong spices, and many other ingredients that enhance meals to our tastes can be so unpleasant to the senses of the young that they cause real distress. Not wanting to deprive the rest of the family of flavors they enjoy, we try to use common sense and creativity to disguise here and separate there—and, in the case of some obviously unnecessary foods, to make some things optional.

Your own child will help determine how you manage this, how

Your own child will help determine how you manage this, how you decide when to yield and when to stand firm. If lentil soup is rejected, the same ingredients in loaf or patty form with home-made ketchup may get pleas for seconds. Cream of vegetable soup, blended in a blender till foamy and light, can cover many otherwise objectionable ingredients. The trick is to decide beforehand what is necessary and what is not. For the necessities, use patient and loving firmness to overcome resistance. If all else fails, try hiding them in attractive snack foods, given when meal-time rules are relaxed.

The joy children this age get from imitating can be put to work here. Children will often try something new—say, a stalk of steamed broccoli—if allowed to cut it carefully into pieces with a table knife beforehand, or if they have been allowed to help prepare the meals they are going to eat. Kneading and baking bread are popular activities at this age. And no learning laboratory is a better place for discovering vegetables than the garden: children love to eat what they have grown and picked themselves.

While it's important to teach good eating habits early on, we want to stress that it can be dangerous to restrict toddlers to an adult diet. Small children need calories, and small stomachs may not hold enough food to meet energy needs on three low-fat meals a day. Whole milk or 2 percent butterfat milk is fine—don't put them on skim—and let them eat between meals when hungry, so long as the food is nutritious. Actually, snack times are a perfect opportunity to slip in all kinds of sources of protein, vitamins, and minerals. We rely mostly on simple foods: raisins, prunes, carrot sticks, hard-boiled eggs, cheese sticks, and apples or bananas with peanut butter are well loved. Peanut Butter Balls, smoothies, and yogurt with fruit can be as simple or as complex as you desire. Cater to your child's sense of delight: at this age, nutritional needs are best met with plenty of variety, freedom to experiment and choose, and adequate calories.

Last, as in other facets of life, it is by your own example that you will do your most effective teaching. Reverence for life, the very basis of vegetarianism as we see it, is really what you are nurturing during these early years. That passionate affection for bugs and kittens, if undisturbed, will slowly expand to embrace all creatures. By the time the teen years roll around, the deep conviction is there that all of life is sacred.

One pediatrician reports that restrictive diets now account for about one fourth of the cases of failure to thrive seen at his hospital. (Time, July 14, 1986)

Controlling Your Weight

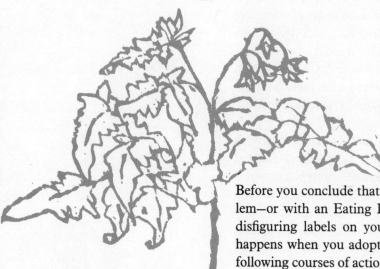

Before you conclude that you are Someone with a Weight Problem—or with an Eating Disorder—before, in fact, you put *any* disfiguring labels on yourself, we urge you to find out what happens when you adopt one or more (ideally, all three) of the following courses of action:

🕭 Move to a diet (not a reducing diet!) of low-fat whole foods.

🕭 Take up a program of daily aerobic exercise.

🕭 Withdraw your attention from food and its consequences, and absorb yourself in activities that really deserve your interest—activities where you have to give of yourself to something truly worthwhile.

All three of these steps, you will observe, are entirely life-supporting. That they help to "normalize" body weight is a happy dividend.

Instead of thinking of yourself as someone who tends to gain weight easily, in other words, think of yourself as a person who lives in a *society* that predisposes its members to gain weight. The difference is subtle, but its meaning won't be lost on anyone who has struggled with the feelings of frustration and self-recrimination that haunt most attempts at weight control.

Consider three facts of normal, everyday life in this country.

First, look at the standard American diet, outrageously high in fat and just as low in dietary fiber. One new "breakfast" touted on billboards by a fast-foods chain provides a perfect symbol: a hot, buttered white-flour biscuit oozing with processed cheese and fried bacon.

Second, there is our extremely sedentary pattern of life. Exercise may be in vogue, but many millions of Americans still use a car for any trip longer than two blocks and "re-create" themselves in front of the television.

Third, from our earliest years we are conditioned to see *consuming*, plain and simple, as the source of life's richest satisfactions.

Add them up and the result is all but inevitable: we put on weight. And the result of that *is* inevitable: embarrassment, chagrin that we can't get into our favorite jeans, and the mounting fear that things really are out of our control.

Any gain in weight triggers that most emotionally loaded of concerns, personal attractiveness—because in our society, having the Body Beautiful ranks right up there with consumerism itself as a reigning obsession. As if it's not enough that we're always beleaguered to eat more food (and more unhealthy food) than we have any desire for, we're battered ceaselessly with the notion that being thin is the key to human happiness. The pincer effect of these two contradictory messages is enough to drive one to madness—certainly to the subclinical everyday sort of madness that has us taping mean notes to ourselves on the refrigerator. The whole business is degrading.

When we put on weight, moreover, the body is telling us something—something much more vital than "Don't buy that bathing suit!" Becoming overweight is an early warning of life-threatening problems further down the line. Once we recognize this and think through to the consequences, we begin to draw upon motivation deeper than personal vanity, stronger even than that conditioned passion for consuming. It's a life-and-death question now: will we live long enough to make the full contribution to life that we're capable of making? Will we be around in later years to love our grandchildren and make the best of the experience we've gained? In this light, certain critical choices become a little easier to make—such as the ones we suggested at the outset of this chapter, starting with a thorough-going change in diet.

Why not a restricted-calorie "reducing" diet? Well, for one thing, because it won't work. Current research indicates that when there is a drastic and sustained reduction in the calories coming in, the body labels the situation an emergency and responds by lowering its basal needs.[1] In other words, it simply burns less fuel. You not only feel lethargic, *you use fewer*

[1] *J. C. Waterlow 1986, "Metabolic adaptation to low intakes of energy and protein," Annual Review of Nutrition 6:495–526;*

F. Grande & A. Keys 1980, "Body weight, body composition and calorie status," in R. S. Goodhart & M. E. Shils, Modern Nutrition in Health and Disease, 6th ed. (Philadelphia: Lea & Febiger), pp. 3–34 (p. 29)

calories. If you limit yourself to 1000 calories a day, therefore, you may lose weight for a few weeks, but by then your metabolism will have adjusted so that weight loss diminishes or stops altogether. When you go back to a normal diet, you gain back all the weight or even more, because your metabolism is still thinking 1000 calories a day. (Just as you always suspected, but no one ever believed you!)

Instead of launching upon a "reducing diet," then, move to a diet of whole-grain breads and cereals, fresh vegetables, legumes, and fruits—the foods that foster a long, healthy life—as outlined in the Food Guide on page 354. Reduce the fat you eat to 30 percent or less of your total calories. Your cardiovascular system will be strengthened, digestion will improve, and you'll have reduced your risk of cancer. *And,* many of us have found, you will lose some weight. As time goes on, you will find that this high-bulk food sends you away from the table satisfied, proof against the next "snack attack." That's not all, either. Fat has twice as many calories per gram as carbohydrates and protein, so eating less fat allows you larger, more filling quantities of food with fewer calories.

Second, start giving your body the active, energetic movement it was designed for. With regular aerobic exercise, your energy level will rise dramatically and your blood pressure will drop. A hundred and one other good things start to happen too—among which typically is loss of weight, and a wonderfully flattering firming up and redistribution. (See page 366 on exercise.)

Third, we can all reject outright the dogma of consumerism by standing it on its head. "It is in giving that we receive," St. Francis said, and no one has ever said it better. Both the "Eat Up" and "Get Thin" commands assume that the only real and wonderful things in life are physical. It's nonsense. The satisfaction that no amount of getting and spending can purchase flows freely into our lives when we give ourselves to what *is* real and wonderful—namely, other people.

Not many people we know have mastered all three of these areas of choice. But by getting a good handle on them—on any two, in fact!—many of our friends have brought their weight down to where they like it to be without really concentrating on weight loss itself. The ripple effect, moreover, has been most gratifying: the parent or sister or child who sees it all happening and realizes, "Hey, *I* have a choice too. . . ."

Is it really so easy? Well, no. After all, our conditioning goes very deep. The following suggestions, though, have helped us and many of our friends. Like the three points just mentioned, they are life-enhancing for anyone; but carried out faithfully, they have a gratifying effect on weight as well.

CHANGING HABITS

[1] *Slow down.* One of the features in our society that conduces to poor eating habits is what Drs. Friedman and Rosenman call "hurry sickness": the pathological drive to get as much done as we can in as short a time as possible. When we're really caught in this kind of behavior, we even try to do as many things as we can *at the same time*—and expect others to do the same. Our culture seems to place a premium on such self-induced stress. No wonder people complain of job burnout—and no wonder most people don't take the time to sit down for family meals.

Such habits are an important and neglected aspect of nutrition. There are studies indicating that speeded-up eating habits are linked with the development of chronic diseases[2] and that stress interferes with the absorption and metabolism of nutrients.[3]

Fast eating is particularly common among those who are overweight. Besides causing you to eat more at one time than you need, rushing through a meal makes it hard to listen to your appetite, since the body needs about twenty minutes for satiety to register.[4] As you learn to eat more slowly, in a calm environment, you will begin to sense when your body has had enough—often quite different from when your mind thinks it's time to stop.

It may seem awkward at first, but with practice you will find that leisurely eating is essential for really enjoying your food. Take time to savor each bite and enjoy the company. Your meals are guaranteed to be more calming and satisfying.

[2] *Unify attention.* Another way people detract from the legitimate satisfaction of mealtimes is by combining other activities with eating: watching television, listening to the radio, reading a book or newspaper. Splitting attention like this means that part of what we are doing is unconscious, so we end up eating more without even being there to enjoy it.

Warm conversation, on the other hand, provides a good sauce. Put your fork down and really listen; then join in the talk. Natural breaks in conversation will provide time for you to eat, and you

[2] *M. Friedman et al. 1982, "Feasibility of altering Type A behavior pattern after myocardial infarction," Circulation 66:83–92*

[3] *D. Kipp 1984, "Stress and nutrition," Contemporary Nutrition 9(7) (Minneapolis: General Mills);*

E. A. Newsholme & A. R. Leech 1983, Biochemistry for the Medical Sciences (N.Y.: Wiley), p. 285

[4] *E. M. Stricker 1984, "Biological basis of hunger and satiety: Therapeutic implications," Nutrition Reviews 42(10):333–340;*

J. Meyer, L. Monello, & C. Seltzer 1965, "Hunger and satiety sensations in man," Postgraduate Medicine 37(6): A97–A102

will enjoy both the conversation and the food a lot more when you give each your full attention.

Whatever you are doing, try to give your full attention to just one thing at a time. With practice, you'll find that you are making your day more mindful: you're more awake, and even routine things will seem less dull. You're gaining control over your attention—less likely to fall into unconscious habits, better able to pull your mind back from them when you do.

[3] *Reduce temptations.* As you learn about nutrition, your kitchen will reflect a better understanding of which foods are helpful and which ones have no place in your life. It's not very helpful to keep tempting but unnutritious foods around. Out of sight may not be out of mind, but it helps.

[4] *Eat only when you're really hungry.* For some people, this means making a rule of eating only at mealtimes, because when you have been snacking most of the time, you forget what "hungry" feels like.

Incidentally, there is nothing dangerous about feeling hungry; it's just the body's way of reminding you that you're on your reserve tank and should replenish your energy before long. Many thin people say they feel especially alert when a little hungry—the opposite of how most of us feel after a big meal. This is no reason to court hunger, but we can learn from such people not to panic when the stomach starts grumbling. Hunger comes in waves. You don't have to respond right away; it will go away. If it is a legitimate need for food, the hunger will also return.

To repeat: we are *not* advocating skipping meals or eating too little to satisfy physical hunger. Moderation and steadiness are more effective in losing weight than swinging between extremes of starving and stuffing.

Other sensations and needs often get mistaken for hunger. When you feel hungry, for example, you might really be thirsty. Try drinking a full glass of water or a hot drink; often that does the trick. Tiredness can also present itself as hunger, and a nap can solve the problem. If you are at work, try to find a place to rest briefly with eyes closed during a break.

Nutrition in Later Years

It is in the latter half of life that carefully cultivated good eating habits pay extra dividends.

For one thing, after the mid-twenties, your need for nutrients remains about the same but your calorie requirement gradually goes down. Beyond middle age, the food you eat has to count nutritionally; there isn't much room for empty calories. The care you have put into cultivating a taste for nutritious food really pays off now, because you have plenty of scope for an interesting and varied diet without danger of adding unwanted weight or skimping on nutrients you really need.

If you have always exercised regularly, your general health will have benefited many ways. Even if you have been sedentary, however, you will find that gradually building up a period of regular exercise still offers a good deal of protection against the ravages of time. Plain old walking is one of the most beneficial of all forms of exercise. The brisker the better, of course, but if you aren't up to brisk, walk slowly and work up. But move! Regular, rhythmic physical activity strengthens the heart and lungs, protects against extra pounds, and helps circulation, all of which boosts your energy and adds zest to life.

In addition, weight-bearing exercise like walking helps maintain strong bones, because bones strengthen themselves in response to stress. Walking every day—or, if you can, a more strenuous activity like tennis or jogging—goes a long way to protect against brittle bones. If you exercise outside, your bones will get help in another way too: the sunshine enables you to build up a sure, safe dose of vitamin D so that your body can make good use of the calcium it needs for strong bones. (If out-

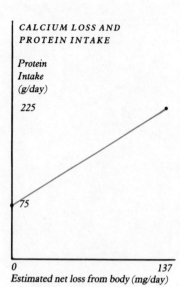

CALCIUM LOSS AND
PROTEIN INTAKE

Protein
Intake
(g/day)

225

75

0   137
Estimated net loss from body (mg/day)

DATA FROM *L. H. Allen et. al., 1979*[1]

side exercise is impossible, be sure you are getting enough vitamin D from fortified milk or supplements.)

Besides calcium, an additional dietary problem associated with softening of the bones or osteoporosis is protein: not too little, but too much. Excess dietary protein, such as 100 grams per day or more, robs calcium from the body and sends it down the drain.[1] However, this doesn't mean you don't need protein; you do. Everybody does, whether old, young, or in between. Aging gradually diminishes the body's ability to absorb protein, so it is wise to keep to the recommended levels—easy with a naturally varied diet of whole foods. (Fast foods and convenience foods, by contrast, often contain excessive amounts of protein along with extra fat, sodium, and sugar.)

Curbing your sweet tooth—if possible, early on—helps too. You'll have healthier teeth and gums, and in addition, a high level of dietary sugar puts added stress on the mechanism which regulates blood sugar levels. This mechanism grows less resilient with age, so blood sugar levels stay high longer after a sugar load than they do in younger people. High blood sugar doesn't usually make a person feel bad, but it can cause damage to small blood vessels all over the body.

Over one third of white women in the U.S. develop osteoporosis.

Osteoporosis leads to over 700,000 bone fractures every year in the U.S. in women 45 years or older.

Hip fractures are the second leading cause of death in people 47 to 74 years of age.

R. Daview and S. Saha 1985, American Family Physician 32:107–114

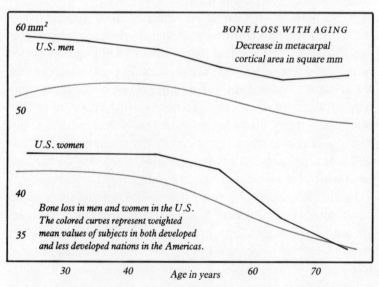

BONE LOSS WITH AGING
Decrease in metacarpal cortical area in square mm

U.S. men

U.S. women

Bone loss in men and women in the U.S. The colored curves represent weighted mean values of subjects in both developed and less developed nations in the Americas.

60 mm²

50

40

35

30   40   Age in years   60   70

REDRAWN FROM *Garn et al. 1969, "Population similarities in the onset and rate of adult endosteal bone loss," Clinical Orthopedics 65:51–60*

Dietary fat leads to the same kinds of problems for older people as it does for anyone else. In really advanced years, however, one of the biggest nutrition problems is simple loss of appetite. Fat does add flavor, and if food does not taste good, it may be hard for some people to eat enough to stay well. If you are in this category, or are caring for someone in this category, use your own judgment: a little butter or Better-Butter, or mayonnaise, or a chunk of cheese can go a long way. Almost all the recipes in this book are low in fat; you can follow them safely at any age.

Many people find as they grow older that their digestion changes. The process slows, and certain foods—milk, or vegetables such as coles and crucifers (broccoli, cabbage, kale, and their relatives) or legumes—may be harder to digest. Fortunately, most people only develop such problems with one or two types of food, so it's still possible to get plenty of variety. (If you have trouble digesting many kinds of food, though, check with a physician; there may be an underlying problem.) A food mill or blender will prove invaluable: many foods that are hard to chew or digest can be turned into tasty soups, or blended and combined with egg to make delicious mini-quiches and such.

If you are caring for an older person, you'll find that your most helpful asset is an alert imagination, always on the lookout for ways to make food (and life in general) more interesting. Older people, like the very young, require special attention to their food problems; but no less than with children, the time you give is an investment. Young, old, and middle-aged all need each other. Our society has almost forgotten this: generations are isolated from each other, and most older Americans, by choice or chance, live in their own world. In our own close-knit neighborhood, which includes every age from infancy to eighties, the regular course of daily interaction means that each person has a part to play in others' lives. This mixing of the generations is unusual in today's world, but it is worth seeking—and not really hard to attain.

[1] L. H. Allen, E. A. Oddoye, & S. Margen 1979, "Protein-induced hypercalciuria: A longer term study," American Journal of Clinical Nutrition 32(4):741–749

GENERAL REFERENCES:

M. D. Hodsworth & L. Davies 1984, "Nutrition at retirement age," Proceedings of the Nutrition Society 43:303–313;
L. Davies 1984, "Nutrition and the elderly: Identifying those at risk," Proceedings of the Nutrition Society 43:295–302

Sports

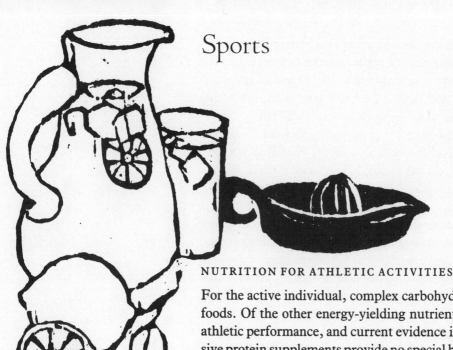

NUTRITION FOR ATHLETIC ACTIVITIES

For the active individual, complex carbohydrates are the best of foods. Of the other energy-yielding nutrients, fat does not help athletic performance, and current evidence indicates that expensive protein supplements provide no special benefit to the athlete. On the other hand, diets high in carbohydrates appear to be helpful during training for endurance events such as long distance running or cycling.[1]

Yet there is some controversy regarding optimal levels of protein in the athlete's diet. Some recognized experts strongly favor high protein intakes—on the order of 1 or even 1½ grams of protein per pound of body weight (2 to 3 grams per kilogram)—for endurance athletes. Three reasons are given for this high recommendation: to prevent a condition called sports anemia, to help increase muscle mass, and to replace protein losses that occur in prolonged periods of exercise.

The evidence supporting the use of very high protein intakes to achieve these goals, however, is equivocal. Some studies show positive results; others show no benefit. On the other hand, there *is* evidence that such high protein intakes harm kidney function over time.[2] Even if athletic performance were improved by very high protein intake, therefore, our own feeling is that it would not be worth the cost. In summarizing the evidence concerning protein and physical activity, J.V.G.A. Durnin of the University of Glasgow concluded that levels above 1 gram per kilogram of body weight (about ½ gram per pound) are not necessary.[3]

Furthermore, several studies have shown that while a balanced diet is important for an active person, special foods and extra

[1] M. H. Williams 1983, *Nutrition for Fitness and Sport* (Dubuque: William C. Brown)

[2] B. M. Brenner & T. W. Meyer 1982, "Dietary protein intake and the progressive nature of kidney disease," *New England Journal of Medicine* 307(11):652–659 (September 29)

[3] J. V. G. A. Durnin et al. 1973, "How much food does man require?" *Nature* 242:418–419 (Apr. 6)

vitamin supplements do not improve performance.[4] In this connection, it has been said that American athletes have the most expensive urine in the world, because of all the supplements they take. Companies making these products are glad to support the myth that athletes need extra nutrients to perform well.

One critical nutrient for the performing athlete *is* known to affect performance dramatically: water. When you sweat heavily, a considerable amount of fluid is lost from the body over time. It is necessary to replace this fluid, and athletes who fail to do so will suffer. There is no need for special liquids: studies comparing various juices and specially formulated "electrolyte replacement" beverages have not shown any advantage over pure water, and concentrated sugar solutions (such as soft drinks) may put the athlete at a physiologic disadvantage because they slow down the absorption of the critical ingredient, water. One common sweetener, fructose, causes blood levels of lactic acid to go up even without increased exertion.[5] Since the body's lactic acid burden can be high during and after exertion, it makes sense to avoid soft drinks at this time, since most are sweetened with high-fructose corn syrup (HFCS).

Any watery fluid—tea, milk, dilute juice, a commercial electrolyte beverage, or water itself—helps maintain circulatory stability and heat balance, and will therefore help prevent a decrease in endurance. Especially if you plan to exercise in hot weather, a pre-event pint of cold fluid fifteen to thirty minutes beforehand will keep you feeling much better, and should improve your performance.

PRE-EVENT NUTRITION

Ideally, the concept of pre-event nutrition includes much more than just the meal before the event. An athlete needs to eat well all season long. Consult the Food Guide on page 354, and instead of vitamin pills, use the leafy greens as your nutritional powerhouse. If after that you still want a supplement, use wheat germ, which is full of B vitamins and vitamin E, and take megadoses of citrus fruits instead of ascorbic acid pills. Remember, excessive amounts of one nutrient can disrupt the body's balance and alter nutrient requirements, which could conceivably harm athletic performance. When it comes time for the event, long-term good eating habits will help your stamina much more than any crash dietary program.

[4] D. W. Barnett & R. K. Conlee 1984, "The effects of a commercial dietary supplement on human performance," American Journal of Clinical Nutrition 40(3):586–590

[5] L. Sestoff 1983, "Fructose and health," in J. Weininger & G. M. Briggs, Nutrition Update, vol. 1 (N.Y.: Wiley) pp. 39–53 (p. 45)

There are a few basic rules, though, to follow for the meal you eat just before competition. The meal should be small enough to allow the stomach to be nearly empty at the start of your event, but satisfying enough that you don't feel ravenously hungry. You need something that will stick with you, such as a good whole-grain pasta dish. And the meal should provide an adequate amount of water, though not so much that you need to find a bathroom during competition.

A light meal three to four hours before competition allows ample time for digestion. Avoid high levels of fat in the meal, since fat keeps everything in the stomach longer than is desirable; and remember that excess protein increases the need for water. Sugary snacks should be avoided, since they can cause deleterious swings in blood sugar levels. So the pre-event meal should be high in complex carbohydrate and low in fat and protein.

Finally, of course, emotional tension can affect digestion, and emotions are often tense before a sporting event. Treat your digestive system kindly at this time, and avoid known irritants such as highly spiced foods, excessively hot or cold foods or drinks, and alcohol.

More information on pre-game nutrition and sports nutrition in general can be found in Melvin H. Williams's excellent book *Nutrition for Fitness and Sport* (Boston, Wm. C. Brown, 1983).

The Vegan Diet

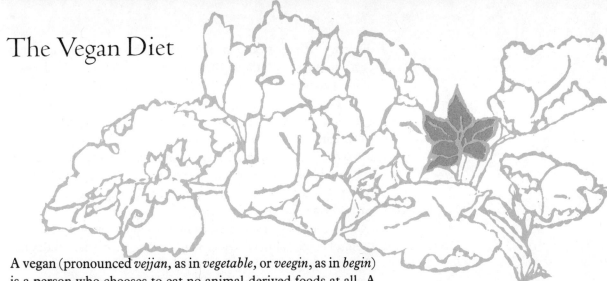

A vegan (pronounced *vejjan*, as in *vegetable*, or *veegin*, as in *begin*) is a person who chooses to eat no animal-derived foods at all. A strict vegan avoids not only red meats, fish, and poultry, but also dairy products and eggs. Some even eschew honey, since it is made by bees, but most vegans consider this unnecessarily orthodox.

Although the term *vegan* is new, the concept has been around for thousands of years. In ancient Greece the ranks of well-known vegans included the philosopher and mathematician Pythagorus, a remarkable athlete from Sparta named Charmis, the philosopher and astronomer Thales, and two great mystics, Apollonius of Tyana and Philo of Alexandria.[1] Each of these men was a prominent figure who attracted many students, and since the custom was for students to live with their teacher and follow his way of life, these examples probably represent not just isolated instances but several ancient vegan communities.

A vegan meal looks simple, austere, and timeless, as if it had been the typical fare of people close to the earth since the dawn of time. But this impression is probably not accurate. Archaeologic findings in Turkey and elsewhere show that certain animals were domesticated as much as nine thousand years ago,[2] and the Leakeys' findings in Africa show that animals have figured in the dietary habits of mankind since the early days of human ancestry.[3] No traditional society that we know of, past or present, has been consistently vegan, except in cases of abject poverty or cataclysmic disruption when no alternative was available.

Vegans in our own society were once rare and adhered generally to an explicit philosophy. In the last two or three decades, though, their number has increased markedly, for reasons that reflect real

[1] *F. R. Ellis & V. M. E. Montegriffo 1971, "The health of vegans," Plant Foods for Human Nutrition 2:93–103*

[2] *M. N. Cohen 1977, The Food Crisis in Prehistory (New Haven: Yale Univ. Press), pp. 140–141*

[3] *Cohen 1977, p. 94*

diversity. There are also many vegetarians who, though not rigid vegans, eat very little in the way of dairy products and eggs. Some people are vegans or near-vegans for health reasons: all-plant diets tend to be very low in fat, and commercial milk and eggs may contain harmful residues of hormones and other additives. Others don't like the way the animals producing these foods are treated on large-scale commercial farms; avoiding animal products eliminates one's own participation in this trade. And many simply find that eggs and milk begin to taste heavy and fatty next to vegetables and grains.

Whatever the reason, just as many omnivores today describe themselves as "almost vegetarians," many vegetarians today are almost vegans. (One of our friends calls himself a "pancake-o vegan": he faithfully avoids all other sources of milk and eggs, but draws the line at ruling out an occasional buckwheat or buttermilk pancake.) Nutritionists are now reporting on the first generation of vegan kids in the schools, children of the experimenters of the sixties. What was a fad is becoming acknowledged as one of many acceptable ways of eating. This trend translates into a real need for up-to-date guidelines on the special nutritional problems of an all-plant diet.

CURRENT KNOWLEDGE OF VEGAN NUTRITION

Despite the example of Pythagoras and the rest, it is only today, with a scientific knowledge of nutrition and the available array of special foods and dietary supplements, that it is easy to be a vegan and stay healthy. Uninformed experimentation can be dangerous, because dairy foods are the usual source of certain nutrients that otherwise can only be assured by careful planning.

The main problem areas of a vegan diet are calcium, which is best supplied by milk, and vitamin B-12, which is not supplied by any plant food. In addition, vegans reportedly have high incidence of dental disease and higher than normal risks of iron deficiency anemia.[4] Despite these potential problems, though, a majority of modern-day vegans seem to manage quite well on their austere diet. "Provided vegans supplement their diet with vitamin B-12, either in the form of tablets or suitably fortified plant foods," Frey Ellis said in a review of the literature in 1971, "they can apparently remain in normal health indefinitely."[5] T.A.B. Sanders goes so far as to suggest that a vegan-type diet supplemented by vitamins B-12 and D may be the diet of choice

[4] J. Bergan & P. Brown 1981, "Studies of nutrient status of vegetarians in the United States: Young Boston adults," in J. J. B. Anderson, ed., Nutrition and Vegetarianism (Chapel Hill: Health Science Consortium), pp. 91–102 (p. 94)

[5] Ellis & Montegriffo 1971, p. 93

for victims of ischemic heart disease, angina pectoris, and certain hyperlipidemias (conditions of excess fat in the blood). "The few clinical studies made so far in Britain and the United States," he adds, "have not been able to identify any real differences in the health of vegans compared with omnivores."[6]

Yet as we have said, care and intelligence are necessary in adopting the vegan eating style. Reports of multiple nutrient deficiencies have surfaced periodically in the literature, especially among children in poorly informed vegan communities.[7] It is not difficult to avoid such problems, as you can see in the suggestions below.

VITAMIN B-12

Since it is not supplied by plant foods but comes ultimately from microorganisms, Vitamin B-12 is usually considered the critical nutrient in the vegan diet. B-12 deficiency is a very serious problem, which over time can harm the spinal cord. The problem proceeds unnoticeably and very slowly, but can cause irreversible damage.[8]

Despite this danger, some popular writers today are discounting the vegan's need for vitamin B-12, since deficiency problems have been quite rare in this country. We can't go along with this attitude. The risks involved are so serious, and preventive measures so simple, that it seems foolhardy to disregard them. *Please do not court a B-12 deficiency!* If you work into your diet the suggestions below, and make them a habit, you can be a vegan without fuss or worry.

One simple way to get your B-12 is by using fortified soy milk. However, commercial soy milk products are often designed not for vegans, but for meat-eating children who are allergic to milk, so the amount of B-12 supplied may be too low to be practical. Check the label to see what percent of the recommended dietary allowance (RDA) for B-12 is met by one glassful. If it is as little as 10 percent, you'll need ten glasses to meet the RDA, and you can suspect that the manufacturer had the allergic omnivore in mind. In any case, commercial soymilk is expensive and so heavily sugared that you may want to make your own, which you can flavor and fortify yourself. Our recipe is given on page 105.

Another way to get vitamin B-12 is to eat tempeh or miso every day. Of the two, tempeh is the more reliable source of B-12, but only if it has been specifically fermented with *Klebsiella* bacteria

[6] T. A. B. Saunders, F. R. Ellis, & J. W. T. Dickerson 1978, "Studies of vegans," American Journal of Clinical Nutrition 31:805–812 (p. 805)

[7] E. D. Shinwell & R. Gorodischer 1982, "Totally vegetarian diets and infant nutrition," Pediatrics 70(4):582–586

[8] V. Herbert, N. Colman, & E. Jacob 1980, "Folic acid and vitamin B-12," in R. S. Goodhart & M. E. Shils, eds., Modern Nutrition in Health and Disease, 6th ed. (Philadelphia: Lea & Febiger), pp. 229–258

along with the usual mold. Other fermented foods, such as natto and even shoyu, may contain B-12, but this should not be counted on.

Some types of nutritional yeast are grown on B-12 enriched media, and these too are reliable sources. Regular nutritional yeast has no B-12 at all, so be sure to check the label.

Finally, you can take a vitamin pill. B-12 supplements generally come in high dosages, so you may need only one a week. The RDA level might also be supplied by daily multiple vitamin pills: again, check the label to see that it lists at least 2 micrograms of B-12.

CALCIUM

Calcium intake is commonly listed among the vegan's problem nutrients, and our own experience tallies with this. One of our good friends avoided dairy products for fifteen years until he discovered that his bones had deteriorated with severe osteoporosis. As is often the case with this disease, there was no sign of a problem until trivial stress on a bone resulted in a painful fracture. He was under forty years old at the time, very active physically and very well informed about nutrition. While aware that his calcium intake was low compared to the RDA, he had believed that this low intake would be adequate. Now he is using milk and calcium supplements in an attempt to strengthen his compromised bones.

It is not unlikely that this friend has an unusual hormonal problem which causes his body to waste calcium. Most people, evidence suggests, *can* adjust over time to very low levels of calcium in the diet, by absorbing it with greater efficiency.[9] But which of us knows whether he or she is in that fortunate majority? As with B-12, we advise caution: the consequences of error are painful, and the remedies simple. We suggest that every vegan monitor calcium intake and make sure that it stays at RDA levels. (See pages 460–461.)

PROTEIN AND ENERGY NEEDS

The medical information available on vegans indicates that they have no trouble getting enough protein. The key, though, is getting enough calories. In our experience, it is possible for a vegan to develop a marginal protein deficiency if he or she simply gets too little food. To be a healthy vegan, in other words, you

[9] *L. V. Avioli 1980, "Calcium and phosphorus," in Goodhart & Shils, pp. 294–309 (p. 301)*

have to be a big eater. The sheer volume of a vegan's normal meals can give the impression of gluttony. Yet according to the literature, very few vegans are overweight—certainly none we know. It simply takes a lot of food to run a vegan body.

Vegans we know tend to have a sweet tooth. We suspect that this is partly due to a need for *calories*—plain energy. Some of the medical cautions against too much sugar may not apply here, since the available literature on vegans' blood lipids and ability to handle glucose show that as a group, they are at very low risk for obesity,[10] heart disease,[10] and diabetes.[11] However, as noted earlier, vegans reportedly do have more dental caries than normal.[12] (You can't have *every*thing.)

Actually, the most important threat that sweets pose for vegans may be simply letting sugar, even in fruits, crowd out more nutritious foods. Fortunately, most vegans probably stay clear of junk foods like candy, soft drinks, commercial potato chips, doughnuts, and fast-food items, the worst offenders in nutrient crowd-out.

[10] F. M. Sacks 1981, "Vegetarian diets and cardiovascular risk factors," in J. J. B. Anderson, ed., Nutrition and Vegetarianism (Chapel Hill: Health Science Consortium) pp. 134–142 (p. 137)

[11] D. A. Snowdon & R. L. Phillips 1985, "Does a vegetarian diet reduce the occurrence of diabetes?" American Journal of Public Health 75(5):507–512

[12] Bergan & Brown 1981, p. 94; W. Price 1947, Nutrition and Physical Degeneration (Santa Monica, Calif.: Price-Pottinger), p. 279

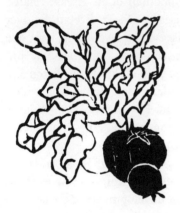

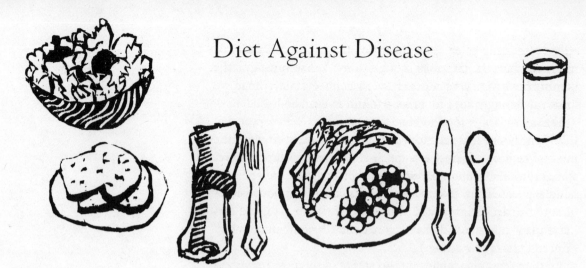

Diet Against Disease

Today it is generally agreed that some of the major chronic diseases of industrialized societies—cancer, diabetes, diverticular disease, certain heart and blood vessel diseases, hypertension, and osteoporosis, for example—are connected with dietary habits. In the United States, one person in every four has cancer or is likely to develop it. Nearly one half of all disease-related deaths are from cardiovascular disease. One in five adults over the age of sixty has diverticular disease of the colon. At least one in five adults has been diagnosed as having hypertension, and another fifth might have the disease without knowing. From 3 to 5 percent of adults have clinically identifiable diabetes, the incidence of which has tripled over the last thirty years. A large percentage of deaths among the elderly follow upon accidents involving fractured bones due to osteoporosis.[1]

These bleak trends are widely known, at least in a general way. The good news is that a sound diet significantly reduces these risks. In one of the most remarkable developments of the last two decades, experts now recommend much the same diet for preventing or treating each of these diseases. To avoid chronic disease, a well-rounded, low-fat, whole-foods vegetarian diet seems to be ideal.

Cancer

By conservative estimate, diet is now thought to be an important factor in 40 to 60 percent of all cancers.[2] This realization has prompted many groups of scientists and policymakers to issue guidelines on diet and cancer. Those of the National Re-

[1] J. Weininger & G. M. Briggs, eds., 1985, Nutrition Update, vol. 2 (N.Y.: Wiley), Sect. I: Nutrition in health and disease, pp. 3–103;

R. S. Goodhart & M. E. Shils 1980, Modern Nutrition in Health and Disease, 6th ed. (Philadelphia: Lea & Febiger), Part VI: Nutrition in the prevention and treatment of disease, pp. 853–1243

[2] S. Palmer 1985, "Public health policy on diet, nutrition, and cancer," Nutrition and Cancer 6(4):274–283

search Council, listed in the margin, are typical. To date, the massive diet survey conducted recently in China—without doubt the largest and most detailed epidemiological study in history—strongly supports the validity of the NRC guidelines[3] (see page 345).

Of all these recommendations, the clearest and most consistent is the one concerning fat: eat less fat, and of the fat you *do* eat, reduce the proportion of saturated fats (usually supplied by animal products) in favor of unsaturated fats. In practical terms, this translates into three simple words: eat less meat. Studies of Seventh-day Adventists, an unusually health-conscious community which includes both vegetarians and nonvegetarians, tend to underline this conclusion: cancer rates for Adventists in general are 50 to 70 percent lower than average in the United States, and among Adventists, vegetarians are less likely to develop cancer than are nonvegetarians.[4] Avoiding excess calories, and expending more calories in exercise, also seems to help prevent cancer.[5]

Diabetes

The term "diabetes mellitus" really refers to two different diseases, called Type I and Type II diabetes. They were given the same name because both are characterized by high levels of blood sugar which the body cannot utilize. Diet is related differently to each of these ailments, but it has been estimated that in 80 percent of all cases of diabetes, obesity, inactivity, and inappropriate diet play major roles.[6]

In Type I diabetes (also called, somewhat misleadingly, "juvenile-onset diabetes") the body is unable to produce enough insulin, the hormone that takes sugars from the blood into the cells for use as fuel. A low-fat, high–complex carbohydrate diet has been found to lessen the risk of serious complications like heart disease and to increase insulin sensitivity in Type I diabetics, but diet is not a causal factor in this kind of diabetes.

Type II diabetes, much more common, is generally associated with obesity and often responds dramatically when excess weight is shed. Blood sugar levels tend to be high for a different reason than in Type I diabetes: the body produces enough insulin, but the cells have grown insensitive to its action. Diet is very probably involved in causing this disease, which is primarily a disease of excess: too many total calories for the amount of energy a

N.R.C.
RECOMMENDATIONS FOR
PREVENTING CANCER

🍂 *Eat less fat (30% or less of total calories)*

🍂 *Eat fruits, vegetables, and whole-grain cereal foods every day, especially fruits and vegetables high in vitamins A and C*

🍂 *Avoid high-dose supplements of vitamins or other nutrients*

🍂 *Alcohol only in moderation*

National Research Council 1982, Diet, Nutrition and Cancer (Washington: National Academy Press)

[3] *T. C. Campbell 1984, "A status report on diet, nutrition, and cancer," Contemporary Nutrition 9(8)*

[4] *R. L. Phillips 1975, "Role of life-style and dietary habits in risk of cancer among Seventh-day Adventists," Cancer Research 35:3513–3522*

[5] *M. W. Pariza 1986, "Calories and energy expenditure in carcinogenesis," Contemporary Nutrition 11(4)*

[6] *G. J. Friedman 1980, "Diet in the treatment of diabetes mellitus," in Goodhart & Shils, pp. 977–997 (p. 983)*

[7] "Exercise and diabetes," 1984, Nutrition and the M.D. 10(7)

[8] J. W. Anderson 1986, Nutrition Management of Metabolic Conditions: A Professional Guide to HCF Diets (Lexington, Kentucky: HCF Diabetes Research Foundation)

[9] A. M. Cohen 1978, "Genetically determined response to different ingested carbohydrates in the production of diabetes," Hormone and Metabolic Research 10(2):86–92

[10] "Diet change and obesity among modernizing Polynesians," 1984, Nutrition Reviews 42(10):347–350;

A. E. Renold, I. Burr, & W. Stauffache 1978, "On the pathogenesis of diabetes mellitus," in M. Katzen & J. Mahler, eds., Diabetes, Obesity and Vascular Disease (N.Y.: Wiley), pp. 215–231 (pp. 219, 220)

[11] Anderson 1986, p. 36

[12] Anderson 1986, p. 15

[13] D. A. Snowdon & R. L. Phillips 1985, "Does a vegetarian diet reduce the occurrence of diabetes?" American Journal of Public Health 75(5):507–512

[14] F. Q. Nutall 1980, "Dietary recommendations for individuals with diabetes mellitus, 1979: Summary of report from the Food and Nutrition Committee of the American Diabetes Association," American Journal of Clinical Nutrition 33:1311–1312

[15] D. P. Burkitt 1972, "Varicose veins, deep vein thrombosis, and haemorrhoids," British Medical Journal 2(813):556–561 (June 3)

[16] S. A. Broitman & N. Zamcheck 1980, "Nutrition in diseases of the intestine," in Goodhart & Shils, pp. 912–952 (p. 943)

[17] Consensus conference, 1985, "Lowering blood cholesterol to prevent heart disease," Journal of the American Medical Association 253(14):2080–2086 (April 12)

[18] R. I. Levy 1984, "Causes of the decrease in cardiovascular mortality," American Journal of Cardiology 54(5):7C–13C

person uses up in physical exercise.[7] Too much fat in the diet also plays a role: it may hasten the onset of diabetes and makes diabetics' blood sugar levels harder to control.[8]

While it has become unfashionable to blame high sugar intake in our society for the increasing incidence of diabetes, award-winning studies by A. M. Cohen have shown such effects in rats genetically predisposed to diabetes.[9] Natural experiments in human populations also generally support an association between sugar consumption and diabetes.[10]

Diets high in complex carbohydrates—starch, oligosaccharides, fibers—definitely help the diabetic keep blood sugar levels under control.[11] Fiber in the diet helps to control blood sugar levels by slowing down carbohydrate absorption in the intestine; it probably also cuts down on the absorption of fats and helps to draw down blood cholesterol levels.[12] (More on fiber on page 424.)

The best diet for the diabetic, therefore, is one that emphasizes vegetables, whole grains, and legumes, and plays down fatty foods, especially those of animal origin—in other words, the same diet that is recommended for reducing the risk of cancer. Studies of Seventh-day Adventists support this conclusion as well, showing that vegetarians are less likely to get diabetes than are omnivores.[13]

Surprisingly, despite the endorsement of the American Diabetic Association,[14] many diabetics have not heard of this kind of diet and are still trying to manage their disease on the old low-carbohydrate, high-fat regimen, exposing themselves to all the risks that entails. If you are diabetic, or have a diabetic in your family, we strongly recommend Dr. James W. Anderson's book *Diabetes: A Practical New Guide to Healthy Living* (London: Dunitz, 1981), and *The Peripatetic Diabetic,* by Barbara Toohey and June Biermann (available, with many other helpful books and products, from Sugarfree Center, P.O. Box 114, Van Nuys, Calif. 91408; write for their catalog).

Diverticular Disease

There is a collection of health problems that might be caused in part by constipation: appendicitis, diverticulosis, hemorrhoids, varicose veins, and bowel cancer. These diseases are rare in societies where diets are high in fiber and people normally get plenty of exercise, while they are common in countries where the vast majority of people are sedentary and eat food that is highly refined.[15] Constipation and its related disorders largely stem from lack of exercise and lack of enough fiber and fluids in the diet.

Over time, the stress of constipation can force little pockets of intestinal tissue to bulge out from weak areas of the intestinal wall.[16] These pockets are called *diverticula* or "detours," and the condition is called diverticular disease—a problem which afflicts an estimated forty million Americans. The way to keep diverticular disease from developing, and the best remedy for it in its early stages, is to change to a whole-foods diet.

Cardiovascular Disease

Cardiovascular diseases such as heart attack and stroke have declined dramatically in this country since the early seventies, but they are still at epidemic levels in most Western nations, accounting for more than twice as many deaths as cancer—in the United States, more deaths than from all other causes combined.[17] One prominent cardiologist, referring to the fact that the cardiac death rate in Japan is about one-tenth what it is in this country, maintains, "There is no reason that [rate] cannot be matched in the United States."[18]

Underlying cardiovascular disease is the condition called atherosclerosis, in which fatty accumulations on the walls of the arteries narrow the passageways through which blood must pass. Calcium deposits and scar tissue gradually collect at the site of this narrowing, and eventually this and other factors cause the arteries to become rigid. When sudden stress on the heart calls for more oxygenated blood than the diseased arteries can deliver, or when an artery leading to the heart is clogged suddenly by a clot, the heart muscle can go into uncontrolled spasms. If this is not quickly brought under control, part of the heart muscle dies—a "heart attack."

The landmark Framingham study described on page 340 showed that incidence of heart disease is closely associated with high levels of cholesterol in the blood. For more than thirty years since then, prevention and therapy of heart disease have focused on reducing saturated fats and cholesterol in the diet, since these fatty substances tend to raise blood cholesterol levels. Generally,

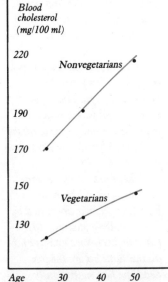

BLOOD CHOLESTEROL IN VEGETARIANS AND NONVEGETARIANS

Blood cholesterol (mg/100 ml)

DATA FROM: *F. M. Sacks et al. 1975, "Plasma lipids and lipoproteins in vegetarians and controls," New England Journal of Medicine 292(22):1148–1151, and R. O. West & O. B. Hayes 1968, "Diet and serum cholesterol levels," American Journal of Clinical Nutrition 21(8):853–862*

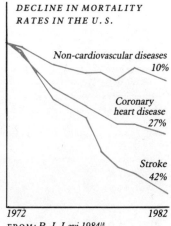

DECLINE IN MORTALITY RATES IN THE U. S.

FROM: *R. I. Levi 1984*[18]

[19] *R. S. Smith 1984, Nutrition, Hypertension and Cardiovascular Disease (Gilroy, Calif.: Lyncean Press)*

[20] *Salt Institute 1982, Nutrition and Blood Pressure: The Effect of Diet on Hypertension, Symposium Proceedings (Alexandria, Va.: Salt Institute), pp. 2–7*

[21] *L. Langseth, ed., 1985, "Hypertension: 1982–1984, Nutrition research literature review," Nutrition Research Newsletter 4(1):1–10 (p. 1)*

[22] *Salt Institute 1982, pp. 4–5*

both can be reduced by eating less animal fat, found in meats, cheese, butter, egg yolks, and full-fat dairy products.

Other dietary factors have shown assocations with heart disease, and some of them may turn out to be more important than cholesterol and saturated fat: trace mineral imbalances, lack of vitamins B-6, E, and C, too little dietary fiber and complex carbohydrates, too much alcohol, and toxic food components created by modern methods of processing, such as, perhaps, *trans* fatty acids and oxidized cholesterol.[19] It is on these areas that future diet–heart disease research will probably focus. Again, a low-fat, high-fiber, whole-foods vegetarian or near-vegetarian diet meets the needs and avoids the problems.

Hypertension

Hypertension (high blood pressure) is a major factor in stroke, congestive heart failure, atherosclerotic heart disease, and kidney failure. It is called a "silent" disease, since people who have it do not necessarily feel any ill effects until severe damage has occurred. In the vast majority of cases, no specific cause for hypertension can be found. Dietary factors that can affect blood pressure include sodium, potassium, calcium, and magnesium, alcohol intake, dietary fats, and plant fiber.[20]

Reducing sodium intake (a low-salt diet) is the most familiar way of trying to manage hypertension through diet. At a reasonable level of restriction—to 1600 milligrams of sodium per day, or about ½ teaspoon of salt—modest reductions in blood pressure do take place in those hypertensives who are salt-sensitive, perhaps one third to one half of the total. However, for the rest, and for those who do not have hypertension, restricting sodium moderately does not lower blood pressure.[21]

Potassium can counteract the blood pressure–raising effects of sodium in salt-sensitive hypertensives.[22] Even so, it would be unwise for anyone to take potassium in pill form unless under a physician's guidance, since these supplements can have harmful side effects. A diet rich in fruits and vegetables provides ample potassium, and is low in sodium unless salt is added.

Inadequate calcium intake may be linked with hypertension, and calcium supplements have been shown to reduce the incidence of hypertension in pregnant women[23] and mildly hypertensive adults in general.[24] Magnesium too appears to have a protective influence against hypertension, probably in concert with calcium. Plant fiber helps to lower high blood pressure, as do lower levels of dietary fat.[20] Leafy green vegetables provide both calcium and magnesium in abundance; dairy products contain plenty of calcium, and most nuts are rich in magnesium. Again, a well-rounded, low-fat diet of whole foods would seem to supply the right minerals and other protective dietary factors.

Finally, some experimental reports suggest that meat-eating itself raises blood pressure. In two studies, omnivores showed lower blood pressures when placed temporarily on a vegetarian diet;[25] other experimenters report that the blood pressure of vegetarians went up when they voluntarily added meat to their meals.[26] Epidemiological evidence too—for example, studies among Adventists and in third-world populations[27]— suggests a connection between meat-eating and hypertension, but the case is scarcely conclusive.

Alcohol, by contrast, consistently raises blood pressure.[28] Caffeine too can raise blood pressure briefly, but apparently has no long-term adverse blood pressure effects on mildly hypertensive adults.[29]

Osteoporosis

Osteoporosis, a progressive loss of bone tissue leading to fragile bones, is another chronic disease of uncertain cause which is widespread in industrialized countries and relatively rare in traditional societies. The first sign is often a sudden fracture, usually in the spine, hip, or wrist—evidence that the disease has already progressed to an advanced stage. Diagnostic tests are not sensitive enough yet to detect the disease until substantial bone loss has occurred.

In a sense, osteoporosis is not a disease but part of the normal process of aging. Bones go on growing much longer than we realize: vertebrae do not reach their maximum density until about age twenty-five, while the bones of the arms and legs continue to add density and strength until age forty-five or so. Once growth stops, however, the process reverses itself, and our bones progressively lose density from then on. It is during the long period of growth in early life that osteoporosis can be prevented; for as long as bone tissue is growing, its density can be increased —through weight-bearing exercise, exposure to sunshine, and

23 J. Belizán & J. Villar 1980, "The relationship between calcium intake and edema-, proteinuria-, and hypertension gestosis: An hypothesis," American Journal of Clinical Nutrition 33:2202–2210

24 J. Belizán et al. 1983, "Reduction of blood pressure with calcium supplementation in young adults," Journal of the American Medical Association 249(9):1161–5 (March 4)

25 I. L. Rouse et al. 1983, "Blood-pressure–lowering effect of a vegetarian diet," Lancet 1(8314–5):5–10 (Jan. 1);

P. Burstyn 1982, "Effect of meat on BP" (letter), Journal of the American Medical Association 248(1):29–30, (July 2)

26 H. Sacks, A. Donner, & W. P. Castelli 1981, "Effect of ingestion of meat on plasma cholesterol of vegetarians," Journal of the American Medical Association 246(6):640–644 (Aug. 7);

A. N. Donaldson 1926, "The relation of protein foods to hypertension," California and Western Medicine 24(3):328–331

27 F. M. Sacks, B. Rosner, & E. H. Kass 1974, "Blood pressure in vegetarians," American Journal of Epidemiology 100(5):390–398

28 T. Gordon & J. T. Doyle 1986, "Effects of alcohol and smoking on weight, blood pressure, and blood lipids," Archives of Internal Medicine 146(2):262–265

29 D. Robertson et al. 1984, "Caffeine and hypertension," American Journal of Medicine 77(1):54–60;

P. B. Dews 1982, "Caffeine," Annual Review of Nutrition 2:323–341 (p. 326)

Dietary factors associated with calcium loss from bones:

Lack of calcium,
  magnesium,
  fluoride,
  vitamin D

Excess protein,
  phosphorus,
  sodium,
  alcohol

Life-style factors associated with calcium loss from bones:

  smoking,
  sedentary habits,
  lack of sunshine

[30] O. Mickelson 1983, *"Nutritional considerations in planning for food production: Nutrition and vegetarianism," in D. Knorr, ed., Sustainable Food Systems (Westport, Conn.: AVI), pp. 402–403;*

A. G. Marsh et al. 1980, *"Cortical bone density of adult lacto-ovo-vegetarian and omnivorous women," Journal of the American Dietetic Association 76:148–51;*

F. R. Ellis, S. Holesh, & J. W. Ellis 1972, *"Incidence of osteoporosis in vegetarians and omnivores," American Journal of Clinical Nutrition 25:555–558*

[31] R. Ferrando 1981, *Traditional and Non-traditional Foods (Rome: Food and Agriculture Organization), pp. 42–51, "Hormones and antihormones";*

J. B. Labov 1977, *"Phytoestrogens and mammalian reproduction," Comparative Biochemistry and Physiology A: Comparative Physiology 57(1):3–9*

enough dietary calcium. Greater bone density means stronger bones throughout life, and insurance against fracture as we age.

In women, the female hormone estrogen slows down the loss of bone tissue, but this protection is lost after menopause. Prematurely menopausal women, and those who have their ovaries removed before the natural menopause, have especially rapid rates of bone loss. If you are in one of these categories, it is important to adopt a life-style that protects against osteoporosis, and to consider any preventive treatment your physician advises. If you are small, slender, or light-skinned, you are more at risk than those who are not.

Even if you already have osteoporosis, you can improve your condition under a physician's guidance by vigorous dietary treatment, calcium supplements, and possibly supplements of fluoride and vitamin D. Hormone treatment may also be included. Each person's case is unique, and must be diagnosed and treated under careful guidance.

As with other chronic diseases related to life-style, however, no amount of treatment can match prevention. There are two steps anyone can take to help prevent osteoporosis. First, get plenty of weight-bearing exercise throughout your life, starting now. Walking fast, rowing, hiking, jogging, and cycling all put stress on the bones, and bones strengthen themselves in response to stress. Second, get enough dietary calcium and exposure to sunshine throughout life—again, starting now.

To date, studies of vegetarians have shown that they tend to have denser bones than omnivores,[30] suggesting a lower than normal risk of developing osteoporosis. This is surprising, for vegetarian diets are high in phytates and oxalates which should theoretically make it more difficult for calcium to be absorbed (see page 426). Several explanations for this have been offered, based on bone-strengthening factors such as those mentioned above. The most intriguing possibility, however, is hormonal. Vegetables and legumes contain plant estrogens, which produce some of the same effects as human estrogens in the body.[31] Since low doses of synthetic estrogens are used medically to treat osteoporosis, it seems plausible that a diet rich in vegetables and legumes might supply similar estrogen activity in a natural way, without the unfortunate risks of synthetic hormones. Whatever the explanation, the evidence indicates that risk of osteoporosis is lower on a whole-foods vegetarian diet.

The Nutrients

The nutrients veil a mystery, the interaction of matter and energy that sustains life. Although we know that life-forms can trap, store, and utilize energy from their environment, no one can say how. We know, for instance, that the chlorophyll molecule in the leaves of plants captures energy from sunlight. We know the shape of that molecule (like hemoglobin, which transports oxygen in the blood of mammals, it contains a circular structure called a porphyrin ring) and we know each step in the cascade of reactions by which chlorophyll combines water, carbon dioxide, and energy from sunlight to create the basic structural material of plants, carbohydrate. The biologist who elucidated these steps earned a Nobel prize for the elegance of his work. Yet the central question—how chlorophyll captures *energy*—eludes us.

It is the same in animal cells, when carbohydrate is broken down and its energy released. We know every step of how that energy is stored and tapped in the electrochemical "batteries" of a molecule called ATP; yet how this process drives metabolism—how ATP energy is translated into the millions of chemical processes that characterize and accompany life—remains a mystery.

Besides carbohydrate, two other energy-yielding nutrients, fats and proteins, also represent stored forms of energy, unavailable to plants but available to animals as fuel. Similarly, where plants use only carbohydrates as structural components, animal bodies use fats and proteins as well. Thus the body's three basic sources of energy are also the building blocks from which its cells and tissues are made.

The amount of energy stored in carbohydrates, fats, and proteins can be measured; protein and carbohydrate each yield about 4 kilocalories (popularly just "calories") of energy per gram, and fat yields about 9. These are fixed, known quantities, like the amount of energy available in a gallon of gasoline. But just as the efficiency of using this gasoline—the gas mileage—varies from car to car, there is a good deal of rather startling evidence that human bodies vary in the efficiency with which they can use energy from foods.[1] Moreover, this efficiency is not fixed, but can change in response to the availability of food, the level of a person's physical activity and physical condition, and probably other factors as well.

One intriguing illustration is provided by studies of heavy laborers in India, an impoverished and ill-nourished group of men and women who carry very heavy loads over a long workday. Careful surveys have shown that these workers use more energy than they should have been able to get from what they ate, according to the customary understanding of how food energy is used.

Another particularly careful study compared the food intake and energy output of pregnant women in Cambridge, England, and Keneba, the Gambia, in West Africa. The groups were well matched for comparison, quite similar in their average height and weight and in their orientation toward breast-feeding. The Cambridge women got over 2000 calories per day. The Gambian women got 1500 calories during the wet season, when food is more plentiful, and a mere 1300 calories—virtually a reducing diet—during the dry season. Throughout pregnancy the Gambian women engaged in strenuous agricultural labor. Yet at the end of the study, the researchers found with surprise that "the gestational and lactational performance of the women in Kaneba is comparable to that of the women in Cambridge, in spite of a substantial difference in energy intake."[2] George Beaton, commenting on the many energy-use studies with similar results, exclaimed, "Either our concepts and understanding are wrong or the data are wrong!"[3] Evidently, as we know takes place with other nutrients, the human body can learn to adapt: to extract food energy much more efficiently than is normal when the human organism is well fed.[4]

Similarly, scientists are beginning to find that the body's efficiency in using dietary proteins for making and repairing structures is not fixed but varies from person to person, and can be altered by varying circumstances of food intake and activity.[5] These are very new realizations, whose implications are unexplored.

[1] J. C. Waterlow 1986, "Metabolic adaptation to low intakes of energy and protein," Annual Review of Nutrition 6:495–526

[2] A. M. Prentice 1984, "Adaptations to long term low energy intake," in E. Pollitt & P. Amante, eds., Energy Intake and Activity (N.Y.: Alan Liss), pp. 3–30

[3] G. Beaton 1984, "Adaptation to and accommodation of long term low energy intake," in Pollitt & Amante, pp. 395–402

[4] S. Margen 1984, "Auto-regulatory processes to maintain energy balance in the individual," in Pollitt & Amante, pp. 57–76

[5] P. V. Sukhatme & S. Margen 1978, "Models for protein deficiency," American Journal of Clinical Nutrition 31:1237–1256

There are six types of nutrients in foods: carbohydrates, fats, proteins, vitamins, minerals, and water. The nutrients which provide energy or structure are called macronutrients, because we need them in large quantities. Besides carbohydrates, fats, and proteins, the minerals calcium and phosphorus could be placed in this category: we need them daily in gram amounts to form bodily structures like bones and teeth. The remaining minerals such as iron, zinc, and potassium, and all of the vitamins, are called micronutrients.

All the nutrients interact in a fluid process of give and take. The energy used in all biochemical reactions comes from the three macronutrients, carbohydrate, fat, and protein; but the energy-yielding nutrients cannot be processed without the help of micronutrients, and energy is required to assimilate the micronutrients from foods.

Micronutrients function in our bodies at the interface between matter and energy. This is perhaps why there is still an air of mystery surrounding vitamins and minerals. Vitamins are incorporated in the enzymes which guide biochemical reactions. The particular shape of the vitamin governs the shape of the enzyme, and it is largely the shape of these keylike enzymes which determines their function. Minerals, which have magnetic charge, alter the shape and electrical properties of enzymes. For instance, copper activates an enzyme called cytochrome oxidase by twisting it into a particular shape, and by charging part of the molecule to create a magnetic attraction. Without that shape and electric charge, the enzyme could not perform its function—the last oxidase in the chain of reactions making ATP.[6]

Scientists find great beauty in such interactions, in the unending interplay of nutrients, gases, acids, and bases, of the structural members and energy-yielding molecules that make up the huge and ever-active engine of life. This beauty has to do with the vast web of relationships that make up the grand design of biology, the "wheels within wheels" that continually churn out life. Boundaries in this engine are difficult to draw. If we remove one small part to analyze it—such as, for example, a particular vitamin or enzyme or trace mineral—it is no longer part of the machine; its very nature is not the same. Life can be understood and appreciated best in terms of processes and interactions instead of as an assemblage of parts, and that is how we shall try to present the nutrients in this book.

[6] R. Cavalieri 1980, "Trace elements," in R. S. Goodhart & M. E. Shils, Modern Nutrition in Health and Disease (Philadelphia: Lea & Febiger), pp. 408–441 (p. 414)

Protein

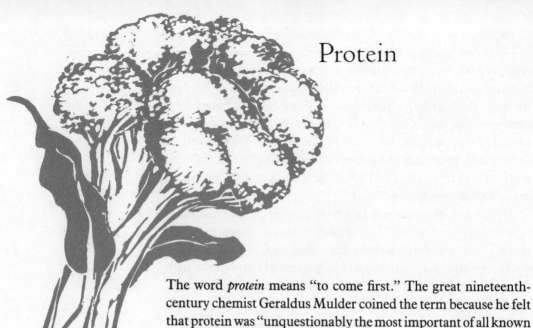

The word *protein* means "to come first." The great nineteenth-century chemist Geraldus Mulder coined the term because he felt that protein was "unquestionably the most important of all known substances in the organic kingdom."[1] Proteins perform a fabulous variety of roles in the body—as regulators of fluid balance, as components of DNA and RNA and of hormones, as nutrient transporters in blood, as components of the bone matrix, and so on almost infinitely. Protein is best known as the basic structural unit our bodies are made of, and this role alone would give it a central place in our view of life on earth.

In the hundred years since its discovery, however, our understanding of protein has evolved considerably. The course of this evolution can be seen in the estimates of dietary need, which have dropped again and again in recent decades.

The first scientific recommendation for adults, 118 grams of protein per day, was set by the German chemist Karl Voit in 1880, and was based simply on the average amount eaten by healthy men in Voit's studies.[2] In 1902, with an enthusiasm for protein that seems to typify our countrymen, the American nutritionist W. A. Atwater hiked this recommendation to 125 grams per day[3]—again, on the basis of what people were eating. By 1941, however, when the National Research Council issued the first of its "recommended daily dietary allowances" or RDAs, the figure was down to 70 grams per day for the average man, 60 for the average woman, reflecting the first experimental work that attempted to define our actual need.[4] Today the RDA is just 56 grams per day for an adult man and 44 for a woman, and the actual minimum from which these figures were calculated is just

[1] E. D. Wilson, K. H. Fisher, & M. E. Fuqua 1965, *Principles of Nutrition* (New Delhi: Wiley Eastern), p. 53

[2] I. Leitch 1942, "The evolution of dietary standards," *Nutrition Abstracts and Reviews* 11:509

[3] L. J. Roberts 1944, "Scientific basis for the recommended dietary allowances," *New York State Journal of Medicine* 44(1):59–65

[4] E. V. McCullom 1957, *A History of Nutrition* (Boston: Houghton Mifflin)

[5] Food and Nutrition Board, National Research Council, 1980, *Recommended Dietary Allowances*, 9th ed. (Washington, D.C.: National Academy of Sciences), p. 46

[6] P. V. Sukhatme & S. Margen 1978, "Models for protein deficiency," *American Journal of Clinical Nutrition* 31:1237–1256

slightly over half that much.[5] Very recently it has even been suggested by some experts that the threshold of need may be dynamic rather than fixed, and may go much lower than has ever been suspected.[6]

While the estimates of need have been dropping, though, the amount of protein that people actually eat has not fallen at all. For nearly a century, Americans of both sexes—including the vegetarians surveyed![7]—have been getting an average of about 100 grams of protein per day, almost double the RDA. Moreover, as G. T. Molitor points out, "it must be borne in mind that the RDAs themselves overestimate human nutrition needs, since a 'margin of safety' has been built into RDA calculations. These discrepancies suggest that protein consumption [in the United States] probably is excessive."[8]

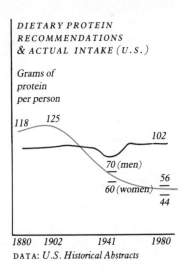

DATA: *U.S. Historical Abstracts*

HOW MUCH PROTEIN DO WE NEED?

Proteins are chains of amino acids, chemicals which can link on to each other because of a characteristic nitrogen atom at one end. It is nitrogen that makes protein unique among the nutrients, for this linking facility is what enables proteins to fasten together in constructing the innumerable, complex structures of living tissue. Like carbohydrate and fat, protein can be burned for energy. But the body needs protein for two purposes which no other nutrient can meet: first, to supply certain amounts of eight essential amino acids; second, to supply more nitrogen for building and repair.

In a sense, the question of how much protein the human being needs is easy to answer: however much is required to grow, to repair tissues, and to carry on the other biological functions that can be performed by protein alone. Since this is essentially a need for nitrogen, scientists reasoned, we should be able to measure how much protein we need by finding experimentally the point of *nitrogen balance*: the level of dietary protein such that nitrogen going in equals nitrogen going out. When protein intake falls below that level—negative nitrogen balance—more nitrogen is excreted than is taken in, suggesting that the body is making up the deficit by tearing down proteins in its own tissues.

The minimum amount of protein required to avoid negative nitrogen balance, then, represents the human requirement for protein. These measurements are the basis for the RDA.

Today, however, it appears that the body is capable of much

[7] *U. S. Department of Agriculture 1984, Nutrient Intakes: Individuals in 48 States, Year 1977–78 (Washington: Government Printing Office);*

J. T. Dwyer 1981, "The Wonderful world of vegetarianism: Benefits and disadvantages," in J. J. B. Anderson, ed., Nutrition and Vegetarianism: Proceedings of Public Health Nutrition Update 1981 (Chapel Hill, N.C.: Health Sciences Consortium), Table 1, p. 7;

J. G. Bergan & P. T. Brown 1981, "Studies of nutrient status of vegetarians in the United States: Young Boston adults," in J. J. B. Anderson, pp. 91–102 (table 4);

B. F. Harland & M. Peterson 1978, "Nutritional status of lacto-ovo vegetarian Trappist monks," Journal of the American Dietetic Association 72:259–264

[8] *G. T. Molitor 1980, "The food system in the 1980s," Journal of Nutrition Education 12(2):103–111 (supplement)*

greater flexibility. Research shows that energy and protein needs vary in direct response to each other, so that instead of one fixed requirement for protein and another for energy (calories), it is more accurate to talk about a continuum of protein-calorie needs.

One aspect of this relationship is not new: if there are adequate calories in the diet, less protein is needed; if calories are low, protein needs go up. This is because protein itself can supply energy, and energy needs are the body's highest priority. On a low-calorie diet, the body burns protein for energy as well as carbohydrate and fat; it then needs more protein to make up its nitrogen requirement. When calories are actually inadequate—as on a crash diet, or among the very poor—even muscle protein is burned for fuel, so that the body begins to waste away. This *is* a protein deficiency, but the real problem is inadequate calories: not too little protein, but too little food.

Calories, therefore, are said to *spare* protein: if your diet supplies enough calories, it need supply only a minimum of protein.

Much more remarkable, however, is the recent realization that this minimum is not fixed. Energy and protein needs are not static; one or both can change, much more widely than has been thought, as the body adapts to its environment.

Nitrogen balance studies, on which the RDA is based, assume that human beings reach protein–energy equilibrium in about ten days. But it now appears that the body is much more adaptable, and can adjust to higher or lower intakes of protein or calories over a period of thirty to sixty days or longer. Over longer periods —years, or even generations—there is evidence that humans can adjust to lower intakes than have been thought possible.[9]

It is difficult to understand these trade-offs between energy balance and protein utilization, and the variability that protein–calorie needs display, in terms of traditional models. As Margen puts it, the very concept of a *requirement* for either protein or energy now appears misleading—or, at least, the requirements are not static but dynamic. Contrary to what has been assumed for decades, there simply is no fixed or genetically determined amount that is required.[10]

In practical terms, this means that it is quite possible—in fact, in poorer populations it is probably commonplace—for an individual to adjust *biologically* to a diet that supplies much less than the RDA of protein and energy. Really poor populations, however, are probably at the extreme end of adaptability; any

[9] *J. C. Waterlow 1986, "Metabolic adaptation to low intakes of energy and protein," Annual Review of Nutrition 6:495–526*

[10] *Sheldon Margen, Prof. of Public Health Nutrition, Univ. of Calif., telephone conversation, May 20, 1986; Sukhatme & Margen 1978*

event disrupting food supply can suddenly precipitate wide-spread famine.[11]

The RDA, then, is really a national standard, not a biological requirement. It reflects the body's adjustment to the levels of consumption people are used to. Yet, as we said earlier, even this standard does not reflect what most people actually eat, which is almost twice that amount. In fact, as you can see if you add up the protein content of your diet, it is actually rather difficult in this country to meet your energy needs and *not* get more protein than the RDA, even if you are a vegetarian.

What's the conclusion? Unless you're pregnant, very sick, or still growing, don't worry about getting more protein. If your resistance is good and you're not always feeling run down, you're probably getting all you need. If you *are* always feeling run down, it's probably still not a protein problem.

HOW ABOUT VEGETARIANS?

Vegetarians often encounter the objection, "But plant proteins aren't complete, as animal proteins are. Vegetarians don't get the *kind* of protein they need."

The question of completeness, or protein quality, refers to the fact that most plant proteins do not supply the eight essential amino acids in the proportion that the human body needs.* This tired bugbear has been ingeniously laid to rest by showing that different plant foods complement each other's proteins: rice and beans, for example, are each high in the essential amino acid that the other is low in. Eating such foods together is biologically the same as eating complete proteins.

However, protein quality is not an issue if you are getting enough calories from a varied diet.[12] *There is no need to calculate complementarity at all.* By conservative consensus, only 20 percent of the RDA needs to be complete protein:[13] that is, about 11 grams for an adult man and 9 for an adult woman, an amount small enough that it is really very easy to get. If you are following our Food Guide, your need for complete protein is met (and exceeded) right in Step 1—not by planning for protein, but simply as a natural bonus of a normal whole-foods diet.

The adult requirement for amino acids is covered by just 11 grams of "completed" protein a day—a little more than is supplied by 1 glass of milk. But even so-called incomplete protein foods can meet this requirement; it just takes larger quantities. Any one of the following servings—for illustration only!—meets the essential amino acid requirement without any other source of protein:

2⅔ cups cracked wheat
3 cups cooked rice
5¾ slices Basic Bread
3 cups diced potatoes
⅓ cup Soy Spread
½ cup wheat germ
2¾ cups rice with ⅓ cup cooked peas

[11] *S. Margen 1984, "Auto-regulatory processes to maintain energy balance in the individual," in E. Pollitt & P. Amante, eds., Energy Intake and Activity (N.Y.: Alan Liss), pp. 57–76 (p. 74)*

[12] *D. M. Hegsted et al. 1946, "Protein requirements of adults," Journal of Laboratory and Clinical Medicine 31:261–284*

[13] *Food and Nutrition Board 1980, p. 43*

---

*There are exceptions: soybeans, quinoa, and even spinach supply protein effectively as high in quality as that of milk.

[14] G. E. Butterfield-Hodgdon & D. H. Calloway 1977, "Protein utilization in men under two conditions of energy balance and work," Federation Proceedings 36(3):1166

[15] D. H. Calloway 1982, "Energy–protein relationships," in C. E. Bodwell et al., eds., Protein Quality in Humans: Assessment and In Vitro Estimation (Westport, Conn.: AVI), p. 148; D. H. Calloway & H. Spector 1954, "Nitrogen balance as related to caloric and protein intake in active young men," American Journal of Clinical Nutrition 2:405–11

[16] E. S. Nassett 1972, "Amino acid homeostasis in the gut lumen and its nutritional significance," World Review of Nutrition and Dietetics 14:134–153

[17] Hegsted et al. 1946

In addition, the body has other fascinating homeostatic mechanisms for ensuring that its protein needs are met. One is that as the caloric value of the diet goes up, so does the efficiency with which protein is utilized.[14] If you are getting plenty of calories, the *effective* quality (biological value) of the protein you eat actually goes up.[15] Second, on a short-term basis, dietary deficiencies in protein quality can be made up by drawing on a pool of amino acids right within the digestive tract, where some 80 to 90 grams of complete protein are supplied daily from the breakdown of cells in the normal course of metabolism.[16]

When you remember that the RDA figure has safety factors which almost double the experimentally measured needs, let alone all the body's mechanisms for adaptation, you will see why we say that protein is not an issue even for vegetarians. The clinical data support this conclusion: protein deficiency problems are as uncommon among ordinary vegetarians as they are among omnivores.[7] There is no evidence that even vegan diets, which avoid dairy products and eggs, have any failing in protein quantity or quality so long as they are reasonably varied. After a classic study of such diets, the noted Harvard nutritionist Mark Hegsted remarked with apparent surprise, "It is most unlikely that protein deficiency will develop in apparently healthy adults on a diet in which cereals and vegetables supply adequate calories."[17]

IS PROTEIN DEFICIENCY EVER A CONCERN?

Despite the body's resourcefulness, protein deficiencies do occur even in the United States. The poor are the most vulnerable: children in poor families, single pregnant women not getting enough food, the elderly with low income or disabilities or both. Deficiencies are also not uncommon among people who are institutionalized, depressed, or on an unusually restrictive diet—a low-calorie weight loss regimen, for example, or a diet of only raw foods or brown rice. But again, the real problem is generally not protein but calories: the protein in the diet is being burned to meet energy needs.

For similar reasons, children and pregnant women in vegan households are also at some risk for protein deficiency, because of the additional needs imposed by rapid growth. Although health can be maintained with very careful planning, we prefer to recommend against a vegan diet for children and pregnant women. (More on special requirements of vegans on page 398.)

ARE THERE HAZARDS IN TOO MUCH PROTEIN?

Since most Americans eat more protein than is biologically necessary, it is reasonable to ask if too much protein is actually harmful.

First, concerns have been voiced about increased risk of cardiovascular disease and cancer due to high protein intake. However, this primarily refers to *animal* protein; plant proteins may actually guard against these problems.[18]

Boston researchers working with both rats and humans have found that "unrestricted intake of protein-rich foods"—specifically, meat proteins—is accompanied by increased pressures in the kidneys.[19] Over time, this may contribute to the progressive loss of kidney function and higher blood pressures which are associated with aging, at least in industrialized countries. (In traditional societies, high blood pressure is rare at any age.)

Additionally, in several studies with human volunteers, it has been shown that high protein intakes cause loss of calcium in the urine. The correlation is direct: the more protein eaten, the more calcium lost. At levels of 100 grams and over, the threat to calcium becomes significant. With osteoporosis (brittle bone disease) of increasing concern, any factor that depletes the body's calcium stores should be avoided, or at least compensated for.[20]

Most experts today believe that the danger of excess dietary protein to normal, healthy people is small. Our own suspicion is that this consensus will change. If only because of the calcium-depleting effect of extra protein, we believe it is safe and prudent to urge adults *not* to go out of their way to "enrich" their diet with high-protein foods.

This holds particularly for protein and amino acid supplements: they are generally unnecessary, and might even be harmful to a healthy adult. In connection with severe dieting or fasting, liquid protein products have been implicated in several deaths due to cardiac arrest.[21] Since many of these reports reached the national papers, such products have declined in popularity, but variations are still on the market as adjuncts to "lose weight fast" schemes.

Single amino acids seem to be the latest fad in nutrient supplementation. So far, very little is known about their nutritional and

[18] R. Smith 1984, Nutrition, Hypertension and Cardiovascular Disease (Gilroy, Calif.: Lyncean Press), pp. 121–125

[19] T. M. Meyer, S. Anderson, & B. M. Brenner 1983, "Dietary protein intake and progressive glomerular sclerosis," Annals of Internal Medicine 98(5, pt. 2):832–838

[20] R. P. Heaney & R. R. Recker 1982, "Effects of nitrogen, phosphorus, and caffeine on calcium balance in women," Journal of Laboratory and Clinical Medicine 99(1):46–55;

L. H. Allen, E. A. Oddoye, & S. Margen 1979, "Protein-induced hypercalciuria: A longer term study," American Journal of Clinical Nutrition 32(4):741–749;

H. Spencer et al. 1978, "Effect of high protein (meat) intake on calcium metabolism in man," American Journal of Clinical Nutrition 31:2167–2180

[21] R. R. Michiel et al. 1978, "Sudden death in a patient on a liquid protein diet," New England Journal of Medicine 298(18):1005–1007 (May 4);

J. M. Brown et al. 1978, "Cardiac complications of protein-sparing modified fasting," Journal of the American Medical Association 240(2):120–122 (July 14)

22 *N. J. Benevenga & R. D. Steele 1984, "Adverse effects of excessive consumption of amino acids," Annual Review of Nutrition 4:157–181*

pharmacological effects. Since little is known, claims abound: lysine is considered a herpes cure, tryptophan a sleep aid, DL-phenylalanine an analgesic. Some of these claims may turn out to be valid, and other pharmacologic uses may be found. But when used in these ways, single amino acids are drugs. They should be used with the same respect and caution as prescription drugs, since purified amino acids can be quite toxic in unnatural doses.[22] In any case, single amino acids are the very opposite of whole foods. It's doubtful that anyone needs these products to lead a healthy life.

NATIONAL DIETS AND NATIONAL WEALTH

How personal income affects food choices: calories from fats, carbohydrates, and proteins as percentages of total calories in the diet, according to national income (gross domestic product per person per year in 1980 U.S. dollars). Correlation based on 85 countries, 1962. REDRAWN FROM: *Périssé et al. 1969, Energy and Protein Requirements (Rome: FAO, 1973)*

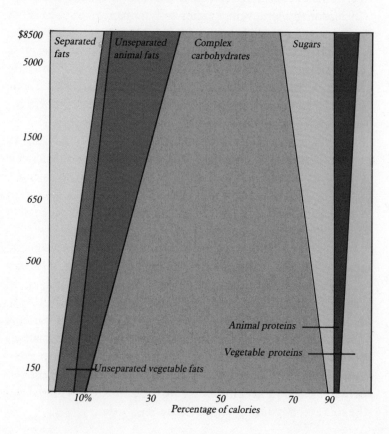

Carbohydrates

For almost all of recorded history, man's staple foods have been carbohydrates—usually a grain, such as wheat, rice, or barley, or a root or tuber, such as yam or potato. With affluence and industrialization, however, such foods tend to fall from favor, giving way to meat and fats. Several factors seem responsible for this, chief among them being wealth and status—traditional staple foods are often considered poor people's fare. The popular myth that carbohydrates are fattening reinforces this trend.

Wealth has almost always meant a richer diet, but in earlier times, only for a few. Today, however, most of us are wealthy by historical standards. In terms of possessions and conveniences, the average American maintains a level of consumption inaccessible even to the ruling elite of earlier times. This enables us to live comfortably, but it also enables even the common person to suffer from diseases that in former times only the rich would get.[1] The diminishing role of complex carbohydrates has a great deal to do with this.

Simple or Complex

Starch, cellulose, cotton, table sugar, and pure glucose are all carbohydrates. The term encompasses all substances that are made up of one or more sugar molecules. Chemically, such substances consist only of carbon and water. But some, such as table sugar, are small, simple molecules, while others (such as cellulose) are long and complicated. This basic distinction between simple and complex makes for important differences in the role carbohydrates play in the human body.

[1] R. T. Steinbock 1976, Paleopathological Diagnosis and Interpretation (Springfield: Thomas), p. 310;

E. Ashtor 1975, "An essay on the diet of the various classes in the medieval Levant," in R. Forster & O. Ranum, eds., Biology of Man in History (Baltimore: Johns Hopkins Univ. Press), p. 162;

M. Reffer 1921, Studies in the Paleopathology of Egypt (Chicago: Univ. of Chicago Press)

Percentage of carbohydrate calories per
person

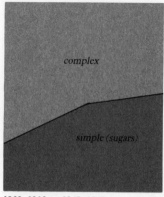

1909–1913   1947–1949   1980

[2] *D. A. Jenkins et al. 1984, "Glycemic
response to foods," American Journal of
Clinical Nutrition 40(5):971–981;*

*A. M. Coulson et al. 1984, "Effect of
source of dietary carbohydrate . . . in
subjects with noninsulin-dependent
diabetes mellitus," American Journal of
Clinical Nutrition 40:965–970;*

*F. Q. Nutall et al. 1983, "The glycemic
effect of different meals . . . ," Diabetes
Care 6:432–440*

[3] *Betty Dismukes, Research Dept., Sugar
Association, letter, Aug. 29, 1985
(unpublished data based on Economic
Research Service and USDA estimates)*

[4] *Physician Task Force on Hunger in
America 1985, Hunger in America:
The Growing Epidemic (Middletown,
Conn.: Wesleyan Univ. Press), p. 42*

Glucose (the body's primary fuel), galactose, and fructose are examples of the simple sugars, the irreducible units of which carbohydrates are made. They cannot be broken down any further without turning back into carbon and water. One step up is table sugar or sucrose, which is made of two simple sugar units—glucose and fructose—bound together. All these sugars are called simple carbohydrates. Starch, cellulose, and all other carbohydrates are called complex, for they are made up of long chains of these simple sugar units.

The body can burn carbohydrate, fat, or protein for energy, but carbohydrate is unique in having virtually no other role. Glucose is the body's preferred source of energy, and life depends on a constant supply of glucose in the blood, readily available to all tissues at all times. Pure glucose goes straight into the circulation, which is why it is used to nourish the body in intravenous solutions during surgery. Table sugar, which needs only to be broken into glucose and fructose, enters the blood almost as fast. But the complex carbohydrates in whole grains, for instance, supply energy not in one quick rush but steadily, over a period of time. For this reason, such starchy carbohydrates make a longer-lasting fuel.

However, the effect that a carbohydrate-rich food has on blood sugar levels—whether it is a steady source of energy, or produces a quick spike and subsequent drop—depends on more than whether that food is simple or complex. In general, as Dr. David Jenkins discovered in 1982, the most easily digested carbohydrates (including those that are highly processed) enter the bloodstream fastest; those that enter more slowly, such as lentils and other legumes, are not only steadier sources of energy but help to stabilize the blood-sugar effects of other foods eaten at the same time.[2] These studies have captured considerable interest and controversy. Our own feeling is that while Jenkins's "glycemic indexing" of foods may be helpful to diabetics, it means little to most of us on a whole-foods diet, where it is the whole meal that really counts.

Interestingly enough, the nutrient "packaging" around the starch in whole grains, legumes, and vegetables makes a perfect vehicle for their carbohydrate fuel, helping to supply other nutritional requirements while satisfying our need for energy. The very nutrients required for carbohydrate metabolism—B vitamins in balanced proportions for burning glucose as fuel, and chromium, a trace mineral crucial to blood sugar control—are generally found right in whole foods themselves. In addition, the fat and protein in the package, along with the indigestible fiber covering, slow down the digestive process, giving the sugars from carbohydrate digestion a little more time to enter the blood. These benefits are lost in highly processed carbohydrates like white flour, and the most refined carbohydrate of all—table sugar—provides fast fuel but nothing else.

Sugars: Health Effects

Sugar consumption in the United States averaged 126.8 pounds per person in 1984,[3] roughly *one-third pound* per day. This figure includes all kinds of carbohydrate sweeteners, but sucrose (table sugar) provides the major share, slightly over half—about 6 tablespoons a day. Since this is an average, many people must be eating a good deal more.

If these amounts don't tally with your experience, remember that roughly three quarters of this is "hidden sugar," sweeteners that are added in food processing. Only one quarter is added by us intentionally. These figures include what is used in the food industry and what is just plain wasted, so they do overestimate what we actually eat: some of the sugar used in the baking industries, for example, is consumed by yeast and not by us. Even allowing for such considerations, however, it is clear that Americans eat a *lot* of sugar—more in the last decade, in fact, than at any other time in the nation's history, as you can see from the chart in the margin. (The apparent exception during Prohibition is due to the sugar used in illegal stills.)

Researchers have been taking a long, hard look at sweeteners to determine their health effects, but no strong associations have been found linking sugars with any disease other than tooth decay. The main problem with refined sugars is that they contribute virtually nothing other than calories. Since the body's appetite is satisfied by calories alone, large amounts of empty-calorie foods crowd out other foods needed for decent nourishment. The result is often bad teeth, obesity, and marginal deficiencies,[4] especially troublesome where sugar consumption is greatest: among children and teenagers.

In any case, it is too soon to conclude that the case for or

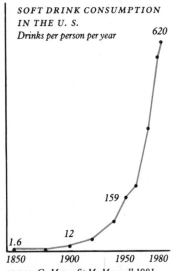

SOFT DRINK CONSUMPTION IN THE U. S.
Drinks per person per year

620

159

12

1.6

1850   1900   1950   1980

FROM: *G. Moyer & M. Maynell 1981, Nutrition Action (Aug.), p. 8*

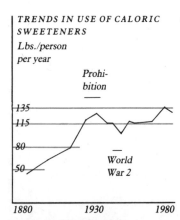

TRENDS IN USE OF CALORIC SWEETENERS
Lbs./person per year

Prohibition

135
115

80

50

World War 2

1880   1930   1980

SOURCES: Sugar Association; U.S. Statistical Abstracts

[5] R. A. Anderson & A. S. Kozlovsky 1985, "Chromium intake, absorption, and excretion of subjects consuming self-selected diets," American Journal of Clinical Nutrition 41(6):1177–1183

[6] S. Langård, ed., 1982, Biological and Environmental Aspects of Chromium (Amsterdam: Elsevier);

W. Mertz et al. 1974, "Present knowledge of the role of chromium," Federation Proceedings 33:2275–2280;

H. A. Schroeder 1973, The Trace Elements and Man (Old Greenwich, Conn.: Devin-Adair), pp. 26, 77–84

RELATIVE SWEETNESS OF SUGARS

Expressed as percentages of sucrose or table sugar

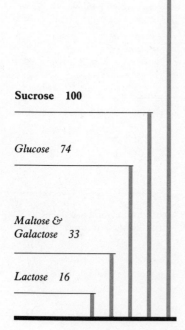

Fructose   173

Sucrose   100

Glucose   74

Maltose & Galactose   33

Lactose   16

against sugar is closed. Sugar consumption seems to increase the loss of chromium.[5] In our society, most people gradually lose blood sugar control as they grow older, and it has been suggested this might be due to depletion in the body's chromium stores through a lifetime of eating too much refined sugar. When blood sugar control gets fragile, severe stress can precipitate frank diabetes. In societies where sugar intake is much lower than ours, blood sugar control does not decline with age,[6] and this kind of diabetes is uncommon. To us, these considerations are enough to warn against adding much sugar to our food—as a rough rule of thumb, not more than 1 to 2 tablespoons a day.

Sometimes honey, brown sugar, or molasses is offered as an answer to white sugar. Molasses may contain significant amounts of iron, depending on how it is processed, but because of its strong flavor it can't really substitute for table sugar. Natural and less refined sugars do contain chromium, but no sweetener is a *good* source of this nutrient or any other. Sugar is sugar; its contribution is calories. Honey, for all practical purposes, is still straight sugar. Real raw sugar is no longer available on the market, and for a very good reason: it is notoriously full of impurities such as sand, waxes, bacterial colonies, insect parts, and dirt. The brown sugar you see in stores is actually white sugar colored with burnt white sugar (which gives it a butterscotch flavor) or molasses. The slight advantage the second kind of brown sugar may have over straight white sugar is entirely due to the little molasses that colors it. (More about these sweeteners on page 446).

Our feeling about sugars and sweeteners is not that they are *bad;* they just aren't particularly good—and who needs empty calories? Even though there is no nutritional advantage, however, we do use honey, molasses, or brown sugar in place of white sugar. The reason is practical: unlike white sugar, these products have characteristic flavors which place a natural limit on how much you add. They can't hide, so you don't use as much.

Since most of the sugar in the American diet is added in processing, the simplest way to cut back on sugar is to stop buying processed foods. Simply following the Food Guide will take you a long way. Another step is to reduce empty-calorie items to a minimum. We serve fruit after ordinary meals, saving sweetened desserts for special occasions—and even then we expect desserts to have something of nutritional value to offer.

Alcohol

Alcohol is not a carbohydrate, but since alcoholic beverages are made from carbohydrate-rich foods, their impact on nutrition deserves mention here.

Fermented beverages like beer and wine have been with us for thousands of years. Distilled drinks, on the other hand, are a recent innovation. In the process of making hard liquor, ethyl alcohol is distilled from a fermenting slurry, retaining only minute traces of the original food. Distilled alcoholic beverages are like white sugar or separated oils in their level of refinement. All they offer is calories stripped of nutrients.

Alcohol is, if possible, even more an empty-calorie food than sugar, for each gram yields 7 calories of energy as opposed to sugar's 4. This high caloric content easily satisfies the appetite, so that alcoholic beverages crowd out other foods needed for nourishment, sometimes leading to deficiencies in heavy drinkers.

Alcohol abuse also damages the liver, whose task is to detoxify any poisons that enter the blood supply. Alcohol is such a poison, which the liver can handle in moderate doses; but when the alcohol in the blood goes above a certain level, the liver gets overwhelmed. Drunkenness is not the only result: more alcohol than the liver can handle actually kills liver cells, so that scar tissue and then fatty deposits from the blood begin to take the place of living tissue. When protein intake is low, as is often the case when alcohol intake is high, this poisoning process is accelerated. Over time, the accumulation of fat and scar tissue leads to the condition known as cirrhosis, in which the liver becomes enlarged with hardened, fat-laden, nonfunctioning tissue.

There is, of course, a place for a little alcohol in a healthy life-style. Sometimes you see reports that moderate consumption of wine or beer is even beneficial to health,[7] though the claim continues to raise controversy.[8] In one recent study, which supports the theory that moderate alcohol intake lowers the risk of heart attack, researchers added that "there are other potential costs that have not been addressed, e.g., auto accidents and cancer risks."[9] Perhaps the main nutritional claim for wine and beer is that they are close to their sources—fruit juices and grains—in nutrient content. Hard liquor has no redeeming nutritional value at all.

[7] *E. Mezey 1985, "Metabolic effects of alcohol," Federation Proceedings 44(1, pt. 1):134–138;*

J. McDonald 1982, "Moderate amounts of alcoholic beverages and clinical nutrition," Journal of Nutrition Education 14(2):58–60

[8] *Mezey 1985;*

L. Koski 1983, "Alcohol and nutrition," Journal of Nutrition Education 15(2):40

[9] *D. S. Siscovick, N. S. Weiss, & N. Fox 1986, "Moderate alcohol consumption lowers risk of cardiac arrest," American Journal of Epidemiology 123(3):499–503*

Fiber

Among all materials scrutinized by nutritionists, dietary fiber is unique. As one distinguished researcher says, it is "understood but not defined."[10] No definition covers all the literally hundreds of substances that come under this term, yet everyone agrees that fiber is a beneficial food component with well-defined roles in promoting health.

The only generality that holds true for all types of fiber is that they derive from plants. When people talk about fiber or "roughage," they usually mean the insoluble, bran-type fibers from the husks and seed coatings of grains. But soluble fiber, though less familiar to most of us, is equally important in nutrition. It includes fruit and vegetable pectins, gums, mucilages, and related substances, which often have beneficial effects on digestion, blood cholesterol levels, and other factors affecting health.

Roughly speaking, dietary fiber is everything in plant foods that our digestive enzymes cannot break down. "Crude fiber," the term used on labels, is the amount of dietary fiber that someone was actually able to measure in a lab. The problem is that laboratory methods are much more destructive than digestion is, so crude fiber measurements generally report much less fiber than a food actually has—with some foods, as little as one tenth.[11] "Crude fiber" is an outdated and misleading term, yet this is still what is reported in most food composition lists, since accurate methods for estimating dietary fiber are not yet in wide use.

For thousands of years, people have known that dietary roughage helps to prevent and treat constipation and related problems. Until recently, it was assumed that the beneficial effect of fiber in the intestine comes from its ability to absorb water, like a sponge. But bran fiber, the most effective of the dietary fibers for treating constipation, has the *least* ability to hold water. Recent research has resolved this puzzle. We know now that the health benefits of insoluble fibers like bran come largely from the fact that they nurture aerobic bacteria and yeasts which do a lot of helpful work: they create the soft bulk that moves intestinal contents along without strain, adjust acidity and alkalinity, and detoxify chemicals in the gut that can cause cancer and other problems.[12] Without dietary fiber, *anaerobic* bacteria take over, and their effects are quite the opposite. Some cancer-producing toxins in

---

To convert "crude" fiber values to approximate dietary fiber, multiply by:

6 for Whole Grains
3 for High-carbohydrate
 Vegetables
3 for Legumes
3 for Nuts and Seeds
3 for Fruits
2 for Super-vegetables
2 for Low-calorie Vegetables

---

[10] *D. Kritchevsky 1982, "Dietary fiber in health and disease," in D. R. Lineback & G. E. Inglett, eds., Food Carbohydrates (Westport, Conn.: AVI), pp. 296–311*

[11] *J. W. Anderson 1986, Plant Fiber in Foods (Lexington, Ken.: HCF Diabetes Research Foundation), p. 2*

[12] *P. Greenwald & E. Lanza 1986, "Dietary fiber and colon cancer," Contemporary Nutrition 11(1)*

the gut, in fact, are produced by bacteria that flourish when the diet is deficient in fiber.

So constipation is not just the homely concern it seems. It is the precursor, and perhaps cause, of some much less tolerable complaints: diverticular disease (a very common and sometimes painful disease of the colon), bowel cancer, appendicitis, varicose veins, and hemorrhoids. All of these diseases are virtually unknown in societies where people eat a high-fiber diet.[13]

In discussions like this, most of the attention goes to bran and other insoluble fibers. But soluble fibers—the pectins, gums, and mucilages from fruits and vegetables—also make important contributions to health. For one, they act in the blood to smooth out the ups and downs of sugar metabolism. Diabetics who eat plenty of this kind of fiber can often reduce their insulin dosage. Even more dramatic, certain soluble fibers lower cholesterol by removing it from the intestine in bile acids.[14]

The problems of a low-fiber diet are well recognized today, thanks to the popular press. Yet no great nationwide increase in fiber consumption has taken place. Instead, commercial interests are still cashing in on the discomforts that come from too little fiber, filling aisles in every drug store and supermarket with remedies for constipation.

Often doctors too take a prescription approach to fiber, recommending that people on low-fiber diets take 2 or 3 teaspoons of bran with each meal to relieve symptoms of constipation and diverticular disease. Although this may be useful, we can't help wishing that everyone could discover how satisfying and healthful it is to eat whole foods. We probably wouldn't even know about some of these diseases if it weren't for refined foods. Before the roller mill and white flour took over in the 1880s, Americans were probably getting 10 to 15 grams of crude fiber a day. With white-flour bread and other refined foods, the figure would be closer to 2 grams.

However, excessive amounts of dietary fiber *can* cause problems for those who are not used to it. People just switching to whole foods may find that their digestive system needs time to learn how to handle all the complex carbohydrate. If your body complains, go more slowly.

Some kinds of indigestible carbohydrates and other compounds listed as fiber—particularly phytic and oxalic acids—can

[13] D. Kritchevsky 1985, "Dietary fiber and cancer," Nutrition and Cancer 6(4):213–219;
Cummings 1984, p. 813;
Kritchevsky 1982, p. 306;
D. P. Burkitt 1972, "Varicose veins, deep vein thrombosis, and haemorrhoids: Epidemiology and suggested aetiology," British Medical Journal 2(813):556–561 (June 3);
D. P. Burkitt 1971, "The aetiology of appendicitis," British Journal of Surgery 58(9):695–699

[14] B. O. Schneeman 1986, "Dietary fiber: Physical and chemical properties, methods of analysis, and physiological effects," Food Technology 40(2):104–110

[15] M. Cheryan 1980, "Phytic acid interactions in food systems," Critical Reviews of Food Science and Nutrition 13(4):297–336 (pp. 316–319)

[16] Judy R. Turnlund, U.S.D.A. Western Regional Research Laboratory, Albany, Calif., interview, March 3, 1986

[17] J. R. Turnlund 1982, "Bioavailability of selected minerals in cereal products," Cereal Foods World 27(4):152–157

[18] T. Shultz et al. 1985, "Vegetarianism and health," in J. Weininger & G. M. Briggs, eds., Nutrition Update, vol. 2 (N.Y.: Wiley), p. 138;

"Phytate and rickets," 1973, Nutrition Reviews 31(8):238–239

[19] A. R. El-Mahdy 1982, "Changes in phytate and minerals during germination and cooking of fenugreek seeds," Food Chemistry 9:149–158;

A. Caprez & S. J. Fairweather-Tait 1982, "The effect of heat treatment and particle size of bran on mineral absorption in rats," British Journal of Nutrition 48(3):467–475

[20] Y. Lopez, D. T. Gordon, & M. L. Fields 1983, "Release of phosphorus from phytate by natural lactic acid fermentation," Journal of Food Science 48(3):953–954, 985;

D. Fardiaz & P. Markakis 1981, "Degradation of phytic acid in oncom (fermented peanut press cake)," Journal of Food Science 46(2):523–525;

[21] El-Mahdy 1982, p. 149; Cheryan 1980, p. 323

[22] J. A. Maga 1982, "Phytate," Journal of Agriculture and Food Chemistry 30(1):1–7;

D. Oberleas 1973, "Phytates," in Food and Nutrition Board, National Research Council, Toxicants Occurring Naturally in Foods, 2d ed. (Washington, D.C.: National Academy Press), pp. 363–371 (p. 365)

[23] A. Hodgkinson 1977, Oxalic Acid in Biology and Medicine (London: Academic Press), pp. 208–210

actually reduce human absorption of nutrients. These latter two are chelators, which means they can grab and hold minerals because of their shape and electrical properties. This serves a useful purpose in living plants, where phytic acid stores the phosphorus needed for growth. In our digestive systems, however, phytic acid continues its trapping and holding act with such minerals as zinc, iron, magnesium, and calcium, keeping them from being absorbed into the body.[15] Since whole foods are generally high in phytic and oxalic acids, this is sometimes mentioned as a potential problem for vegetarians.

Except at bare subsistence levels, however, current evidence indicates that this worry is unfounded. For one thing, researchers point out that past experimental work has ignored the differences between lab conditions and living systems: purified phytic acid added to foods in laboratory experiments chelates minerals much more than the phytic acid actually found in foods.[16] Also, while refining does remove the problematic chelators, it also removes the minerals themselves. One recent study comparing the availability of zinc in white and whole wheat bread, for example, found that although zinc was less available in whole wheat, the *net* zinc absorption was greater with whole wheat bread than with white, since much more zinc is present in the whole grain.[17]

Finally, although phytic acid does contribute to serious deficiencies of zinc and other minerals in impoverished third-world populations, where parasites and intestinal diseases are endemic, there is no evidence that vegetarians in developed nations are any more deficient in these minerals than omnivores.[18]

We believe that phytic acid is not a significant problem on an adequate and varied whole-foods diet. Those who are concerned might be interested to know that grains, nuts, and legumes have less phytic acid when they are cooked,[19] fermented (as in miso, natto, and tempeh),[20] or sprouted,[21] and that yeast-raised bread benefits from microbial destruction of phytic acid.[22]

Oxalic acid has a similar binding or chelating effect in foods that contain it, especially on calcium. Again, this can be a problem in marginal third-world diets, but as one researcher says, it "appears to have little deleterious effect provided there is an adequate supply of calcium and vitamin D." Even in developing countries, he adds, "many rural communities . . . manage to survive on high-oxalate, low-calcium diets."[23]

Fat

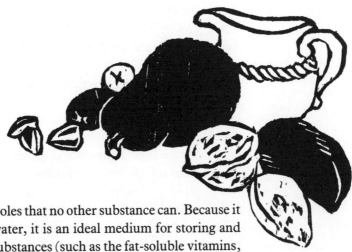

In the body, fat plays roles that no other substance can. Because it does not dissolve in water, it is an ideal medium for storing and transporting certain substances (such as the fat-soluble vitamins, A, D, E, and K) which otherwise could not be carried by the blood. It is also an ideal medium for storing energy, since it packs 9 calories of energy per gram where carbohydrate and protein supply only 4. Body fat is continually being burned for energy and replaced; it does not accumulate unless the body goes on getting more energy (calories) from all food sources than it can deal with.

However, fat to serve these functions does not have to come from food; it can be made within the body from any source of calories. The body needs *dietary* fat only to supply a small amount of linoleic acid—about as much as is present in a teaspoonful of vegetable oil. Since all vegetables, grains, fruits, and nuts contain this essential fat in their cell walls, the requirement is easily met from a normal day's meals of whole foods.

Reasons for eating excess fat are understandable. First, fat tastes good: in fact, taste itself is a phenomenon of fats, since the flavor essences of foods are almost always fat-soluble compounds. Fat is also very satisfying, not only because of those 9 calories per gram, but also because it slows down digestion, making us feel full longer. Finally, there are economic reasons why fat in our food is simply hard to avoid. Fats and oils are cheaper today than ever in history, due to modern processing methods and the fact that oils are virtually a by-product of the cattle-feed industry. Since deep-fat frying is a fast, cheap way to

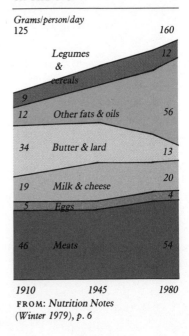

TRENDS IN FAT CONSUMPTION IN THE U. S.

Grams/person/day

125		160
9	Legumes & cereals	12
12	Other fats & oils	56
34	Butter & lard	13
19	Milk & cheese	20
5	Eggs	4
46	Meats	54
1910	1945	1980

FROM: *Nutrition Notes*
(Winter 1979), p. 6

FAT   427

[1] J. T. Dwyer 1981, "The Wonderful world of vegetarianism: Benefits and disadvantages," in J. J. B. Anderson, ed., Nutrition and Vegetarianism: Proceedings of Public Health Nutrition Update 1981 (Chapel Hill, N.C.: Health Sciences Consortium), pp. 5–25 (table 2)

[2] H. Engleberg 1983, "Serum lipemia: An overlooked cause of tissue hypoxia," Cardiology 70(5):273–279;

P. E. Droubay & D. L. Puppione 1980, "Dietary fat–induced postprandial lipemia . . . in subjects with angina pectoris," American Journal of Clinical Nutrition 33(6):1199–1207;

M. Friedman et al. 1965, "The effect of unsaturated fats upon lipemia and conjunctival circulation," Journal of the American Medical Association 193(11):882–886 (Sept. 13)

[3] Engleberg 1983

[4] Friedman 1965

[5] E. A. Newsholme & A. R. Leech 1983, Biochemistry for the Medical Sciences (N.Y.: Wiley), p. 288

[6] Newsholme & Leech 1983, p. 288
[7] Newsholme & Leech 1983, p. 234

[8] F. G. Perkins & W. J. Visek, eds., Dietary Fats and Health (Champaign, Ill.: American Oil Chemists Society)

[9] A. Keys 1986, "Food items, specific nutrients, and 'dietary' risk," American Journal of Clinical Nutrition 43(3):477–479

[10] K. K. Carrol 1983, "The role of dietary fat in carcinogenesis," in Perkins & Visek, pp. 710–720

make things tasty, it is perfectly suited to cooking for convenience or profit: "fast foods" are very often fried, and almost always fatty.

The result, as probably everyone knows, is that Americans eat far more fat than is healthy. About 40 percent of the calories in the average American diet comes from fats and oils. Only two fifths of this—butter, salad oil, mayonnaise, and the like—is actually added in the kitchen or at the table. The rest is "hidden fat": either naturally present, as in meat (even if trimmed), nuts, and milk, or lurking as added fat in processed convenience foods. Vegetarians are not exempt; there is no evidence that they eat less fat than omnivores.[1]

ADVERSE EFFECTS OF A HIGH-FAT DIET

Why should a high-fat diet be a source of trouble? No one can say precisely. Population data can only show the strong associations of fat with disease, not causal links. The biggest problem with a high-fat diet may prove to be not fat as such, but that fat crowds out the complex carbohydrates to which the human body has adapted in the course of evolution.

However, specific adverse effects of dietary fat have been suggested, based on available evidence. One of the more intriguing explanations is that excessive amounts of fat in the blood might form a film over cell surfaces, inhibiting such functions as oxygen uptake from blood and sensitivity to insulin. In heart patients, for example, angina attacks—chest pain due to constricted blood supply to the heart—can be brought on by eating a fatty meal.[2] Angina is associated with a lack of oxygen in the heart muscle, and as one researcher puts it, excess fat in the blood limits oxygen diffusion into tissues and thereby interferes with oxygen delivery to the heart.[3]

A high-fat diet is also known to increase the tendency of red blood cells—the very cells that deliver oxygen—to clump together or clot. Meyer Friedman observed that an increase in platelet aggregation follows a high-fat meal[4]—again, perhaps because the red blood platelets become coated with a sticky, fatty film. (It is interesting that this is a phenomenon of excess: in appropriate quantities, polyunsaturated oils actually *reduce* platelet adhesiveness, by means of important biochemicals called prostaglandins.) When blood cells clump like this, they are likely to form clots, which can block small arteries or adhere to any damaged area in arterial walls,[5] narrowing the passage through which blood must pass.

Excess fat in the blood also alters the electrical conductivity of the heart,[6] especially if oxygen delivery to heart muscle cells is impaired. High fatty acid levels are typically found in the blood of heart attack victims,[7] and drastically altered electrical impulses characterize the spasmodic muscular activity of a heart attack. In such instances fat may act as an insulator, like the plastic around a copper wire, inhibiting electrical impulses in the heart muscle.

Whatever the mechanisms, evidence accumulated over the past decade clearly links high levels of fat in the diet with serious chronic diseases—heart and blood vessel diseases, several kinds of cancer, gout and gallstones, adult-onset diabetes, hypertension, and even impaired immunity.[8]

It is not only the amount of dietary fat that is problematic, but also the kind. After decades of public education, for example, most Americans know that the distinction between saturated and unsaturated fats is connected with the risk of getting heart disease. As you can see from the diagram in the margin, a mere hydrogen atom or two is all that differentiates an unsaturated fat from a saturated one—it is hydrogen that they are saturated with. Yet these small molecular differences result in very different physical characteristics. In the kitchen, for example, saturated fats such as butter, cocoa butter, and coconut oil are usually solid at room temperature, while unsaturated fats are usually liquid—oils. In the body also, their effects on health differ. While no one yet knows why this is, it *is* known that saturated fats in the diet often mean higher levels of cholesterol in the blood, and high blood cholesterol is one of the clearest risk factors for heart disease that research has found.

Unsaturated fats (almost all vegetable oils) can actually lower blood cholesterol levels,[9] leading some people to promote actually adding them to the diet. But unsaturated fats now appear far from blameless, even in connection with heart disease. They tend to raise blood levels of other fatty substances called triglycerides—another suspected coronary risk factor—and they are probably linked to cancer even more strongly than saturated fats.[10] It seems there is no "good" kind of fat when there is too much fat in the diet.

One other kind of fat deserves mention here because of the

TYPES OF FATS

Characteristics of fats and oils according to their predominant fatty acids

SATURATED FATS

maximum number of hydrogen atoms

predominant in animal fats

usually solid at room temperature

MONOUNSATURATED FATS

2 hydrogen atoms short of saturation, forming 1 double bond

common in vegetable oils

liquid at room temperature

POLYUNSATURATED FATS

4 or more hydrogen atoms short of saturation, forming 2 or more double bonds

common in vegetable oils

usually liquid at room temperature

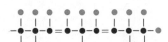

• *carbon atom*
• *hydrogen atom*

PESTICIDE CONCENTRATIONS
UP THE FOOD CHAIN

DDT residues measured 1965–1968
(parts per billion)

• Lard 170   Since most
              pesticides are
              fat-soluble, high-fat
              foods tend to have·
              higher levels of
              contamination than
              lower-fat foods.

• Eggs 100

• Meats 50
  • Cooking oils 40
    • Cheese 30
      • Grains 18
        • Greens 13
          • Root vegs 6

FROM J. Lucas 1974, Our Polluted
Food (N.Y.: Wiley), pp. 56–57

[11] E. A. Emken 1984, "Nutrition and
biochemistry of trans and positional
fatty acid isomers in hydrogenated oils,"
Annual Review of Nutrition
4:339–376
[12] J. E. Kinsella 1981, "Metabolism of
trans fatty acids . . . : An overview,"
American Journal of Clinical
Nutrition 34:2307–2318
[13] J. E. Hunter 1982, "Comments on
metabolism of trans fatty acids" (letter),
American Journal of Clinical
Nutrition 36:376–377; reply by J. E.
Kinsella & G. Bruckner, 377–378
[14] G. T. T. Molitor 1980, "The food
system in the 1980s," Journal of
Nutrition Education 12(2):103–111
(supplement)

public controversy surrounding it. In the process of hydrogen-ating liquid oils to make solid fats like margarine, some of the fatty acid molecules get twisted into strange shapes. These twisted molecules are called *trans* fatty acids. *Trans* fats are almost never present in nature. Since they are unsaturated, they enter the same biochemical pathways as other polyunsaturates, but they behave differently when the time comes to perform.[11] High levels of *trans* fatty acids are used experimentally when scientists want to study essential fatty acid deficiency: the body is fooled into think-ing these twisted fats will do what essential fatty acids do. In such experiments in laboratory animals, the *trans* fats tend to accumu-late in the heart tissue.[12] So far, such characteristics have not been shown to be definitely harmful to human beings in amounts we are likely to consume.[13] However, this argument is heard so often today in connection with newly-introduced environmental factors—*trans* fats, food dyes, BHT, pesticides, solvents, anti-biotics and hormones in animal feeds, industrial wastes, even radiation—that it seems at least reasonable to wonder if it is safe to ignore the unknown effects of all of them together. While waiting for further evidence, we prefer to avoid taking in another chemical of unknown effect on top of the literally thousands of others in today's polluted environment.

CUTTING THE FAT

Whatever the differences in specific fats, it is clear that fat of any kind is harmful in excessive amounts. But what is excessive? What is moderate? What is safe?

The Senate Select Committee, in its *Dietary Goals for the United States,* recommended getting no more than 30 percent of daily calories from fat—a significant reduction from the na-tional average of 40. The same recommendation is made by the American Heart Association, the National Research Council committee on diet and cancer, and other expert bodies in the United States. The Federal Republic of Germany's equivalent of our Food and Nutrition Board advises 25 percent of calories as fat,[14] and Nathan Pritikin built his heart disease rehabilitation program on a goal of 10 percent maximum. None of these num-bers represents anything more than an attempt to balance the clear message of the evidence—eat less fat!—with a goal that people can realistically strive for.

We aim for 25 percent of dietary calories as fat, which is quite within reach for a whole-foods vegetarian. Half the battle is won by avoiding fast foods and convenience foods and limiting the fat you add at the table. Even so, we suggest that you check your diet at least once to see where your calories are coming from.

FAT INTAKE FOR VARIOUS PERCENTAGE TARGETS

Check your fat intake and caloric level to see what percentage of calories come from fat

OR *Pick a percentage target for your calorie level and see how much fat per day it allows*

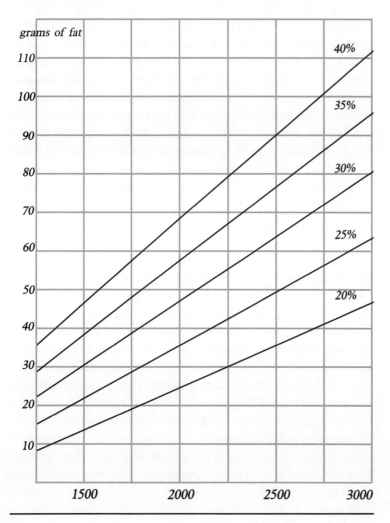

= *piece* 4″ × 4″ × ⅛″
= *two* 1″ *cubes*
= *scant* ⅓ *cup grated*

12.4	Cream cheese
11.8	Cheddar
11.5	Gruyère
11.1	American (processed)
10.9	Roquefort
10.7	Jack, Muenster
10.6	Parmesan, *dry, grated*
10.2	Blue
10.0	Port du Salut
9.9	Edam, Brie
9.7	Swiss, Gouda
9.4	Provolone
9.2	Parmesan, *hard*
8.7	Mozzarella, *full fat, low moisture*
8.3	Neufchâtel
7.7	Mozzarella, *full fat*
7.5	Feta
6.1	Mozzarella, *part skim, low moisture*
5.6	Mozzarella, *part skim*

TO CALCULATE *the percentage of fat calories in your diet, add up the calories and grams of fat in 1 day's food (use tables at back), then convert grams of fat to calories by multiplying by 9. Fat calories divided by total calories, multiplied by 100, gives the percentage of calories as fat. For example:*

1 day = 2250 calories, 72 grams of fat

72 g × 9 cal / g = 648 calories from fat

*648 ÷ 2250 = .288
  = approx. 29% calories as fat*

Vitamins & Minerals

Throughout this book we have stressed the whole diet rather than individual nutrients, since in the body these fifty or so essential chemicals act in concert and not as separate entities. Their functions in the body comingle, joining with other active biomolecules such as hormones and enzymes to regulate metabolic functions and biochemical reactions. Rarely do we find single nutrient deficiencies outside of experimental labs, and rarely can we isolate the functions of one vitamin or mineral from those of other nutrients it interacts with constantly. We are dealing with a complex and marvelous whole, a living, interactive chorus of chemical potencies which is able to adjust and adapt to an extremely wide range of environmental conditions, if we simply provide a variety of wholesome foods with adequate calories.

Of necessity, the science of nutrition began by studying fragments—individual nutrients—one by one. Today a more dynamic view of nutrient interdependence is gaining influence. This approach is reflected in the work of Jean Pennington, whose research provides a comprehensive way of looking at a whole diet through just seven "leader" vitamins and minerals (see margin). According to Pennington's work, if you are getting enough of these so-called index nutrients, together with enough calories, you are assured of filling the need for all the nutrients for which recommended allowances have been established.[1]

The beauty of Pennington's system is that it encourages us to think of our diet as a whole, instead of looking up fifty items in food composition charts and taking pills to compensate for any apparent lack. It is not the roles the index nutrients play in metabolism that makes them special; they are simply indicators of

THE INDEX NUTRIENTS
VITAMINS
A
B-6
Folacin
Pantothenic Acid

MINERALS
Calcium
Magnesium
Iron

[1] *J. A. T. Pennington 1976, Dietary Nutrient Guide (Westport, Conn.: AVI)*

balance and variety. When a whole diet supplies enough of these seven micronutrients, the spectrum of nutrient needs is supplied.

In this spirit, we offer a brief overview of how all the micronutrients work together. The interactions of nutrients in metabolism and the subtle effects of the trace minerals on health are frontier areas in nutrition research. Here we present the aspects of this research which we find most remarkable and relevant, along with a table of vitamin and mineral needs and functions.

The Micronutrients

Vitamins are like hormones and enzymes: active compounds whose functions in the body overlap and interact. The main distinction of vitamins is that the human body cannot make them. We have to get them from the food we eat, and although we need only tiny quantities, they are absolutely essential for life.

In the body, for example, vitamin D actually becomes a hormone—that is, one of the body's metabolic regulators. It is activated in the skin on exposure to sunlight, and from there it goes to the liver and then to the kidney, where further chemical modifications convert it into a hormone which regulates bone formation.

Other vitamins play roles closely allied with those of enzymes, the body's biochemical matchmakers. Life depends on an endless variety of chemical reactions in which one compound combines with another to produce something the body needs. These reactions are much too important to be left to chance, and the purpose of enzymes is to bring the reactants together by means of their shape and physical properties. The enzyme comes out of the reaction unchanged, ready to catalyze another reaction.

Many vitamins are an essential part of particular enzymes: some B vitamins, for example, are part of enzymes that are responsible for energy production in cells. The body can make the enzymes, but not without these vitamin components; so one sign of B vitamin deficiency is a dramatic loss of energy.

Mineral elements too are essential to energy requirements, though they play other life-sustaining roles as well. Of the more than ninety naturally occurring elements in the universe, just four—oxygen, carbon, hydrogen, and nitrogen—account for a full 96 percent by weight. The remaining 4 percent is the inorganic elements of the body, the minerals.

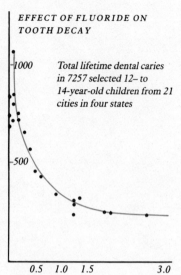

1000   Total lifetime dental caries
        in 7257 selected 12– to
        14-year-old children from 21
        cities in four states

500

0.5   1.0   1.5   3.0

*Fluoride content of public water supply
(parts/million)*

FROM: *H. T. Dean et al. 1942,
"Domestic water and dental caries," U. S.
Public Health Reports 57:1155*

[2] *H. A. Schroeder 1973, The Trace
Elements and Man (Old Greenwich,
Conn.: Devin-Adair), p. 101*

In crystalline form, minerals make up the hard structures of animal bodies, such as shells, bones, and tooth enamel. In solution, mineral atoms or ions carry electrical charge and so are called electrolytes. The physics of attraction and repulsion between these charged ionic particles underlies their usefulness in life's chemistry—in the contraction and relaxation of muscles, the conduction of nerve impulses, and the magnetic attraction that shapes organic chemicals like enzymes, hormones, and the graceful "double-helix" coils of life's genetic record, DNA. The active part of a biomolecule, the "functional group" that actually does the work, often contains a mineral—iron embedded in the center of the hemoglobin molecule in blood, magnesium in chlorophyll, cobalt in vitamin B-12.

The role a mineral can play in the body is governed by its electric charge, its atomic weight, and the arrangement of its electrons. Minerals that are similar in these ways can often double for each other in chemical reactions. Fluoride, for example, is similar to chloride, an ion which normally enters tooth enamel to make it hard; so fluoride in drinking water can take the place of chloride to make the enamel even harder. But not all such substitutions are beneficial. Strontium-90, a radioactive element in atomic fallout, easily substitutes for calcium, and can therefore accumulate in milk and in our bones. Cadmium, which closely resembles zinc in its electron configuration, is present wherever zinc is used to galvanize steel, and acute cadmium poisoning has occurred when acidic fruit drinks were left in galvanized pails or ice trays.[2]

The turnover of minerals in the body is slow compared to that of most vitamins, so mineral deficiencies take longer to show up.

Trace Minerals

Trace minerals, so called because they are required in such minute amounts, are the frontier nutrients in nutrition. Each decade since the 1950s has seen new additions to the list of known essential microelements. In 1976, when the first edition of this book was published, the collection had grown to fourteen, of which half were merely suspected to be essential nutrients because experimental deficiencies had been observed in animals. Since then most of these elements have been confirmed, and a new collection of "possibles" is assembling.

Even minerals like lead, arsenic, and cadmium, once thought of exclusively as poisons, have now joined the list of essential or possibly essential nutrients. Selenium was in the "maybe" list ten years ago; in fact, up until 1969 it was known only as a poison to livestock and, erroneously, as a human carcinogen. Later, however, Keshan's disease, prevalent in an area of China by that name, was found to result from chronic selenium deficiency due to low levels of that element in the soil. Arsenic, still correctly known as a poison, was recently shown to be essential in a nontoxic form in rats, pigs, and goats, and it is very likely that a human requirement will be demonstrated soon. One researcher has even suggested that present levels of arsenic in American diets do not meet the tentatively estimated requirement![3]

How can something poisonous also be essential? In minerals, it is often a matter of form. Trivalent arsenic, with an electrical charge of $^{+++}$, is a poison, and this is the kind found in industrial wastes. But arsenic from organic sources is pentavalent ($^{+++++}$) and not toxic. Chromium comes in two such forms also. Chromium^{++++++} is a deadly poison; chromium^{+++} is not only nontoxic, but known to be essential for blood sugar control in humans.[4]

However, as with other biologically active substances, toxicity is also a matter of amount, and in trace metal nutrition, the difference between what is an essential amount and what is poisonous is sometimes very small—and varies, according to what other elements are present in what amounts. Balance is everything, and balance can be quite fragile.

In some ways, trace mineral research today is reminiscent of physics earlier in the century, when the deterministic picture of matter as a few well-defined building blocks gave way to a flux of elusive, interdependent subatomic events. Current research on the ultratrace mineral environment inside cells has called into question the very idea of individual nutrient needs at the cellular level. The new model, like that of quantum physics, is rigorous yet poetic: a concert of electochemical influences, all interactive and interdependent.

If the *pattern* of trace elements together becomes our focus, it is easier to understand how micronutrients function. Often, one trace ion can substitute for another—manganese for magnesium, for example, in a large number of metal enzyme complexes. Sometimes a trace element can even replace a vitamin (and vice

[3] T. Hazell 1985, "Minerals in foods: Dietary sources, chemical forms, interactions, bioavailability," World Review of Nutrition and Dietetics 46:1–123 (p. 35)

[4] H. Sigel 1986, Concepts on Metal Ion Toxicity, (N.Y.: Dekker; Metal Ions in Biological systems, vol 20)

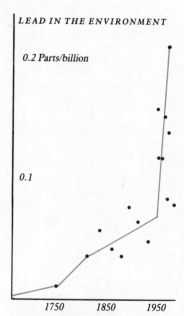

0.2 Parts/billion

0.1

1750   1850   1950

Lead residues in snow at Camp Century, Greenland; the geographical isolation indicates spread of pollution. The rise around 1860 probably reflects the Industrial Revolution; after 1950, probably the sharp increase in use of leaded gas. FROM: *W. Mertz, Nutrition Today, Sept./Oct. 1983, p.28*

[5] *M. Abdulla, B. M. Nair, & R. K. Chandra, eds., 1985, Proceedings of an International Symposium: Health Effects and Interactions of Essential and Toxic Elements (N.Y.: Pergamon)*

versa), as selenium for vitamin E as an antioxidant. In such cases, both nutrients are said to act synergistically, so that their combined effect is much greater than would be expected from adding up the individual potencies.

It is also common for two trace elements—for example, copper and zinc—to act antagonistically, so that an excess of one produces a deficiency of the other. And finally, though trace elements are toxic in excess, some of them can protect against the toxic effects of others. Zinc, for example, reduces the toxicity of cadmium, and iron the toxicity of lead. Alternatively, deficiencies of one such mineral increase the toxicity of the other.

Flexible interdependence is also called for in studying these nutrients. Barriers between the historically separate spheres of chemistry, biochemistry, biology, medicine, and physics crumble with each advance in ultratrace mineral nutrition. The latest field to overlap this study is ecology, for all minerals, essential or toxic, enter our food ultimately from the soil.

In recent years, a new specialty in nutrition has been named: bioinorganic chemistry, which deals with the microelements, the trace and ultratrace mineral nutrients. The frontiers of its research are indicated by some of the topics presented at a recent international symposium on trace elements:[5]

❧ *Trace elements and immunity.* Certain microelements enhance aspects of immune function, while others inhibit it. Further, the same trace mineral can either enhance or inhibit immunity depending on its concentration, and combinations of trace minerals together can affect cellular immunity differently than would be expected from the actions of either element alone.

❧ *Metallo-drug therapy.* Gold, copper, zinc, iron, and other elements have established medical uses, and new applications are being sought. Gold compounds, for example, were known as antimicrobials even to the ancients. Interest was revived by the discovery that gold salts can help to control inflammation in rheumatoid arthritis, and current research is trying to elucidate how.

❧ *Long-term effects of trace element pollution.* Before the advent of large-scale industrial activities, balance and adaptation in nature ensured wide margins of safety in the concentration of trace minerals, both in the body and in the ecological environment. This balance has been upset by the large quantities of lead, cadmium, and mercury that are released daily into our air, water, and soil. The presence of such metals in the environment is being studied as a factor in chronic diseases.

&. *Trace elements in human growth.* Deficiencies or excesses of trace elements can produce birth defects, and play crucial roles in growth and development.

We have got ourselves into double jeopardy with respect to trace minerals. On the one hand, we have found a large variety of ways to strip these minerals from foods by refining. Separated sugars and fats, white flour, hard liquor, extruded protein products, and other achievements of food processing technology retain very little of the trace mineral spectrum of the original foods,[6] with the result that imbalances of essential trace minerals might be contributing to the incidence of chronic disease. On the other hand, our industrial activities concentrate trace minerals—usually the more toxic ones—and dispose of them in rivers, lakes, oceans, or landfills, poisoning the water table, the soil, and marine life.

With the micronutrients, it simply is not clear what the overall effects of such drastic environmental changes will be. What *is* clear is that the impact of technology on food supply is far-reaching and complex, and potentially very grave. The cost of a highly industrialized way of life may not be obvious in the short run, but it is evidently high, and the bills keep coming in.

Toward the end of his life Dr. Henry Schroeder, an original pioneer of trace element research, wrote, "I must emphasize that environmental pollution by toxic metals is a much more serious and much more insidious problem than is pollution by organic substances such as pesticides, weed killers, sulfur dioxide, oxides of nitrogen, carbon monoxide, and other gross contaminants of air and water. Most organic substances are degradable by natural processes; no metal is degradable."[7]

We quote Schroeder not only as an authority, but because he coupled his warnings with specific, practical measures that are entirely within reach. He did not advocate stringent or unrealistic measures such as abolishing the polluting industries. Instead he focused on six industrial pollutants that pose most of the danger to a safe environment: cadmium, lead, nickel, beryllium, antimony, and mercury. If these are controlled soon enough, he felt, we can avert disaster. The knowledge is there; we simply need to get government and industry to apply it.

FIVE ESSENTIAL STEPS FOR CONTROLLING METAL POLLUTION[7]

&. *eliminate nickel and lead additives to gasoline*

&. *treat nickel carbonyl to decompose it in smelter and refinery stacks*

&. *reduce particulate emissions from coal smokes*

&. *regulate factory effluents to eliminate mercury*

&. *find and use less toxic fungicidal compounds for grains, paper, and paint*

[6] *Schroeder 1973, pp. 124–141;*
H. A. Schroeder 1971, "Losses of vitamins and trace minerals resulting from processing and preserving food," American Journal of Clinical Nutrition 24:562–573

[7] *Schroeder 1973, p. 154*

The Micronutrient Universe: Vitamins

	Rich Sources	Function in Body	Helpful Factors	Harmful Factors
Vitamin A	Green and yellow vegetables, fruits, whole milk	Health of skin and mucous membranes, formation of bones and teeth, night vision		
Vitamin D	Egg yolk, sunlight, vitamin D fortified milk	Regulates metabolism of calcium and phosphorus	Exposure to sunlight produces vitamin D in our skin	Living in a dark environment or in most kinds of artificial light
Vitamin E	Vegetable oils, nuts and seeds, whole grains	Antioxidant—protects tissues against "free radicals"	Selenium enhances the antioxidant effects of vitamin E	Air pollution, ionizing radiation. Need increases with increased intake of polyunsaturated fats.
Vitamin K	Green vegetables, cauliflower	Necessary for blood clotting		Loss of gut bacteria through prolonged antibiotic treatment
Vitamin C	Citrus fruit, berries, melon, green vegetables, tomatoes, potatoes	Hydrogen transport, collagen formation, wound healing, antioxidant	Better preserved in acid foods and beverages	Easily destroyed by heat, alkalis, oxygen. Infection, smoking, and stress decrease amount in body
Thiamin (B-1)	Yeast, whole grains, legumes	Conversion of carbohydrates, protein, and fat to energy		Easily destroyed in food handling, leaching, heat and alkalis, and refining of grains
Riboflavin (B-2)	Milk, yeast, green vegetables, legumes	Metabolism of fats, carbohydrates, protein, enzyme component	Protect milk and other sources from light	Easily destroyed by light, or lost by leaching; need is increased by oral contraceptives
Niacin	Legumes, whole grains, green vegetables, milk, coffee	Essential for turning carbohydrates, fats, and protein into energy	The amino acid tryptophan is converted to niacin; alkalis help release otherwise unavailable niacin in corn; very stable to heat	Leaching losses if cooking water is discarded
Pyridoxine (B-6)	Whole grains, legumes, carrots, eggs, bananas	Protein metabolism; making red blood cells and nerve tissue	Need is proportional to protein intake	Need is increased by carbon monoxide exposure, oral contraceptive use, and excess protein

Deficiency Symptoms	Notes on Toxicity	Notes	
Night blindness, blindness, stunted growth	Only from supplements. Headache, vomiting, peeling of skin, diarrhea, blurred vision, loss of hair	Provitamin A intake from vegetables asociated with reduced cancer risks. Vegetarians usually get large amounts in normal diet. Vegetable provitamin is safe; animal form (in pills) highly toxic in excess.	**Vitamin A**
Rickets (bone deformation due to lack of mineralization); growth failure in children, osteomalacia (adult rickets)	Depositing of calcium in blood vessels and kidneys	This vitamin/hormone is responsible for more cases of serious poisoning due to overdose than any other supplement. The body can regulate its own production; exposure to sunlight alone can never cause toxic buildup. Some researchers feel RDA should be expressed as quantity of ultraviolet light exposure.	**Vitamin D**
Very rare—red blood cell fragility leading to anemia	Excess bleeding in some people; formation of blood clots in others. Not very toxic	Very difficult to produce vitamin E deficiency symptoms in adults, but premature infants definitely need extra amounts. Be wary of claims that vitamin E slows aging, heals scars, or cures heart disease.	**Vitamin E**
Blood doesn't clot—hemorrhage		Name comes from German word for "clotting factor." About one-half our vitamin K need is produced in the intestines by microorganisms. Plenty of vitamin K in normal intake of fresh vegetables.	**Vitamin K**
Scurvy, spongy and bleeding gums, listlessness, joint pain, poor wound healing	Urinary stones in some people, acid stomach from pills	Vegetarians usually have high vitamin C intake from vegetables and fruit. Several primates, including humans, need a dietary source; all other animals and even insects make their own.	**Vitamin C**
Mild: reduced stamina, depression, irritability. Severe: beriberi, weight loss, mental breakdown		Deficiency was little known before widespread refining of grains. One of four nutrients added back to white flour in enrichment formula. Alcoholics often deficient. Fever increases metabolic rate and need for thiamin.	**Thiamin (B-1)**
Irritated, watery, bloodshot eyes, scaly rash on face, cracking at corners of mouth, purple tongue		People who avoid milk need alternate sources of riboflavin. Deficiency is not life-threatening, but probably not rare even in U.S. Along with physical symptoms, depression and hypochondria can result.	**Riboflavin (B-2)**
Mild: irritability, insomnia, sore tongue. Severe: diarrhea, dementia, dermatitis, death	"Niacin flush" (hot, prickly skin occurring directly after niacin dose), upset stomach, diarrhea, abnormal liver function	See Goldberger story on page 336. "Niacin flush" is caused by dilating blood vessels in face; this same ability to open up small blood vessels makes niacin a useful drug against angina, when blood supply to heart is constricted.	**Niacin**
Mild: anemia, sore mouth. Severe: dizziness, nausea, confusion, anemia, convulsions	Neurological damage and abnormalities	Considered low in average U.S. diets. Low B-6 in tissues is associated with heart and blood vessel disease. Major B-6 losses in processing are not replaced in "enrichment." Several medical uses.	**Pyridoxine (B-6)**

	Rich Sources	Function in Body	Helpful Factors	Harmful Factors
Folacin	Dark green vegetables, legumes, nuts, fresh oranges, whole wheat	DNA, RNA synthesis	Raw salads	Destroyed by lengthy cooking, holding at high temperatures, and long storage
Cobalamine (B-12)	Milk, eggs	DNA, RNA synthesis	Need is proportional to protein intake	Malabsorption in certain disease states, such as pernicious anemia
Pantothenic acid	Whole grains, legumes	Needed in cell conversions of food to energy	Widely distributed in whole foods	Removed in refining of foods

Minerals

	Rich Sources	Function in Body	Helpful Factors	Harmful Factors
Calcium	Dairy products: milk, yogurt. Leafy greens: broccoli, kale.	Bone and tooth formation, coagulation of blood, muscle contraction	Lactose; vitamin D and sunlight; keeping phosphorus intake low to moderate	Phytic acid, oxalic acid, excess dietary protein
Phosphorus	Milk, cheese, nuts, cereals, legumes	Bone and tooth structure, part of body's "energy coin" used in all energy-releasing reactions		
Magnesium	Nuts, legumes, whole grains, dark leafy greens, milk	Bone and tooth structure, nerve conduction, muscle relaxation, bowel function	Normal zinc intake	
Iron	Legumes, whole grains, potatoes, egg yolk, cocoa, green vegetables, dried fruits	Oxygen transport; part of hemoglobin, myoglobin, cellular enzymes	Absorption improved by vitamin C, cooking in iron pots, iron deficiency	Phytic acid
Iodine	Sea vegetables; plant foods in general, but highly variable depending on soil	Regulates energy metabolism, is part of thyroid hormone, involved in cellular oxidation and growth	Phytic acid, black tea, coffee	
Zinc	Eggs, nuts, cereals; wheat germ is especially rich	Essential for more than 100 enzymes involved in growth, sexual maturation, wound healing, ability to taste, protein synthesis, immunity	Normal copper intake	Phytic acid, excess copper intake

Deficiency Symptoms	Notes on Toxicity	Notes	
Pallor; sore, red tongue; cracking at corners of mouth; diarrhea; megaloblastic anemia		Works with B-12 and can substitute for it partially. Tends to be richly present in the vegetarian diet, to the extent that it can mask anemia of B-12 deficiency. Oral contraceptives lower stores.	**Folacin**
Sore, glossy tongue; digestive disorders; nervous system damage		People who avoid all animal products need alternate sources of vitamin B-12. Humans require miniscule amount, and the body conserves B-12 very well; so deficiency, while serious, takes many years to develop.	**Cobalamine (B-12)**
Fatigue, sleep disturbances, nausea, impaired coordination		Name signifies "found everywhere"; isolated deficiencies found only in experimental situations. Few rich sources; evenly distributed in whole foods.	**Pantothenic acid**
Stunted growth, rickets, osteomalacia	Calcium deposits in soft tissues, urinary stones in susceptible people	May protect against hypertension. Action often complemented by that of magnesium, as in muscle contraction and relaxation. Most "hard water" is rich in dissolved calcium salts.	**Calcium**
Weakness, osteomalacia (adult rickets), decreased heart function, neuro-logical problems		Too much in standard U.S. diets, from soft drinks and meat. Lecithin, a phosporus-containing fat, once touted as a health food, is broken down in digestion, none is needed in the diet.	**Phosphorus**
Growth failure, behavioral disturbances, tremor, weakness, seizures	Diarrhea	May protect against heart disease. Action often complemented by that of calcium, as in muscle contraction and relaxation. Most "hard water" is rich in dissolved magnesium salts.	**Magnesium**
Anemia, pallor, weakness, reduced immune function; yet low blood iron *protects* against certain types of infection	Hemochromatosis, iron deposits in soft tissues	Lost from body whenever blood is lost. Excess (from supplements) can cause constipation. Black tea with meals reduces iron absorption by some 60 percent, coffee reduces it 40 percent. Meat iron is very well absorbed, yet anemia is less prevalent among established vegetarians compared to general population.	**Iron**
Goiter, cretinism (a birth defect)	Depression of thyroid activity, hyperthyroidism in susceptible individuals	Iodization of salt virtually eliminated goiter in the U.S. Iodine is now added to bakery products and other processed foods, so today toxicity is a more likely problem than deficiency.	**Iodine**
Psoriasis-type rash, growth retardation, slow wound healing, delayed puberty, abnormal taste, loss of taste, abnormal sense of smell	Most cases of zinc poisoning result from putting fruit drinks in galvanized steel containers such as buckets	Vegetarians get less zinc than omnivores, and nonmeat zinc is less available to the body. For balance, best to use *foods* for extra zinc rather than supplements: excess zinc interferes with absorption of magnesium and alters the blood's zinc-to-copper ratio, which affects how the body handles cholesterol.	**Zinc**

	Rich Sources	Function in Body	Helpful Factors	Harmful Factors
Copper	Nuts, legumes, whole grains, drinking water	Aids in body's use of iron in hemoglobin synthesis, part of many enzymes in protein fibers and skin pigments	Normal zinc intake	Calcium decreases absorption, requirement increased by excessive zinc
Manganese	Nuts, whole grains, legumes, tea, fruits, non-leafy vegetables	Glucose utilization, enzyme activator, role in synthesis of cholesterol and polysaccharides	Minimal refining	Refining of grains
Fluoride	Naturally or artificially fluoridated water, some kinds of black tea	Included in teeth and bones, effective against dental caries, may reduce osteoporosis		
Chromium	Brewer's yeast, whole grains	Part of "GTF" complex which maintains normal glucose tolerance	Minimal refining	High intake of refined sugar and refined flour products
Selenium	Protein-rich plant foods; however, amount in plants is highly variable depending on soils	Cellular antioxidant, essential constituent of red blood cell enzymes, decreases the toxicity of heavy metals, may inhibit cancer initiation	Wide variety of foods to make up for soil lack in any one area	
Molybdenum	Whole grains and legumes (varies greatly with soils)	Enzyme constituent		Refining of grains
Potassium	Most fruits, starchy root vegetables, dark leafy green vegetables	Main electrolyte inside all body cells	Virtually all fruits and vegetables contain good amounts	Thiazide diuretics increase the loss of potassium in urine
Sodium	Salt: plenty of sodium in food without adding any	Main electrolyte outside all body cells, in the fluid bathing body tissues		Heavy exercise or labor in very hot weather can lead to excess sodium loss in sweat

Deficiency Symptoms	Notes on Toxicity	Notes	
Pallor, infants' anemia, Manke's kinky hair syndrome	Wilson's disease (neurologic problems and liver damage), vomiting	Copper deficiency is unknown outside of starvation, unusual diseases, or experimental laboratories. Intake in this country may be excessive due to the widespread use of copper pipes in plumbing.	**Copper**
Impaired growth, weakness in animals; not well defined in humans.	Generalized disease of nervous system. Least toxic of trace elements.	Manganese-deficient plants do not grow well, so natural deficiency in humans is highly unlikely unless most foods in the diet are overrefined.	**Manganese**
Higher frequency of tooth decay and possibly osteoporosis	Mottling of teeth, increased bone density, neurological disturbances.	Not yet shown to be essential, though helpful in reducing cavities. People who live where water is low in fluoride should seek alternate sources.	**Fluoride**
Impaired glucose metabolism	Low order of toxicity	Can help prevent the loss of blood sugar control that accompanies aging. Best absorbed from natural sources. Hexavalent (Cr^{++++++}) form found in industrial wastes is highly toxic, the trivalent form (Cr^{+++}) is one of the least toxic of ions and an essential nutrient.	**Chromium**
Heart muscle damage; general muscle pain; associated with Keshan disease (heart muscle disease affecting children), hemolytic anemia	Agricultural wastes endanger wildlife with toxicity in U.S.; in humans toxicity results in hair and nail loss, garlic breath, vomiting, labored breathing	Adequate selenium intake from foods is associated with lower cancer risk. Plants need no selenium but pick it up if present in soil. Acts in concert with vitamin E as an antioxidant. Enhances immunity and protects cell membranes and DNA from oxidation and heavy metals, which may explain cancer protection.	**Selenium**
	Gout-like syndrome reported; high intake results in loss of copper	Needed for making uric acid, a protein waste product. Gout, involving excess uric acid, has been associated with high molybdenum intake. Excess wastes copper.	**Molybdenum**
Lassitude, muscle weakness, polyuria	Muscular weakness, arrhythmia, heart failure	Protects against hypertension. Risky to take pills without medical supervision: chronic toxicity is very dangerous to health. Amounts in foods are safe.	**Potassium**
Muscle weakness, cramps, confusion, apathy, anorexia, low blood pressure	High blood pressure, edema, heart failure	Associated with hypertension (high blood pressure), though not in all. Even very high blood pressure can be brought down by strenuous salt restriction; milder restriction helps blood pressure medications work better. Processed foods and fast foods generally contain large amounts of sodium.	**Sodium**

SOURCES: *R. S. Goodhart & M. E. Shils, eds., Modern Nutrition in Health and Disease, 6th ed. (Philadelphia: Lea & Febiger, 1980); J. Weininger & G. M. Briggs, Nutrition Update, vol. 1 (N.Y.: Wiley, 1983), vol. 2 (Wiley, 1985);* *W. R. Faulkner, "Trace elements in laboratory medicine," Laboratory Management July 1981:21–35; "Trace elements in human nutrition," Dairy Council Digest 53(1):1–6 (Jan.-Feb. 1982)*

Food Processing: Oils, Sweeteners & Irradiation

It's hard to avoid processed foods entirely. Oils, fats, sugar, and other sweeteners will continue to find their way into most people's diets, as they have for many thousands of years. In the last few decades, however, the nature of food processing has changed dramatically with new technology. Many people want to be better informed about how these basic foods are manufactured today and whether new terms on the labels indicate processes with consequences for our health.

Food Oils[1]

The technology for separating and refining food oils developed very long ago; today we take oils completely for granted, like salt and sugar. We know that certain oils and fats are better for our health than others, but few of us know much about how oils are produced or what the words on their labels mean.

Virtually all oils available to us are highly processed or they

would not be attractive to most shoppers. Unrefined oil retains the natural flavor and odor of its source, and depending on the amount of heat in its processing, the oil will have darkened and acquired a tendency to go rancid more quickly. Responsible sellers of health-food-label unrefined oils try to handle them carefully so that the quality remains as good as possible. But if the oil you buy is bland and pale, you can be certain that it has been fully refined, bleached, and deodorized.

Above a certain temperature, oils become degraded and darkened and lose much of their vitamin E. Such oils tend to go rancid quickly. For this reason, "cold-pressed" oils are prized— the kind that used to be made in simple stone presses in villages all over the world. This method only works with high-oil-content seeds like sesame or peanuts, or with olives. The press, usually powered by animals, turns slowly, crushing the seeds and letting the oil run out. The oil's quality is protected because the slow turning generates

little heat, so the seed's natural antioxidants are not destroyed.

As far as we know, except for certain gourmet olive oils there is no commercial oil that is really cold pressed. For modern commercial production this method is too expensive, since it leaves too much oil behind in the seed meal.

To compensate for the damage done by the heat and to extract even more oil from the oilseed, a whole world of processing technology has developed. Because each step is separate, one or more of them might be omitted in producing any given oil that you buy.

In the first step, instead of cold pressing, oil is commonly removed directly from "prepressed" seed meal by solvent extraction. Usually hexane, a petroleum derivative, is mixed with the seed meal to dissolve the oil; then the seed meal is settled and filtered out and the solvent evaporated. Compared to most organic solvents, hexane is relatively nontoxic—about as harmful to the body as mineral oil or paraffin would be if we were to drink it. Solvent-extracted oils are still called "unrefined," but except for cheap imported olive oils, they are not usually sold without further processing.

Next the oil is usually "de-gummed" to eliminate substances (like lecithin) that cause cloudiness, sudsing, and the formation of precipitates in the oil. Then the oil is mixed with an alkali like lye or caustic soda, and the soapy mixture is heated until the non-oil substances break out and can be washed away.

Bleaching comes next: not like household bleaching with chlorine, but a purifying process that removes pigments, traces of soap left over from the refining, and moisture that would make the oil go rancid more quickly. Finally, the oil is deodorized—steamed at high temperatures to remove not only odors, but also peroxides that would speed rancidity. Deodorized oil is pale, with virtually no impurities left. It is entirely bland.

However processed it is, food oil can become rancid if exposed to heat, light, or air. To prevent this, two approaches are possible: one is to take great care in storage, transportation, bottling, shelf display, and storage in the kitchen; the other is to add preservatives. Most commercial oils have some preservatives added, and if so the label must list them. The label does not have to say how the oil was extracted or whether it is re-fined, bleached, or deodorized.

RANCIDITY

Unrefined oils smell rancid to most people, "nutty" to those who have developed an appreciation for them. They do tend to go rancid faster, especially soy oil, and their strong flavors can dominate whatever dish or baked good is made with them. (Of course, stong flavor is not always a drawback; in some cases unrefined oils are used as flavoring agents.)

So-called hydrolytic rancidity is the breakdown of a fat by combination with water. The resulting products are glycerin and three "free" fatty acids or FFAs. This breakdown can only take place when moisture is present, and it is greatly accelerated by an enzyme called *lipase,* which is naturally present in plant and animal cells but usually inactive unless the cell is damaged. Oilseeds do not contain much active lipase unless they are improperly stored, but if they become wet enough to germinate, considerable lipase is developed, leading to rancidity in the extracted oil.

Thus the free fatty acid (FFA) content of a fat is one measure of its quality, a high FFA content being undesirable. FFAs can be removed by alkali refining: mixing the oil with an alkali, which combines with the free fatty acids to make a soap that can be precipitated out. The same soap formation can also be an issue in the kitchen. Palm oil and coconut oil in particular undergo hydrolytic rancidity easily, leaving a soapy flavor. For this reason, the shelf-life of imitation "non-dairy" milk substitutes made from coconut oil "is limited even in the absence of lipase."[2]

Another kind of rancidity involves oxidation. A great many substances other than oxygen can act as oxidants; metals, especially copper and iron, are particularly effective, as food processors know. Oil should not be stored in metal containers, or it may go rancid; when oils are sold in soldered steel containers, as olive oil often is, the container has been lined with a plastic polymer to prevent reaction with the oil.*

Oxidative rancidity involves an attack, as it were, on the fatty acid molecule near a site of unsaturation—that is, where no hydrogen molecule is attached. Fully saturated fatty acids, therefore, cannot be bothered by this kind of rancidity—the source of their popularity in the food industries. Have you ever wondered why you can keep shortening out on the shelf indefinitely with no worry about it going rancid? That's why: there is no unsaturated bond to draw an attack.

*Incidentally, oil sold in soldered steel ("tin") cans has been found to contain more lead in it than oil sold in glass or plastic containers, and the longer it stays in the can, the higher the lead content. While the lead never reaches very high levels, it is still worthwhile to transfer your oil to a glass or plastic bottle if it came in a soldered steel container.

saturated bond to draw an attack.

Chemically speaking, the site of unsaturation is a double bond, and double bonds are like tightly compressed springs: they are poised at a high energy level, and compared to single bonds between molecules, they are unstable. They invite trouble. All kinds of invasive marauders—ozone from pollution, hydrogen peroxide, pure oxygen, metal catalysts, even cosmic rays—go straight for the throat, the double bond. That is why unsaturated fatty acids in the body need vitamin E and selenium so desperately, to protect against oxidizers; for when a marauder does get through, it can wreak havoc. If it knocks out an electron at the site of unsaturation, a chain reaction can occur, creating more oxidizing agents or "free radicals" from the unsaturated fats around. This kind of rancidity is a health risk: free radical damage is credited with accelerating the process of aging, and can definitely promote cancer in laboratory animals.[3]

Incidentally, this has an interesting practical application involving acquired tastes. With certain popular fast foods—french fries, potato chips, movie-house popcorn—it has been found that what the public enjoys is actually the flavor of the fat's rancidity. Some fast foods are deep-fat fried in vats of oil that has been used over and over for months, and the stale taste may actu-

ally be what people have come to look for. Yet oils that have been treated like this are bound to be highly rancidified, as well as damaged in other ways that can be very harmful to human beings.

People in the food oils industry admit that taste tests by panels of trained testers actually provide a better measure of oil quality than the other chemical measures that are available. Even without sophisticated training, your own nose can usually tell you what you need to know about the oil in your kitchen: if it smells bad, throw it out.

Rancidity is not the only process that damages fats and results in toxicity. Long exposure to light or heat can lead to reactions which result in brown colors in the oil and the formation of precipitates. The continuous reuse and reheating of an oil, therefore, can lead to the formation of all kinds of unusual by-products, including several known or suspected carcinogens.[4]

In particular, the process of hydrogenation, which is used in making margarine from a liquid oil, results in a geometric change in much of the remaining unsaturated fat molecules—in effect, a twisting, called *trans* isomerization. *Trans* isomers of unsaturated fatty acids are rare in nature. They are used experimentally in nutrition research to induce essential fatty acid deficiencies, in animals or in human volunteers. What other effects they may have is unclear, and for

this reason the presence of *trans* fats in the national diet has caused concern among some researchers. (See p. 430.) Oxidized cholesterol is another fatty substance involved in toxicity, and here the damaging effects in heart disease are well known.[5]

Sugar & Other Sweeteners[6]

Sweeteners are big business now: markets are increasing, product lines expanding, sales pitches proliferating. A far greater variety of sweeteners is available than ever before, from date sugar to crystalline fructose to aspartame.

Since these are commercial products, they are marketed with slogans and claims designed to attract our interest. People who want the sweet taste but not the calories may be caught by the noncaloric sweeteners devised by chemists, such as saccharin, aspartame, and miraculin. Those who respond to health claims may choose honey, date sugar, maple sugar, or perhaps fructose. Each of these products represents a whole industry, dependent on that particular sweetener for its profit.

Meanwhile, though scientific research on the health effects of sweeteners is proceeding rapidly, it is not likely to catch up with trends in our actual use. And since scientific research—often funded by the industry itself—can produce inconsistent results and findings that are confusing and difficult to interpret, half-truths and premature conclusions are easy to find, especially in popular literature.

For ourselves, we ask for a sweetener that is a product of nature, even if highly refined, since very few new organic substances are adequately tested for human safety. Ideally it would have some quality (such as flavor or cost) that would set a natural limit on its use. In normal quantities—granting that no sweetener can be called *beneficial*—it should do a minimum of harm to health. Finally, if possible, we want something that is not harmful to local economies and ecological balance in the way it is produced.

These guidelines, of course, immediately eliminate the chemical sweeteners devised by flavor chemists, which would be difficult to justify in a whole-foods diet in any case. We feel that no amount of testing in laboratories can match the millions of years of adaptation that has tested natural food components, and with this in mind we prefer not to eat any food additives other than those that nature can recognize. This leaves only natural carbohydrates: the sugars.

SUCROSE

Chemically, common white table sugar is crystalline sucrose. As the Sugar Association assures us, this is one of the purest foods available: white sugar is 99 percent sucrose, with no additives, no impurities to speak of, no annoying vitamins or minerals to discolor it. This purity has its advantages, since the darkly colored "raw" sugars available in third world countries generally contain contaminants that most of us do not want to eat, such as insect parts, parasite eggs, and dirt.

However, the main disadvantages of white sugar also stem from its purity. It lacks the "packaging" of nutrients and fiber contained in the original sugar cane or beet, which helps the body regulate sugar metabolism. And since without "impurities" this product has no flavor other than sweetness, one can easily add a great deal of it to foods without dominating them with strong odors or flavors.

In fact, we human beings seem to develop a tolerance for any given level of this purely sweet taste, at which point we need more to get the same taste "rush." Food processors have discovered this fact, finding that extra sugar in their products often provides an easy and cheap way to increase sales. We consumers, in the meantime, grow accustomed—some say addicted—to progressively higher concentrations of sucrose.

To make table sugar, cane or beets are pressed to yield juice which is filtered and clarified, then boiled down in steam evaporators and crystallized in vacuum pans. At this point the product contains solid and liquid fractions together, and the rest of the process is directed toward separating the solid crystals from the liquid molasses. To this end the mixture is centrifuged repeatedly and treated with bone char or activated charcoal to absorb the colored impurities. At each stage, the liquid fraction removed is a particular grade of molasses.

RAW SUGAR

Only when the sucrose is 96 percent pure may it be sold to the public, as *turbinado* sugar. Though this product is alternatively called "natural" or "raw" sugar in the health food industry, it is already one of the most refined foods ever made.

TABLE SUGAR

White table sugar is what then remains after bleaching and further purifying turbinado sugar to 99 percent sucrose.

BROWN SUGAR

Brown sugar represents one further stage in processing, since it is made from this already purified product by adding either molasses or burnt white sugar for coloring and flavor. There are no meaningful nutritional differences between white, brown, or turbinado sugars.

MOLASSES

Molasses, as described above, is a by-product (or, as some in the industry say, a waste product) of table sugar refining. Yet blackstrap molasses is the only sugar with anything to offer of nutritional value. It is the dark, strong-tasting liquid residue from the third stage in the process of refining white sugar, and it does contain some minerals from the original sugar cane plus calcium and iron from the processing. Its iron content can be significant, depending on whether the manufacturer uses iron vats for processing and if so, how long the molasses sits in them. (Most blackstrap today, however, is made in stainless steel vats. Sometimes iron is added in order to match the levels of molasses made in iron vats.) Blackstrap molasses has such a strong taste that it is more a flavoring agent than sweetener, and whether it tastes "rich" or "foul" varies from person to person.

Barbados molasses, the starting material for making rum, is occasionally sold as a sweetener. This kind of molasses is also made from sugar cane, but it differs from blackstrap in that it is not a by-product of the sugar industry. It is made by crushing sugar cane stalks in roller mills to extract the juice, which is then filtered and slowly boiled down to a syrup. This kind of molasses has very low mineral content compared to black-strap.

Sorghum molasses is not to be confused with either black-strap or Barbados molasses, since it is made from a different plant, sweet sorghum, commonly grown in the South. Sorghum generally has a high iron content and a tart, fruity taste compared to blackstrap. It is made much the same way as is Barbados molasses, except that enzymes may be added to increase the sugar content by enzymatic conversion of residual starch. Sorghum molasses is about 65 percent sucrose.

FRUCTOSE

Fructose has always been part of man's diet, since it is found naturally in berries and other fruits, in vegetables, and in certain exotic tubers. Its distribution in such wholesome foods has given fructose a "natural" image in the public mind, and the labels of many products using fructose play upon this image: "Contains only *natural* fruit sugar," or even "Contains *no sugar.*" (Since "sugar" usually means sucrose, table sugar, it is legal for products using only fructose as sweetener to claim that no sugar has been added, even though it has.) But there is very little that is natural about commercially sold fructose. It is made either from corn starch or from sucrose, which makes it yet one more step *less* natural than these totally refined products.

Fructose *is* common in fruit. But so are other sugars. Some fruits, in fact, contain mostly sucrose, and glucose and other sugars are often found in fruits and vegetables.

Chemically, half of both honey and white table sugar is fructose (the other half is another simple sugar called glucose). Fructose is sweeter than sucrose on an equal weight basis, and is especially sweet in cold foods. This makes it possible to get the same sweetness with less sweetener (by weight) than with white sugar—one of the reasons fructose is increasingly popular in the food industry.

The body processes fructose differently from glucose or blood sugar, prompting hopes that fructose would have health benefits over other sugars. Less insulin is required to metabolize fructose, for example, and it enters the bloodstream more slowly than either glucose or sucrose.[7] Using fructose as a sweetener in place of sucrose leads to lower levels of certain fats in the blood (VLDL triglycerides) which have been linked with heart disease. As more studies were completed, though, the initial enthusiasm for fructose dimmed somewhat. For instance, when fructose is compared to glucose or sucrose in long-term studies, at levels similar to those of a normal diet, no differences are seen between these sugars in their effects on blood fats.[8] The hopes that fructose would be beneficial to diabetics have been dampened if not dashed by the discovery that this sugar interferes with insulin's ability to bind to other sugars and reduces by some 30 percent the number of places where insulin can bind to cells.[9] Over the long term, these effects lead to higher levels of insulin circulating in the blood, at all times and to higher levels of glucose and insulin in the blood in response to eating.[10] This means it is not at all clear that longterm use of fructose products is good for diabetics, since high blood glucose and insulin levels are classic laboratory findings in Type II diabetes.

In animal studies, further, fructose at high-dose levels has been shown to overload the body's sugar metabolizing machinery, leading to liver damage; yet glucose fed at similar levels has no such effect.[11] Fructose feeding raises blood uric acid levels, which might increase risks of gout or gouty arthritis in people who are susceptible.[12] It may also have blood–pressure raising effects.[13] Finally, several studies have shown that many people cannot absorb fructose well in amounts that are now common in soft drinks. Symptoms of malabsorption include bloating, gas pains, cramps, and diarrhea,[14] leading to erroneous diagnoses of irritable bowel syndrome. The intestinal distress in these cases is relieved by eliminating high fructose and sorbose foods from the diet, such as soft drinks, pastries, and candies.[15]

Fructose has long been known to speed up the body's rate of metabolizing alcohol, leading to lower blood alcohol levels after drinking. But it does not improve the performance of alcohol-intoxicated subjects, nor does it relieve any of the symptoms of hangover. Drivers should be warned that fructose cannot improve the ability to drive a car after drinking alcohol.

Since fructose is a common sugar in natural foods, it may seem surprising that our bodies cannot handle this sugar too well. Until now, however, we have never had such massive doses. Today children who drink large quantities of soft drinks may be getting as much as one quarter of their dietary calories as fructose.[16] At present no one can say with certainty whether fructose in these quantities poses a threat to the average person's health. But data should be coming in at an accelerating rate, since the continuous rise in soft drink sales to the American public constitutes a truly massive experiment.

Honey

Honey is a fascinating natural sweetener, the only one whose production actually exerts a benign influence on the environment and remains attractive as a small-scale local industry. The folklore of honey goes back five thousand years. But it would be hard to find any substance whose role in folk medicine clashes more with current scientific opinion. While honey does contain small amounts of amino acids, proteins, organic acids, vitamins, minerals, and various other plant-derived compounds, none of these is present in amounts known to influence our nutritional state. Sugar is the main ingredient, accounting for between 81 and 86 percent of the weight; and of the many sugars present, fructose usually predominates at an average of 38 percent.

If *anything* is added to honey—water, sucrose, or (more commonly in recent years) high-fructose corn syrup or HFCS—the product cannot legally be sold as honey. The terms "organic," "natural," or "raw" on honey labels are misleading, therefore, since honey must fit these descriptors to be called honey at all. "Undiluted" is equally unnecessary.

Labels sometimes claim that honey is "uncooked." Since honey is a supersaturated sugar solution, it has a strong tendency to form crystals at room temperature, leaving its liquid fraction liable to fermentation. Heating reduces the tendency to granulate and makes the honey thinner and easier to handle. Too much heat, however, can result in a discolored honey with off flavors. Honey packers are as interested in avoiding this as we are, so most honey you can buy has been minimally processed with heat. There are a few rare brands of honey, though, that have had no heat processing at all, and some people feel this gives the product a better flavor and aroma. (The granulated texture of "buttered" or "creamed" honeys, incidentally, does not mean they are unheated. This kind of honey is commonly made by adding seed crystals, or even sugar granules, to heat-treated honey to produce a very finely granulated product.)

Finally, how about the term "filtered"? If the honey you buy is clear and shiny, you can be sure that it has been filtered, whether the label says so or not. Truly unfiltered honey always contains contaminants such as bee parts, pollen, and dirt. The USDA grades honey according to the degree of filtration: "US Grade A" and "Fancy" refer to the finest screening; the lowest rating is "Substandard." These ratings, however, say nothing about the quality of the honey itself.

A few packers do not filter their honey at all, but instead let it settle in vats to remove the larger particles. This kind of honey is usually more expensive, since the method involves greater waste. But a high price and claims on the label cannot guarantee that the honey has not been filtered, since there is no legal definition of this term for this product.

Blending is a final process that honey often undergoes, and it provides one more confusing variable on labels. The opposite of a blended honey is a single-source honey, such as sage, orange blossom, clover, or buckwheat, made by bees that only had access to that one source of nectar. However, even single-source honeys may be blended. In California, for instance, only 51 percent of the honey need come from a single source to qualify it for that name on its label. Blending need not be bad; often it can improve the flavor if one of the honeys in the blend

is bitter (as orange blossom usually is) or very strong in flavor (like buckwheat honey). Blending is also used to change the moisture content.

Pesticides are not much of a problem in honey, since bees are likely to be killed by the pesticide before they can return to the hive. Of greater concern is the fact that heavy use of pesticides is leading to a shortage of bees to make honey and pollinate crops.

Infant botulism is a concern with honey, since viable spores of *C. botulinum* are often present. Conditions inside infants' immature gastrointestinal tracts are apparently favorable to the growth of these spores, which produce a deadly toxin. We strongly recommend that honey not be given to children under one year of age.

Food Irradiation

Though the idea of irradiating foods with radioactive wastes sounds horrible to most people, the process is likely to become widespread. The reasons for this are mainly economic, since irradiation treatment preserves foods simply and cheaply. When foods are irradiated in hermetically sealed packages, they can remain "fresh" for years without spoiling. Irradiated potatoes, for example, do not sprout eyes; grains can be irradiated instead of treated with the

dangerous insecticide ethylene dibromide (EDB), saving many tons per year from insect infestation. Irradiated fruits spoil less readily, and irradiated foods in general retain more of their vitamin content than if they had been preserved by other methods such as canning or freezing. These are no doubt attractive benefits, but in our opinion they do not make up for some disturbing drawbacks.

Food irradiation has been in use on a limited scale for some thirty years, and there is by now a large volume of scientific work analyzing its practical and health implications. While the data seem clear enough, there are widely differing interpretations. For instance, in the same review, one author states that "numerous papers suggest that irradiated foods are apparently safe for experimental animals,"[17] yet also notes that various potentially harmful radiolytic byproducts are created, including free radicals, reductones, and other unfortunate "secondary degradation products,"[18] many of them never before seen in nature—the so-called Unique Radiolytic Products or URPs. Even the FDA, though in favor of food irradiation, has admitted that foods irradiated above 100,000 rads may contain enough URPs to warrant toxicological evaluation. Accordingly, FDA's maximum allowable level for irradiating grains, fruits, vegetables, and meats is 100,000 rads.[19]

Many scientists working with food irradiation feel that the small quantities of URPs produced in irradiated foods pose no practical danger to people eating them.[20] Other scientists, however, voice an obvious but serious objection: how can anyone testify to the safety of compounds which are unknown? Some of the *known* radiolytic products (RPs) do have measured levels of toxicity—peroxides created from irradiated fats, for example, and reductones from irradiated sugars, but the URPs have simply not been tested. It hardly seems enough to assume they are safe when present in only small amounts, if no one knows how these compounds act in nature. Are the URPs absorbed from the digestive tract? Can they be metabolized? If so, what are the breakdown products, and are any of these harmful? Might certain URPs or their breakdown products remain in our tissues, as do *trans* fats and certain food additives such as BHA and BHT? Do URPs collect in a particular tissue or organ, such as the kidney or liver, perhaps building up to toxic levels over time? How do URPs interact with other food components, with other pollutants, with each other? These very basic questions have simply not been asked, let alone answered, by policy makers.

In many (but not all) short-term experiments with animals, the very small amounts of radiolytic products in foods exposed to less than 100,000 rads caused no evident harm. But such experiments tell little about the long-term effects in humans. In a joint statement about the safety of food irradiation, Samuel Epstein of the University of Illinois Medical Center and John Gofman of U.C. Berkeley's Donner Laboratory of Medical Physics summed up the argument for caution: "Until such fundamental studies are undertaken, there is little scientific basis for accepting industry's assurances of safety. Similarly, there is little or no basis for accepting Food and Drug Administration (FDA) approval of irradiation. . . ."[21]

Some field reports on the health effects of food irradiation have been disturbing. One study followed what happened when irradiated wheat was fed to severely malnourished children. One group received freshly irradiated wheat; another, wheat that had been irradiated and then stored; a third group received wheat that had not been irradiated at all. Polyploid or multiple chromosomes were noted in the white blood cells of the two groups that had eaten irradiated wheat, but not in the group that ate normal wheat, and the children receiving freshly irradiated wheat had significantly more polyploidal blood cells than those whose wheat had been irradiated earlier. "The precise biological significance of polyploidy is not known," the researchers reported, "but polyploid cells have been shown to occur in man in malignancy [i.e., cancer], after exposure to irradiation, during viral infections, and in senility." Similar blood abnormalities were noted when freshly irradiated wheat was fed to a variety of experimental animals.[22]

Another study, examining the effects of irradiated foods on rats, noted that a lifetime of access only to irradiated food resulted in kidney damage.[23] Finally, growth of the mold that produces aflatoxin, a liver carcinogen, is reportedly enhanced by irradiation under certain conditions,[24] while the organism responsible for botulism, an often fatal food poisoning disease, is perversely resistant to gamma radiation.[20]

The cautionary statement of Epstein and Gofman does not rule out food irradiation; it only asks that a responsible testing program be completed before the public is exposed to significant quantities of irradiated foods. Our own argument against food irradiation, however, is based on more than toxicological data. One big issue is the material that is used for irradiating foods. The two sources most commonly used or contemplated, cobalt-60 and cesium-137, are both wastes from producing nuclear power and making weapons. These industries, along with the military, obviously stand to benefit from increased use of food irradiation, since that would provide an outlet for nuclear wastes. The rest of us, however, might well find the implications unsettling. Food processing by irradiation does not solve the problem of radioactive waste, but only locks us into its use. Do we want hot reactor byproducts shipped around the country to food processing plants? What problems will be posed by cases of fire, road accidents, vandalism, and the like, when these involve nuclear wastes? Reactor fuel and nuclear weapons, wastes, tailings, and contaminated equipment are on our highways every day, even now; yet there seems no sense in commiting our vast and vital food industry to this traffic.

Finally, irradiation promises to remove food production further from consumers than it already is, concentrating it even more intensely into a few corporations—a development that can scarcely be expected to benefit either our own farmers or the economies of the poorer food-producing nations. Irradiation is touted as an answer to food problems in the developing nations, but its widespread adoption would lead to further dependence on external suppliers and the spread of atomic wastes and nuclear technology around the world. We strongly prefer to support efforts to bring food production and marketing activities back to the local level, using appropriate technology, both here and in the third world.

[1] T. J. Weiss 1983, *Food Oils and Their Uses*, 2d ed. (Westport, Conn.: AVI)

[2] Weiss 1983, p. 50

[3] L. Balducci et al. 1986, "Nutrition, cancer, and aging: An annotated review," *Journal of the American Geriatric Society* 34:127–136; R. Kroes et al. 1986, "Nutritional factors in lung, colon, and prostate carcinogenesis in animal models," *Federation Proceedings* 45:136–141; D. C. Borg 1976, "Applications of esr in biology," in W. A. Prior, ed., *Free Radicals in Biology*, vol. 1 (N.Y.: Academic Press), pp. 130–131

[4] H. Yoshida & J. C. Alexander 1983, "Enzymatic hydrolysis in vitro of thermally oxidized sunflower oil," *Lipids* 18(9):611–616; J. C. Alexander 1981, "Chemical and biological properties related to toxicity of heated fats," *Journal of Toxicology and Environmental Health* 7:125–138; B. Kantorowitz & S. Yannai 1974, "Comparison of the tendencies of liquid and hardened soybean oils to form physiologically undesirable materials under simulated frying conditions," *Nutrition Reports International* 9(5):331–341

[5] R. S. Smith, *Nutrition, Hypertension and Cardiovascular Disease* (Gilroy, Calif.: Lyncean Press), pp. 13–15

[6] D. R. Lineback & G. E. Inglett, eds., 1982, *Food Carbohydrates* (Westport, Conn.: AVI); G. G. Birch & K. J. Parker 1979, *Sugar: Science and Technology* (London: Elsevier)

[7] L. Sestoft 1983, "Fructose and health," in J. Weininger & G. M. Briggs, *Nutrition Update*, vol. 1 (N.Y.: Wiley), pp. 39–53

[8] B. Bosetti et al. 1984, "The effects of physiologic amounts of simple sugars on lipoprotein, glucose, and insulin levels in normal subjects," *Diabetes Care* 7(4):309–311

[9] Sestoft 1983, p. 46

[10] J. Hallfrisch et al. 1983, "Effects of dietary fructose on plasma glucose and hormone responses in normal and hyperinsulinemic men," *Journal of Nutrition* 113:1819–1826

[11] E. G. Gottschall & D. B. McMillan 1985, "Structural changes in rat hepatocytes following ingestion of sugar solutions," *Acta Anatomica* 123(3):178–188

[12] Sestoft 1983, pp. 44–45

[13] T. Rebello, R. E. Hodges, & J. L. Smith 1983, "Short-term effect of various sugars on antinatriuresis and blood pressure changes in normotensive young men," *American Journal of Clinical Nutrition* 38:84–94

[14] W. J. Ravich, T. M. Bayless, & M. Thomas 1983, "Fructose: Incomplete intestinal absorption in humans," *Gastroenterology* 84:26–29

[15] N. J. Greenburger 1983, "Sugar pains," *Family Practice News*, May 1, p. 4

[16] L. Brewster & M. Jacobson 1978, *The Changing American Diet* (Washington, D.C.: Center for Science in the Public Interest), p. 47

[17] S. Yannai 1980, "Toxic factors induced by processing," in I. E. Liener, ed., *Toxic Constituents of Plant Foodstuffs*, 2d ed. (N.Y.: Academic Press), p. 413

[18] Yannai 1980, p. 414

[19] Food and Drug Administration (FDA) 1984, "Irradiation in the production, processing, and handling of foods," *Federal Register* 49(31):5714–22 (Feb. 14; Docket no. 81N-0004)

[20] FDA 1984, p. 5715

[21] S. S. Epstein & J. W. Gofman 1984, "Irradiation of foods" (letter), *Science* 223(4643):1354 (March 30)

[22] C. Bhaskaram & G. Sadasivan 1975, "Effects of feeding irradiated wheat to malnourished children," *American Journal of Clinical Nutrition* 28(2):130–135

[23] A. I. Levina & A. E. Ivanov 1978, "Pathomorphology of the kidneys in rats after prolonged ingestion of irradiated foods," *Bulletin of Experimental and Biological Medicine* 85(2):236–238

[24] A. F. Schindler, A. N. Abadie, & R. E. Simpson 1980, "Enhanced aflatoxin production by Aspergillus flavus and Aspergillus parasiticus after gamma irradiation of the spore inoculum," *Journal of Food Protection* 43(1):7–9

Conserving Nutrients in the Kitchen

Foods begin to degrade the moment they are harvested or gathered. Those with more moisture, such as greens or milk, decompose very rapidly. Drier foods, such as seeds or nuts, are meant by nature to last until they can bring forth a new plant in another season, so they keep much longer. How foods are handled can make quite a difference in their nutritional value.

In general, nutrients are lost through exposure of foods to heat, light, moisture, and oxygen in the air. Various nutrients are more or less susceptible to these different factors. The trick is to expose foodstuffs as little as possible to the factors which degrade them. Of the lot, cooking in too much water and then discarding the water accounts for the greatest nutrient loss overall.

VEGETABLES AND FRUITS

Freshest is best; time is the culprit. Grow your own for the quickest transit time from soil to table. Green leaves suffer the most nutrient loss in time, so grow these if you have just a little space. If you do buy them, try to keep only a few days' worth on hand.

When you buy vegetables, of course, don't choose any that are wilted or have the tiny gray or black spots that signal the onset of decomposition. Look too at the place where they've been cut from their plant or root. Is the cut new (moist and fresh) or old (dry and withered)? Is the skin still shiny, or has it become dull? Is the vegetable crisp or limp?

Once vegetables are in the kitchen, most of them should be stored in the refrigerator in a closed, airtight container—moist, but not dripping wet. Drier vegetables such as onions, winter squash, garlic, and potatoes like a cool, dry place.

When you prepare vegetables and fruits, trim minimally. Nutrients concentrate on the outside: in the outer leaves of greens, just under the skins of potatoes, carrots, and apples. Wash them well, but don't leave them soaking. Take care not to bruise or crush vegetables, particularly the leafy ones.

In cooking, nutrients are lost mostly through leaching at the cut surfaces, so more nutrients are preserved when pieces are larger. Skins act as a protective barrier to vitamin losses, so the ideal way to cook potatoes or beets is to steam them in large pieces or whole, then remove the skins and cut smaller after cooking.

Leaching losses are greatest when the vegetables cook in too much water. The following cooking methods preserve nutrients *best*, in this order: Pressure cooking, microwaving, steaming, stir-frying, cooking in minimal water, baking. Boiling should always be avoided unless you are using all of the cooking water—a practical method in making soups.

Time is also a factor: the longer vegetables are cooked, the more nutrients are lost. However, cooking does make some nutrients available that wouldn't be if the vegetables were eaten raw.

Leftovers, of course, have fewer nutrients than foods freshly cooked. Time and temperature are the critical factors. Hold leftovers a short time in the refrigerator, then eat them cold or reheat quickly; the nutrient losses will be slighter. If you keep them warm on top of the stove or in a thermos, nutrient loss will be significant, more so the more time elapses. Food safety becomes an issue here, by the way: cooked foods should not be held at temperatures between 50° and 120°F, the range in which bacteria flourish.

GRAINS

Don't wash whole grains before cooking unless they are visibly dirty (buckwheat groats often are). Rinse in cold water only. Cook whole grains in just the amount of water they will absorb (see chart, page 280) so that you don't have to pour off excess water and the nutrients in it.

There are four key words in storing whole grains and whole-grain flours: cool, dry, dark, and airtight. If these conditions are met, whole grains can keep for years. Whole-grain flour or meal, though, must be used fairly quickly. Cornmeal (see

page 50) is the most delicate. Brown rice flour also goes rancid quickly. Whole wheat flour is sturdier: refrigerated, it will keep for a good two months in airtight containers; outside the refrigerator, it will keep for a month provided those four conditions are met. Obviously, you will want to purchase flours and meals from stores where the turnover is very rapid. If you don't have a good source, consider getting a home grinder; the *Laurel's Kitchen Bread Book* has purchasing guidelines.

LEGUMES

Like grains, legumes should be stored in airtight, opaque containers in a cool, dry place. If you presoak them—an otherwise fine way to cut down on cooking time—you should know that a considerable amount of vitamins and minerals will leach out into the soaking water. Cook the beans in the soaking water or soak them in only as much water as they will absorb (usually about their own volume), so you have hardly any left to discard.

MILK

Milk should be stored in opaque or dark containers to avoid loss of light-sensitive riboflavin. Choose cardboard containers over the translucent plastic ones.

FATS AND OILS

Fats undergo destructive chemical changes when overheated. When you are heating oil to sauté vegetables, watch it closely: once oil begins to smoke, it has overheated and should be discarded. Just *before* the smoke point has been reached, the surface of heating oil will take on a rippled look. That's your signal to *quickly* add whatever vegetables you're about to sauté— their moisture will cool the oil sufficiently.

SOURCES

Robert S. Harris & Endel Karmas 1975, Nutritional Evaluation of Food Processing (Westport, Conn.: AVI)

H. A. Schroeder 1971, Losses of vitamins and trace minerals resulting from processing and preserving food, American Journal of Clinical Nutrition 24:562–73.

Suggestions for Further Reading

Beyond the scope of this book lies a much vaster field: the politics and economics of food. Here are some books we think everyone should read, for they help show the way to a hopeful, workable future:

Fukuoka, Masanobu. *The One-Straw Revolution: An Introduction to Natural Farming*. Emmaus, Pennsylvania: Rodale, 1978.

> Not really a book about farming, but practical, provocative philosophy about food growing and land use, distilled from a lifetime of experience.

Gussow, Joan, ed. *The Feeding Web: Issues in Nutritional Ecology*. Palo Alto, California: Bull Publications, 1978.

> A most enjoyable collection of readings on the widest range of food issues, brilliantly conceived and edited.

Lappé, Frances Moore. *Diet for a Small Planet*. Tenth anniversary edition. New York: Ballantine, 1982.

> Be sure you read this edition! Frances Moore Lappé ushered in a whole new way of thinking about vegetarian diet.

Lappé, Frances Moore, and Joseph Collins. *Food First: Beyond the Myth of Scarcity*. Second revised edition. New York: Ballantine, 1978.

> *The* book to start with for learning about the reasons behind food shortages in the world. The approach is very positive and practical.

MacFadyen, J. Tevere. *Gaining Ground: The Renewal of America's Small Farms*. New York: Ballantine, 1984.

> A vivid, well-written introduction to some of the men and women

around this country who are struggling to reinvent agriculture on a human scale.

Schwartz-Nobel, Loretta. *Starving in the Shadow of Plenty*. New York: Putnam, 1981.

A moving account of how one journalist began to unravel the story of hunger in America in the 1980s—personal, persuasive, and essentially hopeful on an issue that concerns us all.

Schumacher, E. F. *Small Is Beautiful: Economics As If People Mattered*. New York: Harper and Row, 1976.

If you haven't yet read Schumacher, do—an impassioned, sparkling-clear, commonsense plea for bringing human values and a human scale into all economic activities. The opening chapter deserves to endure as long as Thoreau's "On Civil Disobedience."

The Recommended Daily Allowances

The Recommended Daily Allowances or RDAs are standards for intake of each known nutrient, revised every four or five years by the Food and Nutrition Board of the National Research Council.

The RDAs are frequently referred to but often misunderstood.[1] They are *not* minimum daily requirements which individuals should meet to avoid falling into deficiency; and although the figures appear precise—for example, "2.2 milligrams of B-6 for men, 2.0 for women"—they are estimates based on research data but derived by committees whose members may differ in how the data should be interpreted. (See note, p. 460.)

As the Food and Nutrition Board itself emphasizes, the RDAs are "recommendations for the average daily amounts of nutrients that *population groups* should consume over time."[2] One person may need very little vitamin C, another a lot, but the RDA for vitamin C is set high enough statistically to cover almost everyone. Public health measures, such as school lunch programs, can then be pegged to these figures with some confidence that they will be adequate for the great majority of the people for which they are intended.

As individuals, do we have an alternative between taking the RDAs literally and just "making our own decisions"? Mark Hegsted has recommended one: a "nutritious mix of foods" in which any individual's needs for particular nutrients would be roughly proportional to the calories required[3]—in other words, just what we aim at with our Food Guide.

One final note: the RDAs are *not* the same as the "U. S. RDAs" on labels. The latter are FDA standards for the nutrient labeling of food products, still based by law on the *1960* RDAs.

(*Continued on page 460*)

The RDA "*is sometimes an unreasonable objective. A few women require 18 mg of iron, for example, but this cannot be achieved with any diet that is currently reasonable. Such a standard forces anyone who uses the* RDA *to make their own decision about what level of iron in the diet they should really try to obtain.*"[3]

If a person's intake of a given nutrient is consistently below the RDA, *that does not necessarily mean that he or she is deficient in that nutrient. "All that can be said is that the further intake falls below the* RDA, *the greater is the risk of nutritional inadequacy.*"[4]

Recommended Daily Dietary Allowances (RDA)

Food and Nutrition Board, National Research Council (Revised 1980)*

	Age years	Weight kg	Weight lbs	Height cm	Height in	Energy needs kcal	Protein g	Vit. A[a] RE[b]	Vit. A[a] IU[c]	Vit. D[d] IU	Vit. E[e] TE
Infants	0 – ½	6	13	60	24	kg×115	kg×2.2	420	1400	400	3
	½ – 1	9	20	71	28	kg×105	kg×2.0	400	2000	400	4
Children	1 – 3	13	29	90	35	1300	23	400	2000	400	5
	4 – 6	20	44	112	44	1700	30	500	2500	400	6
	7 – 10	28	62	132	52	2400	34	700	3300	400	7
Men	11 – 14	45	99	157	62	2700	45	1000	5000	400	8
	15 – 18	61	134	176	69	2800	56	1000	5000	400	10
	19 – 22	67	147	177	70	2900	56	1000	5000	400	10
	23 – 50	**70**	**154**	**178**	**70**	**2700**	**56**	**1000**	**5000**		**10**
	51 +	70	154	178	70	2400	56	1000	5000		10
Women	11 – 14	44	97	157	62	2200	46	800	4000	400	8
	15 – 18	54	119	163	64	2100	46	800	4000	400	8
	19 – 22	58	128	163	64	2100	44	800	4000	400	8
	23 – 50	**58**	**128**	**163**	**64**	**2000**	**44**	**800**	**4000**		**8**
	51 +	58	128	163	64	1800	44	800	4000		8
Pregnant[g]						+300	+30	+200	+1000	400	+2
Lactating[h]						+500	+20	+400	+1000	400	+3

ESTIMATED SAFE & ADEQUATE DAILY DIETARY INTAKES OF SELECTED VITAMINS & MINERALS

Because there is less information on which to base allowances, these figures are not given in the main table of the RDA and are provided here in the form of ranges of recommended intakes.

	Age years	Vit. K μg	Biotin μg	Pantothenic Acid mg	Sodium mg	Potassium mg	Chloride mg
Infants	0 – 0.5	12	35	2	115 – 350	350 – 925	275 – 700
	0.5 – 1	10 – 20	50	3	250 – 750	425 – 1275	400 – 1200
Children	1 – 3	15 – 30	65	3	325 – 975	550 – 1650	500 – 1500
and	4 – 6	20 – 40	85	3 – 4	450 – 1350	775 – 2325	700 – 2100
Adolescents	7 – 10	30 – 60	120	4 – 5	600 – 1800	1000 – 3000	925 – 2775
	11 +	50 – 100	100 – 200	4 – 7	900 – 2700	1525 – 4575	1400 – 4200
Adults		70 – 140	100 – 200	4 – 7	1100 – 3300	1875 – 5625	1700 – 5100

* *Allowances are intended to provide for individual variations among most normal persons as they live in the U.S. under usual environmental stresses. Diets should be based on a variety of common foods in order to provide other nutrients for which human requirements have been less well defined.*

[a] *Assumed to be as retinal in milk during first 6 months of life. All later intakes are assumed to be half as retinol and half as beta-carotene when calculated from international units; as retinol equivalents, three fourths are as retinol and one fourth as beta-carotene.*

[b] *Retinol equivalents. One retinol equivalent = 1 μg of retinol of 6 μg of beta-carotene.*

[c] *International units. One international unit of vitamin A activity is equivalent to 0.3 μg of retinol (0.344 μg of retinyl acetate) and 0.6 μg of beta-carotene.*

[d] *As cholecalciferol. 10 μg cholecalciferol = 400 IU vitamin D.*

[e] *D-alpha-tocopherol equivalents. 1 mg d-alpha-tocopherol = 1 mg d-alpha-tocopherol equivalent.*

[458]

Vit. C mg	Folacin[f] μg	Niacin[g] mg	Riboflavin mg	Thiamin mg	Vit. B-6 mg	Vit. B-12 μg	Calcium mg	Phosphorus mg	Iodine μg	Iron mg	Magnesium mg	Zinc mg
35	50	6	0.4	0.3	0.3	0.5[h]	360	240	40	10	50	3
35	50	8	0.6	0.5	0.6	1.5	540	360	50	15	70	5
45	100	9	0.8	0.7	0.9	2.0	800	800	70	15	150	10
45	200	11	1.0	0.9	1.3	2.5	800	800	90	10	200	10
45	300	16	1.4	1.2	1.6	3.0	800	800	120	10	250	10
50	400	18	1.6	1.4	1.8	3.0	1200	1200	150	18	350	15
60	400	18	1.7	1.4	2.0	3.0	1200	1200	150	18	400	15
60	400	19	1.7	1.5	2.2	3.0	800	800	150	10	350	15
60	**400**	**18**	**1.6**	**1.4**	**2.2**	**3.0**	**800**	**800**	**150**	**10**	**350**	**15**
60	400	16	1.4	1.2	2.2	3.0	800	800	150	10	350	15
50	400	16	1.3	1.1	1.8	3.0	1200	1200	150	18	300	15
60	400	14	1.3	1.1	2.0	3.0	1200	1200	150	18	300	15
60	400	14	1.3	1.1	2.0	3.0	800	800	150	18	300	15
60	**400**	**13**	**1.2**	**1.0**	**2.0**	**3.0**	**800**	**800**	**150**	**18**	**300**	**15**
60	400	13	1.2	1.0	2.0	3.0	800	800	150	10	300	15
+20	800	+2	+0.3	+0.4	+0.6	+1.0	+400	+400	+25	[i]	+150	+5
+40	600	+5	+0.5	+0.5	+0.5	+1.0	+400	+400	+50	[i]	+150	+10

NOTE: *Since the toxic levels for many trace elements may be only several times usual intakes, the upper levels for the trace elements given on this page should not be habitually exceeded.*

Copper mg	Manganese mg	Fluoride mg	Chromium mg	Selenium mg	Molybdenum mg
0.5 – 0.7	0.5 – 0.7	0.1 – 0.5	0.01 – 0.04	0.01 – 0.04	0.03 – 0.06
0.7 – 1.0	0.7 – 1.0	0.2 – 1.0	0.02 – 0.06	0.02 – 0.06	0.04 – 0.08
1.0 – 1.5	1.0 – 1.5	0.5 – 1.5	0.02 – 0.08	0.02 – 0.08	0.05 – 0.1
1.5 – 2.0	1.5 – 2.0	1.0 – 2.5	0.03 – 0.12	0.03 – 0.12	0.06 – 0.15
2.0 – 2.5	2.0 – 3.0	1.5 – 2.5	0.05 – 0.2	0.05 – 0.2	0.1 – 0.3
2.0 – 3.0	2.5 – 5.0	1.5 – 2.5	0.05 – 0.2	0.05 – 0.2	0.15 – 0.5
2.0 – 3.0	2.5 – 5.0	1.5 – 4.0	0.05 – 0.2	0.05 – 0.2	0.15 – 0.5

[f] *The folacin allowances refer to dietary sources as determined by* Lactobacillus casei *assay after treatment with enzymes ("conjugases") to make polyglutamyl forms of the vitamin available to the test organism.*

[g] *1 NE (niacin equivalent) = 1 mg of niacin or 60 mg of dietary tryptophan.*

[h] *The RDA for vitamin B-12 in infants is based on average concentration of the vitamin in human milk. The allowances after weaning are based on energy intake (as recommended by the American Academy of Pediatrics) and consideration of other factors such as intestinal absorption.*

[i] *The increased requirement during pregnancy cannot be met by the iron content of habitual American diets nor by the existing iron stores of many women; therefore the use of 30–60 mg of supplemental iron is recommended. Iron needs during lactation are not substantially different from those of pregnant women, but continued supplementation of the mother 2–3 months after parturition is advisable in order to replenish storers depleted by pregnancy.*

[459]

THE TENTH (1985) EDITION OF THE RDAS

[1] C. W. Callaway 1985, "Nutrition," in "Contempo '85" (annual review), Journal of the American Medical Association 254(16):2338–40 (Oct. 25)

[2] Food and Nutrition Board, National Research Council, 1980, Recommended Dietary Allowances, 9th ed. (Washington, D.C.: National Academy of Sciences)

[3] D. M. Hegsted 1986, "Dietary standards: Guidelines for prevention of deficiency or prescription for total health?" Journal of Nutrition 116(3):478–481

[4] A. E. Harper 1986, "Recommended dietary allowances in perspective," Food and Nutrition News 58(2):7–9

[5] "Lower nutrient levels proposed in draft report on American diet," N. Y. Times, Sept. 23, 1985, p. 1

As a standard for public health policies, the RDAs inevitably have political ramifications, and it should be remembered that they are set by human beings with different ways of interpreting the data and the task before them.

Such divergences came to a head in 1985, when the RDA committee, despite internal disagreement, submitted a draft of the new (tenth) revision of the RDAs which the parent body, the National Research Council, refused to publish. Among other things, the draft called for lower levels of vitamins A and C than the 1980 standards, despite evidence that higher levels of these vitamins protect against cancer. Questioned about this, one member of the committee replied, "We did not concern ourselves with chronic diseases; our task was to focus on specific nutrients."[5] Some nutritionists also expressed concern that such lower values would justify lower standards for school lunch, infant nutrition, and other public health programs, to which the committee replied that scientific standards could not be set in anticipation of public policy.

These disagreements have not been resolved, with the result that the ninth edition of the RDAs, published in 1980, is still current, and the only part of the controversial tenth edition that has been published comes from a copy "leaked" to the *New York Times*.[5]

THE U.S. RDA

"U.S. Recommended Daily Allowances"– Food and Drug Administration standards for nutrition labeling of foods, based by law on the 1960 RDA.

	Adults and children over 4	Infants and children under 4		Adults and children over 4	Infants and children under 4
Protein	65 g	28 g	Vitamin B-6	2 mg	0.7 mg
Vitamin A	5000 IU	2500 IU	Folacin	0.4 mg	0.2 mg
Vitamin C	60 mg	40 mg	Vitamin B-12	6 µg	3 µg
Thiamin	1.5 mg	0.7 mg	Phosphorus	1 g	0.8 g
Riboflavin	1.7 mg	0.8 mg	Iodine	150 µg	70 µg
Niacin	20 mg	9 mg	Magnesium	400 mg	200 mg
Calcium	1 g	0.8 g	Zinc	15 mg	8 mg
Iron	18 mg	10 mg	Copper	2 mg	1 mg
Vitamin D	400 IU	400 IU	Biotin	0.3 mg	0.15 mg
Vitamin E	30 IU	10 IU	Pantothenic acid	10 mg	5 mg

* Labels for nonfood vitamin – mineral supplements follow a slightly different format.

Nutrient Composition of Foods

Except in a few cases—iron in some red-pigmented plants, magnesium in the chlorophyll of green leaves, beta-carotene (provitamin A) coloring foods dark yellow or orange—the nutrient content of foods is not visible. How are we to know what measure of nutrients a food contains? Food composition tables provide the best available approximation.

"Approximation" is, however, the right term. Averages, estimates, missing data, derived data, guesswork, and plain old uncertainty are inherent features of even the most elaborate food composition tables. Yet because they look so complete and precise, this "ballpark guesstimate" feature often goes unsuspected.

It is not that food scientists can't measure nutrient levels accurately; they can. But a great many other factors affect whether the apple in your hand will contain the nutrients listed in USDA Handbook 8 under "Apple, raw, medium, 3″ diameter." Weather conditions while growing, soil type, soil minerals, fertilizer used (if any), variety, water source, storage conditions, and many other factors can significantly alter nutrient levels. With cooked foods a whole new set of variables enters in—cooking times and temperatures, amount of cooking water used, and so on.

With such a wide range of variation, two patty pan squashes, for example, can differ in their nutrient content as much as a patty pan and a crookneck. In practical terms, as Pennington has demonstrated rigorously,[1] this means that average values for a representative food can stand for other foods in the same family. We follow Pennington's principle here, letting one variety of summer squash, say, represent all the others.

[1] *Pennington 1976, Dietary Nutrient Guide (Westport, Conn.: AVI). Pennington's "mini-list" of 300 foods represents all the 3500 foods in the exhaustive USDA Handbook 8 (1964).*

GRAINS AND FLOURS

	Calories Kcal / Protein g	Fiber g / Carbohydrate g	Fat g / Vitamin A IU	Vitamin E mg / Vitamin C mg	Folacin mg / Riboflavin mg	Niacin mg / Vitamin B-6 mg	Pantothenic mg / Thiamin mg	Calcium mg / Magnesium mg	Iron mg / Zinc mg	Sodium mg / Potassium mg
Barley, whole-grain, naked[a]	99	.4	.8			1.74		11.6	.85	.5
½ cup cooked	3.05		0	0	.019		.105			128
pot or Scotch[a]	100	2.3	.8	.85	6	1.05	.186	9.5	.775	.5
½ cup cooked	2.75	22	0	0	.020	.069	.060	16.5	.58	85
pearl, light[a]	98	2.2	.28	.212	5	.85	.125	3	.585	1
½ cup cooked	2.3	22	0	0	.011	.043	.024	6.2	.575	36
Buckwheat, whole grain (kasha)	104	2.55	.8			.8		14	1	.5
½ cup cooked	3.45	24	0	0	.037		.065			153
Buckwheat flour, dark	338	8	2.5	7.75	125	2.75	1.42	32	2.5	1
1 cup sifted	11.5	70.6	0	0	.155	.405	.578	135	2.65	490
light	340	6	1.13	4.5	100	.467	1	11	1	1
1 cup sifted	6.35	77.9	0	0	.047	.090	.091	47	2.56	314
Cornmeal, unbolted[b]	433	1.95	4.75			2.44		24.4	2.92	
1 cup	11.2	89.9	[c]372	0	.134		.463			346
Corn flour	431	1.6	3.04	1.23	19.9	1.64	.643	7	2.1	1
1 cup sifted	9.10	89.9	400	0	.070	.070	.234	124	2.92	140
Corn grits (hominy), degermed	73	.375	.25	.184	1	.98	.041	.5	.775	0
enriched, ½ cup cooked	1.75	15.7	72.5	0	.075	.029	.12	5.5	.087	27
Masa Harina[d]	407	11.5	4.5	2.34	25	9.97	.508	231	8.79	10
1 cup	10.5	82.2	0	0	.739	.427	1.29	123	3	360
Millet, whole-grain	54	1.3	.5	.29	10	.4	.1	3	1.1	1
½ cup cooked	1.4	10.8	0	0	.060	.030	.1	38	.42	64
Oats, rolled	72.5	1.25	1.2	.255	4.75	.15	.234	10	.795	.5
½ cup cooked	3	12.6	19	0	.025	.023	.13	28	.575	66
Popcorn, large kernel, popped, plain	23	1.45	.3		3	.1		1	.27	
1 cup	.8	4.6	8	0	.010	.012	.001	23	.223	
butter and salt added	41	1.45	2		3	.2		1	.27	175
1 cup	.9	5.3	8	0	.010	.013	.001	25	.285	
Quinoa	118	1	1.76			.47		41.1	2.64	2.94
½ cup cooked	5.29	20.5	118	2.11	.1	.294	.088	70.5	.705	209
Rice, brown, long-grain	116	2.25	.78	.55	6	1.35	.342	13	.7	4.5
½ cup cooked	2.45	24.8	0	0	.020	.116	.090	28	.825	68.5
Rice, parboiled (converted)	93	.6	.175	.236	3.35	1.05	.228	16.5	.7	4.5
½ cup cooked	1.85	20.4	0	0	.010	.065	.095	5.55	.281	37.5
Rice flour, brown	432	8.17	2.75	1.94	21.7	5.64	1.56	38.2	2.15	11.0
1 cup stirred	9.01	92.7	0	0	.059	.7	.378	124	2.17	218
Rice bran	16.5	.69	1.15	.893	2.34	1.78	.174	4.56	1.16	0
1 tablespoon	.798	3.04	0	0	.015	.21	.135	4.96	.029	89.7
Rice polishings	17.3	.157	.837	.375	13.2	1.85	.229	4.5	1.05	
1 tablespoon	.793	3.78	0	0	.011	.137	.12			46.8

[a] Pearling removes the hulls and outer portions of the kernel by abrasive action. What remains after the first 3 pearlings is sold as Scotch or pot barley; pearl barley is what remains after 6 pearlings, having lost about 74 percent of the grain's protein, 85 percent of the fat, 97 percent of the fiber, and 88 percent of the mineral constituents of the original barley.

[b] Bolted cornmeal retains 95 percent of the original kernel; the hull is removed by crude sifting but the germ and endosperm remain. Degermed meal and grits are highly refined; both bran and germ are completely removed. Enrichment may then be added.

[c] Values based on yellow varieties. White varieties have only trace amounts of vitamin A.

[d] The Mexican method of preparing cornmeal is to grind it with lime water, which adds calcium. The product shown here is also enriched with niacin, iron, thiamin, and riboflavin.

	Calories (Kcal) / Protein (g)	Fiber (g) / Carbohydrate (g)	Fat (g) / Vitamin A (IU)	Vitamin E (mg) / Vitamin C (mg)	Folacin (mg) / Riboflavin (mg)	Niacin (mg) / Vitamin B-6 (mg)	Pantothenic (mg) / Thiamin (mg)	Calcium (mg) / Magnesium (mg)	Iron (mg) / Zinc (mg)	Sodium (mg) / Potassium (mg)
Rye flour, dark	408	14.4	2.3	3.53	100	3.51	1.4	46	4.21	2
1 cup	17.4	89.6	0	0	.25	.416	.559	107	2.81	543
light	353	2.2	1.3	.95	55	.708	.734	27	1.12	1
1 cup sifted	8.57	78.2	0	0	.091	.092	.172	74	.816	202
whole	428	2.43	2.17			2.04		48.6	3.84	5.12
1 cup	15.4	90.1			.281		.55		7.68	640
Soy bean flour, full-fat	295	1.68	14.2	7.15	298	7.4	1.22	143	5.36	1
1 cup stirred	25.7	21.3	80	0	.218	.43	.573	170	.63	1162
low-fat	313	12	5.9	3.4	383	11.4	1.73	221	8.01	1
1 cup stirred	38.2	32.2	70	0	.318	.596	.761	254	2.75	1711
defatted	326	2.3	.9		400	12.9	1.8	265	1.73	1
1 cup stirred	47	38.1	40	0	.34	.69	1.09	310	4.87	
Triticale, whole-grain flour								39.4	6.19	5
1 cup	19.3		0	0					3.96	526
Wheat berries, hard red spring	42.0	1.05	.3	.528	9.00	.6	.15	4.50	.45	1.50
½ cup cooked	1.42	8.55	0	0	.015	.521	.060	17.5	.66	43.5
hard red winter	97.5	.8	.7	1.9		1.1	0	15.5	1.05	1
½ cup cooked	4	24.1	0	0	.025	.070	.11			121
Wheat, cracked	116	.65	1.1		.9	1.7		1.35	1	1
½ cup cooked	3.4	43.5	0	0	.020		.095		.945	128
Wheat, rolled	71	1.82	.35	.62	13.5	1.1	.182	9.5	.85	1
½ cup cooked	2.1	16.0	0	0	.035	.039	.085	29	.98	101
Wheat, bulgur (parboiled red wheat)	123	3.53	.475	.238	9	2.05	.112	13.5	1.43	1.5
½ cup cooked	4.75	22.1	0	0	.025	.035	.040	28.5	1.40	75.5
Wheat flour, whole wheat	400	11.5	2	4.74	70	5.2	1.2	49	5.16	4
1 cup stirred	16	85.2	0	0	.219	.709	.66	135	3.9	444
whole wheat pastry flour[e]	496	2.8				7.8		53	4.4	4
1 cup stirred	14	110	0		.18		.78			580
gluten flour (45% gluten,	529	.6	2.7					56		3
55% patent flour), *1 cup*	58	66	0				0			84
whole durum flour	398	11.5	4	6.2	87.5	5.28	1.64	44	52	36
1 cup stirred	15.2	84.1	0	0	.14	.63	.79	192	3.3	522
all-purpose (white), enriched, (unsifted), *1 cup*	455	3.75	1	2.89	30	6.6	.544	20	5.5	3
	13.1	95.1	0	0	.5	.225	.8	31	1.5	119
unbleached (white), unenriched	364	.3	1			.9		16	2.9	2
1 cup	10.5	76.1	0	0	.050		.060			95
Wheat bran, crude	4.75	.99	.103	.121	5.8	.607	.054	2.58	.243	.375
1 tablespoon	.36	1.38	0	0	.008	.031	.018	11.3	.292	25.6
Wheat germ, crude	17	.116	.51	.987	15.3	.196	.087	3.37	.281	.125
1 tablespoon	1.25	2.18	0	0	.031	.043	.094	15.7	.687	38.7
toasted	26.9	.168	.768	1.94	29.6	.395	.103	3.12	.544	.25
1 tablespoon	2.05	3.50	0	0	.058	.070	.118	22.6	1.18	66.8
Wild Rice	92	2.56	.2	2	35	1.6	3.86	5	1.1	2
½ cup cooked	3.6	19	0	0	.16	1.31	.11	32.8	1.17	55

DRY LEGUMES

Black beans	85	9.7	.4	.6	49	.4	.126	30	1.7	6
½ cup cooked	5.6	15.3	10	0	.040	.111	.090	80	1	195

[e] *Values adapted from those of whole-grain white wheat, a soft (low gluten content) wheat.*

	Calories Kcal / Protein g	Fiber g / Carbohydrate g	Fat g / Vitamin A IU	Vitamin E mg / Vitamin C mg	Folacin mg / Riboflavin mg	Niacin mg / Vitamin B-6 mg	Pantothenic mg / Thiamin mg	Calcium mg / Magnesium mg	Iron mg / Zinc mg	Sodium mg / Potassium mg
Black-eyed peas (cowpeas)	95	7	.4		71	.5	.207	25	3.75	6
½ cup cooked	6.4	17.2	15	2	.050	.070	.2	58.5	1.61	310
Garbanzo beans (chickpeas)	125	5.5	2.20	1	56.5	.65	.39	45.5	2.55	6
½ cup cooked	6.9	20.5	12.5	0	.052	.173	.095	60	1.31	258
Great northern beans	105	7.5	.55	.975	37	.65	.277	45	2.07	2.5
½ cup cooked	7	19.1	0	0	.065	.199	.125	38	.86	363
Kidney beans	113	9.7	.48	.575	57.5	.68	.205	26.5	3.33	2
½ cup cooked	7.45	20.5	5	.005	.053	.059	.101	41	1.01	355
Lentils	99	4.5	.475	.55	30.5	.585	.294	24.5	3.42	2
½ cup cooked	7.35	17.9	19	0	.052	.104	.076	26.2	.94	253
Lima beans, large or small	135	5.8	.59	3.1	95	.695	.33	26	2.94	2
½ cup cooked	8	25	0	12.5	.059	.146	.131	39.4	1.04	582
Mung beans	70.7	.831	.312			0		16.6	1.14	
½ cup cooked	5.30		0	0	0		0			166
Mung bean sprouts, raw	45	3.2	.2	.21	30	.8		20	1.4	5
1 cup	4	6.9	20	20	.2	.68	.14	22	1.47	234
cooked	42	6.1	.3	.080	17	1.1		22	1.1	6
1 cup cooked	5	6.5	30	14	.21	.48	.17	12.4	1.48	195
Navy beans (small white)	124	7.5	.56	1.02	54	.635	.421	47.5	2.49	1.5
½ cup cooked	7.95	22.5	0	0	.111	.362	.134	44.5	1.00	311
Peas, split	115	6.05	.3	.775	8	.9	.385	11.5	1.7	13
½ cup cooked	8	21	40	0	.090	.066	.14	35	.955	296
Pinto or Calico beans	125	9.39	.5	.475	72.5	.95	.215	47	2.85	2
½ cup cooked	7.3	23.3	5	0	.069	.174	.246	54.5	1.26	461
Soybeans	117	2.6	5.1	5.9	38	.575	.245	66	2.45	2
½ cup cooked	9.89	9.75	25	0	.077	.25	.192	.7	1.05	486
cooked, ground	146	3.23	6.34	7.34	47.2	.715	.305	82.1	3.04	2.48
½ cup	12.3	12.1	31.1	0	.096	.311	.239	.871	1.31	605
tempeh	117	.971	5.14	5.71	42.8	1.14	.342	47.8	1.88	.571
2 oz.	11.2	3.4	22.8	.914	.165	.257	.080	.685	.971	503
tofu	86	.1	5	4.2	55	.1	.212	154	2.23	8
piece 2½" × 2¾" × 1"	9.39	2.9	0	0	.076	.099	.18	133	.876	50
Soy grits	126	2.80	5.49	6.35	40.9	.619	.264	71.1	2.64	2.15
½ cup cooked	10.6	10.5	26.9	0	.083	.269	.207	.754	1.13	524
Soy bean milk, Cornell process,	73		3.3			.4		46	1.8	
unfortified, *1 cup*	7.5	5	90	0	.070		.18			

NUTS AND SEEDS

	Calories Kcal / Protein g	Fiber g / Carbohydrate g	Fat g / Vitamin A IU	Vitamin E mg / Vitamin C mg	Folacin mg / Riboflavin mg	Niacin mg / Vitamin B-6 mg	Pantothenic mg / Thiamin mg	Calcium mg / Magnesium mg	Iron mg / Zinc mg	Sodium mg / Potassium mg
Almonds, whole, shelled	106	2.53	9.56	4.08	17	.625	.098	41.5	.798	.625
2 tablespoons or about 12 nuts	3.25	3.45	0	.000	.163	.017	.044	47.8	.545	137
Almond butter (no salt added)	101	.24	9.46		10.4	.46	.041	43	.59	2
1 tablespoon	2.41	3.39	0	.1	.098	.012	.021	48	.49	121
Almond meal, home-ground	89.7	2.14	8.08	3.45	14.3	.528	.082	35.0	.674	.528
2 tablespoons	2.74	2.91	0	.000	.138	.015	.037	40.4	.46	116
Brazil nuts	52.8	.72	5.42	.52	.368	.142	.018	15.1	.228	0
2 large nuts	1.17	.885	.857	.002	.009	.011	.080	25.4	.382	58
Cashews nuts, roasted	98.1	1.06	7.97	1.92	11.8	.315	.202	6.62	1.12	2.62
2 tablespoons or 11 medium nuts	3	5.12	17.5	.001	.043	.049	.075	46.7	.831	81.2
Chestnuts, fresh, raw	70.5	2.45	1	2.7	24.5	.073	.171	13	.5	2.5
5 nuts	1.05	15.3	0	1	.080	.113	.080	14	.5	166
Cocoanut, fresh meat	157	6.13	15.8	.315	10.6	.134	.118	5.62	.832	9
piece 1⅓" × 1" × ½"	1.68	3.99	0	1.01	.011	.021	.020	22.0	.33	159
dried, shredded	493	23.5	49.5	.98	16	.464	.16	19	3.9	19
1 cup	5	11.5	0	0	.031	.821	.047	70.2	1.4	522

	Calories Kcal / Protein g	Fiber g / Carbohydrate g	Fat g / Vitamin A IU	Vitamin E mg / Vitamin C mg	Folacin mg / Riboflavin mg	Niacin mg / Vitamin B-6 mg	Pantothenic mg / Thiamin mg	Calcium mg / Magnesium mg	Iron mg / Zinc mg	Sodium mg / Potassium mg
Filberts (hazelnuts)	94.5	.914	9.70	3.35	10.8	.134	.172	34.3	1.21	.26
11 nuts	1.89	2.50	15	.000	.082	.084	.069	25.0	.352	99
Macadamia nuts, roasted	104	.915	11.3	2.55	10.2	.195	.137	7.2	.3	
6 whole nuts	1.17	2.38	0	0	.016	.042	.051	18.1	.399	39.6
Peanuts, no salt, *2 tablespoons*	106	1.51	9.23	3.05	20.1	3.20	.391	11.7	.391	1.49
or 18 Virginia or 36 Spanish	4.70	2.53	2.98	0	.024	.074	.212	33.7	.578	130
Peanut butter, commercial	93.6	.288	7.80			2.17		10.5	.384	97.1
1 tablespoon	3.98	3.55	0	0	.019	.001	.063			107
Pecans, *2 tablespoons*	101	.896	10.5	2.92	4.15	.135	.251	10.7	.383	.125
chopped or 12 medium halves	1.36	2.15	18.7	.275	.019	.028	.126	21	.595	89
Pine nuts	170	.252	13.4	1.7	19.2	.95	.256	38	1.5	
1 ounce	8.8	3.3	4	0	.167	.080	.25	75	1.2	208
Pistachio nuts	105	.875	9.43	.912	10.1	.246	.125	23.1	1.17	.625
2 tablespoons or 30 nuts	3.43	3.37	40.6	0	.070	.037	.12	27.5	.415	173
Pumpkin or squash seeds, dried	96.7	.332	8.17	1.87	16	.437	.357	8.87	1.75	5.25
2 tablespoons	5.07	2.62	12.5	0	.034	.015	.043	6.75	.925	173
Sesame seeds, whole, brown	106	1.18	9.21	4.25	25	1.01	.562	218	1.96	11.2
2 tablespoons	3.48	4.05	5.62	0	.045	.015	.183	33.8	1.65	136
hulled	109	1.12	10.0	3.82	18.7	.975	.517	20.6	.462	8.75
2 tablespoons	3.41	3.3	1.5	0	.023	.015	.028	16.8	1.24	142
Sesame seed meal, home-ground	84.5	.945	7.37	3.4	20	.81	.45	174	1.56	9
2½ tablespoons	2.79	3.24	4.5	0	.036	.012	.147	27.1	1.31	109
Sunflower seeds, kernels	101	.688	8.57	9.46	37.5	.993	.25	21.7	1.05	5.37
2 tablespoons	4.37	3.62	8.75	0	.041	.225	.356	6.87	.867	167
Sunflower seed meal, home-ground	83.7	.57	7.09	7.83	31.0	.822	.206	18	.87	4.44
2½ tablespoons	3.62	3	7.24	0	.033	.186	.294	5.68	.717	138
Walnuts, *8 to 13 halves*	97.6	.78	9.60	2.93	11.1	.142	.141	14.8	.525	.25
or 2 tablespoons chopped	2.22	2.37	5	.287	.020	.127	.050	19.7	.371	67.5

VEGETABLES

	Calories Kcal / Protein g	Fiber g / Carbohydrate g	Fat g / Vitamin A IU	Vitamin E mg / Vitamin C mg	Folacin mg / Riboflavin mg	Niacin mg / Vitamin B-6 mg	Pantothenic mg / Thiamin mg	Calcium mg / Magnesium mg	Iron mg / Zinc mg	Sodium mg / Potassium mg
Artichoke, cooked	31	3.7	.2	.018	36	.8	.354	61	1.3	36
1 medium (⅔ pound)	3.4	11.9	180	10	.050	.116	.080	32.4	.385	361
Asparagus, cooked	29	2.17	.3	3	114	2	.619	30	1.5	8
cut in 1½ lengths	3.2	5.2	1310	38	.26	.113	.23	14.5	.877	309
Avocado	457	7.94	43.4	3.79	175	5.44	2.75	30.7	2.83	29.6
one 3¼ diameter	5.62	21.0	1735	22.4	.345	.794	.306	111	1.21	1698
Beans, green lima, cooked	104	1.77	.27			.884	.218	27	2.08	14
½ cup	5.97	20.1	310	8.60	.082	.164	.119	63	.67	485
Beans, snap, green, 1" lengths	31	4.1	.25	1.38	50	.62	.22	63	1.19	5
1 cup	2	6.8	680	15	.11	.078	.090	32.5	.388	370
wax or yellow, 1" lengths	28	4.1	.3	.362	45	.6	.176	63	1.19	4
1 cup	1.8	5.8	290	16	.11	.039	.090	26	.35	189
Beets, cooked, peeled, diced or	56	4.75	.2	.050	133	.59	.204	34	1.34	73
sliced, *1 cup*	2.48	12	30	9.8	.069	.085	.042	31.4	.675	530
Beet greens, leaves and stems,	22.5	5.25	.275	1.57	113	.326	.164	113	1.38	82.5
cooked, *¾ cup*	1.76	4.31	6092	20.2	.174	.109	.064	77.2	.45	980
Broccoli, cooked, ½" pieces	34	9.39	.5	.5	98	1.2	1.08	132	1.37	27
1 cup	4.8	4.75	3880	140	.31	.201	.128	26.3	.4	324
Brussels sprouts, cooked	42	4.5	.6	1.36	56	1.2	.777	50	1.5	15
1 cup	5.42	6.3	715	135	.187	.31	.106	29.4	.589	372
Cabbage, raw, shredded or chpd.	16.8	2.19	.152	1.04	55.2	.24	.168	38	.403	8
1 cup	1.32	3.33	106	34.4	.035	.093	.040	12.8	.207	151
cooked, shredded	26	4.06	.3	.29	32	.4	.217	62	.81	16
1 cup	2.03	4.76	247	48	.052	.145	.052	10.4	.49	234

	Calories Kcal / Protein g	Fiber g / Carbohydrate g	Fat g / Vitamin A IU	Vitamin E mg / Vitamin C mg	Folacin mg / Riboflavin mg	Niacin mg / Vitamin B-6 mg	Pantothenic mg / Thiamin mg	Calcium mg / Magnesium mg	Iron mg / Zinc mg	Sodium mg / Potassium mg
Cabbage, red, raw, shredded or sliced	18	2.38	.12	.14	24	.3	.225	30.3	.392	18
1 cup	1.3	3.8	26	43	.037	.131	.050	11.4	.255	143
savoy, raw, shredded	19	2.2	.19	.14	42	.2	.147	47	.392	12
or sliced, *1 cup*	2.03	3.1	154	39	.046	.128	.039	11.2	.29	189
Cabbage, Chinese, (bokchoy) raw,	11	2	.1	.091	58	.6	.144	116	.392	18
1" pieces, 1 cup	1.1	2	2170	19	.070	.112	.040	9.8	.29	214
cooked	24	3	.3	.114	32	1.19	.092	252	.95	31
1 cup	2.4	4.1	5270	26	.14	.139	.070	11.1	.65	364
Carrot, raw	24.8	3.6	.13	.35	22.9	.481	.192	30.7	.367	34.0
1 medium 7 ½" × 1¼"	.667	5.82	7920	5.99	.039	.107	.044	13.3	.32	231
raw	38	3.2	.2	.535	35	.735	.294	47	.561	52
1 cup grated	1.02	8.89	12100	9	.060	.165	.068	20.4	.49	353
juice, from raw carrots	99		.8		5	1.7		83	1.7	
½ cup	2.5	22.3	25740	17	.080		.17		.31	801
cooked	39	6.8	.3	.744	37	.787	.279	54	.638	64
small cubes	1.16	9	16280	9	.071	.153	.079	14.2	.465	239
Cauliflower, raw, florets	23	2.4	.1	.168	54	.8	.7	29	.667	6
1 cup	2.64	3.9	52	90	.117	.223	.124	23.4	.402	374
cooked, florets	20	2.4	.3	.125	42	.8	.525	26	.619	13
1 cup	2.45	3.05	59	69	.087	.15	.092	16.2	.275	400
Celery, raw	15	7	.1	.66	14.4	.4	.503	50	.576	125
1 cup diced	1.09	3.15	304	11	.037	.116	.045	22.8	.144	340
cooked	14	6	.2	.3	9	.475	.42	62.5	.55	116
1 cup diced	1.05	2.87	390	7.5	.040	.090	.030	13.5	.15	277
Chard, Swiss, cooked, leaves	31	6.8	.4	1.3	57	.7	.23	128	3.2	151
1 cup	3.2	5.8	9450	28	.19	.117	.070	96	.589	961
Chives, raw, chopped	2.12	.193	.025		5	.037	.009	3.5	.137	.437
1 tablespoon	.1	.343	250	3.18	.006	0	.004	1.28	.018	16.2
Collard greens, cooked, leaves	63	7	1.3		89.9	2.28	.79	357	1.5	24
and stems, *1 cup*	6.8	9.7	14820	144	.38	.353	.21	87	.59	498
Coriander, (Chinese parsley,	2.5	.1	.073					12.2	.243	
cilantro), fresh, *¼ cup leaves*	.295	.323	346	1.31	.015		.009	3.25		67.7
Corn, sweet, cooked whole ear	72	4	.8	.493	50	1.1	.3	2	.52	1
one 5" × ¾" diameter	2.5	16.2	308	7	.086	.146	.102	37	.318	364
kernels	89	.49	1.05		38.1	1.32	.72	2	.5	14
½ cup	2.72	20.6	180	5.1	.059	.049	.176	26	.39	204
Cucumber, raw, unpared	3	.126	.022	.042	3.3	.075	.057	5.02	.227	1.5
6 slices from large cucumber	.195	.69	57.7	1.96	.009	.009	.008	2.1	.025	30.7
Dandelion greens, cooked	35	1.37	.63					147	1.89	46
1 cup chopped	2.1	6.72	12280	18.9	.184		.137			244
Eggplant, cooked	38	4.5	.4	.063	32	1	.367	22	1.08	2
1 cup diced	2	8.2	20	6	.080	.158	.1	24.6	.5	496
Endive, Belgian (Wiltloof or	8		.050		0	.265		.26	7	
chicory), raw, *head 5" to 7" long*	.53	1.7	0	5.3	.074	.024	.037	11		4
Endive, curly, or Escarole,	12	.75	.050		165	.35	.154	28	1.12	6
raw, *1 cup small pieces*	.875	1.27	1325	32	.042	.025	.030	5	.17	176
Ginger root, fresh	8	.11	.080		0	.077	.022	2	.050	1
5 slices, ⅛" thick, 1" diameter	.19	1.66	0	.6	.003	.018	.003	5		46
Jerusalem artichoke or Sunchoke,	34	.8	.1	.18	10	1.3	.27	19	2	2
raw, *4 small, 1½" diameter*	1.85	9.7	20	2.85	.060	.071	.142	10	.070	328
Kale, cooked, without stems	43	8	.8	6.93	45	1.8	.888	206	1.8	47
1 cup	5	6.7	9130	102	.2	.221	.11	37.4	.78	244
Kohlrabi, cooked	40	1.65	.2		13.3	.3	.135	54	.5	9
1 cup diced	2.8	8.7	30	71	.050	.125	.1	59.4	.322	426
Lambsquarters, cooked	43	2.1	.8			1.2		309	1.2	
½ cup	4.2	7.3	11600	80	.44		.16			

	Calo-ries Kcal / Protein g	Fiber g / Carbo-hydrate g	Fat g / Vitamin A IU	Vitamin E mg / Vitamin C mg	Folacin mg / Ribo-flavin mg	Niacin mg / Vitamin B-6 mg	Panto-thenic mg / Thiamin mg	Calcium mg / Magne-sium mg	Iron mg / Zinc mg	Sodium mg / Potas-sium mg
Leeks, cooked	24	3.9	.3	.8	7	.4	.1	61	2	6
1 cup	1.8	4.6	40	15	.030	.15	.070	13	.12	280
Lettuce, butterhead	14	1.65	.38	1.15	37.2	.37	.356	34	.9	6
2 cups chopped	1.22	2.44	1082	14.8	.078	.074	.070	12.4	.33	208
romaine or cos	20	1.65	.42	.556	196	.4	.308	74	1.21	8
2 cups chopped	1.4	2.26	2100	20	.080	.070	.060	8.8	.332	198
loose leaf and red	20	1.65	.42	.556	148	.4	.308	74	1.2	8
2 cups chopped	1.4	2.26	2100	20	.080	.070	.060	8.8	.332	198
iceberg	14	1.65	.32	.556	40	.364	.308	24	.628	8
2 cups chopped	1.17	2.26	360	7.4	.076	.076	.066	12	.27	198
Mushrooms (Agaricus), raw	15	4	.31	.1	16.5	2.9	1.54	4	1.19	7
1 cup cut or 3 large to 7 small	1.61	2.85	0	2.53	.303	.056	.070	9.10	.521	256
Mustard greens, cooked, leaves without stems, *1 cup*		7	.6	1.1	90	.8	.23	193	2.1	25
	3.1	5.6	8120	67	.2	.16	.11	35	.3	230
New Zealand spinach, cooked	22	1.1	.31			.702	.461	86	1.19	193
¾ cup	2.34	3.96	6520	28.8	.193		.054	58		183
Okra, cooked	46	5.12	.5		47	1.4	.416	147	1.18	3
1 cup slices or 9 pods, 3long	3.2	9.60	780	32	.29	.12	.21	65.6	.42	513
Onions, raw	3.25	.138	.011	.031	2.62	.018	.015	3	.038	1.06
1 tablespoon minced	.128	.925	4.31	1.06	.004	.010	.003	1.06	.024	17.4
cooked	60	2.8	.2	.55	26	.41	.21	50	.8	15
1 cup sliced	3	12.2	35	15	.065	.126	.060	10.5	.19	231
Onions, young green (scallions)	2.25	.193	.012		3.43	.037	.009	3.18	.125	.437
1 tablespoon chopped	.093	.512	125	2	.004	.003	.004	1.28	.023	16.2
Parsley, raw	1.25	.343	.023	.081	5.06	.045	.011	10	.060	1.87
1 tablespoon chopped	.153	.093	319	6.43	.009	.006	.004	1.74	.080	16.8
Parsnips, cooked	95	3.9	.8	1.55	43	.2	.35	70	.8	19
1 cup diced	2.15	22	50	16	.12	.060	.11	20	.277	588
Peas, green, raw	57	9.10	.295	1.01	65	2.15	.58	15	1.41	1.5
½ cup	4.45	10.1	465	19	.104	.118	.243	22.2	.73	248
cooked	99	17	.62	3.12	120	3.69	.483	29	2.41	2
1 cup	8.3	15.8	860	28	.178	.15	.425	30.9	1.04	314
frozen, cooked, drained	110	17	.57	1.04	120	2.7	.508	30	3	160
1 cup	8.39	19	960	21	.14	.153	.43	35	1.16	216
Peas, edible pods, raw	53	9	.15	2.71	30	.8	.75	43	.7	1
1 cup or 30 pods	3	11.3	680	26	.12	.16	.28	19	.41	170
cooked	47.7	9	.222	2.77	33.3	.762	.683	56.6	.555	1.11
1 cup	3.22	10.5	678	15.5	.122	.118	.244	19.3	.455	132
Peppers, sweet, green, raw	14.8	1.04	.222	.547	14.0	.394	.17	6.90	.641	8.88
1 pod 2¾" × 2½"	.986	2.59	306	94.7	.059	.192	.059	13.3	.091	148
cooked	11.2	.762	.227	.585	7.58	.289	.116	6.50	.292	6.50
1 pod 2¾" × 2½"	.686	2.02	224	51.3	.039	.102	.039	7.22	.146	79.8
red, raw	23.1	2.46	.246	.547	38.6	.394	.2	9.86	.962	8.88
1 pod, 2⅓" × 2½"	1.03	5.27	3295	151	.059	.192	.059	13.3	.091	148
Potato, peeled after boiling	105	3.9	.1	.083	17.4	2	.336	10	.8	4
2.5 diameter	2.9	23.3	1	22	.050	.246	.12	19.3	.411	556
peeled before boiling	90	3	.1	.083	17.1	1.6	.333	8	.7	3
2.5 diameter	2.6	19.6	1	22	.050	.246	.12	19	.383	385
baked in peel	145	4.4	.2	.090	21	2.7	.404	14	1.1	5
4¾" × 2⅓"	4	32.8	1	31	.070	.248	.15	28.4	.89	782
French fried	137	2.9	6.6	.291	11	1.6	.185	8	.7	15
10 strips	2.2	18	1	11	.040	.090	.070	12.5	.125	199
Potato, mashed with milk	135	5.1	1.5	.21	21	2.1	.459	50	.8	632
1 cup	4.4	27.3	40	21	.11	.378	.17	27.4	.56	548
Pumpkin, fresh	49	2.03	.17					37	1.4	3
1 cup cooked, mashed	1.76		2650	11.5	.191		.076	22		564

	Calories Kcal	Fiber g	Fat g	Vitamin E mg	Folacin mg	Niacin mg	Pantothenic mg	Calcium mg	Iron mg	Sodium mg
	Protein g	Carbohydrate g	Vitamin A IU	Vitamin C mg	Riboflavin mg	Vitamin B-6 mg	Thiamin mg	Magnesium mg	Zinc mg	Potassium mg
Pumpkin, canned	80	4.5	.7	1.15	43	1.5	.98	61	1	12
1 cup cooked	2	19	15680	12	.125	.137	.066	24.5	.45	588
Radishes, raw	8	.475	.5	0	10.8	.278	.121	13	.56	6
10 medium, ¾" to 1" diameter	.53	1.6	1	13	.020	.196	.020	6.5	.088	161
Rhubarb, raw	26	3.17	.24	.244	8.7	.366	.104	105	.27	5
1 cup diced	1.09	5.53	122	9.8	.037	.029	.024	14	.13	351
Rutabagas, cooked, cubed or sliced, *1 cup*	60	4.8	.2	.255	36	1.4	.119	90	.5	8
	1.5	13.9	940	36	.1	.204	.1	11.9	.322	284
Salsify, cooked	40	3.8	.8			.3		57	1.71	11
1 cup cubed	3.5	20.4	10	9	.050	.192	.040	18.9		251
Soybeans, fresh, cooked	127	1.67	5.76					131	2.25	
½ cup	11.2	9.95	140	15.3	.14		.234			
Sea vegetables, Arame	24.3	.79	.076			.151		67.6	1.10	96.5
7.8 grams, ¼ cup dry	.724	5.18	57.5	.912	.050	.004	.003			282
Hijiki	18.9	1.01	.074		1.7	.111		60.7	4.96	203
7.8 grams	.67	3.89	184	.608	.036		.003			
Kombu	3.35	.103	.043		14.0	.036		13.1	.222	18.1
2 strips or 7.8 grams	.131	.746	9.35	.158	.011	.015	.003	9.43		6.94
Nori	9		.030			.152		7.6	.18	4
1 sheet or 2.5 grams	.88	1.23	528	2.1	.062		.020			
Wakame	3.51	.042	.049			.124		11.7	.17	68.0
7.8 grams	.236	.712	28.0	.234	.017		.004	8.34	.029	3.9
Spinach, raw	28	7.8	.36	3.02	212	.6	.334	102	2.96	98
2 cups chopped	3.6	4	8920	.56	.22	.25	.116	96.8	.618	518
cooked	30	8.47	.375	2.36	128	.674	.283	125	3	70.5
¾ cup	3.75	4.5	10935	37.5	.195	.243	.096	91.5	.817	437
Sprouts, Alfalfa, raw	9.66	.666	.127		5	.386		8.33	.39	
1 cup	.95	1.08	133	4	.041	.018	.032	3.33	.219	20
Mung bean, raw	45	3.2	.2	.21	30	.8		20	1.4	5
1 cup	4	6.9	20	20	.2	.68	.14	22	1.47	234
cooked	42	6.1	.3	.080	17	1.1		22	1.1	6
1 cup	5	6.5	30	14	.21	.48	.17	12.4	1.48	195
Squash, summer (zucchini, yellow, or scalloped), raw, *1 cup sliced*	25	3.5	.13	.156	40	1.3	.455	36	.559	1
	1.4	5.5	530	29	.119	.089	.070	20	.26	263
1 cup cooked	29	5.8	.2	.252	32	1.7	.147	53	.76	5
	1.9	6.5	820	21	.17	.063	.11	33.6	.434	296
Squash, winter, (all varieties)	93	6.88	.73	1.25	49	1.2	.442	49	1.04	2
1 cup, boiled, mashed	2.7	22.5	8580	20	.245	.122	.098	34	.343	632
baked	130	9.10	.82	1.35	84	1.44	.578	57	1.43	2
1 cup mashed	3.7	31	8610	27	.267	.186	.103	34.8	.65	945
Sweet potato, baked in skin, then peeled, *5" × 2"*	160	4.1	.753	6.04	39	.8	.753	46	1	17
	2.4	37	9230	25	.080	.198	.1	13.7	.185	342
boiled in skin, then peeled	170	4	.753	6.04	38	.9	.997	48	1.1	23
5" × 2"	3	40	11940	26	.090	.196	.14	18.1	.185	367
Tomato, raw	25	2.03	.2	.944	53	.9	.432	16	.648	15
whole 2½" diameter	1	6	1110	28	.052	.141	.075	16.8	.21	300
cooked from raw	63	5.74	.5	1.58	36	1.8	.922	36	1.4	10
1 cup	3.1	13.3	2410	58	.12	.193	.17	31.3	.491	688
canned, with liquid	50	2.2	.491	.53	56	1.7	.471	14	1.46	390
1 cup	2	10	2170	41	.071	.254	.12	28.9	.335	523
paste	26.8	.35	.125	.387	4.5	1.01	.252	8.87	.975	9.5
2 tablespoons or 1 ounce	1.11	6.08	1081	.16	.038	.124	.065	6.5	.062	301
juice, canned	45	.486	.24	1.13	45	1.9	.668	17	2.2	696
1 cup	2	10	1940	39	.073	.464	.121	20.6	.305	552
Turnip, raw	33	4.22	.317	.032	26	.8	.26	64	.623	62
1 cup diced	1.17	6.75	0	40	.078	.13	.052	17.6	.156	320

	Calories Kcal	Fiber g	Fat g	Vitamin E mg	Folacin mg	Niacin mg	Pantothenic mg	Calcium mg	Iron mg	Sodium mg
	Protein g	Carbohydrate g	Vitamin A IU	Vitamin C mg	Riboflavin mg	Vitamin B-6 mg	Thiamin mg	Magnesium mg	Zinc mg	Potassium mg
Turnip, cooked	35	4.1	.382	.023	23	.5	.217	54	.61	48
1 cup diced	1	8	1	34	.080	.093	.060	10.6	.167	291
Turnip greens, cooked	30	5.65	.3	1.5	161	.7	.386	252	1.5	10
1 cup	3.2	4.8	8270	68	.33	.214	.15	44	.7	316
Water chestnuts, Chinese,	6.33	.833	.025		2.5	.112		.666	.107	5
canned, raw, *4 chestnuts*	.1	1.42	0	.275	.003		.002	.976	.069	96.5
Watercress, raw, 10 sprigs	1.92	.329	.030	.099	20	.090	.020	18.5	.176	5.6
	.223	.304	445	7.12	.017	.012	.010	1.84	.017	29.5

FRUITS

	Calories Kcal	Fiber g	Fat g	Vitamin E mg	Folacin mg	Niacin mg	Pantothenic mg	Calcium mg	Iron mg	Sodium mg
	Protein g	Carbohydrate g	Vitamin A IU	Vitamin C mg	Riboflavin mg	Vitamin B-6 mg	Thiamin mg	Magnesium mg	Zinc mg	Potassium mg
Apple, raw with peel	81	4.28	.49	.767	3.9	.106	.084	10	.25	1
2¾" diameter (3 per pound)	.27	21	74	7.8	.019	.066	.023	6	.050	159
cooked, unsweetened	96	4.78	.71	.459	.9	.104	.078	8	.28	1
1 cup	.48	24.5	68	.5	.019	.078	.029	6	.060	159
Apple juice, unsweetened (bottled	116	.52	.28	.025	.59	.248	.001	16	.92	5
or canned), *1 cup*	.15	29	2	2.3	.042	.074	.052	8	.070	296
Applesauce, unsweetened, canned	106	5.12	.12	.122	2.44	.459	.232	7	.29	5
1 cup	.4	27.5	70	2.9	.061	.063	.032	7	.060	183
Apricots, fresh, whole	51	2.23	.41	.944	9.10	.636	.254	15	.58	1
3 medium	1.48	11.8	2769	10.6	.042	.057	.032	8	.28	313
dried, sulfured	49.8	.912	.096	1.08	2.16	.63	.158	9.60	.99	1.8
6 halves	.768	12.9	1520	2.58	.031	.033	.001	9.60	.156	289
Banana, fresh	105	3.85	.547	.393	24	.616	.296	7	.353	1
8¾" × 1¼" diameter	1.18	26.7	92	10.3	.114	.659	.051	32.4	.19	451
mashed	207	7.6	1.08	.776	47	1.22	.585	13	.698	2
1 cup	2.32	52.7	182	20.4	.225	1.3	.101	64	.37	890
Blackberries, boysenberries,	74	10.5	.56	.864	48.9	.576	.346	46	.634	0
youngberries, dewberries, *raw,*	1.04	18.4	237	30.2	.058	.084	.043	29	.39	282
Blueberries, raw	82	4.93	.55		9.3	.7	.135	9	.24	9
1 cup	.97	20.5	145	18.9	.073	.052	.070	7	.16	129
Cantaloupe	79.5	2.65	.728	.485	79.5	1.52	.473	28.1	.556	23.1
½ 5" diameter fruit	2.48	18.0	6921	89.4	.067	.245	.114	40.5	.243	818
Casava	43.4	1.64	.164	.158	38.5	.656	.241	8.68	.656	19.2
7¾" × 2" pieces	1.47	10.1	49.2	26.2	.032	.094	.098	13.5		344
Cherries, sweet	97.5	3.00	1.30	1.21	7.87	.544	.172	19.6	.529	.937
20 fruits	1.63	22.5	291	9.56	.081	.048	.068	15.0	.084	305
Cranberries, raw, whole	46	8	.19		2	.095	.208	7	.19	1
1 cup	.37	12	44	12.8	.019	.062	.029	5	.12	67
Dates, pitted	122	3.87	.2		7.25	.98	.347	14.5	.535	1.25
¼ cup chopped	.875	32.7	22.2	0	.044	.085	.040	15.7	.13	290
Figs, fresh	74	3.72	.3		3	.4	.3	36	.36	2
2 medium	.76	19.1	142	2	.050	.114	.060	16	.14	232
dried, uncooked	95.4	6.91	.436		3.17	.26	.162	53.8	.835	4
2 medium	1.14	24.4	49.6	.32	.033	.083	.026	22.2	.188	266
Gooseberries, fresh	67	4.8	.87	.555	8	.45	.429	38	.47	1
1 cup	1.32	15.3	435	41.6	.045	.12	.060	15	.18	297
Grapefruit, fresh, white	39	1.46	.12	.307	11.8	.317	.334	14	.070	0
½ of 4" diameter	.81	9.92	12	39.3	.024	.051	.044	11	.080	175
Grapefruit juice, fresh	96	.247	.25	.45	52	.494	.467	22	.49	2
1 cup	1.24	22.7	220	93.9	.049	.109	.099	30	.13	400
Grapes, with skin	114	3.2	.92		11.2	.48	.038	17	.41	3
1 cup or 32 fruits	1.06	28.4	117	17.3	.091	.176	.147	10	.090	296
Grape juice, bottled or canned	155	1.26	.19		6.5	.663	.104	22	.607	8
1 cup	1.41	37.9	20	.2	.094	.164	.066	24	.13	334

Food / Serving	Calories Kcal · Protein g	Fiber g · Carbohydrate g	Fat g · Vitamin A IU	Vitamin E mg · Vitamin C mg	Folacin mg · Riboflavin mg	Niacin mg · Vitamin B-6 mg	Pantothenic mg · Thiamin mg	Calcium mg · Magnesium mg	Iron mg · Zinc mg	Sodium mg · Potassium mg
Guava, fresh	90	10.6	1.08		25.2	2.16	.27	36	.56	4
2 fruits	1.48	21.4	1426	330	.090	.258	.090	18	.42	512
Honeydew melon, fresh	45.5	1.39	.129	.129	38.6	.774	.267	7.58	.091	12.9
7″ × 2″ piece	.584	11.8	51.6	31.9	.023	.075	.099	9.10	.111	350
Kiwi fruit, fresh	92	2.32	.68			.76		40	.62	8
2 fruits	1.5	22.6	266	149	.076		.030	46		504
Kumquat, fresh	120	7	.199					80	.7	10
10 fruits	1.7	31.1	600	71	.19		.149	20	.199	370
Lemon, fresh, no peel	17	1.19	.17		7	.058	.11	15	.35	1
one 2¼″ diameter	.64	5.41	17	30.7	.012	.046	.023	1.6	.064	80
Lemon or lime juice, fresh	3.75	.053	0		1.96	.015	.015	1.12	.005	.125
1 tablespoon	.057	1.31	3.06	7	.001	.007	.004	1	.007	18.9
Loganberries, fresh	104	9.25	.462	.447	38.8	1.25	.364	44.7	.955	1.49
1 cup	2.26	19.4	119	52.2	.050	.097	.074	32.8	.507	216
Loquats, fresh	50	.5	.199			.179		20	.299	0
10 fruits	.399	12	1500	1	.020		.020	10	0	260
Mango, fresh	135	3.11	.564	2.32	38.8	1.20	.331	21.3	.263	3.76
1 medium	1.06	35.2	8060	57.3	.117	.277	.12	18.8	.326	322
Nectarine, fresh	67.0	3.26	.62		5.12	1.35	.214	5.91	.204	0
1 medium, 2½″ diameter	1.28	16.0	1001	7.29	.056	.034	.022	10.8	.118	288
Orange, fresh	62	2.62	.16	.314	39.7	.369	.328	52	.136	0
1 medium	1.23	15.4	269	69.7	.052	.079	.114	13	.090	237
Orange juice, fresh	111	1.69	.5	.5	109	.992	.476	27	.3	2
1 cup	1.74	25.8	496	124	.074	.099	.223	27	.13	496
frozen, reconstituted	112	1.69	.14	.2	109	.503	.393	22	.274	5
1 cup	1.68	26.8	194	96.9	.045	.11	.197	24	.13	474
Papaya, fresh	117	3.98	.43		48	1.03	.663	72	.3	8
1 medium, 3½″ × 5″	1.86	29.8	6122	188	.097	.058	.082	31	.22	780
Peach, fresh	74	4.6	.16	1.74	6	1.72	.296	10	.192	0
2 medium, 2½″ diameter	1.22	19.3	930	11.4	.072	.032	.030	12	.24	342
sliced	73	4.5	.16	.17	5.8	1.68	.289	9	.187	1
1 cup	1.19	18.9	910	11.2	.070	.031	.029	11	.183	334
dried, sulfured	124	4.12	.396	.42	2.56	2.27	.2	14.8	1.12	3.6
4 halves	1.87	31.8	1125	2.52	.11	.034	.001	21.6	.3	518
Pear, fresh	98	3.82	.66	.825	12.1	.166	.116	19	.415	1
1 medium 3½″ × 2½″ diameter	.65	25.1	33	6.6	.066	.030	.033	9	.2	208
dried, sulfured	91.8	3.98	.22	.54	4.2	.48	.072	11.8	.415	2
2 halves	.656	24.4	1.2	2.46	.050	.002	.002	11.6	.136	186
Persimmon, fresh	118	3	.31		12.6	.168		13	.26	3
2½″ × 3½″ high	.98	31.2	3640	12.6	.034		.050	15	.18	270
Pineapple, fresh	77	2.95	.66	.163	16.4	.651	.248	11	.574	1
1 cup diced	.6	19.2	35	23.9	.056	.135	.143	21	.12	175
Pineapple juice, canned,	139	.75	.2		57.7	.643	.25	42	.65	5
unsweetened, *1 cup*	.8	34.4	12	26.7	.055	.24	.138	34	.29	334
Plums, fresh	119	8.58	1.35	1.52	10.5	1.09	.396	6.60	.231	0
3 whole, 2″ diameter	1.71	28.3	704	20.8	.208	.175	.092	13.2	.198	373
Prunes, dried, uncooked	117	7.87	.25		1.98	.962	.225	25.0	1.22	1.75
5 large	1.27	30.7	974	1.63	.079	.129	.039	22.1	.262	365
cooked, unsweetened	114	8.60	.245		.050	.765	.113	24	1.17	2
½ cup	1.23	29.7	325	3.1	.106	.231	.025	21.5	.25	354
Prune juice, bottled or canned	90.5	1.5	.040		.5	1.00		15	1.53	2.5
½ cup	.775	22.3	4.5	5.3	.089		.020	18	.26	353
Raisins, seedless	124	2.8	.19	.029	1.65	.337	.018	20.2	.865	4.75
¼ cup not packed	1.33	32.7	3.25	1.37	.036	.102	.064	13.5	.11	310
Raspberries, fresh	61	9.10	.68	.369	32.5	1.11	.295	27	.701	0
1 cup	1.11	14.2	160	30.8	.111	.070	.037	22	.57	187

	Calories Kcal / Protein g	Fiber g / Carbohydrate g	Fat g / Vitamin A IU	Vitamin E mg / Vitamin C mg	Folacin mg / Riboflavin mg	Niacin mg / Vitamin B-6 mg	Pantothenic mg / Thiamin mg	Calcium mg / Magnesium mg	Iron mg / Zinc mg	Sodium mg / Potassium mg
Strawberries, fresh, whole	45	3.38	.55	.298	28	.343	.507	21	.57	2
1 cup	.91	10.5	41	84.5	.098	.088	.030	16	.19	247
Tangerine, fresh	111	4.8	.48		51.3	.402	.504	36	.27	3
3 medium, 2⅜" diameter	1.58	28.1	2319	77.7	.053	.168	.264	30	.252	396
Watermelon, fresh	152	9.60	2.06	.482	10.4	.964	1.02	38	.819	10
slice 1" thick, 10" diameter	2.97	34.6	1762	46.5	.096	.694	.386	52	.34	560
diced	50	3.2	.68	.16	3.4	.32	.339	13	.272	3
1 cup	.99	11.5	585	15.4	.032	.23	.128	17	.11	186

DAIRY PRODUCTS AND EGGS

	Calories Kcal / Protein g	Fiber g / Carbohydrate g	Fat g / Vitamin A IU	Vitamin E mg / Vitamin C mg	Folacin mg / Riboflavin mg	Niacin mg / Vitamin B-6 mg	Pantothenic mg / Thiamin mg	Calcium mg / Magnesium mg	Iron mg / Zinc mg	Sodium mg / Potassium mg
Butter, salted	102		11.5	.224	.437	.006		3.37	.022	117
1 tablespoon	.12	.008	434		.004	.000	.000	.25	.007	3.62
unsalted	102	0	11.5	.183	.437	.006		3.37	.022	1.56
1 tablespoon	.12	.008	434	0	.004	.000	.000	.25	.075	3.62
Cheese: American (pasteurized)	133	0	10.6	.223	3	.024	.171	233	.127	508
1¼ ounces, 2 cubic inches	7.86	.562	429	0	.125	.024	.010	8.12	1.16	42.5
Bleu or Roquefort	105	0	8.95	.179	14	.208	.491	183	.172	513
1 ounces	6.11	.57	297	0	.166	.035	.011	8.14	.57	26
Camembert	106	0	8.58	.223	22.5	.223	.483	171	.127	299
1¼ ounce, 2 cubic inches	6.71	.162	328	0	.172	.080	.010	8.03	.987	52.5
Cheddar	143	0	11.7	.226	6.58	.028	.146	256	.241	220
1¼ ounce, 2 cubic inches	8.81	.454	375	0	.132	.026	.009	9.72	1.1	34.8
Cottage cheese, low fat	102	0	2.18	.725	15	.162	.273	77.5	.18	457
(2% fat), ½ cup	15.5	4.1	79	0	.209	.086	.027	7	.475	109
Cream cheese	99	0	9.52	.179	3.7	.029	.077	22	.338	84
1 ounce or 2 tablespoons	2.1	.75	405	0	.056	.013	.005	2	.125	33
Edam	126	0	9.75	.223	6.25	.028	.099	259	.167	343
1¼ ounce, 2 cubic inches	9.04	.5	325	0	.137	.027	.012	10.5	1.22	51.2
Mozarella	90	0	5.75	.223	3.75	.037	.027	229	.074	165
1¼ ounce, 2 cubic inches	8.75	.974	208	0	.107	.024	.006	8.75	1.03	30
Parmesan, grated	23.0	0	1.51	.031	.357	.015	.026	69.6	.048	94.2
1 tablespoon	2.10	.189	35.5	0	.019	.005	.002	2.51	.217	5.89
Ricotta, part skim	85	0	4.72	.392	7.5	.048	.1	196	.272	76.7
¼ cup	6.37	3.15	266	0	.113	.012	.013	1.07	.822	86.7
Swiss	134	0	9.37	.223	2.25	.032	.152	340	.193	92.5
1¼ ounce, 2 cubic inches	10.0	1.19	300	0	.128	.030	.007	12.5	1.37	37.5
Cream: Half and half (11.7% fat)	39.3	0	3.51	.108	.687	.023	.087	31.7	.021	12.2
2 tablespoons	.895	1.3	131	.26	.045	.011	.010	3.12	.153	39.2
Light (20.6% fat)	58.6	0	5.98	.188	.687	.017	.082	28.8	.012	11.8
2 tablespoons	.81	1.09	216	.227	.044	.009	.009	2.62	.081	36.5
Heavy whipping (37.6% fat)	103	0	11.1	.187	1.25	.011	.075	19.2	.008	11.1
2 tbs. liquid or ¼ c. whpd.	.61	.83	437	.172	.032	.007	.006	2.12	.068	22.3
Egg, chicken's, raw	79	0	5.58	.623	32.5	.031	.864	28	1.04	59
whole, one large	6.07	.6	260	0	.15	.060	.044	6	.61	65
whole	158	0	11.1	1.24	65	.062	1.72	56	2.08	118
½ cup (2 large or 3 medium)	12.1	1.2	520	0	.3	.12	.088	12	1.22	130
white of large egg	16	0	0	0	4	.128	.080	4	.010	50
cooked	3.35	.41	0	0	.090	.001	.002	3	.060	45
yolk of large egg	63	0	5.6	.385	19.4	.012	.753	26	.95	9
cooked	2.79	.040	313	0	.071	.050	.036	3	.55	15
Ice cream, regular (10% fat)	202	0	11.5	.369	2.25	.1	.49	132	.089	87
¾ cup	3.6	23.7	407	.525	.246	.045	.039	13.5	1.05	193
rich (16% fat)	262	0	17.7	.388	1.5	.086	.421	113	.075	81
¾ cup	3.09	24	673	.457	.212	.039	.033	12	.907	166

| | Calories Kcal | Fiber g | Fat g | Vitamin E mg | Folacin mg | Niacin mg | Pantothenic mg | Calcium mg | Iron mg | Sodium mg |
	Protein g	Carbohydrate g	Vitamin A IU	Vitamin C mg	Riboflavin mg	Vitamin B-6 mg	Thiamin mg	Magnesium mg	Zinc mg	Potassium mg
Ice milk (5% fat)	138	0	4.22	.343	2.25	.088	.496	132	.135	78.7
¾ cup	3.87	21.7	161	.57	.26	.063	.056	14.2	.412	199
Kefir, plain	160	0	4.5		20	.3		350	.5	50
1 cup	9.3	8.8	47	6	.44	.087	.45	28	.9	205
Milk, cow's: whole	150	0	8.14	.222	12	.205	.766	291	.12	120
(3.5% fat), 1 cup	8.02	11.4	307	2.29	.395	.102	.093	33	.953	370
low fat (2% fat, 2% nonfat	121	0	4.78	.146	12	.21	.781	297	.12	122
milk solids added), 1 cup	8.12	11.7	500	2.32	.403	.105	.095	33	.963	377
skim	86	0	.44	.001	14	.216	.806	302	.1	126
1 cup	8.35	11.9	500	2.4	.343	.098	.088	28	.915	406
buttermilk, cultured skim	99	0	2.16	.172	12.2	.142	.674	285	.12	257
1 cup	8.10	11.7	81	2.4	.377	.083	.083	25.8	1.03	371
evaporated, canned, skim	198	0	.52	.226	22	.444	1.88	738	.74	294
1 cup	19.2	29	1000	3.16	.788	.14	.114	68	2.18	846
whole	338	0	19.6	.454	18	.488	1.60	658	.48	266
1 cup	17.1	25.2	612	4.74	.796	.126	.118	60	1.98	764
condensed, sweetened, canned	982	0	26.6	.65	34	.64	2.3	868	.58	389
1 cup	24.2	166	1004	7.96	1.27	.156	.275	78	2.88	1136
whey, sweet, fluid	66	12.6	2.09			.182	.942	115	.15	132
1 cup	275	.89	100	.25	.389	.076	.089	20	.32	336
nonfat, instant, powder	244	0	.517		34	.606	2.2	837	.21	373
1 cup	23.9	35.5	1612	3.79	1.19	.235	.281	80	3.06	1160
Milk, goat's	168	0	10.1		2	.676	.756	326	.12	122
1 cup	8.68	10.9	451	3.15	.337	.112	.117	34	.73	499
Milk, human	21.3	0	1.35	.305	1.62	.054	.068	9.87	.008	5.25
2 tablespoons or 1 ounce	.316	2.12	74.1	1.53	.011	.003	.004	1	.052	15.7
Sherbet, orange	203	0	2.86		10.5	.098	.046	77.2	.232	66
¾ cup	1.62	44.0	139	2.89	.066	.018	.024	11.2	.997	149
Sour cream, cultured	61.6	0	5.66	.187	3.12	.019	.103	33.5	.017	14.2
2 tablespoons	.908	1.22	227	.247	.042	.004	.010	3.25	.086	41.3
Half and half, cultured	40	0	3.6	.108	4	.020	.108	32	.020	12
2 tablespoons	.88	1.28	136	.26	.044	.004	.010	4	.16	38
Yogurt, from whole milk	139	0	7.38		17	.17	.883	274	.11	105
1 cup	7.88	10.6	680	1.2	.322	.073	.066	26	1.34	351
from low fat milk	144	0	3.46		25	.259	1.34	415	.18	159
1 cup	11.9	16	150	1.82	.486	.111	.1	40	2.02	531
from skim milk	127	0	.41		28	.281	1.45	452	.2	174
1 cup	13	17.4	50	1.98	.531	.12	.109	43	2.2	579

COMMERCIAL FOODS

YEAST BREADS AND ROLLS

| | Calories Kcal | Fiber g | Fat g | Vitamin E mg | Folacin mg | Niacin mg | Pantothenic mg | Calcium mg | Iron mg | Sodium mg |
	Protein g	Carbohydrate g	Vitamin A IU	Vitamin C mg	Riboflavin mg	Vitamin B-6 mg	Thiamin mg	Magnesium mg	Zinc mg	Potassium mg
Whole wheat bread, firm crumb	84	1.75	1.12	.504	21	.98	.148	35	1.12	185
1 slice	3.63	16.7	1	.001	.042	.059	.084	27.3	.612	95
toasted	84	1.75	1.12	.504	21	.98	.148	35	1.12	185
1 slice	3.64	16.7	1	.001	.042	.059	.084	27.3	.612	95
soft crumb	65	1.4	.7	.434	15.6	.8	.119	24	.896	148
1 slice	2.6	13.8	1	.001	.030	.038	.090	21.8	.532	72
toasted	67	1.4	.7	.372	13	.8	.119	24	.896	148
1 slice	2.6	13.8	1	.001	.030	.028	.070	21.8	.468	72
White bread, enriched, soft	75	.747	.9	.2	11	.9	.122	24	.84	142
crumb, 1 slice	2.4	14.1	1	.001	.070	.011	.11	6.2	.196	29
French bread, enriched white	102	.070	1.1	.2	12.4	1.2	.133	15	.98	203
1 slice	3.2	19.4	1	.001	.080	.019	.14	7.7	.21	33

| | Calories Kcal | Fiber g | Fat g | Vitamin E mg | Folacin mg | Niacin mg | Pantothenic mg | Calcium mg | Iron mg | Sodium mg |
	Protein g	Carbohydrate g	Vitamin A IU	Vitamin C mg	Riboflavin mg	Vitamin B-6 mg	Thiamin mg	Magnesium mg	Zinc mg	Potassium mg
Rye bread (American), light	61	1.01	.3	.285	6.4	.7	.112	19	.675	139
1 slice	2.3	13	0	0	.050	.025	.065	10.5	.4	36
Pumpernickel	79	2	.4	.364	13	.6	.16	27	.928	182
1 slice	2.9	17	0	0	.070	.051	.090	22.7	.365	145

CRACKERS AND TORTILLAS

| | Calories Kcal | Fiber g | Fat g | Vitamin E mg | Folacin mg | Niacin mg | Pantothenic mg | Calcium mg | Iron mg | Sodium mg |
	Protein g	Carbohydrate g	Vitamin A IU	Vitamin C mg	Riboflavin mg	Vitamin B-6 mg	Thiamin mg	Magnesium mg	Zinc mg	Potassium mg
Ak Mak	29.2	.35	.582	.082	3	.262	.045	5.32	.112	
1 piece	1.16	4.72	3.5	.4	.010		.015	10.2	.225	
Graham crackers, plain	28	.7	.65		1	.252	.033	3	.194	47
one 2½" square	.55	5.2	0	0	.040	.002	.010	3.62	.078	27
crumbs	340	8.5	7.89		12.1	3.07	.4	36.4	2.35	571
1 cup, 85 grams	6.67	63.1	0	0	.485	.024	.121	43.9	.947	328
Ritz crackers	36	.266	1.93			.2		10	.2	64.6
2 crackers	.466	4.26		0	.026		.026	1.47		5.33
Ry-Krisp	22	.77	.1		12	.1		2	.3	50
triple cracker	.060	4.9		0	.010		.030	8	.81	33
Saltines	24.6	.022	.666		.666	.206	.016	1.16	.257	104
2 1⅞" squares	.5	4.06	0	0	.025	.005	.025	1.64	.003	6.66
Tortilla, corn, fried	142	1.2	8.10	1.5	.8	.3	.034	139	.855	16
1 tortilla	2.2	19.2	7	0	.020	.018	.010	20	.13	8
white flour	95	.57	1.8	.568	3.4	1.1	.077	35	.84	147
1 tortilla	2.5	17.3	2	.001	.080	.032	.021	6.45	.287	29
Triscuits	42	2	1.5							
2 crackers	.8	6.2		0						
Wheat Thins	36	1.47	1.4							42
4 crackers	.5	5		0						

OILS, FATS, AND COMMERCIAL SALAD DRESSINGS

| | Calories Kcal | Fiber g | Fat g | Vitamin E mg | Folacin mg | Niacin mg | Pantothenic mg | Calcium mg | Iron mg | Sodium mg |
	Protein g	Carbohydrate g	Vitamin A IU	Vitamin C mg	Riboflavin mg	Vitamin B-6 mg	Thiamin mg	Magnesium mg	Zinc mg	Potassium mg
Butter	813		92	1.79	3.5	.048		27	.18	935
1 stick, ½ cup or ¼ pound	.96	.070	3468		.039	.003	.006	2	.057	29
1 tablespoon or ⅛th stick	102		11.5	.224	.437	.006		3.37	.022	117
	.12	.008	434		.004	.000	.000	.25	.007	3.62
Margarine, regular or soft	815	0	91.5	12.5	1.35	.026	.095	30	.2	1070
type, *1 stick, ½ cup, ¼ pound*	1	1	3750	.181	.042	.010	.011	2.95	.227	48
Mayonnaise	98.5	0	10.9	3.37	.375	.001	.036	2.5	.068	78.1
1 tablespoon	.15	.3	38.7		.005	.004	.002	.277	.020	4.68
Oil, corn	1927	0	218	181	.001	0		0	0	0
1 cup	0	0	1	0	0		0		.4	0
1 tablespoon	120	0	13.6	11.3	.000	0	0	0	0	0
	0	0	.062	0	0		0		.025	0
Salad dressings, commercial, Blue cheese, *1 tablespoon*	77.1	.012	8	5	4.37	.012	.056	12.3	.031	8.31
	.737	1.13	32.1	.306	.012	.002	0	11.3	.038	6
French	67.1	.118	6.37	5	0			1.71	.062	214
1 tablespoon	.087	2.72						1.6	.012	12.3
Italian	68.6	.031	7.12	4.68	0			1.43	.031	116
1 tablespoon	.093	1.5							.016	2.18
Russian	75.6	.043	7.81	5	.000	.093		2.93	.093	133
1 tablespoon	.243	1.62	106	.937	.007		.007		.065	24.0
Thousand Island	58.9	.031	5.58	5	.6	.031	.034	1.75	.093	109
1 tablespoon	.143	2.37	49	.5	.005	.004	.003	.875	.025	17.6
Shortening, vegetable	113	0	12.8	4.12	.093	0		0	0	0
1 tablespoon	0	0	0	0	0		0		.006	0

	Calories Kcal / Protein g	Fiber g / Carbohydrate g	Fat g / Vitamin A IU	Vitamin E mg / Vitamin C mg	Folacin mg / Riboflavin mg	Niacin mg / Vitamin B-6 mg	Pantothenic mg / Thiamin mg	Calcium mg / Magnesium mg	Iron mg / Zinc mg	Sodium mg / Potassium mg
SWEETENERS										
Corn syrup, light	951	0	0		12	0		151	.328	223
1 cup	0	246	0	0	0		0	11	0	13
Honey	1031	0	0		34	1	.678	17	1.7	17
1 cup	1	279	0	3	.14	.064	.020	8	.27	173
1 tablespoon	64.4	0	0		2.12	.062	.042	1.06	.106	1.06
	.062	17.4	0	.187	.008	.004	.001	.5	.016	10.8
Malt, dried	104	1.6	.5			2.6			1.1	
1 ounce	.37	21.9			.090		.14			
Malt extract, dried	104		0			2.8		14	2.5	23
1 ounce	1.7	25.3			.13		.1	39.2		65
Maple syrup	800	0	0					528	3.84	48
1 cup	0	205	0	0				75.2	.16	416
1 tablespoon	50	0	0					33	.24	3
	0	12.8	0	0				4.7	.010	26
Molasses, light	688	0		1.31	41.6	.16	1.47	528	17.1	48
1 cup	0	176	0	0	.16	.752	.16	147	0	2928
1 tablespoon	43	0		.082	2.6	.010	.092	33	1.07	3
	0	11	0	0	.010	.047	.010	9.2	0	183
blackstrap	800	0		1.31	41.6	6.4	1.6	2192	70.7	304
1 cup	0	208	0	0	.64	.864	.32	826	0	9360
1 tablespoon	50	0		.082	2.6	.4	.1	137	4.42	19
	0	13	0	0	.040	.054	.020	51.6	0	585
Sugar, brown	821	0	0	0	0	.4		187	5.94	66
1 cup	0	212	0	0	.070	0	.020		.080	757
1 tablespoon	51.3	0	0	0	0	.025		11.6	.371	4.12
	0	13.2	0	0	.004	0	.001		.005	47.3
white, granulated	770	0	0	0	0	0	0	0	.2	2
1 cup	0	199	0	0	0	0	0		.080	6
1 tablespoon	48.1	0	0	0	0	0	0	0	.012	.125
	0	12.4	0	0	0	0	0		.005	.375
BEVERAGES (NONALCOHOLIC)										
Carbonated drinks: cola	136	0	0	0	0	0	0		.238	21.7
12 ounce bottle or can	0	34.8	0	0	0	0	0	.945	.066	2.83
fruit-flavored	156	0	0	0	0	0	0		.228	22.8
12 ounce bottle or can	0	40.7	0	0	0	0	0	0	0	0
Chocolate drink (with low-fat milk)	179	.15	5	1.5	12	.315	.748	284	.6	149
1 cup	8.02	26	500	2.3	.41	.102	.092	33	.91	422
Cocoa powder	14	.279	1.01	.121	2.06	.112	.010	7.75	.731	g1.06
1 tablespoon	.931	2.60	4.25	0	.028	.003	.004	26.0	.408	g62.5
Cocoa powder with dry milk	102	.18	.8	.22	9	.291	.47	167	.75	g149
2 tablespoons	5.3	20.1	10	.78	.21	.053	.040	19.6	.529	g227
without dry milk	98	.36	.6	.27	4	.167	.017	9	.952	g76
2 tablespoons	1.1	25.3		0	.030	.008	.010	20	.23	g142
Coffee, black	2.12	0	0	0	0	.472	.007	3.54	.034	1.41
6 ounces	0	0	0	0	.014		.014	10.6	.027	68.0
instant powder	1.33	0	0	0	0	.279	.004	1.66	.037	.666
1 teaspoon	.003	.353	0	0	.002	.000	0	3.9	.005	36.3
Malted milk, dry powder	116	.175	2.40		13.5	1.44		75.6	.215	130
3 rounded teaspoons or 1 ounce	3.69	20.5	91.8	0	.191	.105	.149	27	.283	215
Milk shake, chocolate, thick	336	.255	7.89	.64	6.13	.434	.561	281	.74	263
large (10 ounce) glass	8.68	57.4	306	2.55	.382	.117	.101	42.8	1.22	510

gWhen cocoa powder is processed with alkalis ("Dutch Process") the sodium content increases and the potassium content decreases from what is shown here.

	Calories Kcal	Fiber g	Fat g	Vitamin E mg	Folacin mg	Niacin mg	Pantothenic mg	Calcium mg	Iron mg	Sodium mg
	Protein g	Carbohydrate g	Vitamin A IU	Vitamin C mg	Riboflavin mg	Vitamin B-6 mg	Thiamin mg	Magnesium mg	Zinc mg	Potassium mg
Tea, clear	2	0	0	.1	10	.1		4	.14	
1 cup	.1	.5	0	0	.050		0		0	

BEVERAGES (ALCOHOLIC)

	Calories Kcal	Fiber g	Fat g	Vitamin E mg	Folacin mg	Niacin mg	Pantothenic mg	Calcium mg	Iron mg	Sodium mg
	Protein g	Carbohydrate g	Vitamin A IU	Vitamin C mg	Riboflavin mg	Vitamin B-6 mg	Thiamin mg	Magnesium mg	Zinc mg	Potassium mg
Beer (alcohol 4.5%)	101	0	0		13.3	1.45	.2	12	.024	16.6
large (8 ounce glass)	.72	9.13	0	0	.072	.084	.006	16.6	.027	60
Gin, rum, vodka, or whiskey, 86 proof, *1½ oz.*	106	0	0	0	0	0	0	0	0	.759
	0	.007	0	0	0	0	0		0	.759
Wine, dessert (alcohol 18%)	91.9	0	0		.097	.078	.029	13.6	.565	4.06
1 glass (3½ ounces)	.195	5.75	0	0	.009	.039		10.7		34.1
table (alcohol 12%)	65.8	0	0	0	.2	.070	.030	9.00	.565	4.16
1 glass (3½ ounces)	.1	.6	0	0	.010	.020		8.00	.010	60.8

MISCELLANEOUS

	Calories Kcal	Fiber g	Fat g	Vitamin E mg	Folacin mg	Niacin mg	Pantothenic mg	Calcium mg	Iron mg	Sodium mg
	Protein g	Carbohydrate g	Vitamin A IU	Vitamin C mg	Riboflavin mg	Vitamin B-6 mg	Thiamin mg	Magnesium mg	Zinc mg	Potassium mg
Agar	5.62							12.0	.157	.75
1 tablespoon	.040	1.3								.5
Arrowroot flour	27.3	0	.007			0		.56	.096	.16
1 tablespoon	.003	6.75	0		0		.003			.16
Baking powder	3	0	0		0	0		147	0	247
1 teaspoon	0	.7	0	0	0		0		0	5
Carob flour	63.7	2.67	.070	.010	0			97.5	1.42	6
¼ cup	1.5	31.5	15		.017	.55	.017		.28	319
Chocolate, bitter for baking	180	1.78	15	1.68	18	.34	.054	22	1.9	1
1 ounce	4	7.47	6	0	.127	.011	.020	82	1.01	230
bittersweet	141	.89	9.75	1.68	14	.318	.050	13	1.04	2
1 ounce	1.9	15.7	10	0	.050	.010	.015	28	1.13	129
milk chocolate	147	.308	9.2	1.4	.28	.952	.198	65	.336	27
1 ounce	2.2	16.1	80	0	.065	.016	.028	16.2	.092	109
Cornstarch	29	.1	.048		0				.040	0
1 tablespoon	.025	7	0	0	.006		0	.16	.002	0
Miso, red	29.7		.352			.033		10.3	.298	902
1 tablespoon	2.03	4.60	9.18	2.01	.234		.007			
white	38.3		.226			.070		4.5	.18	592
1 tablespoon	1.40	7.68	3.06	.3	.017		.003			
Olives, green, pitted	45	1.72	5	.62	.34	.010	.007	24	.6	926
10	.5	.5	120	.001	.001	.008	.001	8.58	.027	21
ripe black, pitted	78	2.08	9.5	1.2	.343	.010	.008	47	.8	385
10	.5	1.2	52	.001	.002	.008	.001	10	.142	13
Pickle, dill	7	.325	.1	0	.7	.010		17	.7	942
1 medium, 1¼″ × 3¾″	.5	1.4	70	4	.001	.005	.001	7.8	.176	589
sweet	22	.075	.045		0	.004	.007	2	.25	255
1 small, ¾″ × 2½″	.090	5.5	10	1	.001	.001	.004	1.5	.001	16
Salt, table	0	0	0	0	0	0	0	14.3	.005	2196
1 teaspoon	0	0	0	0	0	0	0			.333
Soy sauce, shoyu (natural soy sauce), *1 tablespoon*	13		0			.104		44.6	.5	1050
	1.5	1.68	2	.2	.154		.004			
Tapioca, pearl and quick cooking, dry, *1 tablespoon*	33.4	.000	.018		.781	0		1	.066	.312
	.056	8.18	0	0	.009		0	.325		1.75
Vinegar	2.12	0	0		0	0		.875	.087	.125
1 tablespoon	0	.887	0	.000	0		0	.15	.017	15
Yeast: baker's, active dry	12.0	.002	.106	.354	269	2.83	.779	5.67	1.41	3.54
1 scant tablespoon or ¼ oz.	2.52	.248	.236	.000	.387	.141	.167	16.3	.429	142
Yeast, nutritional: brewer's, *1 tablespoon*	23	.136	.090	.4	313	3.16	.676	17	1.39	10
	3.1	3.1	1	.001	.342	.404	1.25	18.5	.632	144
torula, calcium fortified	21.2		.077		225	3.55	.785	32	1.48	1
1 tablespoon	2.9	2.8		.1	.382	.243	1.09	12.2	.512	144

Recipes on pages 54–85

	Calories Kcal / Protein g	Fiber g / Carbohydrate g	Fat g / Vitamin A IU	Vitamin E mg / Vitamin C mg	Folacin mg / Riboflavin mg	Niacin mg / Vitamin B-6 mg	Pantothenic mg / Thiamin mg	Calcium mg / Magnesium mg	Iron mg / Zinc mg	Sodium mg / Potassium mg
BREADS										
Basic Bread Recipe, p. 54	80	2.3	.402	.956	20.3	1.1	.258	11.1	1.06	184
1 slice (15 per loaf)	3.25	17	0	0	.052	.145	.135	27.3	.79	92
French Bread, p. 61	74	2.1	.369	.877	19.1	1.02	.238	10.3	.979	184
1 slice (15 per loaf)	2.99	15.6	0	0	.049	.133	.124	25.1	.725	85
Buttermilk Bread, p. 65	93	2.1	1.22	.899	19.9	1.03	.272	22.3	1	166
1 slice (15 per loaf)	3.34	18.4	33	.125	.066	.137	.128	26.2	.77	102
Yogurt Bread, p. 65	106	2.3	2.29	2.46	21	1.11	.292	20.1	1.08	151
1 slice (15 per loaf)	3.52	19.1	3	.058	.064	.147	.138	28.3	.839	105
Fresh Milk Bread, p. 65	104	2.3	1.48	.981	21.4	1.12	.316	31.2	1.08	200
1 slice (15 per loaf)	3.81	20.1	62	.179	.081	.152	.142	29.6	.857	119
Pine Nut Pinwheels, p. 57	206	4.48	5.64	4.08	43.3	2.16	.544	45.6	2.67	326
1 roll (12 per recipe)	9.24	32.0	118	.714	.138	.312	.313	60.5	1.75	334
Light Rye Bread, p. 71	102	2.73	1.46	1.71	23.9	1.09	.315	22.8	1.13	192
1 slice (15 per loaf)	3.93	19.9	4	.086	.072	.14	.143	29.2	.832	123
Pumpernickel, p. 71	97	3.08	.52	.955	26.7	1.05	.328	14	1.16	184
1 slice (15 per loaf)	3.99	20.9	0	0	.064	.131	.145	28.6	.78	128
Garbanzo Bread, p. 72	88	2.65	.629	.931	25.6	1.02	.273	15.6	1.24	185
1 slice (15 per loaf)	3.65	18.1	2	.012	.053	.144	.126	30.9	.836	112
Soybean Bread, p. 72	105	2.26	2.83	3.09	23.2	1.01	.255	18.4	1.23	184
1 slice (15 per loaf)	4.05	17.2	3	.018	.056	.155	.139	23	.805	143
Oatmeal Bread, p. 73	83	2.08	.495	.832	18.8	.959	.252	10.9	1.01	184
1 slice (15 per loaf)	3.13	17.6	3	.018	.049	.125	.131	26.6	.738	87
Cracked Wheat Bread, p. 73	101	2.34	1.25	.915	20.5	1.17	.279	22.2	1.09	20
1 slice (15 per loaf)	3.66	19.9	33	.125	.068	.139	.131	28.1	.864	107
Sebastopol Pizza, p. 76	459	9.60	16.2	5.31	74.3	2.41	.763	262	2.91	522
1 slice (6 per recipe)	15.6	68.1	346	11.7	.266	.48	.326	81	2.7	499
Puffs, p. 77	120	2.24	2.22	1.1	34.6	1.19	.396	29.1	1.25	275
1 each (12 per recipe)	6.35	19.8	72	.083	.114	.161	.143	29	.911	123
Everyone's Muffins, p. 78, *(Oatmeal) 1 muffin (12 per rec.)*	129	2.39	3.21	2.78	29.6	1.01	.354	14.4	1.28	230
	4.11	22.1	10	.031	.069	.126	.18	35.7	.911	111
Everyone's Muffins, p. 78, *(Buckwheat) 1 muffin (12 per rec.)*	146	2.99	4.23	4.77	49.7	1.51	.402	19.1	1.46	232
	4.55	24.6	2	.229	.093	.21	.23	35.7	1.02	197
Apple Bran Muffins, p. 80	108	2.52	3.41	2.06	18.4	1.25	.311	78.1	2.4	118
1 muffin (24 per recipe)	3.24	18.1	36	2.71	.082	.151	.104	48	.801	339
Cinnamuffins, p. 80	143	1.93	4.82	4.41	6.63	.811	.188	86.9	2.66	165
1 muffin (12 per recipe)	2.22	24.3	1	.269	.046	.116	.090	39.5	.541	365
Lynne's Muffins, p. 81	128	1.9	2.07	.72	15	.588	.452	52	1.13	273
1 muffin (12 per recipe)	5.04	23.4	98	.352	.102	.097	.169	36	.915	141
Corn Bread, p. 81	227	4.61	4.78	4.54	21.5	1.21	.525	48.8	1.35	492
1 square 2" × 3" (6 per recipe)	6.18	40.8	242	.081	.085	.256	.186	55.8	1.17	159
Boston Brown Bread, p. 82	211	3.64	4.03	4.52	32.0	1.66	.555	185	4.46	309
1 slice (12 per loaf)	6.84	39.5	77	.677	.163	.296	.295	76	1.27	671
Oat Crackers, p. 83	44	.544	2.12	.617	4.31	.072	.13	21.8	.372	61
1 cracker (16 per recipe)	1.81	4.85	35	.148	.027	.033	.053	14.3	.286	48
Crispy Seed Wafers, p. 83	64	.959	3.55	.574	4.93	.373	.087	20.6	.478	77
1 wafer (16 per recipe)	1.4	7.34	118	0	.018	.058	.056	14.1	.374	43
Chapatis, p. 84	100	2.87	.5	1.18	17.5	1.3	.3	13.4	1.29	184
1 chapati (12 per recipe)	4	21.3	0	0	.054	.177	.165	33.7	.975	111

	Calories Kcal / Protein g	Fiber g / Carbohydrate g	Fat g / Vitamin A IU	Vitamin E mg / Vitamin C mg	Folacin mg / Riboflavin mg	Niacin mg / Vitamin B-6 mg	Pantothenic mg / Thiamin mg	Calcium mg / Magnesium mg	Iron mg / Zinc mg	Sodium mg / Potassium mg
BREAKFAST										
Light & Bright Cereal, p. 87	98	2.07	.928	.581	8.02	.858	.239	9.91	.998	2
1/6 cup dry	2.74	20.2	5	0	.037	.068	.108	32.0	.683	83
Rice Cream Cereal, p. 87	116	2.25	.78	.55	6	1.35	.342	13	.7	5
1/2 cup cooked	2.45	24.8	0	0	.020	.116	.090	28	.825	69
Stuart's Choice Cereal, p. 87	80	2.23	.67	1.13	14	.857	.275	8.12	.673	1
1/6 cup dry	2.83	16.9	33	0	.025	.12	.113	34.2	1.15	80
Granola, p. 88	148	2.45	4.68	3.05	40.3	.738	.402	23.4	1.66	6
1/3 cup (5 1/2 cups per recipe)	6.17	21.9	23	.121	.115	.128	.279	63.5	1.93	203
Granola with honey, p. 88	180	2.45	4.68	3.05	41.3	.769	.423	23.9	1.71	7
1/3 cup (5 1/2 cups per recipe)	6.2	30.6	23	.214	.119	.13	.279	63.7	1.93	208
Better-Butter, p. 93	112	0	12.5	5.76	.351	.005	.008	4.95	.012	60
1 tablespoon (2 cups per recipe)	.153	.143	223	.014	.007	.001	.001	.437	.028	6
Apple Butter, p. 93	46	1.81	.219	.315	1.88	.062	.039	6.99	.224	1
1 svg., 2–3 tbsp., (makes 2–3 cups)	.131	12	31	3.36	.010	.029	.011	2.96	.032	81
Old Fashioned Pancakes, p. 94	99	1.35	3.36	2.73	26.2	.787	.383	68.9	.968	174
1 pancake (18 per recipe)	4.49	13.5	98	.322	.123	.131	.143	30.3	1.16	142
Fresh Corn Pancakes, p. 94	106	1.87	3.41	2.78	29.4	.925	.417	69.1	1.01	174
1 pancake (18 per recipe)	4.74	15.2	130	.766	.128	.151	.151	32.3	1.19	160
Oatmeal Pancakes, p. 95	98	1.14	3.62	1.66	13.9	.355	.421	61.8	.857	106
1 pancake (10 per recipe)	4.22	12.5	116	.26	.097	.070	.111	23.6	.676	111
Buckwheat Pancakes, p. 95	73	1.08	2.15	1.4	15.7	.469	.328	57.9	.575	109
1 pancake (18 per recipe)	3.1	10.8	84	.257	.082	.080	.084	19.3	.54	104
Potato Latkes, p. 96	81	1	3.39	2.35	54.3	.935	.446	48.8	.843	298
1 pancake (8 per recipe)	3.9	9.28	95	1.54	.153	.118	.134	24.4	.866	152
Stewed Apples, Applesauce, p. 96	76	3.56	.391	.578	3.13	.121	.065	10	.295	1
1/8 recipe (makes 3–4 cups)	.368	19.8	56	6.02	.018	.062	.025	6.18	.051	158
Fresh Fruit Sauce, p. 96	154	5.24	.634	.478	35.8	.804	.394	25.9	.607	2
1/2 cup (2 cups per recipe)	1.86	39.7	162	33.3	.137	.71	.098	39.7	.245	602
Dosas, p. 97	85	1.3	1.56	1.19	2.81	.878	.201	12.4	.735	84
1 pancake (12 per recipe)	2.58	15.5	5	.001	.020	.090	.071	15.9	.282	89
Masala Potatoes, p. 98	163	5.07	3.58	3.09	26.9	2.38	.444	22.6	1.14	8
3/4 cup (makes 3 cups)	3.99	29.3	69	42.2	.077	.327	.156	25.9	.518	699
Yogurt Cheese, p. 104	40	.013	.833		6.46	.054	.228	72.5	.038	25
2 tablespoons (makes 1 cup)	2.75	5.65	36	2.21	.080	.017	.013	7.33	.376	95
Soymilk, p. 105	184	1.71	6.2	7.15	69.9	.793	.619	79.8	3	1
1 cup	11.9	23.3	28	.125	.114	.286	.385	1.2	1.16	633
Soymilk, p. 105	184	1.71	6.2	7.15	69.9	.793	.619	380	3	1
1 cup	11.9	23.3	28	.125	.114	.286	.385	1.2	1.16	633
LUNCH										
Soy Spread, p. 113	79	1.61	4.44	4.45	18.5	.472	.174	41.2	1.37	192
1/4 cup (makes 1 1/2 cups)	4.58	6.28	233	1.39	.045	.135	.097	3.77	.531	290
Garbanzo Spread, p. 114	77	3.31	2.27	1.55	36.2	.41	.219	41	1.43	98
1/4 cup (makes 3 cups)	3.78	11.1	445	10.8	.042	.1	.057	33.5	.803	168
Refrito Spread, p. 114	155	6.48	6.91	2.67	58.4	.79	.221	124	2.33	298
1/4 cup (makes 1 1/4 cups)	7.68	16.4	780	16.2	.108	.142	.173	42.3	1.26	363
Split Pea–Parmesan Spread, p. 115	105	3.02	4.45	3.27	5.11	.468	.222	45.8	.885	151
1/4 cup (makes about 1 cup)	6.02	10.8	43	0	.067	.041	.072	19.1	.622	158
Split Pea–Sunseed Spread, p. 115	151	2.97	9.7	10.1	33.2	1.15	.354	22	1.52	10
1/4 cup (makes about 1 1/4 cups)	6.7	11.3	23	0	.068	.206	.341	19.5	1.08	252
Split Pea–Tofu Dip, p. 115	183	1.99	12.8	12.8	58.2	1.13	.396	87	2.26	77
1/3 cup (makes about 3 cups)	9.77	9.96	17	.033	.090	.256	.423	69.7	1.35	235
Soy Pâté, p. 115	143	1.78	10.1	10.6	43.3	.941	.286	48.2	1.8	280
3 tablespoons (makes 1 1/4 cup)	7.34	7.8	19	1.37	.065	.264	.325	6.1	1.12	338

	Calories Kcal / Protein g	Fiber g / Carbohydrate g	Fat g / Vitamin A IU	Vitamin E mg / Vitamin C mg	Folacin mg / Riboflavin mg	Niacin mg / Vitamin B-6 mg	Pantothenic mg / Thiamin mg	Calcium mg / Magnesium mg	Iron mg / Zinc mg	Sodium mg / Potassium mg
Sesame Spread, p. 116	116	1.18	9.2	4.25	25.3	1.02	.568	218	1.96	57
2 tablespoons (makes ¾ cup)	3.48	6.95	6	.031	.046	.016	.183	34	1.65	138
Tofu Bars, p. 117	170	.62	11.6	9.89	59.2	1.08	.381	161	3.09	605
4 ounces (serves 4)	10.5	8.57	545	1.95	.117	.187	.214	134	1.04	267
Tempeh Bars, p. 117	162	1.31	8.59	8.64	46.9	1.64	.437	56.9	2.38	300
2 ounces (serves 8)	12	6.67	296	2.35	.189	.305	.103	5.4	1.07	616
Swissy Spread, p. 118	81	.147	4.32	.34	6.42	.107	.15	158	.266	153
¼ recipe (makes about 1 cup)	8.05	1.9	179	12	.111	.059	.017	8.97	.684	65
Jack & Dill Spread, p. 118	95	.413	6.17	.634	8.34	.151	.116	133	.349	195
¼ recipe (makes about 1 cup)	7.81	1.79	186	.5	.131	.034	.011	13.2	.621	66
Chili–Cheddar Spread, p. 118	99	.325	6.47	1.24	8.57	.141	.139	126	.295	209
¼ cup (makes 1 cup)	7.7	2.54	455	1.43	.116	.039	.018	7.68	.654	66
Jaji, p. 118	58	.51	1.41	.254	13.4	.157	.326	97.2	.256	146
¼ to ⅓ cup (makes 2 to 2½ cups)	6.82	4.17	176	10.1	.14	.060	.028	11.9	.522	155
Smoothie, p. 119	273	5.21	10.1	2.8	151	2.29	1.29	351	1.54	162
1½ cups	13.2	36	569	10.1	.689	.742	.551	102	1.72	916
Mock Rarebit, p. 119, ⅜ cup	178	2.31	5.26	1.23	28.8	1.2	.559	173	1.2	479
over 1 slice whole-grain toast	11.5	22.2	245	.58	.241	.199	.168	39.9	1.44	223

SALADS

	Calories Kcal / Protein g	Fiber g / Carbohydrate g	Fat g / Vitamin A IU	Vitamin E mg / Vitamin C mg	Folacin mg / Riboflavin mg	Niacin mg / Vitamin B-6 mg	Pantothenic mg / Thiamin mg	Calcium mg / Magnesium mg	Iron mg / Zinc mg	Sodium mg / Potassium mg
Lemon-Parsley Dressing, p. 130	273	4.37	27.6	23.3	49.2	.492	.24	107	.962	566
½ cup	2.08	7.44	2609	102	.103	.134	.070	18.2	.77	244
Blue Cheese Dressing, p. 130	271	0	22.7	11.7	16.8	.364	.726	235	.548	575
½ cup	11.9	4.6	244	.6	.254	.089	.035	14.9	1.5	173
Orange-Parsley Dressing, p. 130	309	3.4	27.4	23.1	49.8	.477	.36	79.7	.361	553
⅔ cup	1.56	16.9	915	85.3	.073	.096	.125	16.9	.318	290
Sesame Dressing, p. 130	366	2.41	33.2	19.8	54.9	2.09	1.33	512	3.96	328
⅓ cup	9.06	12.3	139	7.58	.192	.065	.395	77	3.57	385
Basic Buttermilk Dressing, p. 131	278	.153	27.9	22.6	5.99	.070	.244	99	.061	305
½ cup	2.76	5.49	31	10.3	.127	.038	.033	9.84	.397	145
Fresh Tomato Dressing, p. 131	265	2.16	27.2	4.31	53	.952	.432	33.6	1.06	290
1 cup	1.1	6.45	1180	28.4	.054	.141	.076	19.8	.269	326
Cottage Dressing, p. 131	199	.15	15.2	11.7	13.5	.141	.319	116	.143	513
½ cup	9.89	5.88	168	7.41	.203	.071	.038	11.1	.551	165
Everyday Dressing, p. 131	271	3.4	27.2	4.64	73.2	1.07	.477	60.5	1.08	572
1 cup	1.61	7.26	2385	53.7	.091	.168	.093	23.9	.566	383
Feroz's Dressing, p. 131	309	4.57	27.4	4.79	87.5	1.45	.777	57.1	1.58	1123
¾ cup	2.4	18.5	1685	80.7	.098	.267	.146	28.8	.661	564
Russian Dressing, p. 132	161	.235	12.3	3.73	8.27	.614	.412	113	.77	770
½ cup	5.06	8.60	802	1.07	.175	.102	.067	13.3	.472	309
Avocado Dressing, p. 132	271	4.32	23.5	2.05	97.7	2.96	1.63	91.2	1.58	358
½ cup	5.1	15.5	1083	19.6	.281	.448	.188	66.6	.915	1013
Yogurt Salad Dressing, p. 132	317	.053	28.9	22.6	14.4	.144	.685	210	.095	354
⅔ cup	6	9.31	78	7.91	.244	.063	.054	21	1.06	284
Green Goddess Dressing, p. 132	202	1.49	15.4	11.6	35.8	.337	.733	253	.378	636
¾ cup	6.65	9.85	1395	34.3	.285	.091	.073	28.4	1.37	357
Astonishing Salad, p. 133	304	15.7	17.2	9.72	344	1.67	.848	190	6.25	292
1 serving (4 per recipe)	8.62	30.6	15104	96.4	.399	.584	.244	183	1.49	1217
Greek Salad, p. 133	120	2.66	9.91	1.63	133	.691	.498	155	1.89	431
1 serving (4 per recipe)	4.1	5.7	2148	25.9	.166	.116	.083	20.9	.809	301
Dilled Cucumber & Yogurt Salad p. 134, *1 serving (4 per recipe)*	85	3.17	1.61	1.04	245	1	1.05	246	3.07	334
	6.07	12.2	3432	39.7	.284	.184	.153	34.3	1.16	601
Ceci Salad, p. 134	273	12.8	15	4.67	249	1.89	1.02	136	5.53	361
1 serving (4 per recipe)	10.5	28.2	7476	49.7	.277	.47	.232	152	2.07	927
Mexican Salad Bowl, p. 135	128	6.6	6.15	1.63	207	1.44	.744	78.5	2.8	51
1 serving (4 per recipe)	4.98	14.8	2237	56.5	.145	.245	.153	41.6	.853	583

	Calories Kcal / Protein g	Fiber g / Carbohydrate g	Fat g / Vitamin A IU	Vitamin E mg / Vitamin C mg	Folacin mg / Riboflavin mg	Niacin mg / Vitamin B-6 mg	Pantothenic mg / Thiamin mg	Calcium mg / Magnesium mg	Iron mg / Zinc mg	Sodium mg / Potassium mg
Recipes on pages 135–151										
Chef's Salad, p. 135	336	8.06	20	3.88	405	2.14	1.79	402	5.54	357
1 serving (2 per recipe)	17.5	22.7	5068	112	.443	.479	.283	82.8	2.69	912
California Tossed Salad, p. 135	148	3.42	8.95	4.11	155	1.55	.701	119	2.05	153
1 serving (4 per recipe)	4.79	14.1	2106	25.7	.14	.196	.139	36.8	.849	447
Tomato Pepper Salad, p. 135	36	2.95	.364	1.36	65.7	1.19	.553	27.2	1.11	22
1 serving	1.76	7.79	1527	95.6	.098	.274	.117	26.8	.324	410
Shades of Green Salad, p. 135	151	9.62	6.37	8.89	317	1.87	.817	168	4.27	113
1 serving (4 per recipe)	9.02	16.4	6790	64.5	.272	.377	.392	77.7	1.58	774
Spinach & Mushroom Salad, p. 135	100	10.6	3.12	3.67	240	2.34	1.07	144	4.15	238
1 serving (4 per recipe)	6.75	14	9279	60.5	.377	.32	.195	119	1.22	707
Navy Bean & Cashew Salad, p. 135	140	6.57	7.5	2.01	169	1.29	.923	116	2.62	59
1 serving (4 per recipe)	6.41	13.9	2691	57.7	.223	.28	.174	56.7	1.13	489
Caponata, p. 137	38	1.45	2.55	.509	12.9	.303	.141	14.8	.398	74
¼ cup (4 cups per recipe)	.65	4.01	181	8.56	.024	.055	.028	7.68	.131	135
Coleslaw, p. 138	87	2.32	7.1	6.22	41	.287	.257	59	.412	89
½ cup (2 cups per recipe)	2	4.92	74	41.2	.067	.121	.053	14.6	.33	183
Slaw Chez Nous, p. 138	65	1.62	5.17	3.55	32.0	.382	.192	59.5	.7	98
½ cup (3 cups per recipe)	1.65	3.98	268	24.5	.048	.057	.057	18.5	.456	117
Red Rogue's Delight, p. 139	133	2.25	11.2	10.5	44.2	.803	.327	38.4	.866	307
1 serving (4 per recipe)	3.34	6.68	56	41.7	.054	.219	.231	14.5	.655	228
Carrot Salad, p. 139	106	4.07	.31	.478	41.1	.854	.297	50.5	.9	42
1 serving (4 per recipe)	1.67	26.8	9142	26	.073	.191	.113	25.8	.44	488
Disappearing Carrot Salad, p. 139	162	4.86	5.9	2	40.5	.896	.317	54	1.29	28
1 serving (4 per recipe)	2.75	28.2	6148	26.5	.081	.245	.124	33.9	.601	489
Russian Salad, p. 140	110	4.66	4.03	1.45	66.3	1.29	.336	51.1	1.1	246
1 serving (6 per recipe)	3.48	15.5	294	17.2	.094	.143	.104	24.1	.642	462
Fruity Beety, p. 140	98	4.42	1.74	.28	70.7	.55	.322	55.2	.78	50
1 serving (4 per recipe)	2.02	20.8	215	59	.068	.127	.108	23.5	.342	399
Sweet Potato Salad, p. 141	294	5.18	15.9	9.38	50.8	1.03	1.12	92.2	1.74	222
1 serving (4 per recipe)	5.81	36.2	9213	53.9	.145	.357	.19	44.1	.71	488
Winter Salad, p. 141	140	7.62	6.67	2.19	76.7	1.99	1.16	161	2.19	429
1 serving (4 per recipe)	4.95	18.8	2145	90	.226	.26	.188	37.2	.972	526
Winter Salad with Arame, p. 141	155	7.62	6.72	2.19	76.7	2.09	1.16	204	2.9	490
1 serving (4 per recipe)	5.41	22.1	2182	90.5	.259	.26	.19	37.2	.972	526
Tomato Aspic, p. 142	117	2.73	6.68	2.91	49.8	1.66	.69	60.3	2.45	860
1 serving (6 per recipe)	3.43	13.6	3541	40.3	.089	.455	.141	36.5	.62	564
Finocchio Salad, p. 143	134	4.13	5.03	1.75	26	1.71	.588	25.5	1.52	198
1 serving (6 per recipe)	4.04	20	348	17	.115	.195	.168	35.6	1.01	203
Yogurt Rice, p. 143	201	2.28	5.48	3.37	15.4	1.46	.848	172	.779	614
1 serving (4 per recipe)	6.93	30.9	69	2.11	.203	.16	.127	43.2	1.58	272
Tabouli, p. 144	245	6.28	7.57	1.97	53.8	2.39	.52	36.4	3.13	282
1 serving (6 per recipe)	6.63	39.6	669	21.7	.106	.215	.177	48.2	1.15	287
Pineapple–Bulgur Wheat Salad p. 144, *1 serving (6 per recipe)*	196	5	7.99	2.87	47.8	2.15	.623	21.3	2.31	103
	4.26	29.3	892	37.8	.106	.223	.157	43	.746	358
Sideways Sushi, p. 145	237	5.09	6.76	2.3	24.5	2.67	.731	49	1.46	305
1 serving (8 per recipe)	5.56	39.6	991	3.38	.128	.305	.167	79	1.2	240
Persian Rice Salad, p. 145	245	4.06	9.47	2.24	18.8	1.83	.578	24.4	1.68	7
1 serving (4 per recipe)	4.75	37.7	82	6.25	.063	.178	.155	64.4	1.42	219
SOUPS										
Rasam, p. 150	212	8.2	7.4	7.35	63	1.89	.815	35	2.9	579
1 cup (makes 2 cups)	9.39	29.5	1151	29	.149	.207	.23	56	1.75	657
Golden Broth, p. 151	76	1.93	3.55	3.13	5.92	.408	.286	7.62	.723	6
1 cup (makes 8 cups)	3.1	8.39	17	1.01	.036	.034	.094	17.2	.456	132
Golden Noodle Soup, p. 151	153	6.13	4.97	4.71	28.1	1.44	.621	46.1	1.65	402
1 serving (6 per recipe)	6.1	22.1	2688	16.1	.098	.173	.206	40.5	1.1	395

	Calories Kcal / Protein g	Fiber g / Carbohydrate g	Fat g / Vitamin A IU	Vitamin E mg / Vitamin C mg	Folacin mg / Riboflavin mg	Niacin mg / Vitamin B-6 mg	Pantothenic mg / Thiamin mg	Calcium mg / Magnesium mg	Iron mg / Zinc mg	Sodium mg / Potassium mg
Recipes on pages 152–180										
Gumbo, p. 152	109	5.03	3.96	4.42	70.5	1.32	.507	49.8	1.54	287
1 serving (8 per recipe)	4.1	16.2	853	42.8	.125	.218	.145	38.2	.599	475
Whole Beet Borscht, p. 152	88	6.98	1.92	2.37	101	1.16	.391	101	1.78	626
1 serving (6 per recipe)	3.48	15.9	4325	33.5	.145	.222	.115	55.3	.787	848
Minestrone, p. 153	162	8.02	5.29	2.48	98	2.26	.743	85.5	2.95	847
1 serving (6 per recipe)	6.29	24.1	3751	59.3	.154	.338	.205	53.6	1.09	797
Xergis, p. 154	143	.701	3.06	.285	45.1	.719	1.5	386	.987	510
1 serving (6 per recipe)	11	17.5	213	15.9	.464	.164	.143	52	1.89	683
Old Favorite Green Soup, p. 155	162	12.6	5.16	6.63	176	2.1	.903	124	3.8	458
1 serving (6 per recipe)	9.56	22	6824	55	.313	.276	.323	119	1.53	779
New Favorite Green Soup, p. 156	101	5.7	3.15	.815	40.5	1.4	.307	78	2.1	383
1 serving (4 per recipe)	3.45	16	4838	27	.129	.197	.102	59	.525	788
Asparagus Soup, p. 156	89	4.88	3.26	3.19	123	2.65	.825	58.7	1.92	892
1½ cups (makes 6 cups)	4.47	12.7	1519	46.6	.289	.207	.272	23.7	1.03	538
Creamy Cauliflower Soup, p. 157	51	2.53	1.87	.341	27.8	.862	.375	24.1	.561	291
1 serving (8 per recipe)	2.03	7.53	60	40.6	.061	.141	.076	14.1	.29	352
Lynne's Spiced Pumpkin Soup	116	5.31	3.15	3.09	43.4	1.25	.891	140	1.01	204
p. 158, *1 serving (8 per recipe)*	4.03	20	15181	11.6	.215	.165	.097	28	.746	557
Squash Soup, p. 159	105	6.17	3.47	1.22	50.2	1.04	.38	71	1	1135
1 serving (4 per recipe)	2.72	18.5	7185	29.7	.212	.12	.090	30.2	.442	538
Carrot Soup, p. 159	111	4.31	4.25	.513	24.3	.946	.415	110	.787	364
1 serving (8 per recipe)	3.47	13.2	7360	11.4	.149	.171	.095	21.7	.561	374
Kale-Potato Soup, p. 160	137	7.53	3.44	4.12	44.7	2.42	.816	135	1.76	336
1 serving (4 per recipe)	5.61	22.6	5251	78.6	.168	.353	.175	39.1	.861	506
Potato-Cheese Soup, p. 160	149	3.02	5.66	.306	21.6	1.21	.538	183	.655	665
1 serving (8 per recipe)	6.63	18.1	2394	14.7	.217	.195	.112	26.8	.9	476
Corn Chowder, p. 161	132	4.26	4.66	.583	35.7	1.14	.661	185	.642	646
1 serving (4 per recipe)	6.26	18	1140	20.6	.262	.206	.116	33.7	.899	419
Cream of Celery Soup, p. 161	56	4.34	1.88	2	32	.818	.318	50	.638	461
1 serving (8 per recipe)	1.82	8.74	391	25.1	.049	.138	.061	16.1	.291	319
Tomato Soup, p. 162	90	5.84	3.87	4.69	102	1.84	.886	65.8	1.64	467
1 serving (4 per recipe)	2.52	13.9	4099	53.5	.116	.296	.154	37	.513	649
Cream of Tomato Soup, p. 162	151	5.84	3.99	4.69	111	1.99	1.43	275	1.69	560
1 serving (4 per recipe)	8.49	22.7	4502	54.4	.413	.354	.224	57	1.27	939
Gingery Tomato Soup, p. 163	66	2.64	2.56	3.06	67.6	1.37	.554	27.6	1.16	314
1 serving (8 per recipe)	2.04	10.5	1388	36.2	.077	.184	.107	23.5	.469	443
Fresh Corn & Tomato Soup, p. 163	191	12	4.67	4.72	114	3.45	1.09	30.2	1.6	306
1 serving (4 per recipe)	5.95	38.2	1718	37.5	.159	.517	.232	55	1	667
Catalina Soup, p. 166	184	3.45	7.77	3.24	20.3	2.07	.444	127	1.3	635
1 serving (4 per recipe)	6.57	22.3	680	18.5	.121	.27	.133	23.3	.858	612
Black Bean Soup, p. 166	157	11.8	5.03	4.53	60.1	.897	.281	53.8	2.06	756
1 serving (6 per recipe)	6.68	22.6	1365	12.7	.066	.193	.129	87.4	1.15	374
Hearty Pea Soup, p. 167	168	7.69	.71	1.89	43.8	1.67	.868	48.2	2.67	583
1 serving (8 per recipe)	9.72	32.0	1742	15.4	.119	.226	.283	65.5	1.45	585
Greek Lentil Soup, p. 167	203	7.18	3.99	3.54	56.1	1.31	.781	40.6	4.08	429
1 serving (8 per recipe)	12.1	32.9	1399	7.86	.123	.329	.243	43.4	1.66	491
Early Autumn Fruit Soup, p. 168	133	3.72	.456	.671	14.7	.225	.149	12.2	.324	2
1 serving (4 per recipe)	.451	34.9	104	20.6	.030	.069	.040	8.10	.068	190
VEGETABLES										
Artichokes Tellicherry, p. 176	97	3.46	3.04	.106	26.6	1.23	.343	42.9	1.2	325
¼ recipe (makes 2 to 3 cups)	3.41	18.3	199	17.2	.054	.181	.109	25.8	.386	425
Chinese Asparagus, p. 179	72	3.01	3.38	4.78	95	1.99	.572	59.7	2.07	304
1 serving (4 per recipe)	3.73	8.66	1035	33.7	.227	.135	.219	20.2	1.07	372
Green Beans Hellenika, p. 180	91	7.35	3.88	2.59	80.8	1.39	.577	117	1.89	292
¾ cup (makes 3 cups)	3.83	12.4	2698	60.5	.187	.177	.163	48.1	.863	661

Recipes on pages 181–216	Calo-ries Kcal / Protein g	Fiber g / Carbo-hydrate g	Fat g / Vitamin A IU	Vitamin E mg / Vitamin C mg	Folacin mg / Ribo-flavin mg	Niacin mg / Vitamin B-6 mg	Panto-thenic mg / Thiamin mg	Calcium mg / Magne-sium mg	Iron mg / Zinc mg	Sodium mg / Potas-sium mg
Green Bean Stroganoff, p. 181	182	8.87	8.12	1.51	85.5	3.45	2.27	286	2.61	699
¼ recipe (serves 4 to 6)	10.1	20.5	919	20	.626	.241	.231	67	1.99	1015
Spicy Green Beans, p. 181	39	4.37	.286	1.47	57.6	.77	.297	68.2	1.34	283
1 serving (4 per recipe)	2.29	8.79	828	20.2	.115	.107	.102	33.8	.478	418
Whole Beets, p. 182	70	4.27	3.62	3.37	107	.451	.169	63	1.32	339
1 serving (4 per recipe)	1.97	8.52	2118	16.1	.098	.086	.047	43.8	.521	620
King Cole Curry, p. 184	217	10.7	8.21	6.69	154	2.78	1.45	254	4.26	833
1 serving (4 per recipe)	15.1	25.9	2948	149	.385	.428	.371	149	1.69	726
Brussels Sprout–Squash	187	8.06	6.17	2.01	74.7	1.9	1.	229	2.13	400
Casserole, p. 186, *¼ recipe*	10.6	26.3	4182	111	.46	.402	.216	63.3	1.;4	808
Creamy Brussels Sprouts & Bell	72	5.64	.598	1.31	66.1	1.59	.764	48.2	1.82	292
Peppers, p. 186, *¼ recipe*	5.35	13.6	2195	181	.182	.391	.14	33.5	.588	497
Bubble & Squeak, p. 187	103	5.8	3.88	3.29	1.6	1.37	.39	105	1.76	611
1 serving (4 per recipe)	5.52	13.6	280	77.5	.119	.338	.122	31.9	.858	580
Crumby Carrots, p. 189	214	7.25	6.48	1.65	66	1.99	.901	144	2.36	388
1 serving (3 per recipe)	9.49	32.5	11075	6.41	.229	.256	.223	56.2	1.8	393
Chard Cheese Pie, p. 192	232	11.1	6.13	3.23	129	1.72	1.13	304	6.06	1080
1 serving (4 per recipe)	25.2	22.4	14387	47.2	.591	.326	.199	168	1.97	1644
Eggplant Parmesan, p. 195	362	7.26	12.4	4.52	89.1	3.63	1.16	347	4.24	1239
1 serving (6 per recipe)	19.7	47	2337	16.4	.33	.423	.34	91.7	2.93	817
Colcannon, p. 197	161	7.25	3.7	3.52	50.2	2.92	.882	137	1.6	488
1 serving (4 per recipe)	5.85	27.5	4591	92.5	.201	.352	.198	39.2	.9	768
Tomato Kale, p. 198	131	15.8	3.82	16.4	155	4.52	2.25	385	3.67	411
1 serving (4 per recipe)	10.6	19.4	17661	282	.499	.488	.372	76.6	1.68	893
Crumby Greens, p. 198	133	5.23	4.86	6.03	38.7	1.7	.493	122	2.04	478
1 serving (4 per recipe)	5.73	19.7	3430	40.1	.12	.16	.134	42.9	.925	222
Sesame-Glazed Parsnips, p. 202	114	3.7	3.82	3.19	41.7	.559	.326	87.6	.852	304
1 serving (4 per recipe)	1.68	19.8	5166	23.3	.074	.080	.109	20.6	.463	350
Parsnip Patties, p. 202	292	5.68	12.5	5.8	77	1.57	.83	119	2.79	646
2 patties (12 per recipe)	10	39.7	128	12.1	.204	.234	.238	65.7	1.47	605
Chinese Peppers & Sprouts	105	5.07	3.81	3.54	46.2	1.14	.111	42	2.27	561
p. 204, *1 serving (4 per recipe)*	5.16	11.3	942	80.4	.25	.847	.193	32.5	1.71	377
French Bakes, p. 205	267	7.19	3.73	2.97	34.3	4.41	.66	24.6	1.79	283
1 serving (4 per recipe)	6.54	53.6	2	50.7	.114	.405	.245	46.4	1.46	1279
Parsley Stuffed Potatoes, p. 206	205	5.87	4.13	3.08	48	2.97	.63	102	1.75	579
1 serving (4 per recipe)	6.17	37	1157	52.1	.166	.288	.187	42.1	1.4	948
Green Potatoes for Six, p. 206	178	7.03	5.14	.345	53.1	2.42	.786	171	1.36	472
1 serving (6 per recipe)	8.35	25.5	1465	68.7	.223	.327	.17	33.3	1.02	694
Ishtu, p. 207	216	9.18	12.5	.473	25.8	1.56	.378	28.3	1.78	378
1 serving (6 per recipe)	4.28	22.8	11	22.6	.068	.446	.129	36.5	.723	519
Ishtu, p. 207	448	13.6	14	1.57	37.8	4.26	1.06	54.3	3.17	387
⅙ recipe over 1 cup brown rice	9.18	72.5	11	22.6	.108	.678	.309	92.5	2.37	656
Potatoes Tarragon, p. 208	148	4.44	3.51	.608	22.2	2.07	.375	24.1	1.06	556
1 serving (4 per recipe)	3.47	26.3	8	24.8	.062	.269	.131	21.6	.463	612
Buttermilk Scalloped Potatoes	161	2.91	4.75	.42	19.7	1.65	.494	112	.88	495
p. 208, *1 serving (6 per recipe)*	5.66	24.8	175	17.5	.176	.191	.135	29.3	.969	554
Papas Chorreadas, p. 209	313	7.82	13.1	1.9	96	3.1	.98	288	2.3	888
1 serving (4 per recipe)	16	34.5	1699	53.7	.31	.447	.245	59	1.85	1054
Hijiki Stir Fry, p. 212	154	6.22	8.41	6.91	54.2	.951	.501	137	4.44	454
1 cup (makes 4 cups)	3.94	17.8	5335	43.4	.17	.126	.109	23.9	.559	282
Swiss Chard Stir Fry, p. 212	150	7.27	8.46	7.23	67.4	1.05	.559	130	2.06	361
1 serving (4 per recipe)	4.31	16.8	7579	50	.194	.155	.124	47.9	.707	522
Creamed Spinach, p. 214	129	7.77	7.08	2.36	115	.893	.52	194	2.83	290
1 serving (4 per recipe)	6.39	11.8	9476	32.7	.292	.27	.141	92	1.15	508
Zucchini Provençal, p. 216	94	5.86	3.66	.957	40	1.78	.44	51.3	1.4	291
1 serving (4 per recipe)	2.71	14.1	1443	36.5	.126	.153	.134	31.7	.561	514

[481]

	Calo-ries Kcal / Protein g	Fiber g / Carbo-hydrate g	Fat g / Vitamin A IU	Vitamin E mg / Vitamin C mg	Folacin mg / Ribo-flavin mg	Niacin mg / Vitamin B-6 mg	Panto-thenic mg / Thiamin mg	Calcium mg / Magne-sium mg	Iron mg / Zinc mg	Sodium mg / Potas-sium mg
Baked Zucchini, p. 216	92	4.35	2.63	.707	39.6	1.36	.463	85.5	.919	247
1 serving (4 per recipe)	10.7	7.07	720	15.7	.269	.105	.106	30.1	.715	293
Greek Stuffed Zucchini, p. 217	253	10	10	2.25	102	3.41	1.38	143	2.6	554
⅙ recipe (serves 6 to 8)	8.79	35.2	1741	66.6	.291	.341	.246	73.5	1.53	643
Sandy's Gingered Squash, p. 218	117	5.2	1.98	.965	39.3	.943	.364	38.9	.839	72
1 serving (4 per recipe)	2.11	26.5	6491	20.3	.189	.099	.077	26.5	.272	494
Cranberry Squash, p. 219	163	7.7	.692	.998	41.2	1.04	.401	45.9	1.13	4
1 serving (6 per recipe)	2.49	41.8	5772	25.5	.191	.146	.109	30.9	.309	597
Stuffed Acorn Squash, p. 219	208	10.6	8.37	7.81	100	1.98	.624	121	2.84	460
1 serving (4 per recipe)	6.28	31.9	10279	30.9	.291	.236	.178	80.2	1.05	759
Hungarian Squash, p. 220	167	5.83	7.28	1.2	49	1.13	.698	162	1.22	652
1 serving (4 per recipe)	5.64	22.9	7202	20.9	.331	.142	.113	39.8	.864	669
Squash Malagushim, p. 220	153	7.88	4.87	2.46	36.6	1.27	.645	38.3	1.74	192
1 serving (6 per recipe)	5.8	24.5	5314	12.3	.195	.156	.183	46.8	.833	573
Butternut Tostada, p. 221	233	8.12	11.9	4.89	152	2.14	.817	223	2.56	128
1 serving (4 per recipe)	8.14	32.3	6780	45.3	.3	.244	.199	61.6	1.6	707
South Indian Sweet Potatoes	168	3.46	2.6	4.63	30.2	.852	.557	36.1	1.05	337
p. 222, *1 serving (4 per recipe)*	3.43	32.9	10023	38.6	.077	.129	.078	14.8	.187	287
Ratatouille, p. 225	92	5.42	4.98	1.46	57.4	1.56	.516	44	1.31	381
1 serving (6 per recipe)	2.69	11.3	878	47.8	.135	.228	.142	33.9	.601	540
Ratatouille, p. 225	324	9.92	6.54	2.56	69.4	4.26	1.2	70	2.71	390
⅙ recipe over 1 cup brown rice	7.59	61	878	47.8	.175	.459	.322	89.9	2.25	677
Aviyal, p. 226	293	17.7	13.7	.899	79.6	3.54	.949	205	3.1	634
1 serving (4 per recipe)	9.04	37.1	8967	48	.363	.571	.274	84.7	1.83	1123
Cauliflower-Eggplant Curry	132	8.41	5.17	4.59	79.6	2.49	.805	44.5	1.98	381
p. 226, *1 serving (6 per recipe)*	5.23	18.4	383	69.2	.155	.313	.238	39.3	.813	823
Middle Eastern Vegetables	116	7.45	3.94	3.63	60.1	2	.596	61.2	1.31	576
p. 227, *1 serving (4 per recipe)*	3.45	19.2	3862	59.6	.16	.25	.162	35.5	.59	635
Chinese Vegetables, p. 227	188	7.22	11.9	9.34	89	2.29	.753	211	3.46	1218
1 serving (4 per recipe)	10.3	13	5263	59.4	.279	.399	.267	105	1.91	450
Chinese Vegetables, p. 227	420	11.7	13.4	10.4	101	4.99	1.43	237	4.86	1227
¼ recipe over 1 cup brown rice	15.2	62.7	5263	59.4	.319	.631	.447	161	3.56	587
Mushrooms Petaluma, p. 228	181	8	4.41	.822	46.4	4.25	1.62	60.2	2.74	1029
1 serving (6 per recipe)	4.76	26.1	4747	49.1	.356	.298	.172	35.8	1.12	739
Winter Stew, p. 228	155	7.71	7.59	4.87	52	2.09	.737	191	2.59	935
1 serving (4 per recipe)	5.3	19.8	4882	73	.206	.242	.136	42.7	.98	562

SAUCES & SUCH

	Calo-ries Kcal / Protein g	Fiber g / Carbo-hydrate g	Fat g / Vitamin A IU	Vitamin E mg / Vitamin C mg	Folacin mg / Ribo-flavin mg	Niacin mg / Vitamin B-6 mg	Panto-thenic mg / Thiamin mg	Calcium mg / Magne-sium mg	Iron mg / Zinc mg	Sodium mg / Potas-sium mg
Homemade Ketchup, p. 235	43	.523	.186	.579	6.72	1.51	.377	15.2	1.55	171
¼ cup (makes 1¾ cups)	1.66	10.1	1617	.239	.057	.186	.097	9.89	.113	467
Quick Vegetable Relish, p. 235	13.5	1.01	.089	.395	20.3	.173	.097	20.5	.321	557
¼ cup (makes 2 cups)	.645	3.3	826	22.2	.024	.068	.024	7.35	.131	108
Margarita's Salsa, p. 236	16	1.18	.116	.501	29.1	.482	.232	14	.406	146
¼ cup (makes 2 cups)	.651	4.03	575	15.8	.031	.082	.041	9.96	.133	173
Coriander Chutney, p. 237	73	3.08	6.26	.122	2.49	.073	.023	18.6	.823	141
3 tablespoons (makes ¾ cup)	1.05	4.03	347	3.46	.020	.104	.019	12.2	.177	158
Coconut Chutney, p. 237	74	2.97	7.04	.829	2.36	.069	.022	4.78	.545	72
¼ cup (makes 2 cups)	.729	2.72	1	1.61	.005	.104	.009	8.96	.178	83
Tomato-Ginger Chutney, p. 238	59	2.07	3.63	3.77	53.7	.926	.432	19	.798	290
⅓ cup (makes about 1¼ cups)	1.15	6.87	1110	28.3	.054	.141	.080	18.1	.427	319
Apple Chutney, p. 238	180	3.84	.391	.49	3.61	.239	.068	36	1.24	146
¼ cup (makes 2⅓ cups)	.74	47.6	49	8.31	.033	.083	.043	9.47	.152	325
Mint Chutney/Raita, p. 239	21	.067	.471	0	3.12	.037	.167	60	.174	158
3 tablespoons (makes ⅔ cup)	1.69	2.58	192	1.08	.068	.013	.018	6.6	.252	109
Raita, p. 239	72	.574	2.5	1.19	23.7	.347	.629	165	.366	201
¼ recipe (makes 2½ cups)	4.85	7.81	439	8.66	.201	.079	.061	20.7	.82	301

	Calories Kcal / Protein g	Fiber g / Carbohydrate g	Fat g / Vitamin A IU	Vitamin E mg / Vitamin C mg	Folacin mg / Riboflavin mg	Niacin mg / Vitamin B-6 mg	Pantothenic mg / Thiamin mg	Calcium mg / Magnesium mg	Iron mg / Zinc mg	Sodium mg / Potassium mg

Recipes on pages 240–253

Recipe	Calories/Protein	Fiber/Carbohydrate	Fat/Vit A	Vit E/Vit C	Folacin/Riboflavin	Niacin/Vit B-6	Pantothenic/Thiamin	Calcium/Magnesium	Iron/Zinc	Sodium/Potassium
Mock Sour Cream, p. 240	72	.042	4.45	1.37	6.28	.067	.138	39.6	.093	189
¼ cup (makes 1½ cups)	5.58	2.46	44	3.06	.088	.037	.015	3.91	.21	60
Homemade Mayonnaise, p. 240	101	0	11.2	9.10	1.62	.001	.043	1.84	.060	58
1 tablespoon (makes 1¼ cups)	.303	.118	13	0	.007	.003	.002	.315	.051	5
Tofu Sour Cream, p. 241	78	.067	6.16	5.08	19.1	.195	.086	51.6	.849	297
¼ cup (makes 1½ cups)	3.46	3.31	3	4.71	.033	.041	.061	43.8	.335	39
Russian Tofunnaise, p. 241	39	.031	3.13	2.6	8.85	.042	.033	26.6	.44	67
2 tablespoons (makes 1½ cups)	1.67	1.43	15	.042	.014	.017	.030	21.8	.157	15
French Onion Tofunnaise, p. 241	41	.274	3.11	2.6	10.8	.096	.051	28.5	.481	53
2 tablespoons (makes 1½ cups)	1.75	2.08	636	.966	.021	.025	.034	22.5	.18	37
Cream Sauce, p. 242, Light	62	.179	4.1	.166	4.2	.135	.214	76.7	.116	197
¼ cup (makes about 1 cup)	2.31	4.25	233	.58	.105	.037	.034	10.4	.303	102
Medium	94	.359	7	.296	5.4	.218	.232	78.3	.202	226
¼ cup (makes about 1 cup)	2.59	5.59	342	.58	.11	.048	.044	12.5	.366	110
Heavy	125	.539	9.91	.426	6.6	.3	.25	79.9	.289	256
¼ cup (makes about 1 cup)	2.87	6.92	450	.58	.114	.059	.055	14.7	.428	118
Cream Sauce with Onion, p. 243	63	.571	3.34	.279	6.41	.258	.211	64.4	.262	49
¼ cup (makes 1¼ cups)	2.39	6.14	188	1.21	.093	.053	.046	12.2	.349	104
Cream Sauce without Butter p. 243, *¼ cup (makes 1 cup)*	49	.539	1.28	.258	6.28	.296	.25	76.5	.271	31
	2.78	6.91	125	.58	.111	.059	.054	14.5	.423	115
Basic Buttermilk Sauce, p. 244	79	.050	2.44	.073	7.16	.388	.409	152	.311	452
½ cup (makes 1 cup)	4.57	9.88	250	1.16	.216	.062	.050	19.2	.576	210
Stroganoff Sauce, p. 244	72	.705	4.13	.169	7.72	.344	.348	82.5	.244	199
¼ recipe (makes about 1½ cups)	2.57	6.43	238	2.66	.136	.046	.037	10.4	.309	145
Tomato-Buttermilk Sauce, p. 245	67	.495	2.88	2.09	7.42	.352	.257	83.6	.462	69
¼ cup (makes 1 cup)	2.71	7.83	313	2.62	.114	.067	.044	10.1	.312	203
Sunshine Sauce, p. 245	60	.223	3.22	1.93	6.57	.080	.184	91.9	.206	88
¼ cup (makes about 1 cup)	2.65	5.28	154	2.61	.104	.025	.025	8.54	.342	112
Tangy Cheese Sauce, p. 245	90	.025	3.62	.262	7.2	.099	.294	162	.123	163
¼ recipe (makes about 1½ cups)	7.93	5.94	205	.58	.18	.053	.032	12.5	.635	129
Hungarian Sauce, p. 245	111	.235	5.55	.34	9.22	.13	.309	166	.186	184
¼ recipe (makes about 1½ cups)	8.17	6.85	280	1.7	.185	.062	.036	13.3	.65	147
Potato Dill Sauce, p. 246	35	.7	1.98	1.67	5.16	.27	.064	9.68	.243	159
⅓ cup (makes 2⅓ cups)	.661	3.89	48	5.18	.013	.047	.023	4.48	.125	81
Cheddy Sauce, p. 246	47	1.03	2.92	1.53	7.48	.288	.088	37.3	.276	165
⅓ cup (makes 2⅔ cups)	1.52	4.01	1097	5.09	.029	.053	.026	5.77	.248	89
Mushroom Sauce, p. 246	42	1.17	2.41	2.08	7.05	.811	.316	7.28	.552	198
¼ cup (makes 1½ cups)	1.19	4.47	2	1.23	.067	.044	.038	8.02	.313	87
Wickedly Good Sauce, p. 247	768	6.26	65.1	37.5	125	7.55	1.69	216	6.83	2521
¼ recipe (makes ¾ to 1 cup)	27.7	27.9	233	47.9	.328	.478	.437	300	4.5	693
Yogurt Sauce, p. 247	87	.761	6.75	4	15.4	.473	.382	134	.884	77
¼ cup (makes 1¼ cups)	2.87	4.7	21	3.08	.073	.031	.090	18.8	.886	134
Tomato Sauce, p. 248	45	.958	2.43	2.21	14.6	.785	.21	13.1	.746	256
¼ cup (makes 3 cups)	1	5.28	1572	10.2	.036	.11	.055	9.16	.151	242
Yeast Butter, p. 249	108	.034	11.4	1.66	78.4	.793	.18	8	.372	136
1 tablespoon (makes ½ cup)	.9	.9	469	.022	.090	.102	.313	4.99	.186	42
Lemon Butter, p. 249	52	.038	5.75	.112	.956	.010	.007	2.6	.016	59
1 tablespoon (makes ½ cup)	.087	.558	218	3.1	.003	.003	.002	.562	.006	10
HEARTIER DISHES										
Homemade Vegan Noodles, p. 252	99	2.84	.495	1.17	17.3	1.28	.297	14.4	1.27	363
⅔ cup cooked	3.96	21	0	0	.054	.175	.163	33.3	.963	110
Homemade Egg Noodles, p. 252	125	2.84	2.33	1.37	28	1.29	.58	23.7	1.62	383
⅔ cup cooked	5.94	21.2	86	0	.103	.195	.177	35.3	1.16	131
Hungarian Noodles, p. 253	387	7.3	13.1	2.73	74	2.44	1.31	382	2.46	707
1 serving (4 per recipe)	29.3	41.2	2838	11.3	.593	.424	.348	79.7	2.59	666

| | Calories Kcal | Fiber g | Fat g | Vitamin E mg | Folacin mg | Niacin mg | Pantothenic mg | Calcium mg | Iron mg | Sodium mg |
	Protein g	Carbohydrate g	Vitamin A IU	Vitamin C mg	Riboflavin mg	Vitamin B-6 mg	Thiamin mg	Magnesium mg	Zinc mg	Potassium mg
Vermicelli Florentine, p. 254	328	24.8	7.97	8.72	479	5.06	1.89	296	8.06	304
1 serving (2 per recipe)	17.2	52.8	15992	144	.658	.904	.651	232	2.98	1654
Cannelloni, p. 255	430	7.17	17.3	7.71	143	2.83	1.54	411	4.16	1154
1 serving (6 per recipe)	31.3	38.7	4714	34.5	.572	.547	.366	106	3.23	759
Lasagna al Forno, p. 256	527	8.92	23.7	11.5	110	4.55	1.4	465	5.17	1269
1 serving (8 per recipe)	30.5	52	6841	37.2	.477	.792	.477	121	3.87	1100
Poppyseed Noodles, p. 257	309	5.63	8.60	4.54	42.5	2.57	.774	116	2.78	561
1 serving (4 per recipe)	16.2	44.4	66	4.6	.239	.4	.353	76.9	2.34	316
Lazy Pirogi, p. 257, *over ½ cup*	161	5.3	7.44	6.68	27.2	1.92	.736	47.6	1.74	675
Homemade Noodles (4 per recipe)	4.52	21.2	69	12.3	.154	.252	.17	34	1.33	295
Sandy's Macaroni, p. 258	340	8.14	9.41	3.1	61.9	3.54	1.33	203	3.47	548
1 serving (4 per recipe)	13.6	54.2	1164	35.9	.398	.504	.444	98.7	2.9	568
Blini, p. 258	71	.812	3.32	2.49	28	.53	.299	31.4	.503	65
1 pancake (12 per recipe)	2.75	8.04	63	.198	.092	.068	.073	15.7	.438	88
Crepes, p. 259	48	.718	1.45	.412	10.7	.347	.284	33	.505	112
1 pancake (12 per recipe)	2.68	6.39	85	.193	.072	.063	.056	12.1	.425	70
Dairy-Free Crepes, p. 259	43	.958	1.3	1.33	5.83	.433	.1	10.8	.43	102
1 pancake (12 per recipe)	1.33	7.12	0	0	.018	.059	.055	11.2	.327	37
Cheese Blintzes, p. 260	374	2.84	17.5	2.78	51.6	1.29	1.07	506	2.37	520
1 serving (4 per recipe)	21.6	31.5	895	.686	.466	.221	.207	47.9	3.04	451
Blintzes, p. 260	545	8.62	13.1	4.8	132	4.17	3.43	402	6.05	1345
1 unfilled pancake (15 per recipe)	32.4	76.9	1020	2.4	.807	.749	.671	141	5.06	869
Savory Blintzes, p. 261	268	4.83	11	5.72	53.8	1.48	1.07	256	2.49	701
1 serving (4 per recipe)	14.9	28.2	679	5.85	.321	.234	.235	54.9	2.14	442
Spinach Crepes, p. 261	155	5.95	7.53	2.04	88.7	.987	.701	188	2.43	371
1 filled crepe (12 per recipe)	7.71	15.6	6480	22.1	.301	.255	.161	76.9	1.29	443
Piroshki Crust, p. 262	134	3.45	1.08	1.45	35.6	1.72	.477	46.6	1.63	289
2 crusts (20 per recipe)	5.73	26.9	50	.232	.125	.23	.215	44.6	1.28	179
Artichoke Piroshki, p. 263	196	7.27	2.6	2.94	64.6	2.84	.742	74.1	2.51	631
2 Piroshki (20 per recipe)	8.5	38.6	191	13.3	.175	.36	.321	63.6	1.65	448
Asparagus Piroshki, p. 263	184	5.26	2.55	2.27	71.2	2.69	.723	66	2.37	568
2 Piroshki (20 per recipe)	7.39	34.8	640	20.4	.201	.335	.306	56.1	1.64	393
Spinach Piroshki, p. 263	212	6.14	4.43	3.03	63.6	2.49	.699	113	2.44	613
2 Piroshki (20 per recipe)	8.84	36	1754	23.8	.199	.38	.283	67.3	1.73	417
Spanakopita, p. 264	457	8.55	21.3	4.36	118	2.65	1.33	176	4.21	1224
1 serving (6 per recipe)	27	41.9	5647	16.6	.468	.519	.367	107	2.77	525
Chard Pita, p. 265	489	10.9	19.2	6.74	127	3.66	1.41	252	6.84	1517
1 serving (8 per recipe)	26.4	57.4	7875	38.2	.496	.589	.463	158	3.42	982
Pizza, p. 266	184	4	5.12	3.03	49.4	2.3	.637	153	2.11	560
1 slice (8 per pizza)	9.56	26.5	1299	12.7	.184	.296	.23	47.6	1.7	347
Good Shepherd's Pie, p. 268	180	18.4	5.05	5.2	172	3.15	1.5	224	3.34	964
1 serving (4 per recipe)	8.77	29.2	18816	164	.438	.626	.313	83.4	1.34	978
Potato-Carrot Kugel, p. 269	160	3.61	6.94	4.65	51.4	1.35	.774	81.7	1.59	930
1 serving (4 per recipe)	6.8	18.5	3023	10.3	.157	.236	.218	37.2	1.54	348
Potato Poppers, p. 269	199	4.44	4.73	2.29	25	2.4	.589	124	1.79	676
3 Poppers (12 balls per recipe)	7.35	33.5	624	8.2	.111	.288	.181	43.7	1.17	447
Cabbage Rolls Normande, p. 270	479	11.5	14.5	7.54	61.7	3.65	1.05	148	4.57	906
1 serving (4 per recipe)	10	83.9	2923	50.7	.241	.557	.364	101	2.54	842
Stuffed Chard Leaves, p. 271	255	5.12	5.15	3.19	37.1	1.59	.645	108	2.04	548
1 serving (6 per recipe)	12.5	41.4	2087	15.1	.215	.242	.151	54.5	1.31	485
Simple Cheesy Bread Pudding p. 271, *1 serving (4 per recipe)*	274	2.62	11.8	1.1	47.7	1.59	.872	286	2.07	448
	13.6	31.1	537	1.16	.343	.163	.187	61.9	1.88	359
Quiche, p. 272	431	3.01	29.1	3.32	59.8	1.67	1.17	275	2.33	859
1 slice with Whole Wheat Piecrust	15.6	28.8	1163	.773	.366	.312	.348	74.1	3.07	342
Lighter Whole Wheat Piecrust p. 273, *1 serving (8 per recipe)*	95	1.43	5.35	4.83	8.75	.65	.15	7.02	.645	138
	2	10.6	0	0	.027	.088	.082	16.8	.496	56

	Calories Kcal / Protein g	Fiber g / Carbohydrate g	Fat g / Vitamin A IU	Vitamin E mg / Vitamin C mg	Folacin mg / Riboflavin mg	Niacin mg / Vitamin B-6 mg	Pantothenic mg / Thiamin mg	Calcium mg / Magnesium mg	Iron mg / Zinc mg	Sodium mg / Potassium mg
Oat-Nut Crust, p. 273	127	1.81	6.07	1.85	12	.228	.323	18.8	1.11	138
1 serving (8 per recipe)	4.36	14.7	23	.143	.037	.091	.172	39.8	.805	105
Analee's Crookneck Chiffon Pie	237	6.19	8.14	3.47	71	2.5	.763	179	2.84	369
p. 273, *1 serving (6 per recipe)*	13.2	30.9	822	31.9	.277	.232	.223	69.3	1.71	434
Nori Maki Sushi, p. 274	140	2.83	1.78	1.12	17.1	1.73	.498	49.5	1.12	196
1 serving (6 per recipe)	3.54	27.9	1464	3.87	.075	.202	.139	41.6	.815	116
Chillaquillas, p. 275	346	7.78	17.1	4.54	67.9	2.42	.849	404	2.99	838
1 serving (4 per recipe)	13	54.1	1683	24.5	.42	.219	.256	95.9	2.57	522
GRAINS & BEANS										
Barley Crackers, p. 281	11	.181	.112	.080	.744	.107	.031	6.29	.072	33
one 2½" cracker (54 per recipe)	.399	2.21	2	.044	.008	.015	.006	2.08	.070	15
Spinach & Barley Dumplings	186	5.97	2.78	2.28	59.6	2.05	.639	65.8	2.47	314
p. 282, *1 serving (4 per recipe)*	7.08	36.3	3710	12.5	.134	.345	.137	59.9	1.32	295
Bulgur Wheat Pilaf, p. 284	191	5.3	4.16	3.7	29.4	2.14	.372	26.9	2.68	289
1 serving (4 per recipe)	5.22	34.3	1535	20.8	.085	.15	.145	38.1	.924	174
Uppuma, p. 285	191	4.36	6.45	5.15	34.7	1.8	.61	30.6	1.77	279
1 serving (4 per recipe)	6.3	30.1	200	8.45	.074	.241	.243	77.5	2.6	230
Spoon Bread, p. 286	154	1.83	3.56	1.39	26.7	.499	.928	160	.922	549
1 serving (6 per recipe)	8.85	21.3	497	.631	.29	.162	.13	37.8	1.17	276
Helen's Polenta with Eggplant	187	5.31	7.51	2.42	60.1	1.46	.636	144	1.46	641
p. 287, *1 serving (6 per recipe)*	7.23	24	1273	44.3	.158	.295	.167	48.8	1.23	473
Confetti Quinoa, p. 288	153	1.97	5.69	.947	6.79	.236	.039	57.1	2.24	103
1 serving (6 per recipe)	5.9	20.4	50	8.47	.055	.025	.011	15.1	.172	63
Spanish Rice, p. 289	232	6.4	4.9	4.35	37.7	2.7	.845	55.2	1.74	601
1 serving (4 per recipe)	5.07	43.2	879	32.5	.088	.3	.197	57.2	1.58	355
Teresa's Spanish Rice, p. 290	203	4.27	3.5	2.89	21.6	2.42	.682	26.5	1.32	283
1 serving (4 per recipe)	4.24	39.1	1211	40.6	.057	.334	.174	53.7	.982	169
Pilaf Avgolemono, p. 291	362	4.87	11.3	1.57	25.2	2.92	1.07	167	1.91	497
1 serving (4 per recipe)	10.7	54.7	392	2.91	.163	.292	.228	69.6	2.33	231
Green Rice Casserole, p. 291	337	3.78	13.3	4.09	46.6	1.98	1.34	340	1.95	686
1 serving (4 per recipe)	14.6	39.4	1251	15	.377	.256	.203	65.4	2.6	391
Sarah's Super Curried Rice	383	9.28	4.7	1.53	31.2	3.78	.937	60.5	2.78	319
p. 291, *1 serving (6 per recipe)*	7.51	81.2	230	7.5	.118	.505	.286	84.3	1.42	485
Wild Rice, p. 292	265	6.61	10.1	7.97	66.8	3.05	5.34	50.3	2.57	399
1 serving (6 per recipe)	7.59	37.3	1538	5.13	.315	1.81	.198	81.2	2.22	231
Tempeh a la King, p. 300	283	4.86	17.7	8.35	71.3	2.59	.879	82.8	3.24	76
1 serving (4 per recipe)	14.7	13.5	862	41.6	.363	.374	.154	41.4	1.59	724
Tempeh Cacciatore, p. 300	229	4.16	12.1	7.44	93.7	3.14	1.14	82.4	3.56	607
1 serving (4 per recipe)	13.6	12	972	42.4	.322	.441	.18	27.3	1.56	913
Tempeh a l'Orange, p. 301	273	3.44	15.5	14.5	70.1	1.7	.574	89.9	2.59	709
1 serving (4 per recipe)	12.8	13.8	468	28.6	.213	.348	.158	18.5	1.3	694
Swedish Bean Balls, p. 302	296	9.42	11.4	6.97	75	1.4	.952	206	3.87	540
1 serving (4 per recipe)	14.1	36	332	6.43	.324	.218	.226	69.9	1.93	595
Walnut Oatmeal Burgers, p. 303	178	1.9	12	3.53	25.7	.289	.572	45.7	1.4	205
1 patty (12 per recipe)	6.44	12.8	107	1.32	.094	.173	.166	43	.987	162
Picadillo, p. 303	109	3.6	2.72	.764	5.7	1.04	.257	28.8	1.43	461
1 serving (6 per recipe)	1.75	22.3	972	21.8	.057	.172	.076	17.9	.112	414
Picadillo Burger, p. 303	287	5.5	14.7	4.29	31.4	1.32	.829	74.5	2.83	666
1 serving (6 per recipe)	8.18	35.1	1079	23.1	.151	.345	.241	60.9	1.09	576
Neat Balls, p. 304	159	3.44	3.06	2.34	29.5	1.86	.26	57.8	2.08	348
3 balls (15 per recipe)	8.28	25.2	102	.555	.084	.123	.123	35.6	1.32	237
Sweet & Sour Tofu, p. 304	230	2.82	13.3	9.21	70.8	1.15	.481	162	3.26	808
1 serving (6 per recipe)	11.6	18.7	1905	32.0	.151	.277	.245	144	1.31	272
Rice Lentil Polou, p. 305	305	6.26	4.73	3.83	24.2	2.74	.833	41.9	2.47	559
1 serving (4 per recipe)	7.4	61.1	147	2.79	.078	.416	.245	65.8	1.31	389

	Calories Kcal / Protein g	Fiber g / Carbohydrate g	Fat g / Vitamin A IU	Vitamin E mg / Vitamin C mg	Folacin mg / Riboflavin mg	Niacin mg / Vitamin B-6 mg	Pantothenic mg / Thiamin mg	Calcium mg / Magnesium mg	Iron mg / Zinc mg	Sodium mg / Potassium mg
Recipes on pages 305–321										
Kichadi, p. 305	289	4.74	3.99	2.95	12.4	2.93	.637	56.6	2.98	418
1 serving (8 per recipe)	10.3	53.9	27	2.36	.088	.289	.255	49.5	.875	397
Lentil Nut Loaf, p. 306	116	2.3	5.68	4.71	34.6	.849	.397	38	2.05	110
1 serving (12 per recipe)	6.04	11.7	54	.625	.072	.144	.182	20.2	.941	191
Stuffing, p. 306	167	4.24	5.16	3.71	36.5	1.64	.332	80.9	2.04	577
1 serving (4 per recipe)	6.08	27.3	119	3.6	.080	.122	.14	46.4	.999	240
Tamale Pie, p. 307	398	15.6	11.2	6.49	92.6	2.38	.689	148	4.68	1299
1 serving (4 per recipe)	14.4	62.6	1384	15.3	.18	.469	.429	117	2.53	751
Refritos, p. 307	204	12.5	4.32	.944	97.1	1.27	.3	100	3.84	394
1 serving (6 per recipe)	10.8	31	52	0	.11	.234	.329	74	1.82	619
Chili con Elote, p. 308	229	15.5	5.58	5.16	101	1.68	.52	50.8	4.96	564
1 serving (6 per recipe)	11.5	35.8	584	31.2	.124	.221	.198	68.6	1.65	641
Manybean Stew, p. 308	321	17.7	3.02	4.59	119	2.31	1.1	81.9	6.38	563
1 serving (8 per recipe)	19.6	55.2	300	8.95	.197	.377	.578	140	2.76	1137
Boston Baked Beans, p. 309	307	11.6	6.02	5.95	89.4	1.7	.814	195	7.83	606
1 serving (4 per recipe)	13	52	4	1.87	.225	.641	.232	113	1.68	1038
Tennessee Corn Pone, p. 309	355	12.1	9.76	2.45	94.1	1.6	.963	205	3.73	684
1 serving (4 per recipe)	15.6	52	475	1.2	.322	.37	.391	101	2.47	740
Black-Eyed Peas Virginia Style	141	7.98	3.92	3.23	88.8	.826	.361	38.1	4.06	
p. 309, *1 serving (4 per recipe)*	7.14	20.6	336	19.7	.078	.138	.233	65.1		428
DESSERTS										
Baked Apples, p. 313	282	8.66	6.51	4.75	43.2	.865	.34	41.9	1.81	60
1 apple (4 per recipe)	4.24	57.7	126	15.6	.122	.295	.218	49.6	1.55	517
Diana's Apple Crisp, p. 313	372	7.27	13.3	2.84	33.9	1.02	.384	55.6	2.48	262
1 serving (8 per 9" × 13" recipe)	5.17	63.4	522	11.1	.112	.223	.254	52.6	1.51	452
Appley Bread Pudding, p. 314	316	4.33	5.42	1.1	40.4	1.25	.847	221	1.97	355
1 serving (6 per 8" × 8" dish)	11.9	59	86	7.82	.306	.178	.162	49.9	1.53	498
Fruit Tzimmes, p. 314	1015	39.9	13.4	1.24	67.8	5.32	1.28	260	8.36	2409
½ cup (makes 4 cups)	11.3	241	20036	61.3	.483	1.07	.492	150	1.96	2919
Vanilla Pudding, p. 315	126	.050	2.41	.073	6	.13	.39	161	.45	134
½ cup (makes 2 to 2½ cups)	4.05	22.6	250	1.16	.208	.052	.048	16.5	.485	236
Payasam, p. 315	313	1.62	11.7	1.17	20.7	.759	.932	320	1.38	158
1 cup (makes 4 cups)	10.5	43.6	618	2.66	.439	.174	.178	62	1.52	557
Apple Spice Ring, p. 316	393	7.04	9.08	5.82	28.9	1.74	.481	46.5	2.52	384
1 slice (12 per recipe)	6.23	79.6	38	4.84	.11	.342	.244	56.6	1.29	439
Pound Cake, p. 316	219	2.14	9.08	1.15	21.5	1.04	.448	53.8	1.25	262
1 slice (12 per cake)	4.65	32.2	337	.315	.1	.151	.137	28.5	.916	130
Banana Bread, p. 317	176	2.48	6.71	6.32	25.5	.95	.285	24.9	1.16	140
1 slice (12 per loaf)	3.14	28	24	4.32	.080	.283	.16	35.7	1	231
Gingerbread, p. 317	304	3.89	8.23	1.67	29.6	2.03	.678	239	7.72	343
one 3" square (9 per recipe)	6.42	54.5	294	.643	.183	.326	.241	111	1.31	1043
Figgy Pudding, p. 318	324	6.29	10.9	2.95	38.8	1.46	.604	88.2	2.6	292
1 slice (12 per recipe)	7.68	54.9	166	2.45	.132	.274	.193	57.8	1.26	400
Yogurt Cheese Topping, p. 318	40	.013	.833		6.46	.054	.228	72.5	.038	25
2 tbsp. (makes about 1½ cups)	2.75	5.65	36	2.21	.080	.017	.013	7.33	.376	95
Spicy Pattern Cookies, p. 319	46	.727	1.08	.328	4.85	.364	.091	19	.827	52
1 cookie	1.01	8.47	36	.015	.018	.052	.043	13.6	.247	97
Anise Seed Cookies, p. 319	39	.481	1.19	.233	3.85	.223	.074	12	.328	53
1 cookie	.846	6.54	43	.071	.014	.031	.029	5.82	.181	31
Oatmeal School Cookies, p. 320	144	1.24	6.85	1.41	13.3	.399	.184	25.7	.95	98.5
1 cookie	2.5	19.5	160	.243	.043	.094	.1	21.5	.605	132
Graham Cookies, p. 320	47	.663	2.15	.421	6.64	.358	.081	11.7	.369	47
1 cookie	1.03	6.49	77	.024	.021	.043	.047	10.5	.337	42
Raisin Bars, p. 321	162	2.34	8.7	4.69	12	.541	.214	19.9	1.06	71
1 square	3.34	20.1	9	.573	.041	.147	.123	30	.625	176

Recipes on pages 321–327	Calories Kcal / Protein g	Fiber g / Carbohydrate g	Fat g / Vitamin A IU	Vitamin E mg / Vitamin C mg	Folacin mg / Ribo-flavin mg	Niacin mg / Vitamin B-6 mg	Panto-thenic mg / Thiamin mg	Calcium mg / Magnesium mg	Iron mg / Zinc mg	Sodium mg / Potassium mg
Sunshine Bars, p. 321	146	1.78	6.14	4.8	16.9	.58	.204	17.2	.952	51
1 square	2.62	22	223	5.81	.058	.079	.117	27.7	.653	176
Honey-Peanut Butter Cookies	96	1.18	3.98	1.71	11.5	1.37	.288	7.83	.484	77
p. 322, *1 cookie*	2.89	13.6	7	.083	.029	.064	.047	20	.451	75
Summer Fruit Mold, p. 323	97	3.69	.357	.147	10.5	.829	.157	25.2	.783	3
1 serving (4 per recipe)	.708	24.2	269	13.9	.067	.065	.044	12.6	.227	287
Cashew Cardamom Balls, p. 323	85	2.02	4.96	.882	7.33	.376	.174	7.8	.73	2
1 ball	1.67	10	16	.911	.030	.065	.044	26.3	.437	117
Whole Wheat Piecrust, p. 324	219	2.26	15.2	2.15	29	1.17	.312	18.6	1.27	422
1 serving	4.4	18.1	542	0	.079	.176	.218	41.3	1.42	127
Mock Mince Pie, p. 325	509	7.36	20.8	3.43	48.5	1.88	.538	76.3	3.06	573
1 piece	6.73	80.3	824	19	.151	.331	.353	67	2	534
Berry Pudding Pie, p. 325	310	6.22	16.6	2.5	50.3	1.45	.636	116	1.73	488
1 piece	6.81	36.3	756	11.9	.205	.233	.258	60.5	1.81	350
Yogurt Cheese Pie, p. 327	242	4.3	5.55	.733	19.8	.77	.673	192	1.14	145
1 piece	7.86	43.5	96	3.35	.271	.106	.070	36.1	1.12	374
Peanut Butter Bars, p. 327	118	1.75	8.60	3.17	16.7	2.2	.408	22.8	.51	103
1 bar (3 dozen per recipe)	4.42	7.29	23	.129	.046	.079	.043	30.9	.672	148
Graham Cracker Crusts, p. 327	108	1.88	1.75		4.33	.678	.145	28	.76	123
1 serving (6 per recipe)	1.78	22.6	6	.311	.12	.010	.029	10.8	.276	92

SOURCES: *Most of these values have been taken, with generous permission, from the data bank provided with The Food Processor: Computer Nutrition System (ESHA Corporation, P.O. Box 13028, Salem, Ore. 97309), a careful compilation from USDA Handbooks 8-1, 8-2, etc. (L. P. Posati & M. L. Orr, Composition of Foods: . . . Raw, Processed, Prepared, Washington,* U.S. Govt. Printing Office, 1976–) *and some 250 other sources. Other values have been taken from Food Composition Table for Use in East Asia (U.S. Dept. of Health, Education & Welfare / Food & Agriculture Organization of the United Nations, 1972; DHEW Pub. no. (NIH) 73–465), journal articles, and Standard Tables of Food Composition in Japan* [Nihon shokuhin hyojun seibunhyo], *5th ed. (Tokyo, 1985), the Japanese equivalent of our Handbook 8. Values for many cooked grains are derived from uncooked values, using standard factors for cooking losses. Recipe values assume that low-fat milk products have been used, that optional ingredients have been omitted, and that when alternatives are given, the first option has been followed.*

Index

Apricots *(continued)*
  with yogurt, 312
Arame, 211
  in Winter Salad, 141
Arizona, 116
Armenian foods, 118
Arrowhead Mills, 46
Arrowroot
  in sauces, 244
  uses of, 326
Arsenic, 435
Artery disease, 341, 343, 405, 429.
  See also Arteriosclerosis;
      Cardiovascular disease
Arthritis, 436, 448
Artichokes, 175–77
  sauces for, 131, 176
  steaming of, 176
  trimming of, 175
  RECIPES:
  Artichoke Dressing, 131
  Artichoke Filling, 263
  Artichoke Patties, 177
  Artichokes Tellicherry, 176–77,
      331
  Stuffed Artichoke Hearts, 177
Artichokes Tellicherry, 176–77
Asparagus, 178–79
  and crepes, 259
  folacin in, 371
  guidelines for selection of, 178
  homegrown, 178
  nutrients in, 465
  sauces for, 178, 242, 249
  in spring dinner menus, 331
  steaming of, 178
  RECIPES:
Asparagus and Water Chestnuts, 179
Asparagus Filling, 263
Asparagus Patties, 178
Asparagus Soup, 156, 331
Aspartame, 446
Aspergillis flavis, 299, 451
Aspic, Tomato, 142, 331
Aspirin in pregnancy, 372
Astonishing Salad, 133
Atherosclerosis, 126, 343, 405, 429.
  See also Artery disease
Athletes, 394–96
  effect of dietary fat on, 394, 396
  fluids for, 395, 396
  nutritional supplements for, 395
  pre-event nutrition for, 395–96
  protein requirements for, 394
ATP, 409, 411
Attention, 389–90
Attitudes
  on cooking, 26–28, 30
  on weight control, 386–87
Avgolemono Pilaf, 291
Avgolemono Sauce, 291

Aviyal, 226
Avocado Dip, 132
Avocado Dressing, 132
Avocado oil, 126

B vitamins
  deficiencies of, 433
  effect of toasting on, 86
  in energy metabolism, 420, 433
  in leafy greens, 124
  lost from hulled sesame seeds, 91
Baba Ganouj, 136
Bacteria
  aerobic, 424
  anaerobic, 424
  intestinal, 292, 424
  Klebsiella, and vitamin B-12, 499
  resistant to gamma radiation, 451
Baked Apples, 313, 330
Baked Pears, 311
Baked Zucchini, 216, 329
Baking powder
  home recipe for, 79
  in quick breads and muffins, 79
Balance
  nitrogen, and protein requirement,
      413–14
  of nutrients, 432–33
  of trace minerals, 435–37
  of whole diet, 352, 356
Banana Bread, 317
Banana Raita, 239
Bananas
  for infants, 382
  nutrients in, 469
Barley
  in breads, 51, 73
  cooking time for, 280
  flour, 281
  home milled, 281
  toasting, 282
  types of, 281
  washing, 281, 282
  RECIPES:
  Spinach and Barley Dumplings,
      282, 331
  Uppuma, 285
Barley Bread, 73
Barley Crackers, 281
Bars
  "health food," 321
  Peanut Butter, 327
  Raisin, 321
  Sunshine, 321
Basal metabolism. *See* Metabolism
Basic Bread Recipe, 54, 68, 73, 74
Basic Buttermilk Dressing, 131
Basic Buttermilk Sauce, 244
Basic Vegetable Soup, 147
Basil, 231
  in Italian Blend, 232

Basmati rice, 289
Bay leaves, 230
Beans, 46, 278, 292–309
  adzuki, 86, 293, 296
  in breads, 51, 72
  baby lima, 280
  for breakfast, 86, 293, 328
  cheese served with, 293
  cooking times for, 280, 296
  cooking tips for, 86, 295
  Cuban black beans and rice, 303
  fermented, 293
  fiber in, 293, 424
  flours, 51, 72
  freezing of, 295
  intestinal gas caused by, 292–93,
      294
  kidney, 125, 296, 302
  lima, 280, 297
  marinated, 128
  mung, 120, 121, 204, 297, 305
  navy, 297, 309
  nutrient conservation of, 453
  pinto, 297, 302, 307, 309
  preparation of, 293, 294, 453
  red, 302
  in salads, 125, 128
  for sandwich spreads, 113–15
  soaking of, 294
  sprouts from, 120, 121, 204, 293,
      429
  storage of, 279
  white, 297
  See also Black beans; Garbanzo
      beans; Green beans; Soybeans
  RECIPES:
  Black Bean Soup, 166
  Black-eyed Peas Virginia Style, 309
  Boston Baked Beans, 309
  Chili Con Elote, 308
  Cuban, with Rice, 303
  Greek Beans, 297
  Kichadi, 305
  Lentil Nut Loaf, 306
  Refritos, 307
  Rice Lentil Polou, 305
  Swedish Bean Balls, 302
  Sweet and Sour Tofu, 304
  Tamale Pie, 307
  Tennessee Corn Pone, 309
Beer, 356, 423
Bees, 449–50
Beets, 182
  cooking of, 453
  golden, 182
  leaves of, 182
  sauces for, 182
  RECIPES:
  Braised Beet Greens, 331
  Fruity Beety, 140
  Whole Beet Borscht, 152

Fermented beans, and intestinal gas, 293
Fermented foods, vitamin B-12 in, 399–400
Feroz's Dressing, 131
Fetal alcohol syndrome, 373
Fiber, dietary, 47, 49, 360, 424–26
  in beans, 293, 364
  and blood cholesterol levels, 364, 404, 424, 425
  and blood sugar levels, 404
  in bran, 89, 424, 425
  in breads, 425
  and cancer prevention, 345, 425
  and cardiovascular disease, 406
  characteristics of, 424
  compared with "crude fiber," 424
  and constipation, 424, 425
  for diabetes control, 343, 364, 404, 425
  and "diseases of civilization," 342–43
  in fruits, 365
  health benefits of, 342, 344, 364, 404, 425
  and hypertension, 407
  insoluble, 424
  in legumes, 364
  and nutrient absorption, 426
  soluble, 344, 424, 425
Fiesta, 276–77
Figgy Pudding, 318
Figs, 92
  RECIPES:
  Figgy Pudding, 318
  Yogurt Cheese Pie, 326
Fillings
  for tacos, 277
  RECIPES:
  Artichoke Filling, 263
  Asparagus Filling, 263
  Green Bean Filling, 263
  Mushroom Filling, 263
  Savory Filing for blintzes, 261
  Simple Vegetable Filling for blintzes, 260
  Spinach Filling, 263
Finocchio, 196
Finocchio Salad, 143
Firebrick, 60
Fisher, M. F. K., 18–19, 20, 30
"Flame tamers" for gas stoves, 289
Flatulence, causes and prevention of, 292–93, 294
Flavoring, 230–35
  for adzuki beans, 296
  blends for, 232–33
  and fat, 427, 445–46
  herbs for, 231, 232–33
  Homemade Ketchup for, 235
  for Indian foods, 233

for Italian foods, 323
lemon juice and parsley for, 229
for Mexican foods, 232
miso used for, 165
Quick Vegetable relish, 235
Sesame Salt, 234
shoyu, 234
for spaghetti, 232
Tamari, 234
unrefined oils for, 445
Florence fennel (finocchio), 143, 196
Flour
  barley, 51, 281
  bean, 51, 72
  brown rice, 51, 454
  buckwheat, 51, 283
  corn, 50–51, 243
  "enriched," 358
  millet, 51
  oat, 51
  for pasta, 251
  rye, 51, 69–71
  in sauces, 242, 243, 244, 249
  sources for freshly milled, 45
  soy, 72
  storage of, 48, 279, 453–54
  toasting of, 243, 258
  white, 44, 47, 48, 53, 342, 357, 426, 437
  whole-grain, 279, 453–54
  whole wheat, 48–49, 54–55, 242, 324, 454
Flu, broths for, 149, 150
Fluids
  for athletes, 395, 396
  for breast-feeding, 377
  See also Beverages
Flowers, in salads, 125
Fluoride, 434, 442–43
  and osteoporosis, 408
  RDA for, 459
  and tooth decay, 434
Folacin, 171, 361, 371, 440–41
  effect of toasting on, 86
  food sources of, 124, 361, 371
  in green leafy vegetables, 361
  in legumes, 364
  losses in cooking, 171
  need for in pregnancy, 371
  RDA for, 459
  reduced in hulled sesame seeds, 116
Folic acid, 99. See also Folacin
Food and Drug Administration (FDA), 450, 451
Food, canned, 359, 445
Food chain, pesticides in, 430
Food Guide, the, 43–46, 334, 354, 355–67
  chart, 43, 354, for pregnancy, 375
"variety of whole foods in moderation," 356–59

Food irradiation. See Irradiation of food
Food mills, 154
Food processing. See Processed foods
Ford, Frank, 46
Fortification of soymilk, 108
Fourth of July dinner menu, 331
Framingham study of heart disease, 340–41, 346–47, 405
Freedman, Manuel, 321
Free fatty acids (FFA), 445
"Free radicals," 445, 450
Freezing, 359
  of cooked beans, 295
French Bakes, 205
French Bread, 61–62
French Onion Tofu Mayonnaise, 241
Fresh Corn and Tomato Soup, 163
Fresh Corn Pancakes, 94
Fresh Fruit Sauce, 96
Fresh Milk Bread, 65
Freshness
  of milled grains, 87
  of produce, 358–59
  of rye flour, 69–70
  of soymilk, 107
  of tempeh, 298
  of vegetables, 169, 358–59
  of whole wheat flour, 48–49
Fresh Tomato Dressing, 131, 135
Friedman, Meyer, 349, 350–51, 428
Fructose, 420, 448–49
  and alcohol consumption, 449
  compared with sucrose, 448
  and diabetes, 448
  health effects of, 448–49
  and heart disease, 448
  high-fructose corn syrup, 395, 449
  in honey, 449
  malabsorption of, 448
  physiological effects of, 395
  in soft drinks, 448, 449
  sources of, 448
Fruitarian diet, 365–66
Fruitcake, Carrot, 316
Fruit Compote, 92
Fruited Yogurt, 312
Fruit Mold, Summer, 323
Fruit Pops, 311
Fruits, 24
  added to cereal, 88
  for babies, 382
  glazed, 326
  nutrient preservation of, 453
  preventing discoloration of, 324, 325
  soups from, 168
  RECIPES:
  Carrot Fruitcake, 316
  Early Autumn Fruit Soup, 168,
  Fresh Fruit Sauce, 96

THE END

THE NEW LAUREL'S KITCHEN

*was designed and packaged for publication by
Laurel and her friends at Nilgiri Press. Julia, fondly
featured in Carol's reminiscences of the first edition as
a two-year-old toddler, celebrated her B.A. by doing
the pasteup; Victor and Laurel did the woodcuts;
Brian and Nick designed the charts. And Terry made
it all happen: got things started, kept everyone going,
and (most impressive) managed to bring it to a close.
To all who worked on it,* THE NEW LAUREL'S
KITCHEN *is a work of love. We hope it will serve
you well in your kitchens and your lives.*